HUGHE'S CITY HIGH SCHOOL, CINCINNATI.

SCHOOL ARCHITECTURE;

OR,

CONTRIBUTIONS

TO

THE IMPROVEMENT OF SCHOOL-HOUSES

IN

THE UNITED STATES.

By HENRY BARNARD, LL. D.,

SUPERINTENDENT OF COMMON SCHOOLS IN CONNECTICUT.

FIFTH EDITION.

NEW YORK:
PUBLISHED BY CHARLES B. NORTON.
No. 71, CHAMBERS STREET.
1854.

PREFACE.

At the National Convention of the Friends of Public Education, held in Philadelphia, on the 17th, 18th, and 19th of October, 1849, and of which Hon. Horace Mann was President, Prof. James Henry, Secretary of the Smithsonian Institution in Washington City, Hon. Elisha R. Potter, Commissioner of Public Schools of Rhode Island, and Greer B. Duncan, Esq. of New Orleans, were appointed a Committee to report to the next Convention on the subject of School Architecture, including the location, size, ventilation, warming, and furniture of buildings intended for educational purposes. At the second Convention held in Philadelphia, on the 23d, 24th, and 25th of August, 1850, and of which Rev. Dr. Nott, of Union College, was President, the following Report, prepared by Mr. Potter, of Rhode Island, was submitted by Prof. Henry, with some introductory remarks on the general subject of American Architecture. The Report was ordered to be printed with the Proceedings of the Convention.

REPORT.

The subject of School Architecture has not, till within a comparatively recent period, received that attention from the public generally, or from practical educators in particular, which its important bearings, direct and indirect, on the health, manners, morals, and intellectual progress of children, and on the health and success of the teacher, both in government and instruction, demand. The earliest publication on the subject in this country, which has met the notice of the Committee, may be found in the School Magazine, No. 1, published as an Appendage to the Journal of Education, in April, 1829. In 1830, Mr. W. J. Adams, of New York, delivered a lecture before the American Institute of Instruction, "*on School houses and School Apparatus*," which was published in the first volume of the transactions of that association. Stimulated by that lecture, the Directors of the Institute in the following year offered a premium of twenty dollars for the best "*Essay on the Construction of School-houses.*" The premium was awarded by a committee of the Institute to the Essay by Dr. William A. Alcott, of Hartford, Conn., now residing in West Newton, Mass. This "Prize Essay" was published in the second annual volume of lectures before the Institute, as well as in a pamphlet, and was widely circulated and read all over the country. In 1833, the Essex County Teachers' Association published a "*Report on School-houses*" prepared by Rev. G. B. Perry, which is a searching and vigorous exposure of the evils resulting from the defective construction and arrangement of School-houses. From this time the subject began to attract public attention, and improvements were made in the construction and furniture of school-rooms, especially in large cities and villages.

In 1838, Hon. Horace Mann submitted a "*Report on School-houses*," as supplementary to his First Annual Report as Secretary of the Board of Education in Massachusetts, in which the whole subject, and especially that of ventilation, is discussed with great fullness and ability. This Report was widely circulated in a pamphlet form, and in the various educational periodicals of the country, and gave a powerful impulse to improvement in this department, not only in Massachusetts, but in other states. In the same year, Hon. Henry Barnard prepared an "*Essay on School Architecture*," in which he embodied the results of much observation, experience and reflection, in a manner so systematic and practical as to meet the wants of all who may have occasion to superintend the erection, alteration, or furnishing of School-houses. This Essay was originally prepared and delivered as a lecture in the course of his official visits to different towns of Connecticut, as Secretary of the Board of Commissioners of Common Schools. It was first published in 1841, in the Connecticut Common School Journal, and in 1842 was submitted, with some modifications and numerous illustrations, as a *Report on School-houses*, to the Legislature. It may be mentioned as an evidence of the low appreciation in which the whole subject was regarded at that time, in a State which prides herself on the condition of her common schools, and on the liberality with which her system of public education is endowed, that the Joint Standing Committee on Education, on the part of the Senate and House, refused to recommend the publication of this Essay, although it is by far the most thorough, systematic and practical discussion of the subject which has appeared in this country or in Europe. And it was only through the strenuous efforts of a few intelligent friends of school improvements that its publication was secured, and then, only on condition that the author should bear the expense of the wood-cuts by which it was illustrated, and a portion of the bill for printing. Since its first publication more than one hundred thousand copies of the original Essay have been printed in various forms and distributed in different states, without any pecuniary advantage to the author.

In 1842, George B. Emerson, Esq., in Part Second of the School and Schoolmaster, devoted a chapter to "The School-house," in which sound and practical views of the location, size, and ventilation and warming of edifices for school purposes, are presented and illustrated by appropriate cuts. A copy of this valuable work was presented to each of the 11,000 school districts in the State of New York, and each of the 3,400 districts in Massachusetts. In 1846, Nathan Bishop, Esq., Superintendent of Public Schools in the City of Providence, published a Report on the School-houses of that city, with numerous wood-cuts illustrative of the peculiarities of the furniture and internal arrangements of the buildings devoted to each grade of school. These houses were constructed after an examination of the latest improvements which had been introduced in the School-houses of Boston, Salem, and other large cities and villages in Massachusetts, and have been much consulted by committees and builders as models.

In 1848, Mr. Barnard republished his Essay, with plans and descriptions of numerous School-houses which had been erected under his direction, in Rhode Island and Connecticut, and including by permission all of the plans of any value, which had been published by Mr. Mann, Mr. Emerson, Mr. Bishop, and other laborers in this field—with the title of "*School Architecture, or Contributions to the Improvement of School-houses in the United States.*" As the title conveys a very inadequate view of the fullness and completeness of this valuable work, the Committee feel that they can not better promote the object of their appointment than by calling the attention of the Convention to the general views with which the subject was approached by this Author, and to the table of contents which will be found appended to the extracts which we have been permitted to make from this volume.

"The subject was forced on the attention of the author in the very outset of his labors in the field of public education. Go where he would, in city or country, he encountered the district School-house, standing in disgraceful contrast with every other structure designed for public or domestic use. Its location, construction, furniture and arrangements, seemed intended to hinder, and not promote, to defeat and not perfect, the work which was to be carried on within and without its walls. The attention of parents and school officers was early and earnestly called to the close connection between a good school-house and a good school, and to the great principle, that to make an edifice good for school purposes, it should be built for children at school, and their teachers; for children differing in age, sex, size, and studies, and therefore requiring different accommodations; for children engaged sometimes in study and sometimes in recitation; for children whose health and success in study require that they shall be frequently, and every day, in the open air, for exercise and recreation, and at all times supplied with pure air to breathe; for children who are to occupy it in the hot days of summer, and the cold days of winter, and to occupy it for periods of time in different parts of the day, in positions which become wearisome, if the seats are not in all respects comfortable, and which may affect symmetry of form and length of life, if the construction and relative heights of the seats and desks which they occupy are not properly attended to; for children whose manners and morals, whose habits of order, cleanliness and punctuality,—whose temper, love of study, and of the school, are in no inconsiderable degree affected by the attractive or repulsive location and appearance, the inexpensive outdoor arrangements, and the internal construction of the place where they spend or should spend a large part of the most impressible period of their lives. This place, too, it should be borne in mind, is to be occupied by a teacher whose own health and daily happiness are affected by most of the various circumstances above alluded to, and whose best plans of order, classification, discipline and recitation, may be utterly baffled, or greatly promoted, by the manner in which the School-house may be located, lighted, warmed, ventilated and seated. With these general views of school architecture, this essay was originally written."

The volume will be found on examination to contain:

1. An exposition, from official documents, of common errors in the location, construction, and furniture of School-houses as they have been heretofore almost universally built, even in states where the subject of education has received the most attention.
2. A discussion of the purposes to be answered, and the principles to be observed, in structures of this kind.
3. Descriptions of a variety of plans, adapted to schools of every grade, from the Infant School to the Normal School, in a variety of styles, having a Gothic, Elizabethan, or classic character, and on a large or small scale of expense; either recommended by experienced educators, or followed in buildings recently erected in this country or in Europe.
4. Numerous illustrations of the most approved modes of constructing and arranging seats and desks, and of all recent improvements in apparatus for warming and ventilating school-rooms and public halls generally.
5. A catalogue of maps, globes, and other means of visible illustration, with which each grade of school should be furnished, with the price, and place where the several articles can be purchased.
6. A list of books, with an index or table of contents to the most impor-

tant volumes on education, schools, school systems, and methods of teaching, suitable for school libraries, with reference to catalogues from which village libraries may be selected.

7. Rules and regulations for the care and preservation of School-houses, grounds, and furniture.

8. Examples of exercises suitable to the dedication of School-houses to the sacred purposes of education.

9. A variety of hints respecting the classification of schools.

It will not be necessary to specify further the official reports and periodicals in which the subject has been discussed within a few years past, or to mention in detail the various improvements which have been introduced in the construction of school furniture, and in modes of ventilation and warming. Most of the plans which have been brought before the public, and which have been found on trial to be valuable contributions to plans before published, are embodied in the recent editions of Mr. Barnard's work. In conclusion, the Committee beg leave to present the following summary* of the Principles of School Architecture, which the author of that work has drawn up at their request, as presenting the result of his observations and practical knowledge in this department of educational improvement. He has also placed at the disposal of the Committee numerous plans for schools of different grades, selected from his book, or prepared for subsequent editions, which are herewith communicated as a part of this Report.

Philadelphia, Aug. 23, 1850.

The above Report was published as an Introduction to an abridgment of this work, under the title of Practical Illustrations of the Principles of School Architecture, and is adopted in this revised and enlarged edition, of the original treatise, because it contains not only a brief and accurate sketch of the various publications on the subject of School Architecture, but a summary of the aims and contents of this volume.

HENRY BARNARD.

Office of Superintendent of Common Schools.
HARTFORD, CONN., *February* 1st, 1854.

CONTENTS.

VENTILATION AND WARMING.

SCHOOL FURNITURE.

APPARATUS.

LIBRARY.

CARE AND PRESERVATION OF SCHOOL-HOUSES.

DEDICATORY EXERCISES.

SCHOOL ARCHITECTURE.

In treating of School Architecture, it will be convenient to pre ent—

I. Common Errors to be avoided.
II. General Principles to be observed.
III Plans and directions for erecting and fitting up school-houses adapted to the varying circumstances of country and city, of a small, and a large number of scholars, of schools of different grades and of different systems of instruction.

I. COMMON ERRORS IN SCHOOL ARCHITECTURE.

Under this head it will be sufficient to enumerate the principal features of school-houses as they are.

They are, almost universally, badly located, exposed to the noise, dust and danger of the highway, unattractive, if not positively repulsive in their external and internal appearance, and built at the least possible expense of material and labor.

They are too small. There is no separate entry for boys and girls appropriately fitted up; no sufficient space for the convenient seating and necessary movements of the scholars; no platform, desk, or recitation room for the teacher.

They are badly lighted. The windows are inserted on three or four sides of the room, without blinds or curtains to prevent the inconvenience and danger from cross-lights, and the excess of light falling directly on the eyes or reflected from the book, and the distracting influence of passing objects and events out of doors.

They are not properly ventilated. The purity of the atmosphere is not preserved by providing for the escape of such portions of the air as have become offensive and poisonous by the process of breathing, and by the matter which is constantly escaping from the lungs in vapor, and from the surface of the body in insensible perspiration

They are imperfectly warmed. The rush of cold air through cracks and defects in the doors, windows, floor and plastering is not guarded against. The air which is heated is already impure from having been breathed, and made more so by noxious gases arising from the burning of floating particles of vegetable and animal matter coming in contact with the hot iron. The heat is not equally diffused, so that one portion of a school-room is frequently overheated, while another portion, especially the floor, is too cold.

They are not furnished with seats and desks, properly made and adjusted to each other, and arranged in such a manner as to promote the comfort and convenience of the scholars, and the easy supervision on the part of the teacher. The seats are too high and too long, with no suitable support for the back, and especially for the younger children. The desks are too high for the seats, and are either attached to the wall on three sides of the room, so that the faces of the scholars are turned from the teacher, and a portion of them at least are tempted constantly to look out at the windows,—or the seats are attached to the wall on opposite sides, and the scholars sit facing each other. The aisles are not so arranged that each scholar can go to and from his seat, change his position, have access to his books, attend to his own business, be seen and approached by the teacher, without incommoding any other.

They are not provided with blackboards, maps, clock, thermometer, and other apparatus and fixtures which are indispensable to a well regulated and instructed school.

They are deficient in all of those in and out-door arrangements which help to promote habits of order, and neatness, and cultivate delicacy of manners and refinement of feeling. There are no verdure, trees, shrubbery and flowers for the eye, no scrapers and mats for the feet, no hooks and shelves for cloaks and hats, no well, no sink, basin and towels to secure cleanliness, and no places of retirement for children of either sex, when performing the most private offices of nature.

LEST the author should be thought to exaggerate the deficiencies of school-houses as they have been heretofore constructed, and as they are now almost universally found wherever public attention has not been earnestly, perseveringly, and judiciously called to their improvement, the following extracts from recent official school documents are inserted, respecting the condition of school-houses in states where public education has received the most attention.

CONNECTICUT.

EXTRACT *from the "First Annual Report of the Secretary of the Board of Commissioners of Common Schools for* 1838–39.

"In the whole field of school improvement there is no more pressing need of immediate action than here. I present with much hesitation, the result of my examinations as to several hundred school-houses in different parts of the State. I will say, generally, that the location of the school-house, instead of being retired, shaded, healthy, attractive, is in some cases decidedly unhealthy, exposed freely to the sun and storm, and in nearly all, on one or more public streets, where the passing of objects, the noise and the dust, are a perpetual annoyance to teacher and scholar, —that no play-ground is afforded for the scholar except the highway,—that the size is too small for even the *average* attendance of the scholars, —that not one in a hundred has any other provision for a constant supply of that indispensable element of health and life, pure air, except the rents and crevices which time and wanton mischief have made; that the seats and desks are not, in a majority of cases, adapted to children of different sizes and ages, but on the other hand are calculated to induce physical deformity, and ill-health, and not in a few instances (I state this on the authority of physicians who were professionally acquainted with the cases,) have actually resulted in this—and that in the mode of warming rooms, sufficient regard is not had either to the comfort and health of the scholar, or to economy.

That I have not stated these deficiencies too strongly, I beg leave to refer you to the accompanying returns, respecting the condition of school-houses in more than eight hundred districts in the State, and in more than forty particulars in each. These returns were made from actual inspection and measurement of school-houses by teachers and others. An abstract of them in part will be found annexed, together with extracts from letters received from school officers on the subject. I might accumulate evidence of the necessity of improvement here for every district in the State. Without improvement in many particulars which concern the health, the manners and morals of those who attend school, it is in vain to expect that parents who put a proper estimate, not only on the intellectual, but the physical and moral culture of their children, will send to the district school.

The following extracts are taken from official documents, published in 1846 and 1847, and fair specimens of the manner in which school-houses are spoken of, in the reports of local committees, from different parts of the State.

"In one district the school-house stands on the highway, with eighty pupils enrolled as in attendance, in a room nineteen and a half feet square, without any outbuildings of any kind.

In another in the same town, the school-house is less than seven feet high, and the narrow slab seats are twenty-one inches high, (four inches higher than ordinary chairs.) The walls, desks, &c., are cut and marked with all sorts of images, some of which would make heathens blush.

In another, the room is fourteen feet square, and six feet five inches high. The walls are very black."

"In this town there is one of the most venerable school servants in the State. The room is small, and less than seven feet high. Slab seats extend around three sides of the room, and are too high for men. The skill of several generations must have been expended in illustrating the walls with lamp smoke and coal images. The crevices of the floor will admit any quantity of cold air. The door sill and part of the house sill have rotted away. The day I visited it, the teacher and pupils were huddled around the stove."

"In one district, the house stands near the travelled road, is low and small, being only seventeen feet by seventeen, and seven feet two inches high, for the accommodation of sixty or seventy pupils. The seats on the outside are from seventeen to eighteen inches. The walls, door, and sides of the house are disfigured with obscene images."

"There are only three good school-houses in the society; only three that have any out-houses. The rest of the school-houses are in a miserable condition. One is thirty-five or forty years old. Most of them have only slab seats, with the legs sticking through, upwards, like hatchel-teeth, and high enough to keep the legs of the occupants swinging. They are as uncomfortable to little children as a pillory. Seats and desks are adorned with every embellishment that the ingenuity of professional whittlers can devise."

"Two of our school-houses, those in the two largest districts, are in a bad condition, old, unpainted and inconvenient. They are built and con structed *inside* on the old Connecticut plan. Only one row of desks, and that fastened to the wall of the school-room, running quite around it; and long forms, without backs to rest on, the scholars sitting with their backs to the centre of the room. The other two are in better condition, though one is constructed on the same plan as above. The out-buildings are in bad condition generally. One school-house has no out-building nor wood-house. One school-house only is painted outside."

"Of the nine school-houses in this society, not one is really what they all ought to be, for the morals, health, and intellectual improvement of the pupils. Four of them are considered tolerably good, having one out-building, the other five are hardly passable. The desks in most or all of them are where they never ought to be, against the sides of the room and against one end, and with few exceptions, all of a height, with poor accommodations for loose clothes, hats, &c.; all located on or near some highway; no play-ground attached to any of them, except the highway."

"A part of our school-houses are comfortable buildings, but destitute of every thing like taste or ornament in the grounds, structure, or the furniture of the rooms. Being generally built in the public highway or close by its side, they are, one and all, without enclosures, ornamental or shade trees. But the want of ornament is by no means the greatest defect of our school-houses; a majority of them are not convenient. Although there has been some improvement in those recently built, yet they are not so good as would be desirable. The out-buildings in too many cases are in a neglected condition, and in some districts are not provided at all, indicating an unpardonable neglect on the part of parents and guardians."—*East Windsor.*

"It appears that a great proportion of the school-houses are in a sad condition and of bad architecture. Architectural drawings should, therefore, be scattered over the state, so that in the buildings to be erected those abominations may be avoided which are now so abundant."—*Glastenbury.*

"The internal construction of most of our school-houses is bad, and occasions great inconvenience and hindrance to the prosperity of our schools. Let as much be done as can be, to remove those miserable prison-houses for our children, and in their stead let there be good, large, and convenient school-houses."—*Suffield, 2d.*

"None of our school-houses have play-grounds attached; they generally stand in the highway, and some on a corner where several roads meet."—*Bethany.*

"Another evil is the poor, cold, inconvenient and gloomy school-houses which we find in many districts. There is one in this society not more attractive than a barn, for comfort and accommodation in a cold day: the best I can say about it is, it is thoroughly ventilated."—*Lebanon, 4th.*

"The houses and the internal arrangement are inconvenient; a slanting board the whole length of the house for a desk, and a slab-board for a seat so high that the scholars cannot reach the floor with their feet, constitute the conveniences of half of the schools in this society."—*Easton.*

"We see many a school-house which looks more like some gloomy, dilapidated prison, designed for the detention and punishment of some desperate culprit, than a place designed for the intellectual training of the children of an enlightened and prosperous nation. Instead of being rendered pleasant and attractive to the youthful mind, they are almost as cold and cheerless as an Indian wigwam."—*Chaplin.*

"Many of our school-houses are in a miserable condition, possessing less attractions outwardly than our prisons, while within they are dark, gloomy and comfortless. They are all destitute of an appearance of any out-house."—*Warren.*

"The general plan of all the school-houses is the same. Writing desks are placed around the room against the walls; these are generally so high that it would be inconvenient for adults, much more for children to use them. The seats stand in front of these, so that the pupil has his option to sit with his face or his back to the teacher. In the former case, he has the edge of the writing desk to support his back; in the latter, nothing. An arrangement like this is the worst possible. Of the five school-houses in the society, two may be warmed so as to be comfortable at all times; a third needs nothing but a good stove; but the remaining two cannot be made fit for a school to occupy without thorough repairs. There is but one out-building of any kind connected with the school-houses of this society, and this is entirely unfit for use."—*Winchester.*

"Throughout Middlesex county the school-houses, taken as a whole, are several degrees below respectability—rarely ever painted within or without, and if painted at all, they ever afterward show a worn and weather-beaten coat, like the half starved, half clothed outcast of society. Yet these houses are owned by the public, worth its tens of thousands, and they groan grievously if a small tax is levied to improve them. Of the four locations of school-houses in this town, not one has sufficient land for a private dwelling, and all the land combined would be less than an acre. One stands wholly on the highway; another stands on a bleak and rocky elevation, and during some portions of the winter, almost inaccessible. This location was chosen probably because it was cheaper than the pleasant field on the opposite side of the way. Why should the public school-house which accommodates from thirty to fifty pupils, ten and eleven months in the year, five and a half days of each week, not require as much land as a church or private dwelling?"—*Chester.*

"Our school-houses are not what they ought to be either in their location or construction. In their location they are generally found upon some barren knoll, or too near the highway, forming part of the fence between the highway and the adjoining proprietor, alike destitute of ornament or shade calculated to render them pleasing or attractive. The desks are almost always too high and continuous, instead of single, nor is there generally a gradation in reference to the size of the scholar. Few school-rooms are well ventilated; not more than one or two properly or healthfully warmed; the consequence is unnecessary frequency of colds, head-aches and ill health."—*Tolland.*

The Superintendent (Hon. Seth P. Beers) of Common Schools, thus introduces the subject in his Annual Report for 1848.

"The reports of school visitors from every part of the state speak in strong terms of condemnation of the deplorable condition of many district school-houses. The progress of renovation and improvement in this department has not been as rapid or as thorough, during the past year, as in other sections of New England, or as the true interests of the common schools imperiously demand. Badly located school-houses still "encumber the highway,"—"without shrub or shade-tree around,"—"without play-ground, yard, or out-house, mat or scraper,"—without means of ventilation and uniform temperature,"—"with seats too high and destitute of support for the back,"—"with desks attached to three sides of the room," "with windows destitute of glass,"—"clapboards hanging loose,"—"blinds propped up to be kept in their places,"—"the wood without shelter," and "the stove without a door." These are specimens of the language used by school visitors in describing the places where the children of Connecticut are receiving their early training in taste, manners, morals, and health,—language which it is hoped will touch the pride of the districts, and lead to some efficient action on the subject."

"How surprising and disgraceful is the fact, that a very large proportion of the school-houses of our state present vastly fewer attractions, in point of comfortable arrangement and tastefulness, than are seen about our poor-houses, our jails, and our state penitentiary! This remark is too true of the school-houses in this society. They are all located directly on the road or in it, with hardly a shrub or shade-tree around any one of them; and with no play-ground except the highway, which the children, in several districts, have to share in common with geese and swine. Of their external condition nothing very creditable or gratifying can be said. Six, of the nine school-houses in this society, are wooden ones, and they generally bear a time-honored, weather-beaten aspect. Unpainted and blindless, with clapboards agape to catch the winds of winter, and window-panes rattling, or fallen from the decayed sash, they present a most forlorn and gloomy aspect, which, to say the least, is not very well suited to woo the youthful mind, and fill it with pleasant fancies. One, unacquainted with their original design, might mistake them for the abodes of the evil genii, which would naturally be supposed to haunt the dreary solitudes which surround them.

The internal condition of these school-houses is in perfect keeping with the external. In several of them, the plastering is broken and missing, to say nothing of the dark and dingy color of what remains. The stoves are smoky, and the benches and desks are so high as to be better adapted to the children of a race of giants, than to those of the present generation; and these are hacked and gashed by the pupils, as if in retaliation for the torture suffered from them. My compassion has been deeply moved as I have frequently entered these abodes of suffering, and seen their unhappy inmates—the children of protestant parents—doing penance upon their high seats, with no support to their backs but the soft edge of the projecting board which forms the desk, and with their feet dangling in mid-air several inches from the floor. And when I have looked upon these youthful sufferers, thus seated and writhing with pain, the question has often arisen in my mind, what have these ill-starred children done that they should be doomed to so excruciating torture? What rank offenses have they committed that they should thus be suspended between the heavens and earth for six hours each day? And from deep-felt pity for the innocent sufferers, I have sometimes wished (perhaps it was cruel) that their parents had to sit for one hour in a similar position, that they might learn how to pity their children, and be prompted to attend to their health and comfort in the internal arrangement of the school-room.

Add to all this the fact, so outrageous to common decency, that most of these school-houses have no out-buildings whatever attached to them; and does not the case appeal movingly to the friends of humanity, and demand prompt and decisive measures of reform? Is it not passing strange, that while many parents incur considerable expense in providing themselves with cushioned and carpeted slips in church, where they ordinarily spend, perhaps, but three hours each week, they should be so utterly regardless of the comfort and happiness of their offsprings in the school-room ?"—*Bloomfield.*

"Three of the houses are located in the highway; an excellent device for saving land, but a miserable one for the comfort, safety and improvement of children. In selecting sites for the new houses, recently erected, a good degree of space fronting was provided for. Only two houses have blinds or shutters; all the others give full scope for the sun to see what is going on in the school-room, often to the manifest annoyance of the children and teacher; unless, perchance, the latter has genius enough to convert a stray newspaper, or some other available article, into a temporary curtain to shut him out."—*Manchester.*

"Our school-houses, though not cold and leaky, are very badly constructed within, and are therefore very inconvenient. Two of them stand mostly in the highway, so that one passing in a carriage or on horseback may look in upon the whole school, and as a matter of course the scholars will look at whatever passes. When the school-house is so exposed, it would seem, that *modesty* in our children would require the convenience of good out-houses; but this is not the case with any two school-houses in the town. We have urged the importance of these things, but with poor success."—*Suffield, 2d.*

"There are some houses unfit for their purpose; the weather-boards are starting off, "and the wind enjoys quite freely the luxury of coming in and being warmed by the fire; and the dear children suffer much between a cold northwester and a red-hot stove." It is very common to find the school-houses mutilated by the cuttings of obscene figures; this should draw forth the unqualified censure of proprietors and teachers. Further, there are cases where there are no out-houses for the use of children. This is a sore evil, and ought to be remedied immediately."—*Groton.*

"Among the ten school-houses in this district are several very good buildings; but, taking in view the size and proportions of the edifices, the internal arrangement, the fitness of the seats and desks for the object designed, we feel impelled to say, that in our opinion there are no very good school-houses. In some of the districts it is said the people are obliged to go among strangers to procure teachers, on account of the shabbyness of the school-houses."—*Brooklyn.*

"Not more than one-half of our school-houses in this society are very good, if, indeed, they can be termed more than comfortable. The remainder are bad, some of them very bad, exhibiting nothing of comfort or convenience. In some of them, there are no desks fit to be used for writing purposes. The seats are so constructed as to afford no place to rest the back, or, in some cases, even the sole of the foot. Many of the schools are destitute of out-houses. Some of them have no conveniences for hanging up the hats or clothes of the children, or even to shelter the wood from the weather. And more than half our school-houses are destitute of black-boards, a fact alike discreditable to the district and to the teachers who have served in them."—*Stafford, 1st.*

"It appears from the superintendent's report for 1847, that of 1663 school-houses in the state, 873 have out-houses, and 745 have none! This fact is, undoubtedly, a burning shame and a deep disgrace to the state. It is unworthy of a civilized country, and indicates a state of things that ought to exist only among savages. The committee are happy to say that we have little or no share in this shameful fact: but our school-houses are by no means what they should be, and call for improvement.

They are generally *on* or *in* the street, whereas every building devoted to such a purpose ought to be in a retired situation, with suitable yards for play-grounds, and convenient fixtures. The windows in some do not let down from the top, and therefore are not properly ventilated. In only two out of eight school-houses are the benches what they should be. Large desks running around the room for the older scholars ought to be wholly discarded as intolerable nuisances. The scholars are of necessity always looking into the street; the windows can be opened only by climbing over the benches and desks. The scholars' backs are turned toward the teacher; they sit close together, and of course are often whispering. Large girls can leave their seats only by placing their feet on a level with their hips, which it is not always best that females should do. The smaller benches often have backs that are so *low* as to be of little service. Every school-house ought to be provided with a single desk for each pupil, and every pupil ought to have a slate and books to keep in the desk."—*Vernon.*

The following extracts are taken from the Annual Reports for 1849.

"The *school-houses* are not what they should be. Some of them are decidedly bad. They are neither convenient nor pleasant. The benches and desks are inconvenient. Some of the small scholars are reduced to the miserable necessity of swinging in the air, without being able to either get a foothold or a place to rest their backs against. *Ventilation* is not attended to. Every school-room should be so constructed that it can be freely ventilated, so that the scholars may have pure atmospheric air to breathe. This every one must appreciate, who knows the value of health, and does not wish to see a generation of sickly drones coming on to the stage. As a general thing, the external appearance of the school-houses is bad. A stranger passing through a district, can easily select the school-house. If you see a very unique-looking building, a "squatter" in the highway, or standing by permission on the side of some lot, in a corner rendered useless by a location on the border of some swampy moor, or on some arid field, where no vestige of life is—*that* you may conclude is the district school-house. *That* is the place where our children are to resort, during three-fourths of the first sixteen years of their lives, to get an education. *Such* are the associations with their early, perhaps *all* their education! Why is not the district school the place where correct taste should be demonstrated? Impressions *will* be made, and if they ever yield to good taste, school-house associations, in their present state, will not deserve the credit."—*Enfield.*

"Our school-houses are in a bad condition. Look into the school some warm, comfortable day, when the children are more likely to be in attendance, and if you please, walk in and breathe a specimen of the air in a New England unventilated school-house. If you are a well-bred man, you must do violence to your kind feelings, when you take a seat and look around and find that the teacher has nothing left for his accommodation but a standee; our school-houses are literally jammed full, i. e. the seats—any attempt at improvement is voted down on account of the cost."—*South Windsor, Wapping.*

"One district, for a wonder, occupied a new school-house; but while it is *excellent, compared with the old one*, it is *contemptible*, if not *wicked*, compared with what it *ought* to be. The only plan about it seems to be, the *minimum scale of expenditure.* Its dimensions are too limited even for so small a school. The desk or counter is uniform, and attached to three sides of the room, and almost out of *the tallest scholar's reach!* I have protested to the district, and possibly they will lower the counter, *some time or other.* The other districts *need* new school-rooms, and some *talk* of building."—*Wolcott.*

"In regard to the school-houses in our five districts, only one can be said to be very good. Another, recently repaired, may be called good in a qualified sense; while the remaining three are quite ordinary, if not bad. This neglect to provide neat and comfortable school-houses, doubtless has a tendency to dampen the ardor of children in literary pursuits, and in various ways to retard their progress."—*Plainfield.*

"The school-room in the third district presents the same unsightly appearance which it has in years past; and from the height to which the writing desks, and slabs used for seats, are elevated, some persons would naturally infer that they were originally designed for a race of giants."—*Pomfret, Abington.*

"Most of the school-*houses* are in a bad condition, being old, ill-constructed, and inconvenient. Especially is this the case with regard to the interior of some of them, the seats of which are too high for the comfort of the scholars, with nothing to rest the back against, except the sharp edge of a plank or board, which serves as a writing desk, and this placed so high as to bring the arm to an unnatural and uneasy position when attempting to write. The school-houses, too, with one or two exceptions, stand in the highway, many within a few feet of the traveled path, with windows looking directly upon it, so that the attention of the scholar is necessarily attracted to every passer-by, thus diverting his attention from his studies, retarding his progress, and annoying his teacher."—*Litchfield, Milton.*

The Annual Report of the Superintendent of Common Schools for 1850 contains the following remarks on the condition of the school-houses.

"If any reliance can be placed on the representations made by teachers and school visitors from two hundred and four out of the two hundred and seventeen school societies in the state, as collected from written communications to this department in the course of the last four years, a majority of our school-houses are badly located, badly ventilated, imperfectly warmed in winter, having uncomfortable seats and desks, without apparatus except a black-board, and destitute of the most ordinary means of cleanliness and convenience. To this overwhelming mass of testimony (Appendix G) as to the necessity of immediate and thorough improvement in this portion of the educational field, I will here add an extract from a communication by a teacher of much experience and distinction, who received his education and commenced his experience in teaching in the district schools of this state. His remarks refer to the condition of school-houses in a single county—to three-fourths of which he had just made a personal visit."

"OLD SCHOOL-HOUSES.—These are the Antiquities of Connecticut, rude monuments of art, that must have had their origin coeval with the pyramids and catacombs, for aught we can learn to the contrary, save by the uncertain information of tradition. "It always stood there," says "the oldest inhabitant," when asked the date of the erection of one of them. Little brown structures of peculiar aspect, meek, demure, burrowing in some lone, damp and depressed spot, or perchance perched on the pinnacle of a rock, as if too contemptible and abject to occupy a choice piece of earth,—exposed to the remorseless winds of winter, and the fervid rays of summer,—at one end a narrow and dingy entry, the floor covered with wood, chips, stones, hats, caps, odd mittens, old books, bonnets, shawls, cloaks, dirt, dinner baskets, old brooms, ashes, &c., all thrown together in the order as here catalogued,—the principal room retaining its huge stone chimney, which for generations boasted its ghastly fire-place, affording a ready oblivion to annual piles of green and snow-soaked wood,—the burnt, smoked, scratched and scrawled wainscoting,—the battered and mutilated plastering,—the patched windows,—the crippled and ragged benches,—the desks which have endured a short eternity of whittling,—the masses of pulverized earth in constant agitation, filling the throat, eye and nostrils of the inmates,—the unmistakable compound of odors which come not from "Araby the blest"—all point to the remote antiquity of these buildings, and intimate the veneration in which they are held. That some of these structures are always to remain, does not seem to admit of a "reasonable doubt." The records of their origin, as we have seen, are gone, and the testimony of the past few generations is conclusive that no change has been effected in their appearance from a remote period; hence the deduction that they are among the "things to remain," and never to pass away. Though the "annual miracle of nature" may not be vouchsafed to preserve them, yet, like the monuments of the American Indians which receive their annual votive offering of stones, and are thus rendered imperishable, so these "antiquities," receiving their semi-occasional patches upon windows, upon clapboards, roofs and floors, together with the autumnal embankment of earth around their base, and all these given and received obsequious to the *annual solemn* votes of the district,—stand, despite the advance of public opinion, the "war of elements," and "the tooth of time."

Modern School Architecture.—It is much to be regretted that a work similar to "Barnard's School Architecture" had not been issued and circulated throughout the state some ten years ago, that such as have since that time erected new houses, (that are to stand forever,) might have consulted approved models for the size and forms of their structures, and improved plans for their internal arrangements. It would seem, however, that enough had been said by the author of that work in his annual reports, and occasional addresses in the state, to have excited interest sufficient in those intending to build new houses, to extend their inquiries and observations beyond the limits of their own district, and beyond the pattern of their own recently condemned school-house, and at least to select suitable locations for houses and necessary out-buildings, if not for a yard and play-ground.

The material changes observed in the construction of new houses about the county, consist in placing the *end* of the building toward the street instead of the *side*, and giving a very narrow entry across the end of the building,—affording, in some instances, two entrances into the school-room, with only one into the entry. A portion of the entry is used for wood, which being thrown against the plastering, lays bare the lathing, making the building, while yet new, bear the tokens of age. In a few instances only have two outside doors been observed, giving separate entrances to boys and girls.

In most instances where the building is not erected on the line of the highway, it is placed only so far back as to allow a straggling wood pile just outside the traveled path. An instance is not now remembered where the generosity of the district has given a play-ground to the school, aside from the *public common* or the *traveled highway.*

The internal arrangements of the new houses are, in *many instances*, exactly like those of their immediate predecessors, save that in all cases it is believed the old movable slab benches, are superseded by permanent benches with backs. The windows, in all cases perhaps, in the new houses, have made a sensible step *downward* toward the floor; and the desks and seats of the larger scholars, have also been brought down from their inconvenient and dizzy heights, that their occupants may not be "while *in*, above the world."

Where change has been wrought in the fixtures of the room, the desks are almost always clumsy, occupying unnecessary portions of the room, and rendering them inconvenient for the evolutions of the school.

Ventilation has received a passing thought in the erection of most of the new houses, yet its importance is not probably fully appreciated, nor the best methods of securing it clearly understood. Some ventilate from the windows so successfully, as to part with the warm air almost entirely, and at the same time to retain the offensive gases and odors of the room. Some ventilators are placed in the ceiling in the corners of the rooms, others are placed immediately over the stove pipe,—some are movable, and moved with a cord,—others are simply a scuttle, expected to rise by the expansive power of the gases, as safety valves of engines operate by accumulation of steam.

The substitution of stoves (mainly box stoves,) for the engulphing fire place, as a means of warming school-rooms, is noticed in the new houses.

Of School-Houses generally.—To ascertain if improvement has been effected in this class of structures in the state, we must resort to one or two devices of the astronomer, in observing the motions of the heavenly bodies, viz., to notice their respective positions at different and remote periods of time. The progress of improvement has been so slow, (if improvement has been made in school-houses,) that an observer from year to year only, might be at a loss to know that such was the fact; but a comparison of the structures fifteen or twenty years ago, with the buildings now occupied for schools, will doubtless enable one to say that *progress has been made.* It is stated on very creditable authority that in *some* societies and some towns, *one*, and in some instances, more *than* one house has been built, and one or more has been *painted.*

The contributions upon old hats, upon writing books that are "writ through," &c., &c., are levied less frequently than formerly to repel the winds at the windows; fewer clapboards are now seen swinging gaily by a single nail, than in bye-gone days; the asthmatic wheezing of the winds through the uncounted apertures is hushed, and the pupils enjoy an irrigation through the roof less frequently than formerly. Curtains are occasionally found to protect the eyes of the pupils from the blinding rays of the sun; the comfort of the smaller children is materially increased by the addition of backs to their hard seats; the desks and seats of the larger pupils have descended toward the floor; the use of stoves giving a comfortable temperature to the rooms, instead of the former equatorial heat and the polar cold; in rare instances the ingenious designs in chalk and charcoal upon the walls and ceiling have retired behind a coating of whitewash, and the yawning fire-place has been plastered over. All these movements distinctly indicate that vitality at least exists among the people of this commonwealth, and that *the best good of their children, as they tell us, lies nearest their hearts.*

It is earnestly hoped that all persons will be open to conviction and receive the above statement of facts as a perfect demonstration of the earnestness of the community for the well being of the schools.

When we come to the *et ceteras* of the school-rooms, such as shovel and tongs, brooms, brushes, bells, globes, sinks, wash-basins, towels, pegs, hooks and shelves for hats, clothing, &c., it is feared such great, such momentous changes, such rapid advances, will not appear to have been made; probably not three districts in the county have gone so fast, or so far in advance of the others as to have procured all these articles; probably not more than half a dozen districts have supposed it important, that even a mat and scraper are necessary for pupils to use after walking, perhaps a mile in the mud; yet we should be doing them injustice in not supposing that they really feel this quenchless interest, which they represent themselves as possessing for their children, and should greatly misjudge them if we supposed them not doing all in their power to encourage their children in obtaining useful knowledge, and in cultivating the minor virtues while in school.

OUT-BUILDINGS.---An appalling chapter might be written, on the evils, the almost inevitable results of neglecting to provide these indispensable appendages to school-houses in our state. Who can duly estimate the final consequences of the first shock given to female delicacy, from the necessary exposure, to which the girls in the public schools are inevitably subjected; and what must be the legitimate results of these frequent exposures during the school-going years of youth? What quenchless fires of passion have been kindled within the bosom of the young of both sexes by these exposures, fires that have raged to the consuming of personal happiness, to the prevention of scholastic improvement, and to the destruction of personal character? again, what *disgust* has been created in both sexes by the results of not having the appropriate retirements which nature imperiously demands? and finally, may not the disinclination, the aversion of large numbers of families, of mothers especially, to sending their daughters to the public schools, have been created by the sufferings they themselves have endured, from the above cause; and an unwillingness to subject the delicacy of their daughters to the obnoxious trial? Were the question not so peculiar as almost to defy examination, it is apprehended this would be found to be the truth. Will it not seem incredible, even to Connecticut men, to be informed that less than one-half of the school-houses in this commonwealth are without these necessary buildings? yet such is probably the fact; thus dooming thousands of girls to bear a loathsome burden of mortification, which they cannot remove without withdrawing from the schools. I have no *exact* data for the above estimate, yet it is probably not far below the truth, if indeed it is at all. So filthy are *most* of those that are provided, that they are not only quite useless, but disgusting in the extreme. In one society of nine schools but one out-house was provided, and that, I was informed, could only be reached in *dry* weather, such was its *location;* nor could it be used even then, such was its *condition.* This state of things, it would seem, should be utterly changed, and that speedily."

MASSACHUSETTS.

EXTRACTS *from the "Report of the Secretary (Hon. Horace Mann) of the Board of Education for* 1846."

"For years the condition of this class of edifices, throughout the State, taken as a whole, had been growing worse and worse. Time and decay were always doing their work, while only here and there, with wide spaces between, was any notice taken of their silent ravages; and, in still fewer instances, were these ravages repaired. Hence, notwithstanding the improved condition of all other classes of buildings, general dilapidation was the fate of these. Industry and the increasing pecuniary ability which it creates, had given comfort, neatness, and even elegance to private dwellings. Public spirit had erected commodious and costly churches. Counties, though largely taxed, had yet uncomplainingly paid for handsome and spacious court-houses and public offices.

In 1837, not one third part of the Public School-houses in Massachusetts would have been considered tenantable by any decent family, out of the poor-house, or in it. As an incentive to neatness and decency, children were sent to a house whose walls and floors were indeed painted, but they were painted, all too thickly, by smoke and filth; whose benches and doors were covered with carved work, but they were the gross and obscene carvings of impure hands; whose vestibule, after the oriental fashion, was converted into a veranda, but the metamorphosis which changed its architectural style, consisted in laying it bare of its outer covering. The modesty and chastity of the sexes, at their tenderest age, was to be cultivated and cherished, in places, which oftentimes were as destitute of all suitable accommodations, as a camp or a caravan. The brain was to be worked amid gases that stupefied it. The virtues of generosity and forbearance were to be acquired where sharp discomfort and pain tempted each one to seize more than his own share of relief, and thus to strengthen every selfish propensity.

At the time referred to, the school-houses in Massachusetts were an opprobrium to the State; and if there be any one who thinks this expression too strong, he may satisfy himself of its correctness by inspecting some of the few specimens of them which still remain.

The earliest effort at reform was directed towards this class of buildings. By presenting the idea of taxation, this measure encountered the opposition of one of the strongest passions of the age. Not only the sordid and avaricious, but even those, whose virtue of frugality, by the force of habit, had been imperceptibly sliding into the vice of parsimony, felt the alarm. Men of fortune, without children, and men who had reared a family of children, and borne the expenses of their education, fancied they saw something of injustice in being called to pay for the education of others; and too often their fancies started up into spectres of all imaginable oppression and wrong. The school districts were the scene where the contending parties arrayed themselves against each other; the school-house itself their arena. From time immemorial, it had been the custom to hold school district meetings in the school-house. Hither, according to ancient usage, the voters were summoned to come. In this forum, the question was to be decided, whether a new edifice should be erected, or whether the ability of the old one to stand upon its foundations for another season, should be tried. Regard for the health, the decent manners, the intellectual progress and the moral welfare of the children, common humanity, policy, duty, the highest worldly interests of the race, were marshalled on one side, demanding a change; selfishness, cupidity, insensibility to the wants and the welfare of others, and that fallacious plea, that because the school-house had answered the purpose so long, therefore it would continue to answer it still longer,—an argument which would make all houses, and roads, and garments, and every thing made by human hands, last forever,—resisted the change. The disgraceful contrast between the school-house and all other edifices, whether public or private, in its vicinity; the immense physical and spiritual sacrifices which its condition inflicted upon the rising generation, were often and unavailingly urged; but there was always one argument which the advocates for reform could use with irresistible effect,—the school-house itself. Cold winds, whistling through crannies and chinks and broken windows, told with merciless effect upon the opponents. The ardor of opposition was cooled by snow-blasts rushing up through the floor. Pain-imparting seats made it impossible for the objectors to listen patiently even to arguments on their own side; and it was obvious that the tears they shed were less attributable to any wrongs which they feared, than to the volumes of smoke which belched out with every gust of wind from broken funnels and chimneys. Such was the case in some houses. In others, opposite evils prevailed; and the heat and stifling air and nauseating effluvia were such as a grown man has hardly been compelled to live in, since the time of Jonah.

Though insensible to arguments addressed to reason and conscience, yet the senses and muscles and nerves of this class of men were less hardened than their hearts; and the colds and cramps, the exhaustion and debility, which they carried home, worked mightily for their conversion to truth. Under such circumstances, persuasion became compulsory.

Could the leaders of the opposition have transferred the debate to some commodious public hall, or to their own spacious and elegant mansions, they might have bid defiance to humanity and remained masters of the field. But the party of reform held them relentlessly to the battle-ground; and there the cause of progress triumphed, on the very spot where it had been so long dishonored.

During the five years immediately succeeding the report made by the Board of Education to the Legislature, on the subject of school-houses, the sums expended for the erection or repair of this class of buildings fell but little short of *seven hundred thousand dollars.* Since that time, from the best information obtained, I suppose the sum expended on this one item to be about *one hundred and fifty thousand dollars annually.* Every year adds some new improvement to the construction and arrangement of these edifices.

In regard to this great change in school-houses,—it would hardly be too much to call it a *revolution,*—the school committees have done an excellent work,—or rather, they have begun it;—it is not yet done. Their annual reports, read in open town meeting, or printed and circulated among the inhabitants, afterwards embodied in the Abstracts and distributed to all the members of the government, to all towns and school committees have enlightened and convinced a State.

Notwithstanding the great *revolution* actually wrought in the condition of school-houses in certain villages and cities of Massachusetts, the following picture of these buildings in the rural towns is drawn by Mr. Leach, one of the agents of the Board of Education, in 1853:

Since the commencement of my agency, I have examined more than one thousand school-houses, and have noticed the following defects in their location and construction. I have found very many school-houses situated in the highways, but a few feet from the traveled road, and without any yard for the scholars to play in. Some I have found in wet and marshy places, which were often surrounded by standing water. Some were quite near ponds or streams, which was the cause of very great annoyance, both in summer and winter. Some were near stores and public places of resort, which were frequently visited during the intermission. Some were near workshops, or manufactories, or railroads, or depots, exposing the children to interruption and accidents. Some were on eminences, surrounded by dangerous declivities. Not one in fifty have I found with suitable backyards, well-fenced, and with decent water closets. But very few have two entrances, one for each sex. In consequence of this arrangement, teachers are compelled to sacrifice thirty minutes each day, one-twelfth of the whole school time, or commit the gross impropriety of sending out boys and girls into the same yard at the same time. Very few houses are constructed with any regard to external beauty or internal convenience. Many are quite too small, not affording, in some instances, more than forty or fifty cubic feet to each pupil, instead of one hundred and fifty, which is regarded as the minimum. Very many are not more than eight feet in height, instead of eleven or twelve feet. A very common and serious defect is the want of good blackboards, placed at the proper height. In very many cases, instead of a blackboard in the rear of the teacher's desk, there is a window to admit light directly in the face of the pupils. In many houses of recent construction there are no blackboards, except in the rear of the pupils, so that they were obliged to stand or sit on the top of the desks to witness any illustration from the teacher. Where such arrangements existed, I found that but very little use was made of the blackboard by the teacher. Very many schools I have found badly lighted, some admitting too much light, and others too little, and quite often the light was admitted directly in the faces of the pupils. In consequence of too little light, the pupils become short-sighted, and contract a stooping posture by bringing the head near the book. The cases are quite numerous where pupils have become short-sighted and round-shouldered, by being compelled to study in an improper posture. By an excess of light, the sight of pupils has been very much impaired, and, in some cases, entirely lost.

In a large majority of cases, the stairs leading to the upper rooms have been badly constructed, endangering the lives and limbs of pupils. Very many cases of serious injury I have found, which have resulted from this cause. But very few houses are furnished with large closets, or book-cases, to preserve maps, globes, and books of reference. But few are provided with a well, pump, and sink, a very necessary appendage to every good school. In but few instances have there been any attempts to beautify the grounds, by setting out trees, shrubbery, &c. Globes, clocks, thermometers, mats and scrapers, have not been introduced extensively into the country schools. In school districts in the country, when the pupils live some distance from the school, there is seldom any provision for the pupils who wish to stop at noon, or who come in the morning before the time of commencing the school. Many houses have been built, and some recently, with large rooms, containing from one hundred to two hundred pupils each. I have made it a particular point of inquiry to ascertain the advantages and disadvantages of large rooms, as compared with small ones. I have consulted more than one hundred experienced teachers on this subject, and have found but four or five who do not much prefer small rooms to large ones.

In all my examination, I have found but few houses well ventilated. In a large majority of cases, there are no means of ventilating but by opening the windows and doors. And where attempts have been made, it has been but imperfectly accomplished. The ventilating tubes have almost invariably been too small.

NEW-YORK.

EXTRACT *from the "Annual Report of the Superintendent (Hon. Samuel Young) of Common Schools, made to the Legislature, January* 13, 1844."

"The whole number of school-houses visited and inspected by the county superintendents during the year was 9,368: of which 7,685 were of framed wood; 446 of brick; 523 of stone, and 707 of logs. Of these, 3,160 were found in good repair; 2,870 in ordinary and comfortable repair, and 3,319 in bad repair, or totally unfit for school purposes. The number furnished with more than one room was 544, leaving 8,795 with one room only. The number furnished with suitable play-grounds is 1,541; the number not so furnished, 7,313. The number furnished with a single privy is, 1,810; those with privies containing separate apartments for male and female pupils, 1,012; while the number of those not furnished with *any privy* whatever, is 6,423. The number suitably furnished with convenient seats, desks, &c., is reported at 3,282, and the number not so furnished, at 5,972. The number furnished with proper facilities for ventilation is stated at 1,518; while the number not provided with these essential requisites of health and comfort is 7,889.

No subject connected with the interests of elementary instruction affords a source of such mortifying and humiliating reflections as that of the condition of a large portion of the school-houses, as presented in the above enumeration. One-third only of the whole number visited, were found in good repair; another third in ordinary and comfortable condition only in this respect—in other words, barely sufficient for the convenience and accommodation of the teachers and pupils; while the remainder, consisting of 3,319, were to all intents and purposes unfit for the reception of man or beast.

But 544 out of 9,368 houses visited, contained more than one room; 7,313 were destitute of any suitable play-ground; nearly six thousand were unfurnished with convenient seats and desks; nearly eight thousand destitute of the proper facilities for ventilation; and upwards of six thousand without a privy of any sort; while of the remainder but about one thousand were provided with privies containing different apartments for male and female pupils! And it is in these miserable abodes of accumulated dirt and filth, deprived of wholesome air, or exposed without adequate protection to the assaults of the elements, with no facilities for necessary exercise or relaxation, no convenience for prosecuting their studies; crowded together on benches not admitting of a moment's rest in any position, and debarred the possibility of yielding to the ordinary calls of nature without violent inroads upon modesty and shame; that upwards of two hundred thousand children, scattered over various parts of the State, are compelled to spend an average period of eight months during each year of their pupilage! Here the first lessons of human life, the incipient principles of morality, and the rules of social intercourse are to be impressed upon the plastic mind. The boy is here to receive the model of his permanent character, and to imbibe the elements of his future career; and here the instinctive delicacy of the young female, one of the characteristic ornaments of the sex, is to be expanded into maturity by precept and example! Is it strange, under such circumstances, that an early and invincible repugnance to the acquisition of knowledge is imbibed by the youthful mind; that the school-house is regarded with unconcealed aversion and disgust, and that parents who have any desire to preserve the health and the morals of their children, exclude them from the district school, and provide instruction for them elsewhere?

If legislation could reach and remedy the evil, the law-making power would be earnestly invoked. But where the ordinary mandates of humanity, and the laws of parental feeling written by the finger of heaven on the human heart, are obliterated or powerless, all statutory provisions would be idle and vain. In some instances during the past year, comfortable school-houses have been erected to supply the place of miserable and dilapidated tenements which for years had been a disgrace to the inhabitants. Perhaps the contagion of such worthy examples may spread; and that which seems to have been beyond the influence of the ordinary impulses of humanity, may be accomplished by the power of example or the dread of shame.

The expense of constructing and maintaining convenient buildings, and all other proper appliances for the education of the young, is a mere trifle when contrasted with the beneficial results which inevitably follow.

Of all the expenditures which are calculated to subserve the wants or gratify the caprices of man, there are none which confer such important and durable blessings as those which are applied to the cultivation and expansion of the moral and intellectual powers. It is by such cultivation that human happiness is graduated, and that from the most debased of the savage tribes, nation rises above nation in the scale of prosperity and civilization. The penuriousness which has been manifested on this subject, and the reckless profligacy exhibited on others, is strongly characteristic of the past. In future times, when the light of science shall be more widely diffused, and when the education of the young shall claim and receive the consideration it deserves, a retrospection to the records of the past will exhibit preceding generations in no enviable point of view

The following remarks and extracts from the Reports of the special visiters appointed by the State Superintendent (Hon. John C. Spencer) in each of the counties, for 1840, and for 1841, are taken from Part I of that admirable work, the "School and the Schoolmaster," Part I, by Prof. (now Bishop) Potter, and Part II, by George B. Emerson, Esq., of Boston.

"I ask, then, *first*, are our common schools places of agreeable resort, calculated to promote health, and to connect pleasant associations with study?

Ans. Say the visiters, in one of the oldest and most affluent towns of the south-eastern section of the state, 'It may be remarked, generally that the school-houses are built in the old style, are too small to be convenient, and, with one exception, too near the public roads, generally having no other play-ground.' Twelve districts were visited in this town.—*See **Report** of Visiters* (1840), p. 47.

Say the visiters of another large and wealthy town in the central part of the state, 'Out of the 20 schools they visited, 10 of the school-houses were in bad repair, and many of them not worth repairing. In none were any means provided for the ventilation of the room. In many of the districts, the school-rooms are too small for the number of scholars. The location of the school-houses is generally pleasant. There are, however, but few instances where play-grounds are attached, and their condition as to privies is very bad. The arrangement of seats and desks is generally very bad, and inconvenient to both scholars and teachers. Most of them are without backs.'—P. 28 (***Rep.***, 1840.)

From another town in the north-western part of the state, containing a large population, and twenty-two school districts, the visiters report of district No. 1, that the school-house is large and commodious, but scandalously cut and marked; the school-room but tolerably clean; the privies very filthy, and no means of ventilation but by opening the door or raising the window. No. 2 has an old school-house; the room not clean; seats and desks well arranged, but cut and marked; no ventilation; the children healthy, but not clean. No. 3 has an old frame building, but warm and comfortable. No. 4 has a very poor, dilapidated old frame school-house, though the inhabitants are generally wealthy for that country. No. 5 has a frame school-house, old and in bad condition; school-room not clean; seats and desks not convenient; No. 6 has a frame school-house, old and in bad condition; the school-room is not clean; no cup or pail for drinking water. No. 7 has a log school-house, in a very bad condition; desks and seats are inconvenient. 'Here, too,' say the visiters, 'society is good, and people mostly in easy circumstances, but the school-house very unbecoming such inhabitants. It does not compare well with their dwellings.' No. 8, say the visiters, is 'a hard case.' No. 9 has a frame house in good condition and in a pleasant location, but is 'too small for the number of children.' No. 10 has a log school-house. No. 11 has a 'log shanty for a school-house, not fit for any school.' No. 12 a log house. No. 13 has a log shanty, in bad condition, not pleasantly located, school-room not clean. 'The school-house or *hovel* in this district is so cold in winter, so small and inconvenient, that little can be done towards preserving order or advancing education among so many scholars; some poor inhabitants and some in good circumstances; might have a better school-house.' No. 14 has a good frame house, in good condition, pleasant location, with ample and beautiful play-ground; school-room in clean condition. The visiters add, 'In this district the inhabitants are poor, and the scholars attend irregularly; *the house was built by one man in low circumstances, who has a large family of boys to educate; a noble act.'* No. 15 has a frame house, in a good, warm, and comfortable condition, with a pleasant and retired location and a play-ground. No. 16 has a log shanty for a school-house. No. 17, 'no regular school-house other than some old log house.' No. 18, no school-house. No. 19, a log shanty. No. 20 and 21 are new districts. No. 22 has a frame school-house, in good repair and pleasantly situated. Thus, out of twenty-two school-houses, not more than *five* are reported as respectable or comfortable; none have any proper means of ventilation; eight are built of logs; and but one of them, according to the visiters, has a privy.—*Report* (1840), p. 142.

It is also a subject of frequent complaint in these reports, that the seats are too high (too high, say the visiters in one case, for a man of six feet, and all alike), and are, therefore, uncomfortable for the children, as well as productive of much disorder. 'We have found,' says the report from one town, 'except in one school, all the seats and desks much too high, and in that one they were recently cut down at our recommendation. In many of our schools, a considerable number of children are crowded into the same seat, and commonly those seated beyond the entering place have no means of getting at their seats but by climbing over those already seated, and to the ruin of all regard to cleanliness.'

'We have witnessed much uneasiness, if not suffering, among the children, from the dangling of their legs from a high seat, and, with the one exception, have seen them attempting to write on desks so high that, instead of the elbow resting to assist the hand in guiding the pen, the whole arm has, of necessity, been stretched out; for, if they did not this, they must write rather by guess than sight, unless some one may have the fortune to be near-sighted, and, from this defect, succeed in seeing his work. This is a great evil, and ought to be remedied before we complain of the incompetency of teachers.'—*Report* (1841), p. 38.

These specimens will serve to show how far many of the school-houses, in this state, are pleasant places of resort, or study, and in what degree they are likely to inspire a respect for education, or a desire to enjoy and improve its advantages. The condition and aspect of the building, with its appendages and surrounding landscape, are inseparably associated, in a child's mind, with his first day at school, and his first thoughts about education. Is it well, then, that these earliest, most lasting, and most controlling associations, should be charged with so much that is offensive? Is it to be expected, that the youthful mind can regard that as the cause, next to religion, most important of all others, which is upheld and promoted, in such buildings, as the district school-house usually is? Among the most comfortless and wretched tenements, which the pupil ever enters, he thinks of it with repugnance; the tasks which it imposes, he dreads; and he at length takes his leave of it, as of a prison, from which he is but too happy to escape.

This seems to me to be the greatest evil connected with our school-houses. But their deleterious effect on health, is also to be considered. Air which has been once respired by the lungs, parts with its healthy properties, and is no longer fit for use. Hence a number of persons, breathing the air of the same apartment, soon contaminate it, unless the space is very large, or unless there is some provision for the introduction of fresh, as well as the exclusion of foul air. This ventilation is especially important for school-houses, since they are usually small in proportion to the number of scholars; the scholars remain together a long while at once, and are less cleanly in their personal habits than adults. Yet, important as it is, probably not one common school in fifty, in this state, will be found supplied with adequate means to effect it. The cracks and crevices, which abound in our school-houses, admit quite enough of cold air in winter, but not enough of fresh. What is wanted at that season, for both health and economy, is a constant supply of fresh warm air; and this is easily obtained by causing the air, as it enters from without, to pass through heated flues, or over heated surfaces.

It is also important, to the health of scholars and teachers in common schools, that the rooms should be larger and have higher ceilings; and that much more scrupulous attention should be paid to the cleanliness of both the room and its inmates. 'An evil,' say the visiters of one of the towns, 'greater than the variety of school-books or the want of necessary apparatus, is having school-rooms so unskilfully made and arranged. Of our 13 school-rooms, only 3 are ten feet high, and of the residue only one is over eight feet. The stupidity arising from foul, oft-breathed air, is set down as a grave charge against the capacity of the scholars or the energy of the teacher. A room for 30 children, allowing 12 square feet for each child, is low at 10 feet, and for every additional ten children an extra foot in elevation is absolutely necessary, to enable the occupants of the room to breathe freely.'—*Report* (1841), p. 38.

Are common schools so conducted, as to *promote habits of neatness and order, and cultivate good manners and refined feelings?*

From the quotations already made from the reports of visiters, it appears that the school-rooms, in many cases, were not clean; and the same thing is often alleged of the children. I will add but one other passage, to which I happen to open on p. 39 of the Report (1840). It relates to a town containing 24 school districts, of which 16 were visited. Of these 16, one quarter are represented to have been almost entirely regardless of neatness and order, viz.: No. 4 'has a dirty school-room, and the appearance of the children was dirty and sickly.' No. 2 'has a dirty school-room, inconveniently arranged, and *ventilated all over*;' the children 'rather dirty,' and no means of supplying fresh water except from the neighbor's pails and cups. No. 3 has 'an extremely dirty school-room, without ventilation, the children not clean, and no convenience for water.' No. 24 'has a school-house out of repair, dirty, and inconvenient in its arrangements.'

It is also a subject of almost universal complaint, that the *school-houses are without privies.* On an average, probably not more than one in twenty, of the school-houses throughout the state, has this appendage; and in these, it was almost invariably found, by the visiters, to be in a bad state. This fact speaks volumes, of the attention, which is paid at these schools, to delicacy of manners, and refinement of feeling. None but the very poorest families think of living without such a convenience at home; and a man, who should build a good dwelling-house, but provide no place for retirement when performing the most private offices of nature, would be thought to give the clearest evidence of a coarse and brutal mind. Yet respectable parents allow their children to go to a school where this is the case; and where the evil is greatly aggravated by the fact, that numbers of both sexes are collected, and that, too, at an age of extreme levity, and when the youthful mind is prone to the indulgence of a prurient imagination. Says one of the visiters (*Report*, 1840, p. 77), 'In most cases in this town, the scholars, male and female, are turned promiscuously and simultaneously into the public highway, without the shelter of so much (in the old districts) as a 'stump' for a covert to the calls of nature. The baneful tendency, on the young and pliant sensibilities, of this barbarous custom, are truly lamentable.' So the visiters of one of the largest and oldest counties: 'We regret to perceive that many of the districts have neglected to erect privies for the use of the children at school. This is a lamentable error. The injury to the taste and morals of the children which will naturally result from this neglect, is of a character much more serious than the discomfort which is obviously produced by it.'—(*Report*, 1840, p. 131.)"

VERMONT.

EXTRACT *from the* "*First Annual Report of the State Superintendent (Hon. Horace Eaton,) of Common Schools, October*, 1846," *made to the Legislature.*

"It might occur to any one in travelling through the State, that our school-houses are almost uniformly located in an uninteresting and unsuitable spot, and that the buildings themselves too generally exhibit an unfavorable, and even repulsive aspect. Yet by giving some license to the imagination it might be supposed that, notwithstanding their location and external aspect were so forbidding, the internal appearance would be more cheerful and pleasant—or at least, that the arrangement and construction within would be comfortably adapted to the purposes which the school-house was intended to fulfil. But an actual inspection of by far the greatest number of the school-houses in the State, by County Superintendents, discloses the unpleasant fact, that ordinarily the interior does but correspond with the exterior, or is, if possible, still worse. A very large proportion of these buildings throughout the State must be set down as in a miserable condition. The melancholy fact is established by the concurrent report of all our County Superintendents, that in every quarter of the State they are, as a class, altogether unsuited to their high purposes. Probably nine-tenths of them are located upon the line of the highway; and as the geographical centre of the district usually determines their situation, aside from the relation with the road, it is a rare chance that one is not placed in an exposed, unpleasant and uncomfortable spot. In some cases—especially in villages—their location seems to be determined by the worth, or rather by the *worthlessness* of the ground on which they stand—that being selected which is of the least value for any other purpose. Seldom or never do we see our school-houses surrounded by trees or shrubbery, to serve the purpose which they might serve so well—that of delighting the eye, gratifying the taste, and contributing to the physical comfort, by shielding from the scorching sun of summer, and breaking the bleak winds of winter. And from buildings thus situated and thus exposed, pupils are turned out into the streets for their sports, and for other purposes still more indispensable. What better results could be expected under such a system than that our 'girls should become hoydens and our boys blackguards?' Indeed it would be a happy event, if in no case results still more melancholy and disastrous than this were realized.

But this notice of *ordinary* deficiencies does not cover the whole ground of error in regard to the situation of school-houses. In some cases they are brought into close connection with positive nuisances. In a case which has fallen under the Superintendent's own personal observation, one side of the school-house forms part of the fence of a hog-yard, into which, during the summer, the calves from an extensive dairy establishment have been thrown from time to time, (disgusting and revolting spectacle!) to be rent and devoured before the eyes of teacher and pupils—except such portions of the mutilated and mangled carcasses as were left by the animals to go to decay, as they lay exposed to the sun and storm. It is true the windows on the side of the building adjoining the yard, were generally observed to be closed, in order to shut out the almost insupportable stench which arose from the decomposing remains. But this closure of windows could, in no great degree, 'abate the nuisance;' for not a breath of air could enter the house from any direction but it must come saturated with the disgusting and sickening odor that loaded the atmosphere around. It needs no professional learning to tell the deleterious influence upon health, which must be exerted by such an agency, operating for continuous hours.

Such cases, it is hoped and believed, are exceedingly rare. But it is much to be feared that the usual exemption enjoyed by teachers and pupils, from even such outrages upon their senses and sensibilities, as have been detailed, is to be attributed to the fact that such arrangements are not ordinarily convenient, rather than to any prevailing conviction of their impropriety, or any general and settled purpose to avoid them. The case is named as at least strong evidence that the pertinency of considerations, involving a regard either to taste, comfort, or even health itself, is generally overlooked or disregarded, in fixing upon a site for a school-house. At all events these purposes are all *exposed* to be violated under the prevailing neglect of districts to secure the possession of sufficient ground for a yard around the school-house. But it would seem unnecessary to urge, beyond the bare suggestion, the importance of providing for school-houses, a comfortable location, a sufficient yard and play-ground, a wood-house and other out-buildings, a convenient access to water, and the surrounding of the premises with shade-trees which might serve for shelter, as well as delight the eye, and aid to render the school-house—what it should be—one of the most attracting and delightful places of resort upon the face of the earth. It should be such, that when the child shall have changed into the gray-haired man, and his memory wanders back through the long vista of vanished years, seeking for some object on which it may repose, this shall be the spot where it shall love to rest.

In the construction of the school-house—embracing its material, style of architecture, and finish—as little care and taste are exhibited, as might be expected from the indifference manifested in regard to its location and surrounding circumstances. Cheapness of construction seems, in most cases, to be the great governing principle, which decides upon its materials, its form, and all its internal arrangements. No complaint on this score could justly be made, if the general condition of these buildings were clearly and fairly attributed to want of ability. But while our other edifices, both public and private, have improved in elegance, convenience, and taste, with the increasing wealth of our citizens, our school-houses linger in the rear and bear the impress of a former age. In this respect.

> 'That which in days of yore we were
> We at the present moment are.'

Low walls might be instanced as *one* of the prevailing defects in school-house architecture. The quantity of air contained in a school-room of the usual height, is so small as to be soon exhausted of its oxygen; and the dullness, headache and depression which succeed to this result, are but too well known and too often felt, although they may fail of being attributed to their true cause. And why should our children be robbed of a comfortable supply of that pure and wholesome air, with which our Creator, in the largeness and richness of his bounty, has surrounded the earth and filled the sky? But if the condition of the house is such, as in part to prevent the injurious effects arising from a deficiency of pure air, by means of broken windows and gaping crevices—then colds. coughs and as the ultimate and crowning result—consumption—

(and of this disease, what thousands of cases have had their foundations laid in the school-house!) must be the consequence of this sort of exposure. This is true in regard to *all* classes and conditions of pupils. But it should be distinctly kept in mind, although it is ordinarily overlooked and forgotten, that children accustomed to be comfortably protected against cold or vicissitudes of temperature, at home, will inevitably suffer the more when exposed to them in the school-house. And here is an additional reason why these structures should be improved, as our dwelling houses are generally becoming more comfortable.

But there is not room here for details—not even to exhibit *this* topic in all its important bearings. And it has been thus hinted at only to prove that the general charge of faulty construction is not wholly unfounded.

It was the purpose of the Superintendent to discuss at some length, the pernicious influence exerted, both upon the health of pupils, and their progress in learning, by the miserable structures in which the State abounds, but the extent of the remarks already made precludes it.

One cause of the prevailing fault in regard to the construction and internal arrangement of school-houses, doubtless, is the want of proper models. Districts, when about erecting a school-house, cannot well do more than follow the examples before them. To form the plan of a proper school-house—one well adapted to all the various ends which should be sought, such as the convenience, comfort, and health of pupils, convenience for supervision and conduct of the school, and facilities for the most successful prosecution of study—would require such an extent of observation and so full an acquaintance with the laws of health, of mind and morals—and then such a skill in designing a structure in which all the necessary conditions should be observed and secured, that it would be unreasonable to expect that a district could command them, without an opportunity to avail itself of the experience and observation of others. And districts have almost universally felt this lack of guidance. But it is believed that hereafter, information on the subject of school-house architecture, will be more accessible; and if, as a first step, some one district in every town in the State would avail itself of the necessary information, and make a vigorous effort to secure the erection of a well located, well planned, and well constructed school-house, they would perform an act of high public beneficence, as well as confer upon themselves an inestimable blessing. And shall not one or two years realize the accomplishment of this noble purpose? What district will lead the van?

NEW HAMPSHIRE.

EXTRACTS *from the* "*Report of the Commissioner, (Prof. Haddock of Dartmouth College) of Common Schools, to the Legislature of New Hampshire, June Session*, 1847."

"The success of our whole system depends as much on a thorough reform in the construction and care of school-houses as upon any other single circumstance whatever.

It is wonderful, and when their attention is called to it, strikes the inhabitants of the Districts themselves as really unaccountable, that careful and anxious parents have been content to confine their children for so many hours a day through a large part of the severest and most trying seasons of the year, in houses so ill constructed, so badly ventilated, so imperfectly warmed, so dirty, so instinct with vulgar ideas, and so utterly repugnant to all habits of neatness, thought, taste, or purity. There are multitudes of houses in the State, not only inconveniently located, and awkwardly planned, but absolutely dangerous to health and morals.

And it has struck me with the greater surprise, that this is true not only of the thinly peopled parts of the State, but of flourishing villages. In one of the largest towns the principal District School was kept, the last winter, in a dilapidated, rickety, uncouth, slovenly edifice, hardly more comfortable than some barns within sight of it. In one enterprising village the school-house, as I looked at it from a little distance, appeared decidedly the shabbiest and most neglected building, not to say dwelling, within reach of my eye. I have been in houses, which no scrubbing could keep clean; they were never made to be clean: and this, in places, where private taste is adorning the town with the ornaments of architecture and enriching the country with the fruits of rural industry.

It is, however, encouraging to find, that a better feeling is coming to prevail on this subject. Many districts are rebuilding, and, in most instances, upon an improved plan. Some examples have been set of good judgment and liberal expenditure for this important object. And it is hoped, that other districts will be stimulated to imitate them.

Whenever a new house is to be erected, it should first be carefully located, so as best to accommodate the whole district, and by all means, on an open, healthy, agreeable site, with ample room about it on all sides, and out of the way of floods of water or of dust.

MAINE.

EXTRACT *from a special "Report of the Secretary of the Board of Education, upon the subject of School-Houses."*

"It is worthy of note, and of most serious consideration, that a majority of the returns speak of ill-constructed school-houses as one of the most prominent 'defects in the practical operation of the law establishing common-schools.' The strength and uniformity of the language made use of, as well as the numerous applications to the members of the board, and their secretary, for information upon this subject, leave no room for doubt as to the existence of a wide-spread evil; an evil, the deleterious influence of which, unless it is reformed, and that speedily, is not to be confined to the present generation, but must be entailed upon posterity. In remarking upon this subject, as long ago as 1832, it was said by the board of censors of the American Institute of Instruction, that 'if we were called upon to name the most prominent defect in the schools of our country; that which contributes most, directly and indirectly, to retard the progress of public education, and which most loudly calls for a prompt and thorough reform, it would be the want of spacious and convenient school-houses.' From every indication, there is reason to believe that the remark is applicable to our school-houses, in their present condition, as it was when made. For the purpose of contributing, in some small degree, towards effecting a reform for which so urgent a necessity exists, and rendering some assistance, in the way of counsel, to those who are about erecting new school-houses, or remodelling old ones, this report is prepared, under the direction of the board. It makes no claim to originality of thought or language; it is, in fact, a mere compilation of the thoughts and language of others who have given the subject a careful investigation, whose opinions are the result of close observation and long experience, and are therefore entitled to our confidence and respect. To save the necessity of giving credit, upon almost every page of this report for borrowed language, as well as ideas, it may here be remarked, that the principal sources from which the information herewith communicated has been compiled, are, the reports upon the subject of school-houses, by Hon. Horace Mann and Henry Barnard, Esq., and 'The School-master,' by Mr. George B. Emerson; gentlemen to whom, for their efforts in the cause, a large debt of gratitude is due from the friends of education; a debt which can be discharged in no manner more acceptable to them, than by entering into their labors, and adopting and reducing to practice their very valuable suggestions."

RHODE ISLAND.

EXTRACTS *from "Report on the condition and improvement of the Public Schools of Rhode Island, submitted Nov.* 1, 1845, *by Henry Barnard, Commissioner of Public Schools."*

"The condition of the school-houses, was, in my circuit through the schools, brought early and constantly under my notice, and to effect an immediate and thorough reform, public attention was early and earnestly called to the subject. The many and great evils to the health, manners, morals, and intellectual habits of children, which grow out of their bad and defective construction and appurtenances, were discussed and exposed, and the advantages of more complete and convenient structures pointed out. In compliance with the request of the Committee on Education, a law authorizing school districts to lay and collect a tax to repair the old, and build new school-houses, was drafted and passed; and in pursuance of a resolution of the General Assembly, a document was prepared embodying the results of my observations and reflections on the general principles of school-architecture, and such plans and descriptions of various structures recently erected, for large and small, city and country districts, and for schools of different grades, as would enable any committee to act understandingly, in framing a plan suitable to the wants of any particular district or school. The same document was afterwards abridged and distributed widely, as one of the '*Educational Tracts,*' over the state. I have secured the building of at least one school-house in each county, which can be pointed to as a model in all the essential features of location, construction, warming, ventilation, seats and desks, and other internal and external arrangements.

During the past two years, more than fifty school-houses have been erected, or so thoroughly repaired, as to be substantially new—and most of them after plans and directions given in the above document, or furnished directly by myself, on application from districts or committees."

"Of these, (three hundred and twelve school-houses visited,) twenty-nine were owned by towns in their corporate capacity; one hundred and forty-seven by proprietors; and one hundred and forty-five by school districts. Of two hundred and eighty school-houses from which full returns were received, including those in Providence, twenty-five were in very good repair; sixty-two were in ordinary repair; and eighty-six were pronounced totally unfit for school purposes; sixty-five were located in the public highway, and one hundred and eighty directly on the line of the road, without any yard, or out-buildings attached; and but twenty-one had a play-ground inclosed. In over two hundred school-rooms, the average height was less than eight feet, without any opening in the ceiling, or other effectual means for ventilation; the seats and desks were calculated for more than two pupils, arranged on two or three sides of the room, and in most instances, where the results of actual measurement was given, the highest seats were over eighteen inches from the floor, and the lowest, except in twenty-five schools, were over fourteen inches for the youngest pupils, and these seats were unprovided with backs. Two hundred and seventy schools were unfurnished with a clock, blackboard, or thermometer, and only five were provided with a scraper and mat for the feet."

"Such was the condition of most of the places where the public schools were kept in the winter of 1843–44, in the counties of Kent, Washington and Newport, and in not a few districts in the counties of Providence and Bristol. In some districts, an apartment in an old shop or dwelling-house was fitted up as a school-room; and in eleven towns, the school-houses, such as they were, were owned by proprietors, to whom in many instances, the districts paid in rent a larger amount than would have been the interest on the cost of a new and commodious school house. Since the passage of the Act of January, 1844, empowering school districts to purchase, repair, build and furnish school-houses, and since public attention was called to the evils and inconvenience of the old structures, and to better plans of construction and internal arrangement, by public addresses, and the circulation of documents, the work of renovation in this department of school improvement has gone on rapidly. If the same progress can be made for three years more, Rhode Island can show, in proportion to the number of school districts; more specimens of good houses, and fewer dilapidated, inconvenient and unhealthy structures of this kind, than any other state. To bring about thus early this great and desirable result, I can suggest nothing beyond the vigorous prosecution of the same measures which have proved so successful during the past two years.

1. The public mind in the backward districts must be aroused to an active sense of the close connection of a good school-house with a good school, by addresses, discussions, conversation and printed documents on the subject, and by the actual results of such houses in neighboring districts and towns.

2. Men of wealth and intelligence in their several neighborhoods, and capitalists, in villages where they have a pecuniary interest, can continue to exert their influence in this department of improvement.

3. School committees of every town can refuse to draw orders in favor of any district which will not provide a healthy and convenient school-room for the children of the district; and to approve plans for the repairs of an old, or the construction of a new house, which are to be paid for by a tax on the property of the district, unless such plans embrace the essential features of a good school-house.

4. The Commissioner of Public Schools must continue to furnish gratuitously, plans and directions for the construction and arrangement of school-houses, and to call the attention of builders and committees to such structures as can be safely designated as models.

Districts should make regulations to preserve the school-house and appendages from injury or defacement, and authorizing the trustees to make all necessary repairs, without the formality of a special vote on the subject."

MICHIGAN.

Extracts *from "Annual Report of the Superintendent (Hon. Ira Mayhew,) of Public Instruction of the State of Michigan, submitted December* 10, 1847."

"The *place* where our country's youth receive their first instruction, and where nineteen twentieths of them complete their scholastic training claims early attention. We may then profitably dwell upon the condition of our common school-houses.

In some instances school-houses are favorably located, being situated on dry, hard ground, in a retired though central part of the district, in the midst of a natural or artificial grove. But they are usually located without reference to taste, or the health and comfort of teacher or children. They are generally on one corner of public roads, and sometimes adjacent to a cooper's shop, or between a blacksmith's shop and a saw-mill. They are not unfrequently placed upon an acute angle, where a road forks, and sometimes in turning that angle the travel is chiefly behind the school-house, leaving it on a small triangle, bounded on all sides by public roads.

At other times the school-house is situated on a low and worthless piece of ground, with a sluggish stream of water in its vicinity, which sometimes even passes under the school-house. The comfort and health even of children are thus sacrificed to the parsimony of their parents.

Scholars very generally step from the school-house directly into the highway. Indeed, school-houses are frequently one half in the highway, and the other half in the adjacent field, as though they were unfit for either. This is the case even in some of our principal villages.

School-houses are sometimes situated in the middle of the highway, a portion of the travel being on each side of them. When scholars are engaged in their recreations, they are exposed to bleak winds and the inclemency of the weather one portion of the year, and the scorching rays of the meridian sun another portion. Moreover, their recreations must be conducted in the street, or they trespass upon their neighbors' premises. Such situations can hardly be expected to exert the most favorable influence upon the habits and character of the rising generation. * *

Although there is a great variety in the dimensions of school-houses, yet there are few less than sixteen by eighteen feet on the ground, and fewer still larger than twenty-four by thirty feet. Exclusive of entry and closets, when they are furnished with these appendages, school-houses are not usually larger than twenty by twenty-four feet on the ground, and seven feet in height. They are, indeed, more frequently smaller than larger. School-houses of these dimensions have a capacity of three thousand three hundred and sixty cubic feet, and are usually occupied by at least forty-five scholars in the winter season. Not unfrequently sixty or seventy, and occasionally more than a hundred scholars occupy a room of this size.

A simple arithmetical computation will abundantly satisfy any person who is acquainted with the composition of the atmosphere, the influence of respiration upon its fitness to sustain animal life, and the quantity of air that enters the lungs at each inspiration, that a school-room of the preceding dimensions does not contain a sufficient quantity of air to sustain the healthy respiration of even *forty-five* scholars, three hours, the usual length of each session; and frequently the school-house is imperfectly ventilated between the sessions at noon, or indeed, for several days in succession.

The ordinary facilities for ventilating school-rooms, are opening a door, or raising the lower sash of the windows. The prevailing practice with refrence to their ventilation, is opening and closing the door, as the scholars enter and pass out of the school-house, before school, during the recesses, and at noon. Ventilation, *as such*, I may safely say, has not hitherto been practiced in one school in fifty. It is true, the door has been occasionally set open a few minutes, and the windows have been raised, but the object has been, either to let the *smoke* pass out of the room, or to *cool* it when it has become *too warm*, not TO VENTILATE IT. Ventilation, by opening a door or raising the windows, is imperfect, and frequently injurious. A more effectual and safer method of ventilation, is to lower the upper sash of the windows, or, in very cold or stormy weather, to open a ventilator in the ceiling, and allow the vitiated air to escape into the attic. In this case, there should be a free communication between the attic and the outer air, by means of a lattice window, or otherwise. A ventilator may be constructed in connection with the chimney, by carrying up a partition in the middle. One half the chimney, in this case, may be used for a smoke flue, and the other half for a ventilator.

There are few school-houses the internal construction of which is in all respects alike; yet, by far the majority of them will rank in one of the three following classes:

1. The first class embraces those which are constructed with one or two tiers of desks along each side of the house, and across one end of it; the outer seat having the wall of the house for its back, and the front of each tier of desks constituting the back to the next inner seat. There is usually an alley on each side of the house and at the end of it, leaving the seats of sufficient length to accommodate from five to eight scholars. Those sitting next the alleys can pass to and from their seats without discommoding others. All the rest, (usually not less than three-fourths the entire number,) disturb from one to five or six scholars every time they pass to or from their seats; unless, (which is about as commonly practiced, especially with the scholars most distant from the alleys,) they *climb over the desks* in front of them.

Occasionally the desks are shorter, accommodating three or four scholars; and, sometimes, they are intended to accommodate two scholars only, so that each of them, (excepting the outer ones at the end desks,) sits adjacent to an alley, and can pass to and from his seat without disturbing others. There is usually a desk, or table, for the teacher's use, (or at least a *place* for one,) at the end of the house not occupied by the cross seats.

2. The second class embraces those in which the desks extend across the house, with an alley through the middle of it lengthwise, and occasionally one around the outside of the room. All the desks of the second class front the teacher's desk or table.

3. The third class embraces those which are constructed with a row of desks along each side of the house, and across one end of it, the desks fronting the walls of the house, so that the backs of the scholars, while sitting at them, are turned towards the teacher. In this class of houses there are usually three long seats without backs, just within the desks. Sometimes the seats are joined at the corners so as to continue unbroken, twice the length of the house and once its width, a distance of forty-five or fifty feet. There is usually a second tier of seats, and sometimes desks within them, fronting the central part of the room.

There is one impropriety in the construction of a majority of school-houses. The desks are generally constructed with close fronts extending to the floor, whereby a free circulation of air, and consequent equilibrium of temperature, are interrupted, which would take place were the seats and desks so arranged as to allow suitable channels of communication. The scholars behind the desks are necessarily troubled with cold feet, unless the room is kept too warm. Were this evil removed, the first class, with short desks, would constitute a very comfortable and convenient arrangement, except from the circumstance that the children are placed opposite each other, which is a serious evil, especially where both sexes are in the same room, as is the case in nearly all of our common schools.

Another objection to long desks, is the inconvenience to which the scholars are subjected in passing to and from their seats. This objection exists to a considerable extent in the second class of houses, especially where there is not an alley around the outside of the room. Were it not for this inconvenience,—which might be obviated by introducing a greater number of alleys and shortening the desks, so as to accommodate but two scholars, each of whom would sit adjacent to an alley, and could pass to and from his seat without disturbing others—the *second* would, in my judgment, constitute the preferable plan. All the scholars should face the teacher, but none of them should face each other. This is particularly important where both sexes attend the same school.

And what shall I say of the third class?—I can readily enumerate some of its inconveniences, but its real advantages are, in my opinion, few. The following are some of the inconveniences: 1. There is little or no uniformity, usually, in the position of the scholars. Some of them face the walls, others the inner part of the room, and others still sit astride the seat. 2. When the teacher desires the attention of the school, a portion of the scholars must either turn about, or sit with their backs towards him, while he addresses them. 3. In changing their positions in foul weather, the scholars are apt to muddy the seats, and the clothes of those who sit adjacent to them. 4. The change of position is frequently embarrassing to the girls. 5. Front lights are less pleasant, and more injurious to the eyes, than side lights or back ones are. 6. Sitting on a plane seat, without a back, is uncomfortable, and often engenders disease of the spine, especially in childhood and youth.

The principal supposed advantage of this construction is, I believe, that it affords the teacher a better opportunity for detecting the scholars when engaged in mischief. I do not see how any material advantage of this kind can exist, till the bodies of children become transparent.

But were the *supposed* advantage real, it seems to me to be tempting children to do wrong, to give the teacher an opportunity of displaying his skill in detecting them. When children cannot see their teacher, they frequently think he cannot see them, and conduct accordingly.

There are several inconveniences not yet specified, existing to a less or greater extent, in each of the three classes of houses I have described.

1. The height of the seats, although sometimes adjusted with great care, is frequently determined without any apparent regard to the size and comfort of the scholars who are to occupy them. I have visited many schools in which the majority of the scholars reverse the ordinary practice of *standing up* and *sitting down*. They literally *sit up* and *stand down*, their heads being higher while *sitting* than when *standing*.

2. The desks, with their close fronts, are frequently several inches too high. I have visited many schools in which all that could be seen of a majority of the scholars occupying the back seats, was a *part of their heads*, and that, too, when they sat erect upon their seats. The desks, moreover, are frequently inclined twenty-five or thirty degrees, so that a book laid upon them immediately slides off. An inclination of one inch to the foot will be found more convenient than greater obliquity. A space of three inches on the most distant portion of the desk, should be left horizontal, for inkstands, pencils, pens, etc.

3. The floor is sometimes considerably inclined, for the purpose, I suppose, of giving the teacher a better opportunity of seeing the more distant scholars. The whole school is not only subjected to the inconvenience of walking up and down an inclined plane, but what is much worse, when scholars sit upon their seats, and rest their feet upon the floor, when within reach, they are constantly sliding from under them.

School-houses are not generally furnished with suitable conveniences for disposing of the loose wearing apparel of the scholars, their dinners, etc. There are sometimes a few nails or shelves, in a common entry, through which all the scholars pass, upon which a portion of their clothes may be hung or laid, and where dinners may be deposited. But in such cases, the outside door is usually left open, the rain and snow beat in, and the scholars, in haste to get their own clothes, frequently pull down as many more, which are trampled under foot. Moreover, the dinners are frozen, and not unfrequently they are devoured by dogs, and even by the hogs that run in the street. But the majority of school-houses are not furnished with an entry; and where there is one, frequently not even a nail can be found in it, upon which a single article of clothing may be hung. Neither are there nails or shelves for this purpose within the school-room. Scholars generally are obliged to throw their clothes across the desks, upon the seats, or into the windows.

School-houses are generally warmed by means of stoves, some of which are in a good condition, and supplied with dry wood from the wood-house. The instances, however, in which such facilities for warming exist, are comparatively few. It is much more common to see cracked and broken stoves, the doors without either hinges or latch, and rusty pipe of various sizes. Green wood, and that which is old and partly decayed, either drenched with rain or covered with snow, is much more frequently used for fuel, than sound, seasoned wood, protected from the weather by a suitable wood-house. With this state of things, it is difficult to kindle a fire, which burns poorly, at best, when kindled. The room is filled with smoke a considerable part of the time, especially in stormy weather. The school is frequently interrupted two or three times a day, to fasten together and tie up the stove pipe. This may seem a little like exaggeration. I know there are many exceptions. But in a majority of instances some of these inconveniences exist, and the most of them are united in more cases than people are aware of. I have heard trustees and patrons who have visited their school with me, for the first time in several years, say, "We ought to have some dry wood to kindle with;" "I did'nt know as it was so smoky;" "We must get some new pipe; really our stove is getting dangerous," etc. And some of the boys have relieved the embarrassment of their parents by saying, "It don't smoke near as bad to-day as it does sometimes."

The principal reason why the stoves in our school-houses are so cracked and broken, and why the pipes are so rusty and open, lies in the circumstance that *green wood from the snow bank*, is used for fuel, instead of *dry wood from the wood-house.* There are at least three reasons why this is poor policy.

1. It takes at least double the amount of wood. A considerable portion of the otherwise sensible heat becomes latent in the conversion of ice, snow and moisture into steam.

2. The steam thus generated cracks the stove and rusts the pipe, so that they will not last one half as long as though dry wood from the wood-house were used. And,

3. It is impossible to preserve an even temperature. Sometimes it is too cold, and at other times it is too warm. Several teachers have informed me that in order to keep their fires from going out, it was necessary to have their stoves constantly full of wood, that a portion of it might be seasoning while the rest was burning. Moreover, very offensive and injurious gases are generated in this manner.

There are, perhaps, in the majority of school-houses, a pail for water, cup, and broom, and a chair for the teacher. Some one or more of these are frequently wanting. I need hardly say every school-house should be supplied with them all. In addition to these, every school-house should be furnished with the following articles:—1. An evaporating dish for the stove, which should be supplied with clean pure water. 2. A thermometer, by which the temperature of the room may be regulated. 3. A clock, by which the time of beginning and closing school, and conducting all its exercises, may be governed. 4. A shovel and tongs. 5. An ash-pail and ash-house. For want of these, much filth is frequently suffered to accumulate in and about the school-house, and not unfrequently the house itself takes fire and burns down. 6. A wood-house, well supplied with seasoned wood. 7. A well, with provisions not only for drinking, but for the cleanliness of pupils. 8. At last, though not least, in this connection, two privies, in the rear of the school-house, separated by a high close fence, one for the boys and the other for the girls. For want o. these indispensable appendages of civilization, the delicacy of children is frequently offended, and their morals corrupted. Nay, more, the un natural detention of the *fæces*, when nature calls for an evacuation, is frequently the foundation for chronic diseases, and the principal cause of permanent ill health, resulting not unfrequently in premature death.

In architectural appearance, school-houses have more resembled barns, sheds for cattle, or mechanic shops, than Temples of Science,—windows are broken—benches are mutilated—desks are cut up—wood is unprovided—out buildings are neglected—obscene images and vulgar delineations meet the eye without and within—the plastering is smoked and patched—the roof is so open as to let in a flood of water in a storm, sufficient to drown out a school, were not the floor equally open."

We close this mass of testimony as to the deplorable condition of the common, or public school-houses in States where public instruction has received the most attention, with an extract from a "*Report on School-houses published by order of the Directors of the Essex County Teachers' Association in* 1833."

"There is one subject more to which we must be permitted to refer. One in which the morals of the young are intimately connected, one in which parents, instructors, and scholars, should unite their efforts to produce a reform; there should be nothing in or about school-houses, calculated to defile the mind, corrupt the heart, or excite unholy and forbidden appetites; yet considering the various character of those brought together in our public schools, and considering also how inventive are corrupt minds, in exhibiting openly the defilement which reigns within, we do not know but we must expect that school-houses, as well as other public buildings, and even fences, will continue to bear occasional marks both of lust and profaneness. But we must confess that the general apathy which apparently exists on this subject, does appear strange to us. It is a humbling fact, that in many of these houses, there are highly indecent, profane, and libidinous marks, images and expressions, some of which are spread out in broad characters on the walls, where they unavoidably meet the eyes of all who come into the house, or being on the outside, salute the traveler as he passes by, wounding the delicate, and annoying the moral sensibilities of the heart. While there is still a much greater number in smaller character, upon the tables and seats of the students, and even in some instances, of the instructors, constantly before the eyes of those who happen to occupy them. How contaminating these must be, no one can be entirely insensible. And yet how unalarmed, or if not entirely unalarmed, how little is the mind of community directed to the subject, and how little effort put forth to stay this fountain of corruption. We will mention as evidence of the public apathy, one house which we suppose is this day, it certainly was a few months since, defiled by images and expressions of the kind referred to, spread out in open observation upon its walls, which are known to have been there for eight or ten years. In this building during all this time, the summer and winter schools have been kept; here the district have held their business meetings; here frequently has been the singing-school; here, too, religious meetings have often been held; here, too, the school committee, the fathers, mothers, and friends of the children, have come to witness the progress of their children in knowledge and virtue; all of whom must have witnessed, and been ashamed of their defilement, and yet no effectual effort has been put forth to remove them.

The following views are engraved from "Daguerreotype Likenesses" of two district school-houses in Connecticut, *as they were in* 1852, and in which schools were not taught, but "*kept according to law.*" Although a good work has been accomplished within their walls, in years which go back beyond the memory of the oldest inhabitant, they are now neither attractive without, or convenient within.

Perspective of Mr. John Kingsbury's Female Seminary, Providence, R. I.

II. GENERAL PRINCIPLES OF SCHOOL ARCHITECTURE.

1. A location, healthy, accessible from all parts of the district; retired from the dust, noise, and danger of the highway; attractive, from its choice of sun and shade, and commanding, in one or more directions, the cheap, yet priceless educating influences of fine scenery.

2. A site large enough to admit of a yard in front of the building, either common to the whole school or appropriated to greensward, flowers and shrubbery, and two yards in the rear, one for each sex, properly inclosed, and fitted up with rotary swings, and other means of recreation and exercise, and with privies, which a civilized people never neglect.

3. Separate entrances to the school-room for each sex; each entrance distinct from the front door, and fitted up with scraper, mats, and old broom for the feet; with hooks, shelves, &c., for hats, overcoats, over-shoes, and umbrellas; with sink, pump, basin and towels, and with brooms and duster, and all the means and appliances necessary to secure habits of order, neatness and cleanliness.

4. School-room, in addition to the space required by aisles and the teacher's platform, sufficient to accommodate with a seat and desk, not only each scholar in the district who is in the habit of attending school, but all who may be entitled to attend; with verge enough to receive the children of industrious, thoughtful, and religious families, who are sure to be attracted to a district which is blessed with a good school-house and a good school.

5. At least one spare room for recitation, library, and other uses, to every school-room, no matter how small the school may be.

6. An arrangement of the windows, so as to secure one blank wall, and at the same time, the cheerfulness and warmth of the sunlight, at all times of the day, with arrangements to modify the same by blinds, shutters, or curtains.

7. Apparatus for warming, by which a large quantity of pure air from outside of the building can be moderately heated, and introduced into the room without passing over a red-hot iron surface, and distributed equally to different parts of the room.

8. A cheap, simple, and efficient mode of ventilation, by which the air in every part of a school-room, which is constantly becoming vitiated by respiration, combustion, or other causes, may be constantly flowing out of the room, and its place filled by an adequate supply of fresh air drawn from a pure source, and admitted into the room at the right temperature, of the requisite degree of moisture, and without any perceptible current.

9. A desk with at least two feet of top surface, and in no case for more than two pupils, inclined towards the front edge one inch in a foot, except two to three inches of the most distant portion, which should be level, and covered with cloth to prevent noise—fitted with an ink-pot (supplied with a lid and a pen-wiper,) and a slate, with a pencil-holder and a sponge attached, and supported by end-pieces or

stanchions, curved so as to be convenient for sweeping, and to admit of easy access to the seat—these of varying heights for small and large pupils, the front edge of each desk being from seven to nine inches (seven for the lowest and nine for the highest,) higher than the front edge of the seat or chair attached.

10. A chair or bench for each pupil, and in no case for more than two, unless separated by an aisle, with a seat hollowed like an ordinary chair, and varying in height from ten to seventeen inches from the outer edge to the floor, so that each pupil, when properly seated, can rest his feet on the floor without the muscles of the thigh pressing hard upon the front edge of the seat, and with a support for the muscles of the back, rising above the shoulder-blades.

11. An arrangement of the seats and desks, so as to allow of an aisle or free passage of at least two feet around the room, and between each range of seats for two scholars, and so as to bring each scholar under the supervision of the teacher.

12. Arrangements for the teacher, such as a separate closet for his overcoat, &c., a desk for his papers, a library of books of reference, maps, apparatus, and all such instrumentalities by which his capacities for instruction may be made in the highest degree useful.

13. Accommodations for a school library for consultation and circulation among the pupils, both at school and as a means of carrying on the work of self-education at their homes, in the field, or the workshop, after they have left school.

14. A design in good taste and fit proportion, in place of the wretched perversions of architecture, which almost universally characterize the district school-houses of New England.

15. While making suitable accommodation for the school, it will be a wise, and, all things considered, an economical investment, on the part of many districts, to provide apartments in the same building, or in its neighborhood, for the teacher and his family. This arrangement will give character and permanence to the office of teaching, and at the same time secure better supervision for the school-house and premises, and more attention to the manners of the pupils out of school. Provision for the residence of the teacher, and not unfrequently a garden for his cultivation, is made in connection with the parochial schools in Scotland, and with the first class of public schools in Germany.

16. Whenever practicable, the privies should be disconnected from the play-ground, and be approached from a covered walk. Perfect seclusion, neatness and propriety should be strictly observed in relation to them.

17. A shed, or covered walk, or the basement story paved under feet, and open for free circulation of air for the boys, and an upper room with the floor deafened and properly supported for calisthenic exercises for the girls, is a desirable appendage to every school.

III. PLANS OF SCHOOL-HOUSES.

In determining the details of construction and arrangement for a school-house, due regard must, of course, be had to the varying circumstances of country and city, of a large and a small number of scholars, of schools of different grades, and of different systems of instruction.

1. In by far the largest number of country districts as they are now situated, there will be but one school-room, with a smaller room for recitations and other purposes needed. This must be arranged and fitted up for scholars of all ages, for the varying circumstances of a summer and of a winter school, and for other purposes, religious and secular, than those of a school, and in every particular of construction and arrangement, the closest economy of material and labor must be studied. A union of two or more districts for the purpose of maintaining in each a school for the younger children, and in the center of the associated districts a school for the older children of all or, what would be better, a consolidation of two or more districts into one, for these and all other school purposes, would do away with the almost insuperable difficulties which now exist in country districts, in the way of comfortable and attractive school-houses, as well as of thoroughly governed and instructed schools.

2. In small villages, or populous country districts, at least two school-rooms should be provided, and as there will be other places for public meetings of various kinds, each room should be appropriated and fitted up exclusively for the use of the younger or the older pupils. It is better, on many accounts, to have two schools on the same floor, than one above the other.

3. In large villages and cities, a better classification of the schools can be adopted, and, of course, more completeness can be given to the construction and arrangement of the buildings and rooms appropriated to each grade of schools. This classification should embrace at least three grades—viz. Primary, with an infant department; Secondary, or Grammar; Superior, or High Schools. In manufacturing villages, and in certain sections of large cities, regularly organized Infant Schools should be established and devoted mainly to the culture of the morals, manners, language and health of very young children.

4. The arrangement as to supervision, instruction and recitations, must have reference to the size of the school; the number of teachers and assistants; the general organization of the school, whether in one room for study, and separate class rooms for recitation, or the several classes in distinct rooms under appropriate teachers, each teacher having specified studies; and the method of instruction pursued, whether the mutual, simultaneous, or mixed.

Since the year 1830, and especially since 1838, much ingenuity has been expended by practical teachers and architects, in devising and perfecting plans of school-houses, with all the details of construction and fixtures, modified to suit the varied circumstances enumerated above, specimens of which, with explanations and descriptions, will be here given.

Plans of School-Houses with one School-room.

The largest number of school-houses which are erected with but one school-room, are intended for District, or for Primary Schools.

District School.

By a District School, in this connection, is understood a public school open to all the children of the district, of both sexes, and of the school age recognized by the practice of the district, or the regulations of the school committee of the town to which such district belongs. It is an unclassified school, and is taught in one apartment, by one teacher, usually without any assistance even from older pupils of the school. It varies in the character of its scholars, and its methods of instruction, from summer to winter, and from winter to summer. In summer, the younger children and classes in the elementary studies predominate, and in the winter the older pupils, and classes in the more advanced studies, whilst some of both extremes, as to age and studies, are to be found in both the winter and summer session of the district school. This variety of ages and studies, and consequent variety of classes, increased by the irregularity of attendance, is not only a serious hinderance to the proper arrangement, instruction and government of the school, but presents almost insuperable obstacles to the appropriate construction and furniture of the school-house, which is too often erected on the smallest possible scale of size and expense. A vast amount of physical suffering and discomfort to the pupils is the necessary result of crowding the older and younger pupils into a small apartment, without seats and furniture appropriate to either, and especially when no precaution has been taken to adapt the supply and arrangements of seats and desks according to the varying circumstances of the same school in winter and summer. In every district, or unclassified school, the school-room should be fitted up with seats and desks for the older and younger pupils, sufficient to accommodate the maximum attendance of each class of scholars at any season of the year. And if this cannot be effected, and only a sufficient number of seats can be secured to accommodate the highest number of both sexes in attendance at any one time, then in winter the seats and desks for the smaller children should be removed to the attic, and their place supplied by additional seats and desks for the older pupils; and in summer this arrangement should be reversed.

Primary Schools.

By a Primary School, in our American School Systems, is understood, not generally an Elementary School, embracing a course of instruction for the great mass of the children of the community under fourteen years of age—but specifically, that class or grade of schools which receive only the youngest pupils, and those least advanced in their studies.

Any scheme of school organization will be imperfect which does not include special arrangements for the systematic training and instruction of very young children, especially in all cities, manufacturing villages, and large neighborhoods. Among the population of such places, many parents are sure to be found, who, for want of intelligence or leisure, of constancy and patience, are unfitted to watch the first blossoming of the souls of their children, and to train them to good physical habits, virtuous impulses, and quick and accurate observations; to cleanliness, obedience, openness, mutual kindliness, piety, and all the virtues which wise and far-seeing parents desire for their offspring. The general result of the home training of the children of such parents, is the neglect of all moral culture when such culture is most valuable; and the acquisition of manners, personal habits, and language, which the best school training at a later period of life can with difficulty correct or eradicate. To meet the wants of this class of children, Halls of Refuge and Infant Schools were originally instituted by Oberlin, Owen, and Wilderspin, and now constitute under these names, or the names of Primary Schools, or Primary Departments, a most important branch of elementary education, whether sustained by individual charity, or as part of the organization of public instruction.

No one at all acquainted with the history of education in this country, can doubt that the establishment of the Primary School for children under six years of age, in Boston, in 1818, as a distinct grade of schools, with the modifications which it has since received there, and elsewhere, from the principles and methods of the Infant School system, has led to most important improvements in the quality and quantity of instruction in our public schools, and the sooner a Primary School properly organized, furnished and managed, can be established in every large neighborhood, and especially in the "infected districts" of cities and manufacturing villages, the more rapid and more thorough will be the progress of education.

Location, Yard, and Play Ground.

The site or location of a school-house should be quiet, retired, accessible, attractive, and in all respects healthy. To secure these conditions, no reasonable expense should be spared—for a house thus situated promotes in many ways the highest objects for which a school is instituted.

Noisy and dusty thoroughfares, and the vicinity of places of idle and vicious resort, as well as bleak plains, unsheltered hill tops, and stagnant marshes, should all be avoided, no matter how central, accessible, or cheap the land may be.

In a city or village, a rear lot, with access from two or more streets, will not only be more economical, quiet and safe, but will secure, at the same cost as a narrow front lot, the advantages of a spacious play ground, and admit of the adornments of flower plats, shrubbery, and trees.

In the country, and in small villages, there will be no difficulty, to a liberal and enlightened community or committee, in procuring a spacious lot, attractive from its choice of sun and shade, of trees and flowers, and commanding, in one or more directions, the cheap yet priceless educating influences of fine scenery.

In city or country, a site should be provided, large enough to admit of a yard in front of the building, either common to the whole school, or appropriated to greensward, flowers, and shrubbery, and two yards in the rear, one for each sex, properly graded, inclosed, and fitted up with apparatus for recreation and exercise in all states of the weather, and with privies, which a civilized people never forgets, and in respect to which the most perfect seclusion, neatness, and propriety should be enforced.

The extent to which facilities for gymnastic and calisthenic exercises shall be introduced into the play-ground, must be determined by the circumstances of the school, and mainly by the place which they are to occupy as part of the physical education of the pupils. For purposes of recreation, except in the simplest and cheapest form, and for very young children, and at all times under the direction and supervision of the teacher, who should be specially trained to superintend the exercises and amusements of the play ground, this apparatus has not much value. When pursued at all times, without system, without reference to age, or strength, or the purposes intended, without direction, from day to day for a whole term, the exercises become wearisome, the apparatus is abused, and serious accidents not unfrequently occur. But when gymnastics can be taught and practiced as a regular branch of education—when the more difficult fetes of activity, strength, and endurance, are attained by elementary trials of various sorts, graduated to the age and constitution of each pupil, and so alternated as to keep the interest constantly alive—when walking exercises in the field, or to remarkable places, and even ordinary spots, are occasionally substituted for the military drill, and running, leaping, vaulting, balancing, climbing, and lifting, in the gymnasium—when the incidental acquisition of the moral habits of cleanliness in person, neatness in dress, punctuality, promptitude, and obedience, is made a matter of even greater importance than the direct result of muscular development, an erect and graceful carriage, a firm and regular step, which are the direct objects of these exercises—then, they are truly valuable, and every facility for their introduction should be provided in the play ground. Whenever introduced, the machines and instruments should be constructed of the best material and by the best workmen, for life and limb must not be endangered to save expense in these respects.

The following cuts and description may be useful to an ingenious carpenter, who can not consult a systematic treatise on gymnastics.* The cut which follows, of a play-ground for an infant, or primary school, is copied from Wilderspin's Early Education. We should prefer to see a female teacher presiding over the scene.

* *See* INSTRUCTIONS IN GYMNASTICS, containing a full description of more than eight hundred exercises, and illustrated by five hundred engravings, By J. E. D'Alfonce, late professor of Gymnastics in the Military School in St. Petersburgh, and in Paris. New York: George F. Nesbit & Co., Wall street. 1851.

Play-Ground for an Infant or Primary School.

The house should stand in a dry and airy situation, large enough to allow a spacious play ground. No pains should be spared on this principal and paramount department of a proper infant school. The more extensive the ground may be, the better; but the smallest size for 200 children ought to be 100 feet in length, by at least 60 in breadth. It should be walled round, not so much to prevent the children from straying, as to exclude intruders upon them, while at play: for this purpose, a wall or close paling, not lower than six feet high, will be found sufficient. With the exception of a flower border, from four to six feet broad all round, lay the whole ground, after leveling and draining it thoroughly, with small *binding* gravel, which must be always kept in repair, and well swept of loose stones. Watch the gravel, and prevent the children making holes in it to form pools in wet weather; dress the flower border, and keep it always neat; stock it well with flowers and shrubs, and make it as gay and beautiful as possible. Train on the walls cherry and other fruit trees and currant bushes; place some ornaments and tasteful decorations in different parts of the border—as a honeysuckle bower, &c., and separate the dressed ground from the graveled area by a border of strawberry plants, which may be protected from the feet of the children by a skirting of wood on the outside, three inches high, and painted green, all round the ground. Something even approaching to elegance in the dressing and decking of the playground, will afford a lesson which may contribute to refinement and comfort for life. It will lead not only to clean and comfortable dwellings, but to a taste for decoration and beauty, which will tend mainly to expel coarseness, discomfort, dirt, and vice, from the economy of the humbler classes.

For the excellent and safe exercise afforded by the *Rotary Swing*, erect, at the distance of thirty feet from each other, two posts or masts, from sixteen to eighteen feet high above the ground; nine inches diameter at the foot, diminishing to seven and a half at top; of good well-seasoned, hard timber; charred with fire, about three feet under ground, fixed in sleepers, and bound at top with a strong iron hoop. In the middle of the top of the post is sunk perpendicularly a cylindrical hole, ten inches deep, and two inches in diameter, made strong by an iron ring two inches broad within the top, and by a piece of iron an inch thick to fill up the bottom, tightly fixed in. A strong pivot of iron, of diameter to turn easily in the socket described, but with as little lateral play as possible, is placed vertically in the hole, its upper end standing 4 inches above it. On this pivot, as an axle, and close to the top of the post, but so as to turn easily, is fixed a wheel of iron, twenty-four inches diameter, strengthened by four

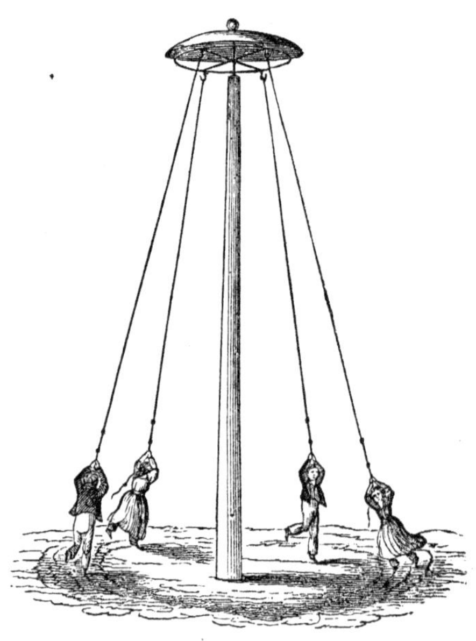

Rotary Swing.

spokes, something like a common roasting-jack wheel, but a little larger. The rim should be flat, two inches broad, and half an inch thick. In this rim are six holes or eyes, in which rivet six strong iron hooks, made *to turn in the holes*, to prevent the rope from twisting. To these hooks are fixed six well-chosen ropes, an inch diameter, and each reaching down to within two feet of the ground, having half-a-dozen knots, or small wooden balls, fixed with nails, a foot from each other, beginning at the lower extremity, and ascending to six feet from the ground. A tin cap, like a lamp cover, is placed on the top of the whole machine, fixed to the prolongation of the pivot, and a little larger than the wheel, to protect it from wet. To this, or to the wheel itself, a few waggoners' bells appended, would have a cheerful effect on the children. The operation of this swing must, from the annexed cut, be obvious. Four, or even six children, lay hold of a rope each, as high as they can reach, and, starting at the same instant, run a few steps in the circle, then suspend themselves by their hands, drop their feet and run again when fresh impulse is wanted ; again swing round, and so on. A child of three or four years old, will often fly several times round the circle without touching the ground. There is not a muscle in the body which is not thus exercised ; and to render the exercise equal to both halves of the body, it is important that, after several rounds in one direction, the party should stop, change the hands, and go round in the opposite direction. To prevent fatigue, and to equalize the exercise among the pupils, the rule should be, that each six pupils should have thirty or forty rounds, and resign the ropes to six more, who have counted the rotations.

Toys being discarded as of no use, or real pleasure, the only *plaything* of the playground consists of bricks for building, made of wood, four inches by two and one and a-half. Some hundreds of these, very equally made, should be kept in a large box in a corner of the ground, as the quieter children delight to build houses and castles with them ; the condition, however, always to be, that they shall correctly and conscientiously replace in the box the full complement or *tale* of bricks they take out ; in which rule, too, there is more than one lesson.

In a corner of the playground, concealed by shrubbery, are two water closets for the children, with six or eight seats in each ; that for the boys is separate from, and entered by, a different passage from that for the girls. Supply the closets well with water, which, from a cistern at the upper end, shall run along with a slope under all the seats, into a sewer, or a pit in the ground. See that the closets are in no way misused, or abused. The eye of the teacher and mistress should often be here, for the sake both of cleanliness and delicacy. Mr. Wilderspin recommends the closets being built adjoining the small class-room, with small apertures for the teacher's eye in the class-room wall, covered with a spring lid, and commanding the range of the place. There is nothing in which children, especially in the humbler ranks, require more training.

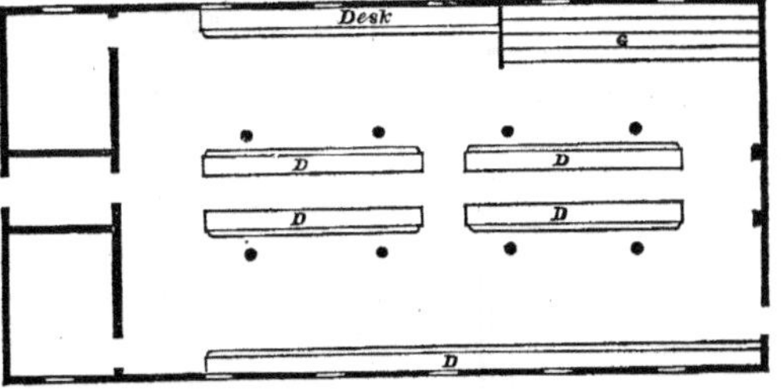

The annexed cut represents an infant school-room, modified in a few unimportant particulars, from the ground plan recommended by Mr. Wilderspin in his "*Early Education*," published in 1840. The original plan embraces a dwelling for the teacher's family, and two school-rooms, one for the boys and the other for the girls, each school having a gallery, class-room, and playground. The school-room is about 60 feet long by 38 wide, and the class-rooms each 13 ft. by 10. D. Desks and Seats. G. Gallery, capable of accommodating 100 children.

The chief requisites in an infant-school play-ground are the following: A Climbing Stand; a Horizontal Bar; Parallel Bars; Wooden Swings; a Double Inclined Plane.

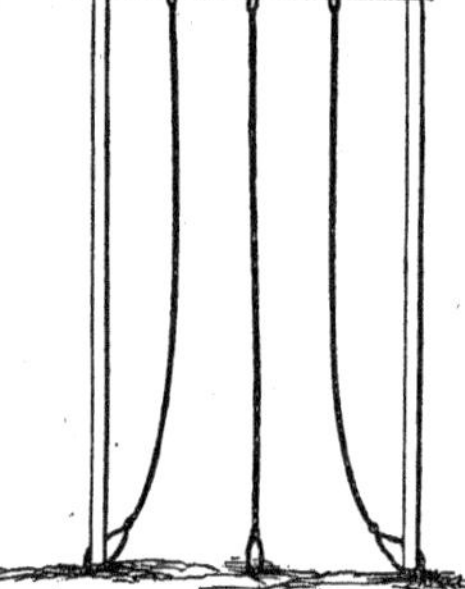

The Climbing Stand consists essentially of a frame-work of poles, which support ropes for climbing. One of the most simple and economical is made of two ordinary scaffold poles, planed smooth and painted, which support a transverse beam having hooks, to which the ropes are attached.

The dimensions may be as follows: Length of perpendicular poles, 15 feet, of which 4 feet are sunk in the ground; circumference of poles at the surface of the ground, 14 inches; length of transverse beam at top, 9 feet. To this beam are attached, by screwing in, two iron hooks, which support the ropes; these are 1½ inches in diameter, to afford a firm grasp to the hand. In order that the ropes may not wear through where attached to the hooks, they are spliced round an iron ring, which is grooved on the outer surface to give a firmer hold to the rope. Both the ropes should be attached to the bottom of the poles so as to hang loosely: if not fastened at the bottom, the children use them as swings while clinging to them, and are apt to injure themselves by falling, or others by coming violently in contact with them.

No apparatus is more advantageous: it is economical in its erection, and not liable to get out of order; it affords exercise to a number of children at the same time, a succession being constantly engaged in climbing and descending the ropes and poles; the muscular exertion is not violent, but decidedly beneficial, expanding the chest, and giving power and freedom of motion to the arms. This exercise is also quite free from danger, the children never advancing higher up the ropes than they feel themselves secure. During the seven years the Home and Colonial Infant-school has been established, 200 children have been the average attendance, but no accidents have occurred from the use of the climbing-stand.

The Horizontal Bar consists of a wooden bar formed of beech, red deal, or some other tough wood not apt to splinter or warp, about three inches in diameter, and usually six feet long, turned or planed round and smooth, in order that the hands may not be blistered by the friction.

Every play-ground should possess two or three of these useful additions; one 6 feet from the ground, another 5 feet, and a third 4 feet high,—each one being supported and fixed firmly by a post at both ends. Or they may be arranged so that four posts will support the three bars. The exercises performed on the horizontal bars consist in the child remaining suspended by the arms and hands; in drawing the body up so as to look over the bar several times in succession; in traversing from one end of the bar to the other (suspended by the hands,) both backwards and forwards; in swinging the body whilst suspended from the bar.

The Parallel Bar consists of two bars placed parallel with one another, each being from 6 to 8 feet long, 4 inches deep by 2 inches wide, with the corners rounded off. The posts that support these bars in their position should be 18 inches apart. The bars should project four inches beyond the post. Two sets of parallel bars are advantageous, one being 2 feet 9 inches high for the younger children, the other 4 feet high for the elder.

The exercises on these bars consist in supporting the body on the arms, one hand resting on each bar, and by moving each hand alternately, proceeding forwards and backwards along the bars; in swinging the body between the arms; and in springing over the bar on each side, both backwards and forwards.

The Wooden Springs afford a kind of exercise extremely popular with the younger children, who are not sufficiently active to take part in the other exercises. Each swing consists of two distinct parts: 1. A piece of 2-inch deal, 1 foot wide and 3 feet long, one end of which is sunk firmly in the ground, the other projecting 18 inches above the surface. At each edge of this piece is screwed on an iron plate, with an eye to receive the iron pivot on which the upper piece works. The upper, or horizontal piece, is made of 2-inch plank, 1 foot wide and 12 feet long. At each end of this piece three handles, formed of 1½-inch deal, are strongly mortised in, 1 foot apart, thus forming seats for three children at each end. Between the handles the plank should be rounded at the edges, so as to form an easy seat. At the under surface of each end a small block of wood is fixed, to prevent the plank wearing by striking the ground.

The above directions should be adhered to. If the support be made lower, the motion of the swing is much lessened; if the plank be made shorter, or the support higher, the swing approaches too nearly to the perpendicular, and serious accidents may ensue from the children being thrown violently from the seats. The whole should be made as stout as recommended, otherwise it is apt to break from the violent action.

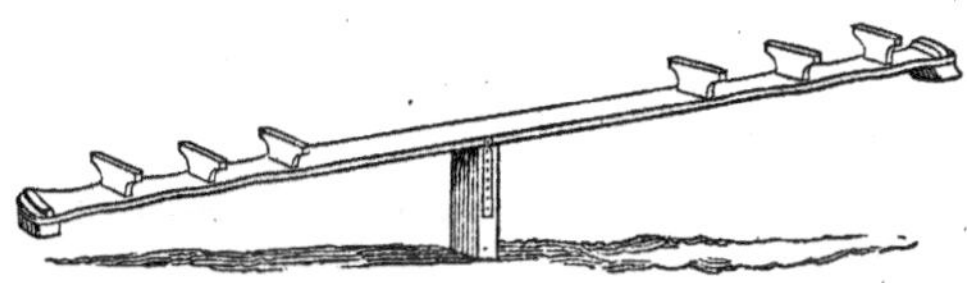

The Double Inclined Plane is adapted more especially for the younger children. It consists merely of a support of two-inch deal, 1 foot wide, and projecting 3 feet from the ground. On this is laid the ends of two planks, each 12 feet long, 1 foot wide, and 1½ inch in thickness. On the upper surface of each plank may be nailed, at intervals of eight or ten inches, small cross-pieces, to prevent the feet slipping.

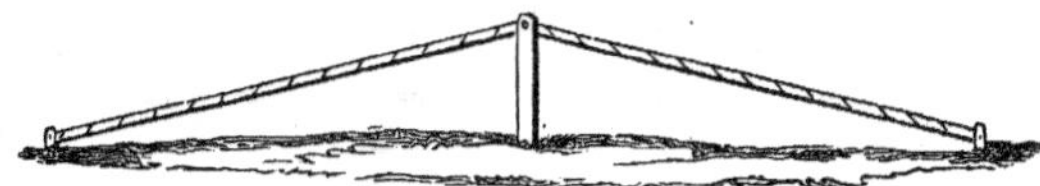

The use of the inclined plane is, that by ascending and descending it, children acquire a facility in balancing themselves. The exercise is beneficial, as it calls into action the muscles of the legs and even of the body. It also furnishes an excellent situation to jump from, as the children can themselves vary the height of the leap at pleasure.

The general use of all these various exercises is, that the different muscles of the body may be strengthened, and the children thus fitted for a future life of labor, and better prepared to escape in case of accidents

In addition to these simple appliances of the playground, and which are particularly adapted to young children, there are a variety of gymnastic machines or apparatus, designed for the systematic exercise of the entire physical organization of scholars, some of which it would be desirable to provide in some sheltered position of the yard, in all city schools, but which should be accessible only under strict regulations, and the instructions of a well-trained master. As an illustration both of the machines and their arrangement, we give below engravings of the ground plan and principal machines of the gymnasium attached to the Collegiate and Commercial Institute—a private school of the highest grade of William H. Russell, of New Haven—which has the best apparatus which has fallen under our observation in this country.

In the large cut, there will be observed a partition running across the building, near the stove and staircase *W*. This marks the limit of a boarded platform at this end, upon which arrangements may be made for a dressing-room, or at least for clothes pegs.

As the letters upon the cuts of single machines designate the same machines in the larger engraving, the descriptions which we will give of them will apply to both.

The *wooden horse*, *A*, is a log, which may be, if preferred, rudely fashioned like a horse's body, and is set upon four legs, about breast high. Two cross-

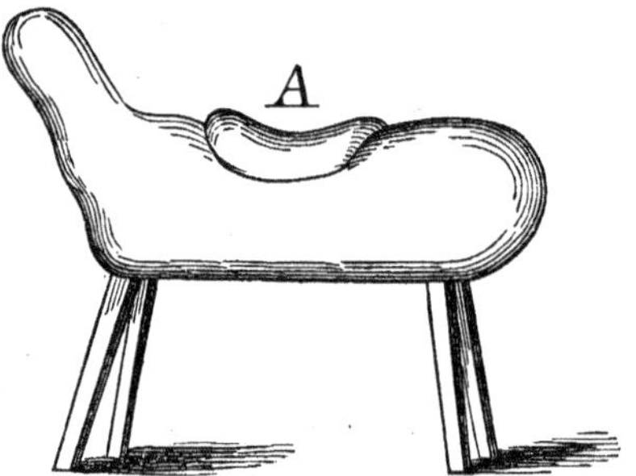

pieces, which do not appear in the cut, should be set transversely in the places of the pommel and cantle of the saddle, raised high enough to allow of being well grasped by the hand, and rounded over the top. The exercises upon this machine are leaps and vaulting with the help of the hands, which are set upon the above cross-pieces, or on various parts of the machine. *B*, is a *spring-board;* an elastic plank raised upon blocks at the ends, to assist the spring. It is, however, doubtful whether such aids are desirable, for they do not habituate the pupil to the unyielding surface from which leaps must generally be taken. The wooden horse exercises give elasticity and spring to the frames and are useful to riders.

C, is a *slanting ladder*, and *D*, a *horizontal* one. The exercises upon these consist in hanging upon or under them, and passing from one end to the other,

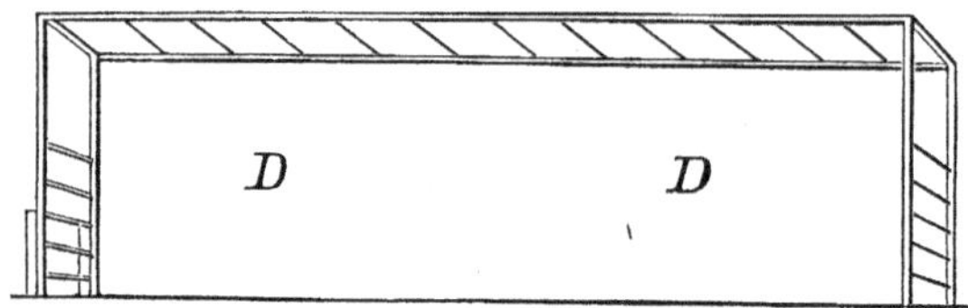

by means of the hands alone, in various ways, and are intended to strengthen the gripe, the arms, and the shoulders. The slanting ladder may run at an angle of about forty-five degrees, from a base about four feet high, to an altitude as great as is convenient.

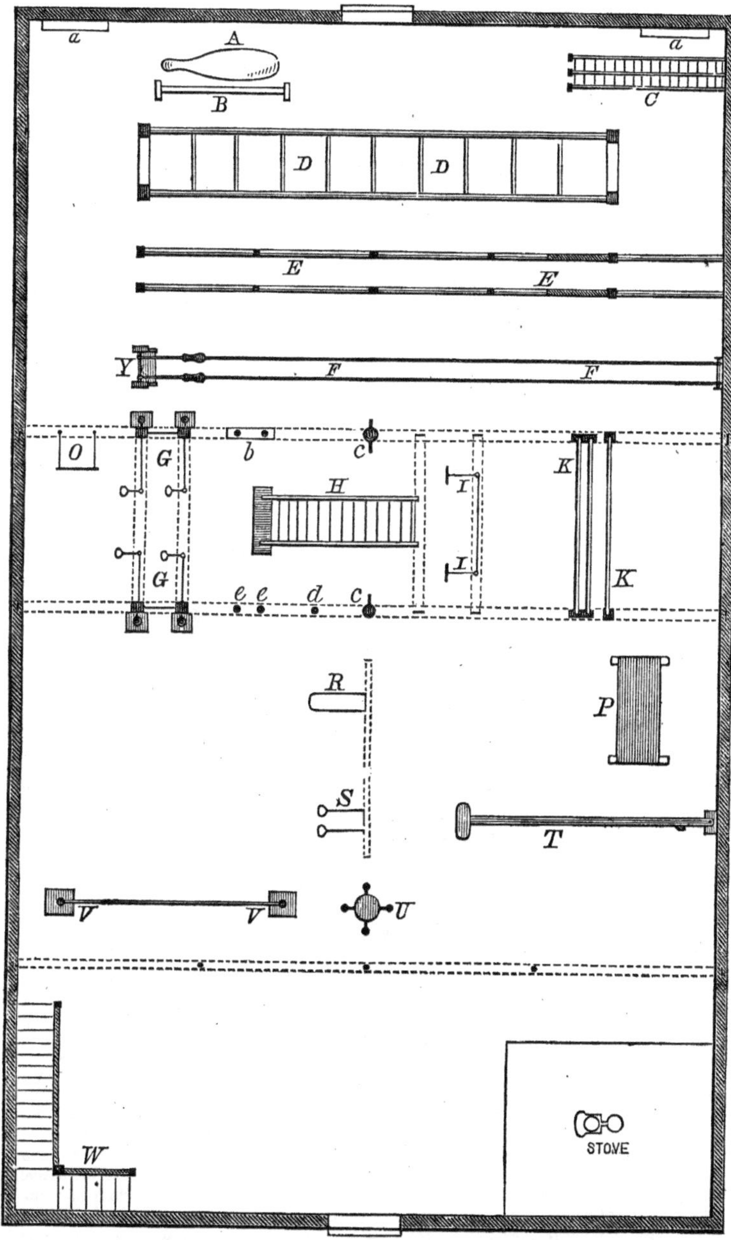

Ground Plan of Gymnasium attached to Russell's Collegiate and Commercial Institute, New Haven.

E, is a pair of *parallel bars*, both horizontal and slanting. The exercises upon this machine widen the shoulders, open the chest, and strengthen that and the

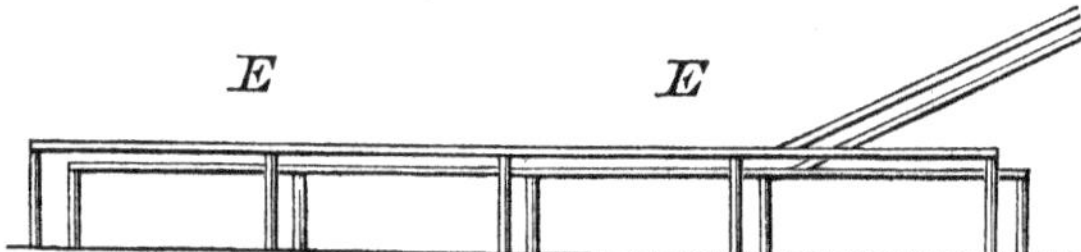

shoulders. They are somewhat difficult, but exceedingly strengthening. The bars are large enough to grasp, say two and a half inches in thickness by three and a half deep, set upon strong uprights, so framed that the uprights at their insertion do not extend beyond the bars. About five feet is a proper height for the upper side of the bars.

F, is a *pair of inclined ropes*, with their sliding-boxes. The windlass at *Y*, with a stout ratchet, is used to keep the ropes strained tight. This machine is not

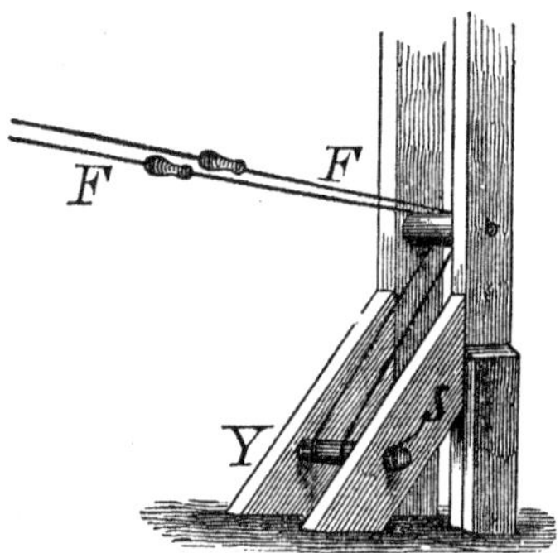

very useful; the principal operation to be performed upon it being to put the sliding-boxes under the arms, and progress up the ropes by swinging the body.

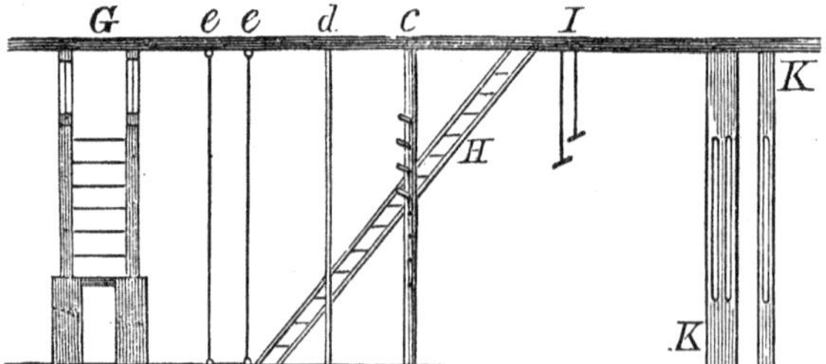

The machines marked *G*, *H*, *I*, *K*, *O*, *c*, *d*, and *e*, are fixed between timbers and cross-pieces, whose places are shown by dotted lines, and the ground. *G*, *G*, are the *weights*. They run in wooden tubes, and are suspended upon ropes, at the other end of which are rings for handles, seen hanging down in the cut. These are used to exercise the arms; and the exercisers upon them are capable of rapidly developing the muscles of the fore arm, upper arm, shoulder and chest. They are performed by drawing or pushing out the weights with the fingers, hands, or feet, in various positions. *H*, is a *slanting ladder*, such as was above described. *I*, is a double running rope, running over two sheaves set in a cross-piece upon

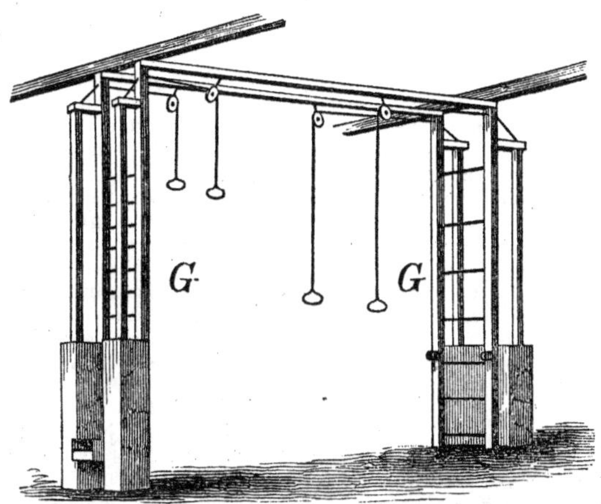

the timbers overhead, and with a stout wooden handle, hung by the middle, at each end; so that these handles hang loose, perhaps six feet apart, and five or six feet from the ground. Two persons, of nearly equal weight, are best fitted to use this machine. One jumps up a few inches, while the other weighs down upon his end of the rope so as to keep it strained tight; and as the first comes down again, the second jumps in his turn; the motion being increased, if desired, until the jumps carry the hands up to the timber overhead, and the lower of the two pupils crouches down to the ground. *K*, is a single and double *vaulting bar*. The bars are movable in slips in the uprights, and are set at any desired height by iron pegs running in holes in the uprights and through the bars. The bars, either alone or together, are used for performing jumps from the ground, with the hands on the bar, and for various other exercises with the feet off the ground. The vaulting exercises strengthen the lower limbs and give elasticity; the remaining ones are chiefly calculated, as indeed are the majority of the apparatus exercises, to strengthen the body above the waist, and the arms. *O*, is a *trapezium* or bar-swing; a hard-wood cross-bar, hung by two ropes, and which should be about five and a half or six feet from the ground. The trapezium exercises are numerous, and consist of jumping, swinging, and turning, in many ways.

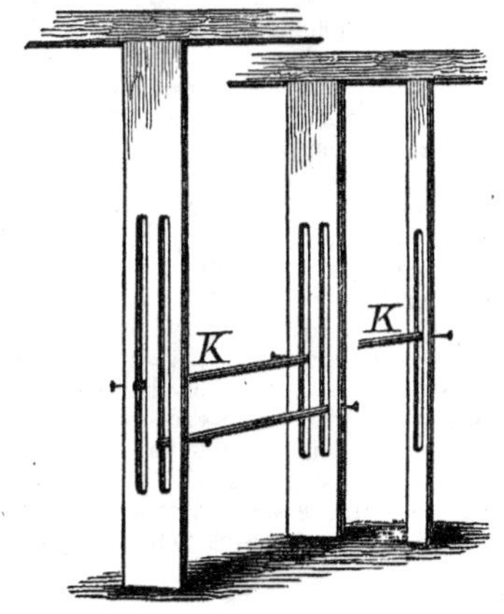

They are not very difficult, and quite pleasant to perform. *e*, *e*, are two upright ropes for climbing, and *d* is a perpendicular pole for the same purpose. These should be as high as the building arrangements will allow. *c*, *c*, are upright poles, with pegs in them fitting loosely into holes. These poles are to be climbed by taking a peg in each hand and setting them one after another into the holes. At *b*, in the large cut, are two upright poles at about the width of the shoulders apart. These may be used for climbing, and for exercising the chest, by holding the poles, one in each hand, nearly shoulder high, and pushing the head and shoulders through between them. *P*, is a wide spring-board for jumping forward. *R*, is a *rope swing*. *S*, is a pair of *iron rings*, hung upon single ropes from a bar overhead, about as high as the trapezium; and the exercises upon them are of the same character, though more varied, difficult, and pleasant. They demand and develope great quickness, and strength of arm and chest, and, if practiced with care, are among the most useful of the gymnastic exercises.

T, is a *spring-beam* set firmly into the wall, and resting upon a fulcrum a short distance from it, so as to furnish considerable elastic force. It is used for perpendicular jumping.

U, is a *flying-machine* or *rotary-swing*, which is described on page 86.

V, is a *movable leaping-stand*, for standing or running jumps. It consists of two light uprights, set in heavy bases, so as to stand firmly, and with a row of holes, an inch or two apart, at corresponding heights in each. Pegs fit into these, over which, at any desired height, may be hung a string with a weight of about five pounds at each end. By this means all danger of catching the feet in jumping is avoided, as a light touch throws the string off the pegs.

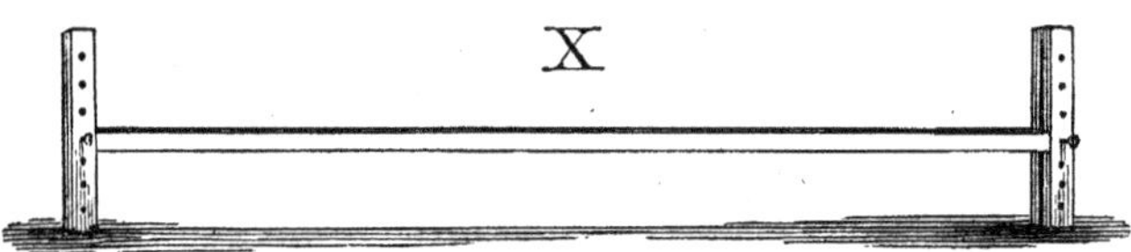

X, (which does not appear on the large cut) is a *horizontal beam;* a stout square stick of hard wood about twenty feet long, with tenons at each end, running in slits in the uprights. Iron pins pass through the uprights, and through holes in the tenons, and hold the beam at any height desired. The uprights may stand about four feet above the surface of the ground, and the holes in them may be three inches apart. The beam should be not less than four inches square. This machine is used for various leg exercises, which are of considerable value.

Exercises in marching, military drill, walking, and running, should be combined with the apparatus exercises, as these latter generally serve as to strengthen and develope the body and arms more than the legs. Mr. Russell has found a most healthy and valuable disciplinary influence in the military drill constantly practiced by his pupils. It gives them promptness, an upright and graceful carriage, and habits of regularity and quick obedience. They exercise with cadet muskets, which are stored in a small loft in one end of the gymnasium, and are organized into a very neat uniform company.

All gymnastic apparatus should be made of the best materials and put together in the best manner, in order to withstand the great strain to which it is subject, and to prevent accidents from breaking. Most or all of the uprights should be strongly framed, and braced into mud-sills at least two feet under ground. No exercises should be ordinarily allowed in the gymnasium, except in the presence and under the directions of a competent and reliable teacher. The exercises should be reduced to a regular and progressive system, and should be performed with as much regularity and care as those of the school recitations; according to the instructor's directions, and by no means according to the caprice of the pupils. This precaution will almost certainly prevent the accidents whose occurrence is so often used as an argument against gymnastics, and ill-directed efforts to perform the harder exercises before the easier are mastered; it will likewise insure a proper amount of drilling thorough acquisition, and the utmost pleasure and advantage to the pupils.

Every school-house should be provided with a room, where the pupils can resort, before and after school and during recess, in unpleasant weather; with a shed, or other suitable place for fuel, which should be supplied of the best quality, in due season, and in the right condition for use; with a well, or other mode of furnishing pure water; and with a bell, large enough to be heard over the district from which the school is gathered.

No department of school architecture among us requires such immediate and careful attention as the arrangement and construction of privies. In none is there now such niggardly economy, or outrageous disregard to health, modesty, and morals, practiced. Over this portion of the school premises the most perfect neatness, seclusion, order, and propriety should be enforced, and every thing calculated to defile the mind, or wound the delicacy or modesty of the most sensitive should be immediatly removed, and any vulgarity in respect to it, on the part of the pupils, should receive attention in private, and be made a matter of parental advice and co-orporation. Neglect in this particular, on the part of the community, in providing suitable buildings and premises, or of the teacher, in enforcing proper regulations, has been followed with the most disastrous results to the health and happiness of thousands of pupils.

There should be one provided for each sex, widely separated from each other—inclosed from the general play ground,—and accessible by a covered walk, and, if practicable, from the basement, or clothes-room appropriated to each sex, and kept locked, except during school-hours. They should be ventilated, and frequently and thoroughly cleansed. Where water closets can be introduced, it will be a wise economy to adopt them. The following plan is copied from "*Richson's School-Builder's Guide.*"

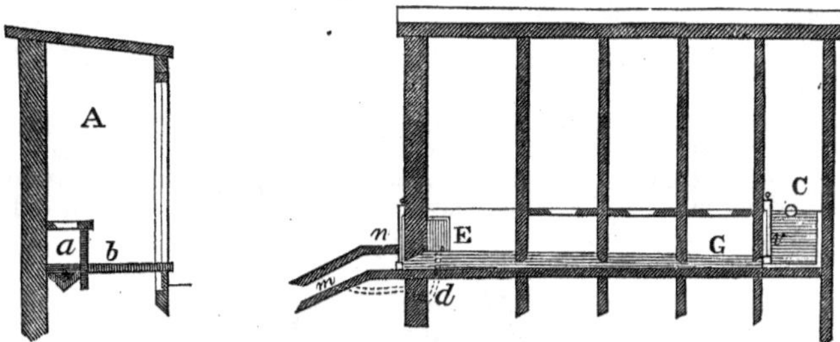

A—Cross sections, without the end wall and entance.

a—The seat, with water channel to the level of the floor. At the back and front of *a*, dipping 1 *inch* into the water, is a Valentia slate, 1 *inch* thick. The channel, although here drawn angular, would be better of an oval form.

b—The level of floor.

B—Longitudinal section.

C—Cistern, supplied by ball tap, with sliding valve to lift and flush the channel G.

E—(With line above) a sloping Valentia slate, $1\frac{1}{2}$ feet high, to form urinal, dipping 1 *inch* into the water.

n—A sliding valve to lift and let off water.

m—An inclined trough or drain to carry off water when the channel is flushed by opening valves *c* and *n*.

d—An escape pipe, bent to form a trap at *d*, fixed at the level of the floor, behind the girt in the corner of E, to carry off superfluous water.

The valves, at *c*, and *n*, being opened *every evening*, or more frequently, will thoroughly cleanse the channel; and the valve at *n* being first shut, the channel G may be filled before *c* is closed.

1. Plans of School-houses recommended by practical Teachers and Educators.

Plan, &c. recommended by Dr. Alcott, and by the American Institute of Instruction.

In 1830 the American Institute of Instruction offered a premium for the best Essay "*On the Construction of School-houses*," which was awarded in Aug. 1831, to Dr. William A. Alcott, of Hartford. The Prize Essay* was published in the proceedings of the Institute of the same year, together with a "*Plan for a Village School-house*," devised by a Committee of the Directors of the Institute.

The plan of the school-room recommended by Dr. Alcott, although less complete in some of its details, is substantially the same as that recommended by Mr. Mann, and can be easily understood by reference to the cut of the latter on the opposite page. The room, to accommodate 56 pupils each, with a separate seat and desk, and from 8 to 16 small children with seats for two, should be 40 ft. long by 30 wide. The teacher's platform occupies the north end of the room, towards which all the scholars face when in their seats. Each scholar is provided with a seat and desk, (each 2 ft. by 14 inches,) the front of one desk constituting the back of the seat beyond. The top of the desk is level, with a box and lid for books, &c. The aisles on each side of the room, are 2 feet wide, and those between each range of seats and desk is 18 inches. A place for recitation 8 feet wide extends across the whole width of the room, in the rear, with movable blackboards. The room can be warmed by stove, placed as in the cut referred to, or by air heated by furnace or stove in the basement. The room is ventilated by openings in the ceiling. A thermometer, library, museum, &c., are to be furnished.

In the "*Plan for a village School-house*," the school-room is 48 ft. long by 35 wide, to accommodate eighty scholars with separate seats. The details of the arrangements are nearly the same as were at that date recommended for schools on the Lancasterian plan, and as are now recommended by the British and Foreign School Society—except that the floor of the room is level, and the seats are provided with backs. In the explanations accompanying the plan, the Directors recommend, that in villages and populous neighborhoods, the children be classified according to age and attainment into a series of schools, and that appropriate rooms for each school be provided.

Plan recommended by Horace Mann.

In 1838, Mr. Mann submitted a Report on School-houses, supplementary to his "First Annual Report as Secretary of the Massachusetts Board of Education," which discusses the whole subject of school architecture with great fulness and ability. This document may be found entire in the Massachusetts Common School Journal, Vol 1., and nearly so, in the Connecticut Common School Journal, Vol. 1., and the New York District School Journal, Vol. 3. It fixed public attention on the defects of these edifices, and has led to extensive improvement all over that Commonwealth. During the five years immediately following its publication, over $516,000 were expended in the construction of 405 new houses, including land, fixtures, &c., and over $118,000, in the substantial repairs of 429 more. The larger portion of the first sum has been expended in the cities and large villages in the eastern part of the state, where may now be seen specimens of the best school-houses, and the best schools, in our country. The following plan embodies substantially the views submitted by Mr. Mann, in his Report.

* This Essay of Dr. Alcott was the pioneer publication on this subject. It was followed in 1833 by a "*Report on School-houses*" prepared by the Rev. G. B. Perry, and published by the Essex County Teacher's Association. This last is a searching and vigorous exposition of the evils resulting from the defective construction, and arrangements of school-houses, as they were at that date almost universally found.

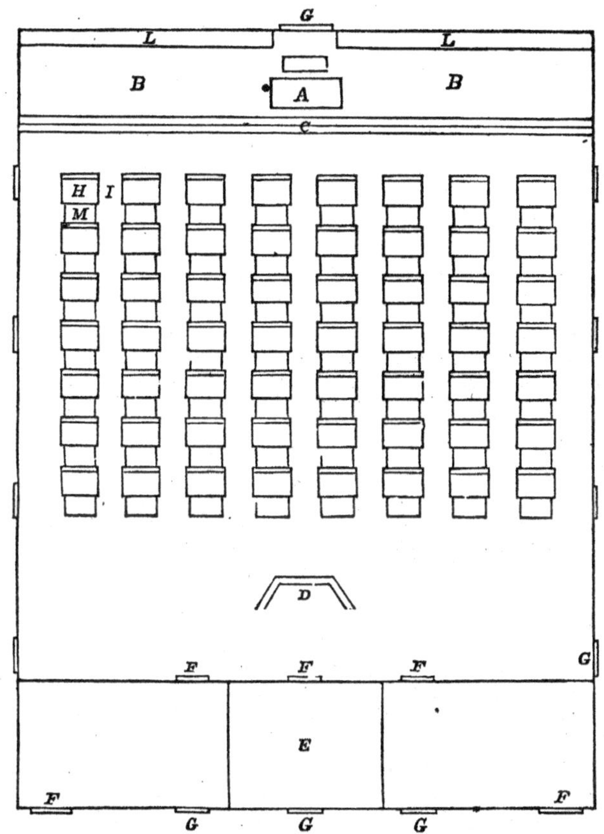

A. Represents the teacher's desk. *B B.* Teacher's platform, from 1 to 2 ft. in height. *C.* Step for ascending the platform. *L L.* Cases for books, apparatus, cabinet, &c. *H.* Pupils' single desks, 2 ft. by 18 inches. *M.* Pupils' seat, 1 ft. by 20 inches. *I.* Aisles, 1 ft. 6 inches in width. *D.* Place for stove, if one be used. *E.* Room for recitation, for retiring in case of sudden indisposition, for interview with parents, when necessary, &c. It may also be used for the library, &c. *F F F F F.* Doors into the boys' and girls' entries—from the entries into the school-room, and from the school-room into the recitation room. *G G G G.* Windows. The windows on the sides are not lettered.

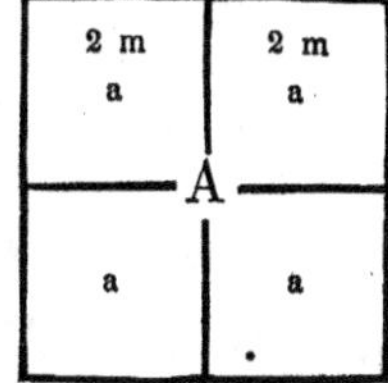

For section of seat and desk constructed after Mr. Mann's plan, see p. 47. To avoid the necessity of fitting up the same school-room for old and young, and the inefficiency of such country schools as we now have, Mr. Mann proposed in this Report a union, for instance of four districts which did not cover more than four miles square, and the erection of four primary school-houses, (a a a a) for the younger children of each district, to be taught by female teachers, and one central or high school, (A) for the older children of the four districts, taught by a well qualified male teacher. This plan is recommended for its wise use of the means of the districts, and the efficiency of the instruction given.

Plans, &c., recommended by George B. Emerson.

The "School and Schoolmaster,"* contains a very valuable chapter on school-houses, by Mr. Emerson, the President of the American Institute of Instruction, illustrated by drawings, which, with the permission of the authors and publishers are introduced here. The whole chapter, as the production of one of the most eminent teachers and writers on education of the age, should be studied by every one who would become thoroughly acquainted with he subject. Most of his valuable suggestions are subjoined.

Situation.—So much do the future health, vigor, taste, and moral principles f the pupil depend upon the position, arrangement, and construction of the school-house, that everything about it is important. When the most desirable situation can be selected, and the laws of health and the dictates of taste may be consulted, it should be placed on firm ground, on the southern declivity of a gently sloping hill, open to the southwest, from which quarter comes the pleasantest winds in summer, and protected on the northeast by the top of the hill or by a thick wood. From the road it should be remote enough to escape the noise, and dust, and danger, and yet near enough to be easily accessible by a path or walk, always dry. About it should be ample space, a part open for a play-ground, a part to be laid out in plots for flowers and shrubs, with winding alleys for walks. Damp places, in the vicinity of stagnant pools or unwholesome marshes, and bleak hilltops or dusty plains, should be carefully avoided. Tall trees should partially shade the grounds, not in stiff rows or heavy clumps, but scattered irregularly as if by the hand of Nature. Our native forests present such a choice of beautiful trees, that the grounds must be very extensive to afford room for even a single fine specimen of each; yet this should, if possible, be done, for children ought early to become familiar with the names, appearance, and properties of these noblest of inanimate things. The border of a natural wood may often be chosen for the site of a school; but if it is to be thinned out, or if trees are to be planted, and, from limited space, a selection is to be made, the kingly, magnificent oaks, the stately hickories, the spreading beech for its deep mass of shade, the maples for their rich and abundant foliage, the majestic elm, the useful ash, the soft and graceful birches, and the towering, columnar sycamore, claim precedence. Next may come the picturesque locusts, with their hanging, fragrant flowers; the tulip-tree; the hemlock, best of evergreens; the celtis, or sweet gum; the nyssa, or tupelo, with horizontal branches and polished leaves; the walnut and butternut, the native poplar, and the aspen.

Of extremely beautiful American shrubs, the number is so great that I have no room for a list. What place intended to form the taste of the young, should be without the kalmias, rhododendrons, cornels, roses, viburnums, magnolias, clethras, honeysuckles, and spiræas? And whoever goes into the woods to gather these, will find a multitude of others which he will hardly consent to leave behind. The hilltop should be planted with evergreens, forming, at all seasons, a barrier against the winds from the north and east.

Of the flower plots, little need be said. They must be left to the taste of the teacher, and of cultivated persons in the district. I can only recommend our wild American plants, and again remind the reader, that there is hardly a

* The "*School and Schoolmaster*," a Manual for the use of Teachers, Employers, Trustees, Inspectors, &c., &c., of Common Schools. Part I. By Alonzo Potter, D. D. Part II. By George B. Emerson. pp. 552. Harper & Brothers, 82 Cliff street, New York. Price, $1.

This excellent treatise, the most valuable contribution yet made to the educational literature of our country, was prepared and published originally at the expense of James Wadsworth, Esq., of Geneseo, N. Y., in 1842. By him a copy was presented to each of the 11,000 school districts of that state. Following this noble example, the Hon. Martin Brimmer, the present mayor of the city of Boston, caused to be printed, at his expense, such a number of copies as would supply one copy each to all the school districts, and one copy each to all the boards of school committee men, in Massachusetts.

The work should be scattered broadcast through every state in the Union. In large orders, or for gratuitous distribution, it can be had of the publishers at a very low rate.

Perspective of School-house, Outbuildings, and Grounds

Front Projection of a Schoolhouse with Trees, Shrubbery, &c.

country town in New York or New England, from whose woods and meadows a hundred kinds of flowers might not be transplanted, of beauty enough to form the chief ornament of a German or English garden, which are now neglected only because they are common and wild. Garden flowers need not be excluded; and if either these or the former are cultivated, the great object, to present something to refine and inform the taste, will be, in some degree, accomplished.

If proper inclosed play-grounds are provided, the master may often be present at the sports, and thus become acquainted with the character, of his pupils. If children are compelled to resort to the highway for their amusements, we ought not to wonder that they should be contaminated by the vices, brawlings, and profanities, which belong to frequenters of highways.

Size.—The room should be sufficiently large to allow every pupil, 1. to sit comfortably at his desk; 2. to leave it without disturbing any one else; 3. to see explanations on his lessons, and to recite without being incommoded or incommoding others; 4. to breathe a wholesome atmosphere.

If the first three objects are fully provided for, the space on the floor will be sufficient. But to secure the advantage of an adequate supply of air, the room must be not less than 10, and, if possible, 12 or 14, feet high.

Arrangement.—For the accommodation of 56 scholars, so as to give ample room for moving, for recitations, and for air, the dimensions of the house should be 38 feet by 25, and 10 feet in height within. This will allow an entry of 14 feet by 7½, lighted by a window, to be furnished with wooden pegs for the accommodation of clothes; a wood-room, 10 feet by 7½, to serve also as an entry for girls at recess, or as a recitation room; a space behind the desks 8 feet wide, for fireplace, passage, and recitations, with permanent seats against the wall 10 or 11 inches wide; a platform, 7 feet wide, for the teacher, with the library, blackboards, globes, and other apparatus for teaching; the remaining space to be occupied by the desks and seats of the scholars. For every additional 8 scholars the room may be lengthened 2½ feet. The desks and seats for scholars should be of different dimensions. A desk for two may be 3½ or 4 feet long. If the younger children are placed nearest the master's desk, the desks in the front range may be 13 inches wide, the two next 14, the two next 15, and the two most remote 16, with the height, respectively, of 24, 25, 26, and 27 inches. The seats should vary in like manner. Those in the front range should be 10 inches wide, in the two next 10½, in the two next 11, in the two last 11½ or 12; and 13½, 14, 15, and 16 inches, respectively, high. All edges and corners are to be carefully rounded.

It is very desirable that the north end of the school-house be occupied by the master's desk; that this end be a dead wall; that the front be towards the south; and that the desks be so placed that the pupils, as they sit at them, shall look towards the north. The advantages of this arrangement are, 1. that the scholars will obtain more correct ideas upon the elements of geography, as all maps suppose the reader to be looking northward; 2. the north wall, having no windows, will exclude the severest cold of winter; 3. the scholars will, in this case, look towards a dead wall, and thus avoid the great evil of facing a glare of light; or, if a window or two be allowed in the north wall, the light coming from that quarter is less vivid, and, therefore, less dangerous, than that which comes from any other; 4. the door, being on the south, will open towards the winds which prevail in summer, and *from* the cold winds of winter.

If, from necessity, the house must front northward, the master's desk should be still in the north end of the room, and the scholars, when seated, look in that direction.

The end of the room occupied by the master should be fitted with shelves for a library and for philosophical apparatus and collections of natural curiosities, such as rocks, minerals, plants, and shells, for globes and for blackboards. The books, apparatus, and collections should be concealed and protected by doors, which may be made perfectly plain and without panels, so as to be painted black and serve as blackboards. They may be conveniently divided by pilasters into three portions, the middle one for books, the others for apparatus and collections. On one of the pilasters may be the clock; on the other a barometer and thermometer; on shelves in the corners, the globes, and over the library in the center, the study card. One of the pilasters may form part of the ventilating tube. The master's platform may be raised eight inches. For all these purposes, the space in front of the ranges of scholars' desks, should be not less than seven or eight feet wide; ten or twelve would be much better. The sides and front of this space should be furnished with seats ten or eleven inches wide, for recitation. By means of a large movable blackboard, this space may be, in case of need, converted into two, so that two classes may recite at a time. In a school intended to accommodate more than 64 pupils, there ought also to be a space for recitation in the south end of the room, separable by movable blackboards into two.

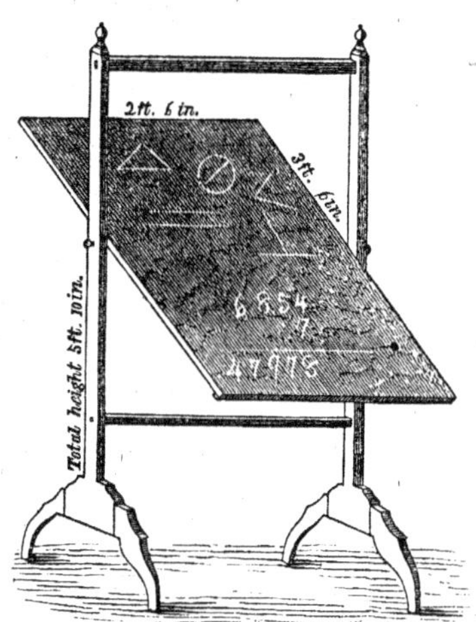

Movable Blackboard.

The entry should be lighted by a window, and be furnished with wooden or iron pins for the accommodation of hats, bonnets, and cloaks; and there should be a wood-closet large enough to contain two or three cords of wood, which may, if it is preferred, be used as a recitation room.

By making the ceiling of the entry and wood-closet only seven feet high, two commodious rooms for recitation may be formed above them, lighted from the window over the front door, and accessible by stairs from within the school-room.

Warming.—In a suitable position, pointed out in the plates, near the door, let a common brick fireplace be built. Let this be inclosed, on the back and on each side, by a casing of brick, leaving, between the fireplace and the casing, a space of four or five inches, which will be heated through the back and jambs. Into this space let the air be admitted from beneath by a box 24 inches wide and 6 or 8 deep, leading from the external atmosphere by an opening beneath the front door, or at some other convenient place. The brick casing should be continued up as high as six or eight inches above the top of the fireplace, where it may open into the room by lateral orifices, to be commanded by iron doors, through which the heated air will enter the room. If these are lower, part of the warm air will find its way into the fireplace. The brick chimney should

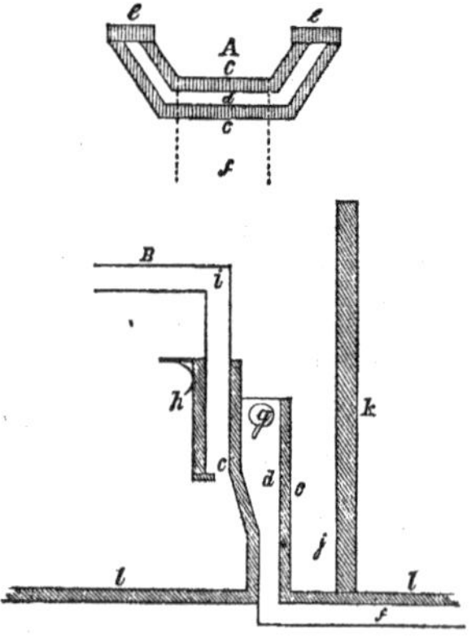

Fireplace.

A. Horizontal section. B. Perpendicular section. *c.* Brick walls, 4 inches thick. *d.* Air space between the walls. *e.* Solid fronts of masonry. *f.* Air box for supply of fresh air, extending beneath the floor to the front door. *g.* Openings on the sides of the fireplace, for the heated air to pass into the room. *h.* Front of the fireplace and mantelpiece. *i.* Iron smoke flue, 8 inches diameter. *j.* Space between the fireplace and wall. *k.* Partition wall. *l.* Floor.

rise at least two or three feet above the hollow back, and may be surmounted by a flat iron, soap-stone, or brick top, with an opening for a smoke-pipe, which may be thence conducted to any part of the room. The smoke-pipe should rise a foot, then pass to one side, and then over a passage, to the opposite extremity of the room, where it should ascend perpendicularly, and issue above the roof. The fireplace should be provided with iron doors, by which it may be completely closed.

The advantages of this double fireplace are, 1. the fire, being made against brick, imparts to the air of the apartment none of the deleterious qualities which are produced by a common iron stove, but gives the pleasant heat of an open fireplace; 2. none of the heat of the fuel will be lost, as the smoke-pipe may be extended far enough to communicate nearly all the heat contained in the smoke; 3. the current of air heated within the hollow back, and constantly pouring into the room, will diffuse an equable heat throughout every part; 4. the pressure of the air of the room will be constantly outward, little cold will enter by cracks and windows, and the fireplace will have no tendency to smoke; 5. by means of the iron doors, the fire may be completely controlled, increased or diminished at pleasure, with the advantages of an air-tight stove. For that purpose, there must be a valve or slide near the bottom of one of the doors.

If, instead of this fireplace, a common stove be adopted, it should be placed above the air-passage, which may be commanded by a valve or register in the floor, so as to admit or exclude air.

Ventilation.—A room warmed by such a fireplace as that just described, may be easily ventilated. If a current of air is constantly pouring in, a current of the same size will rush out wherever it can find an outlet, and with it will carry the impurities wherewith the air of an occupied room is always charged. For the first part of the morning, the open fireplace may suffice. But this, though a very effectual, is not an economical ventilator; and when the issue through this is closed, some other must be provided. The most effective ventilator for throwing out foul air, is one opening into a tube which incloses the smoke-flue at the point where it passes through the roof. Warm air naturally rises. If a portion of the smoke-flue be inclosed by a tin tube, it will warm the air within this tube, and give it a tendency to rise. If, then, a wooden tube, opening near the floor, be made to communicate, by its upper extremity, with the tin tube, an upward current will take place in it, which *will always act whenever the smoke-flue is warm.*

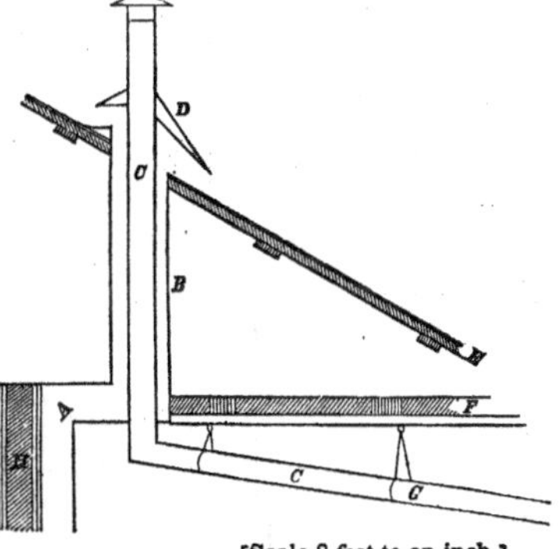

[Scale 8 feet to an inch.]

Ventilating Apparatus.

A. Air box, 1 foot square, or 24 inches by 6, covered by the pilaster, and opening at the floor, in the base of the pilaster. B. Round iron tube 15½ inches in diameter, being a continuation of the air box, through the center of which passes C. The smoke flue, 8 inches in diameter. D Caps to keep out the rain.

It is better, but not absolutely essential, that the opening into the wooden tube be near the floor. The carbonic acid thrown out by the lungs rises, with the warm breath, and the perspirable matter from the skin, with the warm, invisible vapor, to the top of the room. There both soon cool, and sink towards the floor; and both carbonic air and the vapor bearing the perspirable matter are pretty rapidly and equally diffused through every part of the room.

Seats and Desks.—Instead of a seat and desk for each pupil, Mr. Emerson recommends that two seats should be contiguous. In his drawings, the desk is perfectly level like a table, and the back to the seat is perpendicular.

SCHOOL FOR ONE HUNDRED AND TWENTY PUPILS.

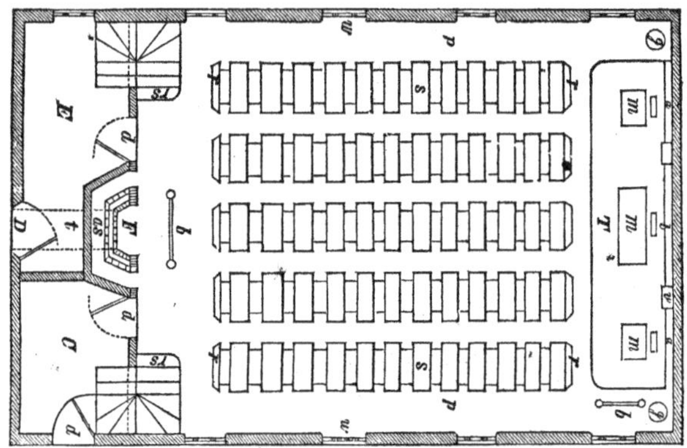

51 feet by 31 feet outside.] [Scale 16 feet to the inch.

D. Entrance door. E. Entry. F. Fireplace. C. Wood closet. T. Teacher's platform. *a.* Apparatus shelves. *t.* Air tube beneath the floor. *d.* Doors. *g.* Globes. *l.* Library shelves. *m.* Master's table and seat. *p.* Passages. *r.* Recitation seats. *s.* Scholars' desks and seats. *r s.* Stairs to recitation rooms in the attic. *v.* Ventilator. *w.* Windows. *b.* Movable blackboard. *a s.* Air space behind the fireplace.

SCHOOL FOR FORTY-EIGHT PUPILS.

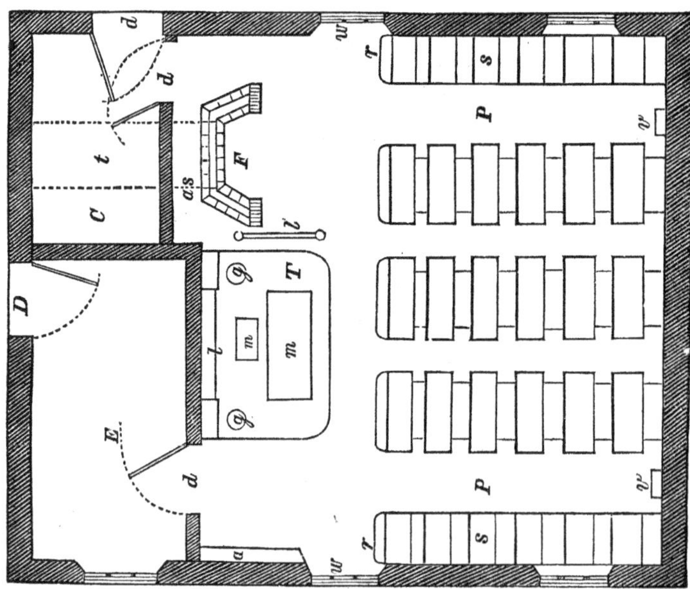

24 feet by 28 feet outside.] [Scale 8 feet to the inch.

D. Entrance door. E. Entry. F. Fireplace. C. Wood closet, or recitation room T. Teacher's platform. *a.* Apparatus shelves. *t.* Air tube beneath the floor. *d.* Doors *g.* Globes. *l.* Library shelves. *m.* Master's table and seat. *p.* Passages. *r.* Recitation seats. *s.* Scholars' desks and seats. *v.* Ventilator. *w.* Windows. *b.* Movable blackboard. *a. s.* Air space behind the fireplace.

Plans, &c., of an Octagonal School-house.

Furnished for the "School and School-master," by Messrs. Town and Davis.

Fig. 1.

This design for a school-house intends to exhibit a model of fitness and close economy. The principles of fitness are, 1. *Ample dimensions*, with very nearly *the least possible length of wall* for its inclosure, the roof being constructed without tie beams, the upper and lower ends of the rafters being helo by the wall plates and frame at the foot of the lantern. The ceiling may show the timber-work of the roof, or it may be plastered. 2. *Light, a uniform temperature, and a free ventilation*, secured by a lantern light, thus avoiding lateral windows (except for air in summer,) and gaining wall-room for black-boards, maps, models, and illustrations. Side windows are shown in the view, and may be made an *addition* by those who doubt the efficiency of the lantern light. (The lantern is not only best for light, but it is essential for a free ventilation.) With such a light, admitted equally to all the desks, there will be no inconvenience from shadows. The attention of the scholars will not be distracted by occurrences or objects out of doors. There will be less expense for broken glass, as the sashes will be removed from ordinary accidents. The room, according to this plan, is heated by a fire in the center, either in a stove or grate, with a pipe going directly through the roof of the lantern, and finishing outside in a sheet-iron vase, or other appropriate cap. The pipe can be tastefully fashioned, with a hot-air chamber near the floor, so as to afford a large radiating surface before the heat is allowed to escape. This will secure a uniform temperature in every part of the room, at the same time that the inconvenience from a pipe passing directly over the heads of children, is avoided. The octagonal shape will admit of any number of seats and desks, (according to the size of the room,) arranged parallel with the sides, constructed as described in specification, or on such principles as may be preferred. The master's seat may be in the center of the room, and the seats be so constructed that the scholars may sit with their backs to the center, by which their attention will not be diverted by facing other scholars on the opposite side, and yet so that at times they may all face the master, and the whole school be formed into one class. The lobby next to the front door is made large, (8 by 20) so that it may serve for a recitation-room. This lobby is to finish eight feet high, the inside wall to show like a screen, not rising to the roof, and the space above be open to the school-room, and used to put away or station school apparatus. This screen-like wall may be hung with hats and clothes, or the triangular space next the window may be inclosed for this purpose. The face of the octagon opposite to the porch, has a wood-house attached to it, serving as a sheltered way to a double privy beyond. This woodhouse is open on two sides, to admit of a cross draught of air, preventing the possibility of a nuisance. Other wing-rooms (A A) may be attached to the remaining sides of the octagon, if additional conveniences for closets, library, or recitation-rooms be desired.

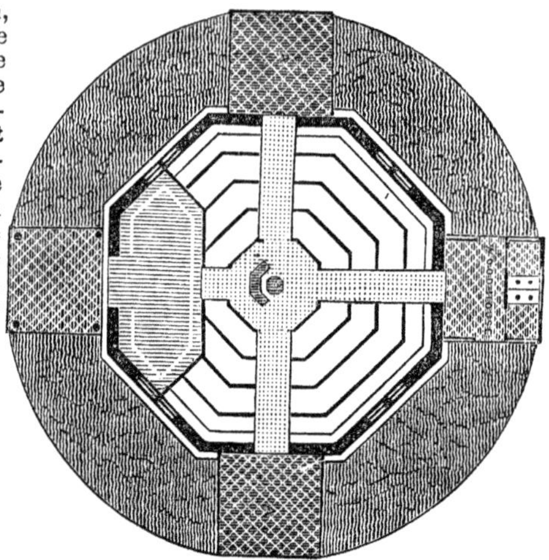

Fig. 2.

The mode here suggested, of a lantern in the center of the roof for lighting all common school-houses, is so great a change from common usage in our country, that it requires full and clear explanations for its execution, and plain and satisfactory reasons for its general adoption, and of its great excellence in preference to the common mode. They are as follows, viz.:

1. A skylight is well known to be far better and stronger than light from the sides of the building in cloudy weather, and in morning and evening. The difference is of the greatest importance. In short days (the most used for schools) it is still more so.

2. The light is far better for all kinds of study than side light, from its quiet uniformity and equal distribution.

3. For smaller houses, the lantern may be square, a simple form easily constructed. The sides, whether square or octagonal, should incline like the drawing, but not so much as to allow water condensed on its inside to drop off, but run down on the inside to the bottom, which should be so formed as to conduct it out by a small aperture at each bottom pane of glass.

4. The glass required to light a school-room equally well with side lights would be double what would be required here, and the lantern would be secure from common accidents, by which a great part of the glass is every year broken.

5. The strong propensity which scholars have to look out by a side window would be mostly prevented, as the shutters to side apertures would only be opened when the warm weather would require it for air, but never in cool weather, and therefore no glass would be used. The shutters being made very tight, by calking, in winter, would make the school-room much warmer than has been common; and, being so well ventilated, and so high in the center, it would be more healthy.

6. The stove, furnace, or open grate, being in the center of the room, has great advantages, from diffusing the heat to all parts, and equally to all the scholars; it also admits the pipe to go perpendicularly up, without any inconvenience, and it greatly facilitates the ventilation, and the retention or escape of heat, by means of the sliding cap above.

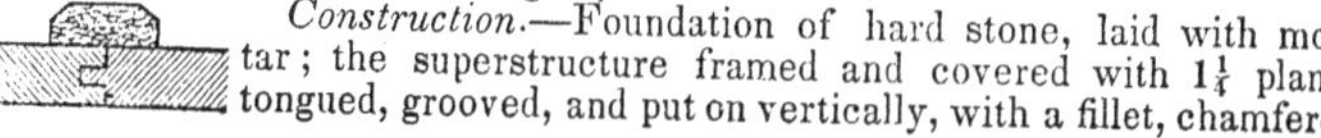

Construction.—Foundation of hard stone, laid with mortar; the superstructure framed and covered with $1\frac{1}{4}$ plank, tongued, grooved, and put on vertically, with a fillet, chamfered at the edges, over the joint, as here shown. In our view, a rustic character is given to the design by covering the sides with slabs; the curved side out, tongued and grooved, without a fillet over the joint; or formed of logs placed vertically, and lathed and plastered on the inside. The sides diminish slightly upward. A rustic porch is also shown, the columns of cedar boles, with vines trained upon them. The door is battened, with braces upon the outside, curved as shown, with a strip around the edge. It is four feet wide, seven high, in two folds, one half to be used in inclement weather. The cornice projects two feet six inches, better to defend the boarding; and may show the ends of the rafters. Roof covered with tin, slate or shingles. Dripping eaves are intended, without gutters. The roof of an octagonal building of ordinary dimensions may with ease and perfect safety be constructed without tie beams or a garret floor (which is, in all cases of school-houses, waste room, very much increasing the exposure to fire, as well as the expense.) The wall-plates, in this case, become ties, and must be well secured, so as to form one connected *hoop*, capable of counteracting the pressure outward of the angular rafters. The sides of the roof will abut at top against a similar timber octagonal frame, immediately at the foot of the lantern cupola. This frame must be sufficient to resist the pressure inward of the roof (which is greater or less, as the roof is more or less inclined in its pitch,) in the same manner as the tie-plates must resist the pressure outward. This security is given in an easy and cheap manner; and may be given entirely by the roof boarding, if it is properly nailed to the angular rafters, and runs horizontally round the roof. By this kind of roof, great additional height is given to the room by *camp-ceiling;* that is, by planing the rafters and roof-boards, or by lathing and plastering on a thin half-inch board ceiling, immediately on the underside of the rafters, as may be most economically performed. This extra height in the center will admit of low side-walls, from seven to ten feet in the clear, according to the size and importance of the building, and, at the same time, by the most simple principle of philosophy, conduct the heated foul air up to the central aperture, which should be left open quite round the pipe of the stove, or open grate standing in the center of the room. This aperture and cap, with the ventilator, is shown by the figure adjoining, which is to a scale of half an inch to a foot. The ventilator is drawn raised, and the dotted lines show it let down upon the roof. It may be of any required size, say two feet wide and twelve inches high, sliding up and down between the stovepipe and an outward case, forming a cap to exclude water. This cap may be pushed up or let down by a rod affixed to the under edge, and lying against the smokepipe.

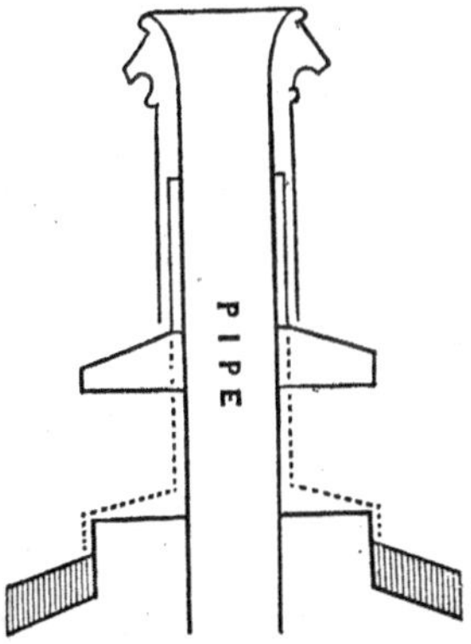

PIPE

In the design given, the side-walls are ten feet high, and the lantern fifteen feet above the floor; eight feet in diameter, four feet high. The sashes may open for additional ventilation, if required, by turning on lateral pivots, regulated by cords attached to the edges above. The breadth of each desk is seventeen inches, with a shelf beneath for books, and an opening in the back to receive a slate. The highest desks are twenty-seven inches, inclined to thirty, and the front forms the back of the seat before it. The seat is ten to twelve inches wide, fifteen high, and each pupil is allowed a space of two feet, side to side.

For the sake of variety, we have given a design in the pointed style, revised from a sketch by ——, an amateur in architecture. Any rectangular plan will suit it; and the principles of light and ventilation dwelt upon in the description of the octagon design, may be adapted to this. The principal light

Fig. 3.

is from one large mullioned window in the rear end. The side openings are for air in summer—not glazed, but closed with tight shutters. The same ventilating cap is shown, and height is gained in the roof by framing with collar beams set up four or five feet above the eaves. The sides, if not of brick or stone, may be boarded vertically, as before described.

The following PLAN OF AN OCTAGONAL SCHOOL-HOUSE represents the *School of Practice annexed* to St. Mark's Primary College, near London. In the cen-

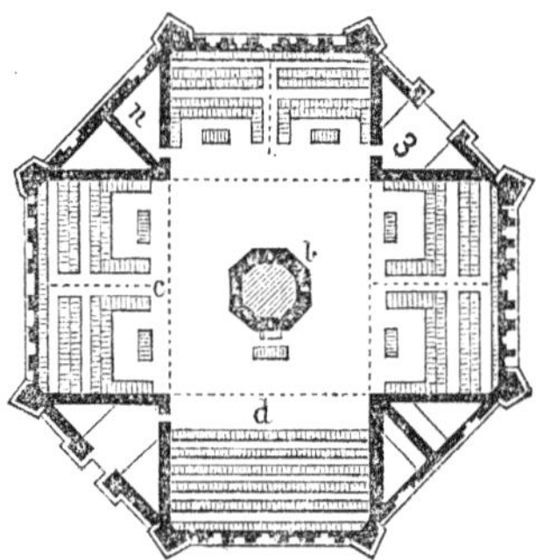

ter (*b*) is the fire-place and ventilating apparatus. On the four sides of the brick-work, forming the ventilating apparatus and the chimneys, blackboards, maps, and musical tablets, are suspended, so as to be seen by the classes in the squares or recesses opposite. Each of the four recesses is 20 feet square, and accommodates about 60 pupils, divided into two classes separated by a curtain (*c*.) In one is a gallery (*d*) for an infant class.

Plan of School-room and Grounds for a Village School.

The following sketch by Dr. Dick, (author of *Mental Illumination*), of the plan and accommodations of a Village School is copied from the *Pennsylvania Common School Journal*, vol. 1, p. 120.

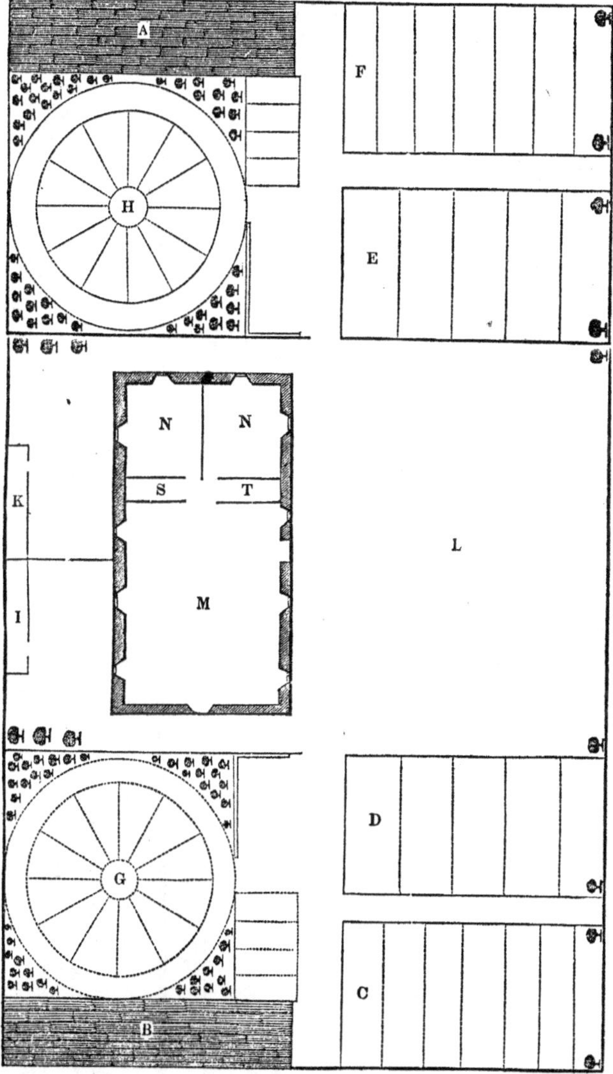

A. B—Covered walks for exercise in winter and rainy days. C. D. E. F—Plats for flowers, shrubs, evergreens, and a few forest trees. G. H—Circles with twelve compartments each, for a different class of plants. I. K—Yards divided with a wall, with suitable accommodations for either sex. L—Portion of ground, smoothed and graveled for play-ground, with circular swing, &c. M—Room, 50 by 30 feet, and 14 feet high. N. N.—Class-rooms, 18 by 15. S. T.—Closets for apparatus, &c.

Plan, &c., of School-room and Grounds for an Infant School.

The following plan and explanations are condensed from a valuable manual for teachers in infant and primary schools, entitled "Infant Education," one of Chambers' Educational Course, published at Edinburgh, in 1840. It is nearly similar to the plan recommended by Mr. Wilderspin in his "Infant School System," and his "Education for the Young," and by Mr. Stow, in the "Manual on the Training System for Infant and Juvenile Schools."

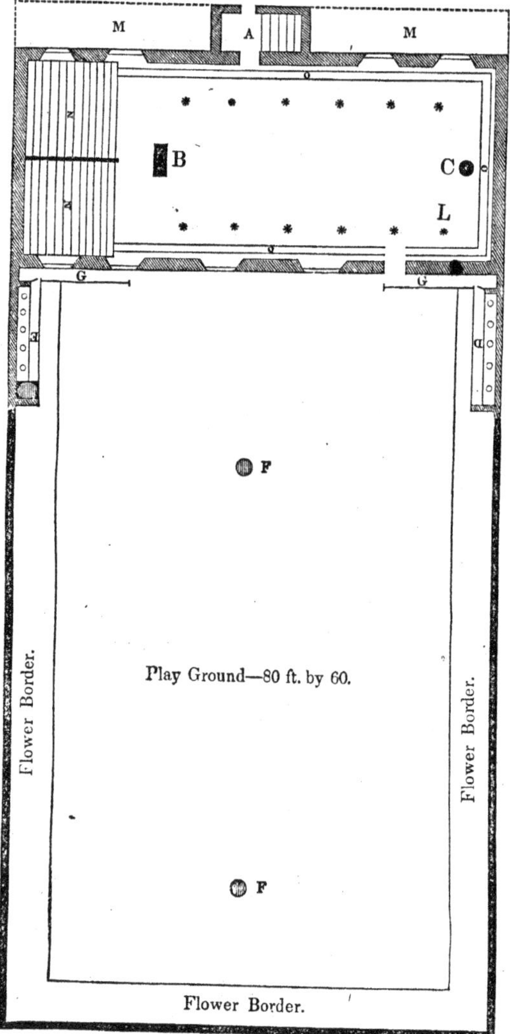

School-room, 60 feet long by 25 wide, and 18 feet high.

A. Porch and lobby, with stairs to the story above, if there should be a second story for a school for older pupils. The infant school should never be higher than the ground story. B. Movable rostrum, or small platform to hold one, two, or three children, when acting as general monitors to the whole school in the gallery. A low rail round it, will prevent them from falling from it. C. Stove, surrounded with a low rail.—(The room should be heated by a furnace.) N. Gallery, consisting of a series of steps the whole width of the room, each eight inches high, and 18 inches wide, divided in the center by a railing, one side for the boys, and the other for the girls. L. Lesson posts, to attach cards, &c. O. Seats round three sides of the room. M. Space for flowers and shrubbery protected by open fence. D. Boys', and C, Girls', water closet, on different sides of the play ground and concealed by a screen and shrubbery, entered by covered way G. F. Gymnastic swing posts

PLAN, &c., OF SCHOOL-ROOMS FOR SCHOOLS OF DIFFERENT GRADES AND DIFFERENT SYSTEMS OF INSTRUCTION.

The plans and remarks for arranging school-rooms thus far, are more particularly applicable to comparatively small, or country schools, where the instruction and government is conducted by one teacher, with at most but one assistant. A few remarks explanatory of the terms used by writers on education, when speaking of systems of organization and instruction, may be useful to a full comprehension of the principles of arrangement embraced in the plans which follow.

1. The *individual* method is the practice on the part of the teacher, of calling up each scholar by himself for recitation, or giving instruction to each scholar in his seat, or calling up classes and hearing each scholar individually, which is practically the same thing. This method will answer a valuable end in a very small school, and must be introduced to some extent in our small country districts where there are children of every age, and in a great variety of studies, and of different degrees of proficiency in each study. It prevails, however, altogether too generally, even in larger districts which admit of a classification of children into schools of different grades, and of the children in each grade of schools. This classification is the first great step towards school improvement.

2. In the *simultaneous* method, the whole school, together, or in successive classes carefully arranged according to their intellectual proficiency, is instructed directly by the teacher. Questions and explanations are addressed to the whole school, or the whole class, as the case may be, and answers are given by all together, or by some one pointed out by the teacher, while all must show by some silent sign, there ability to do so. This method keeps every mind attentive, gives confidence to the timid, admits of the liveliness of oral and interrogative instruction, economizes the time and labor of the teacher, and enlists the great principle of sympathy of numbers engaged in common pursuit. The extent to which this method can be properly carried, will depend not so much on the size of the schools, as on the fact that the school is composed of children in the same studies, and of the same proficiency. This method ought not to exclude entirely individual instruction.

When the number of children increases beyond that which one teacher can conveniently instruct together, or in successive classes, he must adopt the monitorial, the mixed, or the Fächer system, for such classes as he cannot superintend or teach.

3. By the *monitorial* or *mutual* method, is understood the practice of employing the advanced pupils, and many of them very young, to assist in the supervision and instruction of the school, or of particular classes, as systematized by Mr. Lancaster, or Dr. Bell, and as pursued in the schools connected with the National, and the British and Foreign School Societies, England. This method, in different countries, on its first promulgation, attracted much of public favor, on account of its economy, especially in populous districts. In England it still receives the sanction of the two great Societies named above. In Germany it was never adopted in the public schools. In Holland it was tried, and abandoned, but not without modifying very materially the methods of instruction before pursued, and finally leading to the adoption of the *mixed* method. In the large cities of the United States, it was early adopted, but there is hardly a school in the whole country now conducted on the pure monitorial or Lancasterian system, although there are many so called. As pursued in the excellent schools of the New York Public School Society, it is nearly the mixed method as understood and practiced in Holland, and as recommended by the Committee of Council on Education in England.

With these modifications, and the limitation of the duties of the younger monitors to keeping the registers, heading the classes in marching to and from their class-rooms, or the playground, taking charge of books, &c., and in other matters of order and mechanical arrangements, the monitorial system might be advantageously adopted in schools of every grade, and of any system of instruction.

4. The *mixed* method, as the term is generally understood, is a modification of the simultaneous and monitorial system, in which the principal teacher, while he has the superintendence at all times of the whole school, and gives general instruction at certain hours, and in certain studies, to the whole school, as well as to particular classes, employs in the work of class instruction, assistants who are better instructed, and, as a general rule, are older than those employed as monitors under the Lancasterian system, and are not yet qualified to have the whole charge of a school. For example, in Holland, " every school produces two classes of assistants, who are most usefully and economically employed in aiding him in the management and instruction of the school, and may be called *pupil teachers* and *assistant teachers*. By *pupil teacher* is meant a young teacher, in the first instance introduced to the notice of the master by his good qualities, as one of the best instructed and most intelligent of the children; whose attainments and skill are full of promise; and who, having consented to remain at a low rate of remuneration in the school, is further rewarded by being enabled to avail himself of the opportunities afforded him for attaining practical skill in the art of teaching, by daily practice in the school, and by the gratuitous superintendence of his reading and studies by the master, *from whom he receives lessons on technical subjects of school instruction every evening*. He commonly remains in the school in the rank of pupil teacher from the age of 14 to that of 17, daily imbibing a more intimate acquaintance with school management, and all the matter of instruction in elementary schools, and he then proceeds, by attendance at a Normal school, or by further proficiency attained by his own exertions, to qualify himself to act as an assistant teacher. The assistant teacher prepared by these preliminary studies in the elementary Normal school commences his duties at 18 or 20 years of age.

Assistants thus reared in the atmosphere of schools are exceedingly preferable to the best instructed men who are not familiarized by daily habitude with the minutest details of school management. Such assistants constantly replenish the ranks of the teachers with men, all the hopes of whose youth have been directed towards success in the profession of a schoolmaster, and whose greatest ambition is to be distinguished by the excellence of their schools.

5. The *Fächer* system, as it is termed in Germany where it is most popular, consists in employing separate teachers for separate studies, or as we should apply it here, for distinct departments of government, and of instruction. This is the principle on which instruction in our colleges and most of our higher seminaries is given, and is in reality the mixed method carried to its highest perfection. The vital error in our common schools, as they are now organized, is the practice of employing one teacher for the government and instruction of fifty or sixty children of every age, of both sexes, in a great variety of studies, and in different stages of proficiency in each study. It is very rare to find a teacher with the varied qualifications, which success under these circumstances presupposes, while it is not very difficult to find a teacher with talent and experience sufficient to teach some one study, or a few cognate branches, as an assistant, acting under the general direction of a well qualified principal.

Any school organization and arrangements would be imperfect which did not include the systematic training and instruction of very young children, especially in cities and manufacturing villages. Whatever may have been done by others at an earlier date, it seems to be generally conceded now, that to Mr. Wilderspin belongs the credit of having reduced infant education to the science which it now is. It was unfortunate for the improvement of the quality of education given in our schools, that the infant school system was tried in this country, without a full comprehension of its legitimate principles, methods and end, and that the experiment was abandoned so hastily. Its partial and temporary success, however, led to the extension and improvement of our primary schools, and this circumstance renders the success of any well directed effort for their re-establishment more certain.

PLANS, &c., FOR SCHOOLS ON THE MONITORIAL OR MUTUAL SYSTEM.

The "Manual of the System of Primary Instruction pursued in the Model Schools of the British and Foreign School Society," published in 1839, contains the following remarks on the arrangement for schools of mutual instruction connected with that Society.

The school-room should be a parallelogram, the length about twice the breadth.

The height of the walls should be proportioned to the length of the room, and may be varied from 11 to 19 feet. It is recommended that the walls be worked fair and lime whitened, in order to give a neat and clean appearance, reflect light, and contribute to the preservation of health. As it is of great importance to admit as much light as possible into the school, there must be a considerable number of windows, each of which should be fixed in a wooden frame, and movable upon pins or pivots in the center, so that by drawing the upper part into the room, the school may be sufficiently ventilated in hot weather—a circumstance of the utmost importance to be attended to, as the health of the pupils in a great measure depends upon it.

The lower parts of the windows should be at least 6 feet from the floor, in order that the light may not be inconvenient, and the walls be at liberty for the reading lessons, &c., which are to be attached to it; if piers are required, they should be on the outside of the building.

There should be holes in the roof, or in the wall near it, to let foul air escape. This may be effected by a sufficient number of tubes so contrived that they can be opened or shut at pleasure, and at the same time fresh air be admitted from the outside of the building by tubes communicating with the lower part of the room.

All projections in the walls, as well as pillars to support the roof, ought to be avoided; for they interfere with the arrangement of the school, and obstruct the view of the master and of visiters. But if pillars are necessary, they should be placed at each end of the desks, but never in the middle of the room.

Roman Cement, cast into flags, and jointed with the same material, forms a good flooring; it is perfectly dry and durable, and emits but little sound.

In order that all the children may be completely seen by the master, it is of great importance that the floor should be an inclined plane, rising one foot in twenty from the master's desk, to the upper end of the room, where the highest or eighth class is situated.

At the lower end is the platform, elevated in proportion to the length of the room from 2 to 3 feet. The length and breadth of the platform must be in proportion to the size of the room.

The center of the platform is the place for the master's desk; and on each side there may be a small desk for the principal monitors.

The entrance door should be on the side of the platform, in order that visiters on entering the school, may have a commanding view of all the children at once.

Whatever be the size of the school-room, it may be sufficiently warmed by means of one or two stoves placed at the extremities of the apartment. But the most uniform and constant temperature is obtained by steam, when conducted along the lower parts of the room through pipes, or by heated air conveyed into the room through tubes communicating with a stove, which is surrounded by a close casing of iron, leaving a sufficient space for a current of fresh air to be brought in through a tube: this, coming in contact with the stove and the outside of the flue or iron chimney which passes through the casing, is heated, and may be discharged into the room by means of iron pipes. This method has been found to answer extremely well.

The middle of the room is occupied by the forms and desk, a passage being left between the ends of the forms and the wall, 5 or 6 feet broad, where the children form semicircles for reading.

The forms and desks must be fixed firmly in the ground; the legs or supports should be 6 inches broad and 2 inches thick, but cast iron legs are pre-

6

ferable, as they support the desk-board with equal firmness, occupy less room, and have a neater appearance; their number of course will be in proportion to the length of the forms. A form 20 feet long will require five, and they must be so placed, that the supports of the forms may not be immediately opposite to those of the desks; the corners of the desks and forms are to be made round, in order that the children may not hurt themselves.

The general rules for fitting up school-rooms are,—1. One foot for the space or passage between a form and the next desk.

2. Three inches for the horizontal space between a desk and its form.

3. Nine inches for the breadth of a desk, and six for the breadth of a form.

4. Twenty-eight inches for the height of a desk, and sixteen for the height of a form.

5. Eighteen inches in length of the desk for every child to occupy while seated upon his form.

6. From five to six feet for the passage between the walls and the ends of the forms and desks.

The semi-circles for the reading classes are formed opposite to the wall, and are marked by an incision in the floor.

Dimensions of school-rooms for 300 children, length, 62½ ft., breadth, 34 feet; for 200 do. 55 by 28; for 150 do. 52½ feet by 25.

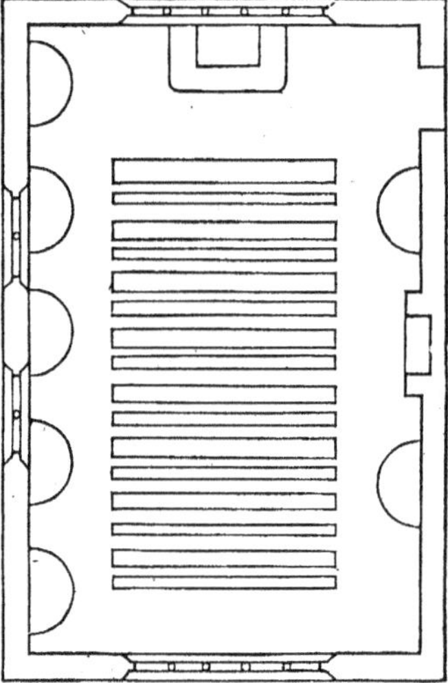

School-room for 56 scholars.

The following suggestions are abridged from the "*General Observations on the construction and arrangements of school-rooms, &c.*," published by the National Society, London.

The form of the room should be oblong. If the room is built large to accommodate boys and girls together, it may be divided by a frame partition, made to slide upon rollers in an iron groove.

The superficial area should include 7 square feet for each child: hence, 50 children will require 350 ft; 80 do. 560 ft.; 100 do. 700 ft., &c.

The desks are generally attached to the wall, and consist of a horizontal ledge two or three inches wide to receive the inkstand, and an inclined plane ten inches wide, made to let down by hinges and movable brackets. The benches or forms are ten inches wide, and supported by standards of cast iron.

The benches for the classes in recitation, are arranged in the floor without desks. The floor is entirely level.

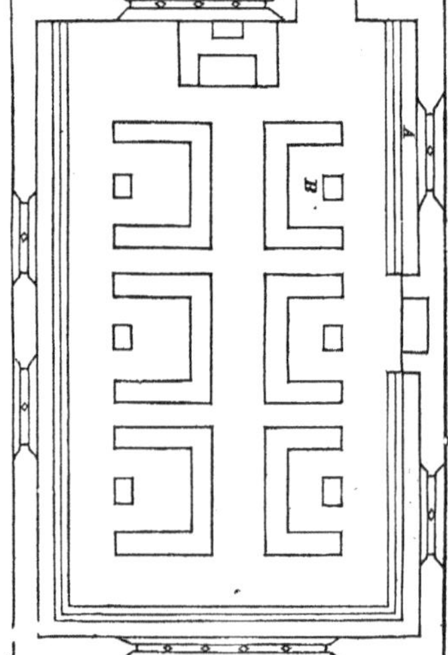

Plans, &c., for Schools on the Mixed and Facher System.

The two plans on the preceding page, for schools of 56 children, arranged on the monitorial or mutual system, are taken from the "Minutes of the Committee of Council on Education, 1840, relative to Plans of School-houses." In each plan, given in the "Minutes," the arrangement of the school-room is delineated, 1. according to the system of *mutual instruction*, distinguishing, as above, that of the National Society from that of the British and Foreign School Society; and 2. according to the *mixed method*, in which a modification of the mutual system, through the agency of better instructed and paid monitors, or pupil teachers, is employed in combination with the simultaneous method. Thus, on the same sheet, with the school-room for 56 children on the mutual system, there is also the following plan on the *mixed* system.

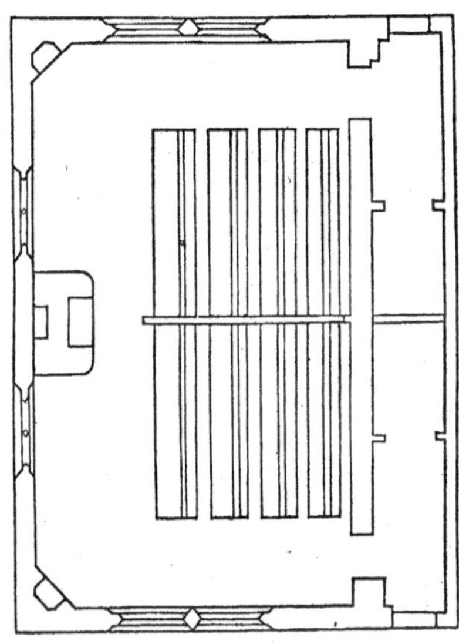

The school-room is 18 feet wide by 31 long, the space (20 feet by 12) occupied by the desks and seats being divided into two parts, one for boys and the other for girls, by a movable partition. The desks and benches are arranged on a series of platforms, rising each 6 inches above the preceding one. The school, if taught on the mixed method recommended would be divided into four classes, the boys of the first class occupying the first bench on one side, and the girls, do. on the other, &c., and employing one pupil teacher and four monitors. The teacher would give general instruction from the platform to the whole school, and hear any class separately, arranged in a circle around him. Two other classes might be heard in the entry, or class rooms attached. (The plan in this cut is modified slightly from the original inprint when it is connected with the dwelling house.)

The "Minutes" contain four *series of plans*, each presenting a different arrangement.

In the *first* series, there are five plans for schools varying from 30 to 56 scholars, each with the classes arranged and seated as above, and two of them presenting additional accommodations for an infant department, one of 20, and the other of 30 children.

In the *second* series, there is a separate range of desks for each class, with five varieties of arrangements, to accommodate 60 to 100 children, with a separate room for an infant school in two. In this series preference is expressed for the plan copied from the model school of the Normal School of Dejon. In this plan, the room is 56 feet by 16, divided into two apartments, each 28 by 16, one for 55 boys and the other for 55 girls. Each department is divided into three classes, one class occupying a group of desks, rising on platforms directly in front of the teacher, and the other two, one on the left, and the other on the right, so that they form a sort of amphitheater around the level portion of the floor occupied by the teacher. Each class can be taught separately, occupying its own group of desks, as arranged around the teacher's desk.

In the *third series* the accommodations ascend from 144 children, and 150 infants, to an indefinitely greater number, by a larger or smaller number of class-rooms arranged on each side of a central school-hall, which is lighted by sky-lights.

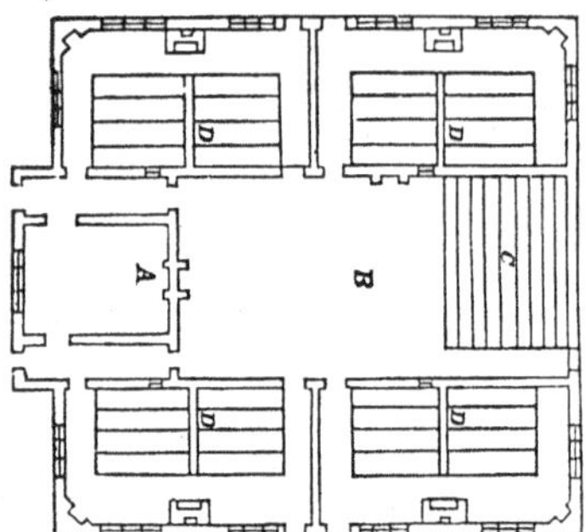

The following plan of a building exhibits the arrangement of a school for three hundred children, including one hundred and fifty in an infant school. A is a private room or study for the principal. B is the school hall (54 ft. by 27) for the assemblage of the whole school for morning and evening prayers, and other general exercises, and for the occupancy of the infant school, and C the gallery of the latter. D, D, D, D, are four class-rooms, (each 19 by 17) each again divided by a partition into two, so that both can be superintended by one assistant teacher, and one pupil teacher. Each subdivision of class-room will accommodate about 40 scholars each. The boys and the girls under eleven years arranged according to attainments, each on separate benches are taught together, while those over eleven years are taught separately in class-rooms appropriated to each. This arrangement affords greater facilities for giving to the instruction of the older children such a particular character as will prepare them for the application of their knowledge to the actual duties of life. Such knowledge must differ, in a class of boys, from that given in a class of girls.

In the *fourth series*, the same principles of arrangements are observed, except that the boys and girls occupy rooms on different floors.

In all of the plans recommended in the "Minutes," of the Committee, accommodations are provided for 1. the technical instruction of the children in classes carefully arranged according to their intellectual proficiency; 2. for the general instruction and exercises of the whole school; and, 3d, for the residence of the teacher. This last feature is common to almost all school houses in Europe, and the use of the same constitutes a part of the teacher's compensation. In the larger structures of Prussia and Saxony, there is an entire room appropriated to each class. Thus in a school-house for 600 children, at Berlin, there are eight rooms, and in these rooms the children are classed according to their ages, capacities and attainments. Eight masters are employed, besides auxiliary masters for special purposes; and two mistresses, for teaching at certain hours sewing and knitting to the girls.

The "Minutes" contain many valuable suggestions respecting the location, ventilation, and warming of school-rooms, similar to what has been already printed. The following section exhibits three forms of desks. The standards are of wrought or cast iron.

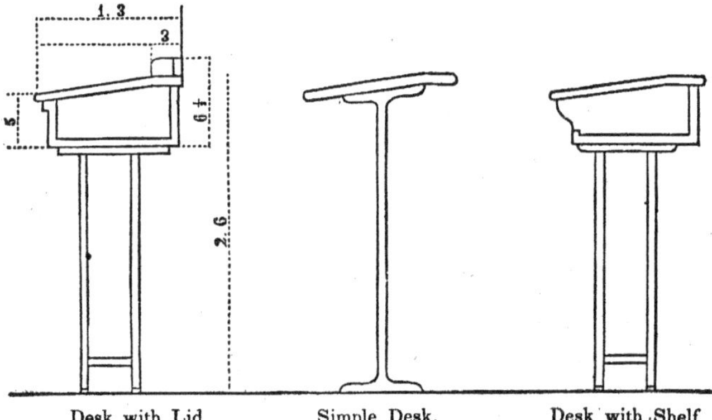

Desk with Lid. Simple Desk. Desk with Shelf.

In the "Minutes of the Committee of Council on Education for 1851–52," under the general head of Organization of Schools, the following memorandum and diagrams "respecting the organization of schools in parallel groups of benches and desks," are published to aid committees in determining the internal dimension of school-rooms, and the best modes of fitting them up, in reference to schools organized on the plan recommended by the committee.

Preliminary Remarks.

"Before a school-room is planned,—and the observation applies equally to alterations in the internal fittings of an existing school-room,—the number of children who are likely to occupy it,—the number of classes into which they ought to be grouped,—whether the school should be "mixed," or the boys and the girls should be in different rooms, should be carefully considered, in order that the arrangements of the school may be designed accordingly.

A. Every class, when in operation, requires a separate teacher, be it only a monitor acting for the hour. Without some such provision it is impossible to keep all the children in a school actively employed at the same time.

The apprenticeship of pupil-teachers, therefore, is merely an improved method of meeting what is, under any circumstance, a necessity of the case; and, where such assistants are maintained at the public expense, it becomes of increased importance to furnish them with all the mechanical appliances that have been found by experience to be the best calculated to give effect to their services.

B. The main end to be attained is the concentration of the attention of the teacher upon his own separate class, and of the class upon its teacher, to the exclusion of distracting sounds and objects, and without obstruction to the head master's power of superintending the whole of the classes and their teachers. This concentration would be effected the most completely if each teacher held his class in a separate room; but such an arrangement would be inconsistent with a proper superintendence, and would be open to other objections. The common school-room should, therefore, be fitted to realize, as nearly as may be, the combined advantages of isolation and of superintendence, without destroying its use for such purposes as may require a large apartment. The best shape (*see diagrams annexed*) is an oblong about eighteen feet in width. Groups of desks are arranged along one of the walls. Each group is divided from the adjacent group or groups by an alley, in which a light curtain can be drawn forward or back. Each class, when seated in a group of desks, is thus isolated on its sides from the rest of the school. The head master, seated at his desk placed against the opposite wall, or standing in front of any one of the classes, can easily superintend the school; while the separate teacher of each class stands in front of it, where the vacant floor allows him to place his easel for the suspension of diagrams and the use of the black-board, or to draw out the children occasionly from their desks, and to instruct them standing, for the sake of relief by a change in position. The seats at the desks *and* the vacant floor in front of each group are *both needed*, and should therefore *be allowed for* in calculating the space requisite for *each class.*

C. By drawing back the curtain between two groups of desks, the principal teacher can combine two classes into one for the purpose of a gallery lesson; or a gallery (doubling the depths of rows) may substituted for one of the groups. For simultaneous instruction, such a gallery is better than the combination of two groups by the withdrawal of the intermediate curtain; because the combined width of the two groups is greater than will allow the teacher to command at a glance all the children sitting in the same line. It is advisable therefore always to provide a gallery.

The drawings annexed to the following rules purport simply to show the best internal dimensions of school-rooms, and the best mode of fitting them up, the doors and windows being placed accordingly. The combination of such rooms with others of the same kind, with teachers' residences, and with the remainder of the school premises, as well as the elevations which may thereby be obtained, depending, as they always must, upon local circumstances, are not intended to be here shown.*

The Committe of Council do not recommend that the benches and desks should be immovably fixed to the floor in any schools. They ought to be so coustructed as to admit of being readily removed when necessary, but not so as to be easily pushed out of place by accident, or to be shaken by the movements of the children when seated at them.

The reasons of the following rules will be readily inferred from these preliminary explanations.

1. In planning a school-room, if it be not more than 18 feet in width, about 8 or 9 square feet will be sufficient for each child in actual attendance. If the width be greater, there must be a proportionate increase of area allotted to each child.

2. A school not receiving infants should generally be divided into at least four classes. (*The varying capacities of children between seven and thirteen years old will be found to require at least thus much subdivision.*)

3. Parallel benches and desks, graduated according to the ages of the children, should be provided for all the scholars in actual attendance, (*see Preliminary Remarks*, B.;) and therefore a school-room should contain at least four groups of parallel benches and desks. (*See Rule* 2.)

4. A group should not contain more than three rows of benches and desks, (*otherwise the distance of the last row is to great for the teacher to see the children's slates, and he must also raise his voice to a pitch which is exhausting to himself and adds inconveniently to the general noise.*)

5. As a general rule, no group of benches and desks should accommodate *more* than twenty-four children, *i. e.* eight children in each of the three rows of the group, (*otherwise the width is too great. See Preliminary Remarks*, C.)

6. The proper lengths are 7 feet 6 inches for five children in a row; 9 feet for six in a row; 10 feet 6 inches for seven in a row; 12 feet for eight in a row; *i. e.* 18 inches for each child.

[The other dimensions and details are shown in the annexed drawings.]

7. Each group of desks must be separated from the contiguous group, either by an alley for the passage of the children, or by a space sufficient for drawing and withdrawing the curtains.

It will be sufficient to provide an alley for the passage of children *at one end only* of each group. At the other end a space of 3 inches will suffice for drawing and withdrawing the curtains.

[Alleys intended for the passage of children must not be less than 18 inches wide in the smallest school, and need not be more than 2 feet wide in any school, unless where a door or fireplace requires a greater interval.]

8. The best width for a school-room, intended to accommodate any number of children between 48 and 144, is 17 or 18 feet. This gives sufficient space for each group of benches and desks to be ranged (with its depth of three rows) along one wall, for the teachers to stand at a proper distance from their classes, and for the classes to be drawn out, when necessary, in front of the desks around the master or pupil-teachers. (*No additional accommodation being gained by greater width in the room, the cost of such an increase in the dimensions is thrown away.*)

9. Where the number of children to be accommodated is too great for them to be arranged in five, or at most, six groups, an additional school-room should be built, and placed under the charge of an additional schoolmaster, who may, however, be subordinate to the head master, or a large school may be built on the plan of diagram No. 6. Where neither of these arrangements can be accomplished, the school-room should not be less than 32 feet wide, and the groups should be arranged along both sides of the room, the children in all cases facing the centre. (*But such an arrangement is very inferior to that of the single row along one wall. The opposite classes see each other, and their several teachers have to stand too close together. See Preliminary Remarks*, B.)

10. A curtain, capable of being readily drawn and withdrawn, should separate

* Specimen of the plans recommended by the committee, combining the foregoing object may be seen on page .

the several groups; but not so as, when drawn, to project into the room more than 4 inches in front of the foremost desk.

11. If the school-room be lighted from above, which is the best possible mode, great care should be taken to prevent the skylights from leaking, and to provide channels for the water which the condensation of the children's breath will deposit on the inside of the glass.

12. All sashes, both upper and lower, should be hung; and all windows, whether in the roof or elsewhere, should be made to open.

13. It is better to have a few large and well placed windows than many small ones.

14. It is important to provide that the faces of the children and teachers, and also the blackboards and diagrams, should be placed in full clear light.

15. If the school-room be not lighted from above, there should be windows, if possible, at each end and on one side of the room. The windows should be carried up as high as possible; and those which are placed at the backs of the children, an arrangement which should be avoided as far as possible, should not come down within 5 feet 6 inches, or at least 5 feet, from the floor.

16. When the benches and desks are arranged on both sides of the room, it should be lighted from above, or there should be, if possible, windows in *each* of the side walls.

17. Except when a school-room is very broad, there should be no fireplace in the center of an end wall.

[A good place for a fireplace is under a window.]

18. The desks should be either quite flat or *very slightly* inclined. The objections to the inclined desks are, that pencils, pens, &c., are constantly slipping from it, and that it can not be conveniently used as a table. The objection to the flat desk is, that it obliges the children to stoop. A raised ledge in front of a desk interferes with the arm in writing.

19. A large gallery for the simultaneous instruction of two or more classes, without desks, may advantageously be provided in a class-room or at one end of the school-room. Such a gallery may be better placed along than across the end of the school-room, for the reason stated in the Preliminary Remarks, B.

20. No such gallery, nor any gallery in an infant school-room, should be placed in front of a window, unless it be very high up above the heads of the children when they stand on the top row of the gallery.

21. No infant gallery should hold more than eighty or ninety infants.

22. An infant school should (besides a large gallery) have a small group of benches and desks, for the occasional use of the elder infants.

23. The alleys leading to a gallery should be at its sides, not in its center. *(See Rules 5 and 6.)*

24. Great care should be taken that the valves which admit the fresh air into the school-room should be placed so as not to create draft where the teachers and children sit.

25. An easel and a blackboard should be provided for each class, and a larger blackboard for the gallery.

26. The dimensions shown in the drawings annexed to this memorandum, are adapted to children of from 11 to 12 years of age. *It is very important that these dimensions should be graduated to suit the sizes of the elder and younger children in a school.*"

Although the following diagrams of the internal arrangements of school-rooms are drawn in reference to schools organized on a peculiar plan, as set forth in the foregoing memorandum, they will suggest valuable hints to a judicious architect or committee. There are some features in them, which we do not approve, and we think will not be found in practice as convenient as several of the more recent plans embodied in this volume.

No. 1. A School for 48 children of one sex, in 4 classes; with a class-room having a gallery capable of containing two of the classes.

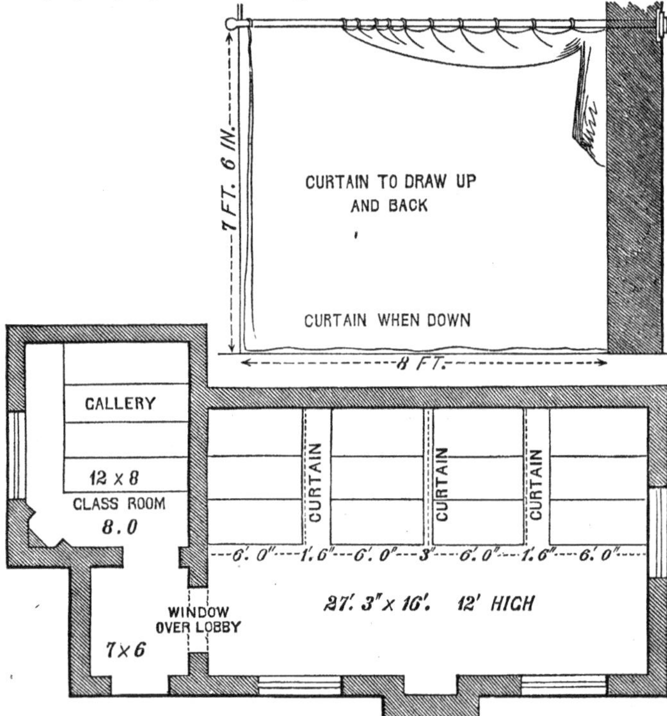

No. 2. A School for 48 boys and girls, in 4 classes; with a class-room having a gallery capable of containing two of the classes.

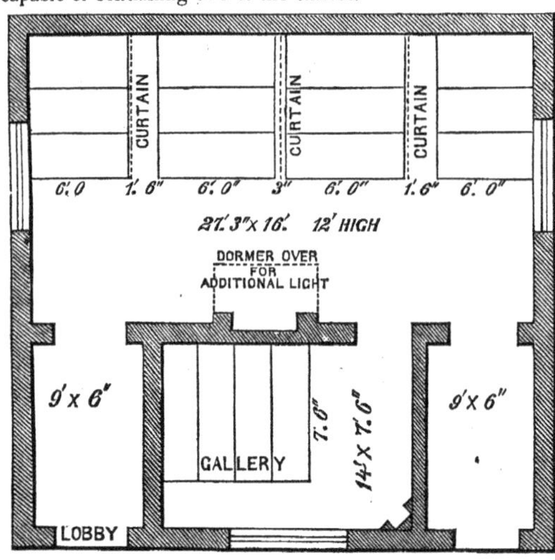

No. 3. A School for 72 children of one sex, in classes; with a class-room having a gallery capable of containing two of the classes.

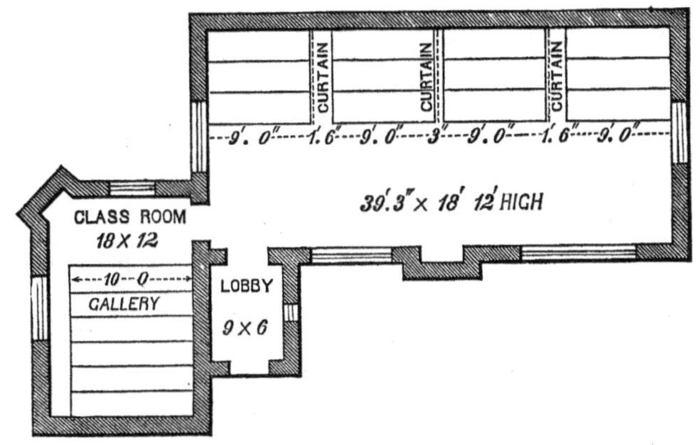

No. 4. A School for 72 boys and girls, in 4 classes; with a class-room having a gallery capable of containing two of the classes.

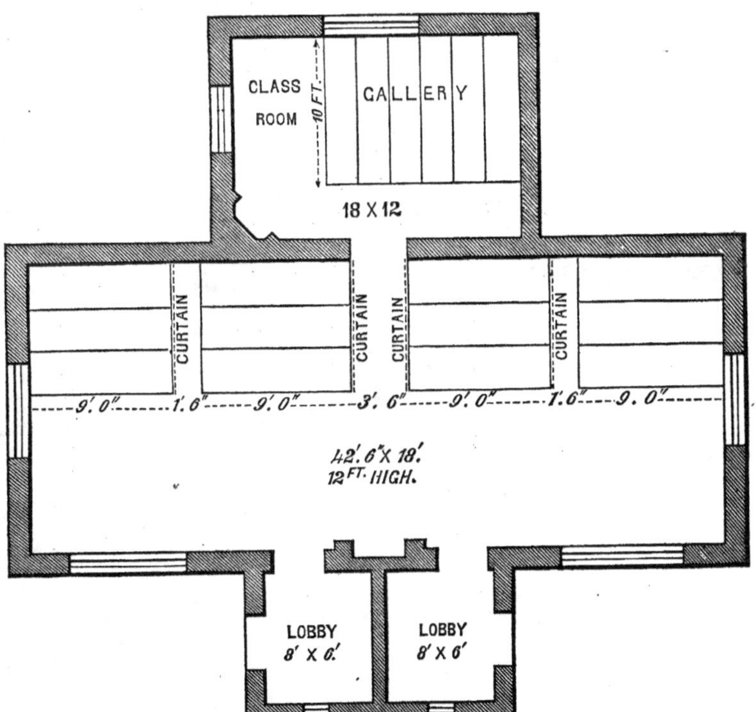

No. 5. A School for 120 children of one sex, in 5 classes; with a class-room having a gallery capable of containing two of the classes.

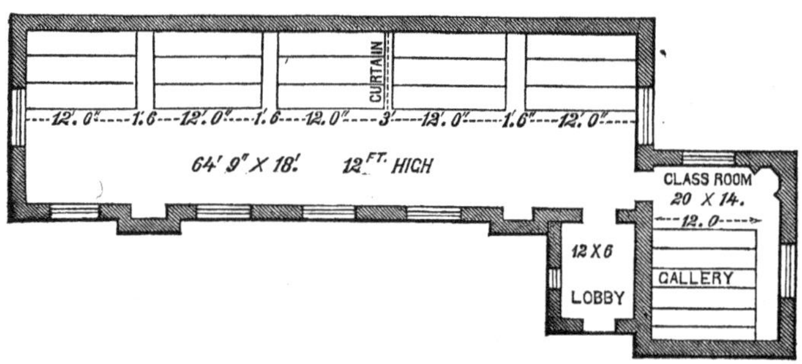

No. 6. A School for 168 children of one sex, in 7 classes, with a gallery; and with a class-room having a gallery capable of containing two of the classes.

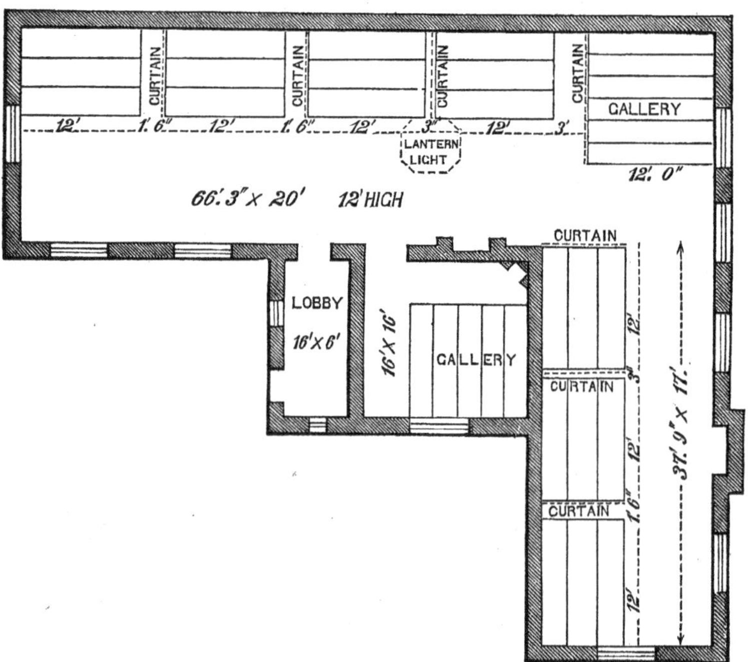

No. 7. A School for 240 children of one sex, in 8 classes, and a gallery; with a class-room having also a gallery capable of containing two of the classes.

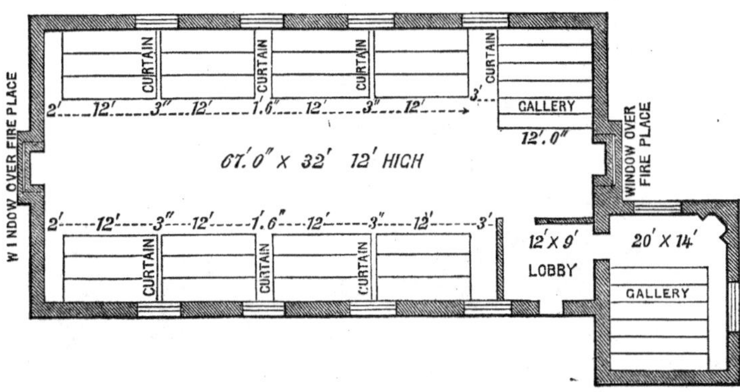

No. 8. Infant Schools for 100 infants, with a gallery capable of accommodating 72 infants, and a group of benches and desks capable of accommodating 15 infants.

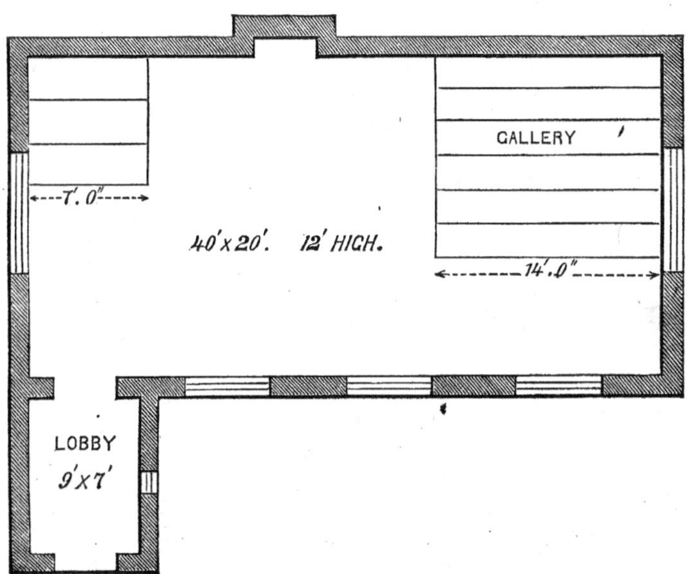

Plan of a Village School-house in England.

Fig. 4.

We are indebted to A. J. Downing, Esq. for the reduced cuts of a plan by J. Kendal, for a National School near Brentwood, in England. It affords accommodation for sixty children. The door is sheltered by a porch, and on the other side is a covered waiting-place for the children coming before school-hours. The cost, with the belfry, was $750. A house in this old English domestic character would give a pleasing variety to the everlasting sameness of our rural school architecture.

Fig. 5. Ground Plan.

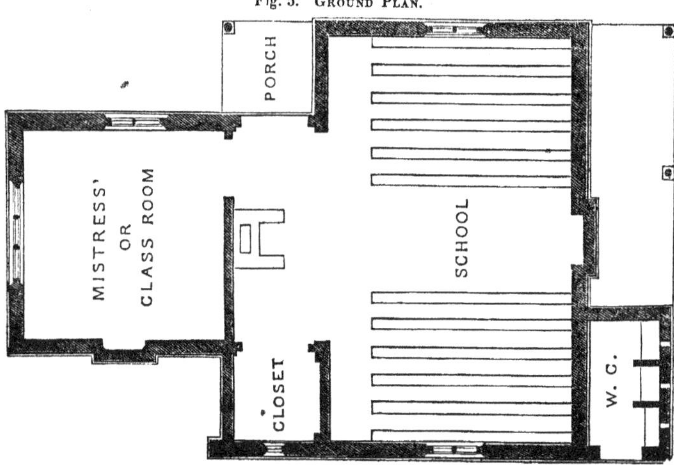

Plans for Rural Towns and Villages, recommended by the Massachusetts Board of Education.

The following Plans were prepared by Mr. Leach, one of the agents employed by the Board of Education in Massachusetts to co-operate with their Secretary in visiting schools in different towns, and in conferring with school officers and teachers in regard to the construction and condition of school-houses, the teaching and governing of the schools, and the action of the towns in relation to them.

Mode of Ventilation.

By your particular direction, I have given considerable attention to the subject of ventilation. In all my examination, I have found but few houses well ventilated. In a large majority of cases, there are no means of ventilating but by opening the windows and doors. And where attempts have been made, it has been but imperfectly accomplished. The ventilating tubes have almost invariably been too small. As the result of my investigations, I would make the following suggestions. To ventilate a room properly containing fifty persons, the ventilating tube should not be less than fifteen square inches inside. The tube should be made of very thin boards, well seasoned, with a smooth inside surface, and it should be perfectly tight. It should be wholly within the room, and opposite to the register or stove. There should be an opening at the top and bottom. The ventilating tubes should be connected in the attic, and conducted through the roof, and furnished with a suitable cap. Another method, which is far preferable, is as follows: The smoke pipes may be conducted into a cast iron pipe resting on soap-stone in the attic floor, instead of a chimney built from the bottom of the cellar. This cast iron pipe may be surrounded by a brick chimney into which the ventilating tubes should lead. The space in the chimney should be equal to the spaces in the tubes, after making suitable allowance for the pipe, and the increase of friction. By this arrangement, the air in the tubes will be rarefied, and a rapid current of air produced. All attempts to ventilate rooms with tubes in the wall, or of less size than fourteen or fifteen square inches for fifty persons, have, so far as I have examined, failed. No artificial means will secure good ventilation when the temperature of the room and that of the outer air are nearly the same, without the application of heat to the air in the tubes. Unless the air is heated before being admitted into the room, it should be let in at the top, and not at the bottom, and always through a large number of small apertures. The quantity of pure air admitted must always be equal to that which is to be forced out.

The expense of introducing a proper ventilating apparatus into houses already built in the country towns, will vary from twenty-five to a hundred dollars, according to the size and character of the house.

Directions for making Blackboards.

To 100 pounds of common mortar, add 25 pounds of calcined plaster; to this add twelve papers, of the largest size, of lampblack. This is to be put on as a skim coat, one sixth of an inch thick to rough plastering, and should be made as smooth as possible by hard rubbing. It may also be put on to old plastering, after it has been thoroughly raked and prepared. This should be covered with a coat of paint, made in the following manner: To one quart of spirits, add one gill of boiled oil. To this add one of the largest papers of lampblack, after it has been thoroughly mixed with spirits. To this add one pound of the finest flour of emery. This paint may also be put on boards or canvas. This should be constantly stirred, when used, to prevent the emery from settling. If too much oil, or if any varnish be used, the board will become more or less glazed and unfit for use. Some prefer to have the board behind the teacher green or bronze, which is more grateful to the eye. This can be done by using chrome green instead of lampblack. None but the very finest flour of emery should be used. Some prefer pulverized pumice-stone to emery.

Note.—All the Plans are drawn on a scale of ten feet to an inch, with the exception of Numbers 9 and 10, which are drawn on a scale of twelve feet to an inch.

PLAN NO. 1, FOR RURAL OR VILLAGE SCHOOL-HOUSE.

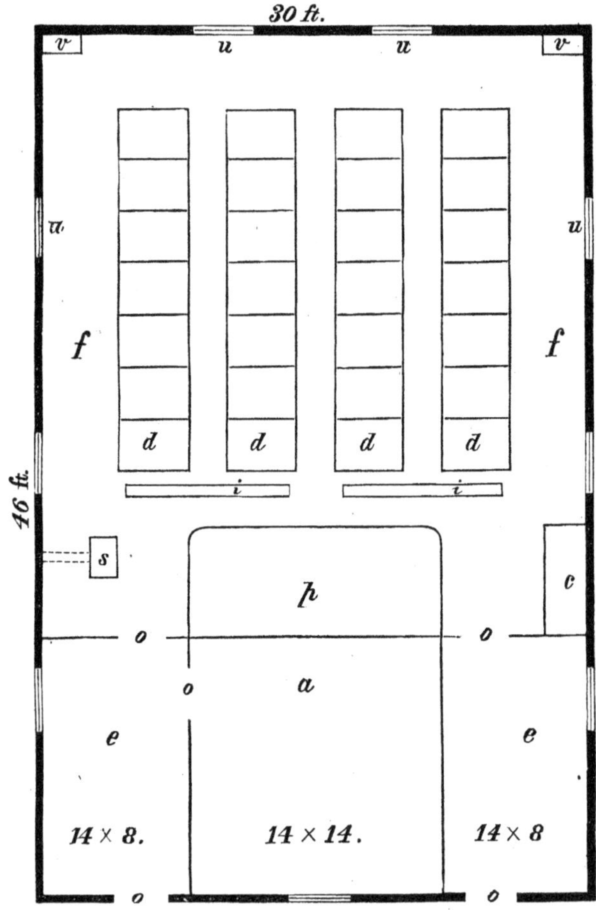

This plan represents the ground floor of a school-house one story high, 46 by 30 feet on the inside.

e, *e*—Entries, one for each sex, 14 by 8 feet. *a*—Anteroom, 14 by 14 feet. This may be used as an assembly-room for the pupils before school and at noon, or for a recitation-room and library. Where it is practicable, there should be separate rooms for the pupils to assemble in. This can usually be provided in the basement at a small expense. *p*—Teacher's platform, 14 feet long and 6 feet wide, and 7 or eight inches high. Behind the teacher's desk there should always be a blackboard the whole length of the platform, from 4 to 5 feet wide, the lower edge of which should be $3\frac{1}{2}$ feet from the top of the platform. *f*, *f*—Aisles. The inner aisles should be from 16 to 18 inches wide. The outer aisles from 36 to 48 inches. *d*, *d*, *d*, *d*—Seats for two pupils each. The desks should be from 40 to 48 inches long; and the desks and seats should be from 30 to 36 inches wide, and adapted in height, to the age of the pupils. *c*—Closet for maps, books of reference, &c. *s*—Stove. The dotted lines an air-box, 10 inches square, to admit pure air. *v*, *v*—Ventilating tubes, 12 by 10 inches each. They should be placed within the room, and made of thin boards, perfectly tight, and smooth on the inside. They should be united in the attic, and lead through the roof.

i, i—Settees for recitations. *o, o, o, o*—Doors. *u, u, u*—Windows.

Blackboards should be placed entirely around the room except in the narrow spaces between the windows. They should be from 4 to 5 feet wide for large scholars, and 3 or 3½ for small ones. The lower edge should be from 2½ to 3 feet from the floor. Every school-house designed for both sexes should have two entrances, one for each sex. There should also be two separate backyards, inclosed with a high tight fence. The entrance to the water-closets should be through the basement, or through doors on the outside which should be kept locked. This is a very important arrangement, and has too generally been overlooked. The best interest of a school can not be secured without it. It is desirable that there should be a basement under every school-house. The bottom may be covered with a floor, with brick, or with hydraulic cement. The basement should be divided into two parts, one for each sex. There should be a well in the center, and a pump and sink in each part. A part of it can conveniently be used for storing fuel, &c. The best mode of heating a school-room is by coal or wood furnaces in the basement. When stoves are used, the pipe may be conducted through the floors, well protected by soap-stone, into a chimney in the attic. In this way valuable room may be saved, which would otherwise be occupied by the chimney. It is also desirable that the teacher's desk be placed at the end of the building at which the pupils enter.

Single desks are generally to be preferred to double ones. The whole expense for room and desks is about twenty per cent. more. When practicable, the house should be so placed, that pupils as they sit, may face the north. In rooms to be used in summer as well as winter, it would be better that there should be no windows* on the south. In all cases there should be outside or inside blinds. Outside blinds are to be preferred to keep a room cool. Inside blinds can be more easily managed to modify the light. The gable end should also be toward the south, since by this arrangement the roofs would be much less heated in summer. On the ceiling of every school-room the four points of the compass should be painted in distinct colors, with letters designating the several points.

PLAN No. 2.

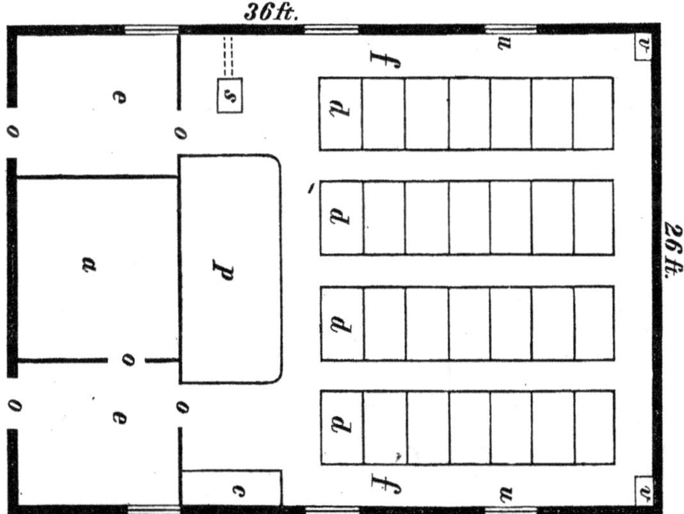

This plan is essentially the same as the preceding one, excepting in size. It is 36 by 26 feet inside. This can be adopted when it is desirable to sacrifice convenience for economy. It will be perceived that the outer aisles are much narrower

* It will be better to provide curtains and shutters to modify, rather than a blank wall to exclude altogether the cheerful sunlight.—H. B.

than those in the Plan Number One. Wide aisles are much more convenient for scholars to stand in during recitations, and to work at the blackboard without being annoyed by others passing them. It is also important that the aisles be wide enough to accommodate settees on days of examination, &c.

PLAN No. 3.

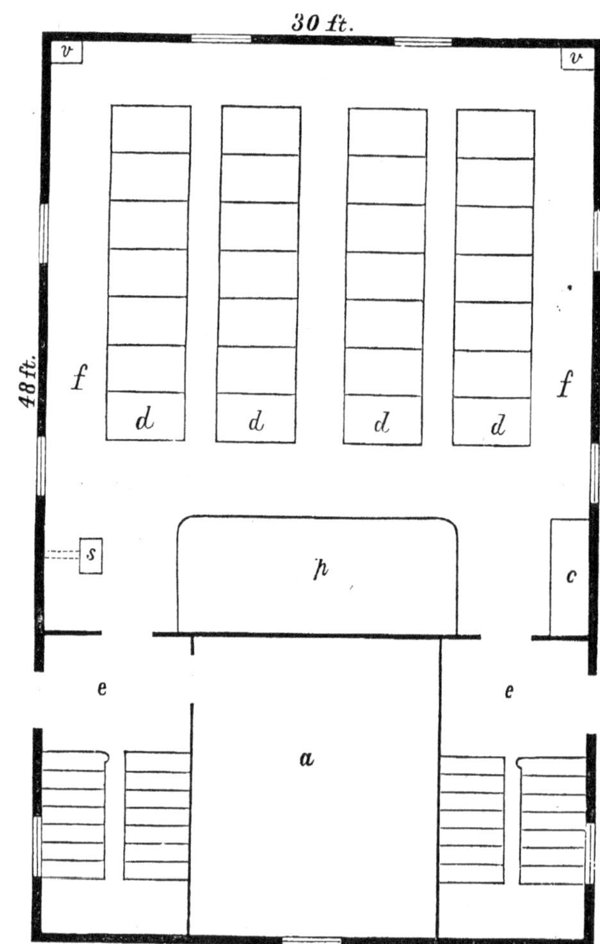

This represents the ground floor of a building two stories high. It is 48 by 30 feet inside. The description of Plan Number One will apply to this, with the exception of the entries.

e, *e*—Entries, one for each sex, 16 by 8 feet. *a*—Anteroom. The one on the lower floor communicating with the boys' entry, the upper one communicating with the girls' entry. There never should be winding stairs in a school-house. They should be made as represented on the plan, or in some form with broad steps. The landing place should never be directly opposite the door. The rooms should be from 11 to 13 feet in height. In large schools the outside door should swing outward, to enable the pupils to rush out easily in case of an alarm.

PLAN No. 4.

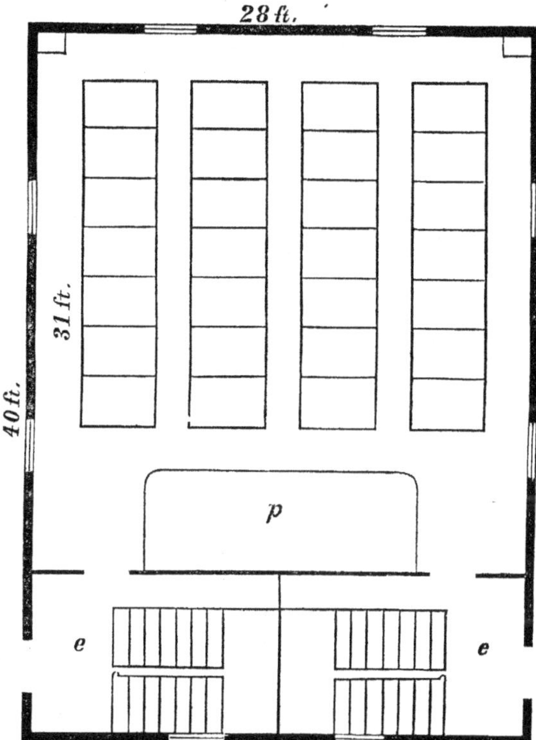

This differs from Number Three chiefly in its size. Its dimensions are 40 by 28 feet inside. It has no anteroom, and the entrances are on the sides. There should always be a basement under houses constructed after this plan. This should be divided into two rooms, which should be well finished, warmed, and lighted.

Plan No. 5.

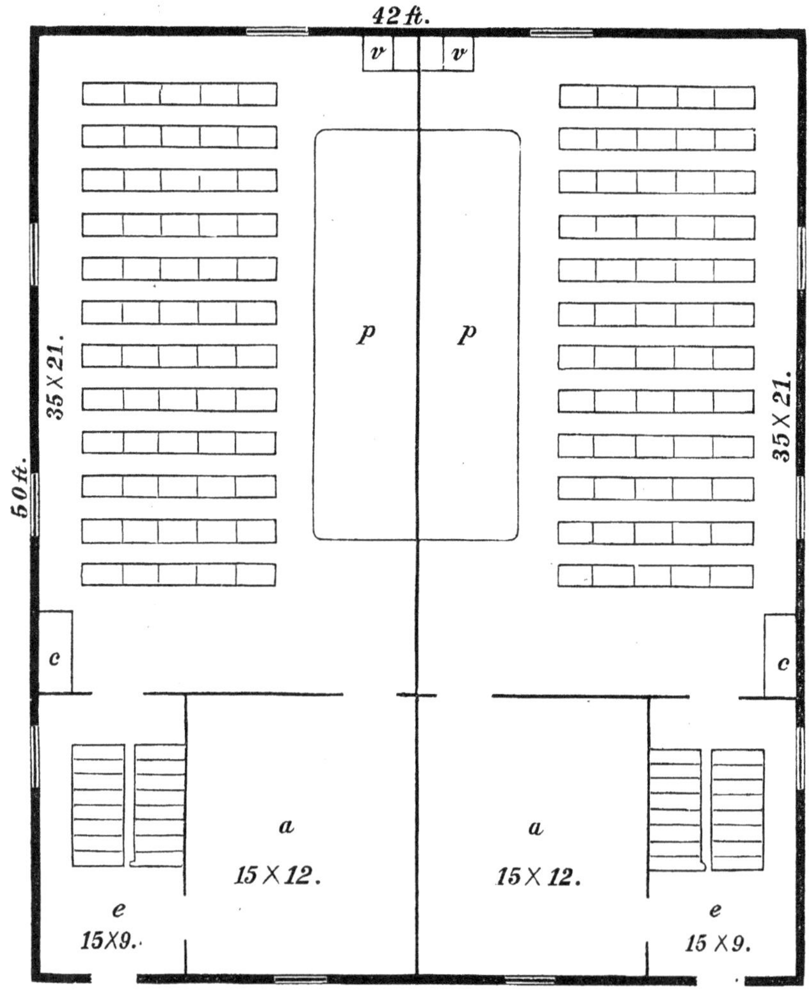

This represents the lower room of a building two stories high. Its dimensions are 50 by 42 feet inside, and contains two rooms and two anterooms that may be used for recitations; and two entries, one for each sex. The doors are at the end, but when it is practicable it would be better to have them on the side.

e, *e*—Entries, 15 by 9 feet each. *a*, *a*—Ante-rooms, 15 by 12 feet each. *c*, *c*—Closets for books and apparatus. The windows should be so placed as not to be directly opposite to the teacher. Neither pupils nor teachers should be compelled to face a strong light.

Plan No. 6.

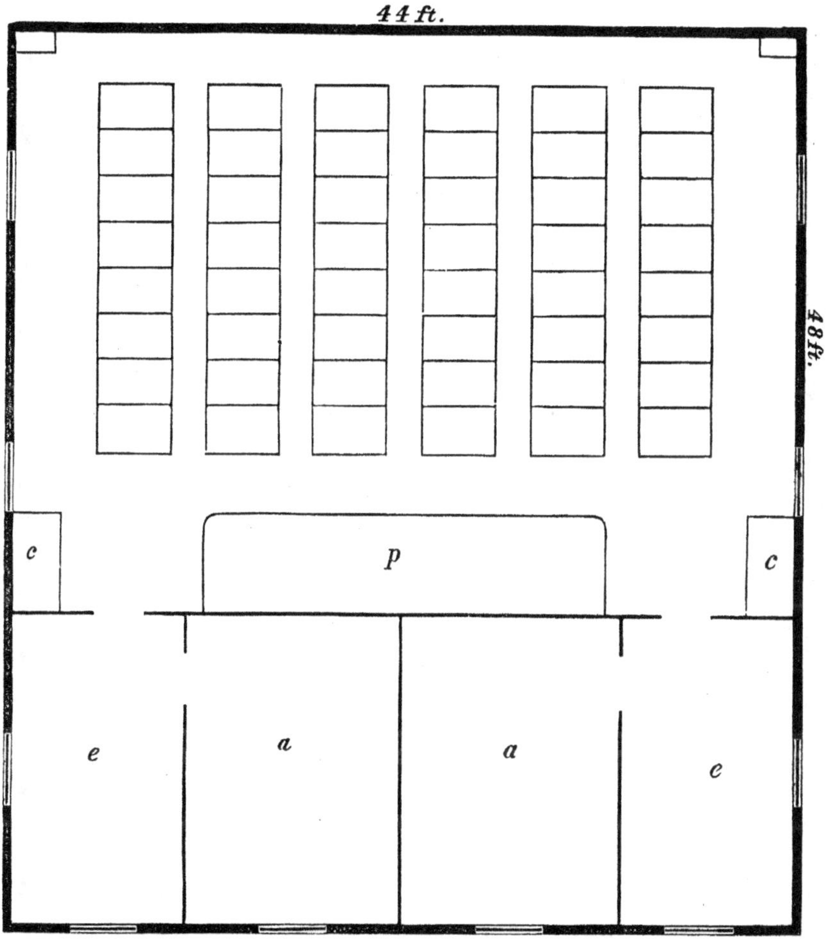

44 ft.

48 ft.

c p c

e a a e

This is a plan of the upper room of a building, the lower floor of which has been described in Number Five. It contains one school-room, 44 feet by 31, two recitation rooms, and two entries. The school-room will accommodate 96 pupils. The recitation rooms can be used as an assembly-room by the pupils, in the morning and at noon. There are many serious objections to large rooms, excepting for advanced pupils, who learn most of their lessons out of school. The testimony of nearly all experienced teachers is against large rooms for schools in which there are numerous classes.

PLAN No. 7.

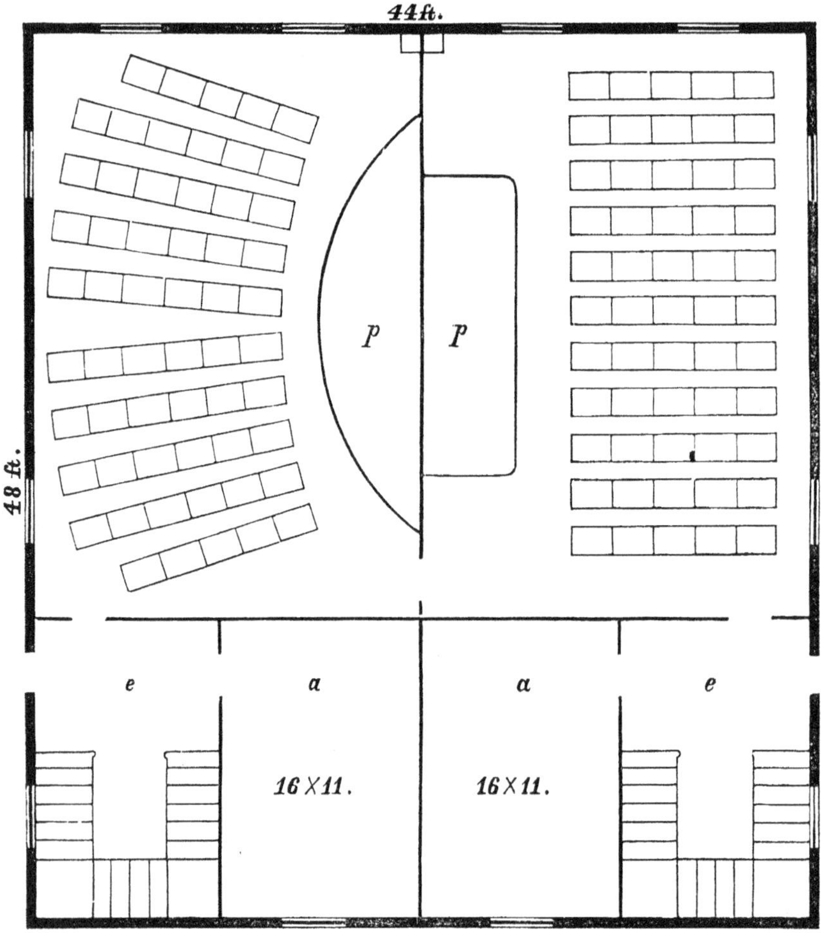

44 ft.

48 ft.

p p

e a a e

16×11. 16×11.

This is a plan of the lower floor of a building 48 by 44 feet. It contains two rooms for primary or intermediate scholars. Two modes of arranging the seats are presented, that either may be adopted. The entrances are on the sides. The form of the stairs differs from the preceding plans, and has some advantages. There are two anterooms, 16 by 11 feet each.

PLAN No. 8.

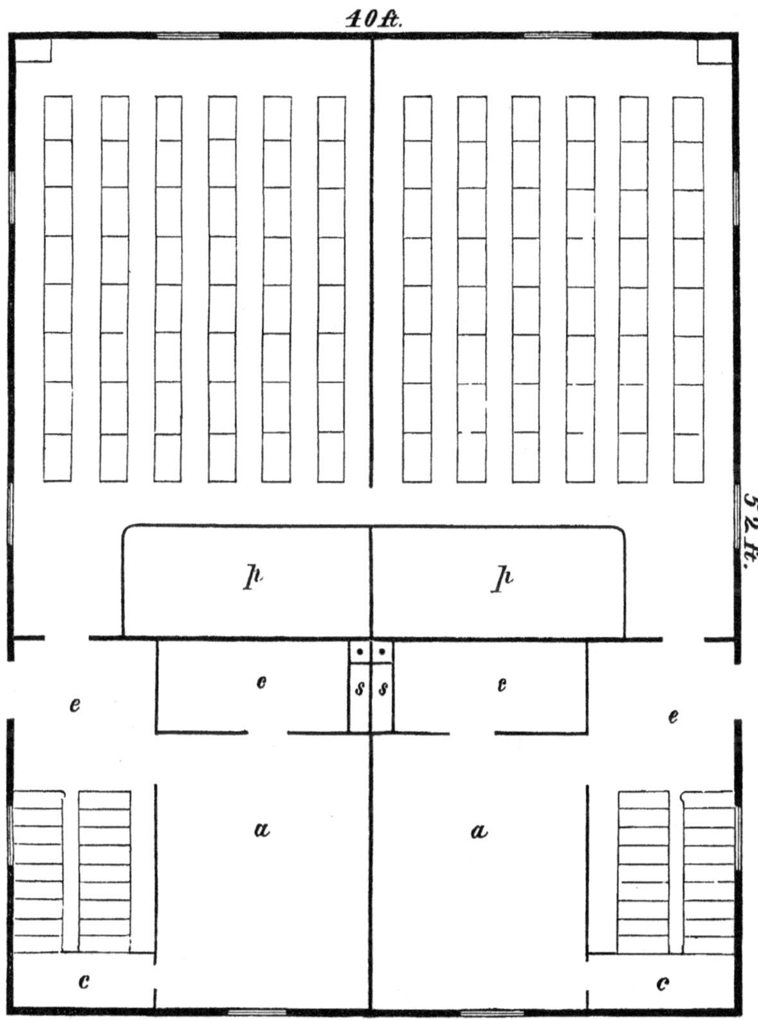

The dimensions of the building represented by this plan are 52 by 40 feet inside. There are two rooms on the lower floor, for small scholars. The entrances are on the sides. There are two anterooms, with closets, in which there is a sink and a pump, communicating with each. This and Number Nine are regarded as the best plans for houses two stories high, containing four rooms each. There are many advantages in having the stairs as represented on the plan, as they occupy less room and there will be much less disturbance by pupils going up and down.

PLAN No. 9.

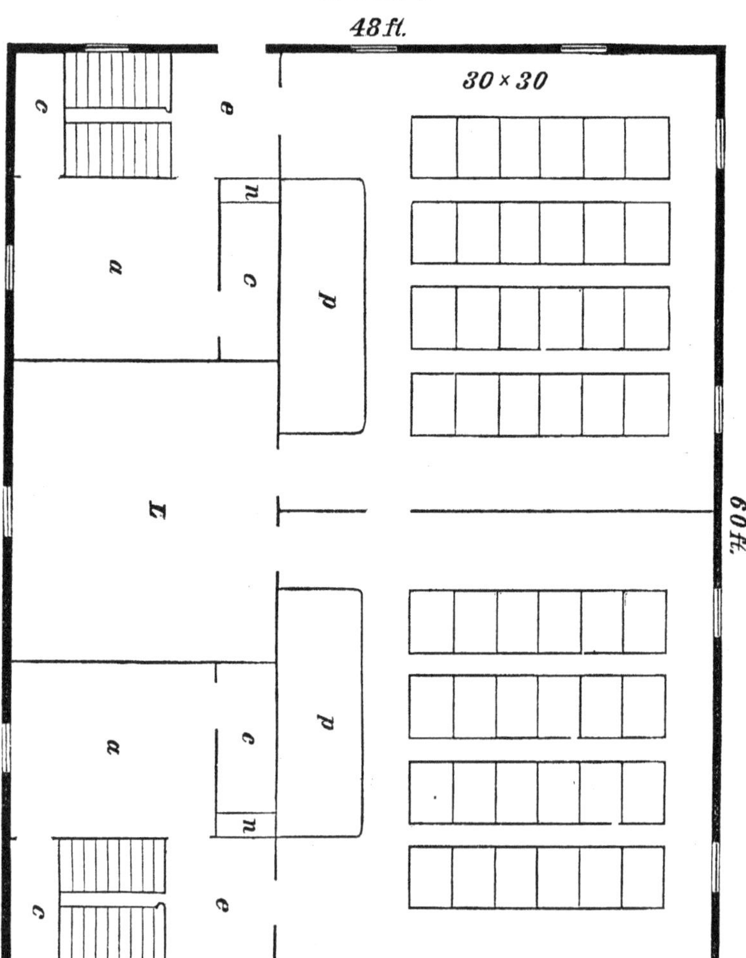

This is similar in its outline to Number Eight. Its dimensions are 60 by 48 feet inside. The entries, anterooms, and closets, are the same in form as Number Eight. It has also a large recitation room or library, (marked *L*) communicating with both rooms. This combines more advantages, perhaps, than are to be found in any of the plans presented. If the building is built two stories and a half high, a large upper room might be finished for assembling the whole school at stated times, or one or both of the partitions might be made to slide up by weights.

PLAN No. 10.

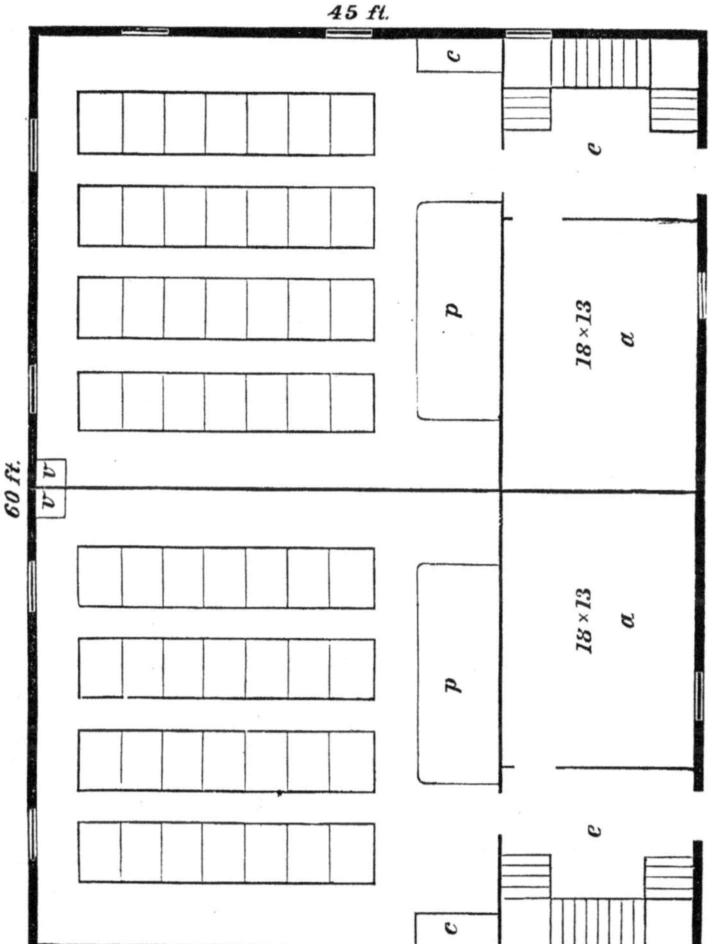

The dimensions of this building are 60 by 45 feet inside. The entrances are on the end. The form of the stairs is similar to Number Seven. In other respects it resembles plans already described.

PLAN No. 11.

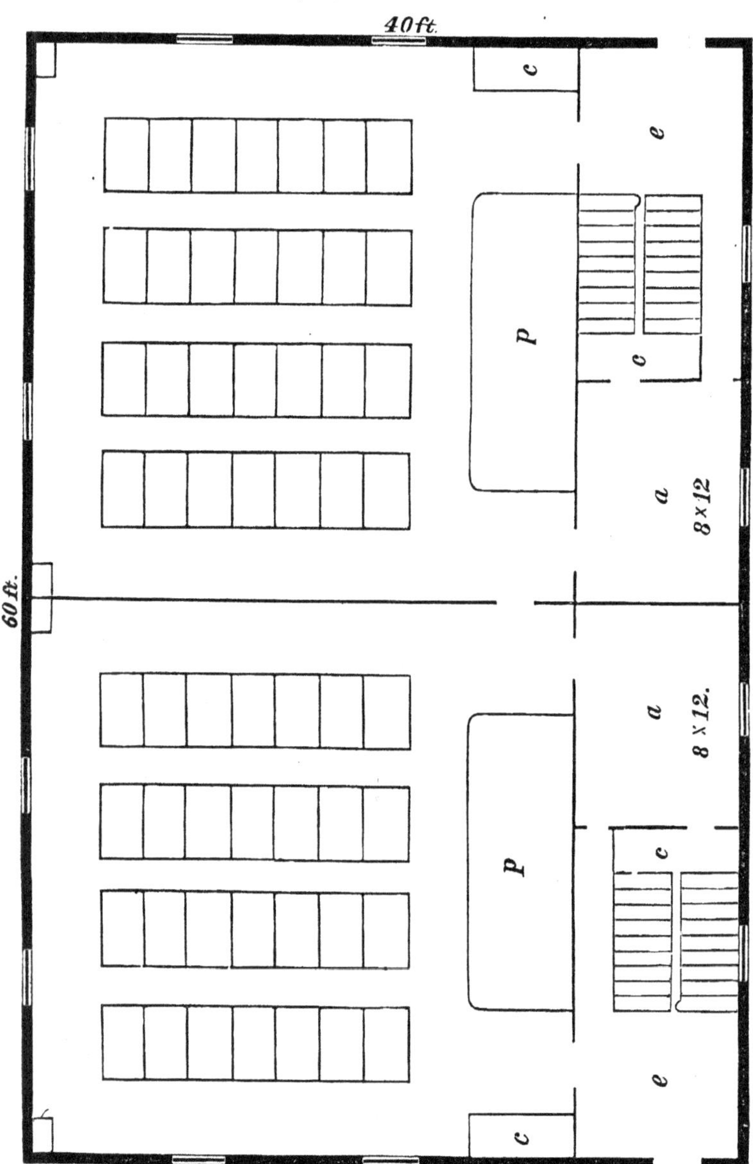

The dimensions of this building are 60 feet by 40. It differs from the preceding chiefly in the size of the entries, and in the form of the stairs; also, in having much smaller anterooms. The entrances are also on the sides.

PLAN NO. 12.

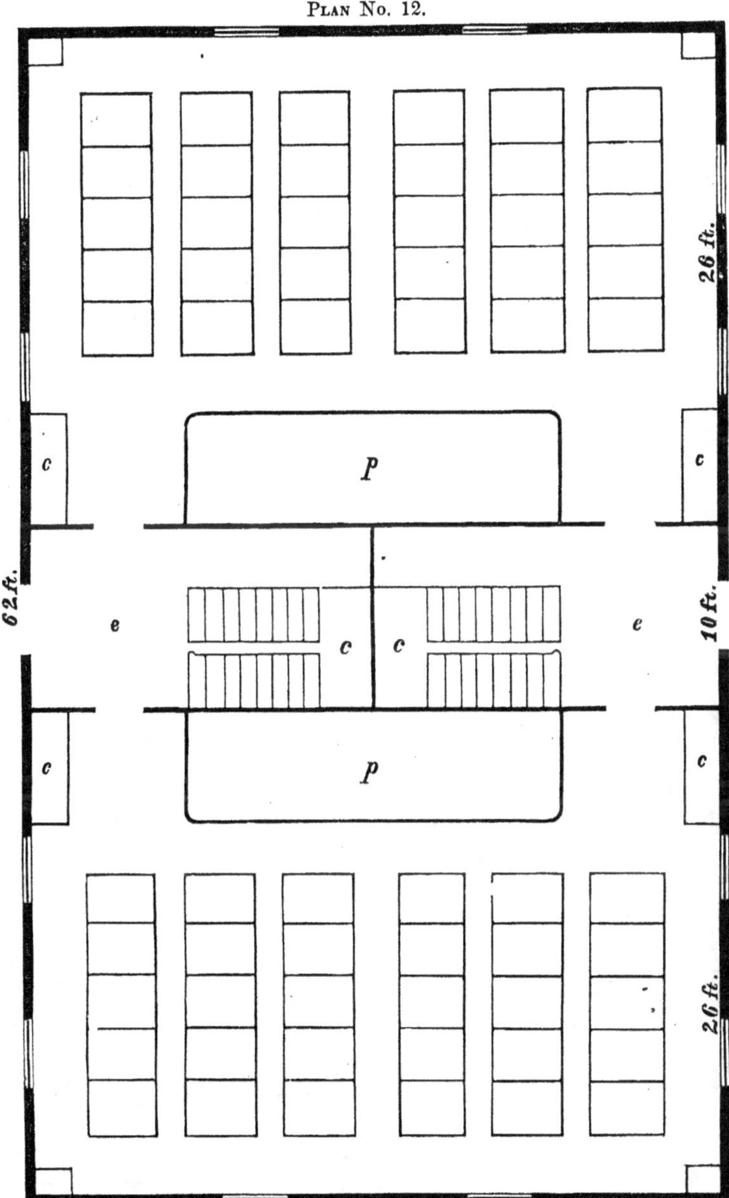

An excellent plan, when furnished with a suitable basement, where pupils can assemble before and after school, and at recess, when the weather is unpleasant. The sexes enter on the opposite sides of the house. The entrances to the water-closets should be from the basement.

Plan No. 13, represents the lower floor of a building, with three rooms on the lower floor. The arrangements of the rooms are the same as already described.

Plan No. 13.

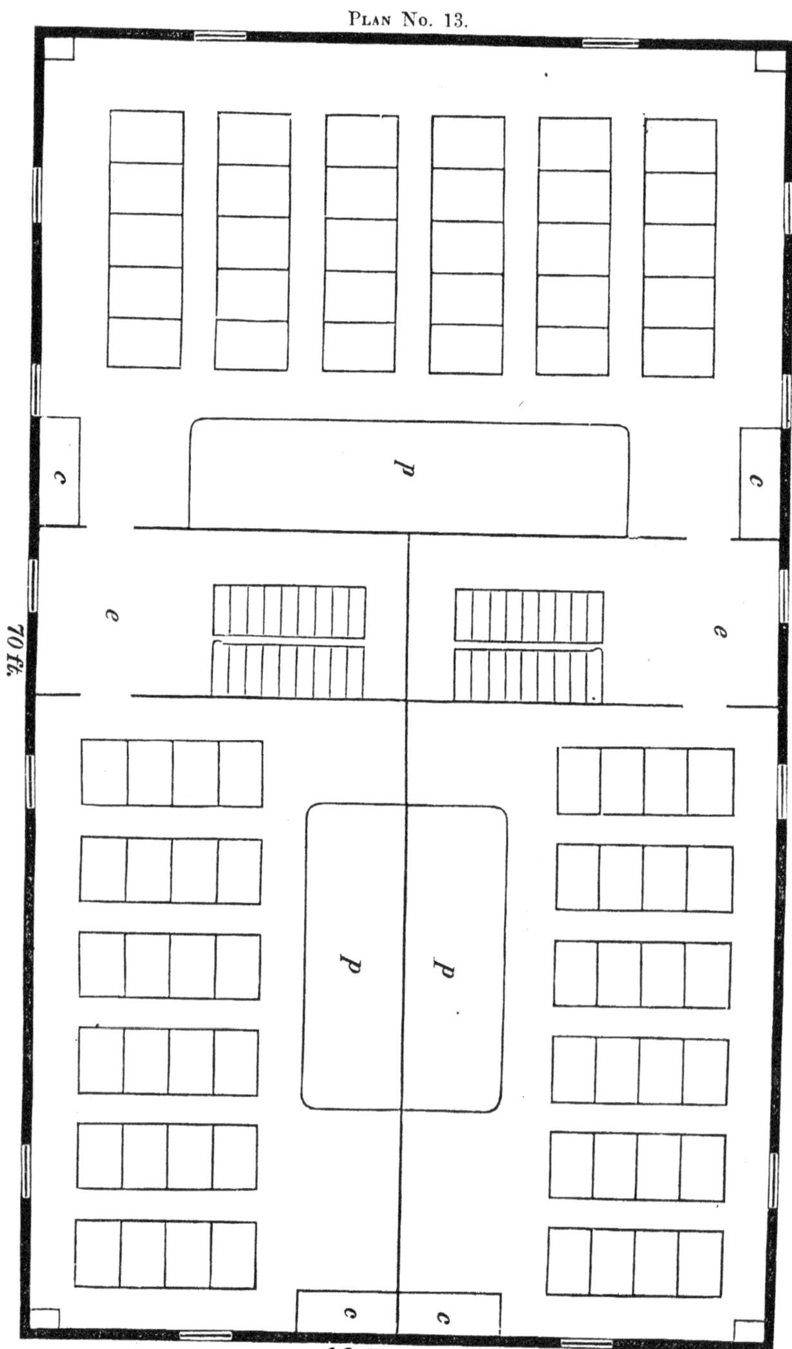

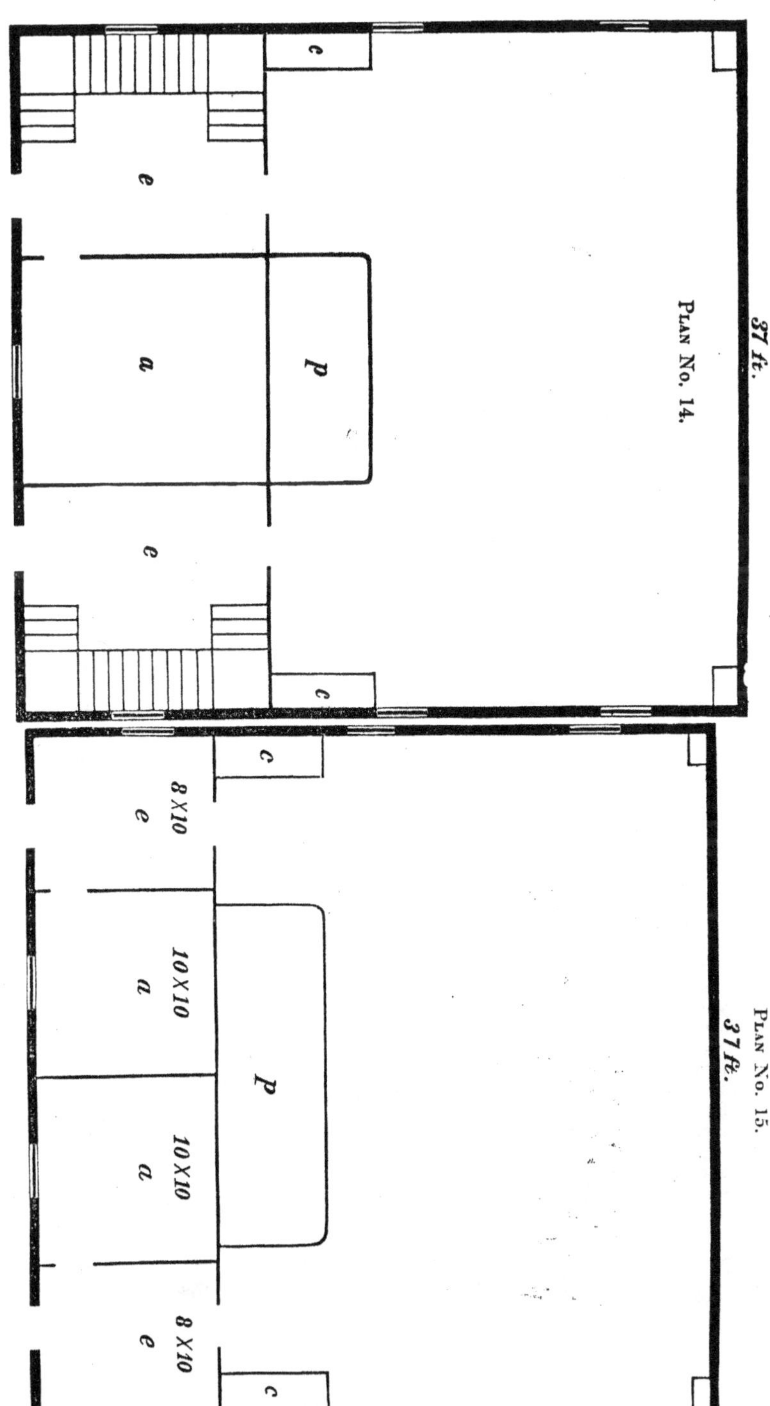
Plan No. 14.
37 ft.
c
e
a
p
e
c
Plan No. 15.
37 ft.
c
8 X 10
e
10 X 10
a
p
10 X 10
a
8 X 10
e
c

PLAN OF VENTILATION.

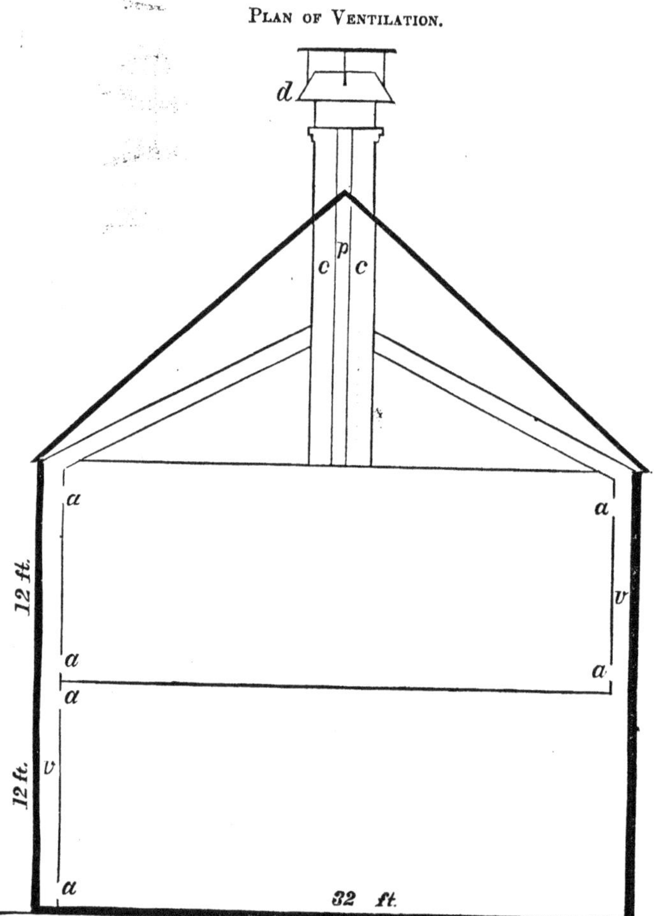

v, *v*—Ventiducts or ventilating tubes. These should be at least 14 inches square for a room containing 50 scholars. *a*, *a*—Apertures into the ventiducts *p*—Cast iron smoke flue, resting on soapstone in the attic floor. *c*, *c*—Chimney surrounding the smoke flue. This should contain as many square inches as the ventiducts leading into it, after deducting the space occupied by the flue. The inside of the chimney should be circular, and plastered perfectly smooth. This mode of ventilating is applicable to any method of heating, either by stoves or by furnaces. The heat of the smoke flue will rarefy the air in the chimney, and produce a strong draught in the ventiducts. This is regarded as the most effective, and, at the same time, the most economical mode of ventilation. The lower aperture should always be kept open. The upper aperture should be closed, excepting near the close of the morning and afternoon session, when it should be opened. It has been ascertained, by repeated experiments, that carbonic gas diffuses itself rapidly into every part of the room. In a room of 50 scholars, from 200 to 500 cubic feet of air are vitiated every minute, and unless some effectual means are devised for expelling the impure air, the most serious consequences must ensue.

Plan of District School-Room, recommended by Dr. A. D Lord, Columbus, Ohio.

The following plan and description are copied from the Ohio School Journal, Vol. II., edited by Dr. Lord, Superintendent of the Common Schools of Columbus, Ohio.

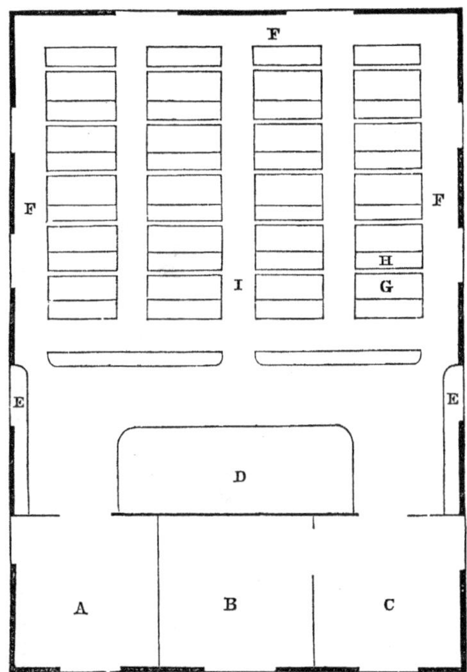

The building here presented should be 26 by 36 feet on the ground, or, at least, 25 by 35 feet inside. The plan is drawn on a scale of ten feet to the inch.

A C—Entries 8 feet square, one for each sex.

B—Library and apparatus room, 8 by 9 feet, which may be used for a recitation room for small sized classes.

D—Teacher's platform, behind which, on the wall, should be a blackboard 12 feet long by 5 feet wide.

E E E E—Recitation seats, those on the sides placed against the wall, those in front of the platform having backs and being movable.

F F F—Free space, at least two feet wide, next the wall on three sides of the room.

G—Desk, for two pupils, four feet long by 18 inches wide.

H—Seat, " " do " " 13 " "

I—Centre aisle two feet wide; the aisles on either side of this should be from 18 to 24 inches wide.

The area on either side and in front of the Teacher's platform, is intended for reading and spelling classes, and any other class exercises in which the pupils stand; and the space next the wall may be used to arrange the greater part of the school as one class in any general exercises requiring it.

Four windows are represented on each side of the house, and two on the end opposite the Teacher's stand. The door to the Library-room opens from one of the entries, and the room is lighted by a large window in the front end of the house.

Plan—No. 14. Front Elevation.

Plans of School-houses recently Erected.

Under this head will be found plans and descriptions of a few of the best school-houses, which have been recently erected in Connecticut and Rhode Island, for schools of different grades, from designs or directions furnished by the author of this treatise. They are not presented as faultless specimens of school architecture, but as embracing, each, some points of excellence, either in style, construction, or arrangement. Although the author, particularly as Commissioner of Public Schools for Rhode Island, was consulted in almost every instance by the local building committee, and was always gratified in having opportunities to furnish plans, or make suggestions,—yet he was seldom able to persuade the committee or the carpenters to carry out his plans and suggestions thoroughly. Something would be taken from the height, or the length, or the breadth ;—some objections would be made to the style of the exterior or the arrangement of the interior ;—and particularly the plans recommended for securing warmth and ventilation were almost invariably modified, and are in many instances entirely neglected. He desires, therefore, not to be held responsible for the details of any one house as it now stands,—for, being thus held responsible, he should probably receive credit for improvements which others are as much entitled to as himself, and should in more instances be held accountable for errors of taste, and deficiencies in internal arrangements, against which he protested with those having charge of the construction. He wishes the reader to bring all the plans published in this volume, no matter by whom recommended, or where erected, to the test of the principles set forth on pages 47 and 48. If in any particular they fall short of the standard therein established, so far they differ from the designs which the author desires to see followed in houses erected under his own eye. But, with some reservation, most of the school-houses recently erected in Rhode Island, (and the same may be said of the new houses in Hartford, described in this volume,) can be pointed to as embracing many improvements in school architecture. Although the last state in New England to enter on the work of establishing a system of common schools, it is believed, she has now a system in operation not inferior in efficiency to any of her sister states. Be that as it may, Rhode Island can now boast of more good school-houses, and fewer poor ones, in proportion to the whole number, than any other State—more than one hundred and fifty thousand dollars having been voluntarily voted for this purpose in less than three years, by school districts, not including the city of Providence.

To Thomas A. Teft, Esq., Architect, of Providence, much credit is due for the taste which he has displayed in the designs furnished by him, and for the elevations which he drew for plans furnished or suggested by the Commissioner. He should, not, however, be held responsible for the alterations made in his plans by the committees and carpenters having charge of the erection of the building. With all their imperfections of execution, Mr. Teft's plans are among the best specimens of School Architecture.

2. Plans and descriptions of School-houses recently erected.

The following school-houses are selected for representation and description, not because they are superior to all others, or are unexceptionable in every respect, but because the plans could be conveniently obtained, and in them all, the great principles of school-architecture are observed.

Plans, &c., of School-house, District No. 6, Windsor, Ct.

The building stands 60 ft. from the highway, near the center of an elevated lot which slopes a little to the south and east. Much the larger portion of the lot is in front, affording a pleasant play ground, while in the rear there is a woodshed, and other appropriate buildings, with a separate yard for boys and girls. The walls are of brick, and are hollow, so as to save expense in securing the antaes or pilasters, and to prevent dampness. This building is 33 ft. 6 inches long, 21 ft. 8 inches wide, and 18 ft. 9 inches high from the ground to the eaves, including 2 ft. base or underpinning.

The entries A A, one for boys and the other for girls, are in the rear of the building, through the woodshed, which, with the yard, is also divided by a partition. Each entry is 7 ft. 3 inches, by 9 ft. 3 inches, and is supplied with a scraper and mat for the feet, and shelves and hooks for outer garments.

The school-room is 24 ft. 5 inches long, by 19 ft. 4 inches wide, and 15 ft. 6 inches high in the clear, allowing an area of 472 ft. including the recess for the teacher's platform, and an allowance of 200 cubic feet of air to a school of 36.

The teacher's platform B, is 5 ft. 2 inches wide, by 6 ft. deep, including 3 ft. of recess, and 9 inches high. On it stands a table, the legs of which are set into the floor, so as to be firm, and at the same time movable, in case the platform is needed for declamation, or other exercises of the scholars. Back of the teacher is a range of shelves *b*, already supplied with a library of near 400 volumes, and a globe, outline maps, and other apparatus. On the top of the case is a clock. A blackboard 5 ft. by 4, is suspended on weights, and steadied by a groove on each end, so as to admit of being raised and lowered by the teacher, directly in front of the book case, and in full view of the whole school. At the bottom of the blackboard is a trough to receive the chalk and the sponge, or soft cloth.

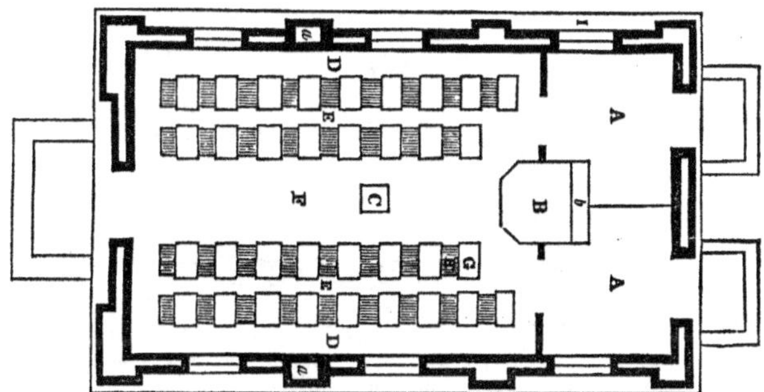

The passages D D, are 2 ft. wide, and extend round the room; E E are 15 inches, and allow of easy access to the seats and desks on either hand. F is 5 ft. 3 inches, and in the center stands an open stove C, the pipe of which goes into one of the flues, *a*. The temperature is regulated by a thermometer.

Each pupil is provided with a desk G, and seat H, the front of the former, constituting the back or support of the latter, which slopes 2½ inches in 16. The seat also inclines a little from the edge. The seats vary in height, from 9½ inches to 17, the youngest children occupying those nearest the platform. The desks are 2 ft. long by 18 inches wide, with a shelf beneath for books, and a groove on the back side *b*, (Fig. 4) to receive a slate, with which each desk is furnished by the district. The upper surface of the desk, except 3 inches of the most distant portion, slopes 1 inch in a foot, and the edge is in the same perpendicular line with the front of the seat. The level portion of the desk has a groove running along the line of the

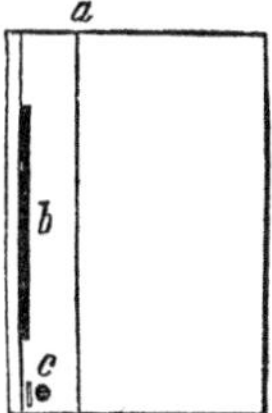

Top of Desk.

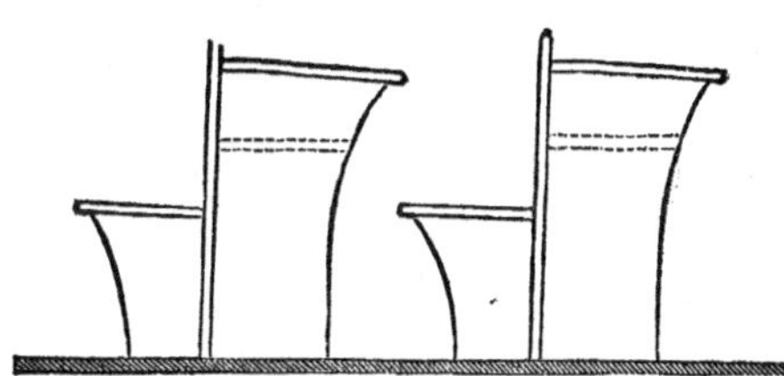
Section of Seat and Desk.

slope *a*, (Fig. 4) so as to prevent pencils and pens from rolling off, and an opening *c*, (Fig 8) to receive an inkstand, which is covered by a metallic lid.

The windows, I, three on the north and three on the south side, contain each 40 panes of 8 by 10 glass, are hung (both upper and lower sash) with weights so as to admit of being raised or lowered conveniently.

PLAN OF SCHOOL-HOUSE IN MEADOW DISTRICT, IN BLOOMFIELD, CONN.

The new school-house in Meadow District, in the town of Bloomfield, for location, neatness, mode of seating, warming, and ventilation, is a good specimen of a cheap, convenient, and attractive edifice for a small country district. It is built of brick, and the cost, excluding the land, and including fences, appendages, and furniture, was about $500. The style and arrangement of the seats and desks are indicated in Figs. 3 and 4. The building is 30 feet by 20. The district is indebted mainly to Hon. Francis Gillette for his zeal and determination in getting up the plan, and superintending the work.

The room is heated by *Mott's Ventilating School Stove*, designed both for wood and hard coal. Fresh air is introduced from outside of the building by a flue beneath the floor, and is warmed by passing along the heated surfaces of the stove as indicated in the following section.

FIG. 2.

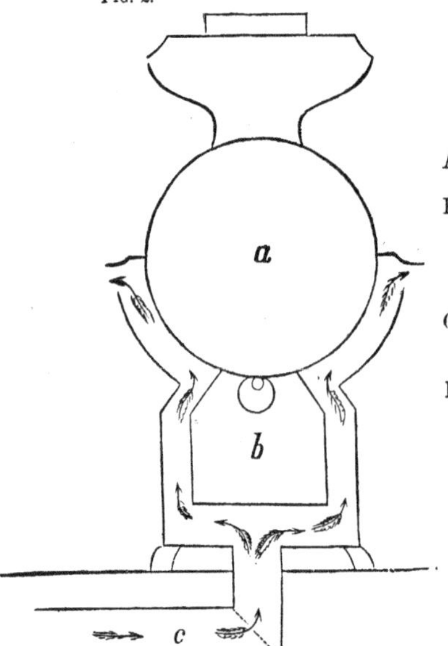

A. A chamber, for coal or wood.

B. A revolving grate with a cam motion, by which the ashes are easily detached and made to drop into the ash-pit below.

C. Ash-pit, by which also the draught can be regulated, and the stove made an air-tight.

D. Duct, or flue under the floor, by which fresh air from without is admitted under and around the stove, and circulates in the direction indicated by the arrows.

The smoke-pipe is carried in the usual way, high enough to prevent any injurious radiation of heat upon the heads of the pupils below, to the centre of the opposite end of the room, where, after passing through the ceiling, it enters the ventilating flue, which, commencing at the floor, is carried up through the attic and out above the roof, as shown in Figures 3 and 4. The heat of the smoke-pipe produces a lively upward current of the air in the upper portion of the ventilating flue, sufficient to draw off the lower stratum of air near the floor, and at the same time draw down, and diffuse equally through the room, the fresh air which is introduced and warmed by the stove at the opposite end.

A—Front entrance.
B—Girls' Entrance and lobby.
C—Boys' do. do.
D—Teachers' platform.
E—Seat and desk, for the pupils.
S—Mott's ventilating school stove.
V—Flue for ventilation.
F—Seats for classes at recitation.
d—Teacher's desk.
e—Library of reference in front of teacher's desk.
c—Closets for school library and apparatus.
f—Fence dividing back yard.

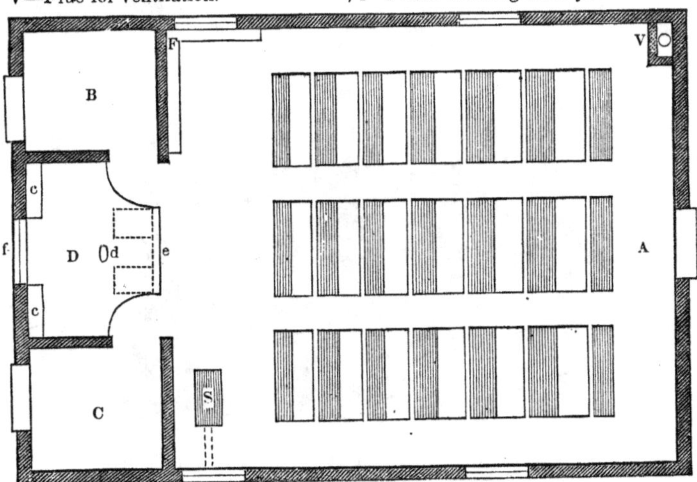

Plan of District School-House in Barrington, R. I.

The above cut represents in perspective the new school-house in District No. 2, in the town of Barrington, Rhode Island—the most attractive, convenient, and complete structure of the kind in any agricultural district in the State—and, it is believed, in New England.

The house stands back from the highway in a lot, of an acre in extent, and commands an extensive view up and down Narraganset Bay, and of the rich cultivated fields for miles in every other direction.

The building is 40 feet long by 25 wide, and 12 feet high in the clear, and is built after working plans drawn by Mr. Teft, of Providence.

The school-room is calculated to accommodate 64 pupils, with seats and desks each for two pupils, similar to the folowing cut, and arranged as in Figure 3.

The end-piece, or supports, both of the desk and seat, are of cast-iron, and the wood-work is attached by screws. They are made of eight sizes, giving a seat from ten inches to seventeen, and a desk at the edge next to the scholar from seventeen to twenty-six inches from the floor.

Each pupil, when properly seated, can rest his feet on the floor without the muscle of the thigh pressing hard upon the front edge of the seat, and with a support for the muscles of the back.

The yards and entrance for the boys and girls are entirely separate, and each is appropriately fitted up with scraper, mats, broom, water-pails, sink, hooks and shelves.

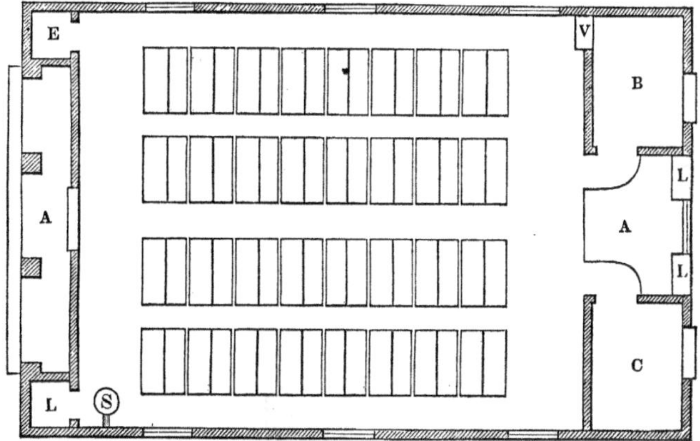

A—Front entrance.
B—Girls' entrance and lobby, fitted up with mats, scrapers, hooks, shelves.
C—Boys' entrance.
D—Teacher's platform.
S—Boston Ventilating Stove.
V—Flue for ventilation surmounted, by Emerson's Ejector.
L—Cases for library.
E—Closets for apparatus, &c.

The school is well supplied with blackboards, maps, globes, and diagrams, and such other instrumentalities as are necessary and useful in the studies usually taught in a district school.

There is abundance of unoccupied space around the sides of the room and between the ranges of desks to allow of the free movements of the teacher and of the pupils, in passing to and from their seats.

There is also a district library of about 600 volumes, containing a large number of books of reference, such as Dictionaries, Encyclopedia, and a variety of the best text books in the several studies of the school, to enable the teacher to extend his knowledge, and illustrate his recitations by additional information.

There are about one hundred volumes selected with reference to the youngest class of children, and about 400 volumes in the different departments of useful knowledge, calculated for circulation among the older pupils, in the families of the district generally.

The maps, apparatus and library were purchased by the Commissioner ot Public Schools at an expense of $250, which was contributed by five or six individuals. The building, furniture and land, cost about $1200.

The school-room is warmed and ventilated under the direction of Mr. Gardner Chilson, Boston, by one of the *Boston Ventilating Stoves*, and by a flue constructed similar to those recently introduced into the Boston Public School houses by Dr. Henry G. Clark, and surmounted by Emerson's Ejector.

A cut and description of this stove, and of *Mott's Ventilating Stove* for burning wood as well as coal, is given on the next page.

The flue for ventilation is carried up in the partition wall, and is constructed of well seasoned boards, planed smooth on the inside.

More than sixty District school-houses have been erected in Rhode Island on the same general plan as that presented in the cuts of the Barrington and Glocester school-house, with some slight variations required by the nature of the site, or the peculiar views of the majority of the district, or of the building committee, in each case. The following plans present some of these modifications. The first is 34 ft. by 25, and the second, 36 ft. by 27.

PLAN OF SCHOOL-HOUSE IN DISTRICT NO. 10, CRANSTON.

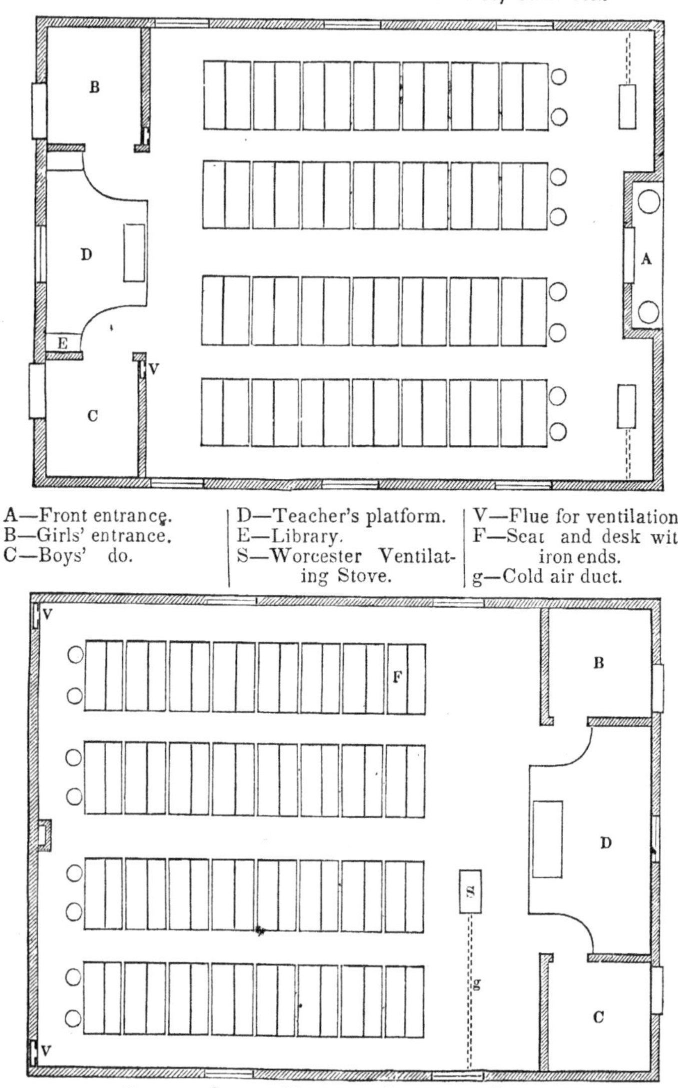

A—Front entrance.
B—Girls' entrance.
C—Boys' do.
D—Teacher's platform.
E—Library.
S—Worcester Ventilating Stove.
V—Flue for ventilation.
F—Seat and desk with iron ends.
g—Cold air duct.

PLAN OF SCHOOL-HOUSE AT CLAYVILLE, SCITUATE.

Plan of School-House in Centreville, Warwick, R. I

The following plan presents a mode of seating a District School-House similar to that adopted in several public school-houses in the city of New York.

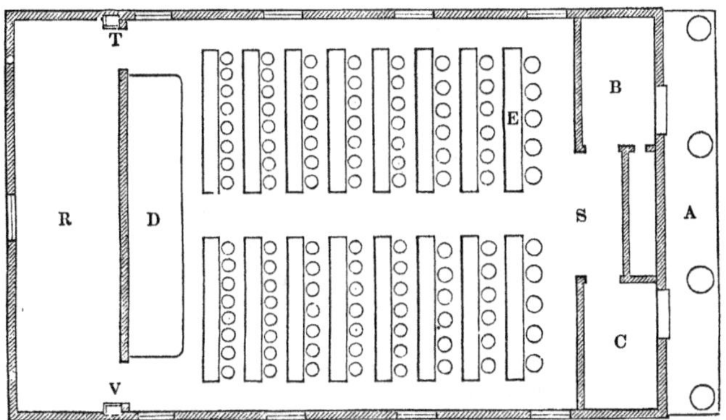

The building is 50 feet long (beside the porch $5\frac{1}{2}$ feet in front) by 30 feet wide

A—Porch.
B—Girls' entrance and lobby.
C—Boys' do.
D—Teacher's platform.
E—Mott's school desk and chair.
R—Recitation-room for assistant.
S—Stove.
T—Smoke flue.
V—Flue for ventilator.

The above mode of seating has been adopted in other districts, and in one instance, with the desks attached at one end to the wall, as in the following plan recommended by Hon. Ira Mayhew. There are serious objections to this arrangement of the seats and desk.

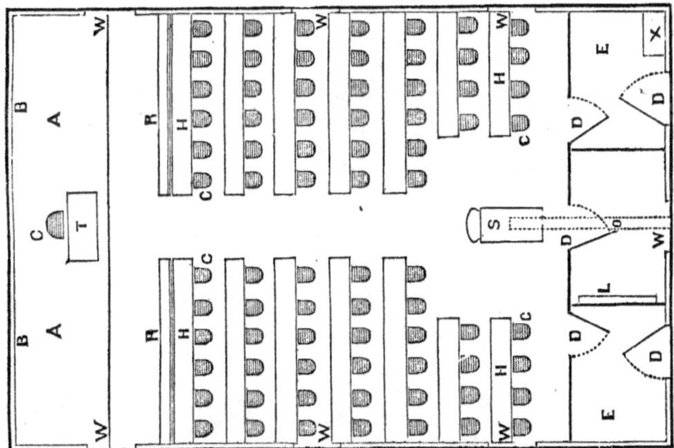

D, entrance and inner doors. W, windows. E, entries, lighted over doors, one for boys and the other for girls. A, teacher's platform. B, blackboard, reaching entirely across the end of the house. T, teacher's desk. H, desks 11 feet long, except the two next the entrance doors. C, Mott's patent cast-iron chairs. S stove. O, an air tube under the floor, through which pure air from without is introduced beneath the stove. L, shelves for library, apparatus, etc.

Plans of School-houses recently erected in New Hampshire.

The following plans, and the descriptions of the same, are taken, by permission, from the "*Third Annual Report of the Commissioner of Common Schools* (Hon. R. S. Rust,) *to the Legislature of New Hampshire, January,* 1849."

Plan of District School-house in Dublin, N. H.

The building is 42 by 32 feet on the ground, and 11 feet high in the clear. The school-room of 29 by 35 feet inside, and is furnished with 64 seats (I,I,I,) and as many desks (H,H,H.) The desks are made of birch board, and painted green, each 2 feet long and from 10 to 18 inches wide, and are all numbered. The supports at the end of the desks are framed down through the floor into the sleepers, or joints under the floor. The seats are in the form of wooden chair bottoms, and are 16 inches down to 10 in height, and are placed at the left hand of the writing desk, so as to make it convenient for the scholar in writing, and give him space to stand within the line of his desk. The outside aisles are 18 inches, the center 24 inches, and the outer 16 inches wide. There are movable seats (N,N,) in front, and on either side of the teacher, for recitation. The entrances (G,G,), one for boys and one for girls, are fitted up for hats, bonnets, &c., and can be used for recitation rooms. Back of the teacher's platform (A,) is a small room for a library, apparatus, and the use of the teacher. The room is heated by one of the Worcester Common School Stoves, which cost about $18. By means of a flue under the floor, the air is introduced beneath the stove, and circulates through heated tubes before it is admitted into the room, on the principle of a furnace.

The ventilation of the room is partially secured by openings into the attic, and hence into the open air.

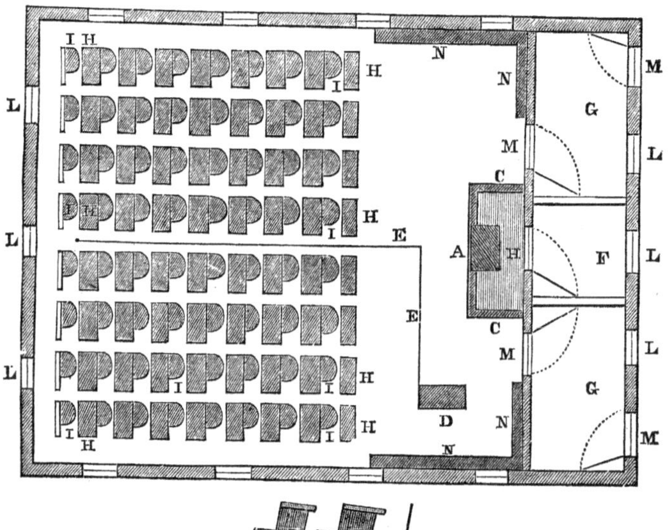

PLAN OF DISTRICT SCHOOL-HOUSE IN GREENLAND, N. H.

The building is 50 feet long by 30 feet wide, and 12 feet high in the clear. It is built of brick. A large entry (E), is partitioned off from the school-room, and fitted up not only to receive the hats, bonnets, &c., of the pupils, but to accommodate all the pupils in rainy weather during recess, as well as those who reside at a distance, when they arrive at the school-house before the school-room is opened, and those who may be obliged to stay during recess. The entry and the school-room is heated by a large stove (S) placed in the partition. The teacher's platform (P) is placed at the end of the school-room, and is raised one step above the floor. Back of the teacher, along the wall, are cases (B) for apparatus, and a well-selected library of 200 vols. There are 48 separate desks of different heights, framed on posts permanently fixed to the timbers of the floor, and fitted with seats of corresponding heights set in cast iron frames secured to the floor; both seats and desks are stained and varnished.

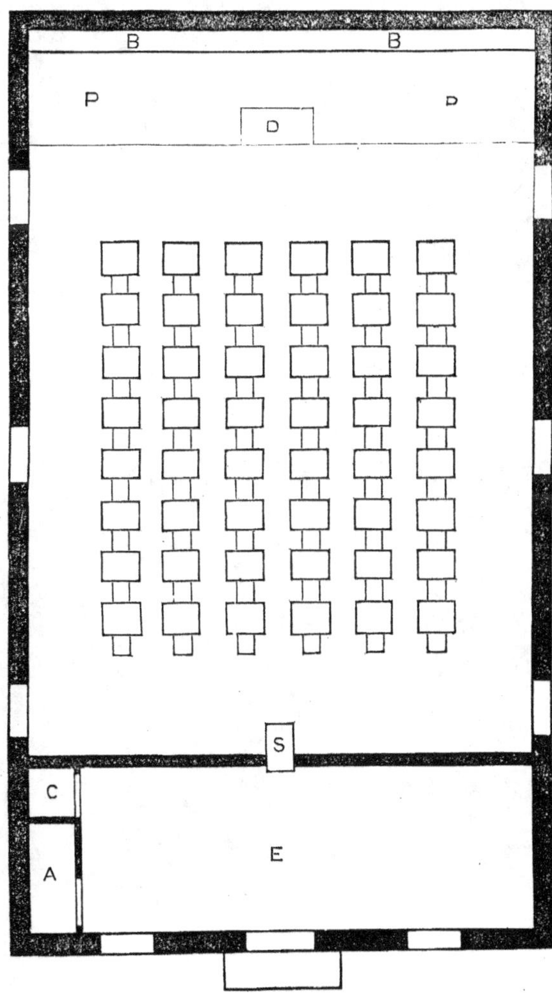

PRIMARY SCHOOL IN WESTERLY, R. I.

VILLAGE SCHOOL-HOUSE IN ALLENDALE, N. PROVIDENCE, R. I.

Plans of School-Houses for Union Schools.

Before describing a few of the best school-houses which have been recently erected in the large villages of Rhode Island, for two or more schools of different grades in the same building, a brief consideration of the importance of classification, or gradation, as applied to the schools of a district, or town, cannot be deemed irrelevant.

To enable children to derive the highest degree of benefit from their attendance at school, they should go through a regular course of training in a succession of classes, and schools arranged according to similarity of age, standing, and attainments, under teachers possessing the qualifications best adapted to each grade of school. The practice has been almost universal in New England, and in other states where the organization of the schools is based upon the division of the territory into school districts, to provide but one school for as many children of both sexes, and of all ages from four to sixteen years, as can be gathered in from certain territorial limits, into one apartment, under one teacher; a female teacher in summer, and a male teacher in winter. The disadvantages of this practice, both to pupils and teachers, are great and manifold.

There is a large amount of physical suffering and discomfort, as well as great hinderances in the proper arrangement of scholars and classes, caused by crowding the older and younger pupils into the same school-room, without seats and furniture appropriate to either; and the greatest amount of suffering and discomfort falls upon the young, who are least able to bear it, and who, in consequence, acquire a distaste to study and the school-room.

The work of education going on in such schools, cannot be appropriate and progressive. There cannot be a regular course of discipline and instruction, adapted to the age and proficiency of pupils—a series of processes, each adapted to certain periods in the development of the mind and character, the first intended to be followed by a second, and the second by a third,—the latter always depending on the earlier, and all intended to be conducted on the same general principles, and by methods varying with the work to be done, and the progress already made.

With the older and younger pupils in the same room, there cannot be a system of discipline which shall be equally well adapted to both classes. If it secures the cheerful obedience and subordination of the older, it will press with unwise severity upon the younger pupils. If it be adapted to the physical wants, and peculiar temperaments of the young, it will endanger the good order and habits of study of the more advanced pupils, by the frequent change of posture and position, and other indulgences which it permits and requires of the former.

With studies ranging from the alphabet and the simplest rudiments of knowledge, to the higher branches of an English education, a variety of methods of instruction and illustration are called for, which are seldom found together, or in an equal degree, in the same teacher, and which can never be pursued with equal success in the same school-room. The elementary principles of knowledge, to be made intelligible and interesting to the young, must be presented by a large use of the oral and simultaneous methods. The higher branches, especially all mathematical subjects, require patient application and habits of abstraction, on the part of the older pupils, which can with difficulty, if at all, be attained by many pupils, amid a multiplicity of distracting exercises, movements and sounds. The recitations of this class of pupils, to be profitable and satisfactory, must be conducted in a manner which requires time, discussion and explanation, and the undivided attention both of pupils and teachers.

From the number of class and individual recitations, to be attended to during each half day, these exercises are brief, hurried, and of little practical value. They consist, for the most part, of senseless repetitions of the words of a book. Instead of being the time and place where the real business of teaching is done, where the ploughshare of interrogation is driven down into the acquirements of each pupil, and his ability to comprehend clearly, remember accurately, discriminate wisely, and reason closely, is cultivated and tested,—where the difficult principles of each lesson are developed and illustrated, and additional information imparted, and the mind of the teacher brought in direct contact with the mind of each pupil, to arouse, interest, and direct its opening powers—instead of all this and more, the brief period passed in recitation, consists, on the part of the teacher, of hearing each individual and class in regular order, and quick succession, repeat words from a book; and on the part of the pupils, of *saying their lessons*, as the operation is significantly described by most teachers, when they summon the class to the stand. In the mean time the order of the school must be maintained, and the general business must be going forward. Little children without any authorized employment for their eyes and hands, and ever active curiosity, must be made to sit still, while every muscle is aching from suppressed activity; pens must be mended, copies set, arithmetical difficulties solved, excuses for tardiness or absence received, questions answered, whisperings allowed or suppressed, and more or less of extempore discipline administered. Were it not a most ruinous waste of precious time,—did it not involve the deadening, crushing, distorting, dwarfing of immortal faculties and noble sensibilities,—were it not an utter perversion of the noble objects for which schools are instituted, it would be difficult to conceive of a more diverting farce than an ordinary session of a large public school, whose chaotic and discordant elements have not been reduced to system by a proper classification. The teacher, at least the conscientious teacher, thinks it any thing but a farce to him. Compelled to hurry from one study to another, the most diverse,—from one class to another, requiring a knowledge of methods altogether distinct,—from one recitation to another, equally brief and unsatisfactory, one requiring a liveliness of manner, which he does not feel and cannot assume, and the other closeness of attention and abstraction of thought, which he cannot give amid the multiplicity and variety of cares,—from one case of discipline to another, pressing on him at the same time,—he goes through the same circuit day after day, with a dizzy brain and aching heart, and brings his school to a close with a feeling, that with all his diligence and fidelity, he has accomplished but little good.

But great as are the evils of a want of proper classification of schools, arising from the causes already specified, these evils are aggravated by the almost universal practice of employing one teacher in summer, and another in winter, and different teachers each successive summer and winter. Whatever progress one teacher may make in bringing order out of the chaotic elements of a large public school, is arrested by the termination of his school term. His experience is not available to his successor, who does not come into the school until after an interval of weeks or months, and in the mean time the former teacher has left the town or state. The new teacher is a stranger to the children and their parents, is unacquainted with the system pursued by his predecessor, and has himself but little or no experience in the business; in consequence, chaos comes back again, and the confusion is still worse confounded by the introduction of new books, for every teacher prefers to teach from the books in which he studied, or which he has been accustomed to teach, and many teachers cannot teach profitably from any other. Weeks are thus passed, in which the school is going through the process of organization, and the pupils are becoming accustomed to the methods and requirements of a new teacher—some of them are put back, or made to retrace their studies in new books, while others are pushed forward into studies for which they are not prepared; and at the end of three or four months, the school relapses into chaos. There is constant change, but no progress.

This want of system, and this succession of new teachers, goes on from term to term, and year to year—a process which would involve any other interest in speedy and utter ruin, where there was not provision made for fresh material to be experimented upon, and counteracting influences at work to restore, or at least obviate the injury done. What other business of society could escape utter wreck, if conducted with such want of system,—with such constant disregard of the fundamental principle of the division of labor, and with a succession of new agents every three months, none of them trained to the details of the business, each new agent acting without any knowledge of the plan of his predecessor, or any well settled plan of his own! The public school is not an anomaly, an exception, among the great interests of society. Its success or failure depends on the existence or absence of certain conditions; and if complete failure does not follow the utter neglect of these conditions, it is because every term brings into the schools a fresh supply of children to be experimented upon, and sweeps away others beyond the reach of bad school instruction and discipline; and because the minds of some of these children are, for a portion of each day, left to the action of their own inherent forces, and the more kindly influences of nature, the family and society.

Among these conditions of success in the operation of a system of public schools, is such a classification of the scholars as shall bring a larger number of similar age and attainments, at all times, and in every stage of their advancement, under teachers of the right qualifications, and shall enable these teachers to act upon numbers at once, for years in succession, and carry them all forward effectually together, in a regular course of instruction.

The great principle to be regarded in the classification, either of the schools of a town or district, or of scholars in the same school, is equality of attainments, which will generally include those of the same age. Those who have gone over substantially the same ground, or reached, or nearly reached the same point of attainment in several studies, should be put together, and constitute, whenever their numbers will authorize it, one school. These again should be arranged in different classes, for it is seldom practicable, even if it were ever desirable, to have but one class in every study in the same grade of school. Even in very large districts, where the scholars are promoted from a school of a lower grade to one of a higher, after being found qualified in certain studies, it is seldom that any considerable number will have reached a common standard of scholarship in all their studies. The same pupil will have made very different progress in different branches. He will stand higher in one and lower in another. By arranging scholars of the same general division in different classes, no pupil need be detained by companions who have made, or can make less progress, or be hurried over lessons and subjects in a superficial manner, to accommodate the more rapid advancement of others. Although equality of attainment should be regarded as the general principle, some regard should be paid to age, and other circumstances. A large boy of sixteen, from the deficiency of his early education, which may be his misfortune and not his fault, ought not to be put into a school or class of little children, although their attainments may be in advance of his. This step would mortify and discourage him. In such extreme cases, that arrangement will be best which will give the individual the greatest chance of improvement, with the least discomfort to himself, and hindrance to others. Great disparity of age in the same class, or the same school, is unfavorable to uniform and efficient discipline, and the adaptation of methods of teaching, and of motives to application and obedience. Some regard, too, should be had to the preferences of individuals, especially among the older pupils, and their probable destination in life. The mind comes into the requisitions of study more readily, and works with higher results, when led onward by the heart; and the utility of any branch of study, its relations to future success in life, once clearly apprehended, becomes a powerful motive to effort.

Each class in a school should be as large as is consistent with thoroughness and minuteness of individual examination, and practicable, without bringing together individuals of diverse capacity, knowledge, and habits of study. A good teacher can teach a class of forty with as much ease as a class of ten, and with far more profit to each individual, than if the same amount of time was divided up among four classes, each containing one-fourth of the whole number. When the class is large, there is a spirit, a glow, a struggle which can never be infused or called forth in a small class. Whatever time is spent upon a few, which could have been as profitably spent on a larger number, is a loss of power and time to the extent of the number who were not thus benefited. The recitations of a large class must be more varied, both as to order and methods, so as to reach those whose attention would wander if not under the pressure of constant excitement, or might become slothful from inaction or a sense of security. Some studies will admit of a larger number in a class than others.

The number of classes for recitation in the same apartment, by one teacher, should be small. This will facilitate the proper division of labor in instruction, and allow more time for each class. The teacher intrusted with the care of but few studies, and few recitations, can have no excuse but indolence, or the want of capacity, if he does not master these branches thoroughly, and soon acquire the most skillful and varied methods of teaching them. His attention will not be distracted by a multiplicity and variety of cares, pressing upon him at the same time. This principle does not require that every school should be small, but that each teacher should have a small number of studies and classes to superintend.

In a large school, properly classified, a division of labor can be introduced in the department of government, as well as in that of instruction. By assigning the different studies to a sufficient number of assistants, in separate class-rooms, each well qualified to teach the branches assigned, the principal teacher may be selected with special reference to his ability in arranging the studies, and order of exercises of the school, in administering its discipline, in adapting moral instruction to individual scholars, and superintending the operations of each class-room, so as to secure the harmonious action and progress of every department. The talents and tact required for these and similar duties, are more rarely found than the skill and attainments required to teach successfully a particular study. When found, the influence of such a principal, possessing in a high degree, the executive talent spoken of, will be felt through every class, and by every subordinate teacher, giving tone and efficiency to the whole school.

To facilitate the introduction of these, and similar principles of classification, into the organization and arrangements of the schools of a town or district, as fast and as far as the circumstances of the population will admit, the following provisions should be engrafted into the school system of every state.

1. Every town should be clothed with all the powers requisite to establish and maintain a sufficient number of schools of different grades, at convenient locations, to accommodate all the children re-

siding within their respective limits—irrespective of any territorial division of the town into school districts.

2. Should provision be made for the creation of territorial school districts, a gradation of districts should be recognized, and every district having over sixty children of an age to attend school, should be obliged to maintain a primary school under a female teacher for the young pupils, and provide a secondary school for the older and more advanced pupils.

3. No village, or populous district, in which two or more schools of different grades for the younger and older children respectively, can be conveniently established, should be sub-divided into two or more independent districts.

4. Any two or more adjoining districts, in the same, or adjoining towns, should be authorized to establish and maintain a secondary school for the older and more advanced pupils of such districts, for the whole, or any portion of the year.

5. Any district, not having children enough to require the permanent establishment of two grades of schools, should be authorized to determine the periods of the year in which the public school shall be kept, and to determine the age and studies of the children who shall attend at any particular period of the year, and also to send the older pupils to the secondary school of an adjoining district.

The extent to which the gradation of schools can be carried, in any town or district, and the limit to which the number of classes in any school can be reduced, will depend on the compactness, number, and other circumstances of the population, in that town or district, and the number and age of the pupils, and the studies and methods of instruction in that school. A regular gradation of schools might embrace Primary, Secondary and High Schools, with Intermediate Schools, or departments, between each grade, and Supplementary Schools, to meet the wants of a class of pupils not provided for in either of the above grades.

1. Primary Schools, as a general rule, should be designed for children between the ages of three and eight years, with a further classification of the very youngest children, when their number will admit of it. These schools can be accommodated, in compact villages, in the same building with the Secondary or High School; but in most large districts, it will be necessary and desirable to locate them in different neighborhoods, to meet the peculiarities of the population, and facilitate the regular attendance of very young children, and relieve the anxiety of parents for their safety on their way to and from school. The school-room should be light, cheerful, and large enough for the evolutions of large classes—furnished with appropriate seats, furniture, apparatus and means of visible illustration, and having a retired, dry and airy play-ground, with a shelter to resort to in inclement weather, and with flower borders, shrubbery and shade trees, which they should be taught to love and respect. The play-ground is as essential as the school-room, for a Primary School, and is indeed the uncovered school-room of physical and moral educa-

tion, and the place where the manners and personal habits of children can be better trained than elsewhere. With them, the hours of play and study, of confinement and recreation, must alternate more frequently than with older pupils. To teach these schools properly,—to regulate the hours of play and study so as to give variety, vivacity, and interest to all of the exercises, without over-exciting the nervous system, or over-tasking any faculty of mind or body,—to train boys and girls to mild dispositions, graceful and respectful manners, and unquestioning obedience,—to cultivate the senses to habits of quick and accurate observation and discrimination,—to prevent the formation of artificial and sing-song tones,—to teach the use of the voice, and of simple, ready and correct language, and to begin in this way, and by appropriate exercises in drawing, calculation, and lessons on the properties and classification of objects, the cultivation of the intellectual faculties,—to do all these things and more, require in the teacher a rare union of qualities, seldom found in one in a hundred of the male sex, and to be looked for with the greatest chance of success among females, "in whose own hearts, love, hope and patience, have first kept school."

The earlier we can establish, in every populous district, primary schools, under female teachers, whose hearts are made strong by deep religious principle,—who have faith in the power of Christian love steadily exerted to fashion anew the bad manners, and soften the harsh and self-willed perverseness of neglected children,—with patience to begin every morning, with but little if any perceptible advance beyond where they began the previous morning,—with prompt and kind sympathies, and ready skill in music, drawing, and oral methods, the better it will be for the cause of education, and for every other good cause.

2. Secondary Schools should receive scholars at the age of eight years, or about that age, and carry them forward in those branches of instruction which lie at the foundation of all useful attainments in knowledge, and are indispensable to the proper exercise and development of all the faculties of the mind, and to the formation of good intellectual tastes and habits of application. If the primary schools have done their work properly, in forming habits of attention, and teaching practically the first uses of language,—in giving clear ideas of the elementary principles of arithmetic, geography, and the simplest lessons in drawing, the scholars of a well conducted secondary school, who will attend regularly for eight or ten months in the year, until they are twelve years of age, can acquire as thorough knowledge of reading, arithmetic, penmanship, drawing, geography, history, and the use of the language in composition and speech, as is ever given in common or public schools, as ordinarily conducted, to children at the age of sixteen. For this class of schools, well qualified female teachers, with good health, self-command, and firmness, are as well fitted as male teachers. But if the school is large, both a male and female teacher should be employed, as the influence of both are needed in the training of the moral character and manners.

Schools of this grade should be furnished with class-rooms for recitations, and if large, with a female assistant for every thirty pupils.

3. High Schools should receive pupils from schools of the grade below, and carry them forward in a more comprehensive course of instruction, embracing a continuation of their former studies, and especially of the English language, and drawing, and a knowledge of algebra, geometry and trigonometry, with their applications, the elements of mechanics and natural philosophy and chemistry, natural history, including natural theology, mental and moral science, political economy, physiology, and the constitution of the United States. These and other studies should form the course of instruction, modified according to the sex, age, and advancement, and to some extent, future destination of the pupils, and the standard fixed by the intelligence and intellectual wants of the district—a course which should give to every young man a thorough English education, preparatory to the pursuits of agriculture, commerce, trade, manufactures, and the mechanical arts, and if desired, for college; and to every young woman, a well disciplined mind, high moral aims, and practical views of her own duties, and those resources of health, thought, manners and conversation, which bless alike the highest and lowest stations in life. All which is now done in private schools of the highest grade, and where the wants of any considerable portion of the community create such private schools, should be provided for in the system of public schools, so that the same advantages, without being abridged or denied to the children of the rich and the educated, should be open at the same time to worthy and talented children of the poorest parent. In some districts a part of the studies of this grade of schools might be embraced in the Secondary Schools, which would thus take the place of the High School; in others, the High School could be open for only portions of the year; and in others, two departments, or two schools, one for either sex, would be required. However constituted, whether as one department, or two, as a distinct school, or as part of a secondary school, or an ordinary district school, and for the whole year, or part of the year, something of the kind is required to meet the wants of the whole community, and relieve the public schools from impotency. Unless it can be engrafted upon the public school system, or rather unless it can grow up and out of the system, as a provision made for the educational wants of the whole community, then the system will never gather about it the warmth and sustaining confidence and patronage of all classes, and especially of those who know best the value of a good education, and are willing to spend time and money to secure it for their own children.

4. Intermediate Schools or departments will be needed in large districts, to receive a class of pupils who are too old to be continued, without wounding their self-esteem, in the school below, or interfering with its methods of discipline and instruction, and are not prepared in attainments, and habits of study, or from irregular attendance, to be arranged in the regular classes of the school above.

Connected with this class of schools there might be opened a school or department for those who cannot attend school regularly, or for only a short period of the year, or who may wish to attend exclusively to a few studies. There is no place for this class of scholars, in a regularly constituted, permanent school, in a large village.

5. Supplementary Schools, and means of various kinds should be provided in every system of public instruction, for cities and large villages, to supply deficiencies in the education of individuals whose school attendance has been prematurely abridged, or from any cause interfered with, and to carry forward as far and as long as practicable into after life, the training and attainments commenced in childhood.

Evening Schools should be opened for apprentices, clerks, and other young persons, who have been hurried into active employment without a suitable elementary education. In these schools, those who have completed the ordinary course of school instruction, could devote themselves to such studies as are directly connected with their several trades or pursuits, while those whose early education was entirely neglected, can supply, to some extent, such deficiencies. It is not beyond the legitimate scope of a system of public instruction, to provide for the education of adults, who, from any cause, in early life were deprived of advantages of school instruction.

Libraries, and courses of familiar lectures, with practical illustrations, collections in natural history, and the natural sciences, a system of scientific exchanges between schools of the same, and of different towns,—these and other means of extending and improving the ordinary instruction of the school-room and of early life, ought to be provided, not only by individual enterprise and liberality, but by the public, and the authorities entrusted with the care and advancement of popular education.

One or more of that class of educational institutions known as "Reform Schools," "Schools of Industry," or "Schools for Juvenile Offenders," should receive such children, as defying the restraining influence of parental authority, and the discipline and regulations of the public schools, or such as are abandoned by orphanage, or worse than orphanage, by parental neglect or example, to idle, vicious and pilfering habits, are found hanging about places of public resort, polluting the atmosphere by their profane and vulgar speech, alluring, to their own bad practices, children of the same, and other conditions of life, and originating or participating in every street brawl and low-bred riot. Such children cannot be safely gathered into the public schools; and if they are, their vagrant habits are chafed by the restraints of school discipline. They soon become irregular, play truant, are punished and expelled, and from that time their course is almost uniformly downward, until on earth there is no lower point to reach.

Accustomed, as many such children have been from infancy, to sights and sounds of open and abandoned profligacy, trained to an utter want of self-respect, and the decencies and proprieties of life, as exhibited in dress, person, manners and language, strangers to those motives of self-improvement which spring from a sense of social, moral and religious obligation, their regeneration involves the harmonious co-operation of earnest philanthropy, missionary enterprise, and sanctified wisdom. The districts of all our large cities where this class of children are found, are the appropriate field of home missions, of unobtrusive personal effort and charity, and of systematized plans of local benevolence, embracing friendly intercourse with parents, an affectionate interest in the young, the gathering of the latter into week-day, infant, and primary schools, and schools where the use of the needle, and other forms of labor appropriate to the sex and age of the pupils can be given, the gathering of both old and young into Sabbath schools and worshipping assemblies, the circulation of books and tracts, of other than a strictly religious character, the encouragement of cheap, innocent and humanizing games, sports and festivities, the obtaining employment for adults who may need it, and procuring situations as apprentices, clerks, &c., for such young persons as may be qualified by age, capacity and character. By individual efforts and the combined efforts of many, working in these and other ways, from year to year, these moral jungles can be broken up,—these infected districts can be purified,—these waste places of society can be reclaimed, and many abodes of penury, ignorance and vice can be converted by education, economy and industry, into homes of comfort, peace and joy.

PLAN AND DESCRIPTION OF DISTRICT SCHOOL-HOUSE IN CENTREMILL, NORTH PROVIDENCE, R. I.

This house was erected after designs by Mr. Teft, of Providence. It stands back from the highway, on an elevated site, in the midst of a grove, and for beauty of design and convenience of arrangement, is not surpassed by any similar structure in New England. It is 26 feet by 51, and 13 feet high in the clear, with two departments on the same floor.

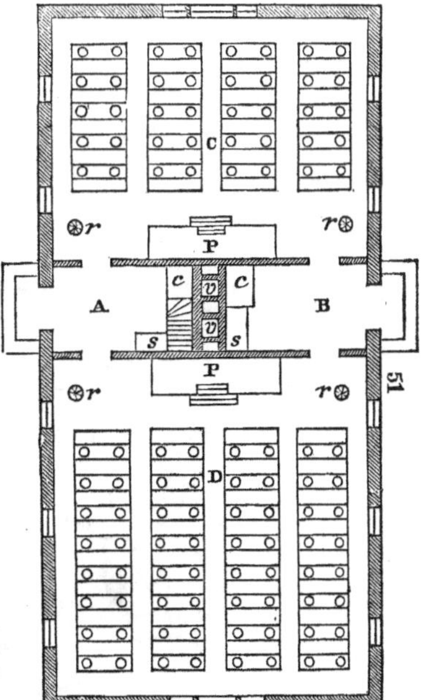

A, Boys' entry, 6 feet by 10.
B, Girls' ditto.
C, Primary department, 20 feet by 25, with desks and seats attached for 70 pupils.
D, Secondary, or Grammar department, 25 feet by 25, with desks and chairs for 64 pupils; *see p.* 120.
r, Register for hot air.
v, *v*, Flues for ventilation.
c, Closets for dinner pails of those who come from a distance
s, Sink.

The smoke pipe is carried up between the ventilating flues, and the top of the chimney is finished so as to accommodate the bell.

PLAN OF SCHOOL-HOUSE AT WASHINGTON VILLAGE IN COVENTRY, R. I.

The following cut presents the ground plan of the new school-house in the village of Washington, in the town of Coventry, R. I. The location is on the high ground in the rear of the village, and commands an extensive prospect in every direction. The site and yard, occupying one acre, was given to the district by Governor Whipple. The whole structure, without and within, is an ornament to the village, and ranks among the best school-houses in Rhode Island.

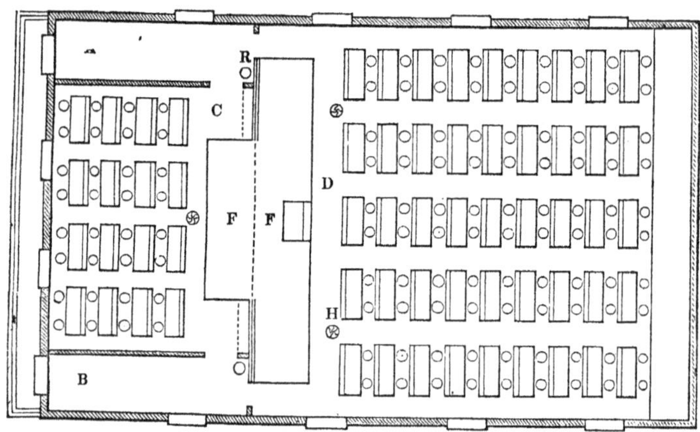

A—Boy's entrance.
B—Girl's entrance.
C—Primary school-room.
D—Secondary, or Grammar Department.
E—Teacher's platform.

F—Desks for two, with iron end-piece.
G—Chairs supported on iron pedestal.
H—Register for hot air.
R—Flue for ventilation, within which is carried up the smoke-pipe.

The two school-rooms can be thrown into one, for any general exercise of the two schools, by sliding doors.

The two rooms are uniformly heated by a furnace in the basement.

There is a well, sink, basin, mats, scrapers, bell, and all the necessary fixtures and appendages of a school-house of the first class.

The cost of the building and furuiture was $2,300.

The district possesses a library of upwards of four hundred volumes, the cost of which was raised by subscription in the District.

ALBANY NORMAL SCHOOL CHAIR AND DESK.

PUBLIC SCHOOL-HOUSE IN WARREN, R. I.

Fig. 1.

THE above cut exhibits a front view of the Public School-house erected in the village of Warren, at the expense of the town, in 1847–48, after drawings made by Mr. Teft, of Providence, under the directions of a committee of the town, who consulted with the Commissioner of Public Schools, and visited Providence, Boston, Salem, Newburyport and other places, in order to ascertain the latest improvements in school architecture, before deciding on the details of the plan. To this committee, and particularly to two of its members, Mr. E. W. Burr and Mr. G. S. Gardiner, is the town largely indebted for the time and personal supervision which they devoted to this public improvement, from its first inception to its completion, without any other reward than the realization of their wish to secure for their town the best school-house, for the amount of money expended, in the State. The Commissioner of Public Schools remarked, in his address at the dedication of the house, in September, 1848, "that, for location, style, construction, means of warming, ventilation, and cleanliness, and for the beauty and convenience of the seats and desks, he had not seen a public school-house superior to this in New England. It is a monument at once of the liberality of the town, and of a wise economy on the part of the committee." The town appropriated $10,000, and the committee expended $8,594.

The opening of the Public School in this edifice was followed by a large increase of attendance from the children of the town.

The lot is 225 deep and 100 feet wide for a depth of 125 feet, and 161 feet wide for the remaining 64 feet. It is divided into three yards, as exhibited in the ground plan, (Fig. 2,) each substantially inclosed, and planted with trees and shrubbery.

The dimensions of the building are 62 feet by 44 on the ground. It is built of brick in the most workmanlike manner.

Most of the details of construction, and of the arrangement in the interior, are similar to those described on page 214.

Each room is ventilated by openings controlled by registers, both at the floor and the ceiling, into four flues carried up in the wall, and by a large flue constructed of thoroughly seasoned boards, smooth on the inside, in the partition wall, (Fig. 3, x.)

The whole building is uniformly warmed by two of Culver's furnaces placed in the cellar.

Every means of cleanliness are provided, such as scrapers, mats, sink with pump, wash basin, towels, hooks for outer garments, umbrella stands, &c.

The tops of the desks are covered with cloth, and the aisles are to be cheaply carpeted, so as to diminish, if not entirely prevent, the noise which the moving of slates and books, and the passing to and fro, occasion in a school-room.

Fig. 2.

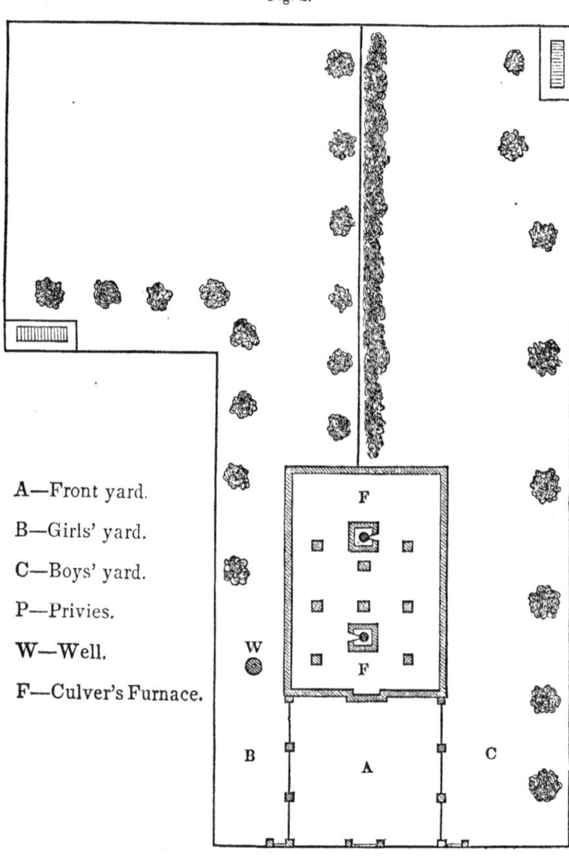

Fig. 3—First Floor.

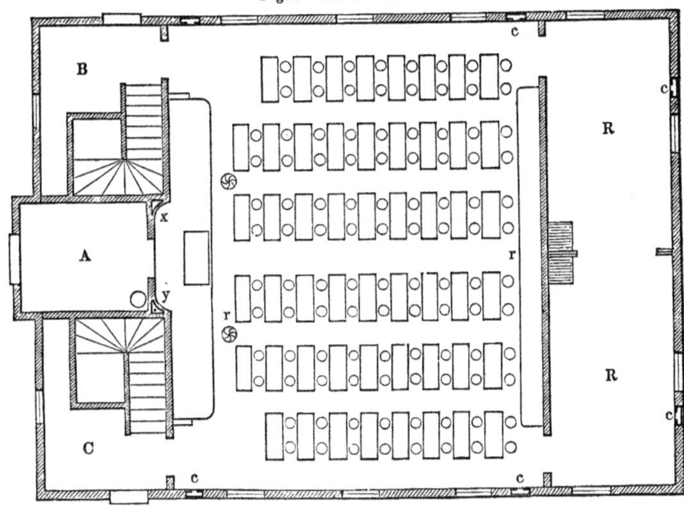

A—Front entrance.

B—Girls' entrance, with mats, scrapers, hooks for clothes, a sink, pump, basin, &c.

C—Boys' entrance do.

R—Recitation rooms, connected by sliding doors.

R, P—Platform for recitation, with a blackboard in the rear.

T—Teacher's platform.

S—Seats and desks; see page 205.

Q—Library and apparatus.

w—Windows, with inside Venetian blinds.

c—Flues for ventilation in the outer wall.

x—Flue for ventilation, lined with smooth, well seasoned boards.

y—Bell-rope, accessible to the teacher by an opening in the wall.

r—Hot air registers.

Fig. 4.—Second Floor.

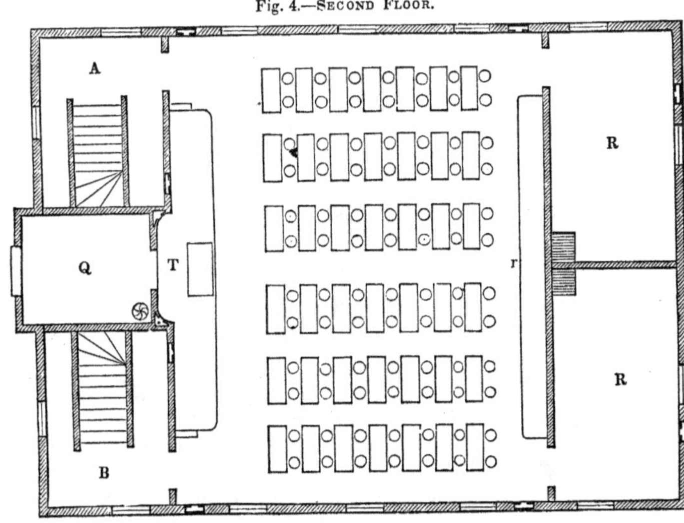

Union School-House, at Woonsocket and Chepachet, R. I.

By the school law of Rhode Island, two or more adjoining school districts in the same, or adjoining towns, may, by concurrent vote, agree to unite for the purpose of maintaining a secondary or grammar school, for the older and more advanced pupils of such associating districts. Under this provision the four school districts in the town of Cumberland, which comprise the village of Woonsocket, voted to unite and provide a school-house for the more advanced pupils, leaving the younger to be accommodated in their respective districts. The Union school-house is located on a beautiful site, the donation of Edward Harris, Esq., and is built substantially after the plan of the Warren Public school-house, already described, at a cost of $7,000. The following are the front and side elevations, as originally drawn by Mr. Teft, but not adopted by the committee.

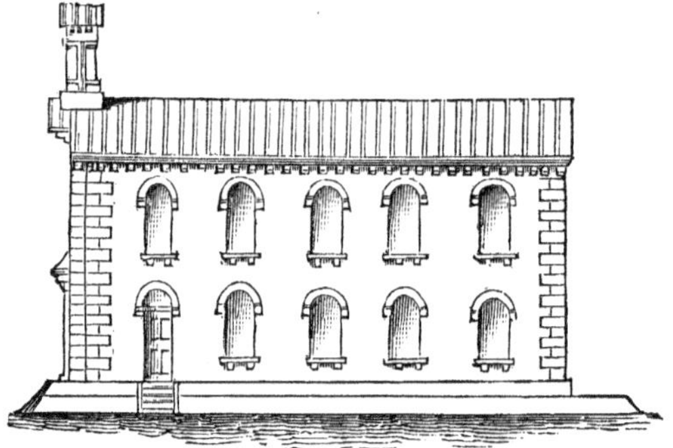

Side Elevation.

Front Elevation.

Under the provision above cited, the three districts into which the village of Chepachet, in the town of Glocester, is divided, voted to establish a Union School, and to provide a suitable house for the same. The building is 50 feet by 34, with two stories, and stands in the centre of a large lot, a little removed from the main street, and is the ornament and pride of the village. The lower floor is divided into two apartments; one for the Primary, and the other for an Intermediate School, for the younger pupils of the village, while the Union or Secondary School occupies the whole of the second floor.

Fig. 1.—Plan of First Floor.

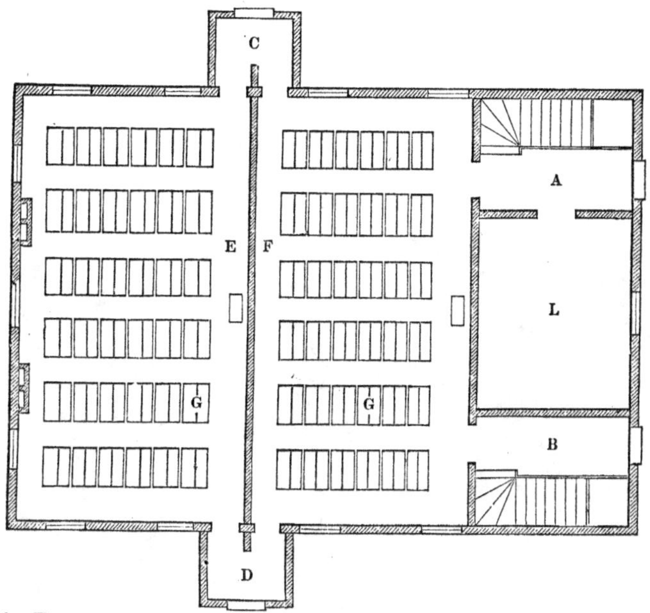

A—Entrance for Girls to Secondary School, U.
B— " " Boys " "
C— " " Girls to Primary, E, and Intermediate School, F.
D— " " Boys " " " " "
E—Primary School-room.
F—Intermediate "
U—Secondary " L—Manton Glocester Library of 900 volumes.
R—Recitation room. S—Stove. V—Flue for ventilation.
G—Seat and desk attached, for two pupils, with iron ends.

Fig. 2.—Plan of Second Floor.

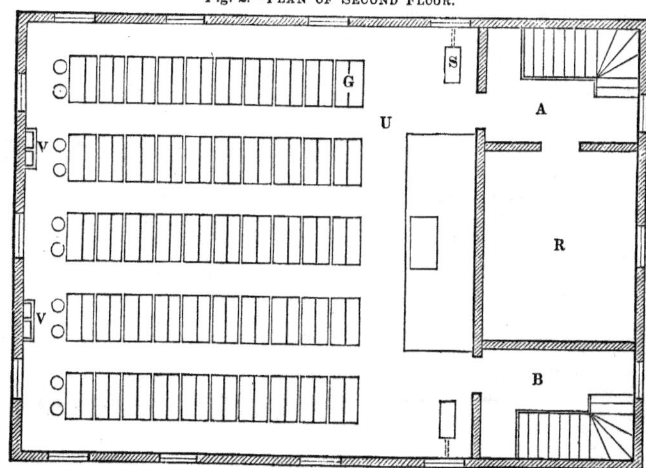

Plan, &c., of Union School-House in Pawtucket, R. I

Fig. 1—Perspective.

This school-house is calculated to accommodate, on the first floor, a Primary School, (D,) with seats and desks for one hundred and sixty pupils; two Intermediate Schools. (E, E,) for sixty-four pupils each; and on the second floor a High School, (F,) for one hundred and seventy pupils.

The building is warmed and ventilated by a furnace in the cellar, from which the hot air is conveyed into the several apartments, as indicated by the registers, (r, r, r, r,) in Figs. 2 and 3, and discharged by flues carried up in the walls, as seen at v, v, v, v.

Each school-room is furnished with an appropriate place for outer garments, and with scrapers, mats and other means of neatness and cleanliness.

The boys and girls have each a separate yard in the rear, and separate entrances into the school-rooms.

The High School is furnished with seats and desk having cast-iron end pieces similar to those described on page 282.

The Primary and Intermediate school-rooms are furnished with the patent Revolving Pivot Chair, and School-desk, manufactured by J. L. Mott, 264 Water street, New York. The seat of the chair is wood; all other parts are of cast-iron. The seat and back turn on a pivot, while the pedestal is screwed fast to the floor. The height of the lower part of the top of the desk is just equal to the highest part of the back of the chair, so as to allow it to pass under. The front edge of the seat is in a perpendicular line with the edge of the top of the desk, so that the scholar is required to sit erect when engaged in writing or studying, and the same time that part of his back which requires support is fully in contact with the chair.

Since the chairs above described were placed in this house, Mr. Mott has modified the patterns—so as to carry the back piece higher, and thus give support to the muscles above the small of the back. The iron can be covered with felt, and thus the rapid conduction of heat from the body, especially from the spinal column, in children thinly clad, and of delicate constitutions may be prevented.

Union School-House in Pawtucket.

Fig. 2.—Plan of First Floor.

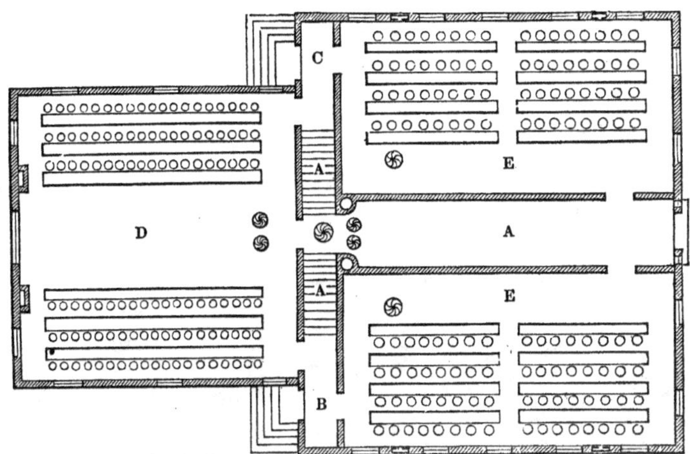

A—Entrance to High School.
B—Entrance for Boys to the Primary and Intermediate Schools.
C—Entrance for Girls to the Primary and Intermediate Schools.
D—School-room, 30 feet by 24, for Primary School.
E, E— " " 40 feet by 16, for Intermediate Schools.
F— " " 40 feet by 40, for High School.
G—Room for Apparatus, &c.
H—Recitation room to High School, 20 feet by 16.
I—K—Entrance room, one for Boys and the other for Girls, fitted up with hooks, shelves, wash-stand, &c.
T—Teacher's desk without any platform.

Fig. 3.—Plan of Second Floor—High School.

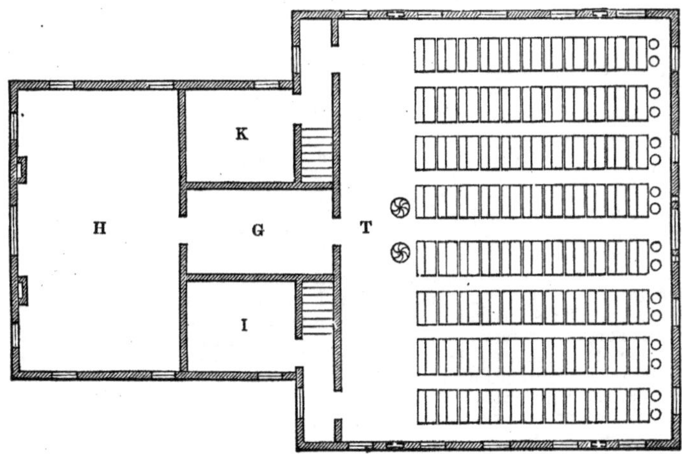

Plans and Descriptions of the Public School-Houses in Providence, R. I.

Primary School-Houses.

These buildings are located in different parts of the city, and are designed for the accommodation of children from four to six or seven years of age, or until they are prepared to enter the intermediate schools.

No. 1.—View of a Primary School-House.

These school-houses stand back from thirty to sixty feet from the line of the street, and near the center of lots varying from eighty to one hundred feet in breadth, and from one hundred to one hundred and twenty feet in length. Each lot is inclosed by a neat and substantial fence, six feet high, and is divided into two yards—one for boys and the other for girls—with suitable out-buildings, shade trees, and shrubbery.

These houses are each forty feet long by thirty-three feet wide, with twelve-feet posts, built of wood, in a plain, substantial manner, and, with the fences, are painted white, presenting a neat and attractive exterior.

The entrance is into a lobby [A] and thence into an open area, where stands the stove [*a*]. A portion of the lobby is appropriated to bins for charcoal [*c*] and anthracite [*d*], which is the fuel used in all the schools; the remainder [B] is occupied by a sink, and as depositories for brooms, brushes, &c. Each room is arched, thereby securing an average height of thirteen feet, with an opening in the center of the arch, two feet in diameter, for ventilation. The ventilator is controlled by a cord passing over a pulley, and descending into the room near the teacher's desk [*b*]. In each end of the attic is a circular window, which, turning on an axis, can be opened and closed by cords, in the same manner as the ventilator.

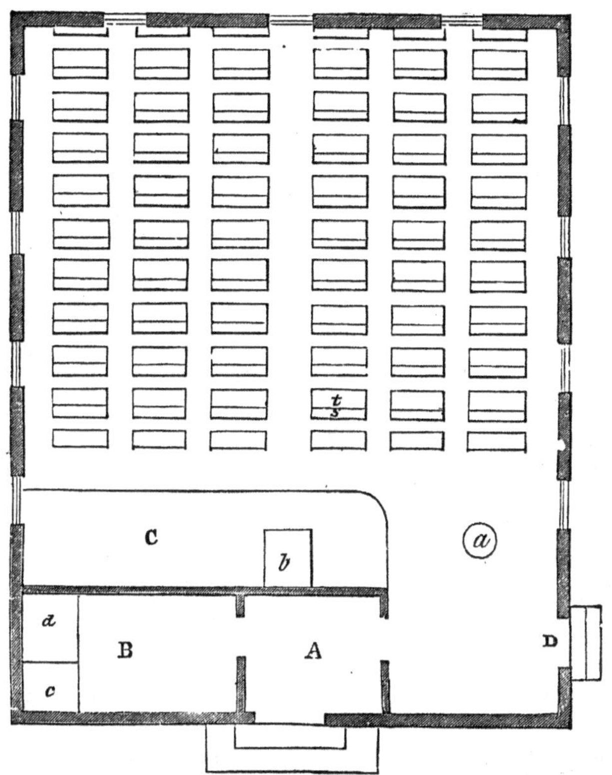

No. 2.—Interior of a Primary School-House.

The teacher's platform [C] is five feet wide, twenty feet long, and seven inches high, with a black-board ten feet long and three feet wide on the wall in the rear.

The floor is of inch and a half plank, tongued and grooved; and, for the purpose of securing warmth and firmness, and avoiding noise, is laid on cement.

The windows, eleven in number, of twenty-four lights, of seven by nine glass, are hung with weights, and furnished with inside blinds. The sides of the room and entries are ceiled all round with wood as high as the window-sills, which are four feet from the floor. The rest of the walls are plastered, and covered with white hard finish. Each room is provided with sixty seats [*s*] and desks [*t*], placed in six ranges; each range containing ten seats and desks, of three different sizes, and each seat and desk accommodating two scholars, or one hundred and twenty in all.

The center aisle is three feet and a half wide, and each of the others about two feet.

The desks are over three feet long, by sixteen inches wide, with a shelf beneath for books. The upper surface of the desk [*a*], except about two inches at the top [*b*], slopes one inch and a half in a foot.

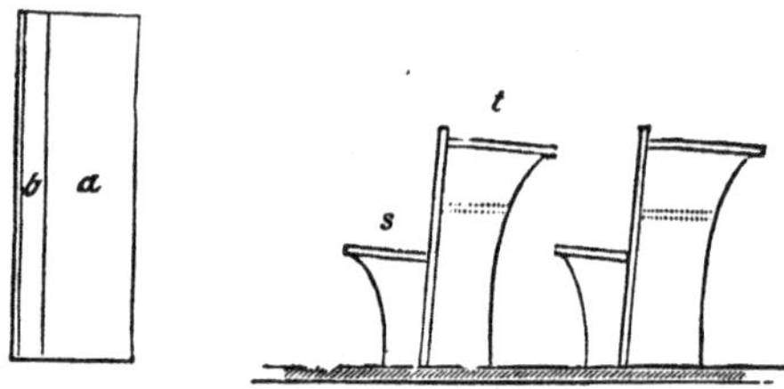

No 3.—View of Top of a Desk, and Sectional View of Primary Seats and Desks.

The front of the desk, constituting the back of the next seat, slopes one inch in a foot. The seat also inclines a very little from the edge. The seats are of four different sizes, varying from seven to ten inches wide, and from nine to fourteen inches in height, the lowest being nearest the teacher's platform.

Intermediate School-Houses.

All the buildings of this class are two stories high, affording accommodations for two schools, a primary and an intermediate. These houses are generally in pleasant situations, on large lots, varying in size from one hundred feet wide by one hundred and twenty feet long, to one hundred and fifty by two hundred feet.

Rows of shade trees, consisting of elms, lindens, and maples, are planted along the side-walks and the fences inclosing the yards; and evergreens, the mountain ash, and other ornamental trees, are placed within the inclosures.

These houses are forty-four feet long, by thirty-three feet wide. Some of them are built of wood, the remainder of brick, and all in a tasteful and substantial style.

The rooms are large, and easily ventilated, being twelve feet in the clear, with large openings in the ceiling of the upper room, and on the sides in the lower room, leading into flues in the walls, which conduct the foul air into the attic, from which it escapes at circular windows in the gables of the buildings. These flues and windows can be opened and closed by cords passing over pulleys, and descending into the rooms below, where the teachers can control them with ease.

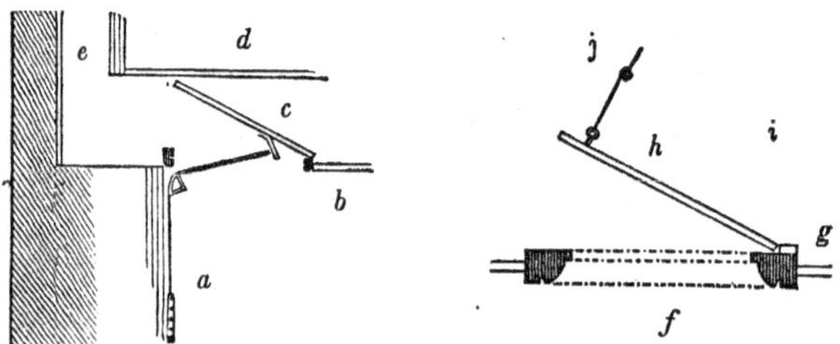

No. 5.—Sections of Ventilators.

In this cut, the cord [*i*], passing over the pulley [*j*], raising [*h*], hung on hinges at [*g*], opens wholly or partially the ventilator [*f*], a circular aperture three feet in diameter. The plan of ventilating the lower rooms is shown on

No. 4.—View of an Intermediate School-House

the other part of the diagram, in which [*a*] represents a cord running over a pulley, and attached to [*c*], a board three feet long by one foot wide, opening the space between [*b*], the top of the lower room, and [*d*], the floor of the upper, leading into the flue [*e*], ascending to the attic.

The windows, nine in number in each school-room, of twelve lights, of ten by sixteen glass, are hung with weights, so as to be easily opened at top and bottom, and furnished with Venetian blinds inside, to regulate the amount of light admitted.

The floors are of hard pine boards, an inch and a half thick, and about six inches wide, tongued and grooved, and laid on mortar, as a protection against fire, for the prevention of noise, and to secure warmth and firmness. All the rooms, entries, and stairways are ceiled up with matched boards about four feet, as high as the window-sills. The remaining portions of the walls are plastered, and coated with white hard finish.

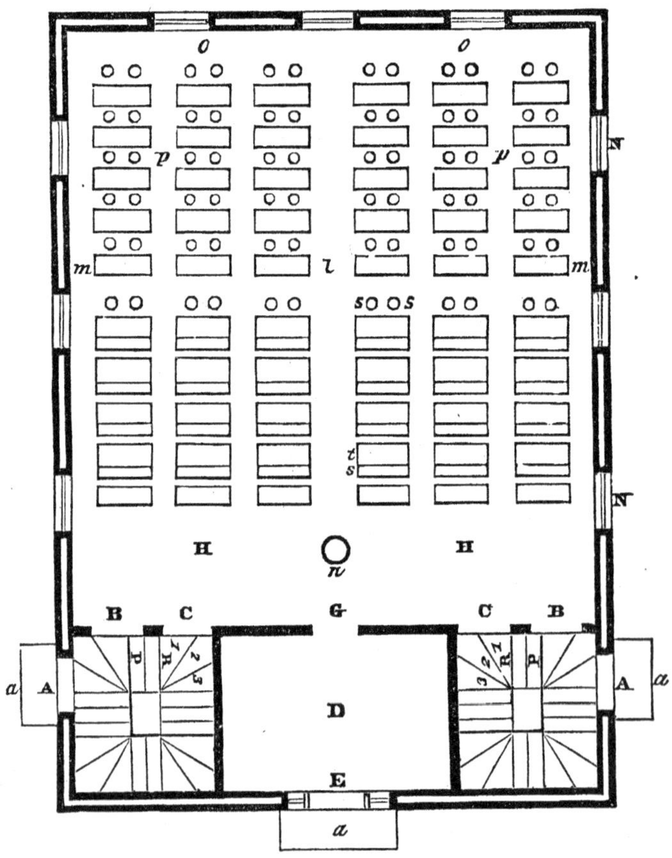

No. 6.—Interior of an Intermediate School-House.

The walls of some of these buildings are solid stone-work, faced with brick; others are built with double brick walls, as above shown, connected by ties of iron or brick.

As the rooms in the lower stories of this class of buildings are appropriated to primary schools, and are furnished in the same manner as those already described, the preceding cut is intended to serve the double purpose of exhibiting on the *first* floor only the improvements on the former plan, and, on the *second*, the whole view of a room for an intermediate school.

The steps [*a*, *a*, *a*] are broad, granite blocks, with scrapers on each end. The side doors [A, A], one for boys, the other for girls, lead into entries, eight feet by ten, from which the pupils of the primary schools pass through the doors [B, B] into the main rooms, which differ from those above described, in having a space [*o*, *o*], two feet wide, on the back part of the rooms, for reading and other class exercises; and the recitation-room, [D], another valuable improvement, as it avoids the confusion arising from having two recitations in one room at the same time.

The flight of stairs in each entry, commencing at the points [R, R], and ascending in the direction of [1, 2, 3], lands on the open space [P] in the upper entry, from which the pupils pass through the doors [C, C] into the school-room.

Coal-bins and convenient closets, for brooms, brushes, &c., are built under the stairs, in the lower entries; and similar closets, for the same purposes, are provided in the upper entries.

The large area [H, H], thirty feet long by seven wide, is the same in both the rooms, and is occupied by the principal teacher in each school, for such class exercises as may be more conveniently managed there than in the other place [*o*, *o*], left for the same purpose. The position of the stove [*n*] is such as not to render it uncomfortably warm on the front seats, and, at the same time, not to interfere with the passage of classes through the door [G] into the recitation-room [D], which is fourteen feet by ten, and, like all the school-rooms, furnished with black-boards. The lower room is lighted by a window over the front door, and by the side-lights; and the upper one by a double or mullion window, of sixteen lights, of ten by sixteen glass.

The side aisles [*m*, *m*] are two feet and a half wide; the others [P, P, &c.] are only eighteen inches wide, except the middle one [C], which is three and a half feet. The passage across the center of the room is about a foot and a half wide, and is very convenient for teachers in passing to the different parts of the room, and also for scholars in going to and from their recitations.

The seats and desks, in the front part of this room, are made and arranged on the same plan as those in the primary school-rooms above described, differing from them only in being one size larger. The lower end, or foot of each perpendicular support, or end-piece, is strongly fastened into a groove in a "shoe," or piece of plank, which, being screwed to the floor, secures the desks in a durable manner, and in a firm position.

The others are constructed upon a different plan, designed especially for the accommodation of pupils while writing. These desks and seats are of three different sizes.

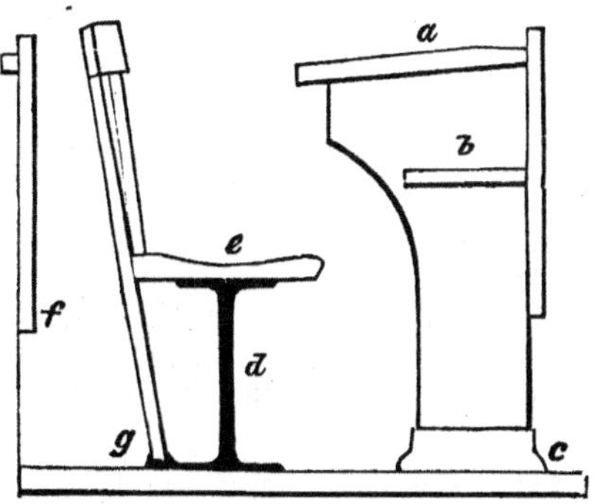

No. 7.—Section of a Writing-Desk and Seat.

The top of the desk [*a*] is of pine, one inch and a half thick, fifteen inches wide, and three feet and a half long. These desks are twenty-seven inches high on the front, and twenty-four on the side next to the seats. A space about three inches wide, on the front edge of the top, is planed down to a level, and an inkstand is let into the center of this, even with the surface, and covered with a small lid. The ends of these desks are an inch and a half thick, and fastened by a strong tenon to the shoe [*c*], which is screwed to the floor. The front of the desk, and the shelf [*b*], for books, &c., are inch boards; the whole desk, made in the strongest manner, is painted a pleasant green, and varnished. In the next smaller size, the same proportion is observed, but all the dimensions are one inch *less;* and in the third, or smallest size, the dimensions are all one inch less than in the second. For each desk there are two chairs, resting on cast-iron supporters [*d*], an inch and a quarter in diameter, with a wide *flange* at each end; the upper one, screwed to the under side of the seat [*e*], is a little smaller than the lower, which is fastened to the floor by five strong screws, rendering the chair almost immovable. The largest size seats [*e*] in these rooms are fourteen inches in diameter and fifteen inches high, with backs, twenty-eight inches from [*g*] to the top, slanting an inch and a quarter to a foot. These backs are made with three slats, fastened by strong tenons into a top-piece, like some styles of common chairs, and screwed to the seat, while the middle one extends down into a socket on the foot of the iron standard. The seats, like the desks, are diminished one inch for the middle size, and two for the smallest, preserving the proportions in the different sizes, which adapts them to the sizes of the desks.

Grammar School-Houses.

There are six buildings of this class, constructed on the same plan, and of the same size. They are seventy feet long by forty wide, with a front projection, twenty-eight feet long by fourteen feet wide. They are located on very large lots, varying from one hundred and fifty to two hundred feet long—from a hundred and twenty to a hundred and fifty feet wide. All of them, except one, are on corner lots, and all have large open spaces around them. These, and all the other public school-houses in the city, are protected with Quimby's lightning-rods, and each is furnished with a bell, which can be heard in the remotest parts of its district.

In the accompanying view, No. 9, the engraver has represented a *few* trees, a little *larger* than any at present around these buildings, because he could not crowd all the trees and shrubbery into the picture, without obscuring the lower part of the house.

The cut on p. 91, No. 10, is a ground plan, on a reduced scale, of a Grammar School-House, including a general view of the cellar, yards, fences, gates, sidewalks, &c.

The yards around each of the grammar school-houses contain from 18,000 to 20,000 square feet, or between a third and half an acre. These grounds are inclosed, and divided into three separate yards, by substantial close board fences [*f, f, f, f*], six feet high, neatly made, and painted white. The boys' play-ground [B], and that of the girls [G], are large; but the front yard [E] is small, and, not being occupied by pupils, is planted with trees and shrubbery. The graveled sidewalks [*s, s, s*], running on two sides of all the grammar school lots, and on three of some of them, are shaded by rows of elms, maples, and lindens, set near the curb-stones. The gates [A, C, D] and the graveled walks [*d, d, d*] lead to the front and the two side doors of the school-house; and [*f*] is a large gate for carting in coal, &c. The out-buildings [*i, i*] are arranged with a large number of separate apartments on both sides, all well ventilated, each furnished with a door, and the whole surrounded with evergreens.

In the plan of the projection [H] the stairway [*r*] leads to the cellar, which is seven feet in the clear, and extends under the whole of the main building. These cellars are well lighted, having eight windows [W, W], with ten lights of seven by nine glass. The windows, being hung with hinges on the upper

No. 9.—View of a Grammar School-House.

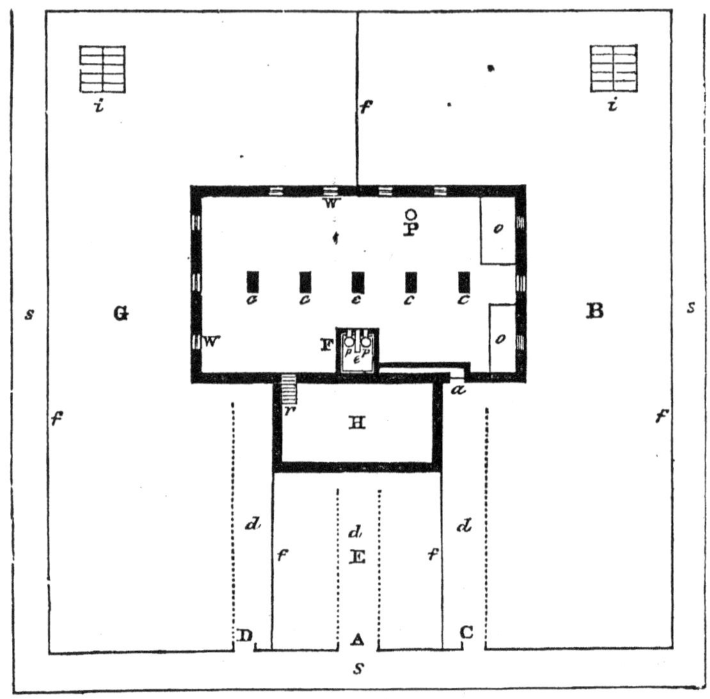

No.10 .—Ground Plan, &c., of a Grammar School-House.

side, and fastened with hooks and staples at the lower edge, may be opened by raising them intc a horizontal position, where they are fastened with hooks as when closed. With this arrangement, it is easy to keep the cellars well ventilated at all seasons. The openings for the admission of coal into the bins [o, o], one for anthracite, and the other for charcoal, are furnished with sheet-iron shutters, fastening on the inside. Every school-house has, in the cellar, an abundant supply of good water, obtained from a fountain, or from a well, which is generally outside of the building, the water being brought in by a pump [P]. A supply of good water for a school-house should not be considered merely as a convenience, but as absolutely necessary.

The horizontal section of a furnace [F] shows merely the ground plan. The cold air passes through [a] to the air-chamber, where it is warmed by the fires in [p, p], two cast-iron cylinders, fourteen inches in diameter. The evaporator [e] holds about fifteen gallons of water, which is kept in a state of rapid evaporation, thus supplying the air-chamber with an abundance of moisture.

In the plan and construction of the various parts of these furnaces, special pains have been taken to remove all danger of fire—an important consideration, which should never be overlooked. The furnace is covered with stone, thickly coated with mortar, and the under side of the floor above is lathed and plastered, not only above the furnace, but at least ten feet from it in every direction.

A full description of the construction and operation of the furnaces used in the public school-houses will be given under another diagram. The cellar walls and the stone piers [c, c, c, c, c] are well pointed, and the whole inside, including the wood-work overhead, is neatly whitewashed, giving this apartment a neat and pleasant appearance.

The walls of all these buildings are of stone, about two feet thick, faced with common brick, and painted a tasteful color.

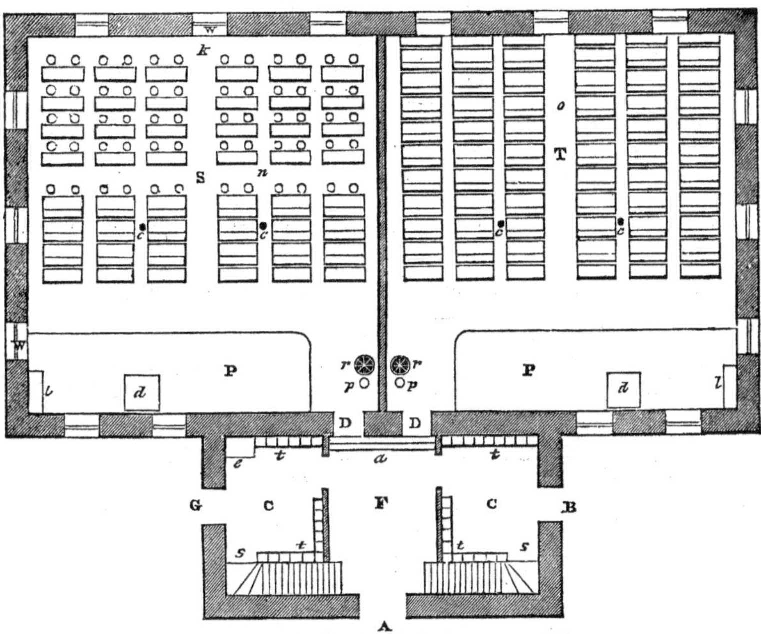

No. 11.—Plan of the First Floor of a Grammar School-House.

There are three entrances to these houses; the front [A], and the two side doors [B], for boys, and [G], for girls, leading into the entries [F, C, C]. The front is a large double door, with a beautiful frontice of fine hammered Quincy granite. At all the outside doors are two or three hewn granite steps, furnished with four or six scrapers at each door.

Pupils belonging to the schools in the lower story pass from the side entries into the middle one, and, ascending two steps at [*a*], enter their respective rooms [T, S], which are rather larger than those in the primary and intermediate school-houses, previously described, being thirty-six feet by thirty-two inside, and eleven feet high in the clear.

In each of the entries [C, C] there is a provision [*t*, *t*, *t*, *t*] for setting up umbrellas. It resembles a ladder placed in a horizontal position, and is fastened to the ceiling on one side, and supported on the other by substantial posts of oak or other strong wood, turned in a tasteful style, and set into the floor.

The seats and desks in the rooms [T and S] are of the same dimensions, and arranged in the same manner as those in the primary and the intermediate school-rooms before described. The small iron posts [*c*, *c*, *c*, *c*], about two and a half inches in diameter, supporting the floor above, are placed against the ends of the seats, so close as not to obstruct the passages at all. Besides the platforms [P, P], twenty feet by six—the tables, three feet by four, for the teachers, and the closets [*l*, *l*], for brushes, &c., there are black-boards, painted upon the walls, extending from the doors [D, D] to the windows, fourteen feet long by four wide, with the lines of a stave painted on one end, to aid in giving instruction in vocal music.

The plan of ventilating these rooms on the first floor is represented by cut No. 5, page 85. Every room is provided with two ventilators, each three feet long by about twelve inches wide, opening into flues of the same dimensions, leading into the attic, from which the impure air escapes at circular windows in the gables. These flues should have extended down to the bottom of the rooms, with openings on a level with the floors, so that, when the rooms are warmed with air from the furnaces above the temperature of the human breath, they might be ventilated by removing the foul air from the lower parts, and thus causing fresh, warm air to be slowly settling down upon the scholars —a very pleasant and healthful mode of ventilation.

These rooms are well warmed by heated air, admitted through registers [*r*, *r*], eighteen inches in diameter, from the furnace below, from which [*p*, *p*] tin pipes, fourteen inches in diameter, convey the air to the grammar school-rooms in the second story.

These rooms are large, with arched ceilings, measuring twelve feet to the foot of the arch, and seventeen to its crown. They are each provided with two ventilators, three feet and a half in diameter, placed in the crown of the arch, about twenty feet apart.

The entrances to the Grammar School-rooms are by two short flights of stairs on a side; from the lower entries to [*s*, *s*], spaces about three feet square,

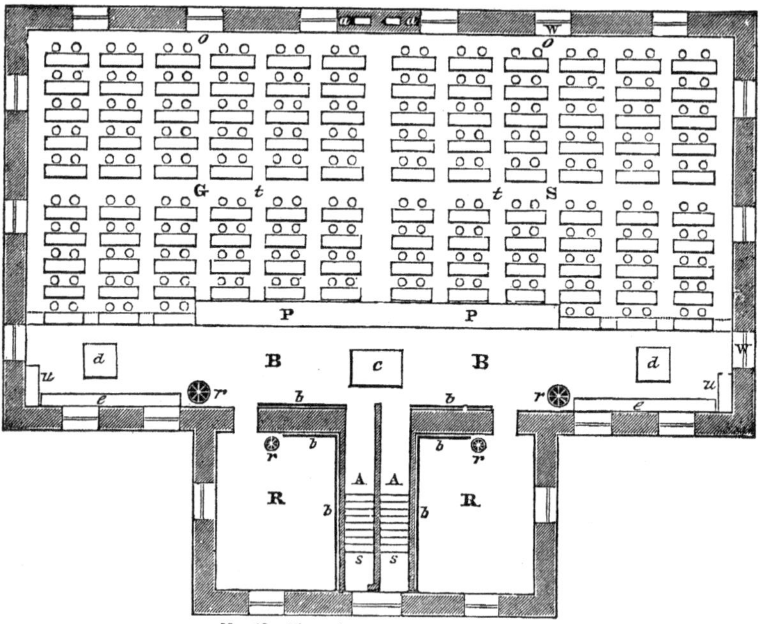

No. 12.—Plan of a Grammar School-Room.

and thence to [A, A], spaces three by five feet, extending from the top of the stairs to the doors opening into the school-room.

The master's table [*c*], as well as tables [*d*, *d*], for the assistants, are movable. The large area [B, B], being fourteen inches above the floor of the room, is eight feet wide by sixty-four long, with large closets [*u*, *u*] at the ends, fitted up with shelves, &c., for the use of the teachers.

The school-room is warmed by heated air, admitted at the registers, [*r*, *r*] and the recitation-rooms [R, R] in the same manner, by the small registers, [*r*,*r*] all of which are connected with the furnace in the cellar by large tin pipes or conductors.

The black-boards, four feet wide, painted upon the hard-finished walls, are indicated by the lines [*b*, *b*, *b*, &c.] in the recitation-rooms, and along the walls behind the master's table, extending on each side to the windows beyond, [*e*, *e*] making, in each Grammar School, about three hundred square feet of black-board.

The long benches [*e*, *e*] are used for seating *temporarily* new pupils on their entering school, until the master can assign them regular seats; also for seating visitors at the quarterly examinations. The space [P, P], a broad step, eighteen feet long and two feet wide, is used for some class exercises on the black-boards. The passage [*t*, *t*], about eighteen inches wide, running the whole length of the room, affords great facility in the movements of pupils to and from the recitations and other class exercises. The master's classes generally recite in the space [*o*, *o*] on the back side of the room, four feet wide and sixty-four feet long, where seats are placed for scholars to sit during recitation, when it is necessary; and the same accommodations are provided in the recitation-rooms.

The windows [W, W, &c.], which are hung with weights, and furnished with inside blinds, in the manner before described, contain twelve lights each, of ten by sixteen glass, of the strongest kind, the Saranac or Redford glass.

The quantity of air furnished for each scholar in the public school-rooms is a matter of no small importance. The rooms for the primary and the intermediate schools—the former designed to accommodate one hundred and twenty, and the latter only ninety-six pupils—contain between fifteen and sixteen thousand cubic feet of atmospheric air. The rooms for the grammar schools, intended to accommodate two hundred pupils, contain over thirty-five thousand cubic feet, after a suitable deduction for the furniture is made.

This estimate allows every child, when the rooms are not crowded, about one hundred and fifty cubic feet of air for every hour and a half, on the supposition that no change takes place, except at the times of recess, and at the close of each session. But the rate at which warm air is constantly coming into the rooms from the furnaces, increases the allowance for every child to about three hundred cubic feet for every hour and a half.

No. 13.—Transverse Section of a Grammar School-House.

The preceding cut is given in order to show an *end view*, the projection, belfry, rooms, seats, desks, and cellar. An imperfect section of the warming apparatus is presented, giving an outline of the plan of its construction. The smoke-pipe, connected with [*a*], the heater, coiled twice around in the air-chamber, passes off in the direction of [*b, b*] to the chimney. The short tin pipes [*c, c*] conduct the warm air into the lower rooms; and the long ones [*e, e*] convey it to the rooms in the second story. On each side of the projection over the door [*d*] is a window, lighting the outside entry, and also the middle entry by another window over the inside door. The end views of seats and desks do not represent the different sizes very accurately, but sufficiently so to give a correct idea of the general plan.

The High School-House.

This building occupies an elevated and beautiful situation, at the head of President street, near the central part of the city. It is a specimen of plain, but tasteful architecture, on which the eye reposes with pleasure. The lot, somewhat irregular in its form, is equivalent to one a hundred feet by a hundred and fifteen, and lies on a gentle hill-side, rendering it easy to construct a basement almost entirely above ground, except on the back side. The extensive grounds in front, and on either side, all planted with trees, and separated from the High School only by the width of the streets, add much to the beauty and pleasantness of its situation. The yards around it are inclosed by a handsome baluster fence, resting in front on heavy blocks of rough granite. The steps are of hewn granite, twelve feet long, making a very convenient entrance.

The High School being designed for both boys and girls, an entirely separate entrance is provided for each department. The front door, at which the girls enter, has a very beautiful frontispiece, with double columns (thus providing for large side-lights), and a heavy ornamented cap, all cut from Quincy granite in the best style.

The door in the circular projection, fronting on another street, has also a fine frontispiece, cut from Quincy granite.

The size of this building is fifty feet by seventy-six, with a projection of seven feet. The walls of the basement are of stone, three feet thick, and faced with rough-hewn granite, laid in courses twenty inches wide. Each stone has a "chiseled draft, fine cut," an inch wide around the face, and all the joints as close and true as if the whole were fine hammered. The remaining portions of the walls, diminishing in thickness as they rise, are faced with the best quality of Danvers pressed brick, giving the building a beautiful appearance. The roof is covered with tin, every joint soldered, and the whole surface kept well painted.

The rooms in the basement story, which is twelve feet high in the clear, are separated from each other by solid brick walls. The pupils in the girls' department, entering the house at [A], pass into the large lobby [C], twelve feet by twenty-eight, from which they can go to all parts of the building appropriated to their use.

The furnace-room [H] has a brick floor, and is kept in as good order as the other parts of the house. The coal-bins [*n, n*] and the furnace [F] are so constructed, that, with an ordinary degree of care, the room may be kept as clean as any of the school-rooms. The arrangements [*m, m*] for setting up umbrellas have been described. The pump [*p*], accessible to all in the girls' department, connected with a nice sink, lined with lead, affords an abundant supply of excellent water. The rooms [E, G, I], each not far from sixteen by twenty-four feet, are appropriated as the Superintendent's Office, and for such meetings of the School Committee, and of its sub-committees, as may be appointed there.

The large lecture-room, on the opposite side of the lobby, is furnished with settees, which will accommodate about two hundred and fifty pupils. On the

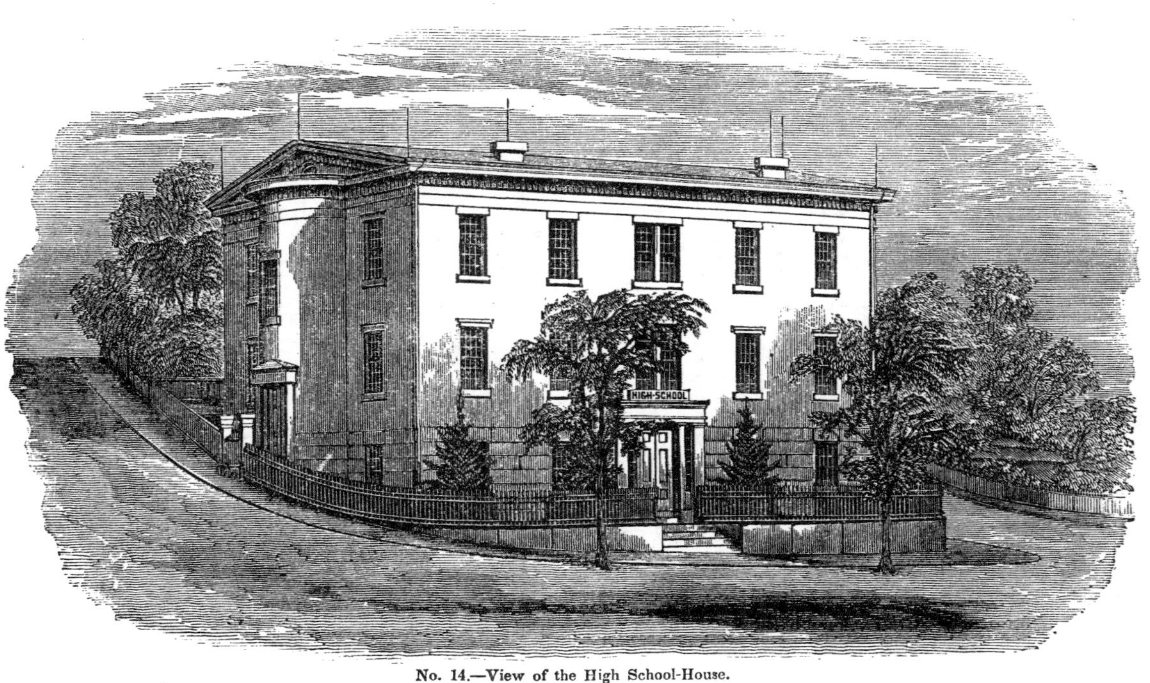

No. 14.—View of the High School-House.

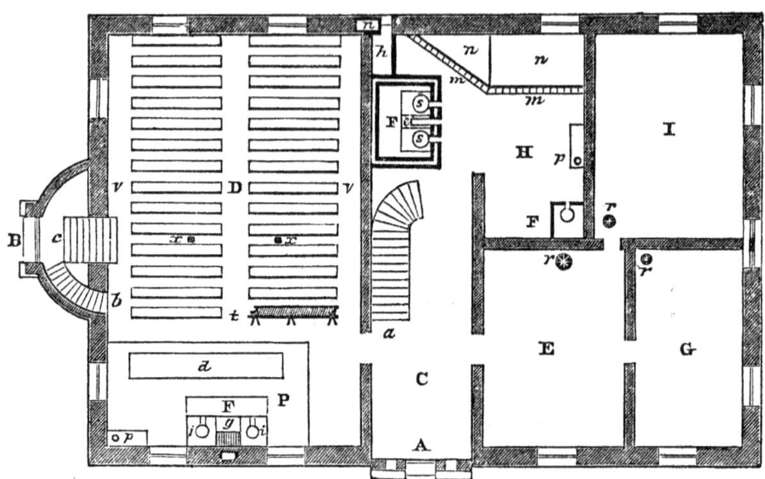

No. 15.—Plan of the Basement of High School.

platform [P], raised seven inches from the floor, a long table or counter [*d*], made convenient for experimental lectures in Chemistry, Natural Philosophy, &c., having pneumatic cisterns for holding gasses. At [F, &c.] are suitable provisions for the fires used in the preparations of chemical experiments. The pump [*p*], with a sink like the other, is used exclusively by the pupils in the boys' department.

In all lectures, and other exercises in this room, the girls, entering at [*a*], occupy the seats on the right of [D], the middle aisle. The boys, entering by descending the short flight of stairs [*b*], are seated on the opposite side of the room. This may seem like descending to useless particulars, but it is done to show that there are no grounds for the objections sometimes made against having a school for boys and for girls in the same building, where the departments are kept entirely separate, except in exercises in vocal music and occasional lectures. The boys enter the house at the end door [B], which is six feet above the basement floor, and, by a short flight of stairs, they reach the first story at [*e*].

The three rooms [C, D, F] are appropriated to the department for girls. They are easy of access to the pupils, who, ascending the broad flight of stairs, terminating at [B], can pass readily into their respective rooms.

The course of instruction in the school occupying three years, the room [D] is appropriated to the studies for the first, [E] to those of the second, and [F] to the course for the third year. In each room there are three sizes of seats and desks, and their arrangement in all is uniform. The largest are on the back side of the room. The largest desks are four feet eight inches long, and twenty-two inches wide on the top; the middle size is two inches smaller, and the other is reduced in the same proportions. The largest seats are as high as common chairs, about seventeen inches, and the remaining sizes are reduced to correspond with the desks. The passages around the sides of the rooms vary from two to four feet wide, and those between the rows of desks, from eighteen to twenty-four inches.

On the raised platforms [P, P, P, P] are the teachers' tables [*d, d, d, d*], covered with dark woolen cloth, and furnished with four drawers each. The registers [*f, f, f, f*] admit the warm air from the furnace, and the pipes [*p, p, p*] conduct it into the rooms in the upper story. The passage [*b*] leads into the back yard, which is ornamented with a variety of shrubbery.

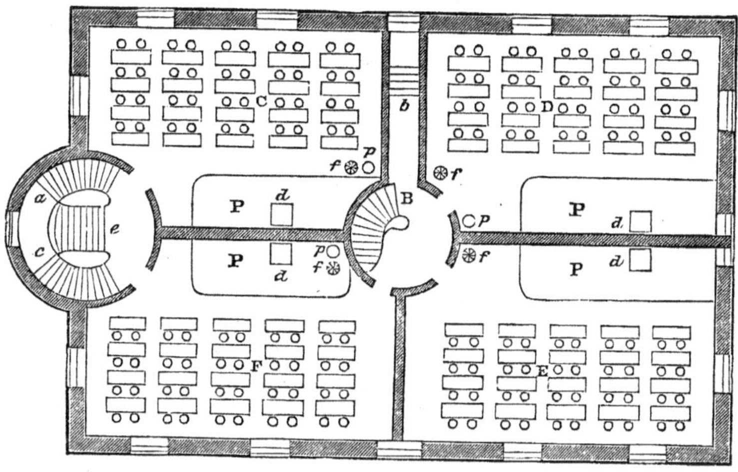

No. 16.—Plan of the First Story of the High School.

The door leading from the room [F] is used only for teachers and visitors, except when the two departments assemble in the hall.

In the room [C] the boys pursue the studies prescribed for the first year; the other rooms in this department are in the next story.

Pupils ascending from the area [e], by two circular stairways, land on the broad space [a, c], from which, by a short flight of stairs, they reach [A], in the following cut, the floor of the upper story, which is sixteen feet in the clear.

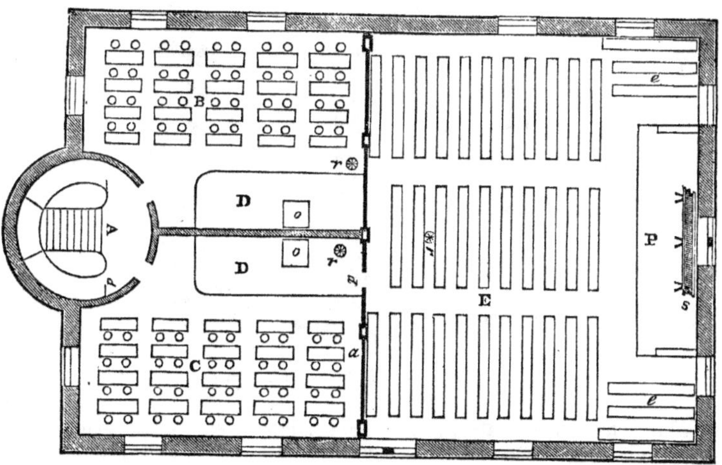

No. 17.—Plan of the Second Story of the High School-House

The room [B] is appropriated to the middle class, and [C] to the senior class. The arrangement of the seats and desks are the same as in the other rooms, except they are *movable*—being screwed to a frame not fastened to the floor, as shown in this cut.

The cross partition [*a*]—see cut No. 17—is composed of four very large doors, about fourteen feet square, hung with weights in such a manner that they may be raised into the attic, thus throwing the whole upper story into one large hall—an arrangement by which one room can be changed into *three*, and three into *one*, as the occasion may require. On all public occasions, such as Quarterly Examinations, and Annual Exhibitions, the rooms are thus thrown together, and the seats and desks turned so as to face the platform [P], in [E], the principal hall.

Observation and experiment, relative to the modes of warming the public school-rooms, have proved that very *large* stoves, eighteen inches in diameter, render the temperature of the rooms *more uniform and pleasant*, and that they are also *more economical*, both in regard to the amount of fuel consumed, and the amount of repairs required. It is a general principle, that a warming apparatus, containing a *large* quantity of fuel, undergoing a *slow* combustion, is better than one containing a *small* quantity of fuel, in a state of *rapid* combustion. The stoves in the small buildings, and the furnaces in the large ones, are constructed on this principle.

In regard to the construction of furnaces for warming public buildings or private dwellings, so much depends upon circumstances, that no specific plan can be given which would be successful in all cases. One familiar with the principles which regulate the motions of currents of air at different temperatures, can, with an ordinary degree of good judgment and mechanical skill, make a furnace in any place, where one can be made at all, that will accomplish all which the laws of nature will permit.

The following cut is intended to illustrate *two* plans for a furnace.

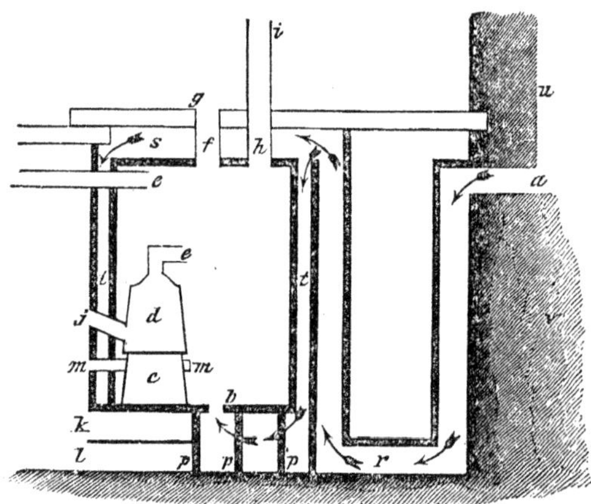

No. 18.—A Vertical Section of a Furnace

In the first, the cold air is admitted at [*a*], through the outside walls of the building, and descends in the direction described by the arrows, to [*r*], and thence rises to the top of the furnace, as shown by the arrows. At this place, the cold air diffuses itself over the whole upper surface, about eight feet by ten, and passes down between the double walls of the furnace, in the spaces [*t*, *t*], which extend all around the furnace, and rises from beneath, through a large opening [*b*], into the air-chamber, where it is heated and conducted to the rooms by large pipes, [*f, h*]. The object of this mode of taking in air is two-fold. In the first place, the constant currents of cold air, passing over the top of the furnace, keep that surface comparatively cool, and also keep the floors above the furnace cool, thus removing all danger of setting fire to the wood-work over the furnace.

In the second place, as the inside walls are constantly becoming heated, and the currents of cold air, passing down on all sides of the walls, become rarified by their radiation, and thus, as it were, take the heat from the outside of the inner walls, and bring it round into the air-chamber again, at [*b*]. This is not mere theory, but has been found to work well in practice. On this plan, the outside walls are kept so cool, that very little heat is wasted by radiation.

In the second plan, the cold air is admitted as before; but, instead of ascending from [*r*] to the top of the furnace, it passes through a large opening, directly from [*r*], to [*p, p, p*], representing small piers, supporting the inside walls, and thence into the air-chamber at [*b*], and also *up* the spaces [*t, t*], to the top [*s*], from which the air warmed by coming up between the walls is taken into the rooms by separate registers, or is let into the sides of the pipes [*f, h*].

By this plan, the air passes more rapidly through the air-chamber, and enters the rooms in *larger* quantities, but at a *lower* temperature. This is the better mode, if the furnace be properly constructed with large inlets and outlets for air, so that no parts become highly heated; otherwise, the wood-work over the furnace will be in some danger of taking fire. The general defects in the construction of furnaces are:—*too small* openings for the admission of cold air—*too small* pipes for conveying the warm air in all horizontal and inclined directions—and defective dampers in the perpendicular pipes. A frequent cause of failure in warming public buildings and private dwellings may be found in the ignorance and negligence of attendants.

A single remark will close this report, which has been extended, perhaps too far by specific details—a want of which is often complained of by mechanics who are engaged in building school-houses.

It is believed to be *best*, and, all things considered, *cheapest*, in the end, to build *very good* school-houses—to make their external appearance pleasant and attractive, and their internal arrangements comfortable and convenient—to keep them in *first-rate* order, well repaired, and *always clean.*

The amount of damage done to school property in this city has uniformly been *least* in those houses in which the teachers have done *most* to keep everything in very good order. The very appearance of school property well taken care of rebukes the spirit of mischief, and thus elevates the taste and character of the pupils.

Respectfully submitted.

N. BISHOP,
Superintendent of Public Schools.

PROVIDENCE, August, 1846.

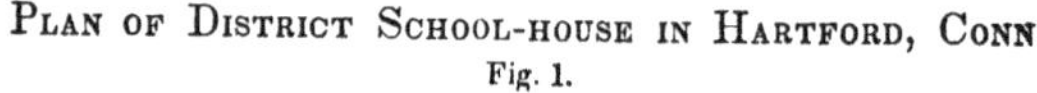

PLAN OF DISTRICT SCHOOL-HOUSE IN HARTFORD, CONN.

Fig. 1.

The above cut represents the front elevation of a new school-house erected in Arsenal District, in Hartford, after designs by Octavius Jordan, Architect. As originally planned there were to be two rooms, as shown in side elevation, (Fig. 3.) The largest (Fig. 2) room is forty-five feet long by twenty-five wide, with a recitation-room (C) fourteen feet by twelve, and two entries, one for boys (A) and one for girls, (B), each twelve feet by six, furnished with sink, hooks, &c. There are thirty-two desks, each for two pupils, with sixty-four chairs, (page 141, Fig. 2), and thirty-two chairs for young children, (Fig. 3, page 30.) The room is warmed by Mott's School Stove, (page 146,) and ventilated by flues in the walls, opening at the top and bottom of the room, which is fifteen feet high in the clear. The material is brick, and the cost **$1800.**

Fig. 2. GROUND PLAN.

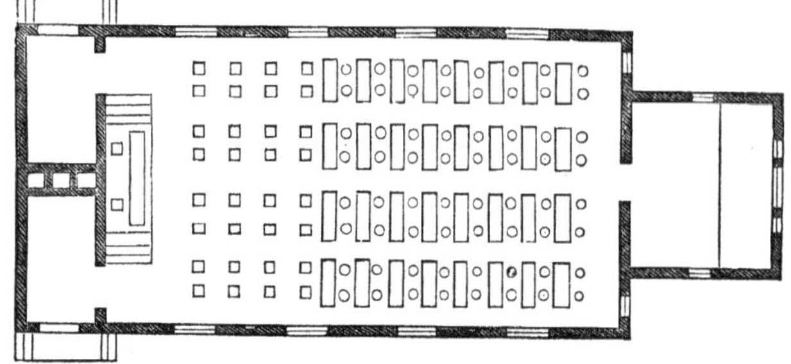

Fig. 3. Side Elevation.

Side elevation of the new School-house in Arsenal District, Hartford, as originally designed for two departments. The flues for smoke and for ventilation are carried up in the belfry, which is of brick

Plans of the South District School-house in the City of Hartford.

The house, illustrated in Figs. 1, 2, 3, 4, 5, and 6, was erected in 1851, after plans by E. D. Tiffany, Esq., at an expense, including lot, inclosure, building, and furniture, of $13,000. The location is both central and retired, on the east side of Wadsworth street, having a front of 320 feet, and depth of 150, and is rendered surpassingly attractive and beautiful by a number of fine old majestic oaks and graceful elms. The building is of brick, 70 feet by 58, exclusive of the towers, and is three stories high, and was designed to accommodate 450 pupils—but owing to the attraction of the house and popularity of the school, provision has been made in it for 500 pupils—classified into five departments.

Fig. 2. Plan of First Floor.

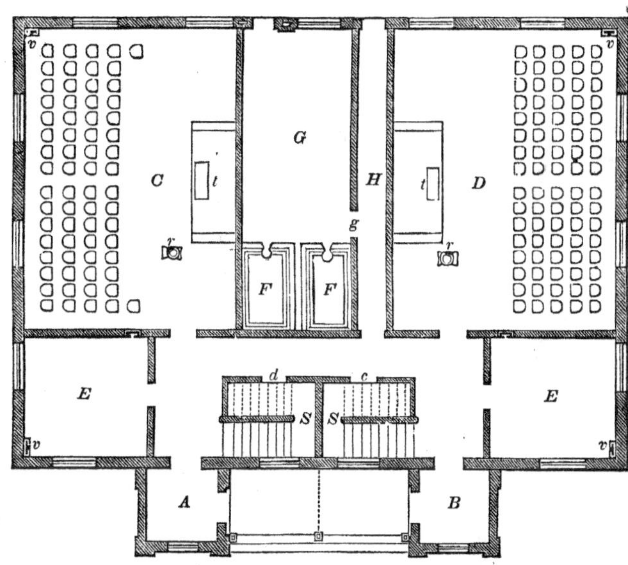

A—Girls' entrance.
B—Boys' do.
C—Primary No. 1. Seated with chairs. (Fig. 5.)
D—Primary No. 2. Seated as No. 1.
E E—Clothes rooms for Upper Department.
F F—Culver's Furnaces in basement.
G—Coal-room, extending under Primary No. 1.
H—Girls' passage to play ground.
S S—Stairs.
c—Clothes room for boys.
d—Clothes room for girls.
g—Stairs to Furnaces, &c.
t t—Teacher's table.
r—Registers for heated air.
v—Flues for ventilation surmounted by Emerson's Ejector.

FIG. 3. PLAN OF SECOND FLOOR.

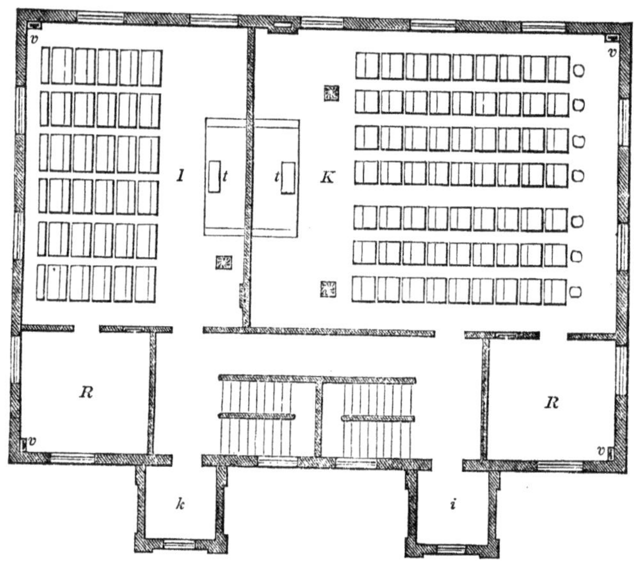

I—Primary No. 3. Seat and desk for two pupils. (Fig. 6.)
K—Intermediate School—seat and desk for one pupil.
i—Clothes room for boys.
k—Clothes room for girls.

FIG. 5. PRIMARY SCHOOL CHAIR.

FIG. 4. PLAN OF THIRD FLOOR.

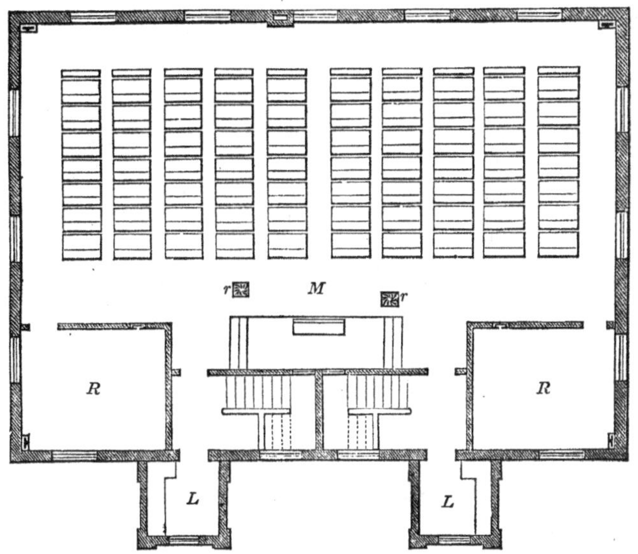

M—Upper Department, seats and desks for two pupils. (Fig. 6.)
L L—Library and Apparatus.

FIG. 6. HARTFORD SCHOOL DESK.

Plans and Description of the Public High School-House, Hartford, Conn.

The Public High School-House of Hartford was built after more than ordinary search for the best plan, (a committee having visited Boston, Lowell, Salem, Newburyport, Worcester, Providence, and Middletown, for this purpose,) under the constant oversight of a prudent, practical and intelligent building committee, and with due regard to a wise economy. The committee were limited in their expenditure for lot, building, and fixtures, to $12,000; and when it was ascertained that a suitable building could not be constructed for that sum, individuals on the committee immediately contributed $2,400 out of their own pockets to complete the house with the latest improvements. The committee have now the satisfaction of knowing that their contributions and personal oversight have been mainly instrumental in erecting and furnishing the most complete structure of the kind in New England, when the aggregate cost is taken into consideration.

The High School is designed for both males and females, and the arrangements of the buildings, and the grounds, are made with reference to the separation of the sexes, so far as this is desirable in the same school.

The lot on which the building stands is at the corner of Asylum and Ann streets, and is at once central, and large enough for the appropriate yards. The yards are separated by a close and substantial board fence, and the grounds are well laid out and properly inclosed; they will also soon be planted with trees and shrubbery. The building is of brick, three stories high, upon a firm stone basement. Its dimensions are 50 by 75 feet. The basement is 13 feet in the clear, six feet of which are above the level of the yard. This part of the building is occupied by furnaces, coal bins, sinks, pumps, entrance rooms, &c. At one end, and on two opposite sides of the building, a stair case eleven feet in width extends from each of the two entrance rooms, to the upper story, with spacious landings on the first and second floors. Two rooms, each 11 by 14 feet, are between the stair cases, the one on the first floor being used for a front entry to the building, and the one on the second floor being appropriated to the Library and Apparatus. Two closets, eleven by four feet on the first floor, and immediately beneath the stair cases, receive the outer garments, umbrellas, &c., of the teachers.

An aisle of four feet four inches in width extends between the desks and outer walls of the rooms, and between every two ranges of desks is an aisle of two feet four inches in width. An aisle of eight feet in width passes through the middle of the rooms, parallel to the narrower passages. A space of five feet in width is likewise reserved between the remote seats in the ranges and the partition wall of the rooms. Around the sides of the rooms, tastefully constructed settees are placed for occasional recitations, and for the accommodation of visiters, and in the upper room for the use of the pupils of the room below, during the opening and closing exercises of the school.

The pupils, when seated, face the teachers' desks and platforms, which occupy the space between the entrance doors of each room.

A blackboard, or black plaster surface, forty feet long, and five broad, extends between the doors leading to the recitation rooms, which are also lined with a continuous blackboard. There is also a blackboard extending the entire length of the teachers' platform in the lower room, and two of smaller dimensions in the room above, a part of the space being occupied by the folding doors leading to the library and apparatus room. Twenty chairs, of small dimensions and sixteen inches in height, are placed around each recitation room, thirteen inches apart and seven inches from the walls, and securely fastened to the floor. A clock, with a circular gilt frame and eighteen-inch dial plate, is placed over the teachers' platform in each school room, in full view of the pupils. A small bell is also placed above the teachers' platform in the lower room, with a wire attached, passing to the desk of the Principal, in the room above, by which the time of recesses, change of recitation classes, &c., are signified to the members of the lower rooms.

The school-rooms in the first and second stories are 50 feet square, and 13 feet in height—to each of which, two recitation rooms 12 by 23 feet are attached. The large rooms are furnished with "Kimball's improved School Chairs and Desks," placed in six ranges, extending back from the teachers' platforms, ten desks forming a range, and two chairs attached to each desk, furnishing accommodations in each room for 120 pupils—60 of either sex. Ample room yet remains in front of these ranges to increase the number of desks when the wants of the school demand them. The desks are four feet in length and one foot four inches in breadth, constructed of cherry, oiled and varnished. The moderately inclined tops are *fixed* to the end supporters, and the openings for books are in front of the pupils. Glass inkstands are inserted in the tops of the desks, and the ink protected from dust and the action of the atmosphere by mahogany covers turning on pivots. The chairs are constructed with seats of basswood, hollowed, and backs of cherry, moulded both to add beauty to the form of the chair, and to afford support and comfort to the occupants. All are neatly stained and varnished, and they, as well as the desks, rest on iron supporters, firmly screwed to the floor.

The entire upper story is converted into a hall, being twelve feet in height at the walls, rising thence in an arch to the height of seventeen feet. This is appropriated to reading, and declamation, and for the female department of the school, to daily recess, and calisthenic exercises. A moderately raised platform is located at one end, above which an extended blackboard is placed, and settees are ranged around the walls; these, properly arranged, together with the settees from the lower rooms, which are easily transported above, speedily convert the open *Hall* into a commodious Lecture room,—and also adapt it to the purposes of public examinations and exhibitions.

In each of the two entrance rooms are placed the means of cleanliness and comfort,—a pump of the most approved construction, an ample sink, two wash basins with towels, glass drinking tumblers, and a looking-glass. Ranges of hooks for hats, coats, bonnets, cloaks, &c., extend around the rooms, and are numbered to correspond with the number of pupils, of each sex, which the capacity of the house will accommodate. In the girls' room, pairs of small iron hooks are placed directly beneath the bonnet hooks, and twelve inches from the floor, for holding the over-shoes. In the boys' room, boot-jacks are provided to facilitate the exchange of boots for slippers when they enter the building—an important article, and of which no one in this department of the school is destitute. A thin plank, moderately inclined by hollowing the upper side, is placed upon the floor, and extends around the walls of the room, to receive the boots and convey the melted ice and snow from them, by a pipe, beneath the floor. A large umbrella stand is furnished in each of the two entrance rooms, also with pipes for conveying away the water. Stools are secured to the floors for convenience in exchanging boots, shoes, &c. Directly under the stairs is an OMNIUM GATHERUM—an appropriate vessel, in which are carefully deposited shreds of paper, and whatever comes under the denomination of *litter*, subject, of course, to frequent removal. These rooms, in common with the others, are carefully warmed. The wainscoting of the entrance rooms, and the stair case, is formed of narrow boards, grooved and tongued, placed perpendicularly, and crowned with a simple moulding. The railing of the stair case is of black walnut. A paneled wainscoting reaching from the floor to the base of the windows, extends around the walls of the remaining rooms. All the wood work, including the library and apparatus cases, is neatly painted, oak-grained, and varnished. The teachers' tables are made of cherry, eight feet in length, and two feet four inches in breadth, with three drawers in each, and are supported on eight legs. A movable writing desk of the same material is placed on each. Immediately in front of the teachers' desk in the upper room, a piano is to be placed, for use during the opening and closing exercises of the school, and for the use of the young ladies during the recesses. Venetian window blinds with rolling slats, are placed inside the windows, and being of a slight buff color, they modify the light without imparting a sombre hue to the room.

The building is warmed throughout by two of Hanks' Improved Air Heater, placed in the basement.

The ventilation of the school-rooms, or the rapid discharge of the air which has become impure by respiration, is most thoroughly secured in connection with a constant influx of pure warm air from the furnaces, by discharging ventiducts or flues, situated on each side of the building at the part of the rooms most distant from the registers of the furnaces. The ventiducts of each room are eighteen inches in diameter, and are carried from the floor entirely separate to the Stationary Top, or Ejector above the roof. The openings into the ventiducts, both at the top and bottom of the room, are two feet square, and are governed by a sliding door or blind.

A flight of stone steps leads to the front and main entrance of the building. The architectural entrance is of simple design, fourteen feet in width, and twenty feet in height. All the parts are wrought from dark colored stone, and on the crowning stone of the entablature, Public High School, appears in plain and prominent relief. Large folding doors, with side and top lights, close the entrance.

A side knob commands a bell suspended in the Library Room, directly behind the Principal.

A broad stone walk reaches from the steps to the street; flagging walks also extend from the street to the side entrances of the building, and thence to the outbuildings.

The Library contains an Encyclopedia, the most approved Dictionaries, both Classical and English, and other important books of reference for the use of the School, together with selected works for the direct professional reading of the teachers.

Several educational and scientific periodicals are furnished to the School, and which at the end of each year will form additional volumes for the Library.

Pelton's and Olney's, together with Mitchell's new series of outline maps, published by J. H. Mather & Co., of Hartford, Ct., and a fourteen-inch terrestrial globe, aid in the department of General Geography.

Mattison's series of sixteen astronomical maps; a fourteen-inch celestial globe; Vale's improved twenty-four-inch celestial globe and transparent sphere; a magic lantern, with sets of slides, containing thirty accurate telescopic and astronomical views; a reflecting telescope of five feet focal distance, with magnifying power of 700, and Chamberlin's best Tellurium, aid in the department of Astronomy.

Historical maps, charts, &c., an Isothermal chart, and set of large drawings to illustrate the anatomical structure, and the physiological functions of the system, will be procured.

The following apparatus has already been procured to aid in illustrating and demonstrating in the studies named:

Mechanics.—Set of mechanical powers, arranged in a mahogany frame, comprising three levers, each sixteen inches long. Five sets of brass pulleys strung with cord and properly balanced. Brass weights from one to sixteen ounces. Screw and lever with nut. Screw as an inclined plane. Ship capstan. Wheel and axle. Wedge in two parts. Inclined plane, with carriage. Movable fulcrum and lever, for combining the power of screw and lever. Machine for illustrating the centrifugal and centripetal forces—thirteen experiments.

Pneumatics.—Air Pump—frame made of rose-wood beautifully polished—barrel twelve by four inches inside; large plate, stop-cock, and barometer in vacuo, and worked with a polished steel lever four feet in length, $85,00. Large swelled, open-top bell glass. Several plain bell glasses of smaller dimensions. Bell glass with brass cap to receive stop-cock. Connector, sliding rod, &c. Revolving jet in vacuo. Bursting squares and wire guard for same. Condensing chamber and condensing gauge. Artificial fountain, with exterior and interior jets. Sheet rubber bag in vacuo, illustrating the rarefaction of confined air by removing the pressure of the external. Mercury tunnel to exhibit the mercurial shower, porosity of wood, pressure of the air, and also the luminous shower. Guinea and feather tube. Philosophical water hammer.

Apparatus illustrating the absurdity of suction, or the necessity of atmospheric pressure to the operation of the lifting pump. Torricellian barometer improved. Bell in vacuo. Apparatus illustrating the buoyancy of air, gas, &c. Weighing air and specific gravity apparatus. Freezing apparatus with thermometer. Condensing syringe. Cylindrical open-top bell glasses, three sizes. Hand and bladder glass, to illustrate atmospheric pressure. Bladder cap, with cap and stop-cock. Double acting exhauster and condenser. Brass hemispherical caps with handles, stop-cock and stand. Apparatus to illustrate the upward pressure of the atmosphere. Connecting screws, guard screws, sliding rod, with packing screws and binding screws. Flexible hose and screw connectors. Hydrogen bottle. Lead hose for conducting gases. Floating bulbs for condensation. Sheet rubber and sheet rubber bags. Glass bells and stems for freezing apparatus. Pair magnetic swans. Detonating glass tubes. Wire gauze, to illustrate Davy's safety lamp.

Hydrostatics.—Hydrostatic bellows, with glass and brass tubes, glass tunnels, weights, &c. Pair of working models of the forcing and lifting pump. Graduated glass jars for cubic inches.

Electricity.—Electrical machine, 24 inch plate, $50,00. Leyden jar of four quarts. Do. do. for suspension with movable rings and points. Do. do. with sliding discharger. Electrometer jar, by which the charge may be measured, &c. Electric batteries with six four-quart jars. Sliding, directing rod. Spiral spotted tube. Jointed discharger, glass handle. Universal discharger. Insulating stand. Electric bells. Wax cylinder. Thunder house with fixtures. Gas pistol. Gas generator and platina igniter, four quarts. Long haired man. Electric float wheel and point. Abbe Noloes' globe. Luminous bell glass. Electric S. Aurora flask. Electric seasons machine. Elastic rubber ball. Ether spoon. Chamberlin's cylindrical gasometers, for oxygen and hydrogen, united, forming a compound blow pipe, $60,00. Iron retort for oxygen gas. Metallic reflectors with stand, iron ball and stands and a thermometer. Glass spirit lamp. Spirit boiler to use with reflectors. Dropping tube. Glass tunnels. Graduated glass hydrometer. Flask with screw-cap admitting thermometer. Platina and copper pendant spoons. Brass pipe for blowing gas bubbles. Hydrogen gas generator, with platina sponge for lighting a long detonating jet. Lamp stand. Flexible hose for transferring and conducting gases. Scales and weights for chemical purposes. Pyrometer with two lamps and rods. Section model of the high pressure engine.

Galvanic Magnetic and Electro Magnetic.—Davis's cylindric battery. Steel U magnet and armature. Magnetic needles and stands. Electro magnet. Electro coil and hemispheric magnets. Terrestrial helix. Primary coil and handles for shocks. Separable helics for analysis of shocks.

Optics.—Models of the human eye in three parts. *Fig.* 1*st.* A dissectible eye four inches in diameter, showing the cornea, iris, ciliary process, choroid tunic, crystalline lens, vitreous humor, retina, black pigment, optic nerve, &c. *Fig.* 2*d.* Showing the eye in its socket, with the muscles. *Fig.* 3*d.* The eye with rays of light passing from an object and forming the image on the retina. The object and the image movable, showing the cause of lens light, short sight, and perfect sight.

An oxy-hydrogen microscope will soon be added in this department.

With the above apparatus more than eight hundred experiments can be performed.

For the purpose of teaching practical surveying, and the elements of engineering, a Theodolite, of approved English manufacture, is provided. Cost $200.

Other apparatus will from time to time be added, as the wants of the School may require.

Building Committee.—A. M. Collins, D. F. Robinson, T. Belknap, J. M. Bunce, W. Pease, Jr., Edward Button, E. D. Tiffany.

Fig. 1—Perspective of High School-House Hartford Conn.

Fig. 2—GROUND PLAN, YARD, BASEMENT, &c.

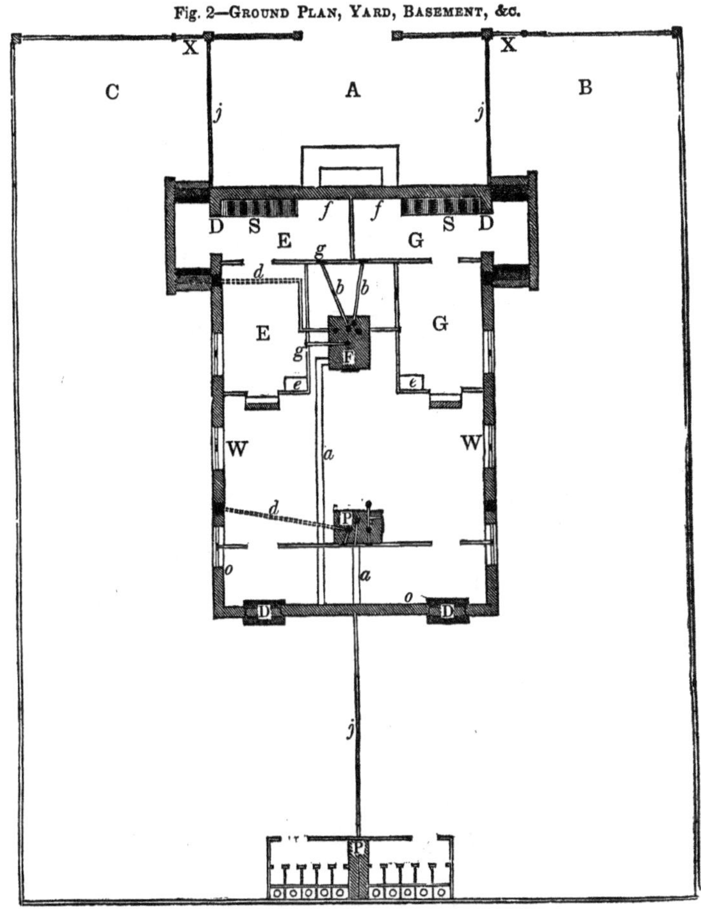

A—Front yard.
B—Girls' yard.
C—Boys' yard.
D—Door.
E—Boys' entrance rooms.
G—Girls' entrance rooms.
F—Furnace.
S—Stairs.
W—Windows.
P—Privies, with screen, doors, &c.
X—Gates.

a—Cold air ducts.
b—Warm air ducts.
c—Foul air ducts or ventilating flues.
d—Smoke pipe.
e—Pump, sink.
f—Umbrella stand.
g—Hollowed plank to receive wet boots, overshoes, &c.
o—Bins for hard coal, charcoal, &c.
j—Close board fence.

Fig. 3—Plan of First Floor.

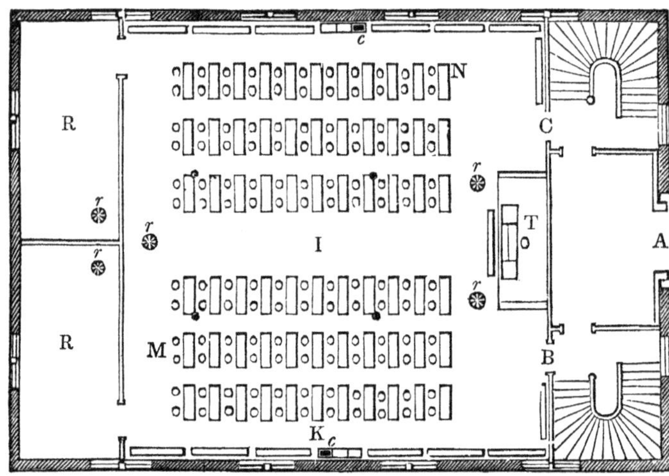

A—Front entrance.
B—Girls' entrance.
C—Boys' entrance.
I—Centre aisle, eight feet.
L—Aisle between each range of seats and desks, two feet four inches.
K—Side aisle, four feet four inches.
M—Space five feet wide.
T—Teachers' platform and desk.
R—Recitation rooms, each twenty-three feet by twelve, furnished with twenty chairs, seven inches from the wall and thirteen inches apart.
Q—Library and apparatus, from eleven feet by fourteen feet.
N—Kimball's desk and two chairs.
O—Piano.
r—Hot air registers.
c—Ventilating flue or foul air duct. N—Settees.

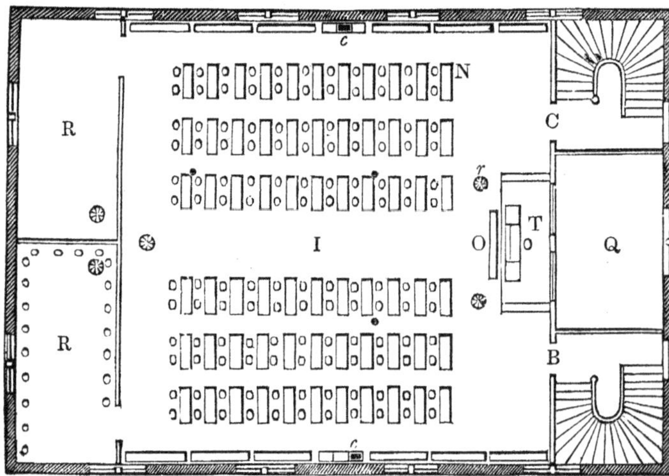

Fig. 4—Plan of Second Floor.

Figs. 5 and 6. PLANS EXHIBITING MODE OF VENTILATION.

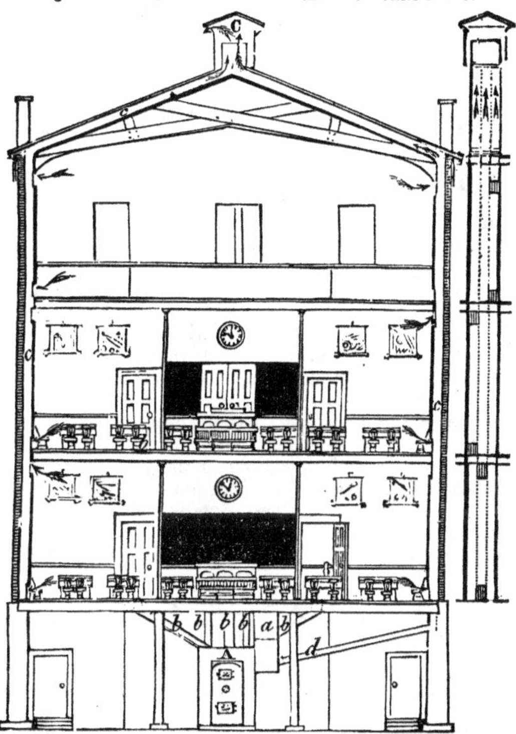

Fig. 5. Transverse section exhibiting the manner in which the ventiducts or hot air flues are carried up on the inside of the walls, under the roof, till they discharge into the Stationary Top or Ejector.

Fig. 6. Lateral section of the ventiducts or foul air flues, showing the manner in which the flues are packed together and carried up separately from the floor of each room until they discharge into the common Ejector. The cut does not represent properly the manner in which the flues are carried under and out of the roof.

Fig. 3.

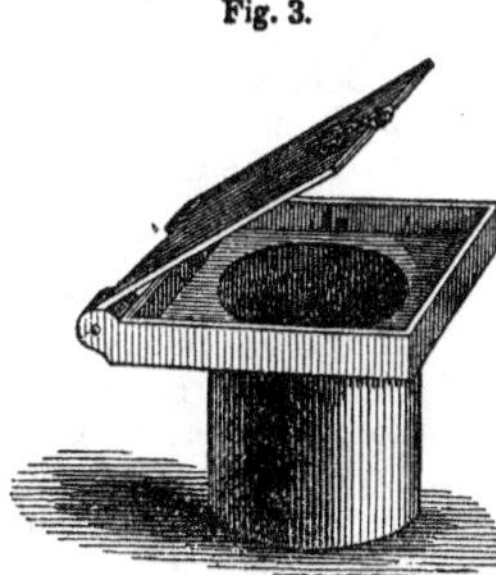

Fig. 2.

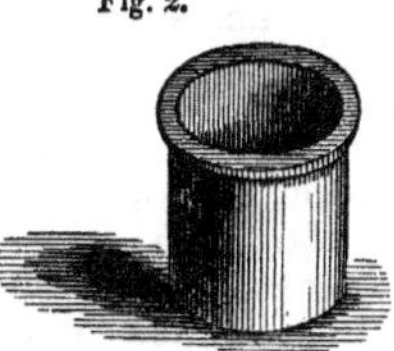

Each desk is fitted up with a glass ink-well (Fig. 2,) set firmly into the desk, and covered with a lid. The ink-well may be set into a cast iron box (Fig. 3,) having a cover; the box being let in and screwed to the desk, and the ink-well being removable for convenience in filling, cleaning, and emptying in cold weather.

Public Schools in Boston.

The system of public schools in Boston originated in a vote of the town, in 1642, by which "Brother Philemon Purmont was entreated to become school-master for the teaching and nurturing of children with us," and the first records of the town contain a sum voted for the "maintenance of a free school-master." By the Act of the General Court passed 1647, "to the end that learning should not be buried in the graves of our forefathers," every town having one hundred householders was required to maintain a "free grammar school; the master whereof being able to instruct youth so far as they may be fitted for the university." In that year the present Latin School was founded, but was known as the Grammar School till 1713, when it took the name of the South Latin School,—a new Grammar school having been established in that year, called the North Latin School, and now known as the Eliot school.

In 1684, a class of free schools called writing schools were founded, to teach children to "read and write." Of this class there were four in 1785.

In 1789, the schools were remodeled. One (the North) of the Latin Schools were discontinued, and "reading schools" (now known as departments under the Grammar master) were established in separate departments from the "writing schools;" and the whole placed under the direction of a School Committee chosen annually by the town. Previous to this, the schools were under the inspection of the Selectmen, "and of such gentlemen of liberal education, together with the reverend ministers" as should be appointed for the purpose.

In 1812, a separate school for colored children was established, and called the Smith School.

In 1818, the School Committee were instructed by a vote of the town to appoint three persons from each ward, whose duty it was made collectively, to provide instruction for children between the ages of four and seven years, out of the sum of $5000, appropriated for the purpose for that year. This was the origin of the Primary Schools of Boston, and of this class of schools in this country. Previous to this date, no child could be sent to the Grammar schools, until he could read the English language.

In 1821 the English High School for boys was begun, and its success was such, as to lead to the establishment in 1825 of the High School for girls. This last school was discontinued in a few years. Its place is in part supplied by allowing the girls to remain two years longer than the boys in the Grammar school. But the fact that near two-thirds of all the scholars in the private schools are females, shows that there is a deficiency in the system of public schools in reference to female education.

In 1828 ten schools, one in each primary district, were designated to receive children who were over seven years, and were not prepared for the Grammar schools.

In 1851, after repeated recommendations of the School Commitee, the City Council authorized that body to elect a Superintendent of Public Schools, whose duty it is made,—"to study the school system, and the condition of the schools;" "to keep himself acquainted with the progess of instruction and discipline in other places, in order to suggest appropriate means for the advancement of Public Schools in this city;" "to examine the schools semi-annually, and report to the Board respecting them;" "to consult with the different bodies, who have control of the building and altering school-houses, and with all those through whom, either directly or indirectly, the school money is expended, that there may result more uniformity in their plans, and more economy in their expenditures." To this office Nathan Bishop, Esq., was elected in May, 1851, and has already signalized his administration by suggesting many practical improvements which have been adopted by the committee.

All of the Public Schools of the city are under the care and superintendence of a Board or Committee, consisting of the Mayor, the President of Common Council, and twenty-four other persons, annually elected, two for each ward.

The Board employs a Superintendent, to act under their control and direction, at a salary of twenty-five hundred dollars; a Primary School Committee, to take particular charge of the Primary Schools; a committee of five members on the Latin and English High School; a committee of three members on each Grammar School, and a committee on school-houses, also of three members. The teachers are elected annually by the Board, and their salaries are fixed for the year.

The system now (1854) embraces 196 Primary Schools, 22 Grammar Schools, 1 English High School, 1 Latin School, and 1 Normal School.

The Primary Schools were instituted in 1818, and now include about 12,000 children, over 4 and under 8 years of age, under female teachers. In these schools, the alphabet, pronouncing and spelling words, numeration and combination of numbers, the stops and marks, mental arithmetic, and reading are attended to. The cost of these schools, in 1853, for the salaries of teachers, was $62,508.82, or $5.45 per scholar; for incidental expenses, $22,231.46, or $1.85 per scholar; or $7.30 per scholar, exclusive of expenditures for school-houses.

There are at present 22 Grammar Schools, (including three independent schools in the same building, and bearing the same name with other schools,) with 10,237 scholars. These schools are not at present organized on a uniform plan; but efforts are making to constitute each Grammar School of about 700 to 800 children, divided into twelve or thirteen equal divisions, of about sixty pupils each, and each division into four large classes. Each school is to be under the charge of one principal teacher, with a requsite number of assistants, one to each room. The course of instruction embraces the common branches of an English education. In these schools the boys remain until they are 15 years of age, or until they pass to the English, High, or Latin School. Girls can remain till they are seventeen. In 1852–3, the cost of the Grammar Schools, for salaries and teachers, was $130,531.18, or $12.63 per scholar; $35,849.82 for incidental expenses; or $3.47 per scholar; or $16.10 per scholar, exclusive of the expenditures on school-houses.

The English High School, was instituted in 1821, and receives pupils who can pass a strict examination in spelling, reading, writing, arithmetic, English grammar, modern geography, and the history of the United States. The course of study embraces three years, and the privilege of remaining one year longer. It embraces ancient geography, general history, algebra, book-keeping, rhetoric, moral philosophy, natural theology, evidences of Christianity, political economy, drawing, English language, and literature, French and Spanish languages, astronomy, higher mathematics, and their applications to surveying, engineering, &c.

The Latin School was instituted in 1635, and receives boys who have attained the age of ten years, and takes them through a course of studies occupying six years, preparatory to entering the most respectable college. It includes the English, as well as the Latin and Greek languages.

The Normal School was instituted in 1852, with the design of furnishing to those pupils who have passed through the usual course of study at the grammar schools for girls, and other girls' schools in the city, an opportunity of qualifying themselves in the best manner for the duties of teachers. Candidates must be over 16, and not more than 19 years of age. The school embraces two departments—one consisting of pupils preparing themselves to be teachers, and the other a model school, composed of children of the age and qualification of pupils in the fourth classes of the Grammar Schools. The course of study embraces two years.

PLANS AND DESCRIPTION OF A PRIMARY SCHOOL-HOUSE, BOSTON.

Three new Primary School-houses were erected in Boston, in 1847, under the direction of, and on plans furnished by, JOSEPH W. INGRAHAM, Esq., Chairman of the Executive Committee of the Primary School Board, and Chairman of their Committee on School-houses. Mr. Ingraham is also a member of the Massachusetts Board of Education. He has devoted himself assiduously, and without compensation, for upwards of twenty-five years, to the Primary Schools of Boston, and the cause of Education generally; and no one is better acquainted than he with what the wants and conveniences of both pupils and teachers require in edifices for this class of schools. The following very minute description and plans were kindly furnished, on application, by him. The plans are copied from those appended to his Address at the Dedication (March 27, 1848) of one of the School-houses,—that in Sheafe street. They will be found worthy the attention of all who are interested in school architecture. The distinguished Secretary of the Massachusetts Board of Education, (Mr. Mann,) who was present at the dedication of this building, in his remarks at the subsequent dedication of another School-house in Boston, referred to *this* as "perfect of its kind," and said it "might well be called the *model* School-house of the State, and in School-houses Massachusetts was a model for the world." The teachers in one of these buildings, after having occupied their rooms for five months, say they "cannot imagine any improvement that can be made."

The City of Boston is so compact, and land is so very expensive, that it is difficult to procure sufficient space for playgrounds and other conveniences; but the Schoolhouses erected during the past year, (1847,) are better provided for, in this respect, than any others in the City.

There were three Schoolhouses erected during the year 1847, on plans devised and furnished by Mr. Ingraham, the Chairman of the Primary School Committee on Schoolhouses. The general features of each are the same, differing only in consequence of the size and location of the lots on which they are erected.

These Schoolhouses are believed to possess greater conveniences, for the comfort and happiness of both teachers and scholars, than any others ever before constructed. In planning them, several objects were had in view. Among these, were,

The desire to allow to each scholar sufficient space, and have the rooms perfectly heated and ventilated, so that no one should suffer from want of room, or comfortable and pure air:

To have all the light in the Schoolrooms come in from one side, and that at the backs of the scholars, to prevent the detrimental effects of *cross*-lights, which are very injurious to the eyes of young children when in a forming state:

To give suitable space, on the walls, for the display of maps, charts, pictures, &c., and provide sufficient recitation-rooms, closets, cabinets, and other necessary conveniences:

To have a separate entrance for each school:

To so arrange the usual out-door conveniences, that the scholars should not have to go out of doors in stormy weather, or down stairs, to gain access to them, and at the same time, by removing them from the play-ground, to obviate the objections which have been made, by some teachers, to having both sexes in the play-ground at the same time, during the recesses:

Ingraham Primary School-House, Boston.

The Schoolhouse, to which the following description and plans more particularly refer, is situated in Sheafe street, at the north part of the City, and on the slope of Copp's Hill, famed in our Revolutionary history. It occupies a space of twenty-six by fifty-three feet, exclusive of the play-ground in front, between it and the street, which is sixteen by fifty-three feet. This front is hardly long enough. Sixty feet would have been much better. The main building is twenty-six by forty-four feet; and there are projections at each end,—one on the west, four and a half by sixteen and a half feet, containing the privies, and one at the east end, three and a half by twenty-one and a half feet, in which is the passage from the lower schoolroom to the play-ground.

The building is three stories in height. Each story contains a Schoolroom, Recitation-rooms, Closets, Entries, and Privies, and is finished twelve feet high, in the clear. Each Schoolroom is lighted by four windows, which are all on one side. The first floor is set eighteen inches above the ground at the front of the building. The Cellar is finished seven and a half feet high, in the clear; and its floor is on a level with the surface of the ground at the back of the building, where is the entrance-door to the first story.

The Schoolrooms in the first and second stories are thirty feet in length, by twenty-two feet and four inches in width, and contain six hundred and seventy square feet of floor. That in the third story is thirty-two feet in length, by twenty-two feet and nine inches in breadth, and contains seven hundred and thirty square feet of floor. Thus allowing from ten to twelve or thirteen square feet of floor, and one hundred and fifty cubic feet of air, to each scholar.

The following diagram will show the arrangement of the ground-floor, with the Play-ground in front.

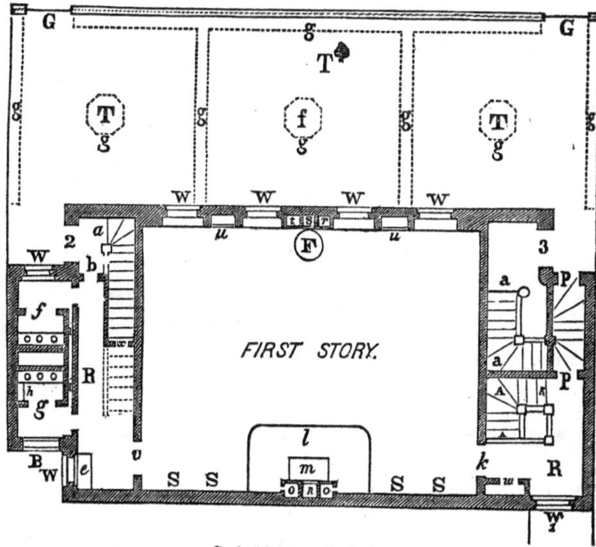

Scale 16 feet to the inch.

The following references will apply to the ground-plan of each of the three stories.

1, Entrance to First Story, by a door under the window W, the back part of the building being eight feet lower than the front.
2, 3, Entrance-doors to the Second and Third Stories.
A, A, A, Stairs to First Story, from the Entrance-door 1.
B, Blinds in Boys' Privies.
F, Fireplace or Furnace-flue, or Stove, when one is used instead of a Furnace.
G, G, Entrance-gates to Second and Third Stories. The Iron Fence extends the whole length of the front on the street, broken only by these two gates.
R, R, Recitation-rooms, or spaces used for that purpose. In the *first story*, that on the right being the entrance-passage to the schoolroom, and that on the left, the passage to the Second Story.
S, S, S, S, Large Slates, measuring four by two and a half feet, affixed to the walls, instead of Blackboards.
T, T, T, Trees in Play-ground. That near the fence, is an old horse-chestnut tree.
U, Umbrella stands. The place of those of the *second story* only are shown. In the other stories, they are also in the entrance-passages.
W, W, Windows.
a, Stairs to Second Story.
b, *b*, *b*, In *second story*, Entry, and place for Boys' Clothes-hooks, also used as a Recitation-room. In *third story*, place for Clothes-hooks.
c, In *second story*, Door into the Recitation-room where are the Sink and Girls' Clothes-hooks. In *third story*, Door into Recitation-room where is the Brush Closet and entrance to Girls' Privy.
d, *d*, *d*, In *second story*, Girls' Clothes-hooks.
e, Sinks.
f, Privy for Girls. *g*, Privy for Boys. *h*, Trough in ditto.
i, *i*, Space between the walls of the Privies and main building, for more perfect ventilation, and cutting off of any unpleasant odor. [This space is here too much contracted, on account of the want of room. It would be much better, if greatly increased.]
k, Entrance-door to Schoolroom, through which, only, scholars are allowed to enter. In *third story*, the passage from the stairs to the Entrance-door is through the Recitation-room.
l, Teachers' Platforms, six feet wide and twelve feet long, raised seven inches from the floors.
m, Teachers' Tables.
n, Ventiduct. That for each room is in the centre of that room. These are better shown in the diagram representing the Ventilating arrangement, (p. 183.)
o, *o*, Closets, in the vacant spaces on the sides of the Ventiducts, in the First and Second Stories. In *first story*, they are on each side of the Ventiduct; in *second story* only on one side. In the *third story*, there are of course none. See the diagram of the Ventilating arrangement, (p. 183.)
p, *p*, Ventiducts for other rooms. In plan of *second story*, *p* shows the position of the Ventiduct for first story. In *third story* plan, *p p* show the positions of those for both the lower stories.
q, *q*, *q*, Childrens' chairs, arranged in the *second story*. Their form is represented in another diagram, (p. 181.)
r, *s*, *t*, Hot-air Flues from the Furnace, Cold-air Flues if Stoves are used, and Smoke Flues. These will be better understood by a reference to the diagram explanatory of the Chimney Pier, (p. 182.)
u, *u*, Cabinets for Minerals, Shells, and other objects of Natural History or Curiosity.
v, Door of Recitation-room. In *first story*, this door leads to the entry in which are the Sink, Brush-Closet, entrance to the Privies, and passage to Second Story. In *second story*, it leads to the Recitation-room where is the Teacher's Press-closet; and in the *third story*, to that in which are the Sink, entrance to the Privies, and Stairs to the Attic.
w, Teacher's Press-closet, fitted with shelves and brass clothes-hooks.
x, Closet for Brooms, Brushes, Coalhods, &c. That for the *first story* is under the Second-Story stairs.
a, a, a, Stairs to the Third Story.
b, b, Doors connecting First and Second, and Second and Third Stories.
f, Place for Fountain, in the centre of the Play-ground.
g, g, g, Grass-plats, or Flower-beds.
p, Passage from the First-Story Schoolroom to the Play-ground.

The Plan of the *second story*, on the next page, is drawn on a larger scale, for greater convenience in showing all the arrangements. The references on this diagram are more copious and minute than on either of the others.

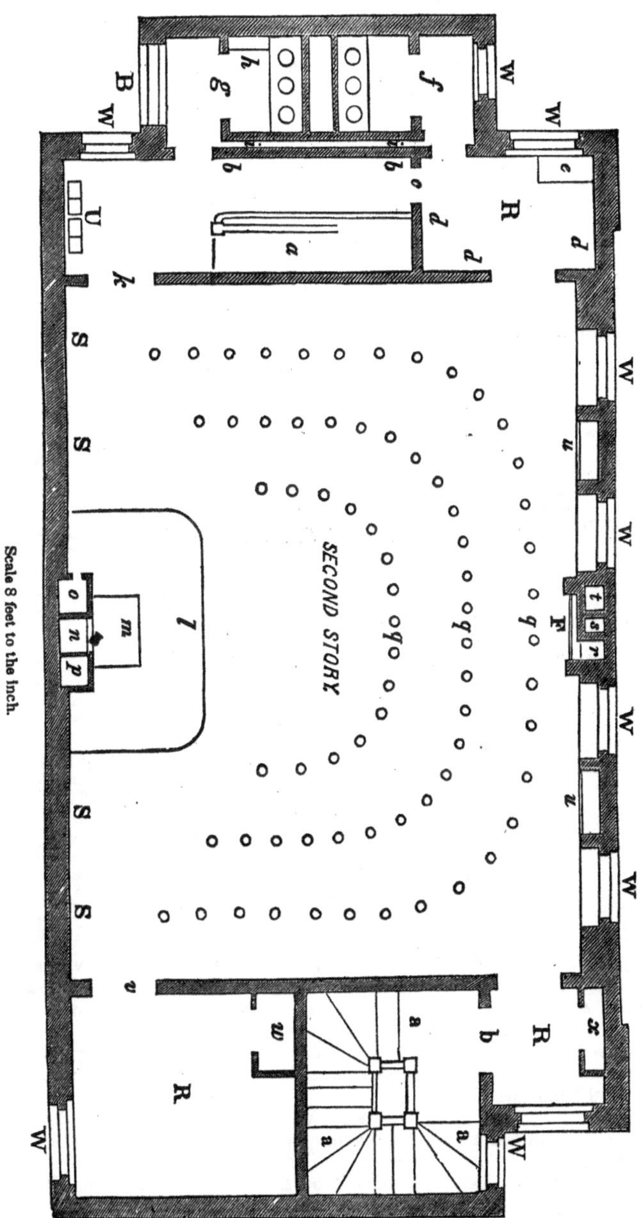

Scale 8 feet to the inch.

The building fronts nearly N. N. E., and of course all the light comes into the Schoolrooms from the North. At the same time, in order to secure the benefit of the winds that prevail in Summer, and the admission of "a streak of sunshine," which adds so much to the cheerfulness of any room, and particularly of a schoolroom, there are windows in the back or southerly wall, opening into the recitation-rooms or entries, through which, and the entrance-doors, the sunlight finds its way into each schoolroom. The Neapolitan proverb, "Where the sun does not come, the physician must," has not been lost sight of; though it must be confessed that we have not been able to pay so much attention to it as would be desirable.

The next diagram, which is on the same scale with the first, will show the arrangement of the *third story*, which differs from the first and second in having a larger schoolroom, and more space for recitation-rooms; less space being occupied for stairways than in the other stories. The partitions at the ends are set one foot each way nearer to the ends of the building, making the Schoolroom thirty-two feet in length, while the others are only thirty.

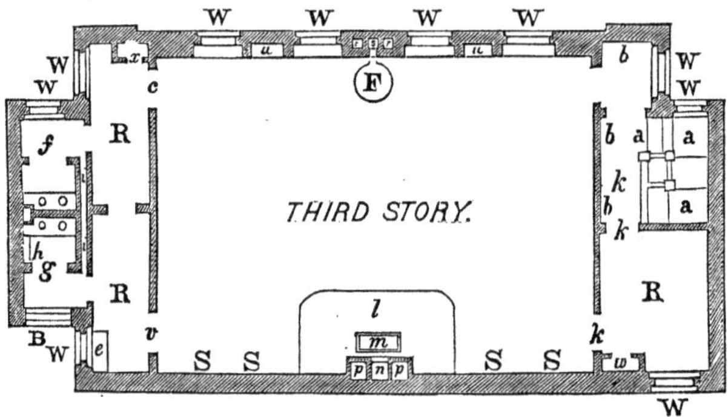

Scale 16 feet to the inch.

It will be seen, that the ends of the building are cut off from the schoolrooms, by entries, stairways, recitation-rooms, &c., and the back and end walls are left blank, for convenience in displaying Maps, Charts, Pictures, &c., and for the large Slates, used instead of Blackboards. As ample provision, as was practicable, has been made for recitation-rooms, closets, and other necessary conveniences.

It will be seen, from the Plans of the different Stories, that the Entrance-door (*k*) to each Schoolroom is in that part of the partition nearest to the back walls; so that, on entering the room, the Teacher's Platform is directly before the scholar or visiter. This Platform is six feet wide and twelve feet long, and is raised seven inches above the floor, that being a sufficient height to give the Teacher a full view of the whole school. In the transverse-sectional elevation, (p. 184,) the raised Platform is shown at P.

On this Platform, is a Table, (*m*,) instead of a Desk, that being the more convenient article for the Teacher's use. On it, are constantly kept, in full view of the scholars, THE LAWS OF THE SCHOOL,—the *Holy Bible*, the Rule and Guide of Life, the Moral and Religious Law; the *Dictionary*, the Law of Language, the Authority for Orthography and Orthoepy; and the *Rules and Regulations of the Committee*. These should be always on every Teacher's table or desk, and should be frequently appealed to. On this Table, also, are the Record Book of the School, Ink-standish, Table Bell, and other necessary articles.

In front of the Teacher's Platform, and facing it, arranged in a semi-circular form, as shown at *q q q*, in the Plan of the Second Story, are the Seats for the scholars. These are comfortable and convenient Arm-chairs, of which the annexed diagram shows the form. Each has a rack at the side (A) for convenience in holding the books or slates of the scholars. These chairs were the contrivance of Mr. Ingraham, and were introduced by him into the Primary Schools, in 1842, since which time, the Primary School Board have recommended their introduction into all their schools, in preference to any other seats, and about one hundred and thirty of the one hundred and sixty schools are now supplied with them. They are *not* fastened to the floor, but can be moved whenever necessary; and this is found to be a great convenience, and productive of no disadvantage. They have been strongly recommended by the Committees on School and Philosophical Apparatus, at the Exhibitions of the Massachusetts Charitable Mechanics' Association, in 1844 and 1847, and premiums were awarded for them in both those years.

The following diagram is an elevation of the Front wall of the Schoolroom, as seen from the Teacher's Platform. It is on the same scale with the preceding Plan of the Second Story,—eight feet to the inch.

Each Schoolroom is lighted by four windows; and in the central pier, between the windows, are the Cold-air and Chimney Flues, or the Furnace Flues. The Fire-place, or Furnace Flue, is represented at F, as in the preceding Plans of the different Stories. The arrangement of the Flues, in this pier, will be seen in the next diagram.

On the mantel-piece, over the Furnace Flue, is, in one room, a Vase of Native Grasses, or Flowers, and in the others, ornamental Statues, or Statuettes, furnished by the Teachers. Above this, suspended on the pier, is the Clock.

Between the other windows, are Cabinets, for the reception of Minerals, Shells, and other objects of Natural History or Curiosity. Their location is seen at *u u*, in the Plans of the respective Stories. There are two of these Cabinets in each Schoolroom, between the windows, above the skirting, and as high as the windows, with double sash-doors, of cherry-wood, hung with brass hinges, fastened with thumb-slides and locks, and fitted with rosewood knobs. There are twelve shelves in each, six of them being inclined, with narrow ledges on each, to prevent the specimens from rolling off. Immediately below them are small Closets, with four shelves in each, and double doors, hung and fastened in the same manner as the sash doors.

The Blinds of the Second Story, represented in this diagram, are framed, two parts to each window, and are hung with weights and pulleys, in the same manner as the window sashes. They run up above the tops of the windows, and behind the skirting of the next story above, in close boxes, and have rings on the bottom rails, to draw them down. In this elevation, they are shown in different positions. The windows in the First Story are fitted with Venetian Blinds, and those in the Third Story with Inside Shutter-Blinds.

All the window-stools are wide, and contain Vases of Native Grasses, or Flowers.

Particular attention has been given to the mode of Heating and Ventilating these buildings; and provision has been made for a copious and constant supply of fresh air, from out-of-doors, which is so introduced, that it is sufficiently warmed before it enters the Schoolrooms.

The Sheafe-street building is heated by one of Chilson's largest-sized Furnaces, though it was originally constructed with a view to using Dr. Clark's excellent Ventilating Stoves, as in the other two buildings.*

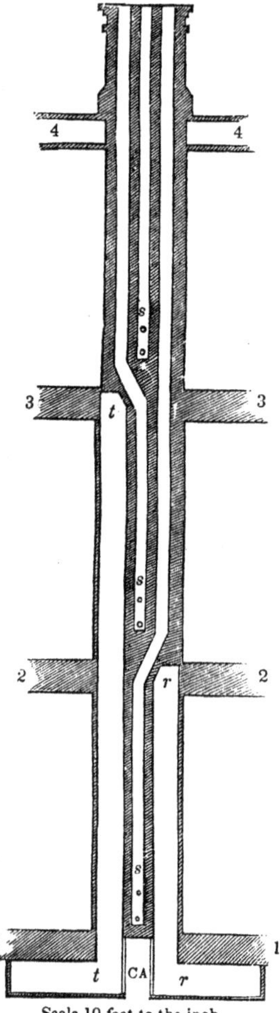

Scale 10 feet to the inch.

The accompanying diagram shows the arrangement of the Cold-air and Smoke Flues, as arranged for the Stoves. It will be well to examine it in connection with the transverse-sectional elevation, (p. 184,) and the Floor Plans of the different Stories, (pp. 177, 179, 180.)

1, 2, 3, Floorings of the First, Second, and Third Stories. 4, Roof.

CA, Cold-air Flue for First Story, which delivers the air from without, under the Stove, as shown at C A, in the transverse-section, (p. 184,) and at F, in the floor-plans.

r, *r*, Cold-air Flue for Second Story, which empties into the box under the Stove, at CA, in the Second Story of the transverse-sectional elevation. It corresponds to *r*, in the Floor Plans of the *first* and *second stories*.

t, *t*, Cold-air Flue for Third Story, which empties into the box CA, under the Stove of that Story, as seen in the transverse-sectional elevation, and at F, in the Floor Plan. It corresponds to *t*, in the Floor Plans.

These Cold-air Ducts are twelve by eighteen inches, *inside*, and are *smoothly* plastered, throughout. This is hardly large enough, however.

s, *s*, Smoke Flues. That of First Story corresponds to *s*, in the floor plan of *first story*, and to *r*, in those of the *second* and *third*. That of Second Story corresponds to *s*, in *second-story* Plan, and to *t*, in *third-story* Plan. That of Third Story corresponds to *s*, on the Plan of that Story.

These Smoke Flues are eight inches square, *inside*, and are *smoothly* plastered, throughout. That of each Story commences in the centre of the pier in the room to which it belongs.

[The pier in which these Cold-air Ducts and Smoke Flues are placed, is wider than the piers between the other windows, in order to allow sufficient width to the Ducts. It must be at least six feet.]

It will be seen, from the transverse-sectional elevation, (p. 184,) (the Smoke Flue in which is represented as continuous, it not being practicable to show the bends,) as well as from the Plans of each Story, that the arrangements for Ventilation are directly opposite the Chimney Flues. The Ventiducts are contained in the projecting pier back of the Teachers' Platforms and Tables shown at *l*, *m*, in the Floor Plans.

It has already been stated, that particular attention has been paid to the

* Descriptions and Plans of this Furnace and Stove will be found on page 155

mode of Ventilation; and it is believed that the system, if not perfect, is better adapted to its purpose than any other. The Ventiduct for each room is of sufficient size for the room; and the three are arranged as shown in the next diagram. It will be seen, that the Ventiduct for each room is in the centre of the pier, thus avoiding any unsymmetrical or one-sided (and of course unsightly) appearance.

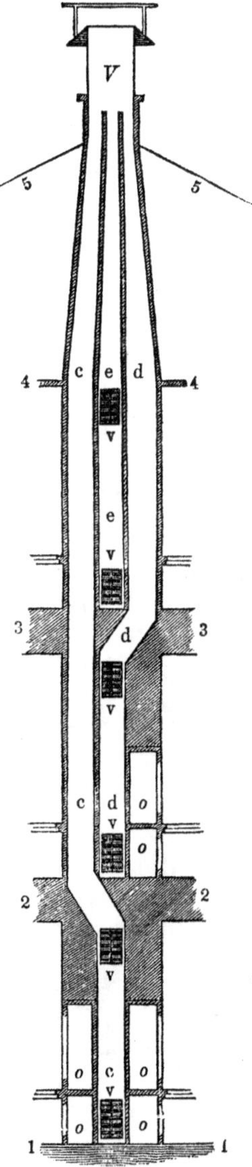

Scale 10 feet to the inch.

1, 2, 3, 4, Floorings of the First, Second, and Third Stories, and Attic. 5, Roof.

c, c, c, Ventiduct of First Story, commencing in the centre of the pier. Between the ceiling of this room and the floor of the Second Story, this flue is turned to the left, and then continues in a straight line to the Attic, where it contracts and empties into the Ventilator *V*, on the Roof.

d, d, d, Ventiduct of Second Story, also commencing in the centre of the pier, and turning to the right, between the ceiling of the Second and floor of the Third Story, whence it is continued to the Attic, and empties into the Ventilator *V*.

e, e, Ventiduct of Third Story, also emptying into *V*.

These Ventiducts are made of thoroughly seasoned pine boards, smooth on the inside, and put together with two-inch screws. Each, as will be seen, is placed in the centre of the room to which it belongs. They are *kept entirely separate from each other*, through their whole length, from their bases to the point where they are discharged into the Ventilators on the Roof. Each is sixteen inches square *inside*, through its whole length to the Attic. where, as will be seen by the diagram, each is made narrower as it approaches its termination, till it is only eight inches in width, on the front, the three together measuring twenty-five inches, the diameter of the base of the Ventilator on the roof. As they are contracted, however, in this direction, they are gradually enlarged from back to front, so that each is increased from sixteen to twenty-four inches, the three together then forming a square of twenty-five inches, and fitting the base of the Ventilator into which they are discharged. The increase in this direction will be better seen in the Elevation on p. 184, where V V represents one Ventiduct, continued from the lower floor to the Ventilator.

V, Ventilator, on the Roof, into which the three Ventiducts from the schoolrooms are discharged. This is twenty-five inches in diameter.*

v, v, Registers, to regulate the draught of air through the Ventiducts. There are two of these in each Ventiduct, — one at the bottom, to carry off the lower and heavier stratum of foul air, which always settles near the floor; and the other near the ceiling of the room, for the escape of the lighter impure air, which ascends with the heat to the top of the room. Each of these Registers has a swivel-blind, fitted with a stay-rod, and may be easily opened or closed by the Teacher.

o, *o*, Closets. The Ventiduct of each Story being in the centre of the projecting pier, affords room for Closets, on each side in the First Story, and on one side in the Second Story, as shown at *o o*. There are four in the First Story, two above and two below the wainscot. In the Second Story, there are two only, one above and the other below the wainscot; the other side of the pier being occupied by the Ventiduct of the First Story. In the Third Story there are of course none.

* A description, and larger plans, of this Ventilator, are given on page 144.

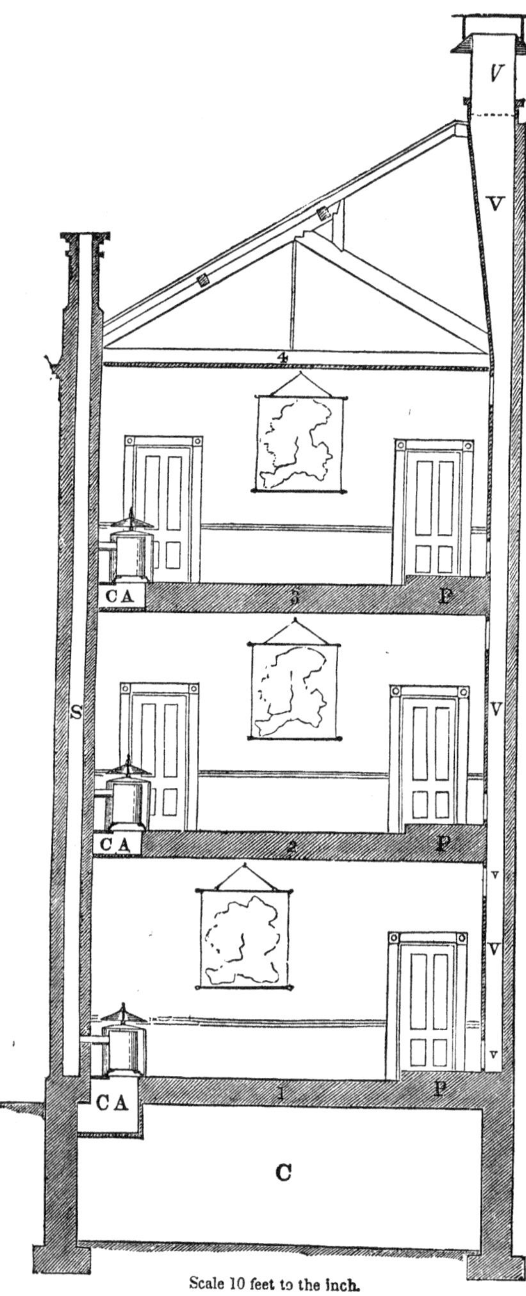

Scale 10 feet to the inch.

1, 2, 3, 4, Floorings of the First Second, and Third, Stories, and the Attic.
C, The Cellar.
C A, Cold-air Boxes, opening under the Stoves.
S, Smoke Flue.
P, Teachers' Platforms.
V, Ventiduct, emptying into the Ventilator on the Roof.
v, v, Ventiduct Registers.
V, Ventilator.

This plan of arranging the Heating and Ventilating apparatus has been adopted by the Committee on Ventilation of the Grammar School Board;* but as their plans and diagrams were taken from Mr. Ingraham's first draughts, before his final arrangement was decided upon, they are not so complete as these.

The preceding diagram gives a transverse-sectional elevation of the building.

It has already been stated, that the children are seated with their backs to the light, and their faces towards the Teacher's Table and the wall above and on either side of it. On this wall, and also on the two end walls, (as shown in the transverse-section,) are suspended Maps, Charts, and Pictures, not only for ornament, but for the communication of instruction. Vases of Flowers and Native Grasses ornament the window-stools and the Teachers' Tables; and Statuettes and other useful ornaments and decorations are placed in various parts of the rooms: so that whatever meets the eyes of the children is intended to convey useful and pleasing impressions, encouraging and gratifying the love of the beautiful, and combining the useful with the agreeable. The Cabinets of Minerals, Shells, and other objects of Natural History and Curiosity, add much to the interest and beauty of the rooms.

On the back wall, on either side of the Teacher's Platform, at S S S S, are four large Slates, in cherry-wood frames, each two and a half by four feet, used instead of Blackboards. These Slates are far preferable to the *best* Blackboards, and cost about the same as common ones. The Teachers greatly prefer them to Blackboards. In using them, slate pencils are of course employed, instead of chalk or crayons, and thus the dust and dirt of the chalk or crayons,—which is not only disagreeable to the senses, but deleterious to health, by being drawn into the lungs,—are avoided. These Slates may be procured in Boston, of A. Wilbur.

Each School has convenient Recitation-rooms; though, in consequence of the space occupied by the stairs to the Second and Third Stories, the lower Story is not so conveniently accommodated, in this respect, as could be desired. It has, however, two good Entries, which are used for this purpose. In the Second and Third Stories, there are three of these rooms, of which much use is made. Their location is shown in the Floor Plans.

In these ante-rooms, are Closets for Brooms, Brushes, and other necessary articles of that description, and also Press-closets, furnished with shelves and brass clothes-hooks, for the Teachers' private use. In these, also, are Sinks, furnished with drawers and cupboards, pails, basins and ewers, mugs, &c. Pipes leading from the Sinks, convey the waste water into the Vaults; and in a short time, the waters of Lake Cochituate will be led into each Story.

Each School has its own separate entrance; so that they will not interfere with each other. And each is provided with sufficient conveniences in its entry, for hanging the clothing of the pupils, thus avoiding the necessity of its ever being brought into the Schoolroom. Each has also two Umbrella-stands in its entry.

In the Cellar, are placed the Furnace, and necessary conveniences attached to it, with Bins for coal and wood. Also two Rain-water Butts, one at each end, which receive all the water from the Roofs. Being connected with each other, by leaden pipes, under ground, the water in both stands at the same level; and a pipe, leading from the top of one of them into the Vault, prevents their ever running over.

The Cellar is paved with brick, and is convenient for a play-room, when the weather is too stormy for the children to go out of doors at recess-time.

Instead of having the usual out-door conveniences in the yard, they are here connected with the entries of the respective schoolrooms, so that no child has to go into the open air, except for play in recess-time, or to go

* See a notice of their plans on page 158.

home. This is considered a very great convenience, and a matter of the highest importance.

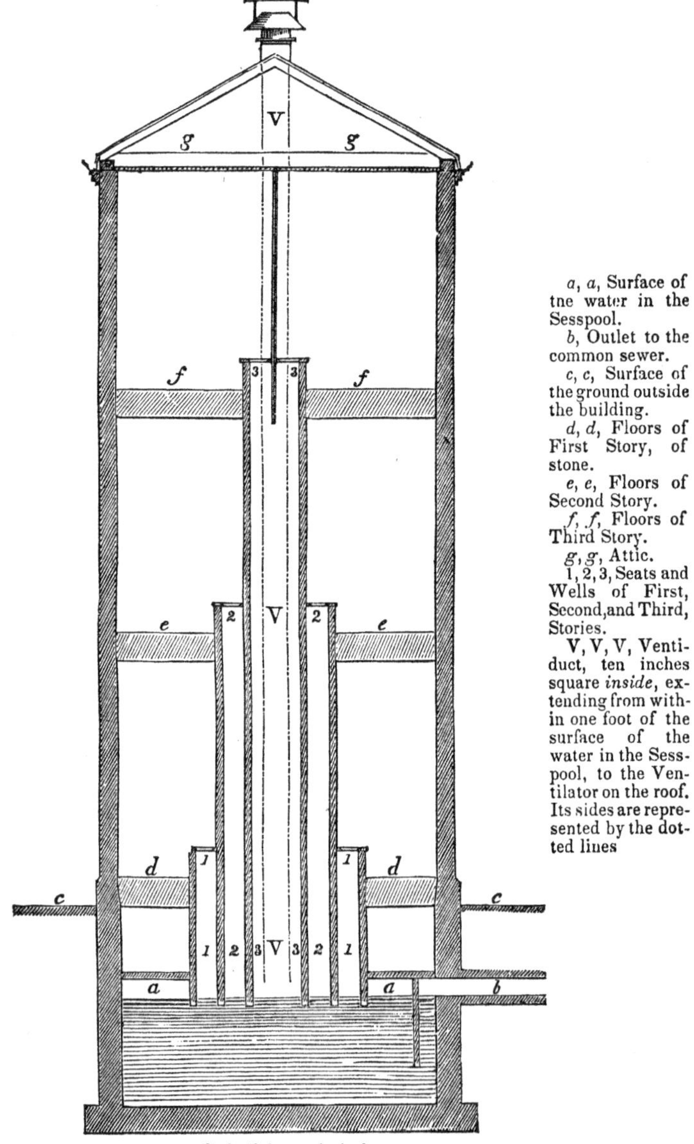

Scale 10 feet to the inch.

The preceding transverse-section will show the peculiar arrangement of the Privies to the different stories, and the manner in which all unpleasant consequences or inconveniences are, it is believed, effectually guarded against.

By the Plans of the different Stories, it will be seen, that the Privies are in a Projection on the western end of the building, the wall of which is separated from that of the main building, by the space *i i*, this space being four inches between the walls, and extending from the floor of the First Story to the Attic. The doors leading from the entries are kept closed, by strong springs; and at B, in the southern wall, is a Blind, through which the air constantly passes into this space, and up to the Attic, whence it is conveyed in a tight box to the Ventilator on the Roof. Except in very cold or stormy weather, the window in the northern side is kept open, (the outer blinds being closed,) and thus the whole of the Projection is cut off from the main building by external air. The space between the Projection and the main building is not, however, so great as it would have been made, had there been more room.

It will be seen, that there is a distinct Well to each Privy, separated from the others by a brick wall ending *below* the surface of the water in the sesspool. Of course, the only odor that can possibly come into either of the apartments, must come from the well of *that* apartment, there being no communication with any other, except through the water. And as every time it rains, or water is thrown in from the sinks, the water in the sesspool will be changed, and washed into the common sewer, it would seem that no danger of unpleasant odor need be feared. When the City water is carried to every floor of the building, the conveniences for frequently washing out the sesspool will be greatly increased.

There are two apartments on each floor; one for the girls, at *f*, and another for the boys, at *g*. In the latter, is a trough, (*h*,) with a sesspool, and pipe leading into the well, under the seat. There is no window in the boys' apartment, but merely the blind, B, which extends from the floor to the ceiling. The girls' apartment, being in the front part of the Projection, is provided with a window similar to the others, and outside blinds.

Each apartment is fitted with pine risers, seats, and covers. The covers are hung with stout duck or India-rubber cloth, instead of metal hinges, which would be liable to corrode, and are so arranged that they will fall of themselves, when left. The edges of the cloth are covered with narrow slats. There is a box for paper in each apartment. The whole finish is equal to that of any other part of the building.

The interior plastering of all the walls of the building is hard-finished, suitably for being painted.

All the Rooms, Entries, Stairways, and Privies, are skirted up as high as the window-stools, with narrow matched beaded lining, gauged to a width not exceeding seven inches, and *set perpendicularly*.

The interior wood-work of the lower Schoolroom, as well as the interior of all the Closets and Cabinets, is painted white. The skirting of the Second Story is of maple, unpainted, but varnished. All the rest of the inside wood-work is painted and grained in imitation of maple, and varnished. The outside doors are painted bronze. The blinds are painted with four coats of Paris green, and varnished.

In some other schoolrooms in the City, the interior wood-work,—even of common white pine,—has been left unpainted, but varnished; with a very good effect; and it is contemplated to have some of the new Schoolhouses soon to be erected, finished in the same way. White pine, stained with asphaltum, and varnished, presents a beautiful finish, and is cheaper than painting or graining.

In the angles formed by the meeting of the walls with the ceiling of each room, and entirely around the room, are placed rods, fitted with moveable rings, for convenience in suspending maps, charts, and pictures, and to avoid the necessity of driving nails into the walls.

It has been stated, above, that the space between the Privies and the main building, in the Sheafe street Schoolhouse, is not so great as is desirable, nor as it would have been, had there been more room. In the Schoolhouse in Tremont street, erected at the same time with that in Sheafe street, there being sufficient room for the purpose, the Projection containing the Privies is nine and a half by twelve feet, and the wells of the Privies are seven feet from the wall of the main building.

The following Plans were prepared for a new arrangement of the Sheafe street Schoolhouse, when it was contemplated to occupy a space eighty feet in depth, extending from Sheafe street to the Avenue in the rear. In these Plans, the Projection for the Privies is about ten by sixteen feet; and the entrance to each of the Privies is six feet from the wall of the main building, and separated from it by three doors. This gives them as much space, and separates them as much from the main building, as is needed.

Plan of First Story. Scale 24 feet to the inch.

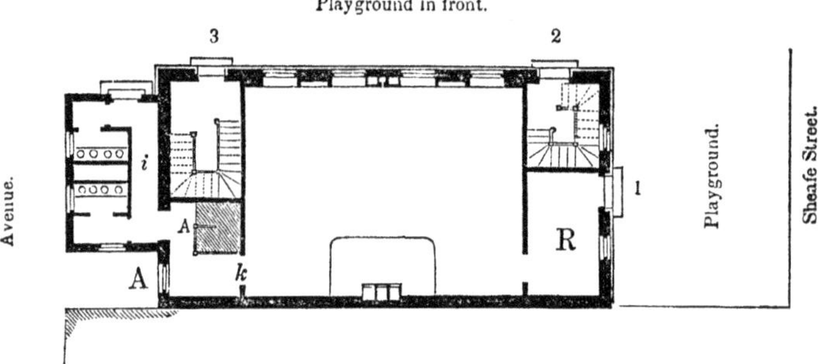

It will be seen, from this Plan, that the building was to have an end fronting on Sheafe street, (from which it was to be set back nineteen feet,) and a side looking into two of the Playgrounds, each of which was to be twenty-seven by thirty feet. The nineteen feet between the building and the street, and on a line with the building, the whole extent of the fifty-three feet on Sheafe street, was to form a third Playground.

It has already been mentioned, that the ground at the rear of the building, on the Avenue, is eight feet lower than at the front, on Sheafe street; and the scholars of the lower room were to enter, as they do now, from the Avenue, by a door under the window A, and pass to their schoolroom up the stairs A, through the door *k*. Their Playground was to have been at the front end, on Sheafe street, to which they were to pass through the Recitation-room R, and out by the door 1. The space between the Privies and the main building, which is a three-feet passage, is shown at *i*, as in the former Plans, pp. 177, 179, 180.

The Entrance-doors for the second and third stories are shown at 2, 3.

Plan of Second Story.

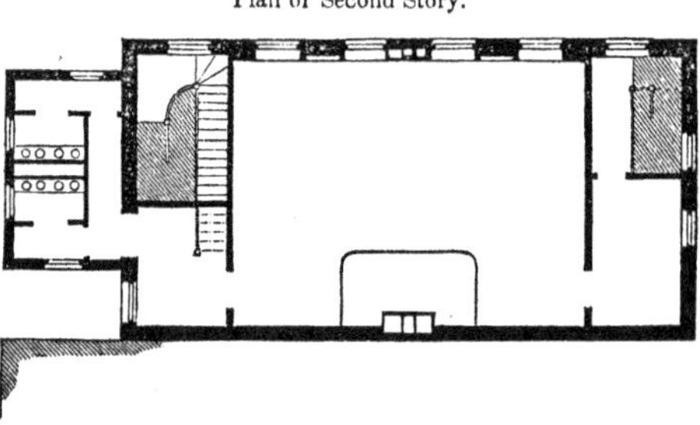

Plan of Third Story.

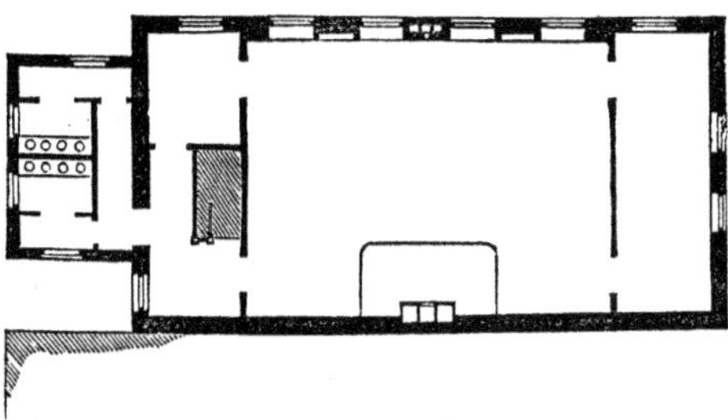

In other respects, these Plans present some improvement over that of the present building in Sheafe street, which is only forty-four feet in length, while that proposed in these Plans is fifty feet. This, of course, allows more space for the stairways, Recitation-rooms, &c.

These three Plans will be easily understood, by comparing them with those on pp. 177, 179, 180, 181, which are there fully explained.

Some persons, perhaps, may think that ornaments and decorations, such as have been here described, are not *necessary* in a Schoolhouse; though none, we presume, will think them out of place. Why should not the places, where both Teachers and children spend so large a portion of their time, be made as pleasant and attractive as possible? The Schoolroom is the Teacher's parlor and drawing-room; and should always, not only be neat and tidy, but exhibit evidences of good taste and useful ornament. Why should blank and naked walls, presenting a cold and cheerless aspect, unrelieved by a single pleasant spot or speck of verdure, be the only or principal objects to meet the eyes of the young inmates of these establishments, who are here to receive those *first impressions*, which, as they are the most lasting, and indeed almost indelible, should always be useful, and promotive of some useful purpose? Everything which will give to young persons "a perception of *the Beautiful*," is of great value; and everything that can be done to render the interior of our schoolrooms pleasant and attractive, is of importance. "Why," says Mrs. Sigourney, in a valuable Essay 'On the Perception of the Beautiful,' "why should not the interior of our schoolhouses aim at somewhat of the taste and elegance of a parlor? Might not the vase of flowers enrich the mantelpiece, and the walls display, not only well-executed maps, but historical engravings or pictures? and the bookshelves be crowned with the bust of Moralist or Sage, Orator or Father of his Country? Is it alleged that the expense, thus incurred, would be thrown away, the beautiful objects defaced, and the fair scenery desecrated? This is not a necessary result. I have been informed, by Teachers who had made the greatest advances towards the appropriate and elegant accommodation of their pupils, that it was not so. They have said it was easier to enforce habits of neatness and order among objects whose taste and value made them worthy of care, than amid that parsimony of apparatus, whose pitiful meanness operates as a temptation to waste and destroy." And it will always also be found that those schools where the most attention has been paid to making the rooms pleasant and attractive to the children, will be the most orderly, and well disciplined, while in those held in ordinary rooms, where no attention seems to be given to refinement in appearances, the pupils are also proportionably unrefined and undisciplined.

"Let the communities," continues Mrs. Sigourney, in the Essay just quoted, "let the communities, now so anxious to raise the standard of education, venture the experiment of a more liberal adornment of the dwellings devoted to it. Let them put more faith in that respect for the beautiful, which really exists in the young heart, and requires only to be called forth and nurtured, to become an ally of virtue and a handmaid to religion. Knowledge has a more imposing effect on the young mind, when it stands, like the Apostle with the gifts of healing, at the 'beautiful gate of the Temple.' Memory looks back to it, more joyously, from the distant or desolated tracks of life, for the bright scenery of its early path." "But when the young children of this Republic are transferred from the nursery to those buildings, whose structure, imperfect ventilation, and contracted limits, furnish too strong an idea of a prison, the little spirits, which are in love with freedom and the fair face of Nature, learn to connect the rudiments of knowledge with keen associations of task-work, discomfort, and thraldom." "I hope the time is coming, when every isolated village schoolhouse shall be as an Attic temple, on whose exterior the occupant may study the principles of symmetry and of grace. Why need the structures, where the young are initiated into those virtues which make life beautiful, be divorced from taste, or devoid of comfort?"

"Do any reply, that 'the perception of the Beautiful' is but a luxurious sensation, and may be dispensed with in those systems of education which this age of *utility* establishes? But is not its culture the more demanded, to throw a healthful leaven into the mass of society, and to serve as some counterpoise for that love of accumulation, which pervades every rank, intrudes into every recess, and spreads even in consecrated places the 'tables of the money-changers, and the seats of such as sell doves?'

"In ancient times, the appreciation of whatever was beautiful in the frame of Nature, was accounted salutary, by philosophers and sages. Galen says, 'He who has two cakes of bread, let him sell one, and buy some flowers; for bread is food for the body, but *flowers are food for the soul.*'"

"If the *perception of the Beautiful* may be made conducive to present improvement, and to future happiness; if it have a tendency to refine and sublimate the character; ought it not to receive culture throughout the whole process of education? It takes root, most naturally and deeply, in the simple and loving heart; and is, therefore, peculiarly fitted to the early years of life, when, to borrow the language of a German writer, 'every sweet sound takes a sweet odor by the hand, and walks in through the open door of the child's heart.'"

We insert Mr. Ingraham's communication, unabridged, although it was drawn up by him as the material out of which we should prepare a description. We have also preserved his system of punctuation and capitalizing, though it differs from that followed in other parts of this work.

We think very highly of the plan of the Sheafe street School-house. Any objections we might entertain to some of the details, could be easily obviated in places where land is not so expensive as in Boston. We prefer, however, to see the Primary School-house with but one story, and in no case with more than two stories. In cities, the basement, under the school room, should always be paved, and fitted up for a covered play-ground, as is the case in Mr. Ingraham's plans.

Mr. Ingraham, in his letter, acknowledges his obligations to Mr. F. Emerson, and Dr. Henry G. Clark, for valuable aid in arranging his system of ventilation, and also to Mr. Joseph E. Billings, the Architect, for aid in the architectural arrangements, and for the manner in which the working plans were drawn.

Having given so minute a description of this School-house, we shall confer a favor upon such of our readers as may wish to erect buildings like it, if we insert, entire, MR. INGRAHAM's original Specification for the workmen, with such modifications as he proposes to introduce into the new buildings, which are to be erected during the present year, (1848.)

SPECIFICATION

Of materials to be provided, and labor performed, in the erection of a Primary School-house, to be built on a lot of land lying upon the southerly side of Sheafe street, according to the plans of JOSEPH W. INGRAHAM, Chairman of the Primary School Committee on Schoolhouses, as exhibited in the Drawings made by Joseph E. Billings, Architect.

DESCRIPTION.

The building is to be three stories high; each Story is to contain a Schoolroom, Recitation-rooms, Entries, and Privies, and to finish twelve feet high, in the clear. The first floor is to be set eighteen inches above the ground, at the front of the building. The Cellar, under the whole building, (except the entrance to the first-story Schoolroom, which is to finish six feet and eight inches,) is to be finished seven and one half feet high, in the clear. The main building is to measure twenty-six by forty-four feet, upon the ground plan, above the underpinning; the Projection on the east end, three and one half by twenty and one half feet; and the Projection containing the Privies, four and one half by sixteen and one half feet. The Roof is to have an inclination of thirty degrees.

The Front and Side Walls of the main building, and the Front Walls of the Projections, above the underpinning, and the Rear Wall of the main building and sides of the Projections, from the level of the ground on the rear of the lot, are to be built of brick

MASON'S WORK.

Excavating.

The Dirt and Rubbish is to be dug out, as required, for the Cellar, the Cellar-Walls, the Vault, and the Drains; and the remainder of the lot is to be graded up, on an inclination of one inch to a foot, from Sheafe street to the front of the building.

All the rubbish, and the dirt that is not required for filling in, is to be removed from the premises. All the Loam is to be carefully taken up, kept by itself, and spread upon the surface of the Playground, as may be directed by the Committee.

Rough Stone.

The Footings to all the walls and piers, and the Cellar and Foundation-walls, are to be built of square-split Sandy-Bay or Quincy cellar-stone. The Bottom or Footing-course is to be puddled and rammed to a perfect bed, and those to the main walls and the piers, are to be laid entirely below the level of the cellar floor. The Walls are to be laid in lime mortar; and those of the Cellar are to be faced and pointed on the inside. The Footings are to be eighteen inches rise. Those to the main walls are to be three feet in width; those to the projections are to be two and one half feet in width; and those to the piers are to be three feet square. The Front Wall of the Cellar is to be two feet thick, and the other Walls twenty inches. Good and sufficient Foundations are to be laid for the Steps, Window Curbs, &c.

Hammered Stone.

The Underpinning to the front walls of the main building and projections, and the Returns at the first-story Entrance-doors, the Steps to the Entrance-doors, the Thresholds to the Entrance-doors and Gates, the Curbs, Sills, and Caps, to the cellar-windows, the Curbs to the sesspool, the Fence-stone, and the Platform steps to the Entrance-doors, are to be of Quincy granite, of even color, free from sap, rust, or flaws, fine-hammered, with all the returns, rabbets, washes, &c., indicated by the Drawings.

The Floors to the Privies on the first-story, a Moveable Cover to the Vault, and Hearth-stone in each Schoolroom, are to be of North-River Flagging-stone. About three quarters of the Playground is also to be laid with North-River Flagging-stone, as may be hereafter directed by the Committee. The rest of the Playground is to be left unpaved, for flower beds, &c.

There is to be an Iron Strainer fitted to the Sesspool-cover. The Hearth-stones are each to be three feet square, with a circular hole in the centre, eighteen inches in diameter, for the admission of the cold air under the stove.

Sand-stone.

There is to be a set of Caps and Sills to each of the windows in the brick walls, and Caps to the entrance-doors. The Caps to the doors are to be four courses rise, and ten inches thick, and those to the third-story front windows eight and one half inches thick: the other Caps are to be four inches thick. The Sills to the windows are to be eight inches wide. The Sills and Caps to the blind-openings, in the rear wall of the privies, are to be of the full thickness of the wall, and finished on all sides. There is to be a Moulded Belt on the front, and over the east and west entrance-doors; and a Base and Cap to the Chimney, of the forms shown by the Drawings. All the above is to be of the first quality of Connecticut free-stone; that in the faced-brick-work is to be sand-rubbed, and the remainder fine-chiselled.

All the stone-work is to be set in lime-mortar, and Cramped, Headed, and Pointed, as required.

Brick-work.

The Front Walls, above the underpinning, the Rear, Side, and Privy Walls, from the rough stone, the Piers in the cellar, the Backing-up of the stone-work, the Lining of the Vault, the Walls between the privies, the Sesspool, the Drains, and the Flues, are to be built of hard-burnt Charlestown (not Fresh Pond) bricks, excepting the Facing of the front and side walls of the main building and the front walls of the projections, the Covings, and the Chimney, which are to be of the first quality of pressed-brick, laid plumb-bond, tied into the other work with bond-irons in every seventh course.

The Front Wall, to the top of the belting, and above the top of the third-story windows, with the corner Piers on each side, and the Rear Wall, from the bottom to the top of the first-story floorings, are to be sixteen inches thick. The remainder of the Front and Rear Walls, the Side Walls of the main building, and the Front Walls of the Projections, are to be one foot thick. The Rear and Side Walls to the Privies, the Side Wall to the easterly Projection, and the Walls of the Sesspool, are to be eight inches thick. The Lining of the Vault, and the Walls between the Privies, are to be four inches thick. The Bottom of the Vault is to be laid three courses thick. The Piers in the cellar are to be sixteen inches square, on the ground.

The Vault, (which is to be of the sesspool plan, and so arranged, that no solid matter shall remain in the vault, but shall all pass off into the common sewer,) Sesspool, Drains, Wall between the privies, and the Hollow Wall between the privies and main building, are to be laid throughout with cement-mortar, and plastered inside, throughout, with the same. The remainder of the brick-work is to be done with lime-mortar. The Drains are to be barrel-form, the larger one to be of sixteen inches bore, and the smaller ones, one foot. The Vaults are to be not less than six feet deep.

The Cellar, and the Passage-way from the east end of the building, out to Margaret Avenue, are to be paved with the best paving-brick, on perfect foundations of gravel and sand.

The Cold-air Flues are to be twelve by eighteen inches, inside, and the Smoke Flues eight inches square, inside, all smoothly plastered, inside and out, with a stout coat of lime-mortar. The Flues are to be arranged as shown in the diagram. [*See p.* 182.]

The Cold-air Flue or Box, leading horizontally into the room to the aperture under the Stove, is also to be thoroughly and smoothly plastered, and made perfectly secure from danger by fire, in case of live coals or ashes dropping into it from the Stove. It is to be fitted with a valve, having a handle in the room, to regulate the admission of air.

Lathing and Plastering.

All the Walls, Ceilings, and Stairways, throughout the first, second, and third stories of the main building and the Projections, and the Ceiling of the Cellar, are to be Lathed and Plastered with a stout coat of lime and hair, and hard-finished, smoothly, with lime and sand, for painting; excepting the Ceiling of the Cellar, which is to be finished on the hair-coat, and the Wall between the main building and the privies, which is to be plastered upon the bricks. The Walls of the Cellar are to be white-washed with three coats.

Care must be taken, that the beads on the corners of the walls and stairways are not plastered. The quirks are to be neatly cut, and the beads kept clean.

Slates, Slating, &c.

Smoothly-polished Slates are to be set into the back wall of each Schoolroom, on each side of the Ventilating Pier, and neatly finished around the edges. They are to be two and a half feet wide, and ten feet in the whole length. They may be in slabs of five feet each, in length.*

The Roof is to be Slated with the best of Ladies' Slates, put on with Composition-nails, and properly secured with flashings of sheet lead, weighing three-and-one-half-pounds to the square foot, and warranted perfectly tight for two years.

Coppering.

There are to be moulded Copper Gutters, on the front and sides of the main building and front and rear of the Projections, worth one dollar and twenty-five cents per foot. They are to run back six inches under the slates.

There are to be two four-inch-square Trunks, from the gutters to the water-butts in the cellar; three-inch ones from the rear of the Projections to the Vault; and a round one from each butt to the vault. The Trunks are to be made of twenty-four-ounce cold-rolled copper, put up, connected with the gutters, and led off in a proper manner, with suitable lead pipes, of three inches in diameter.

Iron-work.

There is to be in each Smoke Flue an Iron Casting, with a funnel-hole twenty-four inches from the floor, and a hole below for clearing out the mouth of the flue; each hole to be fitted with a tight stopper.

There is to be an Iron Fence, on the line of Sheafe street, across the whole front, with two Gates, and an Iron Gate at the entrance of the back passage, on Margaret Avenue. All the Gates are to be fitted with Lever Locks, and Latches, of the best quality, and *small* duplicate keys.

There is to be an Iron Grating to each of the cellar-window curbs, of inch-and-a-quarter by one-quarter-inch bars, set one inch from centre to centre; and wire netting above it in front of the windows.

All the Iron-work is to be painted with three coats of lacker.

There are to be stout Iron Scrapers, placed at each door, where directed by the Committee.

There are to be an Iron Strainer to the Sesspool Cover, and Strong Iron Rings to the Moveable Cover of the Vault.

There are to be Composition Rods, in all the angles formed by the meeting of the ceilings and inner walls, in the Schoolrooms and Recitation-rooms, attached by neat staples, and fitted with Moveable Brass Rings, at suitable distances, for hanging charts, maps, &c.

CARPENTERS' WORK.

Framing.

The Floors and Roofs are to be Framed in the manner indicated by the Drawings, with good sound spruce lumber, of the following dimensions:

Principal Flooring-Joists,	3	by	14	inches.
Short Flooring-Joists,	3	"	11	"
Trimmers and Headers,	5	"	14	"
Partition Studs,	2	"	4	"
Privy-Floor Joists,	2	"	10	"
Attic-Floor Joists,	2	"	10	"
Ties to Roof Trusses,	7	"	10	"
Rafters to Trusses,	7	"	12	"
Collars,	7	"	9	"
Purlins,	8	"	8	"
Wall Plates,	3	"	8	"
Small Rafters,	3	"	6	"

The Flooring-Joists are to be worked to a mould, crowning one inch. They are to have a fair bearing of four inches on the walls, at each end, and to be bridged with two lines of Cross Bridging.

The Trusses in the Roof are to be fitted with Wrought-iron Bolts, one inch in diameter, with Heads, perfect Screws, and large Washers and Nuts.

* These large Slates may be procured in Boston, and cost no more than good Blackboards. When it is not convenient to obtain them, the walls, where Blackboards are needed, may be adapted to the purpose, by mixing the Plastering or Hard-finish with Lampblack, rubbing it down smoothly, and *allowing it to become perfectly dry and hard before it is used.* Or, Blackboards may *be covered* with the composition mentioned on p. 197.

The Floor-Joists are to be framed into the Trimmers, and the Ceiling-Joists of the third story into the Ties of the Roof-Trusses, with Tusk-Tenons, and properly secured with hard-wood Pins.

All the Partitions in the main building are to be set with two-by-four-inch plank Studs, so as to give five nailings to a lath, thoroughly bridged throughout, and trussed over the openings.

There is to be a Lintel, four by eight inches, over each window, and other opening in the walls that requires it, and under the withs of the Privies, with a fair bearing of eight inches at each end.

Enclosing.

The Under-Floors of the Rooms, Entries, Passages, Platforms, and Privies, in each story, and the Floor of the Attic, are to be laid with No. 3 Pine boards, planed, jointed, laid close, and thoroughly nailed. The Roofs are to be covered with Matched boards, of the same quality, and thoroughly nailed.

Furring.

All the Walls, throughout, (excepting the cellar walls, the back walls of the several privies, and the side walls of the privies next to the main building,) and all the Ceilings, Entries, and Stairways, are to be Furred with three-inch Furrings of sound, seasoned, dry No. 3 Pine boards, spaced so as to give five nailings to a lath. They are to be put on the walls with twelve-penny nails, and on the ceilings with ten-pennies.

Grounds, three-fourths of an inch thick, are to be put up for all the finish, and three-quarter-inch Beads on all the angles and corners of the walls and stairways. The Beads are to be kept clean.

There are to be two Strips of Furring put up, (for convenience in driving nails for hanging charts, &c.,) extending entirely around the Schoolrooms, at distances of three and eight inches from the ceilings; and also similar Strips for the same purpose, set perpendicularly, on the rear and sidewalls, as directed by the Committee. Also, Composition Rods, in the angles of the ceiling, all round the rooms, with Moveable Rings at suitable distances, for picture lines.

Cold-air Boxes, and Ventiducts.

The Cold Air is to be taken in at one of the cellar-window openings, which is to be finished outside with a plank frame and coarse iron-wire netting.

The Air is to be conducted into the Brick Cold-air Flue of each Schoolroom, in separate Boxes, each twelve by eighteen inches, inside, made of thoroughly-seasoned Pine boards, smoothed on the inside, and put together with two-inch screws.

The Ventiducts, or Ventilating-Flues, are also to be made of thoroughly-seasoned Pine boards, smoothed on the inside, and put together with two-inch screws. There is to be a separate one for each Schoolroom, and the Privies, and each is to be fitted with two Swivel-blind Openings, or Registers, one at the floor and the other at the ceiling, with Stay-rods to regulate them, as may be directed by the Committee.

There are to be two Closets on each side of this Pier, in the first story, and on one side, in the second story, as shown in the diagram, on p. 183.

The Ventiducts, or Ventilating-Flues, for the Schoolrooms, are each to be sixteen inches square, inside; that for the Privies is to be ten inches square, inside. The Swivel-blind Openings in the Schoolrooms are to be sixteen by twenty-four inches; and those in the Privies are to be ten inches square.

The Ventiducts, or Ventilating-Flues, for the Schoolrooms, are to be brought together in the attic, and connected with the Ventilator on the main Roof.

The Ventiduct, or Ventilating-Shaft, for the Privies, is to be ten inches square, and carried down to within one foot of the surface of the water in the Vault or Sesspool; and the air from this Shaft, and also from the space between the privies and the main building, is to be conducted in a tight box over the ceilings of the third-story privies, to the Ventilator on the ridge.

Windows and Blinds.

All the Windows, (excepting those in the cellar,) are to have Double Box Frames, with two-inch pine plank Sills and Yokes, inch inside and outside Casings, one-and-one-fourth-inch hard-pine Pulley-styles, five-eighths-of-an-inch Inside Beads, and five-sixteenths-of-an-inch Parting Beads.

The Sashes are to be made of pine, one-and-three-fourths-inch thick, moulded and coped. They are all to be double hung with the best White Window Lines, Iron Pulleys with steel axles, and Round Iron Counter-weights. All the Sashes are to be fastened with strong Bronzed Sash-fastenings, of the best quality, to cost five dollars and fifty cents per dozen.

All the Windows in the first and second stories are to be fitted with one-and-one-fourth-inch Framed Blinds, two parts to each window, hung in light Box-frames, with Weights, Lines, and Pulleys, in the same manner as the sashes, excepting that they are to run up above the tops of the windows, in close boxes, and to have satisfactory Knobs, Rings, or Handles, on the bottom rails, to draw them down.

The Windows in the third story are to have Inside Shutter-Blinds, one inch thick, made in eight parts to each window, hung with Iron Butt-hinges, and fitted with Bronzed Hooks and Staples, and Rosewood Knobs.

The Openings in the Rear Wall of the Privies are to have Stationary Blinds, four inches thick, and reaching to the floors. The Windows in the Front Wall are to have Outside Blinds, one-and-three-fourths-inch thick, hung and fastened in the usual manner.

All the Windows, and the Openings in the Privy-Walls, are to be finished with one-and-one-fourth-inch moulded Architraves, with turned Corner-blocks. [Care to be taken to have no Architraves or Corner-blocks omitted on one side, or cut partly off.] Those in the first story are to have panel Jambs, and Soffits and Stools. Those in the second story, and all the Openings in the Privies, are to have Edge and Sill Casings. Those in the third story are to have Elbows to the Shutter-boxes, moulded panel Soffits, and wide Stools.

The Cellar-Windows are to be made with plank Frames, rabbeted for the sashes; and are to have Single Sashes, hung with Iron Butt-hinges to the tops of the frames, fastened with strong Iron Buttons, and fitted with Catches to hold them open when desired.

There is to be a Single Stationary Sash over each Entrance-door, made in six lights.

There are to be two Skylights in the Roof, which are to be made and hung in a neat and substantial manner, and properly fitted to rise and fasten.

There is to be a Scuttle, in the ceiling of the third story, made, cased, and hung, in a neat and substantial manner.

Doors.

All the Doors, throughout, (excepting the Outside ones, which are to be two-and-one-fourth-inches thick, and the Closet doors, which are to be one-and-one-fourth-inch thick,) are to be two inches thick, made in four moulded Panels each, hung with three four-inch iron Butt-hinges, and fastened (excepting the outside ones) with Robinson's best $2,50 Mortise Locks, with Catches and Bolts, Rosewood Knobs, Bronzed Trimmings, and *small* duplicate Keys to each. The Outside Doors are to be fastened with double-bolt Lever Locks of the best quality, having duplicate keys as *small* as practicable. The Privy Doors are to have strong Door-springs, in addition to the other trimmings.

All the Inside Doors, excepting those to the closets, are to be finished with hard-pine Sills, two-inch rabbeted and beaded Frames, and Architraves as described for the Windows, with Plinths. The doors, in every case, to be set so far from the walls, as to give the full Architraves and Corner-blocks on both sides.

The Outside Doors are to be hung to three-inch plank Frames, properly dogged to the thresholds and wall, and finished inside like the Inside Doors.

The Entrance and Cellar Doors are to be four feet by seven feet eight inches. The Inside Doors are to be three feet by seven feet four inches. The Privy Doors are to be two feet six inches, by seven feet four inches.

Stairs.

The Stairs are to be framed with deep plank Stringers and Winders, as shown by the Drawings. They are to be finished with hard-pine Risers, one inch thick, Treads one-and-one-fourth-inch thick, and Balusters one-and-one-eighth-inch diameter. The String and Gallery finish is to be of white pine, and the Posts, Newels, and Rails, of cherry. The bottom Posts are to be seven inches in diameter, turned, and the Rails three inches wide. The Rails are to be not less than three feet high, measuring from the nosing of the Steps.

There are to be two Flights of Stairs to the Cellar, framed with plank Stringers and Winders, and finished with planed pine Risers and Treads, and close Partitions one-and-one-half-inch thick, matched and planed.

There is to be a neat Flight of Portable Steps, to ascend from the third story to the Attic, and others to ascend from the Attic to the Skylight in the Roof.

Skirting.

The Rooms, Entries, Stairways, and Privies, are to be Skirted up as high as the window stools, in the respective stories, (except on the back sides of the Rooms,) with narrow matched beaded Lining, not to exceed seven inches in width, Capped to correspond with the nosing of the window stools. The Lining is to be gauged to a width, and set perpendicularly. That on the back Wall is to be fitted to the Slates in that wall, which are to rest on the Capping. That in the first story is to be of cherry-wood, the second story of maple, and the third story of white-pine, wrought and finished smoothly, suitable for being stained and varnished without painting.

Floorings, &c.

The Platforms are to be furred up, as shown by the Drawings, and the Stairways, Platforms, and Hearths, are to be bordered, and the Floors to be laid, with narrow hard-pine floorings, perfectly jointed and thoroughly nailed. The Strips are to be gauged to a width respectively in the schoolrooms, and the joints are to be broken, at least three feet, so that no two strips of different widths will but on to each other.

Cabinets, Closets, Clothes-Hooks, &c.

There are to be two Cabinets, in each Schoolroom, between the windows, above the skirting, and as high as the windows, with double cherry Sash-doors, each hung with three Brass Hinges, fastened with Thumb-catches and Locks, and fitted with Rosewood Knobs. There are to be twelve Shelves in each, and immediately below them are to be small Closets, with four Shelves in each, and double Doors, hung and fastened in the same manner as the sash doors. The shelves are to be placed as directed by the Committee. Six of them are to be inclined, with two narrow ledges on each.

There are to be two Closets in each side of the Ventilating Pier, in the First Story, and two in one side in the Second Story, as shown at *o o*, in the diagram on page 183. Each Closet is to be fitted with three shelves, and the doors are to be hung and fastened in the same manner as the Closets under the Cabinets.

There is to be for each Schoolroom, where directed by the Committee, a Press-closet, having three Shelves on one side, with six brass double Hat-and-Coat-Hooks, on beaded cherry-wood cleats; the Door to be neatly hung, fastened, and trimmed, similar to the other doors.

There is to be in the entry of each Schoolroom, where directed by the Committee, a Closet, for brushes, brooms, coal-hod, &c., two by three-and-one-half feet, made with matched boards, and fitted with three Shelves on one side, and eight Hooks on the other side and back. The Door is to be made, hung, and fastened, to correspond with the other doors.

There is to be a Sink, attached to each Schoolroom, where directed by the Committee, made of two-inch pine plank, the top hung with stout hinges, and with Drawers and Cupboards below. It is to be fitted with a Composition Sesspool, lined with zinc, and a lead Waste-pipe, leading to the vault. Suitable Pipes, to lead the City water into the sink in each story, are to be provided.

There is to be a Dumb-waiter from the cellar to the third story, opening into each story, for raising coals, wood, &c.

There are to be seventy extra-stout iron double Hat-and-Coat-Hooks, to each Schoolroom, put up on beaded cherry-wood Cleats, as directed by the Committee.

There are to be two Umbrella-stands, in each Entry, to hold six umbrellas each.

Coal-Bins, &c.

There are to be three Coal-Bins in the Cellar, each capable of holding three tons of Coal, having Covers hung with strong wrought-iron Hinges, and sliding Gates, with boxings around them to keep the Coal from the floor. Also, three Closets for Kindlings, the doors to be hung with iron Strap-hinges, and fastened with iron Buttons.

There are also to be in the Cellar, two large iron-bound Water-butts, with metal Faucets.

Privy-Finish.

The Privies are to be fitted with pine Risers, Seats, and Covers. The Covers are to be hung with stout Duck, or India-rubber cloth, instead of metal Hinges; the edges of the cloth to be covered with narrow slats. They are to be so arranged, that they will fall of themselves when left. There is to be a Box for paper in each Privy, and the Boys' Privies are to have Troughs, lined with zinc, with Sesspools. The whole finish of the Privies is to be equal to that of the other parts of the building.

Painting.

All the Hard-wood Finish, (except the Skirting of the first and second stories, which is to be varnished,) is to be oiled, with two coats of boiled Linseed-oil, well rubbed in with cloth.

All the Outside wood-work, the Copper-trunks, and the inner walls throughout, are to be prepared and painted with three coats of Oil-and-Lead paint, of such color as the Committee may direct. The Outside-doors are to be painted Bronze.

The Insides of the Closets and Cabinets are to be painted white, and the Teachers' Platforms in imitation of Marble. The Blinds are to be painted with four coats of Paris Green, and Varnished. The third-story skirting is to be stained with asphaltum, and varnished. The rest of the Inside Pine Finish is to be Putty-stopped, Primed, and Painted and Grained, in imitation of Oak, Maple, or other color, as directed by the Committee, and Varnished.

All the Painting and Varnishing is to be equal to that of first-class dwelling-houses.

Glazing.

All the Sashes, throughout, are to be glazed with Crystal Sheet Glass, of double thickness, and of the best quality. Each light is to be properly Bedded, Sprigged, and Back-Puttied.

The Windows are to have Lights of the following dimensions, as shown in the Drawings:

First Story, Front Windows, eighteen Lights, each eleven by fourteen inches. First Story, Rear Window, twelve Lights, each eleven by sixteen inches. That in the west wall, eight Lights, each eleven by sixteen inches.

Second Story, Front Windows, eighteen Lights, each eleven by fourteen inches. Second Story, Rear Windows, eight and twelve Lights, each eleven by sixteen inches. Front Window in easterly Projection, twelve Lights, each eleven by fourteen inches.

Third Story, Front Windows, twelve Lights, each eleven by nineteen inches. Third Story, Rear Windows, eight and twelve Lights, each eleven by fifteen inches. Front Windows in easterly Projection, eight Lights, each eleven by nineteen inches.

The Cellar Windows, eight Lights, each eight by ten inches.

The Sashes over the Doors, each six Lights.

The Skylights are to be two feet six inches by three feet six inches.

Ventilators.

There are to be two of Emerson's Patent Ventilators, of galvanized iron; one on the Roof of the Main Building, twenty-five inches in diameter, and another on the Roof of the Privies, twelve inches in diameter.

Furniture.

Each Schoolroom is to be furnished with sixty Small Arm-Chairs, of Mr. INGRAHAM's pattern, such as are used in the other Primary Schools in the City.* Also, with a Table, for the Teacher's Platform, four feet by two, (made of Mahogany, Black Walnut, or Cherry-wood, as directed by the Committee,) furnished with two Drawers, and fitted with Locks, Keys, and Rosewood Knobs, of the best quality.

Memorandum.

No bricks, stone, lumber, or other building-materials, of any description, are to be placed on the garden-plat; and the Trees and Garden are to have a rough box built around them, for their preservation from injury. No lines are to be fastened to the Trees, for any purpose whatever.

All the Lumber is to be well and thoroughly seasoned; and all that is in sight is to be free from Shakes, Sap, and Knots; and that and every part of the work is to be equal to any used in first-class dwelling-houses.

MR. INGRAHAM'S COMPOSITION FOR BLACKBOARDS.

Lampblack and Flour of Emery, mixed with Spirit-Varnish.

No more Lampblack and Flour of Emery should be used, than are sufficient to give the required black and abrading surface; and the Varnish should contain only sufficient gum to hold the ingredients together, and confine the Composition to the Board. The thinner the mixture, the better.

The Lampblack should first be ground with a small quantity of Alcohol, or Spirit-Varnish, to free it from lumps.

The Composition should be applied to the smoothly-planed surface of a Board, with a common painter's brush. Let it become *thoroughly dry and hard before it is used.* Rub it down with pumice-stone, or a piece of smooth wood covered with the Composition.

Boards prepared in this way are almost equal to Slates, and will last for years; and they can be used with slate-pencils, which are much better than crayons or chalk, on account of their freedom from dust and dirt. Crayon or chalk dust is deleterious to health, as well as to cleanliness.

This Composition may also be used on the walls.

---

* See pp. and 181.

PLANS, &c., OF BRIMMER GRAMMAR SCHOOL, BOSTON.

This building was erected in 1843. It is situated on Common-street, near Washington. It is 74 feet in length on the street, by 52 feet deep, with three stories. The entrance is in the center of the front into a hall 8 feet wide, leading through into the yard in the rear, which is divided by a wall into three portions. The passage to the second and third floors is by a double flight of stairs near the front door.

The first floor is occupied by two Primary School-rooms, each 30 by 22 feet, and 11 feet high; and the Ward-room, 30 by 50 feet.

The school-room on the *second floor* is 70 feet by 37 feet wide, and 14 feet 6 inches high between the bays. The ceiling is plastered up between the bays, (cross timbers) by which eighteen inches are grained in height, dividing the ceiling into equal compartments. There are two recitation rooms, one

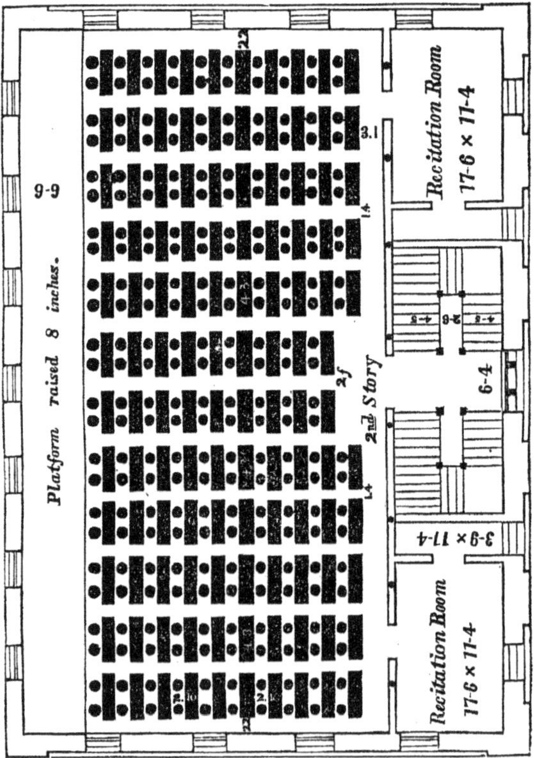

on each side the entrance, 17 feet 6 inches, by 11 feet 4 inches each, with two windows in each room, and benches on all the sides for the pupils. The school-room is lighted on three sides, and contains 118 desks, and 236 chairs, two chairs to each desk, the desks and chairs being of four sizes. The tops of the desks are cherry wood, and the chairs are Wales' patent. The desks are separated by aisles one foot four inches in width, except the center aisle, which is two feet wide.

The aisles on the side nearest the recitation-rooms, are three feet wide, and those at each end, 2 feet 6 inches each. The platform on which are the desks of the master and assistants, is eight inches high, and 6 feet 6 inches wide, and the desks are so placed *that the pupils sit with their backs to the platform;* and the pupils are so arranged at the desks in classes and sections, that when one class is reciting, the desk is only occupied by one pupil. The windows are shaded by inside blinds painted green.

The school-room on the *third floor* is of the same size, having an arched ceiling 13 feet high in the center, with recitation-rooms and other arrangements similar to the school-room on the second floor.

The building is warmed by two furnaces, and ventilated by six flues, discharging into the attic, from which the impure air is carried off by copper ventilators in the roof. The openings into the flues in the school-rooms are controlled by Preston's ventilators.

The frame of Preston's Ventilator is made of a flat bar of iron $2\frac{1}{2}$ by $\frac{1}{4}$ inch, framed at the corners, the end at each corner running by in order to receive a clamp to screw the frame to the brick work; the door is of plate iron, ($\frac{1}{16}$ wire gage), with a rod passing down the center of the plate, on the back side, each end of the rod running by the plate and entering the frame, forming a pivot on which the plate or door of the ventilator turns. The door shuts against a projection in the frame.

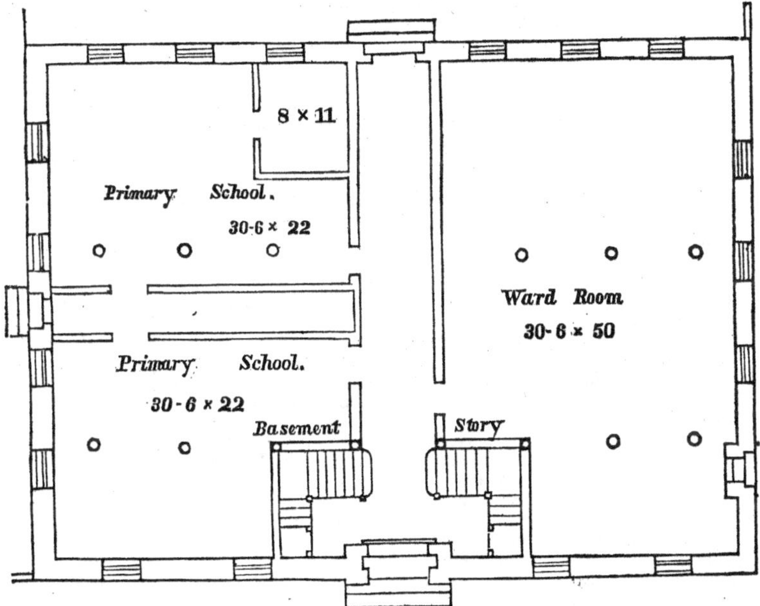

The Brimmer school has two masters, one in each room, and each with an usher and female assistant.

[Since the above description was first published, (in 1843) the seats and desks have been reversed, so that the pupils sit with their faces to the platform. The former method was found by the teacher to be "very inconvenient, and wholly impracticable. The scholar should see the face and hear the voice of the Principal as much as possible."]

Plan and Description of Bowdoin Grammar School-House.

The new Bowdoin School-house, completed in 1848, is situated on Myrtle street, and with the yard occupies an area of about 75 feet by 68 feet, bounded on each of the four sides by a street. It is built of brick with a basement story of hammered granite, and measures 75 feet 9 inches extreme length by 54 feet 6 inches extreme breadth—having three stories, the first and second being 13 feet, and the third, 15 feet high in the clear. The ground descends rapidly from Myrtle street, thereby securing a basement of 15 feet in the rear. One third of which is finished into entries, or occupied by three furnaces, coal bins, pumps, &c., and the remaining two thirds is open to the yard, thereby affording a covered play-ground for the pupils.

The third story is finished into one hall 72 feet long by 38 feet wide, with seats and desks for 180 pupils. On the south side of this hall there are two recitation rooms, each 16 feet by 12 feet, and a room for a library, &c. There are three rooms of the same size on the two floors below.

The second story is divided into two rooms by a partition wall, each of which is 35 feet by 38, and accommodates 90 pupils, and so connected by sliding doors that all the pupils of both schools can be brought under the eye and voice of the teacher.

The first story corresponds to the second, except there are no sliding doors in the partition, and no connection between the room except through the front entry. The two rooms on this floor have each seats and desks for 100 pupils.

Each story is thoroughly ventilated, and warmed by one of Chilson's Furnaces. In each furnace the air chambers, the apertures for conducting the cold air into them, and the flues for constructing the heated air into the rooms in each story, being all large, a great quantity of warm air is constantly rushing into the rooms, and the ventilating flues or ventiducts being so constructed and arranged that the air of the rooms will be frequently changed, and that a pure and healthy atmosphere will at all times be found in each of these rooms, provided the furnaces are properly and judiciously managed. On the top of the building there are two of Emerson's large ventilators, connected with the attic and ventilating flues, through which the impure air passes out into the atmosphere above.

To accommodate pupils who come to school with wet feet or clothes, there is an open fire in a grate in one of the recitation rooms.

Each room is furnished with Wales' American School Chair, and Ross's Desk, and both desk and chair are in material, form and style, as described on page 202 and 205.

This is a school for girls only, and consists of two departments, one of which is called the Grammar department, and the other the Writing department; the master of each department being independent of the other.

The number of assistant female teachers in each department of this school, when full, will be four, the teachers in each department being independent of the master and teacher in the other.

The master of the Grammar department and two of his assistants will occupy the large hall in the third story, and his other two assistants will occupy one of the rooms in the first story.

The master of the writing department and two of his assistants will occupy the rooms in the second story, and his other two assistants will occupy the other room in the first story, each master being the superintendence of his own department.

The school, when full, will be divided into five classes, and each class into two divisions, nearly equal in numbers. The first week after the vacation in August, the first division of each class will attend in the grammar department in the morning, and the second division of each class will attend in the writing department; and in the afternoon, the second division of each class will attend in the grammar department, and the first, in the writing department. The next week, this order of attendance is to be reversed, and this alteration is to continue through the year, the weeks of vacation not being counted.

This house and the Quincy Grammar School-house are built after designs by Mr. Bryant.

PLAN OF FIRST AND SECOND FLOOR.

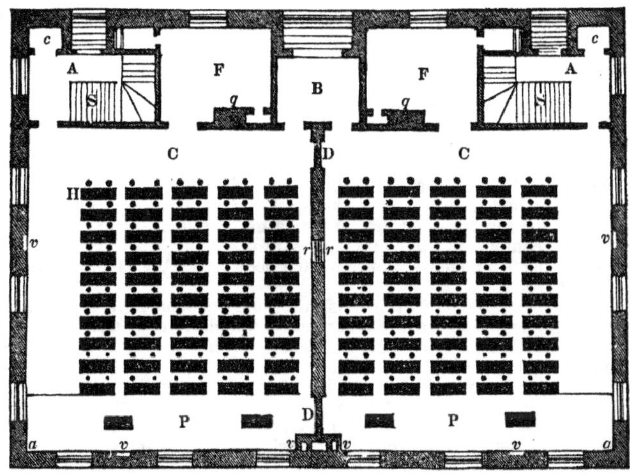

A, A, Entrance for Pupils.
B, Ditto for Teacher.
C, C, Study halls, each 35 by 38 feet; with seats and desks for 100 pupils.
D, Sliding door, by which the two rooms on the second floor are thrown into one.
E, Study hall, 72 feet by 38.
F, F, Two recitation rooms on each floor, 16 feet by 12.
G, Room 10 feet by 12, for library, apparatus, &c.
H, Ross' desk, and Wales' chair.
P, Teacher's platform with desk for teacher and assistants.
S, S, Staircase leading to second and third floors.
a, Case with glass doors for apparatus.
c, Closet for Teacher.
q, Grate.
r, Hot air register.
v, Flues for ventilation.

PLAN OF THIRD FLOOR.

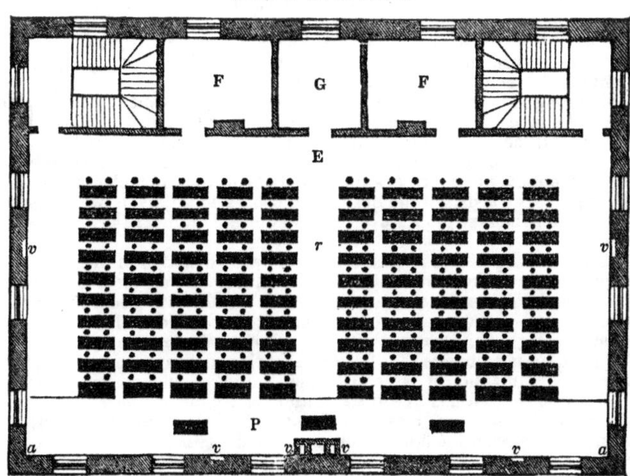

Plan and Description of Quincy Grammar School-House, Boston.

This building, which was commenced in 1847, and dedicated on the 26th of June, 1848, is situated on a lot 90 feet by 130 feet, extending from Tyler street to Hudson street.

The ground plan is in the form of a cross, the exterior dimensions of the body being 80 feet by 58 feet, the end fronting on Tyler street. The wings are 12 feet in front by 36 feet deep. It is four stories high, with a basement 8 feet in the clear, for the furnaces and fuel, and an attic for gymnastic exercises.

Each wing contains a front and back entrance, a flight of stairs from the basement to the attic, and a room on each floor 10 feet by 11 feet, connected with a school-room.

The fourth story of the body is finished in one spacious hall, 16 feet high in the clear, with centre-pieces and a cornice, and a platform at each end 22 feet by 11 feet, and 22 inches high. It is furnished with settees arranged in 4 rows, sufficient to accommodate 700 children.

The third floor is divided by a corridor 8 feet wide, extending across the main body from one wing to the other, having 2 school-rooms on each side.

These four school-rooms are of nearly the same size, averaging about 31½ feet by 26½ feet, and 13 feet high. Each room is lighted by 2 windows at the side, and 2 at the end, and has a platform for the teacher 24 feet by about 5½, with one end towards the entrance from the corridor, and on the other end is placed a book-case of cherry, 3½ feet by 8 feet, with glazed doors, facing the entrance.

The scholars' desks front the platform and the windows on the side of the building, and are separated by aisles 1 foot and 4 inches wide. They are 2 feet in length, made of cherry-wood, and varnished and supported by cast iron stands. J. L. Ross, maker. Each scholar has a desk by himself.

The chair is made by Mr. Wales, of Boston. It has a scroll back and cast iron support.

Each room accommodates 56 pupils, one desk and chair being placed on a small movable platform for a monitor.

The rooms are lined with composition blackboards 3½ feet wide, 2 feet from the floor.

The school-rooms which have not small rooms attached, are provided with closets for the children's clothes. There are 2 sinks in the corridor, with conveniences for introducing Cochituate water. The description of this story will answer for the two below it, as the first three are essentially the same.

The windows are furnished with inside blinds, having revolving slats, so that the light may be regulated with great ease.

The building is warmed by 4 furnaces placed in the basement, 2 being placed at the middle of each end, each being intended to warm the three rooms immediately over it, the cast iron chimnies being relied upon for heating the hall.

Emerson's system of ventilation has been introduced since the building was finished, each room having a separate air-duct to the roof, 14 inches by 14 inches.

The apparatus consists of the Boston Philosophical set, by J. M. Wightman, Eayrs and Fairbanks' globe, 2 sets of Pelton's Outline Maps, and one of Mitchell's.

A library costing $200 has been furnished by the donation of Mayor Quincy.

To protect the desks from injury, the slate-frames are all required to be covered with cloth, and each scholar is to provide himself with a convenient box to contain his pen, pen-wiper, pencils, rubber, &c. Each desk has an inkstand sunk into the right-hand corner, with a revolving metalic cover.

The building is calculated for but one school, and is at present occupied by but one, the organization of which is adapted to the arrangement and construction of the house. When the organization is complete, the school will be divided into 4 classes, each class containing 168 scholars, and each class into 3 divisions. At present the 3 lower classes contain two divisions each, and the first class 3.

On the 3rd floor are the first division of the first class under the instruction of the Principal, and the several divisions of the 2d class instructed by assistants; On the 2d floor is the 2d division of the 1st class instructed by the sub-master, with the several divisions of the 3d class under assistants; and the usher takes the 3rd division of the 1st class, with the several divisions of the 4th class on the 1st floor. By this arrangement the government is rendered comparatively easy. The whole school is brought together in the hall for devotional services, and other general exercises.

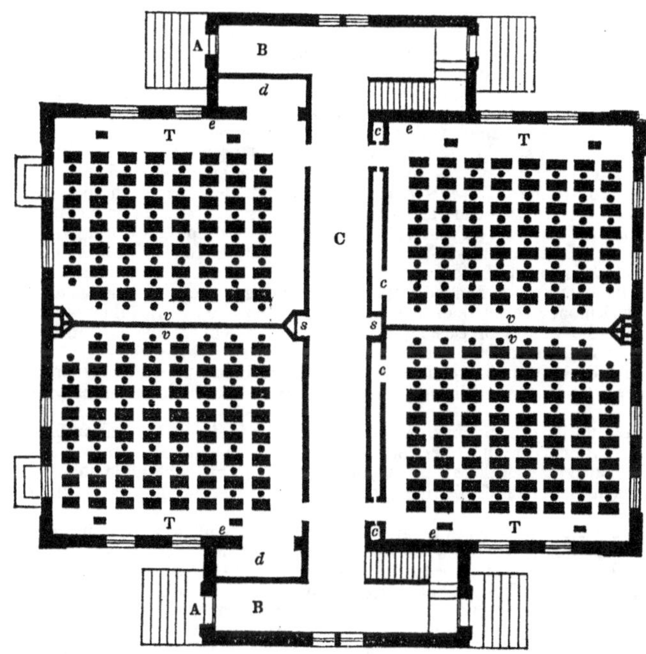

Plan of First Floor.

A, A, Front Door.
B, B, Entries.
C, Corridor or Hall.
T, T, T, T, Teachers' Platform 24 feet by 5½.
r, *r*, *r*, *r*, Hot-air flues.
v, *v*, *v*, *v*, Preston's Ventilators for controlling the flues in the partition wall, which communicate with the iron smoke pipes near the top of the building. This plan is adopted in the first story only.
e, *e*, *e*, *e*, Indicates the location of the flues of Emerson's Ventilators in the second, third and fourth stories.
s, Sink.
c, *c*. *c*, *c*, Closets.
d, *d*, Closets 10 feet by 11 feet.

It is to be feared there are not many communities, even in New England, where the Chief Magistrate, elected annually by the people, would have the courage to utter the following noble sentiments, spoken by Mayor Quincy, at the dedication of the Quincy Grammar School-house, June 26, 1848.

As Chairman of the "City Fathers," he did not hesitate to stand there and tell the tax-paying community that they had, in this manner, just expended $200,000 of their money; and he was confident the question would not be asked, Why spend so much? Why spend more for popular education in the city of Boston, than is expended in the whole of Great-Britain?

He said, if but once in a century, a little being should be sent into this world, of most delicate and beautiful structure, and we were told that a wonderful principle pervaded every part of it, capable of unlimited expansion and happiness, capable of being fitted to associate with angels and becoming the friend of God: or if it should receive a wrong bias, of growing up in enmity against him, and incurring everlasting misery, could any expense of education which would contribute to save from such misery and elevate to such happiness, be too much? But, instead of one such little being, 24,000 were now entrusted to the care of the "City Fathers," and their education, in this world, will determine their future destiny,—of companionship with angels, or with the degraded wretched, enemies of God.

If the community had no responsibility in the matter, how, he asked, could it spend money better than in educating these children? But they would soon control the affairs of Boston, and, to a great extent, of the Commonwealth. Nor would their influence stop here. "No man liveth for himself" Each of these children would form a centre of widening influence, whose circumference might yet embrace millions of minds, and extend through unnumbered centuries.

Here, unlike other countries, every restraint to individual elevation is thrown off. All have the most perfect liberty that can be enjoyed, without infringing upon the rights of others. How important then, that each child should be educated to understand his rights, and the principles and habits of *self-Government.*

We are all, said he, in a partnership, and if one of these little partners suffers in his character, the whole community suffer in consequence.

He believed that nearly half of the 400 boys in that school were not Americans. Many of their parents were not fitted for the duties of a Republic. But these children, educated side by side with our own, would learn self-government, and be trained to become worthy citizens of this free country.

It seemed, he said, the design of Providence to mix races; and this influx of foreigners might constitute the very elements necessary to give to American character its highest excellence. Standing on such a moral elevation, as Boston did, they felt it a duty to provide for the education of all, and thus present to the whole country, *models* of popular education.

These schools are justly the pride and boast of the city; and the sentiment with which they are universally regarded is beautifully embodied in the following extract from an address by George S. Hillard, Esq.

The schools of Boston are the best jewels in her crown. If I were asked by an intelligent stranger to point out to him our most valued possessions, I would show to him—not our railroads, our warehouses, filled with the wealth of all the earth, our ships, our busy wharves and marts, where the car of commerce is ever "thundering loud with her ten thousand wheels," but I would carry him to one of our public schools, would show him its happy and intelligent children, hushed into reverent silence at their teacher's word, or humming over their tasks with a sound like that of bees in June. I would tell him that here was the foundation on which our material prosperity was reared, that here were the elements from which we constructed the State.

Here are the fountains from which flow those streams which make glad our land. The schools of Boston are dear to my heart. Though I can have no personal and immediate interest in them; though no child on earth calls me father; yet most gladly do I contribute to their support, according to my substance; and when I see a father's eyes filled with pleasant tears as he hears the music of his child's voice linked to some strain of poetry or burst of eloquence, I can sympathize in the feeling in which I cannot share. May the blessing of Heaven rest upon our schools. They are an object worthy of all efforts and sacrifices. We should leave nothing undone which may tend to make them more excellent and more useful. For this, we should gather into our own stores all the harvest of experience which have been reaped from other soils. The present is an age of progress. The claims of humanity are now beginning to be heard as they never were before. The movements in favor of Peace, of Anti-Slavery, of Temperance, of Education, of Prison Discipline, all spring from the same root— a sense of sympathy and brotherhood. Is it too much to say that the dawn of a new day is reddening the tops of the mountains? Higher yet may that light ascend, till its golden shafts have pierced the deepest valleys of ignorance and sin! Let us not stand idly on the brink, while the tide of improvement sweeps by us, but boldly launch our bark upon the stream.

We live in a community ready to discern and to do that which is right. It should be a source of gratitude to us that our lot is cast on a spot, where every good and worthy faculty may find appropriate work to do. When I behold this city that we love, seated upon her triple throne of hills with her mural crown of spires and domes glittering in the smokeless air, when I remember how much of that which embellishes and dignifies life is gathered under those roofs, I feel that he has not lived in vain who has contributed, even in the smallest measure, to the happiness and prosperity of Boston. And how can we do this more effectually than by watching over her schools,—by making them as nearly perfect as human institutions can be? For this object let neither wealth nor toil be spared. Here are fountains of life; as they are, so will its issues be. The child is father to the man. Make our schools all that they can be, and all that they should be, and we shall give to the prosperity of our beloved city a permanence like that of moral truth. It will become an inevitable necessity, like that which compels the heart of man to love what is lovely, and venerate what is venerable.

The following statistics are taken from the "*Third Annual Report of the Superintendent of Public Schools, (Nathan Bishop, Esq.,) of the City of Boston,*" submitted Dec. 29, 1853.

Estimated cost of all the Public School Estates to May 1st, 1853.

1. Cost of the Latin and English High School Estate, and of the improvements on the same,	$82,151.51
2. Cost of all the Grammar School Estates, and of the improvements on the same,	797,848.49
3. Cost of all the Primary School Estates, and of the improvements on the same,	448,500.00
Total cost of all the Public School Estates,	$1,358,500.00

Means and Cost of supporting Public Schools.

The City receives annually, from the State School Fund, about,	$5,500.00
The remainder of the means for supporting the Public Schools is drawn from the City Treasury, which is replenished by the annual tax and by other sources of income. During the last twelve years, 21 per cent. of the ordinary city expenditures has been appropriated to the Public Schools.	
In the year 1853, the expenses of the School Department amounted to,	329,800.20
Viz., for Grammar Schools—salaries of teachers,	130,531.18
" " " " incidental expenses,	35,849.82
" " " " new buildings and alterations,	42,991.00
" " Primary Schools—salaries of teachers,	62,508.33
" " " " incidental expenses,	22,231.46
" " " " buildings,	35,823.09

After a variety of experiments in school architecture, the School Committee of Boston have adopted the internal arrangements of the Quincy Grammar School, as the best adapted to that organization which affords the greatest facilities of instruction and government in this class of schools. Although we are not prepared to adopt without qualification the views taken of the subject, we give below extracts from the First Semi-Annual Report of the Superintendent of Public Schools, (Nathan Bishop, Esq.) in which the grounds of this preference are set forth.

The proper size of a school-house in a large city, where the population is dense, must be determined by the number of pupils required in one building in order to make the *best classification.* By classification is meant, the putting together of as many scholars as one teacher can instruct well into one division or group. Experience has shown that between fifty and sixty, all being about equally advanced in their several studies, can be well taught by one teacher. The best classification of pupils in schools is nothing more than a wise application of the principle of the division of labor, which has done so much to advance and to perfect the various branches of industry. A division of labor, made on the right principle, always increases the facilities of performing the process, or improves the quality of the article made, and not unfrequently accomplishes both these objects at the same time. It must constantly be borne in mind, that it is not simply a division of labor which has effected such wonderful improvements in every department of business carried on in the civilized world; but it is a division of a particular kind of labor, on such a principle as will enable the persons engaged in it to perform more of it in a given time without additional effort, and to do it as well as they could before, or even better.

Actual experience has shown, in many instances, that a school containing eight hundred pupils can be classified to better advantage than one containing any smaller number. A school of this size can be managed with but little more labor on the part of the principal than is required for one only half as large. If the difference in the attainments of the children in each division be so small that they can with advantage study the same lessons, then the teacher may instruct them altogether in some recitations and exercises, and, for the others, he may separate them into two sections; and, while he is hearing one recite a lesson, the other may be preparing for the next recitation; and so on, for every school-day in the year, the teacher can give *one half of his time* to one section, and one half to the other; and in this way each pupil will receive a greater amount of personal instruction and assistance from his teacher than on any other plan of dividing the labor of teaching a large school.

The teacher, having but few branches pursued in his division, has ample time to make thorough preparation to explain and illustrate all difficult points in every lesson. Having sufficient time, also, for hearing the recitations of his pupils, a good teacher can awaken in his class a degree of mental activity in the pursuit of knowledge, which will lend to their intellects the best discipline, while it enlarges the fields of their vision on the different branches of study. He will also have time to throw around the more important facts and principles in the text-books such remarks and illustrations as will attract and secure the attention of his scholars, and impress upon their minds a well-defined idea of each leading fact or principle by itself; and then he may group them together into one larger view, showing their connection with the general subject, and making them throw some light on what has gone before, or prepare the way for what comes after, in the study under examination.

The following "Specification of materials to be provided, and labor performed, in the erection of a Grammar School-house," drawn up by Joseph R. Richards, architect, embodies the latest improvements adopted by the School Committee of Boston.

Specifications for a Grammar School.

Description.

The building is to be of brick, it is to measure sixty feet by eighty feet above the underpinning, and to contain three finished stories; the first and second each twelve feet high, and the third story fourteen feet high, in the clear. The roof is to have an inclination of twenty-nine degrees from each side of the building, intersecting in a ridge; there is to be an observatory or belfry immediately upon the center of the ridge 9½ by 9½ feet octagonal form, and thirteen feet in height to top of roof; the cellar will be eight feet deep in the clear. The lot of land is to be inclosed with a brick wall on two sides, and with an iron fence on the front end; the space in the rear is to be divided into yards by board fences, and to contain a block of privies against the rear line of the estate. The first floor of the buiding is to set four feet above the level of the street sidewalk. The building is to set back from the front line of the lot of land ten feet.

Excavating.

The dirt and rubbish is to be dug out for the cellar and cellar walls, and all trenches and footings for the vaults and the drains and cesspools, as required; and all that is not required for grading up the lot, is to be removed from the premises. The yards are all to be filled and graded up to the level of the cellar flooring, with good gravel, where below the same.

Granite Foundations.

Each of the walls are to have a bottom course, three feet long, eighteen inches deep, and two feet wide, laid crosswise of the trenches; upon the same is to be laid a stone wall, eighteen inches thick, built with square split granite blocks, laid in cement mortar, faced on the inside, and thoroughly whitewashed. Good and sufficient foundations are to be laid for the steps, coal hoals, walls of the privies, and furnaces.

The underpinning of the four walls of the building, the steps, platforms and thresholds, gate thresholds, and fence stones, caps and sills to cellar windows, privy thresholds, curbs to vaults, covers to yard cesspools, are all to be of even colored granite, free from rust, sap, or flaws; fine hammered where directed; and set in lime mortar, cramped, leaded, and pointed, as required and directed. Iron strainers are to be fitted to the cesspool covers, with a movable cover, and three stone movable covers are to be fitted to the vaults, having strong iron rings fitted thereto. Properly fit a cold air box to the outside wall, with a grating on the outside thereof.

Sandstone.

There are to be caps and sills to all the windows of the building, and caps to the privy doors, of freestone, rubbed on the three fronts, and tooled on the rear front; the first and second story caps are to be moulded according to the full size drawing.

Brickwork.

Back up the underpinning of the four walls, so as to make a total thickness of twenty inches to the same. The four exterior walls, are to be in two thicknesses, of eight inches each, with an air space of four inches between them, built up the whole height of the building to the roof boarding; and a neat facia fitted to the cornice. The outside facing of three side walls are to be laid with the first quality of pressed bricks, properly tied to the walls every seventh course by "angular brick ties." The interior walls are each to be twelve inches thick, laid from the bottom course to the under side of the attic flooring. The outside walls of the privies, are to be laid eight inches thick each, and seven and a half feet high, and the partition walls four inches thick. The yard walls are each to be twelve inches thick, and eight feet high above the sidewalk level, commenced on solid stone foundations below ground. The above are all to be laid in the best lime mortar. The vaults to be laid in cesspool form, and the drains, cesspools are to be laid in cement mortar of the best quality. The cellars are to be paved with uniform hard bricks all over their surfaces. The exterior walls are to be tied together at suitable distances; the ventilators are to be laid partly in the wall, fourteen by eighteen inches each, smoothly plastered; the iron chimneys are to be recessed in the entry walls and connected therewith; the vaults are to be six feet deep; the yard walls are to be capped with stone, set in cement. All the brickwork is to be built with the best hard burnt brick.

Lathing and Plastering.

The ceilings of the three stories are to be lathed and plastered; the several walls are to be plastered on the walls without lathings, with a stout coat of lime and hair mortar, and finished smoothly with lime putty; the whole work to be done neat and true; a coat of lime and hair mortar is to finish on the walls of the privies and the ceilings also.

Slating.

The roof of the building is to be slated with the best of wide ladies slates, laid not exceeding 6¾ inches to the weather, put on with composition nails, and properly secured with flashings of lead, 3½ lbs. to the square foot; fit heavy zinc, strapped with irons, to the ridges, and warrant the whole perfectly tight.

Iron works and Incidentals.

There is to be an upright, twisted, diamond formed, wrought iron grating to each of the cellar windows, with a heavy frame attached. There are to be two stout iron scrapers at each door. There is to be a stout iron snow fender running around the building on the roof, costing 50 cents per foot. An iron fence, to cost $3 per lineal foot, is to be made and set up complete, with two gates hung and fastened across the front end of the lot with four iron posts, securely set, leaded, and fastened; the gates are each to have a lock. The ends of the fence are to be fastened to a stone post, placed at the ends of the side walls.

The building committee will provide for the furnaces, iron smoke pipes, ventilators, and furnace registers, and hot air pipes complete; set the same as directed. Set and introduce such water pipes in the building as may be required, the building committee furnishing such, and all the furnaces. The committee will also provide such drains and cause such cesspools to be laid as may be required.

An iron cornice with modillions is to be set entirely around the building, costing $2.50 per lineal foot; the gutter of the building is to be made therein; the whole to be braced and properly fastened to the wall. There are to be four conductors to the building, each four inches in diameter, of 18 oz. cold rolled copper, put up, connected with the gutters, and led off in a proper manner with heavy goose necks, and 3½ inch pipes at the bottom to lead water into the drain. To be two copper conductors and a copper gutter to the block of privies. The roof of the privies and observatory are to be covered with sheet X X tin, lapped, soldered and finished in the best possible manner and warranted tight.

Carpentry and Framing.

The roofs and floors are to be framed in the manner indicated by the drawings, with good sound lumber, and timber of the following dimensions. Principal floor joists, of spruce, 3×15 inches; trimmers and headers, of spruce, 6×15 inches; privy floor joists, of spruce, 3×6 inches; attic ceiling joists, of spruce, between tresses, 2×6 inches; tie beams of roof, of pine, 9×12 inches; truss rafters of pine, 9×12 inches; purlines of spruce, 8×8 inches; small rafters of spruce, 20 inches apart, 3×5 inches; wall plates, of spruce, 3×9 inches; ridge plank, 2×10. The floor joists are to be worked to a mould crowning 1 inch, they are to have a fair bearing of 4 inches on the walls, at each end, and to be placed not exceeding 15 inches apart, from center to center of each, and bridged with two rows of cross bridging. The roof tresses are to be fitted with wrought iron bolts, 1 inch in diameter, with heads, screws, washer and nuts, and footings, bolts also of same size. There is to be a lintal 4×8 inches over every opening in the walls that require it, and under the "withs" of the privies, having a fair bearing of eight inches at the end.

Boarding and Furring.

The under floors of the rooms, entries, and platforms, and privies and the roofs, are to be laid with No. 3 pine boards, machine planed, matched, and well nailed.

The ceilings and stairways of the three stories are to be furred with three inch furrings, of sound seasoned, dry pine boards, spaced for five nailings to a lathe. Nail them with tenpennies. Put on three-fourth inch grounds for finish, and irons for corners and angles. There are to be two strips of furring for hanging charts thereto, extending entirely round each of the school-rooms, as directed.

Cold Air Boxes and Ventilating Flues.

There is to be a separate flue for each furnace, 12×20 inches clear, made of thoroughly seasoned pine boards, smoothed on the inside and put together with two inch screws; there is to be a valve and handle to each. The ventilating flues are to have a valve and a handle; they are to be made of thoroughly seasoned pine boards, smoothed inside and outside and put together with screws. There is to be a separate one for each school-room, and each block of ten privies; fitted with blind openings or registers at the floor and ceiling, arranged as shown upon plans, and as now completed in most of the school-houses recently erected by the City of Boston. The ventilating flues are to be connected with two roof ventilators, largest size, arranged as directed. There are to be two roof ventilators over the privies.

Windows and Blinds.

All the windows of the three stories are to have double box frames, hard pine pulley stiles, &c. The sashes are to be made of pine 1¾ inches thick, moulded, coped, and lipped. They are all to be double hung with the best of white window lines, iron pulleys, steel pintels and round iron weights of accurate balance. All the sashes are to be fastened with strong bronzed sash fastenings to cost $4.50 per dozen. All the windows of the three stories are to be fitted with 1¼ inch framed blinds, eight parts to each window, hung and fastened complete with iron butt hinges and bronze hooks, staples, and rosewood knobs, and to fold into flat boxings. They are all to finish with 1¼ inch moulded architraves, 8 inches wide, plain jambs, sofits, and stools. The cellar windows are to be made with plank frames rebated for the sashes, and to have double sashes hung to the tops of the frames, fastened with strong iron buttons and fitted with catches to hold them open when desired. Each privy is to have a movable window in its door. The observatory windows are to be double hung and fastened.

Doors.

The outside doors are to be 2¼ inches thick, all other doors in the building are to be two inches thick, made with four panels each, hung with two four inch butt hinges, and fastened with mortice locks and knobs, to cost $2.50 each, and with catches, bolts, mineral knobs, bronze trimmings, and small duplicate keys. The outside doors are to be fastened with lever locks of the best quality, with mineral knobs and small duplicate keys. The privy doors are to be two feet by six feet one and one half inches thick, four paneled, hung with iron butt hinges, fastened with good knob locks, having duplicate small keys; they are to have two inch rebated and beaded frames, hard pine thresholds, and architraves, as described for the windows, with plinths. Properly hang the outside doors to three inch Southern pine plank frames, properly dogged to the threshold and wall.

Stairs.

The several flights of stairs are to be square frames, with four deep plank stringers; they are to be finished with hard pine risers one inch thick, and treads one and one-fourth inches thick, with moulded nosings. The cellar stairs are to be finished with plain pine risers and treads, and close partitions one and one-half inches thick, matched and planed. There is to be a neat flight of portable steps to ascend to the attic and observatory, and to the roof scuttle, which is to be made and hung complete. All the flights are to have cherry wood hand rail, moulded, three by two and three-fourth inches; turned cherry wood posts, five inches in diameter, at the head and foot and each landing of the flights, and hard pine balusters, one and one-fourth inches diameter, three to each stair tread; the top of the rail is to be three feet above the nosing of the stair tread; the whole to be made and finished in a perfect manner. All the well rooms are to be properly cased and finished.

Skirting

The rooms, closets, entries, and stairways, are to be skirted up as high as the window stools, in the respective stories, with narrow, beaded, matched lining, guaged to a width not exceeding seven inches, and the joints to butt even in every case; cap the same to correspond with the window stools; the lining is to be of clear white pine. One side of the wall of each room is to be fitted for the slates with frames, as directed.

Floorings.

The platforms are to be furred up, as shown by the drawing, and the stairways, platforms, and privies are to be boarded, and the several floorings to be laid with narrow hard pine clear boards, perfectly jointed and thoroughly nailed. The strips are to be guaged to a width respectively, and the joints broken at least three feet, and in no case are strips of a different width to butt on to each other. The entry and privy floors are all to be of hard pine.

Cabinets, &c.

There is to be a cabinet at the wall end of each platform, with shelves and small closets below, and a sash door. There are to be sixty-five clothes hooks hung on strips of pine, as directed, to each room. There are to be two umbrella stands in each entry. To be six sinks placed where directed. To be four coal bins, and two closets for kindlings, in the cellar. Finish the privy seats as directed, complete in every particular. Put up three bells where directed, with "pulls" and tubes complete.

Painting and Glazing.

Oil all the hard wood finish, except floorings. All the outside wood work is to be prepared and painted in imitation of free stone. The outside doors are to be painted bronze. The blinds are to be painted, four coats of Paris green, and varnished. The rest of the inside finish is to be primed, painted, and grained, in imitation of oak, maple, or other color, as directed by the committee, and varnished twice. Paint all the iron work, three coats best black and one coat varnish. All the sashes are to be glazed with the very best quality of German glass, of double thickness, and finish the same complete in every particular, with the sizes of glass as marked upon plans.

Memorandum.

All the timber and lumber is to well seasoned, and all that is in sight is to be entirely free from sap, shakes, and large knots; the finish stock of every kind must be perfectly kiln dried; the labor is to be done in the most faithful manner.

PUTNAM FREE SCHOOL, NEWBURYPORT, MASS.

PLANS AND DESCRIPTION OF THE PUTNAM FREE SCHOOL-HOUSE, NEWBURYPORT, MASS.

We are indebted to W. H. Wells, Esq., the gentleman who has been selected as Principal of the Putnam Free School, and to whom the work of organizing this important institution has been committed, for the following plans and description.

The Putnam Free School was founded by Mr. Oliver Putnam, a native of Newbury. It has a permanent fund of fifty thousand dollars, besides the amount invested in the school-house and its appurtenances.

The number of pupils to be admitted at the opening of the school (April, 1848,) is limited by the Trustees to 80. No pupil can be received under twelve years of age, nor for less time than one year.

The object of the Institution is to lead pupils through an extended course of English study. It is open to students from any portion of the country, who are prepared to meet the requirements for admission. No charge is made for tuition.

This building is situated on High street, directly opposite the Common or Mall. It is constructed of brick, with corners, door-sills, underpinning, steps, etc., of freestone. It is two stories in height, exclusive of a basement story, 85½ feet in length, and 52½ in breadth.

The upper story is divided into two principal school-rooms, each 49½ feet by 40½. There is also a small room in this story for the use of the Principal. The lower story contains a hall for lectures and other general exercises, and four recitation rooms. The hall is 44 feet by 48½. Two of the recitation rooms are 14 feet by 17, and two are 11 by 20.

Each of the principal school-rooms is furnished with 64 single seats and desks, besides recitation chairs, settees, etc. The desks are made of cherry; and both the desks and the chairs are supported by iron castings, screwed firmly to the floor. In form and construction, they are similar to Kimball's "Improved School Chairs and Desks."

The central aisles are two feet and eight inches in width; the side aisles, four feet and four inches; and the remaining aisles, two feet.

The building is warmed by two furnaces. It is ventilated by six flues from the hall on the lower floor, six from each of the school-rooms on the second floor, and one from each of the recitation rooms. Each of these flues has two registers; one near the floor, and the other near the ceiling. The two principal school-rooms are furnished with double windows.

The institution is provided with ample play-grounds and garden plots, back of the building and at the ends. It has also a bell weighing 340 lbs.

The first appropriation of the Trustees for the purchase of apparatus, is one thousand dollars. Other appropriations will probably be made, as the wants of the school may require. In addition to the apparatus procured by the Trustees, the institution is to have the use of an achromatic telescope, which will cost between three and four hundred dollars.

The cost of the building and ground, with the various appurtenances, exclusive of apparatus, has amounted to twenty-six thousand dollars.

The accompanying plans give a correct representation of the arrangements on the two principal floors.

The building was erected after designs and specifications by Mr. Bryant, Architect, Boston.

PUTNAM FREE SCHOOL-HOUSE.—LOWER STORY

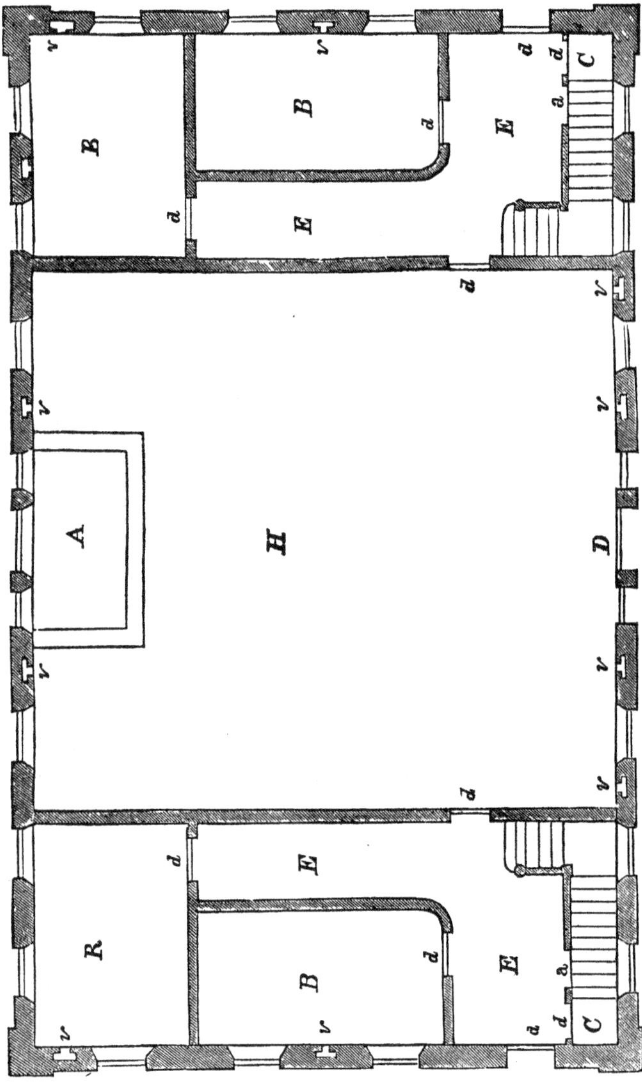

H—Hall for lectures and other general exercises, 44 feet by 48½. A—Raised platform for desk. D—Front door. (The portico in front does not appear in the plate.) B, B—Recitation rooms, 11 feet by 20. R, R—Recitation rooms, 14 feet by 17. E, E, E, E—Entries. C, C—Wash closets, under the stairs. a, a—Doors leading to the basement story. d, d, d, d, d, d, d, d, d, d—Doors. v, v, v, v, v, v, v, v, v, v.—Ventilating flues.

PUTNAM FREE SCHOOL-HOUSE.—UPPER STORY.

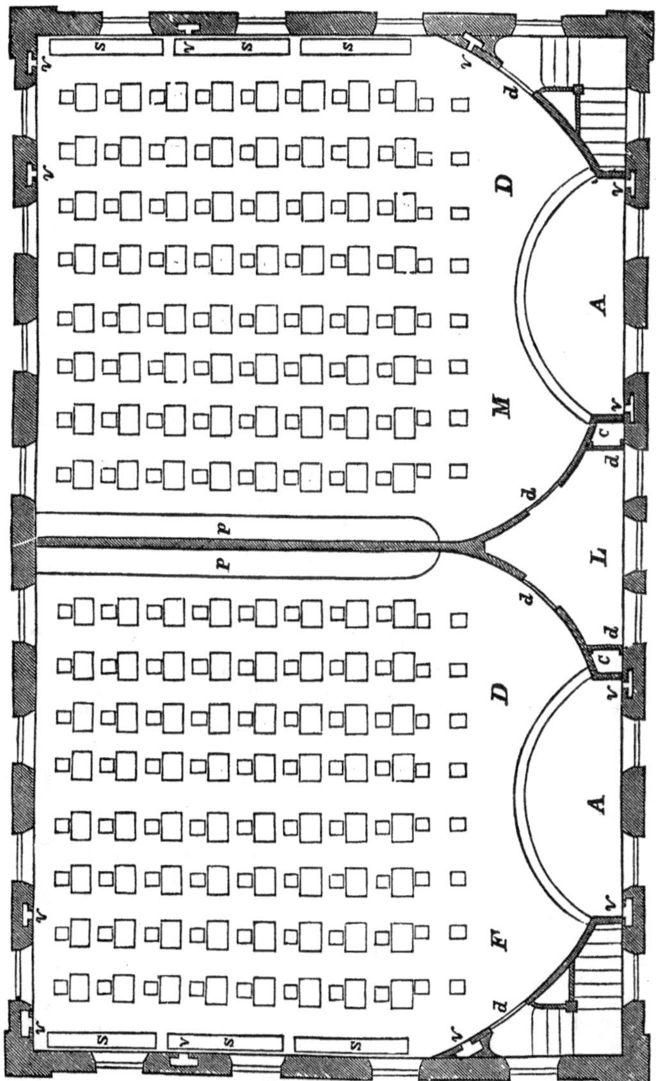

M, D—Room for Male Department. F, D—Room for Female Department. A, A—Raised platforms for teachers' desks. L—Principal's room. C, C—Closets. p, p—Raised platforms under the black-boards. s, s, s, s, s, s—Settees d, d, d, d, d, d—Doors. v, v, v, v, v, v, v, v, v, v, v, v—Ventilating flues

Plan, &c., of East School, Salem, Mass.

The lot on which the house stands extends from Essex street to Bath street.—There is a sufficient passage-way on each side of the house, and access from each street. The north end faces the common, which affords the most ample play-ground, always open.

The exterior dimensions of the building are 136 by 50 ft. The school-rooms are 65 by 36 ft. and 15 ft. high, each: the space in front of the desks, 65 by 4 ft. 6 inches; the space occupied by the desks, 59 by 25 ft.; the space in rear of the desks, 65 by 6 ft. 6 inches; the floor of which is raised 8 inches above the floor of the rooms; the side aisles are 3 ft., and all the other aisles 18 inches in width.

The desks are so placed that the scholars sit with their faces towards the partition which separates the school-room from the recitation rooms, the light being thus admitted in their rear and on one side.

The desks are 4 ft in length, and of four sizes in width, the two front ranges being 16 inches, the two next 15, the two next 14, and the two next 13. The desks are also of four sizes in height; the two front ranges being, on the lower side, 27 inches, the two next 26, the two next 25, the two next 24.

The desks in each school-room are placed in ranges, each range containing eleven desks, and each desk being fitted for two scholars; so that 176 scholars may be received in each department, or 352 in the whole school. The desks are constructed like tables, with turned legs, narrow rails, inclined top and a shelf beneath. The legs and rails are of birch, stained and varnished, and the tops of cherry, oiled and varnished. The legs are secured in the floor by tenons. The tables of the teachers are constructed and finished like the desks of the scholars.

The chairs are also of four sizes; those in the two front ranges being 12 by 12½ inches in the seat, (i. e. extreme width, the sides being of the usual shape of chairs,) and 16 inches in height, and those in the succeeding ranges being reduced in height in proportion to the desks, and also varying proportionally in the dimensions of the seats.

The chairs are constructed with seats of bass wood, and cherry backs; the seats and backs hollowed, and the seats resting on wooden pedestals, secured to the floor by tenons and screws.

Upon the front edge of the raised platform, in the rear of the desks, settees are placed, which are of the same length as the desks, and are placed in corresponding positions, with intervening spaces in continuation of the aisles. The settees are placed with the back towards the desks, and are designed exclusively for the use of classes attending reviews before the principals. The settees in width and height correspond to the largest size of chairs, and are constructed of the same materials, and finished in the same style.

In the center and at the extremities of the range of settees, are placed tables, (of 4 by 2 ft. 6 inches, oval shape,) which are occupied by the assistants, during general exercises, when the station of the principal is in front of the desks, the middle one being used by the principal when attending reviews.

Each recitation room (18 by 10 ft.) is appropriated to a single course of study, as marked upon the plan, and is therefore used exclusively by one assistant. Three sides of the room are appropriated to seats, being lined with cherry wood, (oiled and varnished) to a height reaching above the heads of the scholars. The lining is projected at the bottom, so as to furnish inclined backs to the seats, which are constructed of cherry wood, 13 inches in width, 2 inches thick, with hollowed top and rounded edge, supported on turned legs, the height being 15¼ inches from the top of the seat to the floor. The fourth side of the room, opposite the window, is occupied by a blackboard of 3 ft. in width, which extends across the space upon each side of the door.

All the spaces between the doors and windows upon the four sides of the school-rooms are occupied by blackboards. In the spaces between the windows upon the rear, recesses have been constructed, which are fitted with book-shelves, and are closed by means of covers in front, which are raised and lowered by weights and pulleys. These covers are blackboards, and are so finished as to represent sunken panels. Drawers are constructed beneath the blackboards to receive the sponges, chalk, &c.

Circular ventilators are placed in the ceiling of each school-room and recitation room ; three in each school-room of 3 ft. in diameter, and one in each recitation room of 2 ft. in diameter. These ventilators are solid covers of wood, hung with hinges, over apertures of corresponding size, and raised or lowered by means of cords passing over pulleys, through the ceiling into the room below, the cords terminating in loops, which are fastened to hooks in the side of the room. When the ventilators are raised, the impure air escapes into the garret, the ventilation of which is also provided for by means of the circular windows in the gable ends, which turn on pivots in the center, and are opened or shut by cords passing over pulleys in the same manner as the ventilators.

Each school-room is warmed by a furnace, placed directly under the center of the space in front of the desks, the hot air ascending through a circular aperture of 2 ft. in diameter, which is represented upon the plan. The smoke-pipe, (of galvanized iron) is conducted upward through the center of this aperture, and thence, after passing a considerable distance into the school-room, through one of the recitation rooms into the chimney, which is built in the center of the front wall. The recitation rooms are warmed by means of apertures at the top and bottom respectively of the partitions which separate them from the school-rooms, which being open together, secure a rapid equalization of temperature in all the rooms. These apertures are fitted to be closed, with revolving shutters above, and shutters hung on hinges below.

In the partition wall between the school-rooms, is a clock having two faces, and thus indicating the hour to the occupants in each room. The clock strikes at the end of each half hour. In the ante-rooms, (marked F, F, on the plan Fig. 1) are hooks for caps, overcoats, &c. In each of these rooms, also, there is a pump and sink.

In the *lower story*, there are two primary school-rooms 36½ ft. by 24½ ft., each seating 60 children. Each child has a chair firmly fixed to the floor, but no desk. In the rear there is an appropriate shelf for books, for each pupil, numbered to correspond with the number on the chair. In front of the school, there is a blackboard occupying the distance between the doors, and a desk, at which the several classes stand in succession, and copy appropriate exercises on the slate from the blackboard.

For this school-house, with all its completeness of arrangements and regulations, the city of Salem is indebted mainly to the indefatigable exertions of the late Mayor, the Hon. Stephen C. Phillips. During the three years of his administration, every school-house was repaired or rebuilt, and all the schools brought under an admirable system. On leaving his office, in 1842, he gave to the city for school purposes, his salary for three years, amounting to $2,400, which has been applied to repairing and refurnishing the High School building, which is now a monument of his taste and munificence.

The High School, and one of the new primary schools, are furnished with "Kimball's Improved School Chair," which for strength, comfort, and style of finish, is superior to any other now before the public.

High School Chair.

Primary School Chair.

FIGURE 1 EAST SCHOOLHOUSE, SALEM. *First Story.* [Scale 1-20 inch to a foot.]

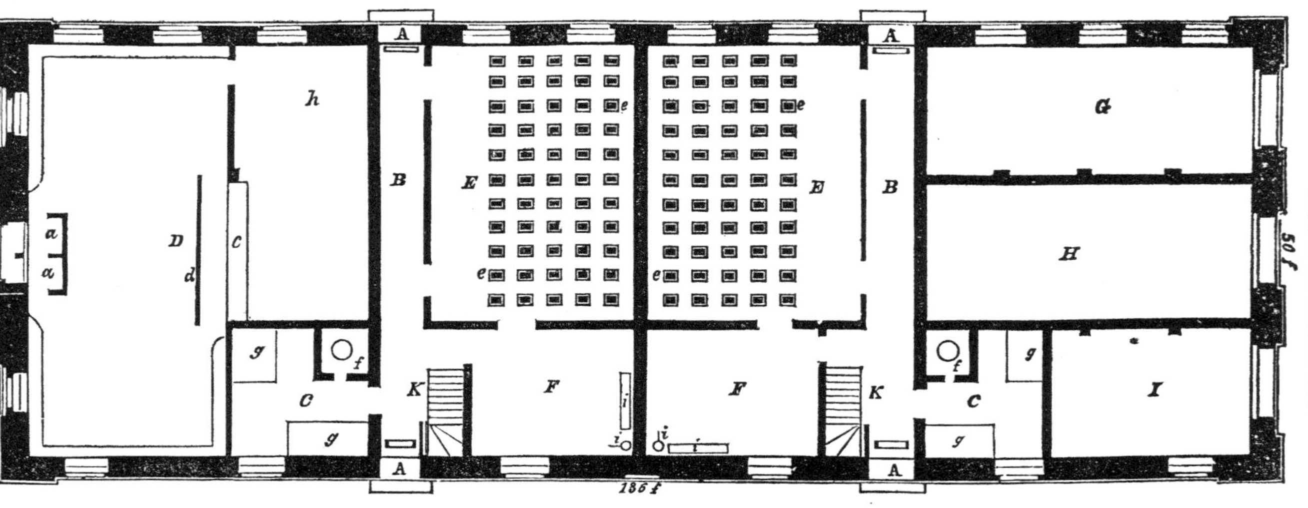

A, A, A, A—School entrances.
B, B—Passages, 5 feet wide.
C, C—Furnace and fuel rooms, 15 by 13 feet.
E, E—Primary schools, 36.6 by 24.3 feet.
e e—Seats in primary schoolrooms.

F, F—Ante-rooms, 15 by 19 feet.
K, K—Stairs to second story.
f, f—Furnaces.
g, g—Fuel and ash bins.
i, i, i, i—Pumps and sinks.

The other apartments in the lower story are occupied for various city purposes, which it is unnecessary here to specify.

FIGURE 2. EAST SCHOOLHOUSE, SALEM. *Second Story.* [Scale, 1-20 inch to a foot

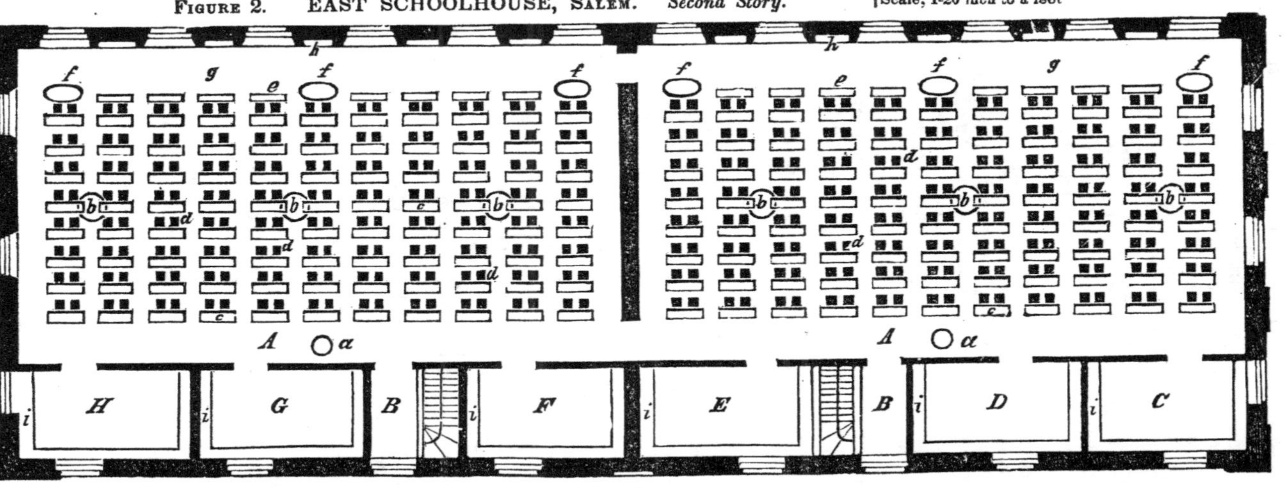

A, A—Schoolrooms, 65 by 36 feet each.
B, B—Entries and stairs from the first story.
C—Recitation room for reading, first course, 17 by 10 feet.
D— " " " grammar, " 18 by 10 "
E— " " " reading, second course, 19 by 10 feet.
F— " " " arithmetic, " 19 by 10 "
G— " " " geography, 18 by 10 feet.
H– ' " " arithmetic, first course, 17 by 10 feet

a, a—Hot air entrances.
b, b, &c.—Ventilators, 3 feet diameter, in the upper ceilings of the rooms.
c, c—Desks.
d, d—Seats.
e, e—Settees.
f, f, &c.—Tables for teachers.
g, g—Platform, raised 8 inches above floor of rooms
h, h—Recesses, containing books.
i, i—Seats occupying three sides of recitation rooms

Description of Latin and English High Schools, Salem.

The interior of this building is fitted up in a style of ornamental and useful elegance which has no parrallel in this country.

The Latin School is believed to be the first Free School established in the United States, and probably in the world, where *every person* within certain geographical limits, and possessing certain requisites of study, has an equal right of admission, free of cost. It was founded in 1637, and has continued without interruption, giving a thorough preparation to students for college, to the present day. The English High School was established in 1827.

The walls of the Latin Grammar School are enriched and adorned with inscriptions in the Greek and Latin language and character. These are not merely apothegms of wisdom, but mementoes of duty; they are fitted to inspire the pupils with noble sentiments, and are the appropriate "*Genius of the Place.*"

The interior of the English High School is adorned in a manner no less appropriate and useful.

In the center of the ceiling is the circle of the zodiac, 29 feet in diameter. The ventilator, 3½ feet in diameter, represents the sun, the spots being designated upon the nucleus in conformity to the latest telescopic observation. The divergence of the solar rays is also fully exhibited. The earth is represented in four different positions, indicating the four seasons. The moon also is described in its orbit, and its position so varied as to exhibit its four principal changes. The globular figure of the earth is clearly shown, and lines are inscribed upon it representing the equator, tropics, and polar circles. The hour lines are also marked and numbered. The border of the circle represents upon its outer edge the signs of the zodiac, with their names, and within, the names of the months. The signs are divided into degrees, and the months into days, both of which are numbered. The thirty-two points of the compass are marked upon the inner edge, the true north and magnetic north both correctly indicated,—the variation of the needle having been ascertained by a recent series of observations.

The circle of the zodiac, as thus described, being enclosed within a square panel, the exterior spaces in the four angles are filled up as follows:

The western angle exhibits the planet Saturn, with his rings and belts, as seen through a telescope, and his true size in proportion to the sun, supposing the circle of the zodiac to represent the size of the sun. The eastern angle exhibits Jupiter, with his belts, of a size similarly proportionate. The other primary planets and the moon are described according to their relative sizes, in the southern angle. In the northern angle is a succession of figures, designed to represent the varying apparent size of the sun, as seen from the different planets. In the ceiling there are also two oblong panels, one towards the western, the other towards the eastern extremity. The western panel contains a diagram, which illustrates, by their relative position, the distance of the several planets, primary and secondary, from the sun, which is placed at one end of the panel. The several planets are designated by their signs, and the figures, placed opposite to each, show how many millions of miles it is distant from the sun. The satellites of the Earth, Jupiter, Saturn, and Herschel, are described as revolving in their orbits around their respective primaries. The eastern panel contains a diagram, which illustrates the theory of the solar and lunar eclipses. The moon is represented in different parts of the earth's shadow, and also directly between the earth and the sun.

Upon the four sides of the room, in the space above the windows and doors, eight panels are described, containing as many diagrams, which illustrate successively the following subjects:—

1. The different phases of the moon. 2. The apparent, direct, and retro grade motions of Mercury and Venus. 3. The moon's parallax. 4. The commencement, progress, and termination of a solar eclipse. 5. The diminution of the intensity of light, and the force of attraction in proportion to the increase of the squares of distance. 6. The transit of Venus over the sun's disc. 7. The refraction of the rays of light by the atmosphere, causing the sun, or other celestial bodies, to appear above the horizon when actu-

ally below it. 8. The theory of the tides, giving distinct views of the full and neap tide, as caused by the change of position and the relative attraction of the sun and moon.

The two small panels over the entrance doors represent, respectively, the remarkable comets of 1680 and 1811, and the theory of cometary motion as described in the plates attached to Blunt's "Beauty of the Heavens."

The diagram in the large panel upon the north side of the recitation platform represents the relative height of the principal mountains and the relative length of the principal rivers on the globe. The mountains and rivers are all numbered, and scales of distance are attached, by which the heights and lengths can be readily ascertained. The relative elevation of particular countries, cities and other prominent places, the limits of perpetual snow, of various kinds of vegetation, &c., are distinctly exhibited. This diagram is a copy of that contained in Tanner's Atlas.

The diagram in the corresponding panel on the south side of the recitation platform represents a geological section, the various strata being systematically arranged and explained by an index.

The space between the windows upon the north and south sides of the room are occupied by inscriptions in which the diameter, hourly motion, sidereal period, and diurnal rotation of the several primary planets and the earth's moon, are separately stated, according to calculations furnished for the purpose by Professor Peirce, of Cambridge. The hourly motion and sidereal period of the four asteroids are also stated in corresponding inscriptions upon the western side. The diameter and rotation of the sun are inscribed upon the edge of the circular recess beneath the ventilator.

Over the frontispiece, which surmounts the recess upon the teacher's rostrum, is a beautifully executed scroll bearing the inscription,

"ORDER IS HEAVEN'S FIRST LAW."

This motto may be regarded as equally appropriate, whether viewed as explanatory of the celestial phenomena which are figured upon the walls, or as suggesting the principle which should guide the operations of the school.

The clock is placed within the recess, upon the wall of which the course of studies prescribed for the school, and arranged into two divisions, is conspicuously inscribed.

Many of the charity schools of Holland contain paintings of no inconsiderable excellence and value. In Germany, where every thing, (excepting war and military affairs,) is conducted on an inexpensive scale, the walls of the school-rooms were often adorned with cheap engravings and lithographs, of distinguished men, of birds, beasts, and fishes;—and, in many of them, a cabinet of natural history had been commenced. And throughout all Prussia and Saxony, a most delightful impression was left upon my mind by the character of the persons whose portraits were thus displayed. Almost without exception, they were likenesses of good men rather than of great ones,—frequently of distinguished educationists and benefactors of the young, whose countenances were radiant with the light of benevolence, and the very sight of which was a moral lesson to the susceptible hearts of children.

In the new building for the "poor school" at Leipsic, there is a large hall in which the children all assemble in the morning for devotional purposes. Over the teacher's desk, or pulpit, is a painting of Christ in the act of blessing little children. The design is appropriate and beautiful. Several most forlorn-looking, half-naked children stand before him. He stretches out his arms over them, and blesses them. The mother stands by with an expression of rejoicing, such as only a mother can feel. The little children look lovingly up into the face of the Saviour. Others stand around, awaiting his benediction. In the back-ground are aged men, who gaze upon the spectacle with mingled love for the children and reverence for their benefactor. Hovering above is a group of angels, hallowing the scene with their presence.—*Mr Mann's Seventh Annual Report.*

Public School Society of New York.

Prior to 1805, the only schools in the city of New York which partook at all of the character of public schools, were one established by the "Female Association for the Relief of the Poor," in 1802, and those sustained by different religious denominations for the gratuitous education ot the children of their own members. These were few, feebly sustained, and the course of instruction altogether inadequate.

In April, 1805, on the petition of De Witt Clinton and other individuals, a "free school" was incorporated by the legislature for the education of children who did not belong to, and were not provided for by any religious society. This school was organized in May, 1806, and taught on the plan then recently originated by Joseph Lancaster.

In 1808, the institution was enlarged by the legislature under the name of the "Free School Society of the City of New-York," and the city corporation presented a site for a school-house, and entrusted to its keeping the education of the children of the alms-house.

In 1809, the first edifice was completed and dedicated to its future purposes in an address by De Witt Clinton, the president of the society.

In 1815, the society received its quota ($3,708) of the first apportionment of the State Fund for the support of Common Schools.

In 1821, a committee of the society were instructed to correspond with distinguished educators, in Europe and the United States, for information on the subject of schools, and especially the education of the poor. This step resulted in some modifications of the plans of the society, and the methods of instruction in the schools.

In 1828, the first primary school was opened in the Duane street building, on the plan of the infant schools, which had been introduced into the large cities of the United States, under voluntary efforts. The result was favorable. It drew off the younger scholars from the other schools in the same building, and facilitated the instruction and government in both classes of schools. This school was for a time under the joint management of the society and a committee of ladies from the infant school society. At this time, Mr. Samuel S. Seton was employed by the society as an agent to visit the families of the poor, to make known the benefits of the schools and secure the punctual attendance of delinquent scholars. This step led to a knowledge of various abuses, and the introduction of several improvements. Mr. Seton has since acted as the Agent of the Society, and in this capacity has given unity to all of the operations of the several committees of the Board.

In 1828–29, the schools of the public school society were placed more on the basis of "Common Schools"—open to all, not as a matter of charity, but of right, and supported in part like other great public interests, by a general tax. This tax was *one eightieth of one per cent.*, and was the first tax raised by the city of New York, for the support of Common Schools; the memorial by which the attention of the Common Council was called to the subject was signed principally by the wealthiest citizens.

In the winter of 1832 a large committee on the part of the society, was appointed to examine into the condition of the schools, and propose such modification and improvement, as might be considered judicious. To aid the committee with the experience of other cities, two of their number were deputed to visit Boston and examine the school system and schools of that city. This committee reported certain modifications, which were concurred in by the board. These modifications were the establishment of primary schools, under female teachers, for the elementary classes, with some simple apparatus for visible illustration; an extension of the studies in the upper public schools, so as to embrace astronomy, algebra, geometry, trigonometry, and book-keeping; an increase of the salaries of teachers, the substitution of assistant teachers for certain class recitations and reviews, and the opening of recitation rooms for this purpose; the more extended use of blackboard, maps, globes, and other apparatus; and the establishment of evening schools for apprentices, and such as leave school at an early age.

In 1834, owing to the increase of the primary schools, a school was opened for the benefit of those who were employed as monitors in that class of schools. This plan has been extended so as to embrace such pupils of the older class of the upper schools, as from their peculiar taste, industry and proficiency, could be recommended as monitors or teachers. While in these normal schools, they are denominated "cadets," and such as are properly qualified are promoted to the station of monitors, under pay, and so on to "passed monitors," from which class the assistant teachers are to be selected. These schools now embrace two hundred pupils, under the charge of nine teachers, and have already furnished the schools with a number of teachers.

In 1836, owing to a want of one or more high schools in the system, a number of scholarships in Columbia College and the University, with their preparatory schools, were opened by those having the management of these institutions, for such scholars of the public schools as were advanced to the limit of the instruction there provided. In 1841–2, similar privileges were opened in the Rutgers Female Institute, for a certain number of girls.

In 1842, an act passed the legislature which altered very essentially the system of public schools in the city of New York, by providing for the appointment of School Commissioners in the several wards, who together constitute a Board of Education.

In 1844, Mr. Josiah Holbrook's system of scientific exchanges and a plan of oral instruction in the natural sciences, were introduced into the schools of the Society. The teachers were authorized to allow the pupils to occupy a limited portion of time weekly in preparing specimens of writing, mapping and drawing, with a view to the exchanging of such specimens for those of other schools in this and other states. These exchanges of the results of mental and artistical labors on the part of the pupils, have excited a most healthful rivalry, greatly favorable to the development of their mental faculties, while its moral influences have been decidedly good. Not the least among its benefits has been the cultivating of a taste for the art of drawing, so necessary and useful a part of common school education, particularly in those pupils designed for mechanical pursuits. Connected with the operations here alluded to, was a plan of instruction by short oral lectures on the natural sciences, from objects collected and placed in the school cabinets by the pupils themselves, formed into associations or "school lyceums."

In 1847, the Free Academy was established by the Board, after an expression in its favor by a direct popular vote. Admission into the Academy is confined to those who have been pupils in the public schools. The range of instruction is equal, if not superior, to that of the best academies in the State.

In 1848, evening schools were established for such pupils as could not attend the public or ward schools by day.

In 1853, the schools and property of the Public School Society were transferred to the Board of Education, and the Society, after years of faithful, disinterested, and useful service, in building up an improved system of public instruction, was abolished.

Plan and Description of Public School, No. 17, New York.

The following plans and explanation of a "Public School" and a "Primary School" are copied from the "Thirty-ninth Annual Report of the Trustees of the Public School Society of New York." The plans after which the school-houses of this Society were originally constructed, as well as the methods of instruction pursued in their schools, were adopted from those recommended by Joseph Lancaster, and the British and Foreign School Society. These plans and methods have been from time to time essentially modified, until they can no longer be characterized as Lancasterian or Monitorial, but the plans and methods of the Public School Society of New York. There are two grades of schools, the higher called the Public Schools, and the lower, called the Public Primary Schools. Those schools of the primary grade, which are in the buildings appropriated to the higher schools, are designated Primary Departments, to distinguish them from the Primaries taught in separate buildings. The system of instruction pursued in the Primary Departments was originally the Infant School system, and still retains many of the methods of that system. The school-rooms were, therefore, constructed and furnished in reference to simultaneous exercises of the whole school, to oral instruction with visible illustrations, and to physical movements of various kinds.

Public School, No. 17, is in 13th Street, between the 7th and 8th Avenues, on the centre of a lot of ground 100 feet front and rear, by 103½ feet deep. The main building is 42 feet front, and 80 feet deep; the stair building (in the rear,) is 21 by 14 feet. The main building is 49 feet high, from the pavement to the eaves. The first story of the front of the main building is of brown stone, polished, as is also the bases and caps of the pilasters. The walls are all of brick (including the front fences); the front being of (what are called) Philadelphia pressed bricks; the front cornice is of wood, and painted white.

The windows of the lower story, contain each 30, and the two upper stories each 40 panes of glass, 12 by 10 inches: the sashes are all hung with weights and cords, so that they may be raised or lowered at pleasure.

The rooms are all wainscoted, as high as the window sills: the wainscoting, doors, and desks are all grained in imitation of oak: the doors, window casings, and sashes are painted white. The rooms are ventilated by means of six blinds, 2 by 3 feet, being placed in the ceiling between the timbers, and two or three bricks being left out opposite the blinds, in the outside walls.

The first story is 11 feet 6 inches high in the clear, and is occupied as a Primary Department, for both boys and girls, and contains seats for 150 children in the Front Room, (marked A on Fig. 1,) and 200 on the Gallery, (marked M on Fig. 1); making in all 350 seats in this department.

The second story is occupied as the Girls' department; the room is 15½ feet high in the clear, and contains seats for 252 scholars.

The third story is occupied as the Boys' department; the room is 16½ feet high in the clear, and contains seats for 252 scholars; making in all 854 seats in the building, exclusive of the seats in the recitation rooms.

The steps in the stair building, by which the scholars enter and retire from school, are of blue stone, 3 inches thick by 12 inches wide, and are expected to last as long as any part of the building. This method was adopted to avoid the necessity of putting in new steps every few years, (which has heretofore been necessary where wooden steps have been used,) and also to lessen the noise consequent on a great number of children going either up or down wooden steps, at the same time; thus far the experiment has succeeded admirably, and is now adopted for both Public and Primary Schools.

Fig 1. Ground plan of Primary Department, yards, &c.

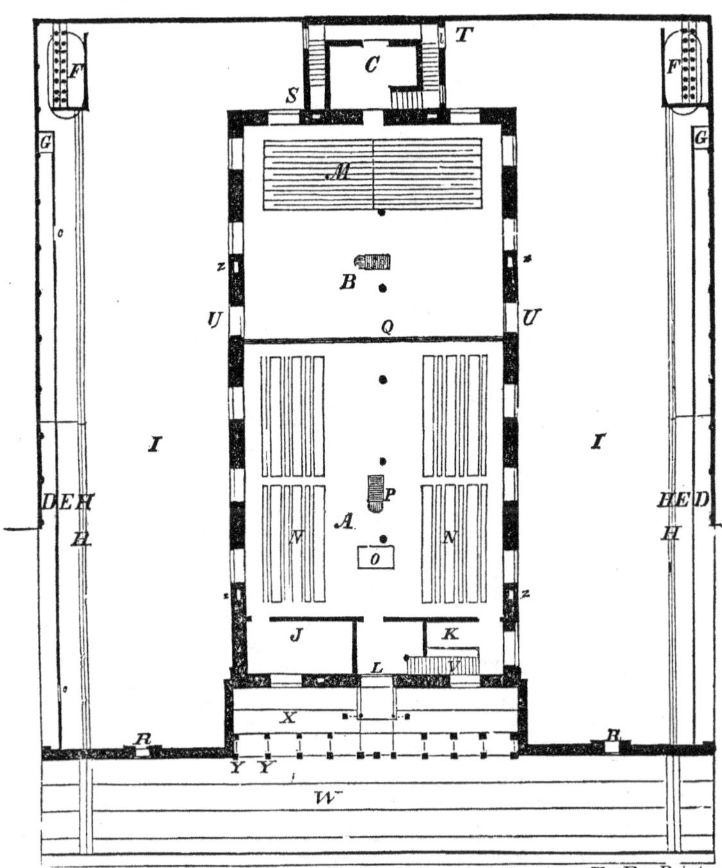

A—Primary School room 39 by 38 feet.
B—Infant do do 39 by 30 feet.
C—Room for brooms, pails, &c.
J—Boys' ward-robe, $16\frac{1}{2}$ by 8 feet.
K—Girls' do $12\frac{1}{2}$ by 8 feet.
M—Gallery, 32 by 11 feet—Seats for 200 children.
N, N—Desks, each $16\frac{1}{2}$ feet long.
O—Teachers' table.
L—Main entrance.
R, R—Entrance to the yard.
U, U do to Primary department.
V—Stairs to Girls' and Boys' do.
S—Scholars' entrance—Boys' do.
T do do Girls' do.
Q—Sliding doors—28 by $9\frac{1}{2}$ feet.
P, P—Stoves.
Z, Z—Flues for stove pipes.
I, I—Play ground, 102 by 26 feet; paved with brick. F, F—Privies, 12 by 8 feet. G, G—Boxes for sand—3 by $2\frac{1}{2}$ feet.
D, D—Wood-houses—83 by $2\frac{1}{2}$ feet, and $6\frac{1}{2}$ feet high; the front of which is made of hemlock strips, 4 by 2 inches, set perpendicularly 2 inches apart, to al low a free circulation of air.
E, E—Roof of wood-houses—projecting $3\frac{1}{2}$ feet beyond the front of the houses; forming a shelter for the scholars in stormy weather.
H, H—Gutters of blue stone to conduct the waste water from the wood houses and yards to the street.
X—Court Yard—$8\frac{1}{2}$ wide; blue stone flagging. Y, Y—Stone foundation blocks, to which the iron railing in front is secured.

Fig. 2. Ground Plan of the Boy's Department, or third story.

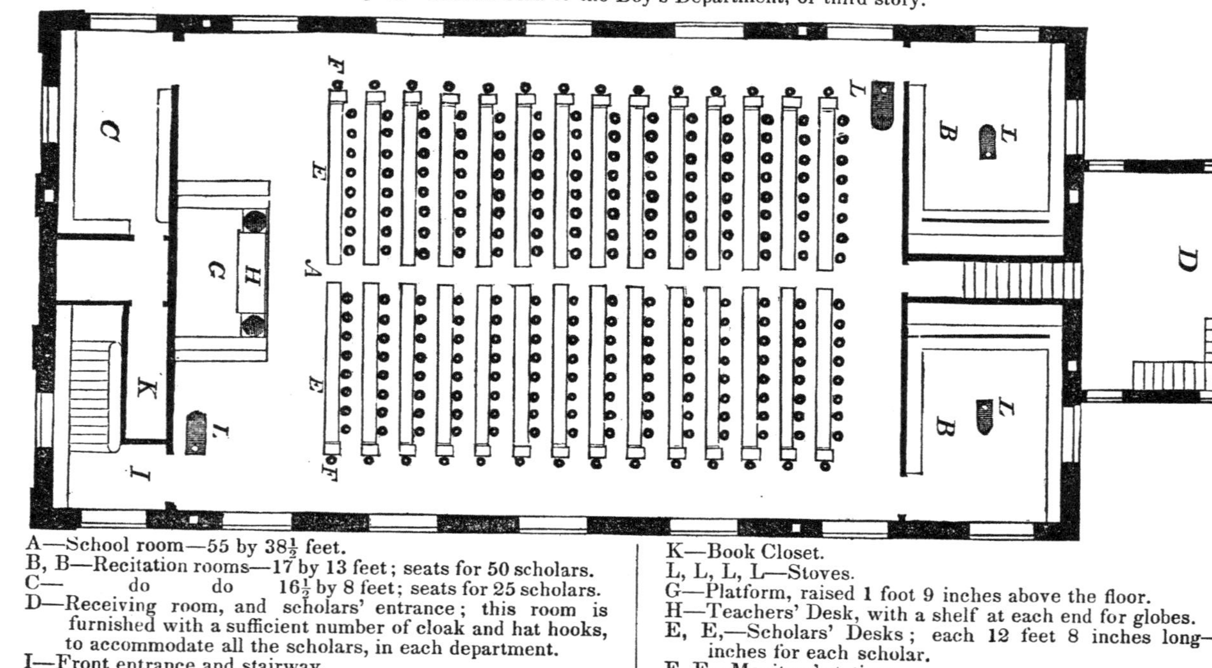

A—School room—55 by $38\frac{1}{2}$ feet.
B, B—Recitation rooms—17 by 13 feet; seats for 50 scholars.
C— do do $16\frac{1}{2}$ by 8 feet; seats for 25 scholars.
D—Receiving room, and scholars' entrance; this room is furnished with a sufficient number of cloak and hat hooks, to accommodate all the scholars, in each department.
I—Front entrance and stairway.
K—Book Closet.
L, L, L, L—Stoves.
G—Platform, raised 1 foot 9 inches above the floor.
H—Teachers' Desk, with a shelf at each end for globes.
E, E,—Scholars' Desks; each 12 feet 8 inches long—19 inches for each scholar.
F, F—Monitors' stations.

The front of the teachers' desk, toward the scholars, is formed by a blackboard 3 feet wide, and extending the whole length of the desk.

PLAN &c., OF PRIMARY SCHOOL, NEW YORK.

The main building is 25 feet front, by 62½ feet deep: the stair building is 27 feet by 11 feet 8 inches. The main building is placed 6 or 8 feet from the line of the street, according to the depth of the lot. The walls above the ground are built entirely of brick. The roof is of tin; and the gutters of copper. The lower doors and windows have iron bars inserted, for safety, and to admit a free circulation of air in the summer, but are closed with sashes in the winter.

Fig. 1. Ground plan of first story, or play-ground.

This story is 7½ feet in the clear, with a partition wall through the middle to give separate play-grounds for the boys' and girls' schools. This wall is 8 inches thick; and about 2½ feet of the upper part is open work for ventilation. C, C — Stairways. L, F — Places for pine (kindling) wood — under stairs. E.—Sand box for both departments. h, h—Piles of wood about 4½ feet high. I, I—Lines on which the scholars are marshaled, previous to entering school. l, l, l—Doors.

Fig. 2 and 3. Ground plan of boys' and girls' department, each 60 by 32.

D—Teachers' platform and table, (movable rollers.) d, d—Desks for scholars—the black dots are iron chairs. a—Cast iron lesson stands—on which two lesson boards are hung, to accommodate classes standing on the line b, b. H—Class Room. g, g, g—Flues, or chimnies, for stove pipes. f, f, f, &c.—Air flues, or recesses for ventilation, extending from the 2d story to the garret. C—Stove—the pipes extend from the stove to the front into the flue, and also to the rear.

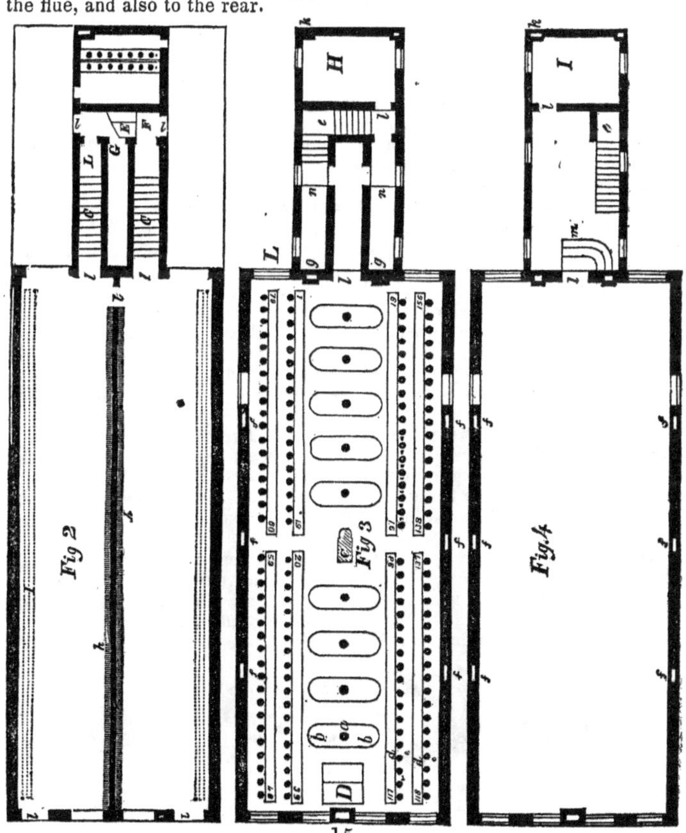

PLANS AND DESCRIPTION OF WARD SCHOOL-HOUSE No. 30, IN THE CITY OF NEW YORK.

Fig. 1. FRONT ELEVATION.

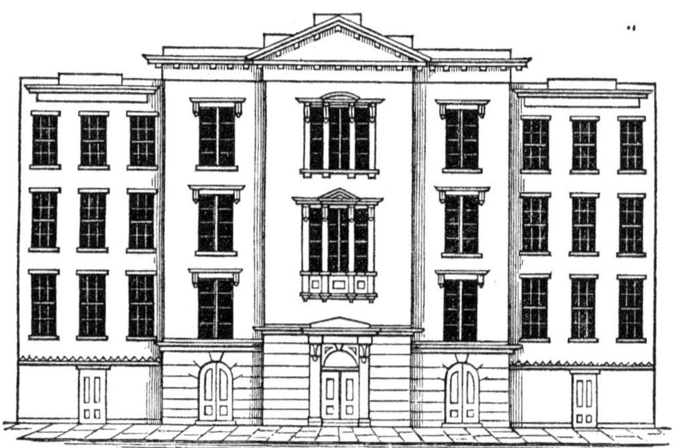

Ward School, No. 30, is located in the Sixteenth Ward of the City of New York, on the north side of Twenty-fourth Street, between the Seventh and Eighth Avenues. The school-house, represented in Figures 1, 2, 3, 4, and completed in 1852, has a front of 54 feet on the street, and is 95 feet deep, with side wings, each 18 by 25 feet. It was built after plans and specifications drawn by T. B. Jackson, Architect.

The basement of the main building in front is built of Connecticut brown stone, as are also the windows and door trimmings, finely cut and polished. The front and side of the main building, as well as the front of the wings, are built with smooth brick, painted and sanded brown-stone color.

The basement story is 8 feet high in the clear, and except such portions as are used for class-rooms, stairs, water-closets, &c., is flagged so as to afford a shelter for the pupils in inclement weather, and is divided by a wall to separate the sexes.

The building is thoroughly warmed by six of Culver's patent furnaces, and ventilated with flues in the walls, with openings at the floor and ceiling in each room.

The second and third stories are occupied respectively by the female and male departments of the upper school. The large rooms are used to assemble the whole school at the opening in the morning, and are so arranged that, by closing the sliding doors they can be used as separate rooms, which, together with the other class-rooms, afford ample accommodations for the several classes pursuing their different studies.

The croton water is brought into the basement and each story of the main building, and every convenience is provided for comfort and cleanliness.

The stair-cases afford ample egress, and are so constructed as to provide against all accidents, and the doors are hung so as to swing outwards.

The windows have inside folding blinds.

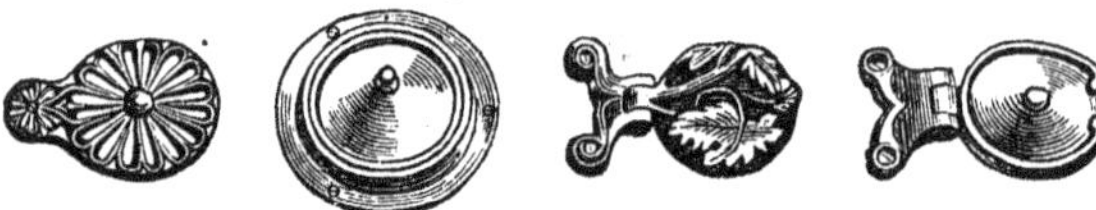

Fig. 2. PLAN OF BASEMENT.

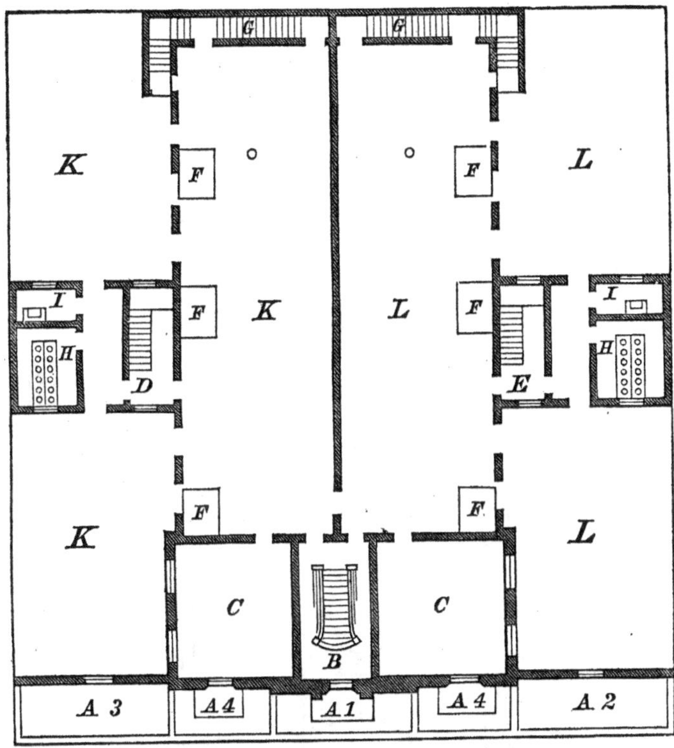

A 1—Entrance for teachers and visitors.

A 2—Entrance for girls.

A 3—Entrance for boys.

A 4—Entrance to rooms C.

B—Principal stair-case, constructed with one wide center flight, and two side flights leading to the top story.

C—Rooms which were intended as vestibules, but have been made into class-rooms, and fitted up with seats.

D—Boys' stairs.

E—Girls' stairs.

F—Culver's furnaces for heating the building.

G—Stairs to primary department for children in the gallery.

H—Children's water-closets.

I—Teacher's water-closets.

K—Boys' play-ground.

L—Girls' play-ground.

The first floor, divided by folding doors into two large rooms and four class-rooms, are occupied by the primary department.

Fig. 3. Plan of First Story.

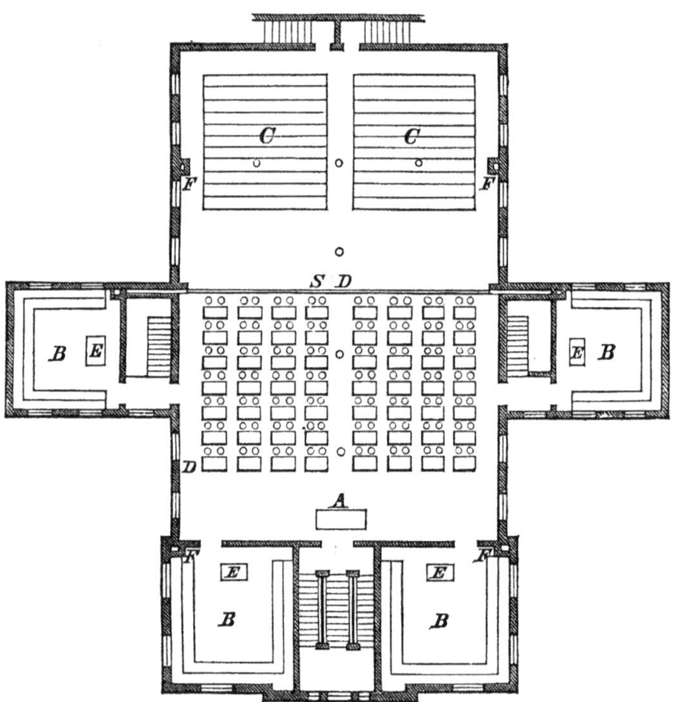

A—Principal's desk.
B—Class-rooms, fitted up with a platform 2 feet 6 inches wide, running round three sides of the room, and two rows of benches.

C—Galleries for small children.
D—Desks in principal school-room.
E—Teacher's tables in class-rooms.
F—Furnace registers for warm air.

No. 5. Ross' Primary Double Desk and Chairs.

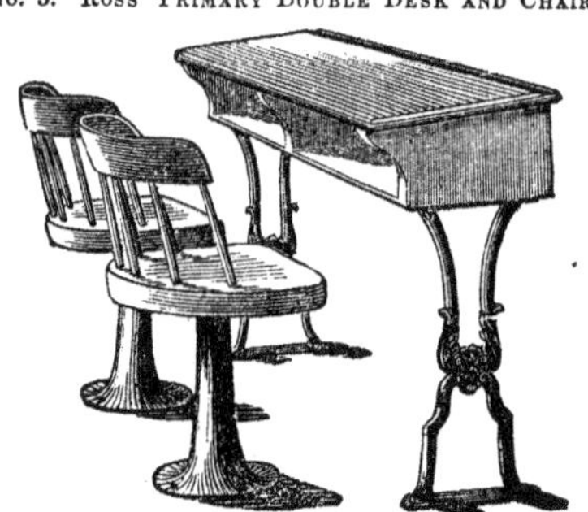

Fig. 4. Plan of Second and Third Story.

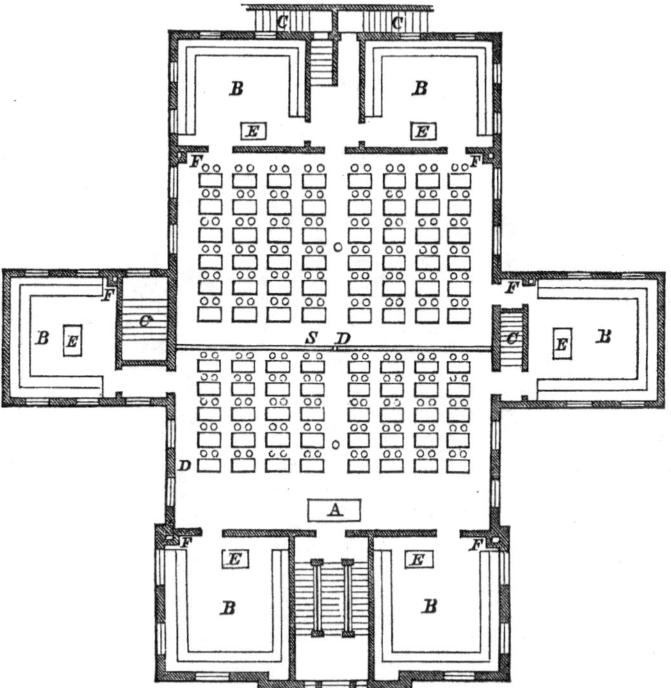

A—Principal's desk. B—Class-rooms, fitted up in the same manner as described in the primary department. C—Stairs to yards. D—Desks in principal school-rooms. E—Teacher's tables in class-rooms. F—Furnace registers, where the warm air is admitted in the rooms.

No. 6. Ross' Primary Double Desk and Chair.

WARD SCHOOL Nº 29.

Plans and Description of Ward School, No. 29, in the City of New York.

Ward School, No. 29, is situated on the southeast corner of North Moore and Varick Streets, in the Fifth Ward of the City of New York. The school-house, represented in Figures 1, 2, 3, was erected in 1852, after designs and specifications by T. B. Jackson, Esq., Architect, New York, to accommodate a primary department of 500 pupils, between the ages of four and eight years; and two departments, one for 500 girls, between the ages of eight and fourteen, and one for the same number of boys, of the same age. The girls enter on North Moore Street, and the boys on Varick Street.

The new building has a front on North Moore Street of 75 feet, and on Varick Street of 87 feet. The basement, ante-bases, and window trimmings are of Connecticut free-stone, cut in the finest manner; and the brickwork is painted and sanded brown-stone color.

The basement, the floor of which is one foot above the level of the side walk, is ten feet high in the clear, and, except such portions as are used for furnaces, committee room, library, &c., is appropriated to a play-ground, for the pupils, and is divided by a wall to separate the sexes, affording a shelter in unclouded weather.

The first floor is 14 feet high in the clear, and is fitted up into a large school-room, 70 feet by 76, with infant class-rooms, for the primary department, and will accommodate over 500 pupils.

The second and third stories, each 14 feet high, are divided in a similar manner, the former to accommodate 300 girls, and the latter 300 boys. One of the class-rooms on each floor is fitted up with seats and desks, to accommodate an advanced class of pupils.

The building is warmed by three of Culver's Furnaces, placed in the basement; and each school-room and class-room is ventilated by one or more flues, carried up in the walls, with openings at the floor and ceilings, controlled by registers, into which the vitiated air escapes. These flues discharge into two larger flues in the attic, which are carried above the roof, and are surmounted by Emerson's Ejectors.

The furniture throughout all the rooms, was manufactured by Joseph L. Ross, of Boston. The desks and seats in the primary department are of four different sizes, and are made after the pattern represented in Figs. 6 and 7, on page 267. The desks and chairs in the two upper rooms, (the wood-work of cherry, and the standards of cast-iron,) are of six different sizes, and are similar to those reoresented in Fig. 6, on page 237.

Each desk has a cast-iron box, with a lid to receive a glass ink-well.

 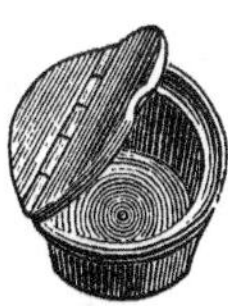 

The Croton water is brought into each story; and in the basement every convenience for cleanly habits are provided, such as scrapers, mats, washbasins, towels, brooms, &c.

There are three stair-cases, and each is so constructed as to afford ample egress, and to provide against all accidents; and the doors are hung so as to swing outwards.

The windows are furnished with inside blinds, having revolving slats, so that the amount of light can be easily regulated.

Fig. 2. Basement.

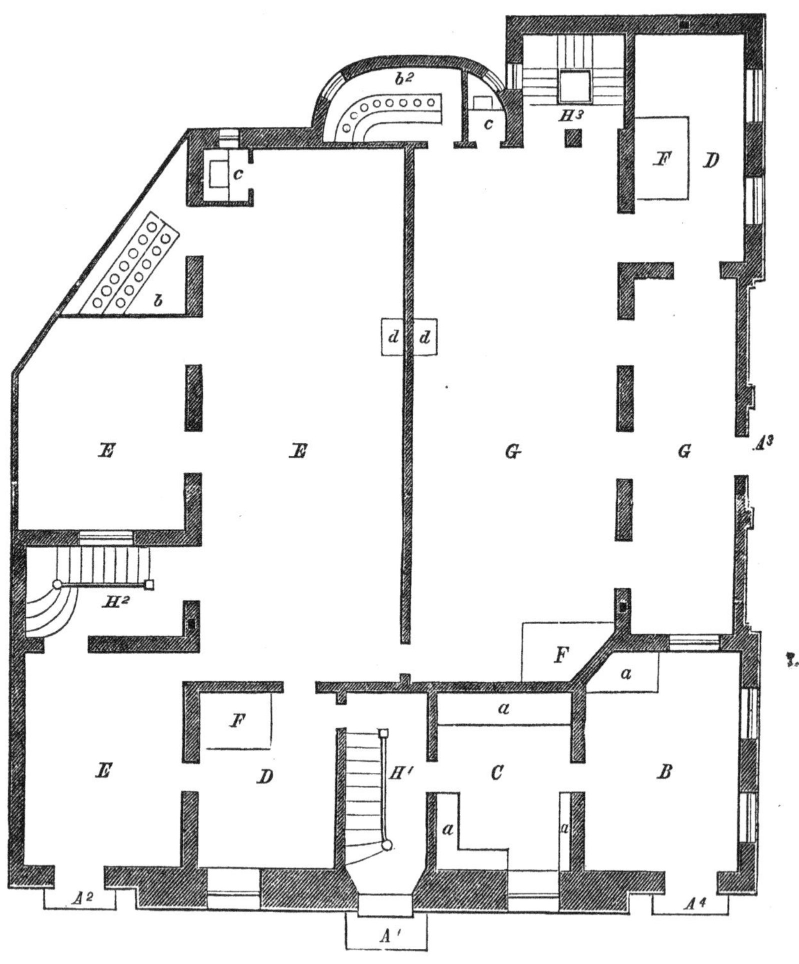

A, 1—Teachers and visitors' entrance.
A, 2—Girls' entrance.
A, 3—Boys' entrance.
B—Committee room.
C—Library.
D—Furnace rooms.
E—Girls' vestibule and play-ground.
F—Culver's furnaces.
G—Boys' play-ground.
H, 1—Teachers' and visitors' stair-case.
H, 2—Girls' stair-case.
H, 3—Boys' stair-case.
a, a, a—Book-cases.
b, b—Water-closets.
C, C—Teachers' closets.
d, d—Croton water, with conveniences for drinking, and cleanliness.

The three stories of the building above the basement are each divided into one large school-room, and five recitation rooms.

Fig. 3. PRIMARY DEPARTMENT.

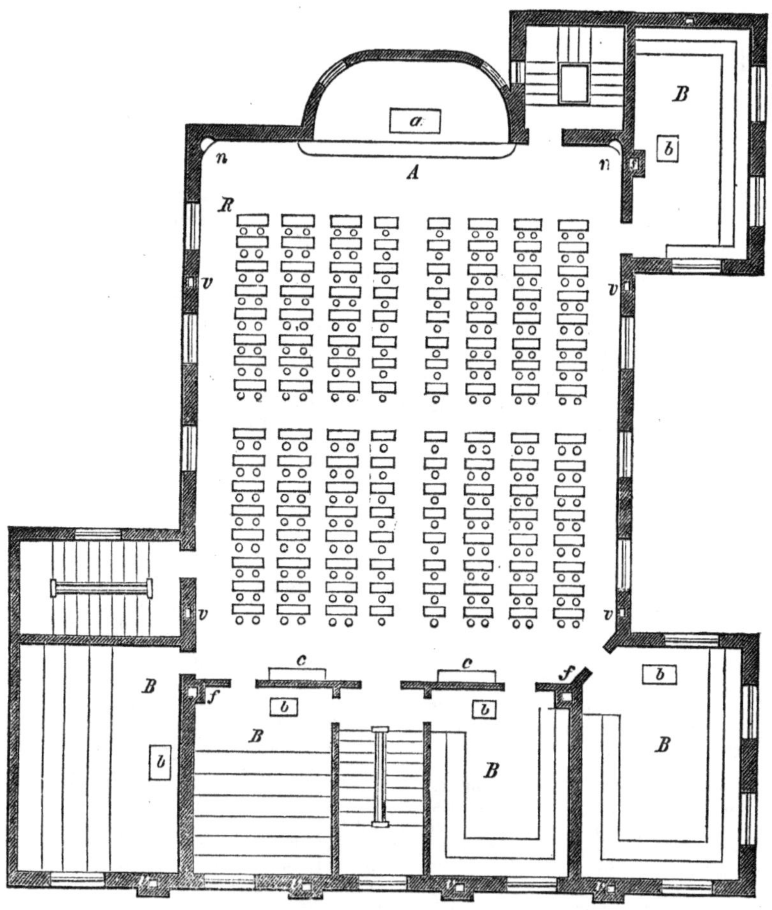

A—Large school-room, with Ross' desks.

B—Recitation or class-rooms, fitted up with platforms, and two rows of benches running round three sides of each room.

a—Principal's desk in the alcove, the floor of which is raised 16 inches above the floor of the school-room.

b, b—Teachers' tables in class-rooms.

c, c—Book-cases.

n, n—Niches for globes, busts, or statues.

f, f—Registers, supplying warm air from furnaces.

v, v—Ventilation flues.

The Female and Male Departments, fitted up in the same manner, with the exception of the N. W. class-rooms, which have desks to accommodate an advanced class.

The Free Academy of the city of New York was established by the Board of Education, in 1847, in pursuance of authority granted by the Legislature on the memorial of the Board, and on condition that the question of its establishment should be submitted to the people of the city, and a majority of the votes given should be in favor of the proposition. The question was so submitted on the first Monday of June, 1847, and 19,904 votes were given in favor of the same to 3,409 against. The act of the Legislature authorized the Board to erect a building at an expense of $50,000, and to raise by tax annually for its support, the sum of $20,000, exclusive of a proportion of the State Literature Fund, and any other means from other sources than those of taxation. Admission into the Academy is confined to those who have been pupils in the public schools of the city. The character and design of this institution may be gathered from the following extracts from the Memorial of the Board:—

"It cannot be denied that the unavoidable expense of a regular course of education at this time, is greater than can be borne by the heads of families in this city pursuing the various trades and occupations, whose business occupies the great mass of the people.

"If the number of highly educated men can, with a trivial addition to the public expense, be greatly multiplied; if these benefits can be rendered accessible to the great mass of young men who cannot now indulge the hope of enjoying them at all, if pecuniary inability to defray the present expenses of a collegiate education can cease to be a barrier to the acquisition of it, it is but reasonable to expect that in a brief period the number liberally educated in this city will be increased at least four-fold.

"One of the important objects designed to be secured by establishing a Free Academy, is to bring the advantages of the best education that any school in our country can give, within the reach of all the children of the city whose genius, capacity, and desire of attainment are such as to render it reasonably certain that they may be made, and by such means would become, eminently useful to society.

"The permanency of our free institutions, the future state of society, the extent to which the laws of the country will be regarded, and social quiet and order preserved, depend essentially upon the virtue and intelligence of the people.

"It is believed that a liberal education of the largest practicable number of the young men who may propose to seek the means of subsistence in agriculture, mechanical, or other productive occupations, would exercise a genial influence upon all the varied relations of social and political life: and that such an education would not tend to dissatisfy them with such pursuits.

"One object of the proposed Free Institution is, to create an additional interest in, and more completely popularize the Common Schools. It is believed that they will be regarded with additional favor, and attended with increased satisfaction, when the pupils and their parents feel that the children who have received their primary education in these schools, can be admitted to all the benefits and advantages furnished by the best endowed college in the state, without any expense whatever. It is believed that such an institution as the proposed Free Academy is designed to be, in addition to the great benefits it will confer by annually graduating a large number of highly educated young men, destined to pursue some of all the various pursuits of life, would stimulate tens of thousands, who might never enter this academy, to additional industry and greater advances while in the common schools. The certainty to a young man of good abilities, and desirous of making large acquisitions in knowledge, of having the opportunity of gaining as extensive an education as can be acquired in any institution in the State, if his parents can only furnish him the means to subsist at home, is in the highest degree cheering, while the certainty that the limited earnings of his parents will preclude him, in the existing state of things, from having any such advantages, tends to repress all such generous aspirations, paralyze effort, and prevent the full development of his ability to become extensively useful to the class in which his lot may be cast, or to society at large."

Plan and Description of the Free Academy in the City of New York.

The Free Academy is situated on the S. E. corner of Twenty-third street and Lexington avenue, in the upper part of the city, being convenient of access from all the great thoroughfares. The style of architecture, in which the building is erected, is the same as that of the town halls and colleges of the 14th century, in Europe. This style attained its greatest perfection in the Low Countries, and especially in Belgium, which at that period was the great seat of learning, science and the arts, as well as the great centre of the commercial enterprise of Europe. It was the opinion of the architect, therefore, apart from the economy in construction, of the Gothic style, when properly managed, that this style would be peculiarly appropriate for the High School of the city of New York, and was also well adapted to the materials of which it was proposed to construct the building, many of the old halls and colleges being built of brick. The architect, Mr. Renwick, of New York, in a letter to the President of the Board of Education, remarks,

"I am confident that the style I have adopted is, at the same time the strongest, the cheapest, and the one best adapted to the purposes of heat and ventilation, being the only one, except the Norman, in which chimneys and flues become ornamental, and a roof of high pitch, necessary for external beauty, and capable of being intersected by dormer windows, which latter will add to the beauty of the building and to the convenience of lighting and ventilating the great hall, in the roof.

"As you (the Board) have proposed, with perfect correctness, to make the great hall in the Gothic style, for it can be in no other order, placed in such a position immediately beneath the roof, and is capable of being made highly ornamental in such a place, I was of opinion that the exterior of the whole building should accord with it, as, if it were planned in any other style, it would appear inharmonious, and therefore produce an unpleasant effect on the mind by its incongruity. The height of the building, too, the great pitch of the roof, and the numerous chimneys and ventilating flues necessary to render the arrangement perfect, would entirely preclude the adoption of the Grecian, Roman, or modern Italian styles, with any good effect, apart from their being much more expensive, and less beautiful.

"I have entered at length into the reasons which guided me in the adoption of a style for the building, because it might at first sight appear expensive, and therefore improper for such an institution. You will at once perceive the great strength which the buttresses impart to the building, and the consequent reduction in the thickness of the walls. These buttresses will also serve for ventilating flues, which in such a building should be of large size, in order to prevent, as far as possible, any friction from interfering with the passage of the currents of air, an end which can only be attained by large and smooth flues."

The dimensions of the building are as follows: The length of the building, exclusive of all projections, is 125 feet, and the breadth 80 feet. The height, to the eaves, 65 feet, and to the top of the gable, 100 feet. The height of the towers, 110 feet

The building is divided into a basement, three stories, and a great hall under the roof. The basement is nine feet in height, and is arched to afford ground for exercise in bad weather. In it, also, are the janitors' lodgings, the chemical laboratory, and the closets for the hats and clothes of the students. The first, second and third stories are divided into four great rooms by two wide, spacious halls, which are carried through the centre of the building longitudinally and transversely. Two of these rooms, on each floor, are again divided, affording smaller rooms for recitation, &c. Above these stories is the great hall, 125 feet long by 60 feet in breadth, divided by the king and queen posts of the roof, which are made ornamental, into three aisles, the centre one of which is 40 feet in height, and the two side aisles each 20 feet in height. The ceiling of this room is of wood immediately under the roof, of which it forms part, and it is ornamented with carved ribs of wood, in the manner of the old college halls at Oxford and Cambridge. It is lighted by windows at the ends and by dormers in the roof, and when finished, will probably be the largest and finest collegiate hal. in this country.

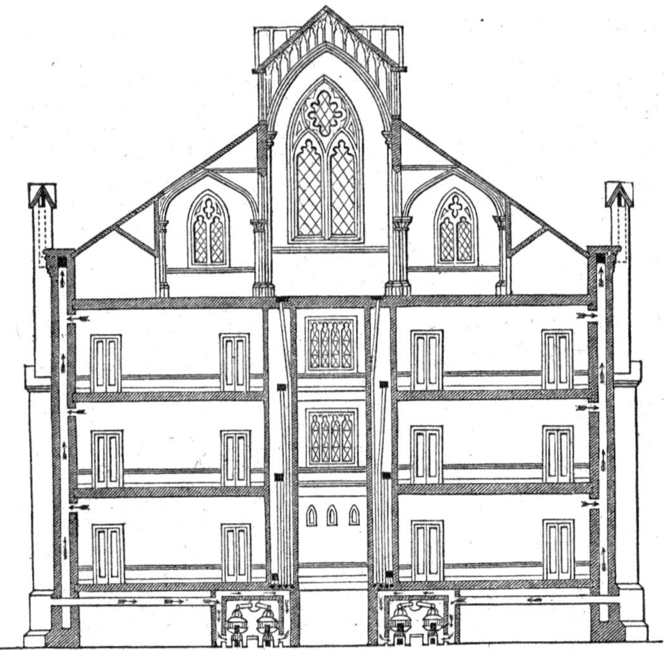

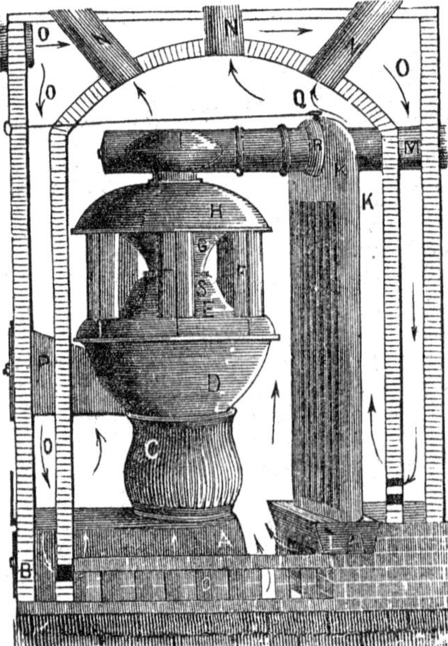

A. Iron or brick ash-pit.
B. Ash-pit door.
C. Pot, or coal Burner, with or without *soap-stone* lining.
D. Fire chamber.
E. Lower half of tubular drum.
F. Elliptical tubes.
G. Upper half of tubular drum.
H. Top of tubular drum.
I. Cap and smoke-pipe.
K. Flat radiator.
L. Water basin or evaporator.
M. Smoke pipe to chimney.
N. Conductors of hot air.
N. Cold air conductor and chamber.
P. Feed door.
Q. Hot air chamber.
R. Damper in globe with rod attached.
S. Pendulum valve for cleaning.
⟵ Shows the direction of the currents of hot or cold air.

Fig. 3.—Culver's Furnace.

The mode of warming and ventilating the several apartments of the Free Academy can be easily understood by consulting Figures 2, 3 and 4. Four of Culver's furnaces are set in the basement, as shown in Fig. 3. A large quantity of fresh air from out of doors, after being warmed by these furnaces, is carried up to the several stories by pipes in the division walls, (Fig. 2,) and is admitted into the rooms at a convenient point, as indicated in Figures 5 and 6. The air of each room, as it becomes vitiated by respiration, is discharged by openings near the ceiling into the buttresses, which are constructed hollow and finished smooth, so as to constitute large ventilating flues. Each opening is fitted with one of Culver's Ventilators or Registers, with cords attached, by which the capacity of the opening for the discharge of vitiated air can be enlarged and diminished at the pleasure of the teacher. The practical working of the furnaces and flues for ventilation, secures the object aimed at—a genial and pure atmosphere at all times.

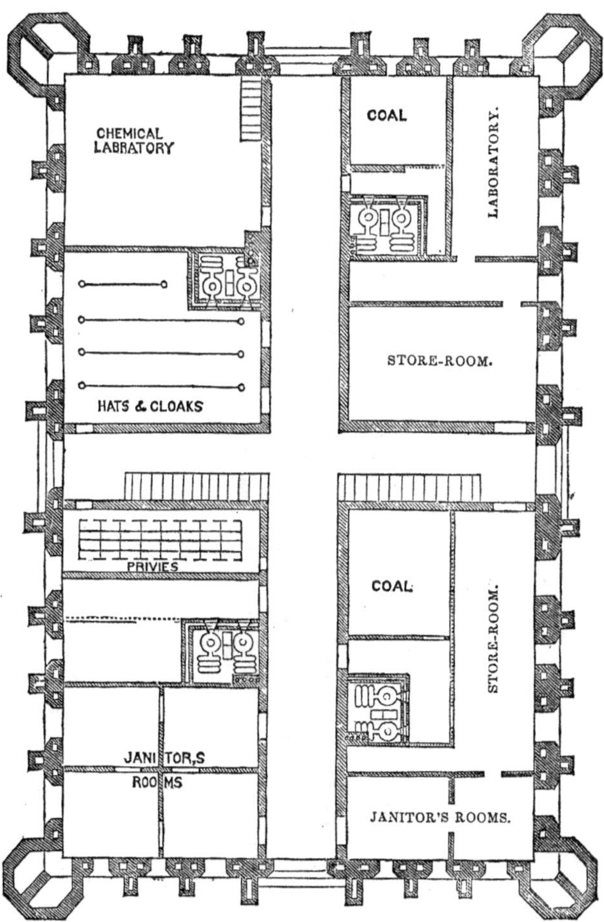

Fig. 3.—Basement Floor.

The above cut gives an incorrect view of the exterior of the building, but a good idea of the internal arrangement of the basement story.

Fig. 5.—PLAN OF FIRST STORY.

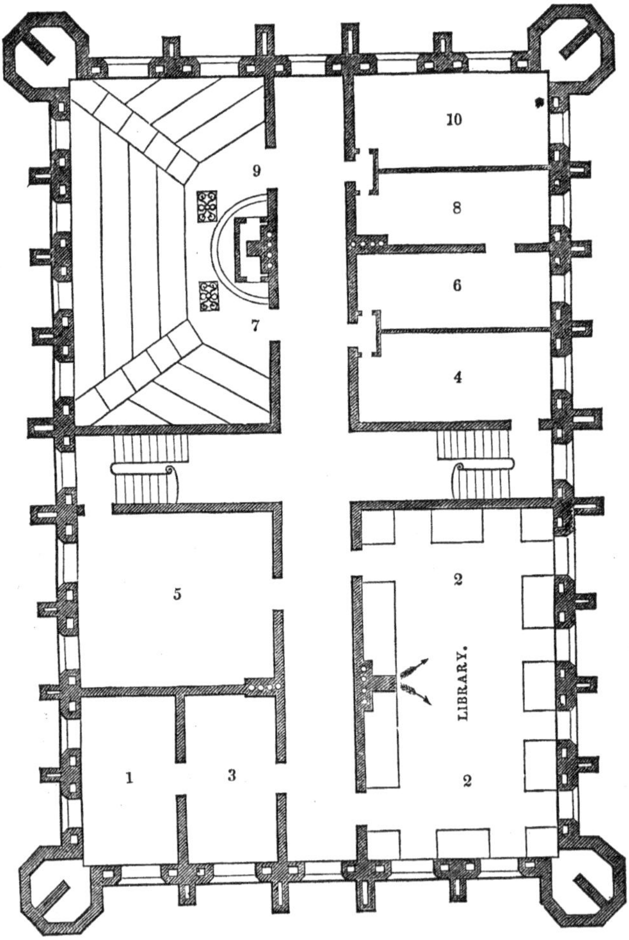

Nos. 1. Office of Principal.
2. Library.
3. Depository of Text-Books.
4. Class Room in Mathematics.
6. Professor in French.
7 and 9. Lecture Room.
8. Class Room in Mathematics.
10. Professor of History and Belles Letters.

Fig. 6.—PLAN OF SECOND STORY.

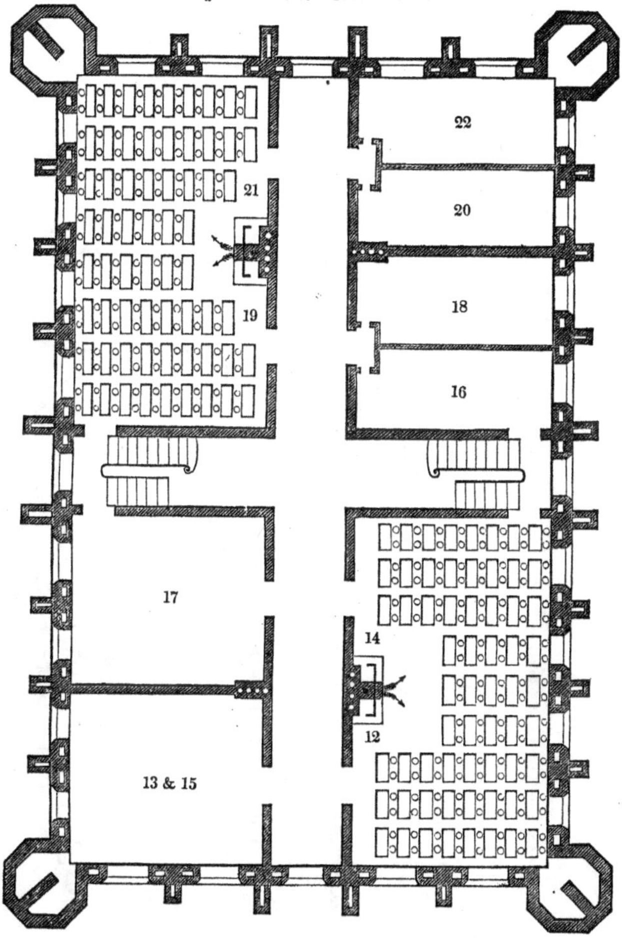

Nos. 13 and 15. Professor of Civil Engineering.
12 and 14. Study Hall.
16. Class Room for Tutor in Mathematics.
17. Study Hall.
18. Class Room for Tutor in Moral Philosophy.
19 and 21. Drawing Hall.
20. Professor of Ancient Languages.

Fig. 7.—Plan of Third Story.

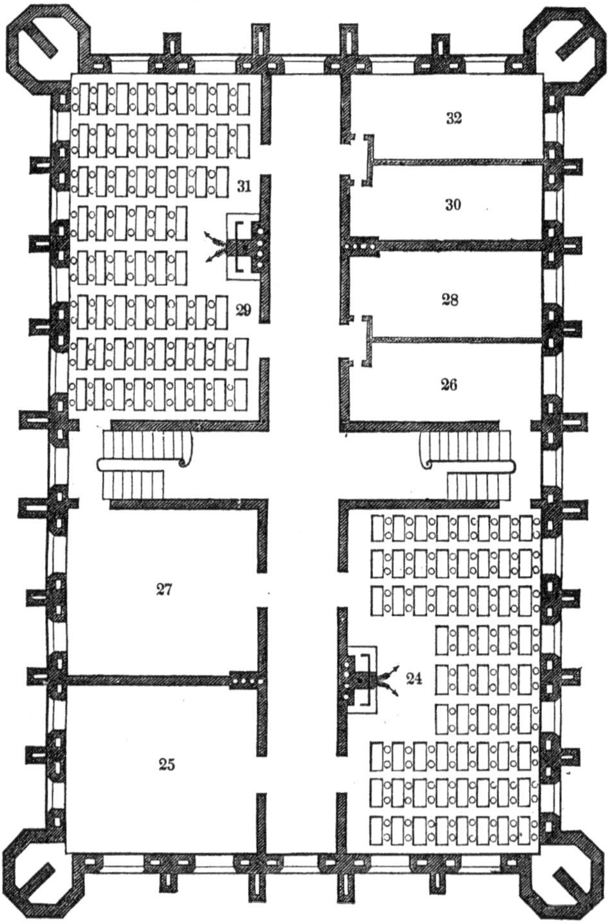

32
30
31
28
29
26
27
24
25

Nos. 24. Study Hall.
25. Professor of Mathematics.
26. Class Room for Tutor of Moral Philosophy.
27. Study Hall.
28. Class Room for Tutor of Rhetoric.
29 and 31. Study Hall.
30. Class Room for Tutor of Rhetoric.
32. Professor of English Literature.

PLAN—No. 12. FRONT ELEVATION.

PLAN—No. 13. FRONT ELEVATION.

Plans and Description of the Academy Building, Rome, N. Y.

We are indebted to Edward Huntington, Esq., for the following plans and description of the new Academy building recently erected in Rome, N. Y., under his supervision. The building is 70 feet by 44 feet on the ground.

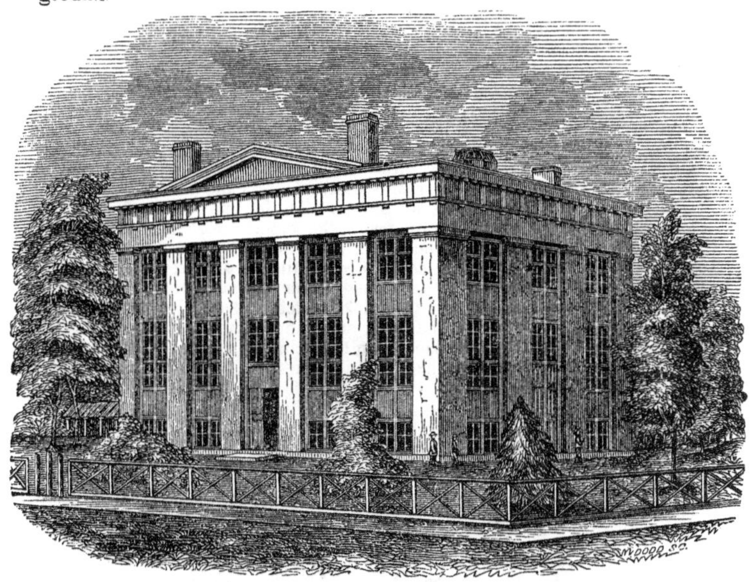

Fig. 2. Basement.

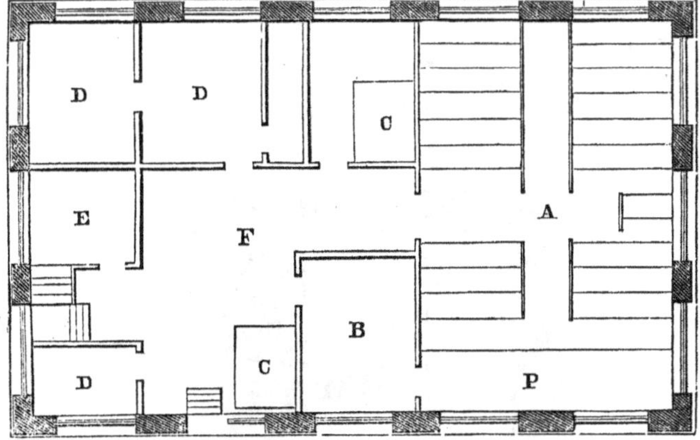

A—Lecture-room and Chapel. B—Laboratory. C, C—Furnaces. D, D, D—Janitor's rooms. E—Entry. F—Hall.

The building was erected in 1848, on a lot 198 by 170 feet, on the corner of Court and James streets, fronting the public square, and is of brick, 70 by 44 feet on the ground. The basement wall, up to the water table, is of stone, laid in hydraulic cement. The roof is covered with tin, laid in white lead.

The basement, 10 feet high in the clear, contains a lecture-room (which serves also as a chapel,) 26½ by 40 feet, with comfortable seats to accommodate conveniently 200 pupils. The floor descends 2 feet from the rear of the room to the platform, giving 12 feet height immediately in front of it. A laboratory, 12 by 15½ feet, adjoins the lecture-room, with which it communicates by a door at the end of a platform. The remainder of the basement floor is occupied by the furnaces for warming the building, and by the rooms of the Janitor.

The First Floor is occupied by the male department, and consists of a school-room about 30 by 54 feet, and nearly 15 feet in clear height, with two recitation-rooms, entries, &c. There are 62 desks, each four feet long and accommodating two pupils.

On the Second Floor are the girls' school-room, about 28 by 40 feet, with seats for 76 pupils, 2 recitation-rooms, library, hall, and room occupied by Primary department. There is a large skylight in the centre of the girls' school-room, and another in the library. The rooms are 15 feet in height.

The building is thoroughly and uniformly warmed by two furnaces in the basement, and a change of air is secured by ventilators at the top of the rooms, and also near the floor, opening into flues which are carried up in the chimneys. The warmth imparted by the smoke which passes up in the adjoining flues secures a good draft. In the upper story additional means of ventilation are furnished by the skylights, which can be partially opened.

The desks are of varnished cherry, similar in form to Ross's school desk.

Fig. 5.

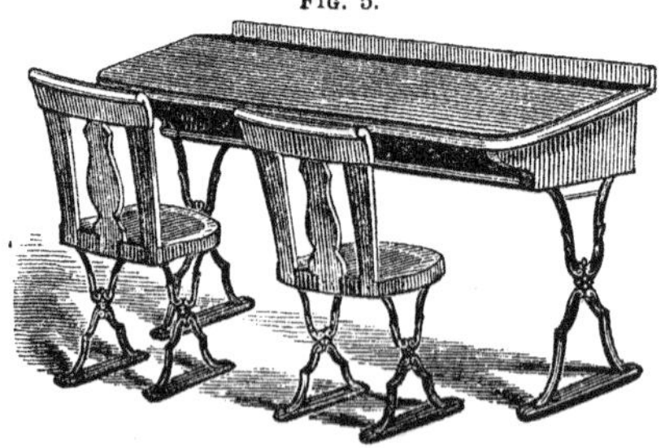

The supports are of wood, however, instead of cast-iron, and the seats are easy Windsor chairs. Both seats and desks are firmly secured to the floor by small iron knees and screws.

The school and recitation rooms are all furnished with large slates set in the wall, in the room of blackboards.

The teachers' desks in the school-rooms are similar to Fig. 6.

Fig. 6.

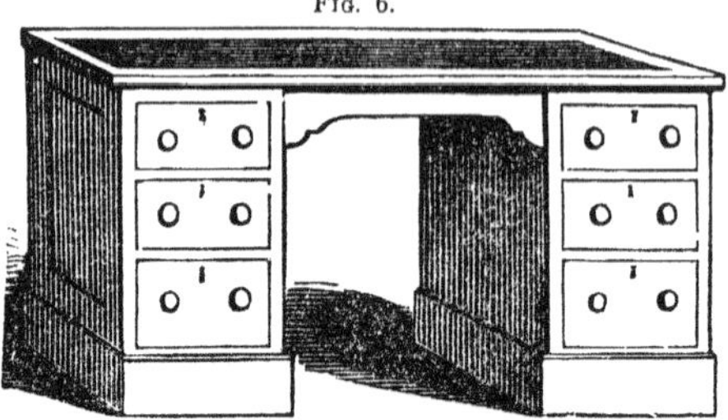

The whole cost of the building, including furnaces, scholars' desks and chairs, slates and inkstands, was about 6,000 dollars.

FIG. 3. PLAN OF FIRST FLOOR.

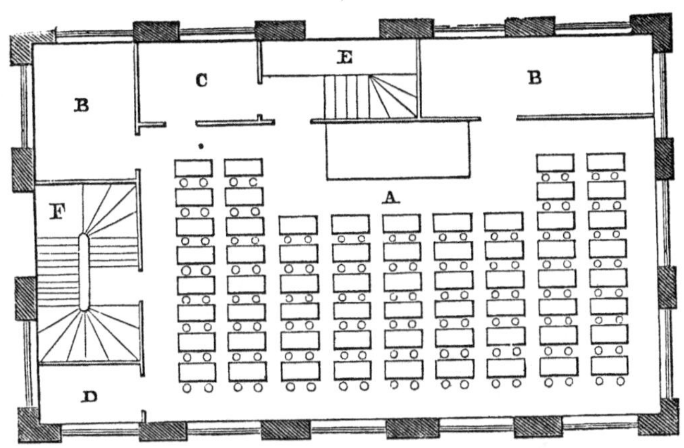

A—Boys' School-room, with 124 seats.
B, B—Recitation-rooms.
C—Dressing-room.
D—Closet for Apparatus.
E—Entrance for Boys.
F—Entrance for Girls.

FIG. 4. PLAN OF SECOND FLOOR.

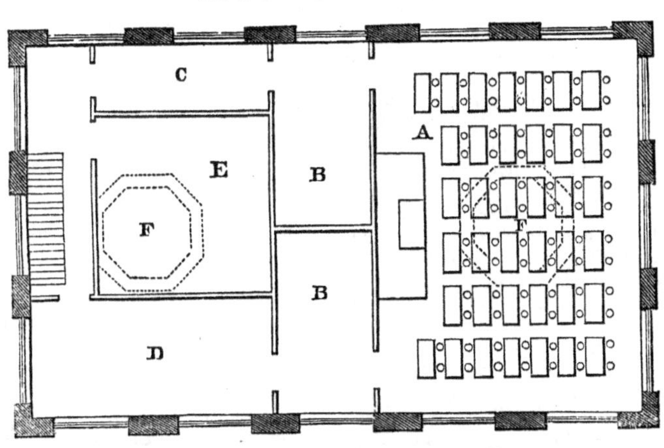

A—Girls' School-room, with 76 seats.
B, B—Recitation-rooms.
C—Dressing-room.
D—Primary Department.
E—Library, lighted by skylight.
F—Skylight in ceiling.

System of Public Schools in Philadelphia.

The system of public schools in Philadelphia has grown up, from very small beginnings, into its present gigantic yet harmonious proportions, in a comparatively brief period of time, and is a monument of the disinterested zeal, intelligence, and fidelity of the men who have been intrusted with its administration, and of the liberality of the citizens generally, in providing the means for its support and expansion.

Prior to 1818, a system of charity schools was maintained by a society of benevolent individuals, which had been aided by a small appropriation from the city, from 1808. In these schools 2,600 poor children were educated in 1817, at the cost of $11 per scholar.

In 1818, against violent and interested opposition from various quarters, the present system was commenced, and the first school opened in a hired room under the Lancastarian method of instruction.

In 1819, there were six schools established, one school-house built, ten teachers employed, and 2,845 children instructed in reading, writing, and arithmetic, at an aggregate expense of $23,049 45, of which near $19,000 was invested in land, and building, and furniture.

In 1823, the first school for colored children was established.

In 1826, there were 4,144 children in nine schools, at an aggregate expense of $22,444.

In 1833, an infant model school was organized. There were at this date 5,768 children in thirteen schools, under twenty-three teachers, instructed at an aggregate expense of $53,042, of which $23,000 was for school buildings and fixtures.

In 1836, twenty-six primary schools were established. A committee of the board of Controllers, visited the public schools of Boston and New York, and at their suggestion the system of instruction was modified, and additional teachers, at a higher compensation, were employed, and the services of juvenile monitors dispensed with. At this date, 11,127 children were instructed, in forty-eight schools of different grades, at the aggregate expense of $75,017, of which $23,000 was for land and buildings. Thirteen school-houses had been erected up to this date.

In 1837, sixty primary schools were in operation, with nearly six thousand scholars. These schools were eminently successful in gathering up the young children who would otherwise not be at school, and in relieving the higher schools of a class of pupils, who only embarrassed the teachers and retarded the more advanced learners. During this year, the corner stone of the Central High School building was laid, with an astronomical observatory attached. The monitorial system was still further dispensed with or modified. At this date, 17,000 children were in all the schools, and the expenditure amounted to $191,830, of which $112,000 was for land, buildings, and furniture. Of this last amount, $89,000 was received from an appropriation by the State of $500,000 for school-houses.

In 1830, the Central High School was opened, with professors in various branches of Classical, English, Belles Letters, Mathematical, Astronomical, and Physical sciences, and before the close of the year, reorganized on a plan submitted by President Bache, of the Girard College of orphans. More than 18,000 children were in regular attendance at school, and the expenditure for the year amounted to $188,741, of which $82,000 was for land, buidings, and furniture. The ordinary expense of the system was about $6 for each pupil.

In 1848, a Normal School was opened under the charge of A. T. W. Wright, "for the thorough training of female teachers in such practical exercises as will discipline and develope the mind, adorn and elevate the character, insure the best modes of imparting knowledge, and prevent fruitless experiments, manifold mistakes. and inseparable loss of time."

In 1850, evening or night schools were opened by the Controllers in different parts of the city, to accomodate those to whom circumstances may have denied the advantages of education in early life, as well as to enable those whose necessities will not permit to attend the day school, to share the benefits of that mental training so necessary to fit them to become useful citizens. The attendance in these schools, during the winter of 1852–53, was 7,772; of which number, 5,776 were males, and 1,995 females. The average age of the males was 17 years 4 months, and of the females 16 years 9 months. Of the whole number, 3,235 were born in Philadelphia; 1,452 in other parts of the United States; and 3,085 were of foreign birth. Of the 7,772, when admitted, 943 could not read, 1,581 could not write, and 1,943 were entirely ignorant of the use of figures. The cost of supporting the night schools, in the winter of 1852–53, was $16,907 or $2.17½ for each pupil.

The system of public instruction embraced, in 1853:

I. Classified schools, viz.: 152 primary schools; 35 secondary schools; 55 grammar schools; and 1 high school for boys—each grade having its appointed course of study and requisites of admission.

II. Unclassified schools, viz.: 42 day schools and 30 night schools, scattered through the less populous portions of the district, or where the habits or circumstances of the population are not favorable to regularity of attendance. The pupils of these schools are classified, but not according to the rules applicable to the schools in the first division.

III. Normal school, for training female teachers for the different grades of schools.

The attendance in all the schools was as follows: in the 286 day schools, 50,085, of which number 25.836 were males, and 24,249 females; in the 20 night schools 7,772, of which number 5,776 were males, and 1,990 females—making an aggregate attendance of 57,857 scholars.

The entire expense of supporting the system, for the year ending June 30, 1853, including text-books and stationary, was $386,122.32, exclusive of the sum of $25,181, paid for rent of ground and houses, and of the estimated interest on $932,290.02, the cost of grounds and buildings now belonging to the Controllers. Of the entire expense, the sum of $31,307 was derived from the State appropriation, and the balance from a tax on the property of the city.

Exclusive of rent and interest on cost of school-houses, the cost of educating 57,857 pupils, in the day and night schools, was $6.67 for each pupil; and including rent and interest, $7.06.

The cost of supporting the unclassified, primary, secondary, Grammar, High, and Normal Schools, with an attendance of 50,085 pupils, was $358,714.70, including the cost of books and stationary furnished by the Controllers, and exclusive of the rent of school-room and the interest on the cost of grounds and buildings—or $7.16 to each pupil.

The cost of the night schools, with an attendance of 7,772 pupils, was $16,907.02, or $2.17½ to each pupil.

The cost of the High School with an attendance of 519 pupils, was $17,449.53, or $32.97 for each pupil.

The cost of Normal School, and School of Practice, with 519 pupils, (including pupil-teachers and children,) was $6,796.72, or $10.98 to each pupil.

The cost of the grammar, secondary, primary, and unclassified schools, with an attendance of 49,052 pupils, was $335,468.45, or $6.84 to each pupil.

The cost of furnishing books and stationary, included in the foregoing calculations, was 75½ cents for each pupil for the year.

The progress and influence of the Central High School, is thus set forth by Dr. Hart, its present accomplished principal. [*See* page 258.]

Fig. 1.—Perspective of Jefferson Grammar School, Philadelphia.

Plan and Description of Jefferson Grammar School-house in Philadelphia.

Jefferson Grammar School is located in Fifth-street above Poplar, and was erected in 1836. The lot is 100 feet on the street, and 120 feet deep, and the space not occupied by the building and the walks, is planted with the choicest shrubs and flowers, which are kept in beautiful condition by the teacher and pupil. For these, the fountain, and other embellishments, the children and the public owe a large debt of gratitude to Daniel S. Beideman Esq., who has thus introduced a new element of physical, moral, esthetical education into the public schools of this section of the city.

The children of the school exhibit a commendable pride in taking care of the grounds, and in protecting the shrubbery, flowers, and other embellishments from the depredations of the "outside barbarians." The influence, direct and indirect, of these decorations, and of the daily care and interest in their preservation by the pupils, was soon manifest in their improved manners and tastes, and in the improved habits of the whole neighborhood. And why can not every city school-house, even when located in the most crowded neighborhood, have its plat of flowers, and its attractions of verdure and foliage, if it must be on a small scale, and if no other place can be afforded, on the walls of the inclosures? Why may not a vase of flowers always adorn the table of the teacher, and bust of orator, poet, patriot, and philanthropist, fill, each its appropriate nich around the school-room? As has been justly remarked by Mrs. Sigourney, in a valuable "Essay on the Cultivation of the Beautiful in Common Schools"—the expense of such decorations will not be thrown away, the beautiful objects will not be defaced, and the fair scenery will not be desecrated. It will be easier to enforce habits of neatness and order among objects whose taste and value make them worthy of care, than amid that parsimony of apparatus and adornment, whose pitiful meanness operates as a temptation to waste and destroy.

The building is 100 feet by 50, and three stories high. Each story is divided into one large school-room, with four class rooms in connection. The first story is occupied by a Primary School; the second, by the girls department of the Grammar School, and the third, by the boys' department.

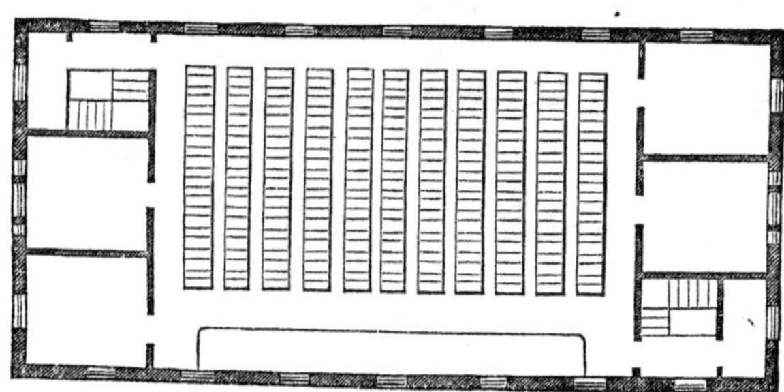

Fig. 2.—Second Floor.

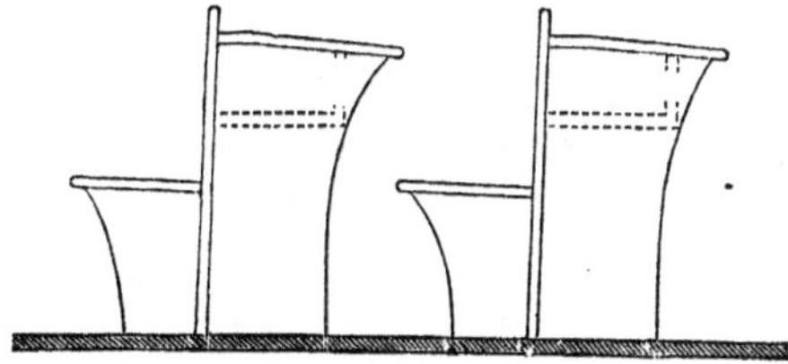

PLAN AND DESCRIPTION OF NORTH-EAST GRAMMAR SCHOOL-HOUSE, PHILADELPHIA.

Fig 1.—PERSPECTIVE.

The Grammar School-house on New street, between Second and First-streets, in Philadelphia, was erected after plans and specifications made by Samuel Sloan, Architect, in 1852. It is 81 feet 6 inches front, by 65 feet 6 inches deep, and three stories high, each story being fifteen feet in the clear. The basement, windows, and door trimmings are of the best blue marble, finely cut and polished, and the walls are of the best pressed brick. All the outside walls are laid with a hollow space of four inches—the inner and the outside walls being tied together with alternate bricks in the heading courses.

The building is warmed by three of Chilson's furnaces, of the largest size, and ventilated by a shaft, extending from the cellar to the top of the roof, with lateral flues and openings from each story, with a stove at the base in the cellar, to warm the shaft, to quicken the discharge of the foul air, both in winter and summer.

The peculiarity of this, and the more recently constructed school-houses in Philadelphia, is in the plan of the school-rooms. Instead of one large room, with two or more class rooms in connection on each floor, each story is divided into four apartments, of suitable size to accommodate the number of pupils assigned to one teacher, with movable glass partitions. By this arrangement, the Principal can have a full view of all the pupils and assistants on the same floor, while each division is protected from annoyance or interruption from the exercises of the other. By removing the glazed partitions,—one half of which is admitted into the wainscotting below, and the other, into the wainscotting above, and are so hung as to balance each other,—the several apartments are thrown into one, and the whole school is then within the hearing and voice of the principal.

The following cut, Fig. 2, represents the first floor of the North-east Grammar School, and gives a good idea of the new plan of arranging the school-rooms.

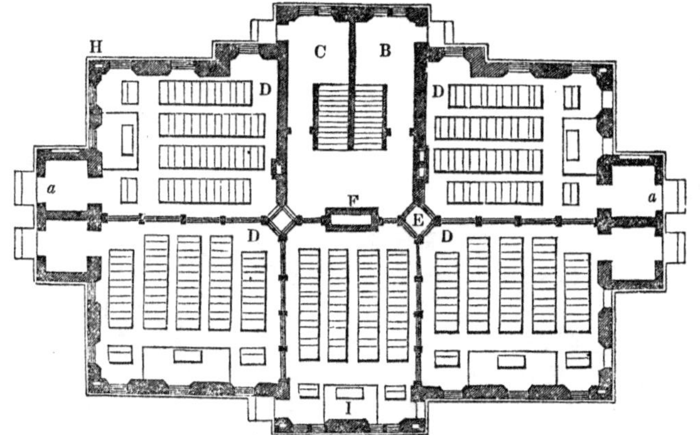

Fig. 2.—First Floor of North-east Grammar School.

a, a, a, a—Entrance lobby to the rooms on the ground plan.

B—Entrance and stairway leading to the second story.

C—Entrance and stairway leading to the third story.

D, D, D, D, D—Class rooms to accommodate 60 pupils each.

E, E—Vestibules, which afford a communication from one room to the other, having glazed doors on its four sides.

F—A shaft, which contains all the hot-air pipes, from which they branch to the various rooms on each story and discharge through register in the floor.

The vestibules E, E, on the second and third stories, are also the entrances to the class rooms from the outer gallery or landing of the stairs.

H, H, H, H, H, H—The ventilating flues, which are placed in the angles of the rooms opposite to that of the hot-air registers.

I, I, I, I, I—The teachers desk, with a small platform 6 feet broad by 8 feet long.

Fig. 2.—Second Floor of the Warren Grammar School.

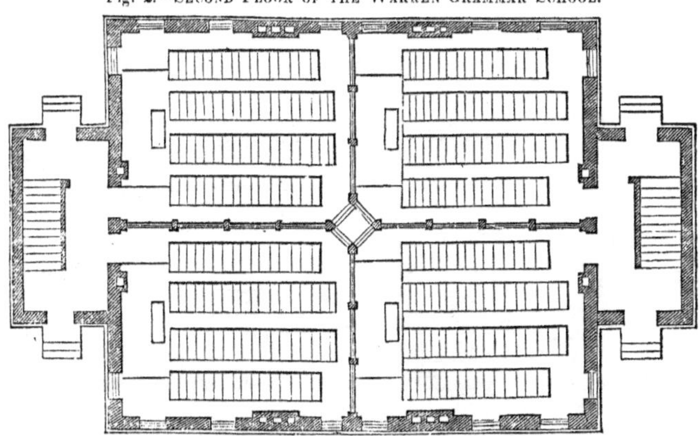

The Warren Grammar School-house is situated on Robertson-street, was built in 1852, on the same general plan as the North-east Grammar School, the description of which is applicable to this.

PLAN OF WARREN GRAMMAR SCHOOL-HOUSE.

Fig. 1.—PERSPECTIVE OF WARREN GRAMMAR SCHOOL-HOUSE.

The Warren Grammar School-house is situated on Robertson-street, was built in 1852, on the same general plan as the North-east Grammar School, the description of which is applicable to this.

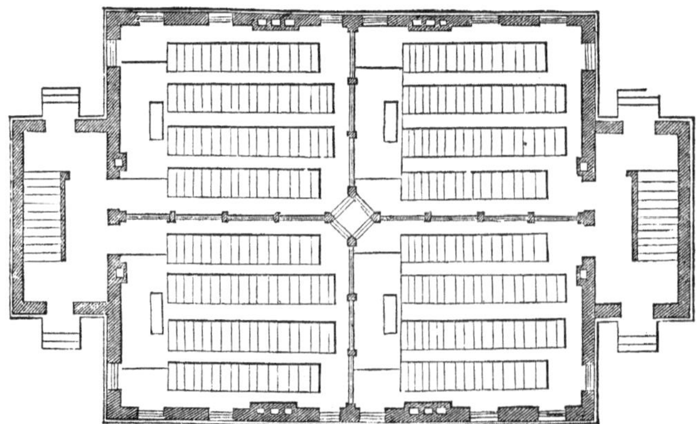

Fig. 2.—PLAN OF THE INTERIOR.

Plan of Glenwood School-house, Philadelphia.

Fig. 1.—Perspective of Glenwood School-house.

Glenwood School-house is situated on Ridge-road, and is intended for an Unclassified school. The building is 66 by 46 feet, besides the projection, and is two stories high. Each story is divided into two apartments, separated by a glazed partition.

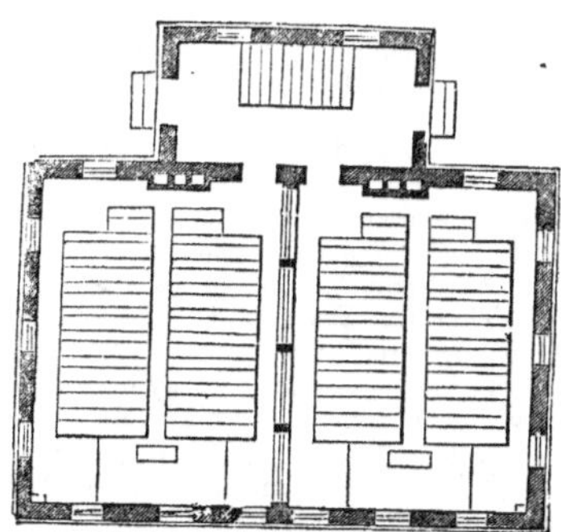

Fig. 2.—Plan of First Floor.

PLANS AND DESCRIPTION OF THE CENTRAL HIGH SCHOOL, PHILADELPHIA.

Fig. 1.—PERSPECTIVE.

In 1853, a new building was erected for the accommodation of the Central High School, in Spring Garden, on the east side of Broad street. The lot is one hundred and fifty feet on Broad street, by ninety-five feet deep, having Green street for a boundary on the north, and Brandywine street on the south.

The building is constructed throughout in a substantial manner, with good materials, and with a main reference to utility rather than ornament, although the latter has not been altogether lost sight of. The walls throughout are built hollow, to prevent dampness; the outside walls and those on each side of the transverse hall have an average thickness of eighteen inches, while those separating the various class rooms have a thickness of thirteen inches. The exterior is built of the best quality of pressed brick. The plainness of the extended façade is relieved by projections and recesses in the line of the outer wall, by a horizontal line of marble work separating the first story from those above, by a large main entrance in the middle, by the cornice, and by the dome of the observatory above. Though simple in design, and constructed in an economical manner, the building presents externally quite an ornamented appearance.

The observatory is built upon two piers of solid masonry. These piers stand isolated from all the rest of the structure, being inclosed within the walls on each side of the front entrance. They are sixteen feet wide by two and a half feet thick, and extend upwards, without material change, from below the foundation to the top of the third story. There they are connected by iron girders, and on these girders the instruments rest. The dome of the observatory rests upon the other walls of the building, and has no connection with the piers that are used to support the instruments. The height of the dome above the level of the pavement, is one hundred and twelve feet.

Throughout the building, careful provision has been made for light. The windows are all large, and are as closely placed as a due regard to the strength of the walls would permit. Four out of six of the class rooms on each floor, are corner rooms, admitting light from two sides. The large lecture room on the first floor, is lighted on three sides.

There are two main stairways, one at each end of the large hall. That in front runs in a well, from the first floor to the arch of the observatory. That in the rear connects only the first and second stories. The building has also a double flight of stairs in the rear, connecting the main hall with the basement, a double flight of outside stairs into the basement from each end of the building, and a small stairway connecting the chemical laboratory with the class room above. The main stairways are all six feet wide, each stair having a rise of seven, and a tread of twelve inches. The door into the main entrance in front, is a folding-door, opening outwards, eight feet wide and eighteen feet high. That in the rear is also folding, opening outwards, eight feet wide and fourteen feet high. The main entrance into the lecture room is likewise a double door, seven feet wide, opening freely both ways. The class rooms are all severally connected by doors, with each other, as well as with the main hall. These doors are all three and a half feet wide. The building thus has admirable facilities for the movements of the classes, as well as for being instantly cleared in case of panic.

The general plan of the building is exceeding simple. It is in shape an oblong parallelogram, fronting lengthwise on Broad street, being one hundred feet long by seventy-two deep. There are three stories besides the basement. The plan in each story is nearly the same. A hall, sixteen feet wide, runs east and west, dividing the building on each floor into two equal parts; these parts are again severally subdivided by walls running north and south, into three rooms, averaging thirty-eight feet by twenty-two. This gives six rooms on a floor, except on the first floor, where the whole of the north side is reserved for a lecture-room. There is also an additional small room in the third story, occupying the space in the hall over the rear stairway. The lecture room on the first floor is sixty-eight feet long by thirty-eight feet wide, and twenty feet high, and is capable of seating eight hundred persons.

The height of the several stories, in the clear both of the floor and the ceiling, is as follows: the basement story ten feet; the first story twenty feet three inches; the second story sixteen feet six inches; the third story sixteen feet. The basement in front is five feet three inches above the level of the curbstone; and, as the lot descends considerably in the rear, the basement is, on an average, more than one-half above ground. It is divided into six rooms, with a transverse hall, on the same plan as the stories above, the rooms being intended for a chemical laboratory, clothes room, wash room, storage, &c.

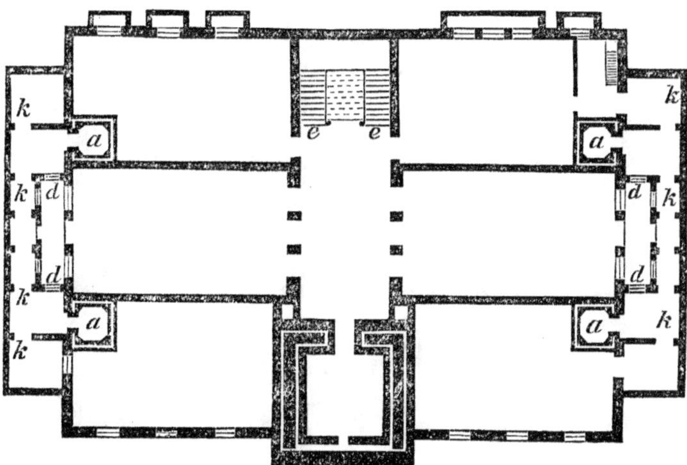

Fig. 2.—Basement.

In regard to the important matter of heating and ventilation, two methods engaged the attention of the controllers. The first was, to generate all the heat in one large chamber in the center, and send it thence, north and south, to the ends of the building. The objection to this plan was the difficulty of producing, in connection with it, a proper ventilation. To secure good ventilation in an apartment, it is necessary to establish a current through it. The air must be brought in at one end and carried out at the other end. The ventiducts for carrying off the air, after it has been used, must be, as nearly as possible, opposite to the warm flues by which the pure air is introduced; consequently, if the hot air chamber were placed in the centre of the building, the ventiducts would have to be in the extreme ends. But the end walls, in a building standing apart from others, and en-

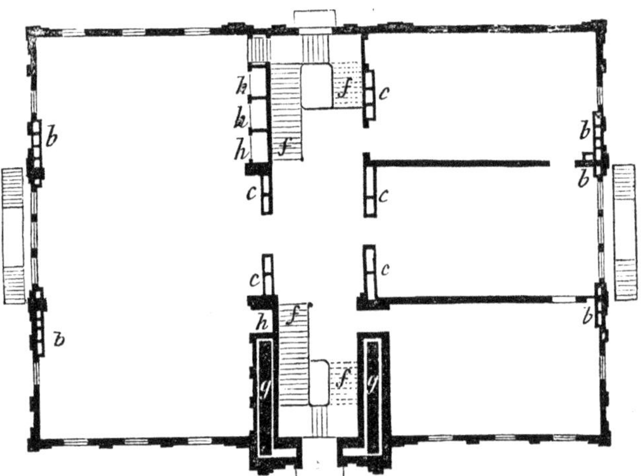

Fig. 3.—First Floor.

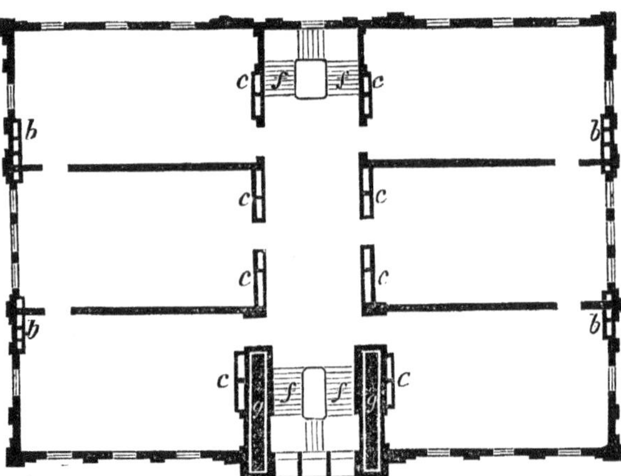

Fig. 4.—Second and Third Floor.

tirely exposed to the external atmosphere, are naturally colder than those in the center; they would consequently chill the ventiducts, and thereby greatly impair their efficiency in carrying off the foul air.

Besides this, in order that the ventiducts may be perfectly reliable in all weathers, it is necessary that some artificial means should be used for increasing the current by rarefying the air within them. This is ordinarily done by introducing, within the ventiduct, a jet of burning gas, or a small stove. The trouble and expense of such an apparatus is greatly increased by multiplying the number of places where it must be applied. It was, therefore, very desirable, that the ventiducts should be all brought together into one general tube before going out of the roof. One good fire maintained within it would then suffice for the whole building. But this arrangement would be impracticable if the warm-air flues were to radiate from the center, and the ventiducts be placed at the extremities.

It was, therefore, determined to take the other method, namely, to centralize the ventilating apparatus, and generate the heat at the extremities. This is done by four of the largest size furnaces, two being placed at each end of the building, and the heat sent inwards towards the center. This is indicated by the position of the hot air flues, which are all placed in the north and south walls of the several apartments. The ventiducts being at the opposite ends of these apartments, all occur in the walls that line the central hall, and are all brought together into one large tube or duct in the loft. This tube, which is about seven feet in diameter, is equal in capacity to that of all the separate ducts combined. It passes out ten feet beyond the roof, and is surmounted by one of Emerson's ventilating caps, with a disc of about ten feet diameter. Into this large tube or chamber, just below the roof, a coal stove is introduced, by which a large amount of hot air may be generated, and an impetus may be given to the ascending current to any extent that is desired.

This part of the arrangement is deemed especially important. In clear, cold weather, when the furnaces are in action, and a current of warm air is constantly setting into one extremity of an apartment, it is not difficult to establish and maintain an ascending exit current from the other end. The air is forced into the ventiduct by the constant pressure from the other end. Moreover, it enters the ventiduct already warmer than the external air. The ventiduct itself becomes warmed; and so the current, once established, perpetuates itself. But when the furnaces are not in operation, nothing of this sort takes place. And yet, this occurs precisely in those parts of the year, when ventilation in a school-room is most needed, viz.: in moderate weather, when it is not warm enough to open the doors and windows, and yet not cold enough to maintain a fire. At such times, the stove in the loft, acting directly and powerfully upon the ventiduct, will at all times create an ascending current, sucking the foul air up, as it were, from the several apartments, and thereby causing fresh air to enter from the other extremities. The position of the windows, directly opposite the ventiducts, gives a special facility for this purpose, when the furnaces are not in action. The windows, at such times, take the place of the warm air flues in supplying a stream of fresh air.

The following additional particulars may be mentioned in regard to the apparatus for heating and ventilation. The flues are all made large, both those for the admission, and those for the exit of the air. The dimensions of the several ducts are given in the engravings. In the large lecture room, the two warm air flues have together a capacity of about six square feet; and the two ventiducts for the same have, together, a capacity of twelve square feet. In the class-rooms, which are thirty-eight feet by twenty-two, the warm air flues average one and one-sixth square feet, and the ventiducts two and one-third square feet. In all the rooms, the warm air is introduced at the bottom of the apartment, as near as possible to the level of the floor; and the ordinary opening for the escape of the foul air is also on the level with the floor, at the opposite extremity, so as to sweep constantly the lower stratum of air, in which the pupil is immersed. The ventiducts are also supplied with openings at the ceiling, to be used, not in ordinary, but whenever needed, to get rid of excessive heat. In reckoning the advantages of the buiding, in respect to pure air, especial emphasis should be given to the commendible height of the ceilings. Each apartment has a large volume of air at its disposal, in proportion to the area of its floor; and it is obvious, that the air of a room eight or ten feet high, is much more rapidly vitiated than that of one fifteen or twenty feet high.

Commencing from small beginnings, in 1838, with only sixty-three students and four professors, and with a character not much beyond that now attained by our best Grammar Schools, the High School has gradually enlarged its corps of professors, its number of students, and its course of studies, until it has assumed, in public estimation, the rank, as from the Legislature of the Commonwealth, it has received the distinctive attributes of a college. The minimum age for admission was originally twelve, and few students were then admitted much beyond that age. The minimum age for admission is now thirteen, while the actual age of those admitted, averages nearly fifteen. The preparatory studies at the same time have been nearly doubled, raising thereby, in a corresponding degree, the character and studies of the Grammar Schools, and of the whole connected series of schools below them.

The number of students in attendance on the High School, during the last six years, has been constantly a little over 500, and it is at this time 516. During the fifteen years that the High School has existed, 2,805 students have been admitted to its privileges, of whom 2,289 have entered upon the active duties of life, and are to be found in almost every walk of professional, commercial, and mechanical business. These young men, it is true, did not all complete the full course of study. Some of them were not more than a year, a few not more than six months, in the school. Yet, of the great majority of them, it is evident that they were long enough in the institution to have received from it an abiding moral and intellectual influence. The average time of their continuance in the school, was over two years, while many of them completed the full course of four years. The institution, therefore, young as it is, may justly claim to have conducted through a liberal course of study, more young men, even in this infancy of its career, than some of our most honored colleges, which have already celebrated their hundredth anniversary. The graduates of the High School are admitted, without further preparation, to the study of law, medicine and divinity. As teachers, they are rapidly placing themselves in the front ranks of the profession. Our own public schools have felt the benefit of their influence, and applications are constantly received for their services, in organizing and conducting important educational establishments in other states. The alumni of the High School have furnished the most successful reporters for the United States Senate and House of Representatives. Large numbers of them are engaged in civil engineering, and not a few of them are connected with that important scientific undertaking, the United States Coast Survey. They are engineers in the Japan Expedition, surgeons in the navy of the United States, miners and merchants in California, and engaged, it is believed, in some capacity, in every State in the Union.

All these young men are bound together by a tie of affection for the public schools, and particularly for the High School, the strength of which is even more than proportionate to the benefit they have received. I have been often surprised at the liveliness and fervor of the interest which they have shown towards their Alma Mater. A large part of them, all who were in the school as long as two years, are united in a general society, known as the "Alumni Association," numbering now 760. Besides this, there are numerous smaller associations, meeting weekly as literary or debating societies, for the purposes of following up the intellectual culture which they commenced at school. These associations differ from the ordinary literary societies in colleges, inasmuch as they do not consist of the undergraduates, but are made up entirely of those who have left school. They discuss literary and scientific subjects, prepare essays and lectures, appoint committees to report on questions of science or art, submitted by the members, and receive communications on these subjects from such of their members as have removed to other parts of the country.

When it is recollected that the vast majority of this number settle in our midst, that they are to be found in every walk of honorable enterprise, professional, mercantile and mechanical, and that from the character of the education which they have received, they will naturally acquire positions of greater influence than others who have had less favorable advantages, it is difficult to overestimate their growing importance as a body. There are certainly not less than eighteen hundred of these young men now engaged in active life in the city of Philadelphia, at ages varying from fifteen to thirty. Such is the character which they have acquired among the citizens for successful attention to whatever they undertake, that not a week passes without applications being received at the school for some of its alumni. Eligible situations in the very best stores and counting houses in the city are offered to them without solicitation. They are constantly advertised for, hoc nomine, in the public papers. These facts would seem to indicate that the course of instruction and discipline provided by the controllers has been such as to fit the students of the High School for the actual wants of life. It is gratifying to observe, also, that the habits and the moral training, even more than the intellectual instruction, are constantly mentioned as among the qualities that have brought our alumni into request.

OCCUPATIONS *of the* 2,107 *pupils who graduated or left during thv eleven years ending July* 22*d*, 1853.—Architects 5, Bakers 5, Blacksmiths 48, Blind Makers 2, Bookbinders 19, Brewer 1, Bricklayers 47, Brickmakers 5, Brushmaker 1. Cabinetmakers 14, Cadets 3, Carpenters 166, Carvers and Gilders 2, Chairmakers 3, Chemists 12, Clergymen 9, Clerks 199, Coachmaker 1, Coachtrimmers 2, Conveyancers 76, Coopers 10, Copper-plate printers 2, Copper-smiths 2, Cordwainers 62, Curriers, 14, Cutlers 2. Dentists 10, Druggists 69, Dyers 2. Engineers 51, Engravers 55. Farmers 95. Gas fitters 7, Gilders 4, Glasscutters 3, Goldbeater 1, Grocers 27. Hatters 13. Ironfounders 2, Iron railing maker 1. Jewellers 21. Lawyers 29, Locksmiths 3. Machinists 91, Manufacturers 13, Mariners 48, Masons 4, Miller 1, Millwrights 3, Morocco dresser 1, Moulders 2. Painters 13, Paper hanger 1, Patternmakers 2, Physicians 34, Plasterers 2, Ploughmaker 1, Plumbers 3, Potter 1, Printers 76. Saddlers 19, Sailmakers 2, Ship Carpenters 9, Shipjoiners 2, Shipwrights 40, Silversmiths 2, Stereotypists 2, Stone cutters 9, Storekeepers 439, Surveyors 3. Tailors 15, Tanner 1, Teachers 72, Tinsmiths 8, Tobacconists 5, Turners 6, Type founders 4. Umbrellamakers 4, Upholsterer 1. Watchmakers 6, Weavers 5, Wheelwrights 8. Not ascertained 29. Deceased while pupils 10.—Total, 2,107.

OCCUPATIONS *of the Parents or Guardians of the pupils admitted, from the opening, October* 22*d*, 1838, *to July* 16*th*, 1853.—Agents 6, Aldermen 2, Artists 3, Auctioneers 2. Bakers 24, Barbers 2, Blacksmiths 37, Blindmakers 2, Boarding-house keepers 13, Boilermaker 1, Bonnet pressers 3, Bookbinders 12, Booksellers 5, Bottlers 3, Brassfounders 6, Brewers 11, Bricklayers 29, Brickmakers 14, Bridlebit makers 2, Brokers 28, Brushmakers 12, Button-maker 1, Butcher 1. Cabinetmakers 35, Cap-maker 1, Carder 1, Car-builder 1, Carpenters 245, Carrier 1, Carters 24, Carvers and Gilders 3, Caulker 1, Chairmakers 6, Chaise-driver 1, Chemists 4, Clergymen 41, Clerks and Accountants 159, Coachmakers 6, Coachtrimmer 1, Coal dealers 8, Coal viewer 1, Coffee roaster 1, Coiners 2, Collectors 6, Combmakers 13, Comedians 2, Commission Merchants 11, Conductors 3, Confectioners 10, Contractor 1, Conveyancers 9, Coopers 16, Copper-plate printer 1, Copper-smiths 1, Corders 3, Cordwainers 128, County Commissioner 1, Curriers 18, Custom-house officers 3, Cutlers 2. Daguerreotypists 2, Dealers 22, Dentists 14, Distillers 10, Draymen 4, Drovers 3, Druggists 29, Dry goods Merchants 12, Dyers 10, Dye-sinkers 1. Editors 2, Engineers 11, Engravers 21. Farmers 42, Fishermen 7, Flour Inspector 1, Frame maker 1, Furriers 3. Gardeners 4, Gentlemen 4, Gentlewomen, (widows) 134, Gilders 4, Glass-blowers 5, Glove-maker 1, Goldbeaters 2, Grocers 100, Guager 1, Gunsmith 1. Hardware Merchants 12, Hair-dresser 1, Hatters 34, Hay Merchants 2, Horse dealers 2, Hose-makers 2, Hucksters 2. Ice-dealers 3, Importers 3, Inn-keepers 54, Iron-founders 8. Jewellers 16, Judges 6. Laborers 59, Lamp-maker 1, Lapidary 1, Lastmakers 3, Lawyers 35, Lime burner 1, Livery Stable keepers 3, Locksmiths 4, Lumber Merchants 9. Machinists 47, Mantuamakers 35, Manufacturers 73, Marble Mason 1, Mariners 36, Mast-Makers 2, Mathematical Instrument makers 6, Measurer and Surveyor 1, Merchants 145, Military Cap maker 1, Millers 12, Milliners 10. Millwrights 3, Miners 2, Morocco-dressers 4, Musical Instrument maker 1, Moulder 1. Organ builder 1, Oystermen 2. Painters 13, Paper Box makers 4, Paper-hangers 2, Paper manufacturer 1, Pattern-makers 3, Paviors 2, Pawnbrokers 4, Pedlars 2. Physicians 62, Piano forte makers 3, Plane makers 2, Plasterers 20, Plumbers 6, Porters 2, Portrait Painters 2, Potters 2, Printers 42, Prison-keeper 1, Publisher 1, Pumpmakers 4. Reedmaker 1, Refiner 1, Reporter 1, Rigger 1. Saddlers 31, Sailmakers 4, Sailing Masters 2, Salesmen 4, Sashmaker 1, Saw-makers 2, Sawyers 2, Scale maker 1, Seamstresses 28, Shipchandler 1, Shipjoiners 5, Shipsmiths 3, Shipwrights 29, Shuttle-maker 1, Silver-platers 3, Silver-smiths 4, Skin dresser 1, Slater 1, Soap boilers 2, Spar makers 2, Spectacle makers 2, Spinner 1, Spooler 1, Spring makers 2, Stage drivers 3, Starch manufacturer 1, Stereotype-founders 2, Stockmakers 2, Stone cutters 17, Stone Masons 5, Storekeepers 139, Stove finisher 1, Stove maker 1, Superintendent of Gas Works 1, Surgical Instrument makers 10, Surveyors 2, Suspender maker 1. Tailoresses 7, Tailors 86, Tallow Chandlers 4, Tanners 5, Teachers 49, Tinsmiths 16, Tobacconists 16, Traders 4, Tube maker 1, Turners 9, Type-founders 4. Umbrella makers 8, Undertakers 2, Upholsters 4. Varnisher 1, Victuallers 22. Warpers 2, Watchmakers 12, Watchmen 13, Weavers 39, Weigh Master 1, Wheelwrights 14, Whipmaker 1, Worker in Metal 1.—Total, 2,805.

HUGHES' CITY HIGH SCHOOL CINCINNATI.

Fig. 1.—PERSPECTIVE.

PLANS OF HUGHES' CITY HIGH SCHOOL OF CINCINNATI.

The Hughes City High School is one of two Public High Schools, sustained partly out of two trust estates, known as the "Woodward" and "Hughes" Funds, by the City of Cincinnati, as part of its system of public instruction. This system has grown up to its present extent and usefulness since 1828-9, when Col. Andrew Mack carried through the Legislature of Ohio, a bill for a special act, imposing a tax of $7,000 upon the city, for the erection of suitable buildings in the several wards, and an annual tax of $7,000 in each subsequent year, which, together with the State appropriation, was to be applied to the support of common schools. Under this act, the system was commenced, and in 1834, it was better grounded and greatly extended by an act authorizing the City Council to build substantial school-houses, and to provide for the support of common schools therein at the expense of the city. Accordingly, the city was divided into districts, and in the course of four years nine buildings were erected, at an expense of $96,000—which, in location, size, and arrangement, were greatly in advance of the then generally received notices of school architecture. From year to year the number of houses has been increased, to meet the demands of the growing population, and the style and fixtures greatly improved. The care of the schools is committed to a Board of Trustees and Visitors, one for each ward, elected by the legal voters thereof.

In 1845, the board were authorized to establish schools of different grades, and in 1847, a Central High School was organized under the charge of Prof. H. H. Barney, who has just (1853,) been elected State Superintendent of Common Schools.

In 1850, the Legislature authorized the appointment of a Superintendent of Common Schools, "whose duty it should be to visit and superintend all the common schools of the city, and, under the direction of the board of trustees and visitors of common schools, to establish such course of studies, rules, and regulations as may be deemed best calculated to promote the progress and well being of said schools."

In 1852, the Woodward and Hughes Funds, amounting to $300,000, and yielding an annual income of over $6,000, were united for the purpose of sustaining two High Schools, in different sections of the city—with the same requisites for admission and course of study, and open to both sexes.

For the Hughes City High School a lot on Fifth-street was purchased for $18,000, and a building, of which the following diagrams present the size, and internal accommodations, was completed in 1853, at an expense of $20,000.

The system of Public Instruction in Cincinnati, embraces:

I. District schools—one for each of the twelve districts, into which the city is divided for school purposes. Each school is classified into four sections or grades, and the pupils pass from the lowest to the next highest on examination, which is held twice a year. In 1850, there were 6,740 pupils, under 148 teachers, of whom 124 were females.

II. German English Schools—three in number, are intended for the special accommodations of children born of German parents—and who are taught both the German and English language. In 1850, there were three schools, twenty-four teachers, and twenty-three hundred pupils.

III. Evening Schools. Cincinnati was one of the first cities to provide this class of schools for children who could not attend the day schools, and for adults whose early education had been neglected. In 1850, there were six schools, open five evenings in the week from October to February, with about six hundred pupils.

IV. High Schools—of which there are now (1853) two.

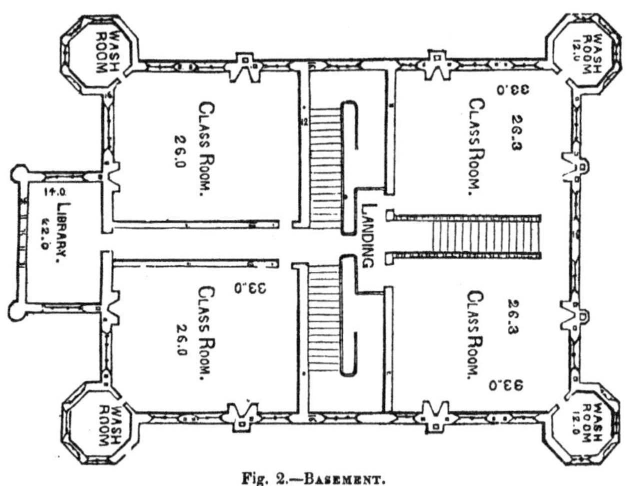

Fig. 2.—Basement.

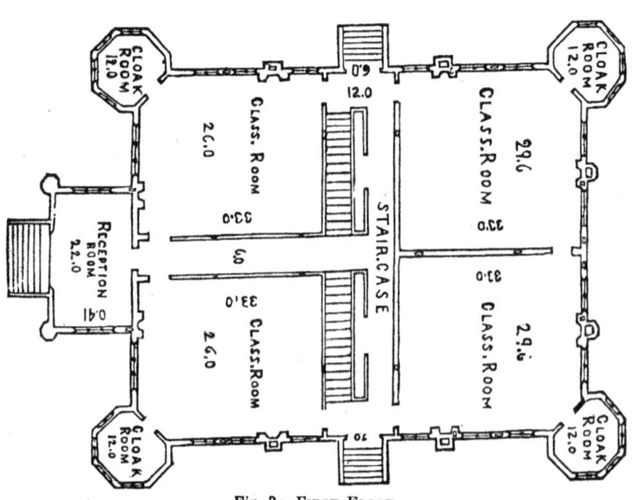

Fig. 3.—First Floor.

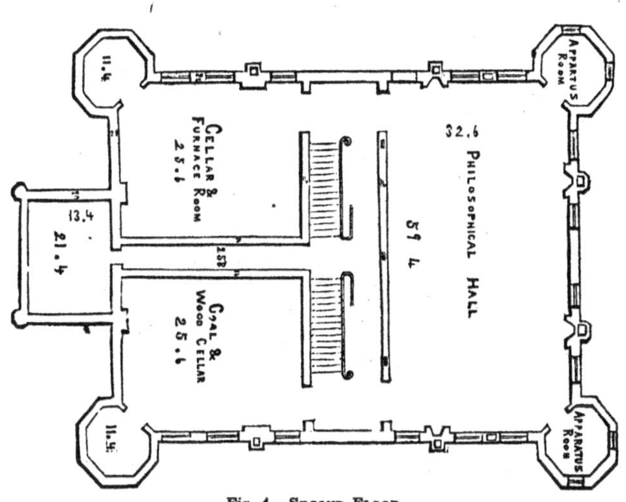

Fig. 4.—SECOND FLOOR.

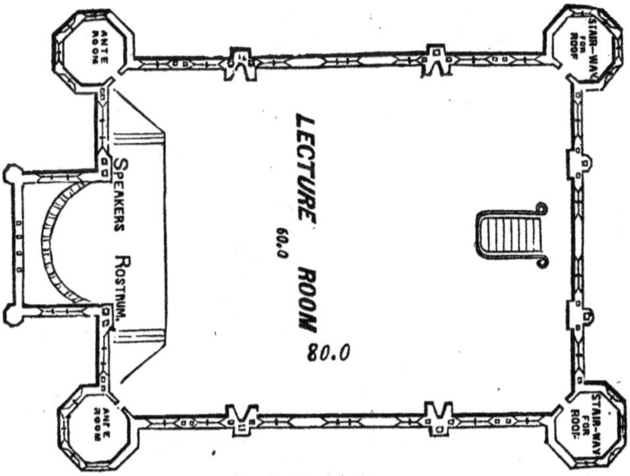

Fig. 5.—THIRD FLOOR.

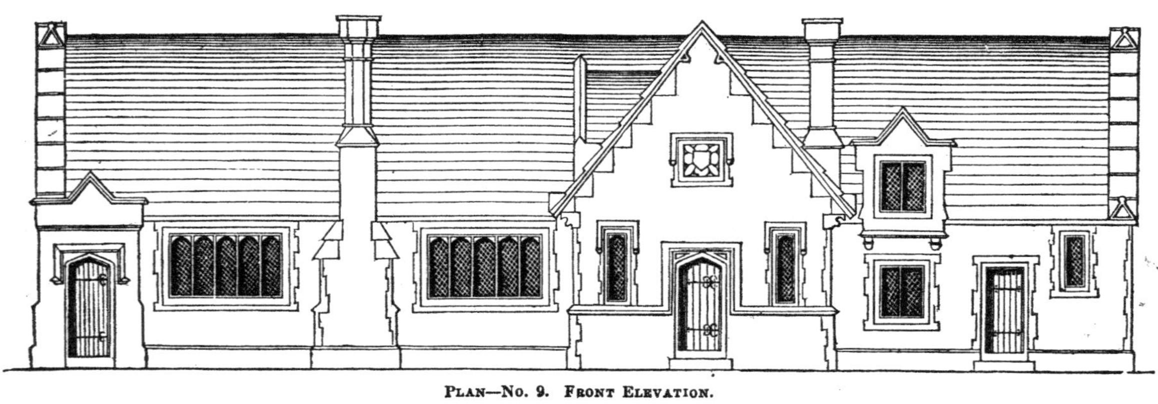

Plan—No. 9. Front Elevation.

Public High School.

In the preceding pages we have presented a variety of plans for the construction and internal arrangements of buildings designed and erected for Public High Schools. Whenever and wherever the interest of the community can be sufficiently awakened to call for a public school of the grade generally understood by the term High School, there will be no difficulty in raising the funds necessary to erect and furnish a suitable edifice for the accommodation of the school. It may not, then, be amiss in this place to present a few considerations and facts bearing upon the establishment of a school of this grade in every large village and city in our country.

By a Public or Common High School, is intended a public or common school for the older and more advanced scholars of the community in which the same is located, in a course of instruction adapted to their age, and intellectual and moral wants, and, to some extent, to their future pursuits in life. It is common or public in the same sense in which the district school, or any lower grade of school established and supported under a general law and for the public benefit, is common or public. It is open to all the children of the community to which the school belongs, under such regulations as to age, attainments, &c., as the good of the institution may require, or the community may adopt. A Public High School is not necessarily a free school. It may be supported by a fund, a public tax, or an assessment or rate of tuition per scholar, or by a combination of all, or any two of these modes. Much less is it a public or common school in the sense of being cheap, inferior, ordinary. To be truly a public school, a High School must embrace in its course of instruction studies which can be more profitably pursued there than in public schools of a lower grade, or which gather their pupils from a more circumscribed territory, and as profitably as in any private school of the same pretensions. It must make a good education common in the highest and best sense of the word common—common because it is good enough for the best, and cheap enough for the poorest family in the community. It would be a mockery of the idea of such a school, to call it a Public High School, if the course of instruction pursued in it is not higher and better than can be got in public schools of a lower grade, or if it does not meet the wants of the wealthiest and best educated families, or, if the course of instruction is liberal and thorough, and at the same time the worthy and talented child of a poor family is shut out from its privileges by a high rate of tuition. The school, to be common practically, must be both cheap and good. To be cheap, its support must be provided for wholly or mainly out of a fund, or by public tax. And to justify the imposition of a public tax, the advantages of such a school must accrue to the whole community. It must be shown to be a common benefit, a common interest, which cannot be secured so well, or at all, except through the medium of taxation. What, then, are the advantages which may reasonably be anticipated from the establishment of a Public High School, properly organized, instructed, and supervised?

First. Every thing which is now done in the several district schools, and schools of lower grade, can be better done, and in a shorter time, because the teachers will be relieved from the necessity of devoting the time and attention now required by few of the older and more advanced pupils, and can bestow all their time and attention upon the preparatory studies and younger children. These studies will be taught in methods suited to the age and attainments of the pupils. A right beginning can thus be made in the lower schools, in giving a thorough practical knowledge of elementary principles, and in the formation of correct mental and moral habits, which are indispensable to all sound education. All this will be done under the additional stimulus of being early and thoroughly fitted for the High School.

Second. A High School will give completeness to the system of public instruction which may be in operation. It will make suitable provision for the older and more advanced pupils of both sexes, and will admit of the methods of instruction and discipline which cannot be profitably introduced into the schools below. The lower grade of schools—those which are established for young children,—require a large use of oral and simultaneous methods, and a frequent change of place and position on the part of the pupils. The higher branches, especially all mathematical subjects, require patient application and habits of abstraction on the part of the older pupils, which can with difficulty, if at all, be attained by many pupils amid a multiplicity of distracting exercises, movements, and sounds. The recitations of this class of pupils, to be profitable and satisfactory, must be conducted in a manner which requires time, discussion, and explanation, and the undivided attention both of pupils and teacher. The course of instruction provided in the High School will be equal in extent and value to that which may be given in any private school, academy, or female seminary in the place, and which is now virtually denied to the great mass of the children by the burdensome charge of tuition.

As has been already implied, the advantages of a High School should not be confined to the male sex. The great influence of the female sex, as daughters, sisters, wives, mothers, companions, and teachers, in determining the manners, morals, and intelligence of the whole community, leaves no room to question the necessity of providing for the girls the best means of intellectual and moral culture. The course of instruction should embrace the first principles of natural and mechanical philosophy, by which inventive genius and practical skill in the useful arts can be fostered; such studies as navigation, book-keeping, surveying, botany, chemistry, and kindred studies, which are directly connected with success in the varied departments of domestic and inland trade, with foreign commerce, with gardening, agriculture, the manufacturing and domestic arts;

such studies as astronomy, physiology, the history of our own state and nation, the principles of our state and national constitutions, political economy, and moral science; in fine, such a course of study as is now given in more than fifty towns and cities in New England, and which shall prepare every young man, whose parents may desire it, for business, or for college, and give to every young woman a well disciplined mind, high moral aims, refined tastes, gentle and graceful manners, practical views of her own duties, and those resources of health, thought, conversation, and occupation, which bless alike the highest and lowest station in life. When such a course is provided and carried out, the true idea of the High School will be realized.

Third. It will equalize the opportunities of a good education, and exert a happy, social influence throughout the whole community from which it gathers its scholars. From the want of a public school of this character, the children of such families as rely exclusively on the district school are isolated, and are condemned to an inferior education, both in quality and quantity; they are cut off from the stimulus and sympathy which the mingling of children of the same age from different parts of the same community would impart. The benefits, direct and indirect, which will result to the country districts, or poor families who live in the outskirts of the city, from the establishment of a school of this class, cannot easily be overestimated. The number of young men and young women who will receive a thorough education, qualifying them for business, and to be teachers, will increase from year to year; and the number who will press up to the front ranks of scholarship in the school, bearing away the palm of excellence by the vigor of sound minds in sound bodies, of minds and bodies made vigorous by long walks and muscular labor in the open air, will be greater in proportion to their number than from the city districts. It will do both classes good, the children of the city, and the children of the country districts, to measure themselves intellectually in the same fields of study, and to subject the peculiarities of their respective manners, the roughness and awkwardness sometimes characteristic of the one, and the artificiality and flippancy of the other, to the harmonizing influence of reciprocal action and reaction. The isolation and estrangement which now divide and subdivide the community into country and city clans, which, if not hostile, are strangers to each other, will give place to the frequent intercourse and esteem of individual and family friendship, commenced in the school-room, and on the play-ground of the school. The school will thus become a bond of union, a channel of sympathy, a spring-head of healthy influence, and stimulus to the whole commnnity.

Fourth. The privileges of a good school will be brought within the reach of all classes of the community, and will actually be enjoyed by children of the same age from families of the most diverse circumstances as to wealth, education, and occupation. Side by side in the same recitations, heart and hand in the same sports, pressing up together to the same high attainments in knowledge and character, will be found the children of the rich and poor, the more and the less favored in outward circumstances, without knowing or caring to know how far their families are separated by the arbitrary distinctions which divide and distract society. With nearly equal opportunities of education in childhood and youth, the prizes of life, its best fields of usefulness, and sources of happiness will be open to all, whatever may have been their accidents of birth and fortune. From many obscure and humble homes in the city and in the country, will be called forth and trained inventive talent, productive skill, intellectual taste, and God-like benevolence, which will add to the general wealth, multiply workshops, increase the value of farms, and carry forward every moral and religious enterprise which aims to bless, purify, and elevate society.

Fifth. The influence which the annual or semi-annual examination of candidates for admission into the High School, will operate as a powerful and abiding stimulus to exertion throughout all the lower schools. The privileges of the High School will be held forth as the reward of exertion in the lower grade of schools; and promotion to it, based on the result of an impartial examination, will form an unobjectional standard by which the relative standing of the different schools can be ascertained, and will also indicate the studies and departments of education to which the teachers in particular schools should devote special attention. This influence upon the lower schools, upon scholars and teachers, upon those who reach, and those who do not reach the High School, will be worth more than all it costs, independent of the advantages received by its pupils.

Sixth. While the expenses of public or common schools will necessarily be increased by the establishment of a school of this class, in addition to those already supported, the aggregate expenditures for education, including public and private schools, will be diminished. Private schools of the same relative standing will be discontinued for want of patronage, while those of a higher grade, if really called for by the educational wants of the community, will be improved. A healthy competition will necessarily exist between the public and private schools of the highest grade, and the school or schools which do not come up to the highest mark, must go down in public estimation. Other things being equal, viz., school-houses, teachers, classification, and the means and appliances of instruction, the public school is always better than the private. From the uniform experience of those places where a High School has been established, it may be safely stated, that there will be an annual saving in the expenses of education to any community, equal to one half the amount paid for tuition in private schools, and, with this saving of expense, there will be a better state of education.

Seventh. The successful establishment of a High School, by improving the whole system of common schools, and interesting a larger number of families in the prosperity of the schools, will create a better public sentiment on the subject than has heretofore existed, and the schools will be regarded as the common property, the common glory, the common security of the whole community. The wealthy will feel that the small additional tax required to establish and sustain this school, if not saved to them in the diminished tuition for the education of their own children in private schools, at home and abroad, is returned to them a hundred fold in the enterprise which it will quicken, in the increased value given to property, and in the number of families which will resort to the place where it is located, as a desirable residence, because of the facilities enjoyed for a good education. The poor will feel that, whatever may betide them, their children are born to an inheritance more valuable than lands or shops, in the free access to institutions where as good an education can be had as money can buy at home or abroad. The stranger will be invited to visit not only the institutions which public or individual benevolence has provided for the poor, the orphan, the deaf mute, and the criminal, but schools where the children and youth of the community are trained to inventive and creative habits of mind, to a practical knowledge of the fundamental principles of business, to sound moral habits, refined tastes, and respectful manners. And in what balance, it has well been asked in reference to the cost of good public schools, as compared with these advantages, shall we weigh the value of cultivated, intelligent, energetic, polished, and virtuous citizens? How much would a community be justified in paying for a physician who should discover or practice some mode of treatment through which many lives should be preserved? How much for a judge, who, in the able administration of the laws, should secure many fortunes, or rights more precious than fortunes, that might else be lost? How much for a minister of religion who should be the instrument of saving hundreds from vice and crime, and persuading them to the exertion of their best powers for the common good? How much for the ingenious inventor, who, proceeding from the first principles of science onward, should produce some improvement that should enlarge all the comforts of society, not to say a steam-engine or a magnetic telegraph? How much for the patriotic statesman, who, in difficult times, becomes the savior of his country? How much for the well-instructed and enterprising merchant who should suggest and commence the branches of business that should bring in a vast accession of wealth and strength? One such person as any of these might repay what a High School would cost for centuries. Whether, in the course of centuries, every High School would produce one such person, it would be useless to prophesy. But it is certain that it would produce many intelligent citizens, intelligent men of business, intelligent servants of the state, intelligent teachers, intelligent wives and daughters, who, in their several spheres, would repay to any community much more than they and all their associates had received. The very taxes of a town, in twenty years, will be lessened by the existence of a school which will continually have sent forth those who were so educated as to become not burdens but benefactors.

These results have been realized wherever a Public High School has been opened under circumstances favorable to the success of a private school of the same grade,—wherever a good school-house, good regulations, (for admission, attendance, studies, and books,) good teachers, and good supervision have been provided.

The Principal of the Latin High School of Boston, in a letter written 1846, says,—

"There is no institution so truly republican as such a school as this. While we, the present teachers, were undergraduates of the school, the rich sent their sons to the school because it was the best that could be found. They ascertained that it was not a source of contamination, but that their boys learned here to compare themselves with others, and to feel the necessity of something more that mere *wealth* to gain consideration. At that time, poor men sent their sons hither because they knew that they here would get that education which they could afford to give them in no other way. They gained too by intercourse with their wealthier mates a polish of exterior manners, and an intellectual turn of mind which their friends could appreciate and perceive, although they could not tell what it was that had been acquired. Oftentimes also the poor boy would take the lead of his more pampered classmate, and take the honors of the school.

In a class lately belonging to the school were two boys, one the son of a man of extreme wealth, whose property cannot be less than $500,000; and the other the son of an Irish laborer employed by the city at a dollar a day to sweep the streets. The latter boy was the better scholar."

The Principal of the English High School in a letter writes,—

"The school under my charge is pricipally composed of what are called the middling classes of our city. At present, about one third of my pupils are sons of merchants; the remaining two thirds are sons of professional men, mechanics and others. Some of our best scholars are sons of coopers, lamplighters, and day laborers. A few years ago, he who ranked, the last year of his course, as our third scholar, was the son of a lamplighter, and worked three nights per week, during his whole course, to save his father the expense of books, &c., while at school. This year my second (if not the first,) scholar, is a cooper's son. We have several sons of clergymen of distinction and lawyers of eminence. Indeed, the school is a perfect example of the poor and the rich, meeting on common ground and on terms quite democratic."

The Principal of the High School for girls in Newburyport, writes,

"The Female High School was established by the town of Newburyport nearly three years since, under great opposition. It was the desire of its principal advocates to make it such a school, in respect to the course of instruction, and facilities for acquiring knowledge, and laying the foundation for usefulness, as should so successfully compete with our best private schools, as to supersede their necessity."

"A few days after we were organized, a gentleman came into the schoolroom to make some inquiries respecting the classes of society most fully represented amongst us. I was totally unable to give him the desired information, and judging from the appearance of the individuals of my charge, I could form no idea as to who were the children of poor parents, or of those in better circumstances. I mentioned the names of the parents of several, which I had just taken, and, amongst others, of two young ladies of seventeen or eighteen years of age, who, at that moment, it being recess, were walking down the room, with their arms closely entwined about each other's necks. 'The first of the two,' said the gentleman, 'is a daughter of one of our first merchants, the other has a father worse than none, who obtains a livelihood from one of the lowest and most questionable occupations, and is himself most degraded' These two young ladies were classmates for more than two years, and very nearly equal in scholarship. The friendship they have formed, I am confident no circumstances of station in life can ever impair.

"We have had in our number many from the best families, in all respects, in the place. They sit side by side, they recite, and they associate most freely with those of the humblest parentage, whose widowed mothers, perhaps, toil day after day, at a wash-tub, without fear of contamination, or, as I honestly believe, a thought of the differences which exist. I have, at present, both extremes under my charge—the child of affluence and the child of low parentage and deep poverty. As my arrangements of pupils in divisions, &c. are, most of them, alphabetical, it often happens that the two extremes are brought together. This never causes a murmur, or look of dislike.

A member of the School Committee of Worcester, Mass., writes:

"Our High School is exceedingly popular with all classes, and in the school-rooms and on the play-grounds, the children of the richest and poorest mingle with perfect equality. No assumption,—no jealousy are seen among them. I have been charmed with this republican and Christian character of the school. I have seen the children of parents whose wealth was estimated by hundreds of thousands, in the same school-room with children (and those last among the best scholars of their class) whose parents have been assisted year after year by individual charity. The manners, habits, and moral sentiments of this school are as pure and high as in any academy, or female seminary of the same grade in the commonwealth.

"To the improvements of our public schools, which has been going steadily forward since 1825, does this town owe more of its prosperity, its large accession of families from abroad, especially of industrious and skillful mechanics, than to all other causes combined. As a mere investment of capital, men of wealth everywhere cannot do better with a portion of their property than to build elegant and attractive school-houses, and open in them free schools of the highest order of instruction. They will then see gathering around them men, it may be, of small means, but of practical skill, and moral and industrious habits; that class of families who feel that one of the great ends of life is to educate their children well."

A correspondent from Brattleboro', Vt., writes:

"In the same school-room, seated side by side, according to age and attainments, are eighty children, representing all classes and conditions in society. The lad or miss, whose father pays a school tax of thirty-five dollars, by the side of another whose expense of instruction is five cents *per annum*. They play cordially and happily on the same grounds, and pursue the same studies—the former frequently incited by the native superiority and practical good sense of the latter. While the contact corrects the factitious gentility and false ideas of superiority in the one, it encourages cleanliness and good breeding in the other."

The history of the High School in Providence is the history of almost every similar institution.

"The High School was the only feature of our system which encountered much opposition. When first proposed, its bearings on the schools below, and in various ways on the cause of education in the city, was not clearly seen. It was opposed because it was "aristocratic," "because it was unconstitutional to tax property for a city college," "because it would educate children above working for their support," "because a poor boy or girl would never be seen in it"—and for all such contradictory reasons. Before it became a part of the system, the question of its adoption, or rejection, was submitted directly to the people, who passed in its favor by a vote of two thirds of all the legal voters of the city. Even after this expression of popular vote in its favor, and after the building for its accommodation was erected, there was a considerable minority who circulated a petition to the City Council against its going into operation. But the school was opened, and now it would be as easy to strike out the whole or any other feature of the system as this. Its influence in giving stimulus and steadiness to the workings of the lower grade of schools,—in giving thoroughness and expansion to the whole course of instruction,—in assisting to train teachers for our city and country schools,—and in bringing together the older and more advanced pupils, of either sex, from families of every profession, occupation and location in the city, many of whom, but for the opportunities of this school, would enter on the business and duties of life with an imperfect education—has demonstrated its own usefulness as a part of the system, and has converted its opponents into friends."

Testimony of the same character might be adduced from Philadelphia, Lowell, New Orleans, and every place where a school of this grade has been established.

The growth and influence of a Public High School, when liberally sustained, is admirably illustrated in the history of the Central High School of Philadelphia.

Normal Schools, or Teachers' Seminaries.

By a Normal† School, or Teachers' Seminary, is meant an institution for the training of young men and young women who aim to be teachers, to a thorough and practical knowledge of the duties of the school-room, and to the best modes of reaching the heart and intellect, and of developing and building up the whole character of a child. It aims to do for the young and inexperienced teacher, all that the direction and example of the master-workman, and all that the experience of the workshop do for the young mechanic—all that the naval and military schools do for those who lead in any capacity in the army or navy—all that the law school, or the medical school, or the theological seminary do for the professions of law, medicine, or theology. In every department of mechanical, artistic, or professional labor, the highest skill is attained only after long and appropriate training under wise superintendence; and the Normal School aims to impart this previous training by providing a thorough course of instruction, under competent teachers, with reference to teaching the same things to others. This course of instruction involves the whole art of teaching—a knowledge of human nature, and of a child's nature in particular—of the human mind, and especially of a child's mind, and of the order in which its several faculties should be called into exercise; of the best motives by which good habits of study can be cultivated in the young; of the arrangement and classification of scholars, and of the best means and appliances for securing obedience and order, and keeping alive an interest in the daily exercises of the school. And this art of teaching must be illustrated and exemplified by those who are to apply it, in a model school. The idea of such a school is not a mere speculation of ardent benevolence—it is an existing reality in this country as well as in Europe.

The first school specially destined for educating and training teachers in the principles and practice of their profession, was instituted by the Abbé de La Salle, while Canon of the Cathedral at Rheims, in 1681, and was perfected into the Institute of the Brothers of the Christian Schools, in 1684.

In 1697, Augustus Herman Franké founded, in connection with his orphan school at Halle, a teacher's class composed of poor students, who assisted him certain hours in the day in his schools, in return for their board and instruction. Out of these, he selected, about the year 1704, twelve, who exhibited the right basis of piety, knowledge, and aptness to teach, and constituted them his "Seminarium Præceptorum" or Teachers Seminary. These pupils received separate instruction for two years, and acquired a due degree of practical skill, in the classes of the same general establishment. Teachers thus trained, and hundreds of others, who resorted to Halle, to profit by the organization and spirit of the schools of Franké, disseminated a knowledge of better methods of school organization and instruction throughout Europe, in the course of the next half century.

In 1735, the first regular seminary for teachers in Prussia was established in Pomerania, and the second at Berlin, in 1748, by Hecker, a pupil of Franke. By a royal ordinance in 1752, Frederic 2d enjoined that all vacancies in the country schools on the crown lands, in certain sections of his kingdom, should be supplied by pupils from Hecker's Seminary. The King at the same time allowed an annual stipend for the support of twelve alumni of this establishment, a number which in 1788 was raised to sixty. In 1773, the chools established at Rekahn, in Brandenburg, became the model schools to which young men resorted from every part of Germany to be trained in the principles and practice of primary instruction. Prior to 1800, there were but six of these institutions in Prussia. But it is the pride and glory of this monarchy, that in periods of the greatest national distress and disaster, when the armies of France were desolating her fields, occupying her citadels, and diverting her revenues, the great work of improving her schools was never lost sight of. The establishment of teachers' seminaries still went forward; that at Konigsburg in 1809, at Branersburg in 1810, and at Breslau in 1812. But not content with establishing these seminaries at home, the most promising young teachers were sent into other countries to acquire a knowledge of all improvements in the science and art of education.

Normal Schools were introduced into Hanover in 1757; into Austria in 1767; into Switzerland in 1805; into France in 1808; into Holland in 1816; into Belgium in 1843, and into England in 1842.

In Prussia and most of the German States, there are now enough of these institutions to supply the demand for teachers in the public schools. Saxony, with a population less than that of the State of New York, supports five Normal Schools, and Saxe-Weimar, with a population less than that of Connecticut, supports two. Prussia, with a population of fourteen millions, has at this time forty-nine seminaries, in which there are nearly three thousand teachers. At the end of three years after leaving the seminary, the young teachers return for a re-examination.

In Great Britain, after years of strenuous effort on the part of the friends of popular education, the importance of Normal Schools as the chief means for improving the qualifications of teachers, has been recognized by the Government. The Training School at Chelsea, (called St. Mark's College,) under the management of the National Society, the Normal and Model School of the British and Foreign School Society, the Battersea Training School, and the Model School of the Infant School Society in England, the Model School of the National Board for Ireland, the Normal Schools at Edinburgh and Glasgow in Scotland, are all aided out of the annual parliamentary grant for education.

In this country, the claims of these institutions were first distinctly presented by Rev. Thomas H. Gallaudet, of Hartford, Conn., in 1825, and by James G. Carter, of Lancaster, Mass., in a series of essays on the subject, and by William Russell, of Boston, in the Journal of Education for 1826. One fact is certain, the improvement of schools in every country has followed hand in hand with the establishment, multiplication, and improvement of Normal Schools.

Plans and Descriptions of the Massachusetts Normal School-Houses.

The following plans and descriptions are copied from the "Tenth Annual Report of the Secretary of the Massachusetts Board of Education," with the permission of the Hon. Horace Mann, by whose indefatigable labors these institutions were founded, seconded as his efforts were by the munificent donation of the sum of ten thousand dollars, from the Hon. Edmund Dwight, of Boston.

These buildings were erected partly out of the contribution of $5000, subscribed originally by the friends of Mr. Mann, as a testimony of their esteem for his public services, and, at his suggestion, invested in this way—thus converting these edifices into the monuments of their generosity, and of his self-sacrifice.

Bridgewater State Normal School-House.

Fig. 1.—Front Elevation.

This edifice is constructed of wood, and is sixty-four feet by forty-two, and two stories in height. The upper story is divided into a principal school room, forty-one feet by forty, and two recitation-rooms, each twenty feet by twelve, and is designed for the Normal School. The lower story is fitted up for a Model School.

BRIDGEWATER STATE NORMAL SCHOOL-HOUSE.

Fig. 2.—LOWER STORY.

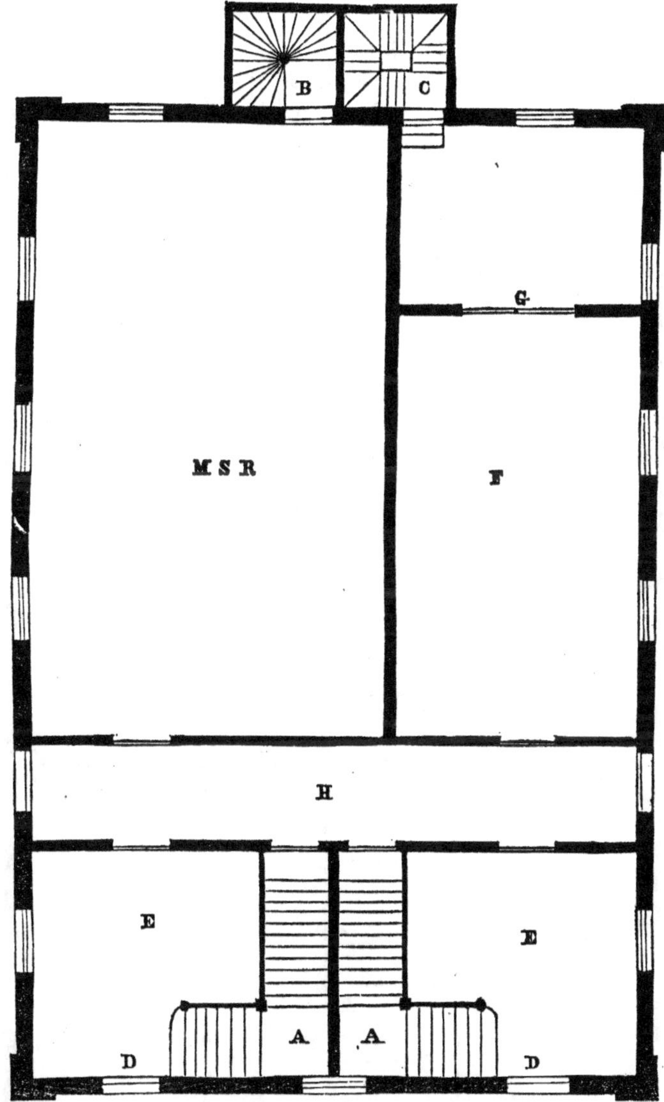

D, D—Doors, one for males, the other for females. E, E—Hall-entries, into which the doors D, D open, 19 feet by 15. A, A—Stairways, leading from the entries to the Normal School-room. M, S, R—Model School-room, 40 feet by 24, with single seats and desks. H—Entry-way, 6 feet 8 inches wide, for Model School scholars. At each end of this entry is an outside door, for the entrance of the Model School scholars—a separate entrance for each sex. G, F—Laboratory and chemical room, or lecture-room, connected by folding doors. The two rooms 40 feet by 16. B, C—Back stairways.

Bridgewater State Normal School-House.

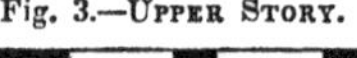

Fig. 3.—Upper Story.

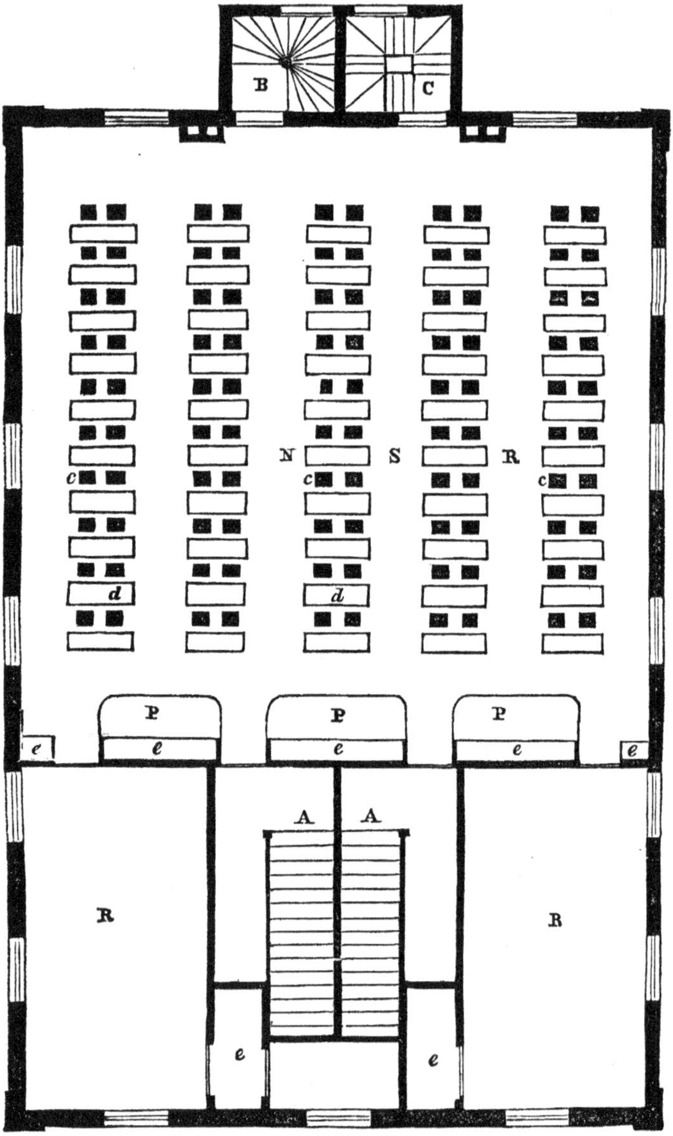

A, A—Separate stairways, for the different sexes, leading from the lower entries, or halls, to the Normal School-room. N, S, R—Normal School-room 41 feet by 40. c, c, c—Single seats. d, d—Double desks. P, P, P—Teachers' platform. e, e, e, e, e—Behind the platform are recesses in the partition for a library. e, e—Between R, R, are closets for apparatus. R, R—Recitation-rooms, 22 feet by 12. B, C—Back stairways.

WESTFIELD STATE NORMAL SCHOOL-HOUSE.

Fig. 4.—FRONT ELEVATION.

This edifice is of brick, of the size of sixty-two feet by forty feet, with a portico of eight feet at each end of the building, and is two stories in height. The Normal School-room is about forty feet square, and is provided with two recitation-rooms. The first story is fitted up with a room large enough to accommodate a Model School, which is composed of the children of one of the districts in the town of Westfield, the district having paid the sum of $1500 towards the erection of the building, and being obligated to pay an agreed proportion of the expenses of fuel, instruction, &c.

Westfield State Normal School-House.

Fig. 5.—Lower Story.

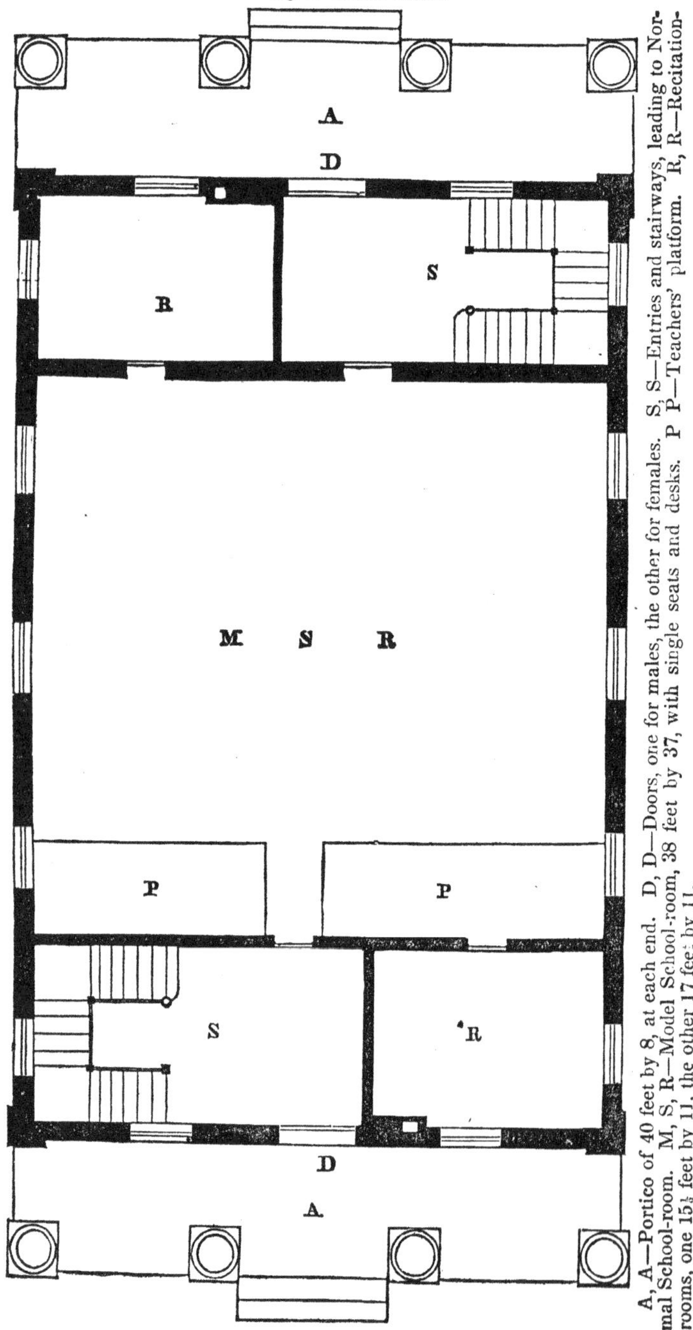

A, A—Portico of 40 feet by 8, at each end. D, D—Doors, one for males, the other for females. S, S—Entries and stairways, leading to Normal School-room. M, S, R—Model School-room, 38 feet by 37, with single seats and desks. P P—Teachers' platform. R, R—Recitation-rooms, one 15½ feet by 11, the other 17 feet by 11.

Westfield State Normal School-House.

Fig. 6.—Upper Story.

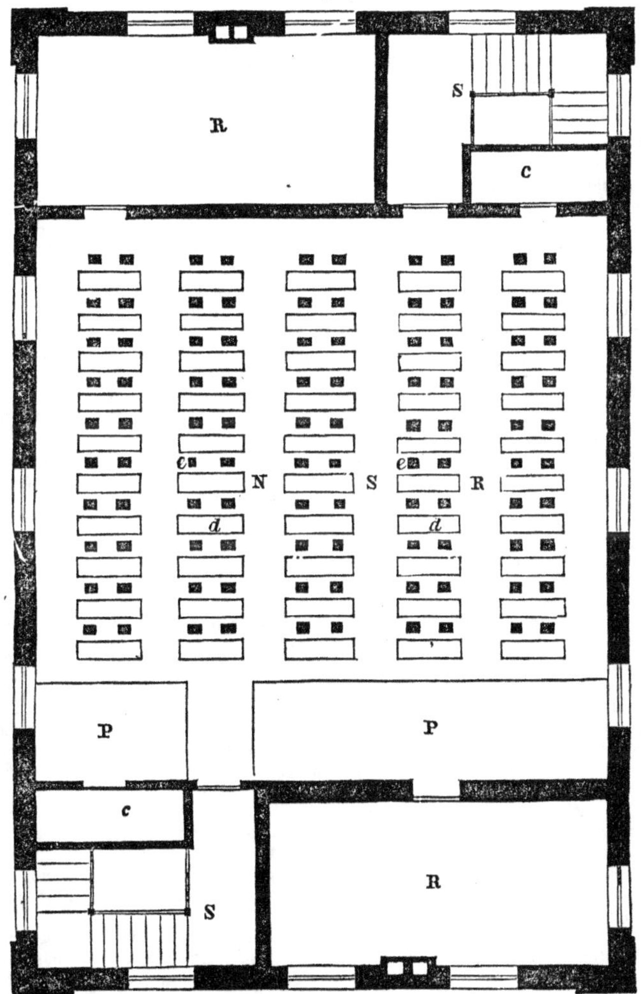

S, S—Stairways, leading from entry to Normal School-room. N, S, R—Normal School-room, 38 feet by 37. e, e—Single seats. d, d—Double desks. P, P—Platform, with recesses in the partition behind for a library. c, c—Closets for apparatus. R, R—Recitation-rooms, one 22 feet by 11, the other 22 feet by 10½.

Framingham State Normal School-house.

The State Normal School at Framingham is designed for female teachers, and was originally established at Lexington, in July, 1838, and removed to West Newton in 1846, and to Framingham in 1853. In each instance, as larger and better accommodations were demanded, the location was determined mainly by the liberality of the citizens, in offering greater facilities than other towns for the improvement of the pupils.

In 1852, the legislature appropriated six thousand dollars, to defray the expenses of providing a more commodious site and building, and the necessary appurtenances and apparatus for the accommodation of the Normal School, established at West Newton, to be expended for that purpose by the Board of Education, which was directed to receive propositions from towns or individuals in aid of the object, and to make such selection as would best subserve the interests and accommodate the wants of the school. The Board selected a site in the town of Framingham, offered to them by several of its citizens, the town itself having voted the sum of two thousand five hundred dollars toward the erection of the building, and the Boston and Worcester Railroad Company having also contributed the further sum of two thousand dollars for the same object.

The lot contains four and three-quarters acres of land, situated a few rods south of the central village of the town, on the south-western slope of a hill of gentle declivity, protected on the north by a grove of forest trees, and commanding a view of the surrounding country of wide extent and great beauty. The neighboring village is retired and quiet, containing three churches of different denominations, and a sufficient number of inhabitants to afford homes for the pupils, while the character of the people, owing to the absence of large manufacturing establishments, to the predominance of agricultural pursuits, and the residence in the neighborhood of many gentlemen who have either retired from business, or pursue it in the city at a distance from their dwellings, is calculated to exercise a favorable influence upon the young ladies who will compose the school.

The building is in the Norman style of architecture, sixty feet square, two stories high, with an entrance arcade, of the same height, thirty-two feet in length and fourteen in width.

The first story is finished, ten feet six inches in height, containing entrance halls and stair-cases, a commodious lecture room, which can also be used as a recitation room, an apparatus room adjoining the latter, a large recitation room, a dressing-room, with rooms adjoining, containing water-closets and other conveniences.

The second or principal story is finished, seventeen feet high, and is reached by two wide stair-cases, with two entrances to the school-room, which measures fifty-seven feet by thirty-six feet six inches, and has accommodations for one hundred and twenty pupils, which may be extended to one hundred and fifty, with a recitation room, a library, and the principal's room adjoining. The three last-mentioned rooms are finished, eight feet six inches in height, and over them is a large recitation room, and a room for the water cistern and storage.

The entire interior of the two stories is heated by furnaces in the cellar, and ventilated in a manner to insure a circulation of pure air at all times.

The house, (with furniture, fence, and appurtenances,) cost $15,750.00, and was dedicated by an appropriate address, by George B. Emerson, which is published in the Seventeenth Annual Report of the Board of Education, of which he is one of the most efficient members.

It may be mentioned here, to the credit of the legislature of Massachusetts in 1853, that, besides making an appropriation for the Normal School building above described, and for the erection of a fourth Normal School-house at Salem, and to aid pupils to prolong their attendance at these schools, forty-eight State scholarships in the colleges of Massachusetts were established, to provide for the education and training of young men for the office of principal teacher in the High Schools of the State. To each scholarship the sum of $100 per annum, for four years, is guarantied. The appointments are made by the Board of Education. To George B. Emerson, Esq., belongs the credit of bringing this subject before the committee of the legislature in a manner to command their unanimous approval. Mr. Emerson was the author of the memorial to the legislature, in behalf of Normal Schools, in 1835.

Fig. 2.—First Floor.

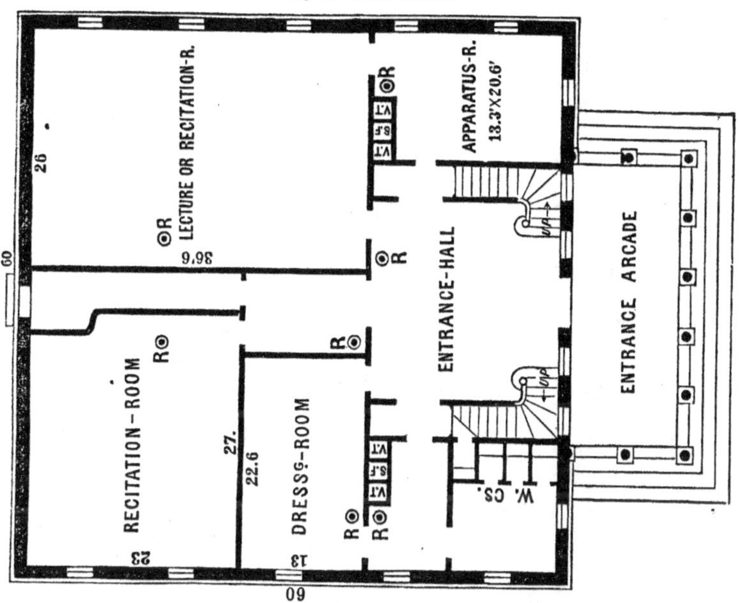

V. T—Ventilating Ducts. S. F—Smoke Flue. R—Registers for Hot Air.

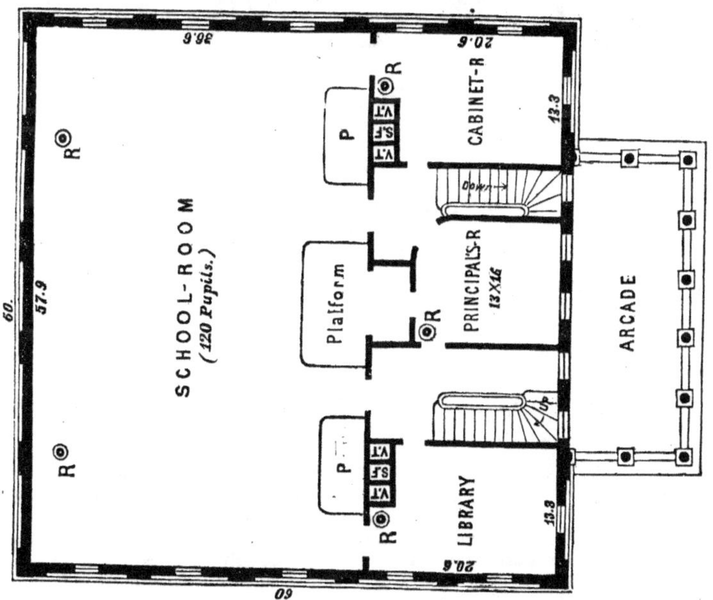

Fig. 3.—Second Floor.

Plans and Descriptions of State Normal School at Albany, New York.

Fig. 1.—Perspective.

The Normal School for the State of New York was established by an act of the Legislature, in 1844, "for the instruction and practice of Teachers of Common Schools, in the science of Education and the art of Teaching,"—such an institution, having been first recommended to the Legislature by Governor De Wit Clinton, in his message to the Legislature in 1825, and again, in 1826, "as the best plan of obtaining able teachers that could be derived," and because it was well calculated to have "most benign influence on individual happiness and social prosperity." After an experiment of seventeen years, in trying to train teachers in departments connected with certain academies—aided for this purpose out of the Literature Fund—on the recommendation of Samuel Young, Superintendent of Common Schools, and through the efforts of Calvin T. Hulburd, Chairman of the Committee on Colleges, Academies, and Common Schools, in the House of Representatives, Samuel S. Randall, Deputy Superintendent, Francis Dwight, Editor of the District School Journal, Prof. (now Bishop) Potter, the sum of $10,000 annually, for six years, was appropriated in 1844, for the support of a Normal School. It went into operation on the 18th of December, 1844, in a building provided gratuitously by the city of Albany, and temporarily fitted up for that purpose.

In 1848, an act was passed by the Legislature "for the permanent establishment of a State Normal School," appropriating $15,000 toward the erection of a suitable building. The following year an additional appropriation of $10,000 was made for its completion. A large and commodious edifice, (*see* Figs. 1, 2, 3, 4, 5, 6,) containing a dwelling-house for the Principal, has accordingly been erected on the corner of Lodge and Howard-streets, adjoining the State Geological and Agricultural Rooms. To this building the school was removed on the 31st of July, 1849.

FIG. 2. PLAN OF BASEMENT.

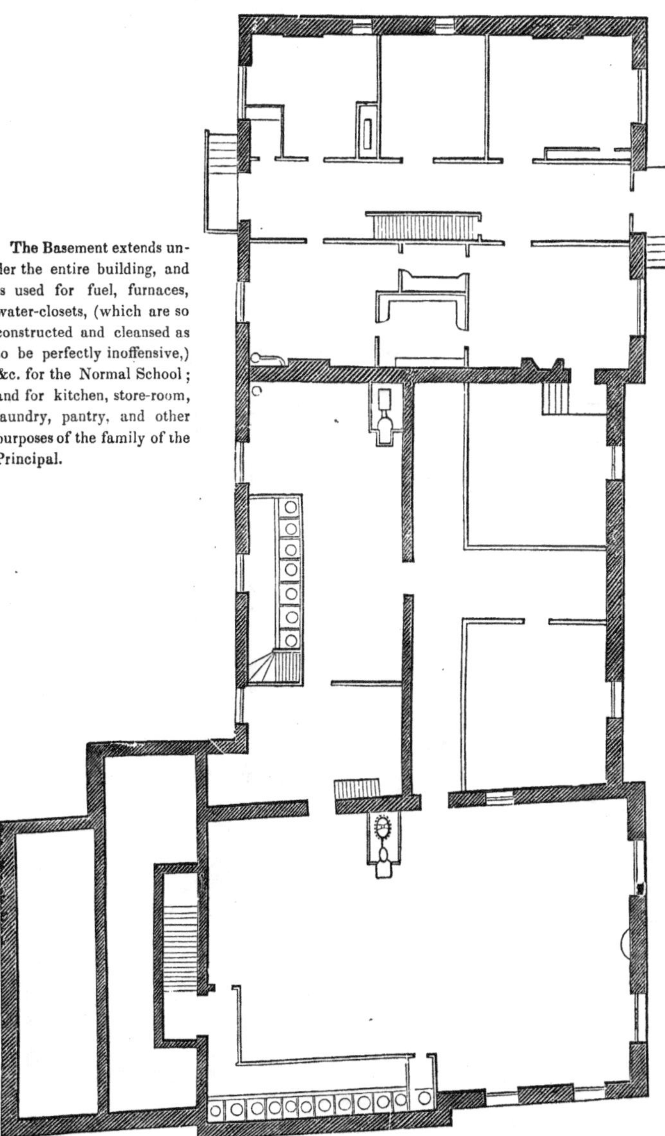

The Basement extends under the entire building, and is used for fuel, furnaces, water-closets, (which are so constructed and cleansed as to be perfectly inoffensive,) &c. for the Normal School; and for kitchen, store-room, laundry, pantry, and other purposes of the family of the Principal.

Fig. 3. Plan of First Floor.

FIG. 4. PLAN OF SECOND FLOOR.

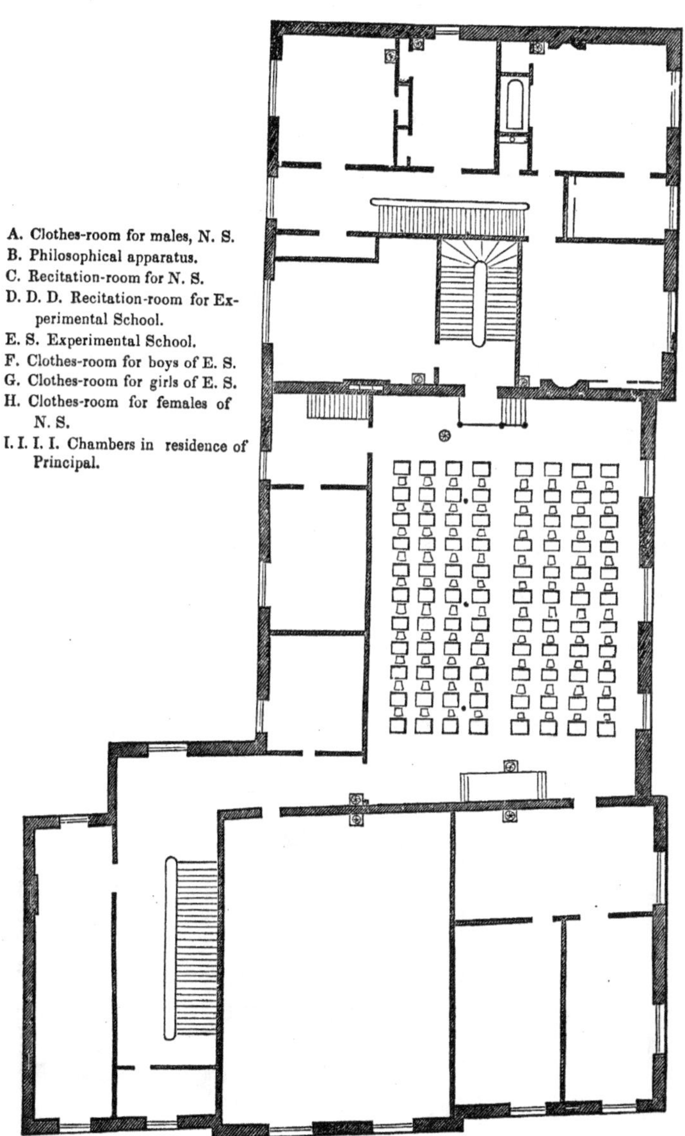

A. Clothes-room for males, N. S.
B. Philosophical apparatus.
C. Recitation-room for N. S.
D. D. D. Recitation-room for Experimental School.
E. S. Experimental School.
F. Clothes-room for boys of E. S.
G. Clothes-room for girls of E. S.
H. Clothes-room for females of N. S.
I. I. I. I. Chambers in residence of Principal.

FIG. 5. PLAN OF THIRD FLOOR.

A. Text book library.
B. Study-room of Normal School.
C. Desk and chairs for two pupils.
D. D. D. D. Recitation-rooms for N. S.

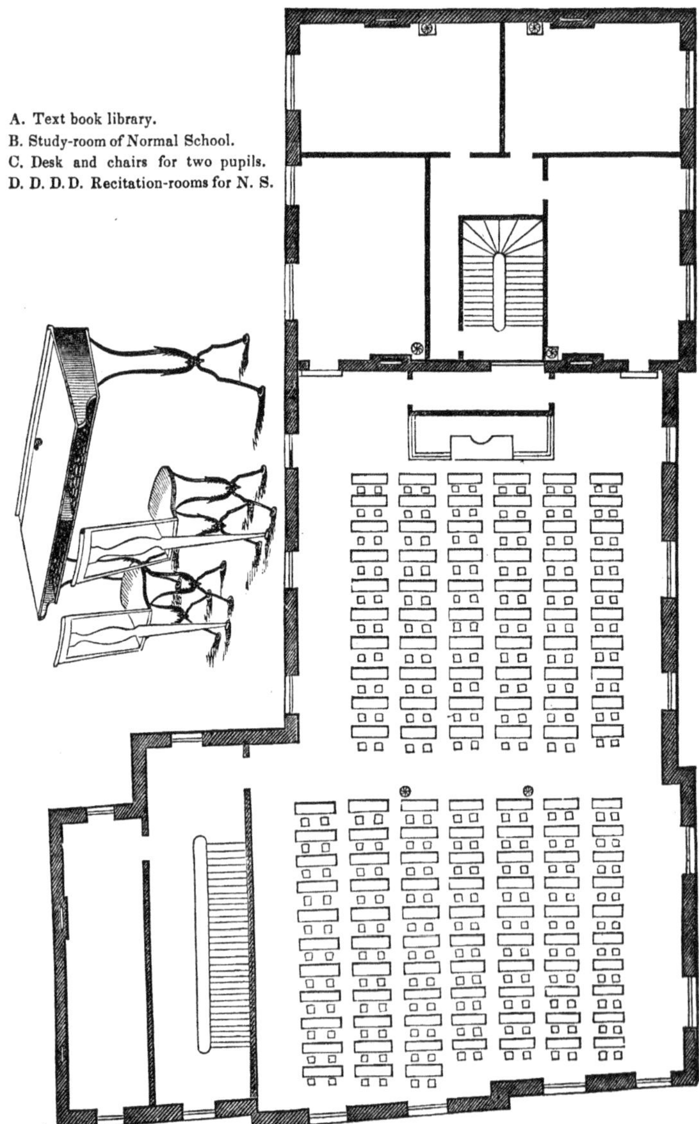

FIG. 6. PLAN OF FOURTH FLOOR.

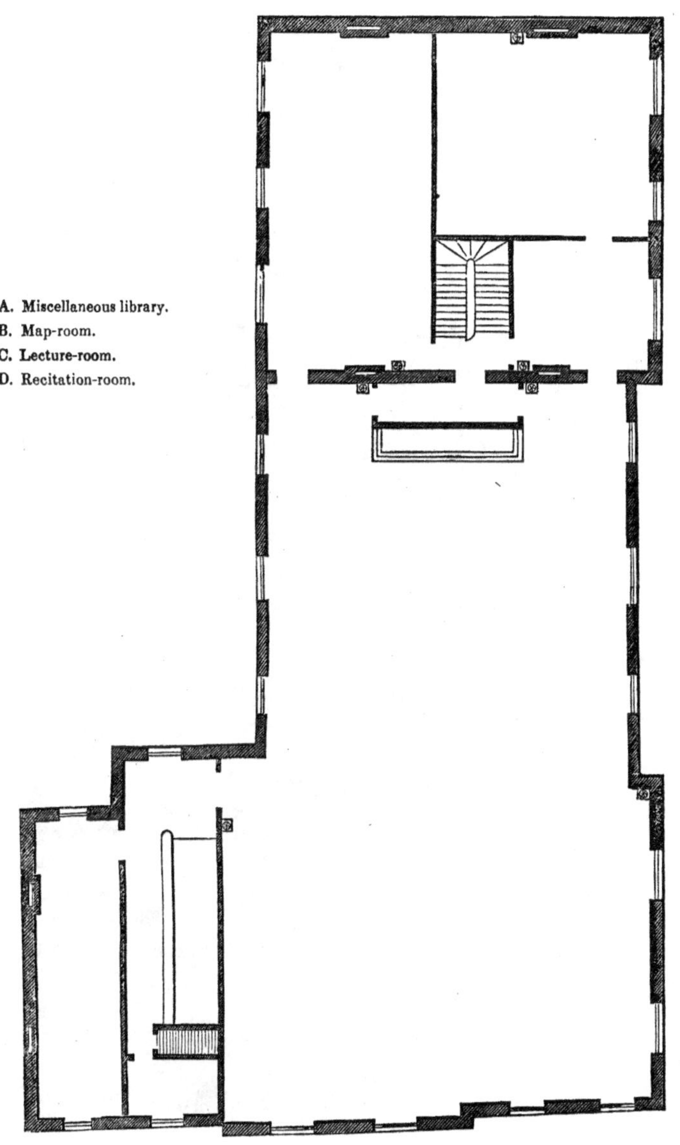

FIGURE 1.—PERSPECTIVE VIEW OF STATE NORMAL SCHOOL.

Plans and Description of the State Normal School at New Britain, Connecticut.

The Normal School at New Britain, was incorporated in 1849, by an "*Act for the establishment of a State Normal School,*" "for the training of teachers in the art of instructing and governing the Common Schools of the State." It was located at New Britain, by the Board of Trustees charged with its management, on account of the central position of the town, and its accessibility from every section by railroad; and also in consideration of the liberal offer, on the part of its citizens, to provide a suitable building, apparatus, and library, to the value of $16,000, for the use of the institution, and to place all the schools of the village under the management of the Principal of the Normal School, as Schools of Practice.

The building provided for the accommodation of the Normal School and Schools of Practice was erected by an association of citizens of New Britain, who were incorporated under the general law relating to "Joint Stock Corporations," with the name of the "New Britain Educational Fund Association."

The Normal School building consists of a structure, 70 feet long by 42 feet broad, commenced for a town hall before the location of the Normal School in New Britain, (and since purchased,) and an additional structure, 76 feet by 48. The original building is three stories in height; the new part, four.

The basement embraces two passages, one for males and one for females, to the yard; two large and convenient dressing-rooms; four entrance halls, furnished with hooks for clothes, &c. There are also in the basement story a room for the accommodation of the Intermediate School; a room for one of the Primary Schools; a chemical laboratory; a spacious wood and coal room; three furnace rooms, with furnaces and their fixtures complete, and so arranged that the heat from all the furnaces can be thrown into either one of the large apartments, while, in mild weather, the heat of either one of the furnaces can be diffused through the whole building. Connected with this story is a yard, two hundred feet long by one hundred wide; three-fifths of it for the use of males, the remainder for females. The yard is surrounded and divided by a substantial, painted fence, six feet high. It is also provided with out-buildings of the most approved and convenient structure, and a well, from which water may be drawn in either yard.

The second story, besides the continuation of the above-named entries, contains a room for the Trustees, which, when not occupied by them, is used as a reception room; five recitation rooms and a hall, divided into two apartments, for the accommodation of the upper and lower divisions of the High School of the village.

The third story is occupied by the normal school-room, 50 feet by 40, with two large class-rooms, each 40 feet long by 35 broad, and a library and cabinet, 35 feet long by 13 feet broad, and an office for the principal. The fourth story, besides a hall, 72 feet by 20, which can be used for declamation, reading, &c., and a passage to the observatory, which is directly above it, contains four large recitation rooms. The whole of the third and fourth stories are designed for the Normal School proper.

The building was completed and opened, for the accommodation of the State Normal School and the schools of the village, as Model Schools and Schools of Practice, on the 4th of June, 1851, in the presence of the Governor, and other State officers, and both branches of the Legislature, with an address from the Superintendent of Common Schools, and a "Speech for Connecticut" by Rev. Horace Bushnell, D. D.

The building and grounds cost about $25,000, toward which the State has appropriated a bank bonus of $4,500, the balance (save $4,000) having been contributed by citizens of New Britain, of whom Seth J. North subscribed $6,000.

To those who should consult the plans of this building, with a view of adopting any features of the same in the construction of other buildings, it may be well to remark, that the mode of warming and ventilation has not proved satisfactory, owing to the position of the furnaces, and the position and smallness of the ventilating flues. It has been found necessary to place one of Chilson's portable furnaces in both the Primary and Intermediate school-rooms, (S, S, Fig 2,) to warm the school-room, recitation room, and library, on the first and second floors immediately above.

The State appropriates $4,000 a year toward the current expenses of the institution.

FIGURE 2. PLAN OF BASEMENT STORY.

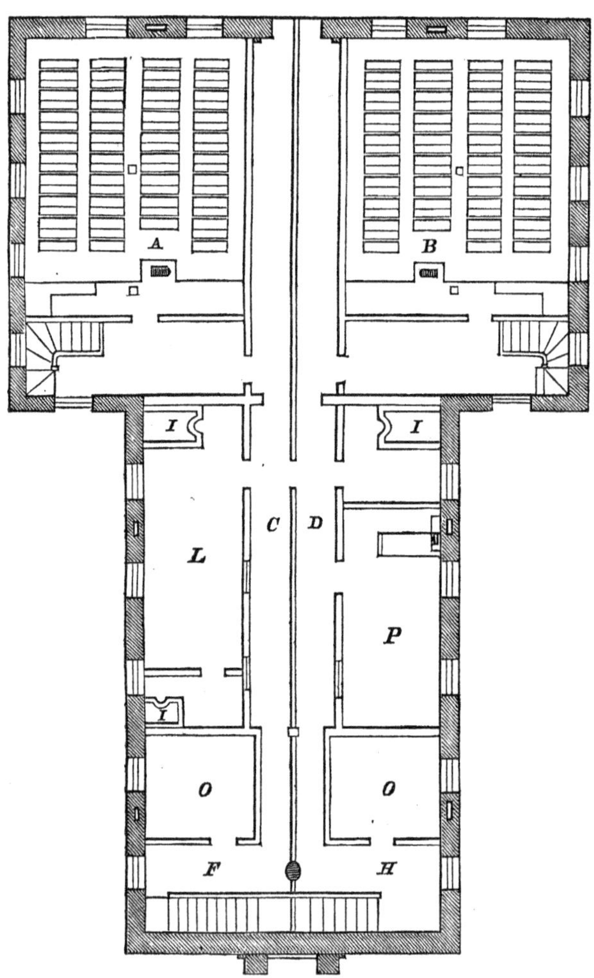

A.—Primary School-room.
B.—Intermediate School-room.
C.—Hall leading to yard for females.
D.—Hall leading to yard for males.
E.—Entrances to Normal School, one for males and the other for females.
F.—Entrance to High School, for girls.
H.—Entrance to High School, for boys.
I. I. I.—Furnaces.
J.—Stove to dry wet feet, accessible on each side.
O. O.—Clothes rooms, one for boys and the other for girls.
P.—Laboratory.
L.—Coal, &c.

FIGURE 3. PLAN OF FIRST FLOOR.

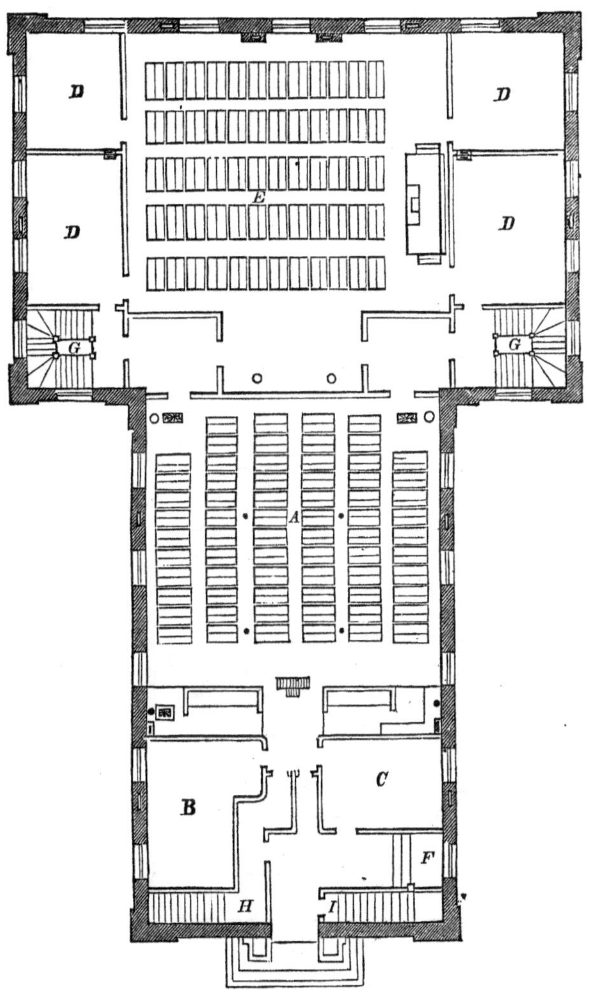

A.—High School-room, with seats and desks for 120 pupils.
B.—Office of Principal of Normal School, and Class-room.
C.—Reception room.
E.—Grammar School-room, with seats and desks for 120 pupils.
D. D. D. D.—Recitation rooms.
F.—Front stairs to Hall.
G.—Side stairs to Normal School-room.
H.—Stairs for girls from basement to High School-room.
I.—Stairs for boys from basement to High School-room.

FIGURE 4. PLAN OF SECOND FLOOR.

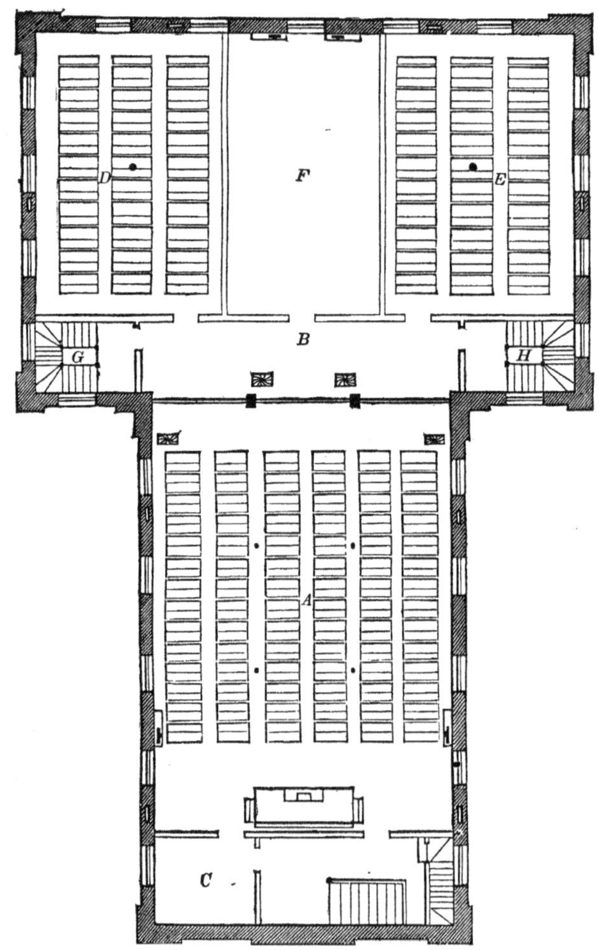

A.—Normal School-room, with seats and desks for 120 pupils, and capable of seating with corridor, 220 pupils.

B.—Corridor; connecting with Normal School-room by folding doors.

C.—Office for Trustees of Normal School, and occupied by Associate Principal as an office.

D.—Recitation and Lecture room, 34 feet by 29, for Junior Class of Normal School.

E.—Recitation and Lecture room, 34 feet by 29, for Middle Class of Normal School.

F.—Library. 34 by 13.

G.—Stairs to Normal School, for Females.

H.—Stairs to Normal School for Males.

FIGURE 5. PLAN OF THIRD FLOOR.

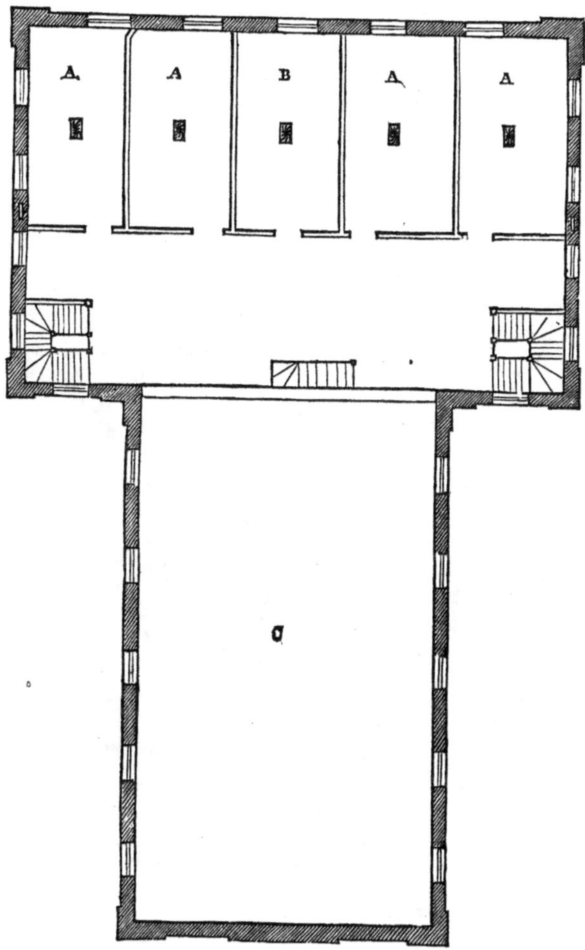

A. A. A. A.—Recitation study rooms for Normal pupils.
B.—Library of Text-books.
C.—Attic.
D.—Hall for Calisthenics.

Plans of City Normal School-house in Philadelphia.

The Normal School of Philadelphia was instituted in 1848, "for the thorough training of female teachers of the public schools, in those branches of a good English education, and in such practical exercises as will discipline and develop the mind, adorn and elevate the character, insure the best mode of imparting knowledge, establish uniformity in teaching, prevent fruitless experiments, manifold mistakes, and irreparable loss of time, with all their consequences to teachers and pupils." The building will accommodate 150 Normal pupils, and a School of Practice of 350 pupils, distributed in eight classes.

Fig. 1. Perspective.

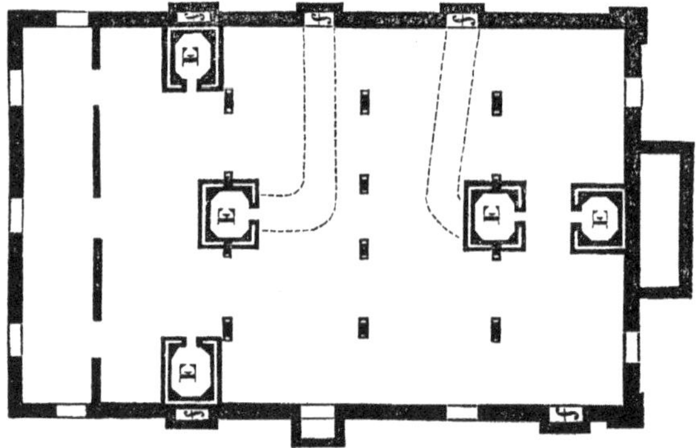

Fig. 2. Plan of Cellar.

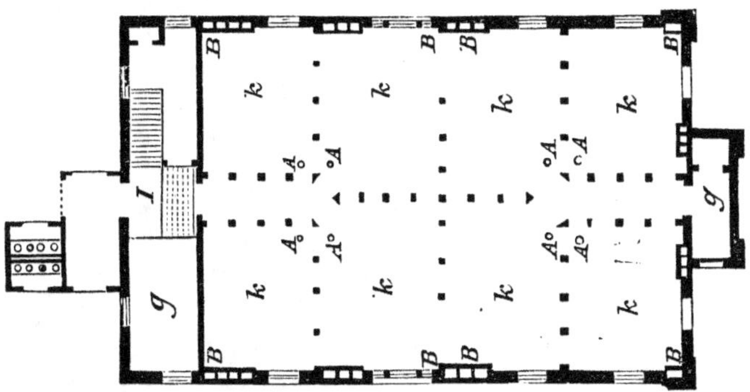

Fig. 3. FIRST FLOOR.

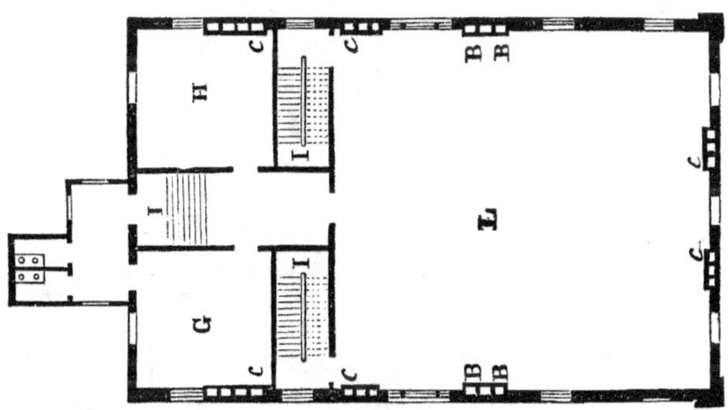

Fig. 4. SECOND FLOOR.

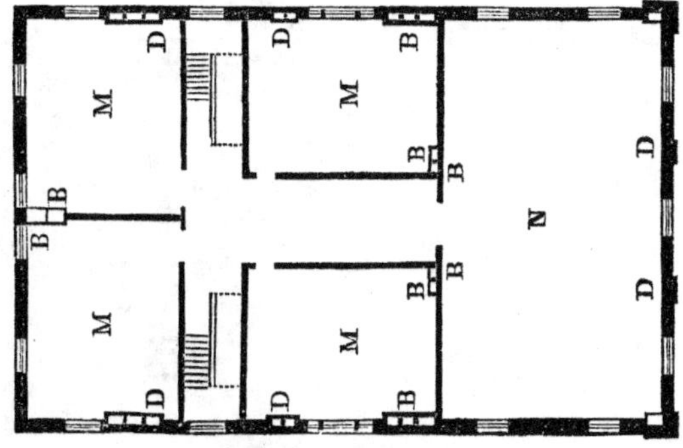

Fig. 5. THIRD FLOOR.

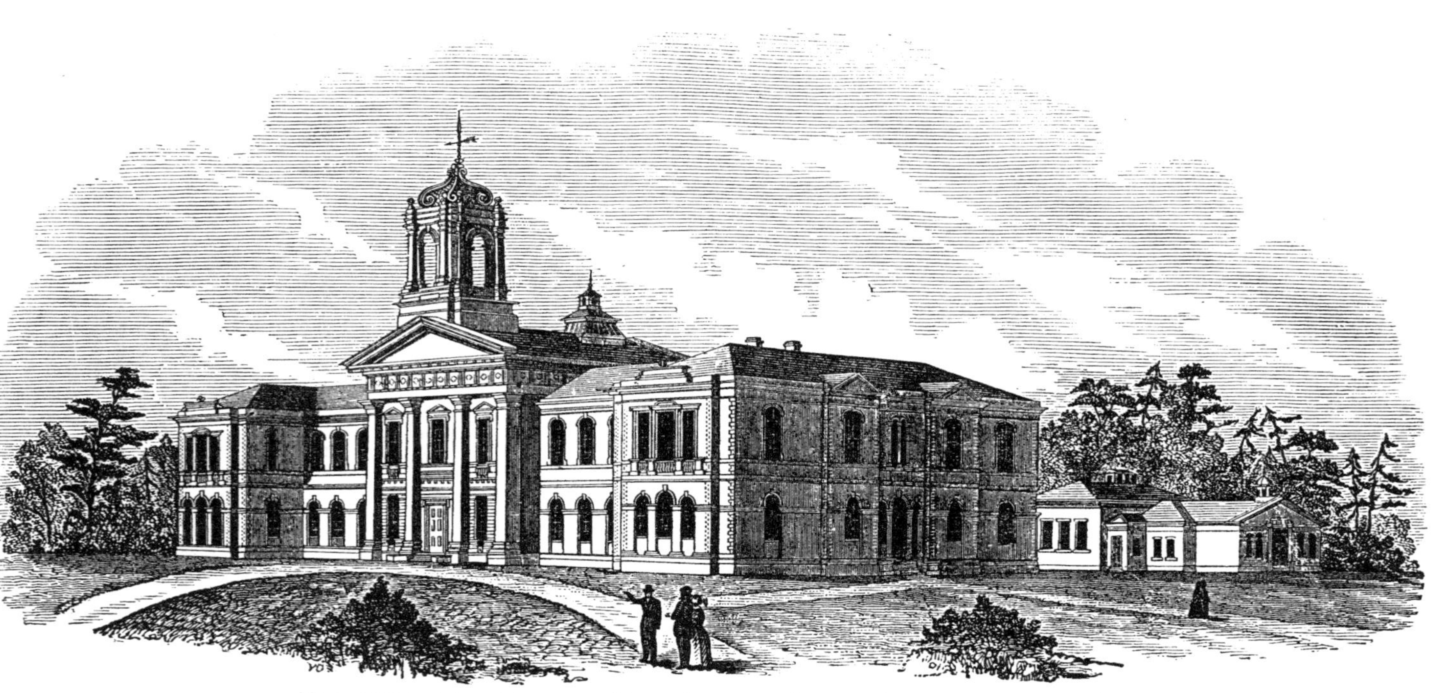

Fig. 1. Front and Side View of the Normal School and Education Offices for Upper Canada.

Plan and Description of the Normal and Model School-building at Toronto, Upper Canada.

The Normal and Model Schools for Upper Canada, are situated upon the center of an open square, bounded on the north by Gerrard Street, on the east by Church Street, on the south by Goold Street, and on the west by Victoria Street, in the city of Toronto. The distance from the bay is about three quarters of a mile. The situation is very beautiful, being considerably elevated above the business parts of the city, and commanding a fine view of the bay, island, and lake. The square, which contains seven acres and a-half of ground, was purchased in August, 1850. The amount of the legislative grant for the purchase of the site and the erection of the buildings, was £15,000.

The principal normal school building, as seen in the perspective, Fig. 1, is 184 feet 4 inches frontage, by a depth on the flanks, east and west, of 85 feet 4 inches.

The front is in the Roman Doric order of Palladian character, having for its center, four pilasters of the full height of the building, with pediment, surrounded by an open doric cupola, of the extreme height of 95 feet. The principal entrance (to the officers of the educational department, &c.,) is in this front; those for the male and female students being placed on the east and west sides respectively, C and D. In the center of the building is a large central hall, (open to the roof, and lighted by a lantern) with a gallery around it, at the level of the upper floor, at B, in Fig. 3, approached on each floor by three corridors—south, east, and west—and opening on the north to the Theatre or Examination Hall.

On the east side, the accommodation on the ground floor is as follows:

School of Art and Design, No. 1,	36′ :	0″	by	28′ :	0″
School of Art and Design, No. 2,	36 :	5	"	28 :	0
Male Students' Retiring Room,	36 :	0	"	30 :	0
Council Room,	39 :	0	"	22 :	0
Male Students' Staircase A,	17 :	6	"	11 :	0

On the west side:

Waiting Room,	22′ :	8″	by	14′ :	8″
Ante-Room,	22 :	0	"	14 :	3
Chief-Superintendent's Room,	28 :	0	"	21 :	0
Depository for Books, Maps, &c.,	28 :	0	"	21 :	0
Depository for Apparatus, &c.,	22 :	8	"	14 :	8
Female Students' Retiring Room,	36 :	0	"	26 :	10
Recording Clerk's Office, with fire proof vault,	37 :	11	"	22 :	0
Second Clerk's Office,	22 :	0	"	14 :	3
Female Students' Staircase A,	17 :	6	"	11 :	0

North of the Central Hall is the Theatre, with Lecturer's entrance in the center, and side entrances east and west, *d*, *d*, for male and female students respectively. Here the aisles are marked *a*, *b*, and *c*, with seats arranged between them: the Lecturer's platform being placed between *B* and *e*. This portion of the Theatre will accommodate 470 persons, and including the galleries, 620. Around the Theatre, and beneath its gallery, are east and west corridors, by which the students reach the Model School.

By this arrangement, except when actually in the presence of the masters, the male and female students are entirely separated.

Passing (by the corridors last named) to the Model School, which is 175 feet 6 inches frontage, by 59 feet 6 inches, the students enter the boys and girls' schools by doors to the east and west, each of which has a large school-room at its center, 56 feet 6 inches by 33 feet, capable of accommodating 300 children, with four smaller class-rooms adjoining it, about 17 feet by 15 feet 6 inches each. The boys and girls' entrances (like those for the students of the normal school already described) are at the east and west ends of the building—such entrances having each a hat and cloak room and master's (or mistress') room on either side. These schools accommodate 600 children.

Returning to the Normal School, and passing to the upper floor: on the landing of the staircases A, A, are entrances to the gallery of the Theatre, which is designed to accommodate 150 persons.

On the upper floor is the Central Hall, with its gallery B, connecting the east and west corridors, communicating with the following rooms:

Class Room, No. 1,	56′ :	0″	by	36′ :	0″

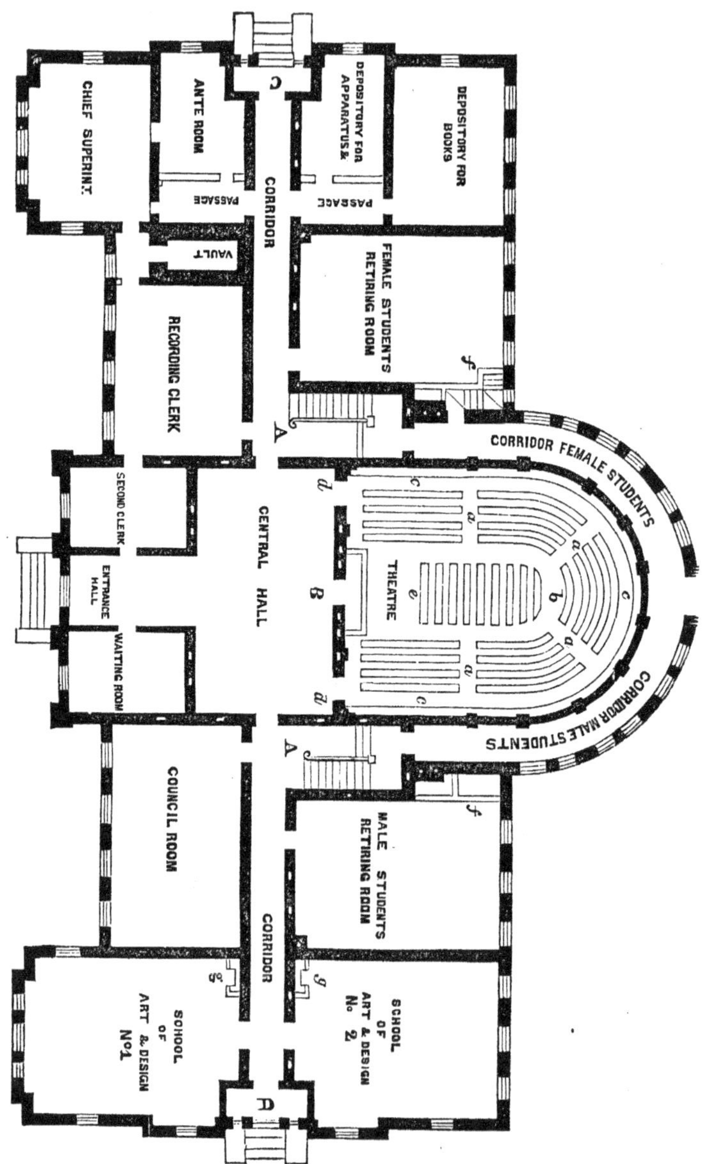
CHIEF SUPERINT.
ANTE ROOM
PASSAGE
CORRIDOR
C
DEPOSITORY FOR APPARATUS &
PASSAGE
DEPOSITORY FOR BOOKS
VAULT
FEMALE STUDENTS RETIRING ROOM
RECORDING CLERK
A
f
CORRIDOR FEMALE STUDENTS
SECOND CLERK
ENTRANCE HALL
WAITING ROOM
CENTRAL HALL
B
THEATRE
a
b
c
d
e
CORRIDOR MALE STUDENTS
A
COUNCIL ROOM
MALE STUDENTS RETIRING ROOM
f
CORRIDOR
g
SCHOOL OF ART & DESIGN No 1
SCHOOL OF ART & DESIGN No 2
D

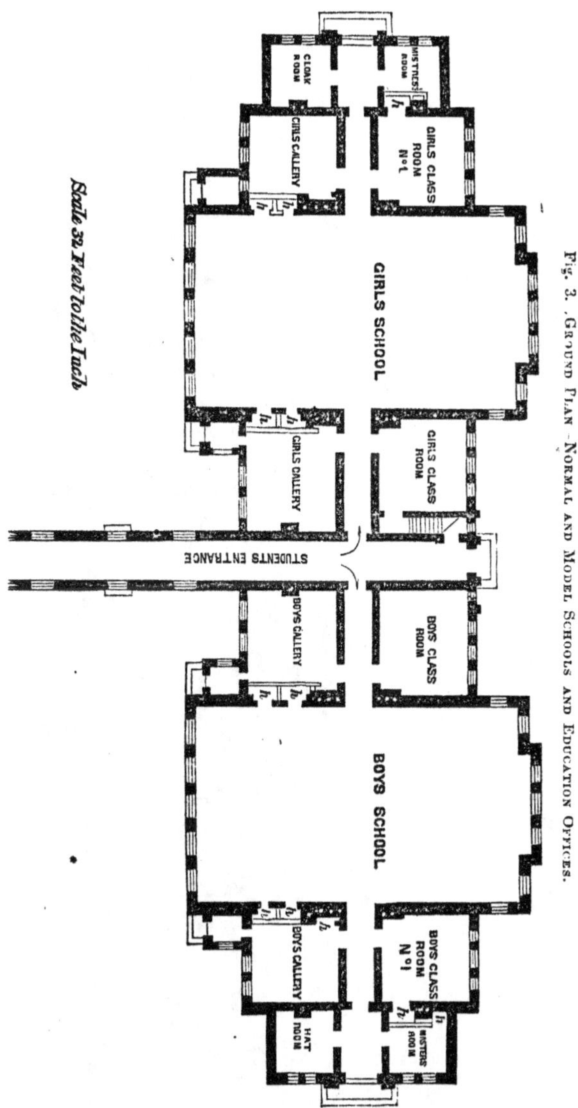

Fig. 3. Ground Plan.—Normal and Model Schools and Education Offices.

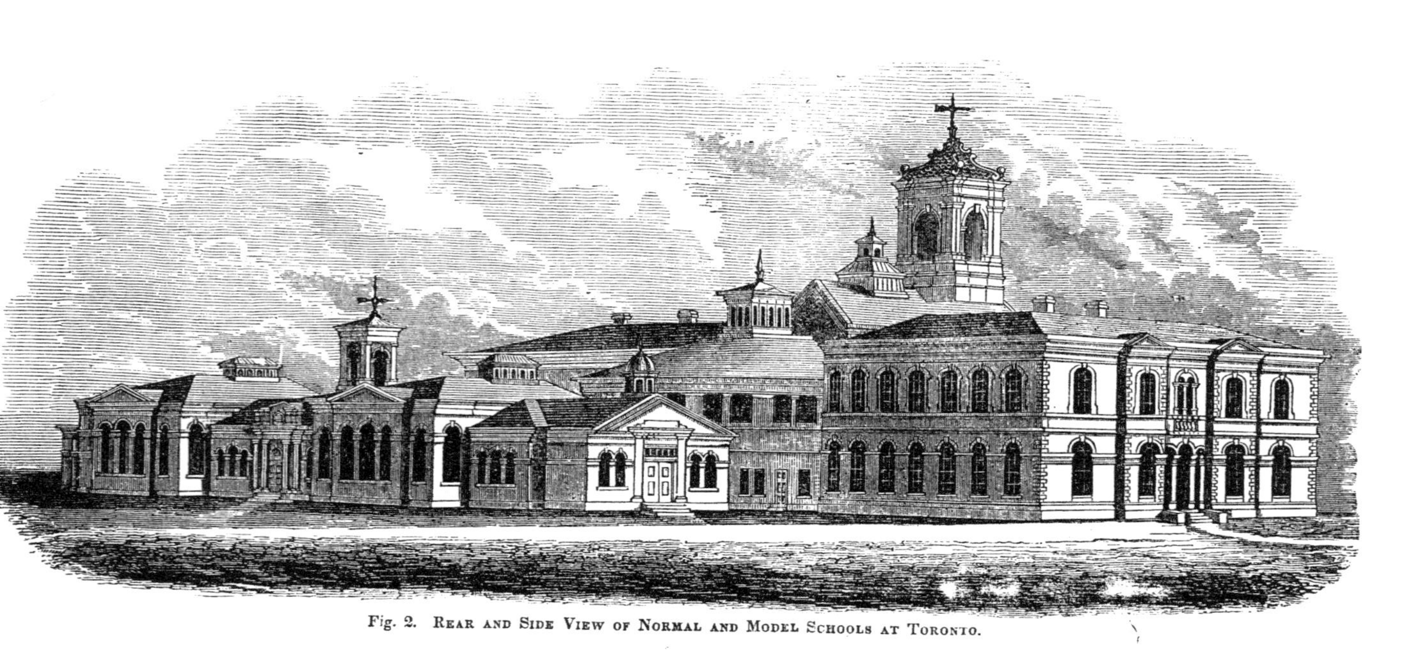

Fig. 2. Rear and Side View of Normal and Model Schools at Toronto.

Class Room, No. 2,	56	:	0	by	36	:	0
Class Room, No. 3,	45	:	2	"	28	:	0
Class Room, No. 4,	32	:	8	"	28	:	0
1st. Master's Room,	22	:	0	"	19	:	5½
2nd. Master's Room,	22	:	0	"	19	:	5½
Museum,	42	:	0	"	22	:	0
Library,	39	:	5	"	22	:	0
Laboratory,	21	:	6	"	12	:	0

In addition to the accommodation thus enumerated, there are, in the basement, rooms for the residence of the Janitor, together with furnace rooms, from whence warm air is conducted to the whole building.

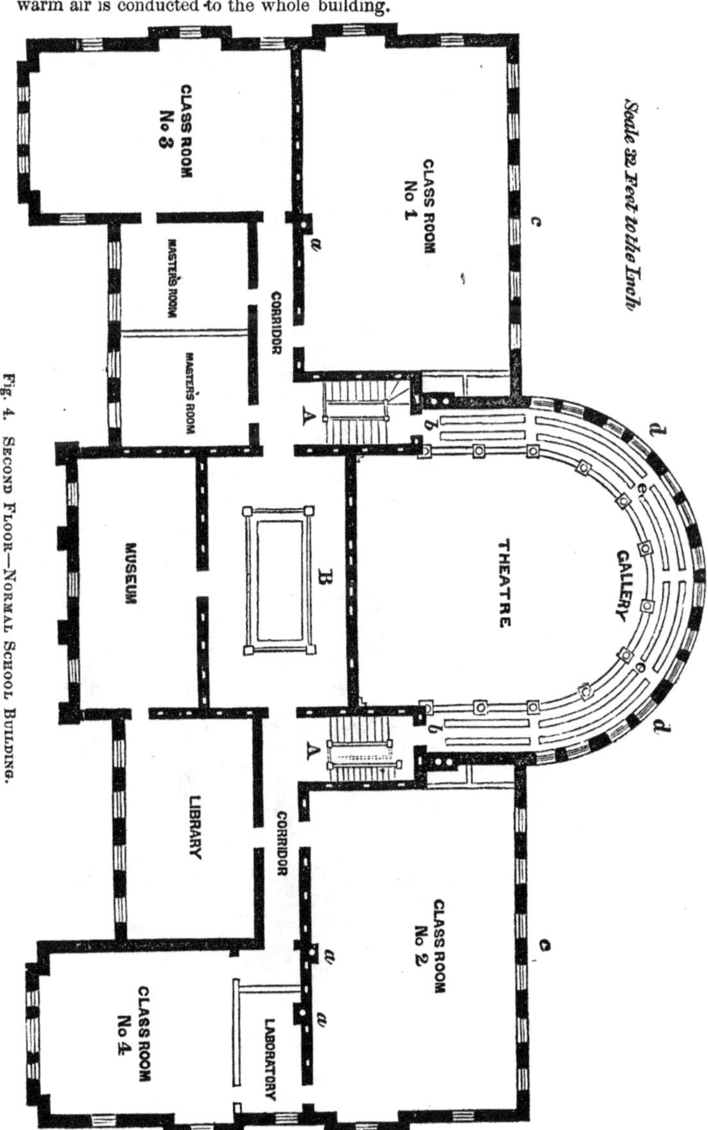

Fig. 4. Second Floor—Normal School Building.

W. H. DODD Sc.

VENTILATION.

EVERY apartment of a school-house should be provided with a cheap, simple, and efficient mode of ventilation, by which the air, which is constantly becoming vitiated by respiration, combustion, or other causes, may be constantly flowing out of the room, and its place filled by an adequate supply of fresh air drawn from a pure source, and admitted into the room at the right temperature, of the requisite degree of moisture, and without any perceptible current. These objects may be attained by attention to the following particulars:

1. The location of the school-house must be healthy, and all causes—such as defective drains, stagnant water, decaying animal or vegetable substances, and manufactures, whose operations evolve offensive and deleterious gases—calculated to vitiate the external atmosphere, from which the air of the school-room is supplied, must be removed or obviated.

2. The means provided for ventilation must be sufficient to secure the object, independent of doors and windows, and other lateral openings, which are intended primarily for the admission of light, passage to and from the apartment, and similar purposes. Any dependence on the opening of doors and windows, except in summer, will subject the occupants of the room near such points to currents of cold air when the pores of the skin are open, and when such extreme and rapid changes of temperature are particularly disagreeable and dangerous.

3. Any openings in the ceiling for the discharge of vitiated air into the attic, and hence to the exterior of the building, or by flues carried up in the wall, no matter how constructed or where placed, can not be depended on for purposes of ventilation, unless systematic arrangements are adopted to effect, in concert with such openings, the introduction and diffusion of a constant and abundant supply of pure air, in the right condition as to temperature and moisture.

4. All stoves, or other heating apparatus, standing in the apartment to be warmed, and heating only the atmosphere of that apartment, which is constantly becoming more and more vitiated by respiration and other causes, are radically defective, and should be altogether, without delay, and forever discarded.

5. Any apparatus for warming pure air, before it is introduced into the school-room, in which the heating surface becomes *red-hot*, or the air is warmed above the temperature of boiling water, is inconsistent with good ventilation.

6. To effect the combined objects of warming and ventilation, a large quantity of moderately heated air should be introduced in such a manner as to reach every portion of the room, and be passed off by appro-

priate openings and flues, as fast as its oxygen is exhausted, and it becomes vitiated by carbonic acid gas, and other noxious qualities.

7. The size and number of the admission flues or openings will depend on the size of the school-room, and the number of persons occupying the same; but they should have a capacity to supply every person in the room with at least five cubic feet of air per minute. Warm air can be introduced at a high as well as a low point from the floor, provided there is an exhaustive power in the discharging flues sufficient to secure a powerful ascending current of vitiated air from openings near the floor.

8. Openings into flues for the discharge of vitiated air, should be made at such points in the room, and at such distances from the openings for the admission of pure warm air, that a portion of the warm air will traverse every part of the room, and impart as much warmth as possible, before it becomes vitiated and escapes from the apartment.

These openings can be made near the floor, at points most distant from the admission flues, provided there is a fire-draught, or other power operating in the discharging flues, sufficient to overcome the natural tendency of the warm air in the room to ascend to the ceiling; otherwise they should be inserted in or near the ceiling.

Openings at the floor are recommended, not because carbonic acid gas, being heavier than the other elements of atmospheric air, settles to the floor, (because, owing to the law of the diffusion of gases among each other, carbonic acid gas will be found equally diffused through the room,) but because, when it can be drawn off at the floor, it will carry along with it the cold air which is admitted by open doors, and at cracks and crevices, and also the offensive gases sometimes found in school-rooms.

9. All openings, both for the admission and discharge of air, should be fitted with valves and registers, to regulate the quantity of air to pass through them. The quantity of air to be admitted should be regulated before it passes over the heating surface; otherwise, being confined in the air chamber and tubes, the excessive heat will cause much injury to the pipes and the woodwork adjoining.

10. All flues for ventilation, not intended to act in concert with some motive power, such as a fan, a pump, the mechanism of a clock, a fire-draught, a jet of steam, &c., but depending solely on the spontaneous upward movement of the column of warm air within them, should be made large, (of a capacity equal to at least 18 inches in diameter,) tight, (except the openings at the top and bottom of the room,) smooth, (if made of boards, the boards should be seasoned, matched, and planed; if made of bricks, the flue should be round, and finished smooth,) and carried up on the inside of the room, or in the inner wall, with as few angles and deviations from a direct ascent as possible, above the highest point of the roof.

11. All flues for the discharge of vitiated air, even when properly constructed and placed, and even when acting in concert with a current

of warm air flowing into the room, should be supplied with some simple, reliable exhaustive power, which can be applied at all seasons of the year, and with a force varying with the demands of the season, and the condition of the air in the apartment.

12. The most simple, economical, and reliable motive power available in most school-houses is heat, or the same process by which the natural upward movements of air are induced and sustained. Heat can be applied to the column of air in a ventilating flue—

1. By carrying up the ventilating flue close beside, or even within the smoke flue, which is used in connection with the heating apparatus.

2. By carrying up the smoke-pipe within the ventilating flue, either the whole length, or in the upper portion only. In a small school-room, the heat from the smoke-pipe carried up for a few feet only in the ventilating flue before it projects above the roof, is a motive power sufficient to sustain a constant draught of cool and vitiated air, into a opening near the floor.

3. By kindling a fire at the bottom, or other convenient point in the ventilating flue—

If the same flue is used for smoke from the fire, and vitiated air from the apartment, some simple self-acting valve or damper should be applied to the opening for the escape of the vitiated air, which shall close at the slightest pressure from the inside of the flue, and thus prevent any reverse current, or down draught, carrying smoke and soot into the apartment.

4. By discharging a jet of steam, or a portion of warm air from the furnace, or other warming apparatus, directly into the ventilating flue.

Any application of heat by which the temperature of the air in the ventilating flue can be raised above the temperature of the apartment to be ventilated, will cause a flow of air from the apartment to sustain the combustion, (if there is a fire in the flue,) and to supply the partial vacuum in the flue, which is caused by the rarefaction of the air in the same.

In all school buildings, when several apartments are to be ventilated, the most effectual, and, all things considered, the most economical mode of securing a motive power, is to construct an upright brick shaft or flue, and in that to build a fire, or carry up the smoke-pipe of the stove, furnace, or other warming apparatus; and then to discharge the ventilating flues from the top or bottom of each apartment, into this upright shaft. The fire-draught will create a partial vacuum in this shaft, to fill which, a draught will be established upon every room with which it is connected by lateral flues. Whenever a shaft of this kind is resorted to, the flues for ventilation may be lateral, and the openings into them may be inserted near the floor.

13. With a flue properly constructed, so as to facilitate the spontaneous upward movement of the warm air within it, and so placed that the air is not exposed to the chilling influence of external cold, a turncap, constructed after the plan of Emerson's Ejector, or Mott's Exhausting

Cowl, will assist the ventilation, and especially when there are any currents in the atmosphere. But such caps are not sufficient to overcome any considerable defects in the construction of the ventilating flues, even when there is much wind.

14. The warming and ventilation of a school-room will be facilitated by applying a double sash to all windows having a northern and eastern exposure, or on the sides of the prevailing winds in winter.

15. In every furnace and on every stove, a capacious vessel, well supplied with fresh water and protected from the dust, should be placed.

16. Every school-room should be furnished with two thermometers, placed on opposite sides in the room, and the temperature in the winter should not be allowed to attain beyond 68° Fahrenheit at a level of four feet from the floor, or 70° at the height of six feet.

17. The necessity for ventilation in an occupied apartment is not obviated by merely reducing the atmosphere to a low temperature.

18. No apparatus, however skillfully constructed or judiciously located, can dispense with the careful oversight of a thoughtful teacher.

Although much has been said and printed on the principles and modes of ventilation, there is much to be done by educators, committees, and teachers, to enlighten and liberalize the public mind and action on this important subject—not only in reference to school-rooms, but to halls of justice and legislation, to churches, lecture rooms, and workshops,—to all places where human beings congregate in large numbers, for business or pleasure.

Mr. D. Leach, one of the agents employed by the Board of Education in Massachusetts, to visit schools and confer with committees in regard to the construction of school-houses, remarks in 1853:

In a large majority of school-houses, there are no means of ventilating but by opening the windows and doors. And where attempts have been made, it has been but imperfectly accomplished. The ventilating tubes have almost invariably been too small. As the result of my investigations, I would make the following suggestions. To ventilate a room properly containing fifty persons, the ventilating tube should not be less than fifteen square inches inside. The tube should be made of very thin boards, well seasoned, with a smooth inside surface, and it should be perfectly tight. It should be wholly within the room, and opposite to the register or stove. There should be an opening at the top and bottom. The ventilating tubes should be connected in the attic, and conducted through the roof, and furnished with a suitable cap. Another method, which is far preferable, is as follows: The smoke pipes may be conducted into a cast iron pipe resting on soap-stone in the attic floor, instead of a chimney built from the bottom of the cellar. This cast iron pipe may be surrounded by a brick chimney, into which the ventilating tubes should lead. The space in the chimney should be equal to the spaces in the tubes, after making suitable allowance for the pipe, and the increase of friction. By this arrangement, the air in the tubes will be rarefied, and a rapid current of air produced. All attempts to ventilate rooms with tubes in the wall, or of less size than fourteen or fifteen square inches for fifty persons, have, so far as I have examined, failed. No artificial means will secure good ventilation when the temperature of the room and that of the outer air are nearly the same, without the application of heat to the air in the tubes. Unless the air is heated before being admitted into the room, it should be let in at the top, and not at the bottom, and always through a large number of small apertures. The quantity of pure air admitted must always be equal to that which is to be forced out.

Methods of Ventilation and Warming, recently introduced into the School-Houses of Boston.

In February, 1846, the School Committee of Boston appointed Dr. Henry G. Clark, E. G. Loring, Esq., and Rev. Charles Brooks, a Committee "to consider the subject of ventilation of the school-houses under the care of this Board, and to report at a future meeting some method of remedying the very defective manner in which it is now accomplished." The Committee were further "authorized to ventilate any three school-houses, in such manner as they may deem expedient." Under these instructions, the Committee visited, and carefully examined all the school-houses under the care of the Board, and instituted a variety of experiments, for the purpose of determining on the best method of ventilation, to be generally introduced. In December, 1846, this Committee made a Report, for a copy of which we are indebted to the author, Dr. Clark, by whose agency and ingenuity mainly, these great improvements, both in ventilation and warming, hereafter detailed, have been introduced into the Public Schools of Boston. We are also indebted to Dr. Clark for the use of the cuts by which this Report, and a subsequent Report, are illustrated. We shall extract largely from these valuable documents, with the permission of the author. It will be seen that the views here recommended are substantially the same with those presented under the head of Ventilation, in this Treatise.

"Your Committee desire to call the attention of this Board, chiefly to the consideration of such general and well established Physiological and Philosophical principles, as have a distinct and intimate relation to the subject of this Report, and may be useful in its elucidation.

In doing this, there are two things of which they hope to satisfy the Board.

First. The necessity of a system of ventilation, which shall furnish, for all the pupils in the Public Schools of Boston, at all times, an abundant supply of an atmosphere entirely adapted, in its purity and temperature, to the purposes of respiration.

Secondly. The entire failure of the measures heretofore adopted to accomplish this desirable end.

The function of Respiration, is that process, by whose agency and constant operation, atmospheric air is admitted to the internal surface of the lungs, and there brought into close contact with the blood, for the purpose of effecting certain changes in it, which are essential to the continuance of life, and to maintain the integrity of the bodily organs. During this process, the atmosphere is constantly losing its oxygen, which is carried into the circulation, while, at the same time, it is becoming overcharged with the carbonic acid gas, which is continually thrown off from the lungs by respiration. This effete and deadly poison spreads itself rapidly into all parts of the room.

'M. Lassaigne has shown, by a series of investigations, that, contrary to a common opinion, the air in a room which has served for respiration without being renewed, contains carbonic acid alike in every part, above as well as below; the difference in proportion is but slight; and, where appreciable, there is some reason to believe that the carbonic acid is in greater quantity in the upper parts of a room. These experiments establish the very important fact, that all the air of a room must be changed, in order to restore its purity.'*

Dr. Wyman makes the following remarks on this point: 'Although carbonic acid is a much heavier gas than atmospheric air, it does not, from this cause, fall to the floor, but is equally diffused through the room. If the gas is formed on the floor without change of temperature, this diffusion may not take place

*Silliman's Journal for September, 1846.

rapidly. In the celebrated *Grotto del Cane*, carbonic acid escapes from the floor, and rises to a certain height, which is pretty well defined to the sight on the walls; below this line, a dog is destroyed, as if in water; above it, he is not affected. An analysis of the air above and below a brazier has been made, and it was found equally contaminated,—the former containing 4.65 per cent., and the latter 4.5 per cent. of carbonic acid.

'From the experiments of M. Devergie, who has devoted much attention to the poisonous effects of these gasses, it appears, that the heat disengaged from the combustion of charcoal, produces an equable mixture at all elevations in the apartment; and this state of things continues *as long as the room remains warm;* but after twelve hours or more, the carbonic acid sinks, and while that near the ceiling contains only a seventy-eighth, that near the floor contains nearly four times as much, or a nineteenth.' (*See Prac. Trea.* p. 77.)

If further proof be needed, to establish this position, we have other testimony. During respiration, a considerable quantity of vapor is discharged from the lungs. With regard to this, Mr. Tredgold says: 'if the air did not contain this mixture of vapor, it would not rise when expelled; and we have to admire one of those simple and beautiful arrangements, by which our all-wise Creator has provided against the repeated inhalation of the same air; for a mixture of azote, carbonic acid gas, and vapor, at the temperature it is ejected, is much lighter than common air even at the same temperature. Hence, it rises with such velocity, that it is entirely removed from us before it becomes diffused in the atmosphere. But as all gaseous bodies and vapors intimately mix when suffered to remain in contact, we see how important it is that ventilation should be continual; that the noxious gasses should be expelled as soon as generated; and that the ventilation should be from the upper part of a room.' (*See Tredgold on Warming, &c.,* p. 70.

If, to the foul effluvia ejected from the lungs, and accumulating in an apartment as badly ventilated as one of our school-rooms, be added the fouler matter thrown into the air from the insensible perspiration of so many individuals, many of whom are of uncleanly habits in person and apparel, it is apparent, that, in a very limited period of time, the air, in a perfectly close room, would become so entirely unfit for respiration, that, to all who were exposed to its influence, submersion in water could not be more certainly fatal.

The terrible effects of continued exposure to carbonic acid gas in a concentrated form, have been graphically described by Howard, in his account of the Black Hole of Calcutta. Of one hundred and forty-six persons, shut up in this place for only ten hours, without any other means of ventilation than one small opening, but twenty-six were found alive, when it came to be opened; and most of these suffered afterward from malignant fevers.

The fainting of feeble persons in crowded assemblies, and the asphyxia, so often produced in those who descend into deep wells without suitable precaution, are familiar examples of the same noxious effects of this poison.

In has been usually estimated, that every individual, by respiration, and the various exhalations from the body, consumes or renders unfit for use, at least from four to five cubic feet of air per minute. This is probably a low estimate; but authors of good repute differ considerably on this point. Mr. Tredgold's remarks, in this connection, are interesting and pertinent. 'The Physiological Chemists,' says he, 'have placed in our hands a more accurate means of measuring the deterioration of air in dwelling rooms, than by the best eudiometer; for they have shown, by repeated experiments on respiration, that a man consumes about thirty-two cubic inches of oxygen in a minute, which is replaced by an equal bulk of carbonic acid from the lungs. Now, the quantity of oxygen in atmospheric air is about one fifth; hence it will be found, that the quantity rendered unfit for supporting either combustion or animal life, by one man, in one minute, is nearly one hundred and sixty cubic inches, by respiration only. But a man makes twenty respirations in a minute, and draws in and expels forty inches of air at each respiration; consequently, the total quantity contaminated in one minute, by passing through the lungs, is eight hundred cubic inches.'* The other sources of impurity, which should be considered, will increase the estimate to the amount above stated. The amount of vapor discharged from the lungs, and thus added to the impurities of the air, is said to exceed six grains per minute. It has also been shown

*Tredgold on Warming, &c., p. 69

that air, which has been some time in contact with the skin, becomes almost entirely converted into carbonic acid.

In estimating the amount of fresh air to be supplied, we ought not merely to look at what the system will tolerate, but that amount which will sustain the highest state of health for the longest time. Dr. Reid recommends at least ten cubic feet per minute, as a suitable average supply for each individual; and states that his estimate is the result of an 'extreme variety of experiments, made on hundreds of different constitutions, supplied one by one with given amounts of air, and also in numerous assemblies and meetings, where there were means for estimating the quantity of air with which they were provided.' (*Illustrations of Ventilation*, p. 176.)

These calculations refer to adults; but the greater delicacy of the organization of children, and their feebler ability to resist the action of deleterious agents, together with their greater rapidity of respiration, demand for them at least an equal supply. Proceeding upon this basis, and multiplying the amount required per minute, by the minutes of a school session of three hours, we have eighteen hundred cubic feet for each pupil, and for two hundred and fifty pupils—the average maximum attendance in one of our large school-rooms,—450,000 cubic feet, as the requisite quantity for each half-day. The rooms contain about 22,500 cubic feet only: so that a volume of air, equal to the whole cubic contents of each room, should be supplied and removed, in some way, ten times every three hours, in order to sustain the atmosphere in them at a point which is perfectly wholesome and salubrious. For such a purpose, the present means are so entirely inadequate, that it was found that the air of a room became tainted in ten or fifteen minutes. In ordinary cases, four per cent. of the air expelled from the lungs is carbonic acid. The presence of five or six per cent. will extinguish a lamp, and with difficulty support life. It is therefore certain, that the air would become deprived of all its best properties in one school session.

Le Blanc,—who examined many public and private buildings, in France and elsewhere,—speaking of the Chamber of Deputies, where sixty-four cubic feet of fresh air *per minute*, were allowed to each individual, states, that of 10,000 parts escaping by the ventilator, twenty-five were carbonic acid; while the quantity of this gas ordinarily present in the atmosphere, is but $\frac{4}{10000}$. Dr. Reid states, that he never gave less than thirty cubic feet of air a minute, to each member of the House of Commons, when the room was crowded; and once he introduced, for weeks successively, sixty cubic feet a minute, to each member.

The very earliest impressions received by your Committee, in their visits to the school-houses, satisfied them of their lamentable condition in regard to ventilation. In some of them, they found the air so bad, that it could be perceived before reaching the school-rooms, and in the open entries; and the children, as they passed up and down the stairs, had their clothes and hair perceptibly impregnated with the fœtid poison. And these circumstances existed in houses, where the open windows testified, upon our entrance, that the Masters had endeavored to improve the atmosphere by all the means placed at their disposal. To this custom,—*that of opening windows in school hours*,—the Instructors are compelled to resort, for relief; and this expedient, certainly, is the lesser of two very great evils. Your Committee found in their visits to the school-houses, during the severest days of last winter, that no school-room had less than three, and that more than half of them had at least seven windows open for the admission of pure air. Yet this dangerous and injurious practice only mitigates the evils of bad air, by creating others. It produces colds and inflammatory complaints, and the air still remains impure, offensive, and highly deleterious; sufficiently so, to affect the delicate organization of childhood, to blight its elasticity, and destroy that healthful physical action, on which depends the vigor of maturer years.

We have already referred to some of the more violent and sudden effects of exposure to air highly charged with these noxious gasses. There are others, which are more remote, and, to a superficial observer, less noticeable. But they are not, therefore, of less importance. The grave consequences of a long-continued exposure to an atmosphere but a little below the standard of natural purity, although not immediately incompatible with life, can hardly be overstated. These effects are often so insidious in their approach, as hardly to attract notice; they are therefore the more necessary to be provided against in advance.

Children, confined in the atmosphere of these schools, soon lose the ruddy and cheerful complexions of perfect health which belong to youth, and acquire the sallow and depressed countenances which might reasonably be expected in over-worked factory operatives, or the tenants of apartments unvisited by the sun or air. We noticed in many faces, also, particularly towards the close of a school session, a feverish flush, so bright that it might easily deceive an inexperienced eye, and be mistaken for a healthy bloom. Alas! it was only a transient and ineffectual effort of nature to produce, by *overaction*, those salutary changes which she really wanted the *power* to accomplish.

The condition of the pupils, depressed as they are by these influences, is constantly demanding increased exertions from their Instructors, while the requirements of the age place the standard of education at an elevation sufficiently difficult of access under the most favorable circumstances.

Your committee are satisfied, therefore, that the present state of the school-houses daily impairs the health of the pupils and Instructors, and the efficiency of the schools for the purposes of instruction. That its continuance will produce, not only immediate discomfort and disease, but, by its effect on the constitutions of the children, who must pass in them a large portion of those years most susceptible to physical injury, will directly and certainly reduce the amount of constitutional vigor hereafter to be possessed by that large mass of our population, which now and hereafter is to receive its education in these schools.

Although the atmosphere in the different school-houses varied very much in particular cases, either owing to the time of the visits, or from the amount of attention and intelligence of the Masters, yet in none of them was it at all satisfactory; not one of them was furnished with any useful or systematic means of ventilation. Every one, in order to be kept in a tolerably comfortable condition in this respect, required the frequent and laborious attention of the Instructors, and often to a degree which must have seriously interfered with their legitimate duties.

All of the rooms are provided with registers, in or near the ceiling, ostensibly for the purpose of discharging the foul air, but which your Committee believe to be almost entirely useless. The openings through the roof into the open air, where they exist, are so small, as to be quite inadequate to relieve the attics; so that the bad air must accumulate there, and, after becoming condensed be gradually forced back again, to be breathed over by the same lungs which have already rejected it. The condition of the apartments, after undergoing a repetition of such a process, for any length of time, can easily be imagined."

A reference to the subjoined diagram will explain at once the present state of the Ventilation of the School-Houses.

a. Heated air from furnace.
b. Hot air escaping through open window.
c. Cold air entering through open window.

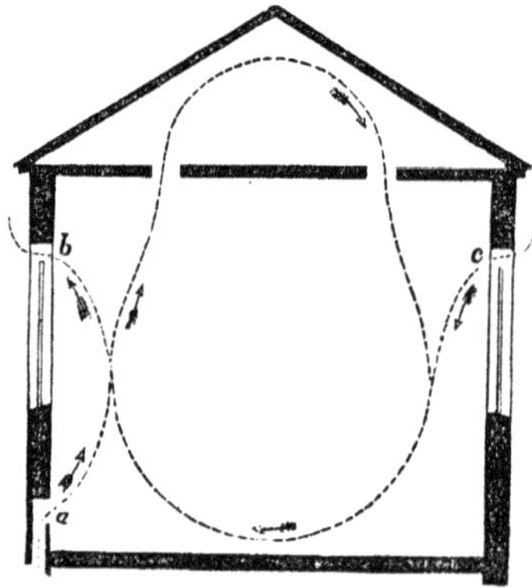

It may be a matter of surprise, to some, perhaps, that the subject of ventilating our school-rooms has not long ago received the consideration necessary to remedy, or even to have prevented altogether, the evils of which we at present complain. But these evils have not always existed. It should be recollected, that the stoves and furnaces now in common use, are of comparatively modern date; and moreover, that the ample fireplaces, which they have displaced, always proved perfectly efficient ventilators, although, it is true, somewhat at the expense of comfort and fuel. But in closing the fireplaces, and substituting more economical methods of warming, evils of far greater magnitude have been entailed upon us.

It is evident, that, in order to carry into operation any complete system of ventilation, there must be connected with it some apparatus to regulate the temperature of the air to be admitted, as well as to ensure its ample supply. Your committee have accordingly examined, with much care, this part of the subject. A majority of the buildings are furnished with 'hot-air furnaces,' situated in the cellars; the remainder with stoves, placed in the school-rooms themselves. Most of the furnaces possess great heating powers,—indeed much greater than is necessary, if the heat generated by them were properly economized, or could be made available;—but, as now constructed, they are almost worse than useless, consuming large quantities of fuel, and, at the same time, so overheating the air which passes through them, as to deprive it of some of its best qualities, and render it unsuitable for respiration. It is difficult to define, with precision, and by analysis, the changes which take place in air subjected to the action of metallic surfaces, at a high temperature. The unpleasant dryness of the air can be detected, very readily, by the senses; and the headache, and other unpleasant sensations, experienced by those who breathe such an atmosphere, would seem to prove a deficiency of oxygen and electricity. The rapid oxydation and destruction of the ironwork of the furnaces themselves, also tends to confirm this supposition.

It has been ascertained, by repeated examinations, that the temperature of the air, when it arrives at the rooms, is often as high as 500° and 600° Fahrenheit. Of course, it is entirely impossible to diffuse air, thus heated, in the parts of the room occupied by the pupils. Much of it passes rapidly out of the windows, which may be open; the rest to the ceiling, where it remains until partially cooled, gradually finding its way down by the walls and closed windows, to the lower parts of the room. The consequences are, that, while much more caloric is sent into the apartment than is requisite, many of the pupils are compelled to remain in an atmosphere which is at once cold and stagnant.

The source of the cold air for supplying the furnaces, is not always free from objection; some being drawn from the neighborhood of drains, cesspools, &c. This is a radical defect, as it must inevitably affect the whole air of the building. The boxes, which admit the cold air to the furnaces, are much too contracted; some of them being only a few inches square, when their capacity ought to be nearly as many feet. The air enters the 'cold-air' chamber of the furnace, at its top, whence it is intended to be carried down between thin brick walls, (which *should be cold*, but which are often heated to 300° Fahrenheit,) to the lower part of the furnace, and thence into the 'hot-air' chambers, and so on to the rooms above. It is obvious that the 'hot-air' chamber must be heated to a temperature far beyond that of the 'cold-air' chamber, in order to compel the air, against its own natural tendencies, to pass into it with any velocity or volume, and the very attempt to accomplish this, almost defeats itself; as, by driving the fire for this purpose, the 'cold-air' chamber becomes still hotter, so that at last the contest is decided only by the greater calorific capabilities which the iron plates possess over the brick wall. At any rate, the temperature of the iron is frequently raised to a *red* and even a *white heat*, by running the furnaces in the ordinary way. This soon destroys them, and they require consequently to be frequently renewed. In addition to all this waste of fuel and material, the folly of attempting, in any way, to warm school-rooms whose windows are freely opened to the admission of an atmosphere, at the low temperature of our winter climate, may well claim a passing notice.

The following diagrams will exhibit the mode in which the two houses already referred to, are now ventilated.

PLAN OF THE VENTILATION OF THE ELIOT SCHOOL-HOUSE.

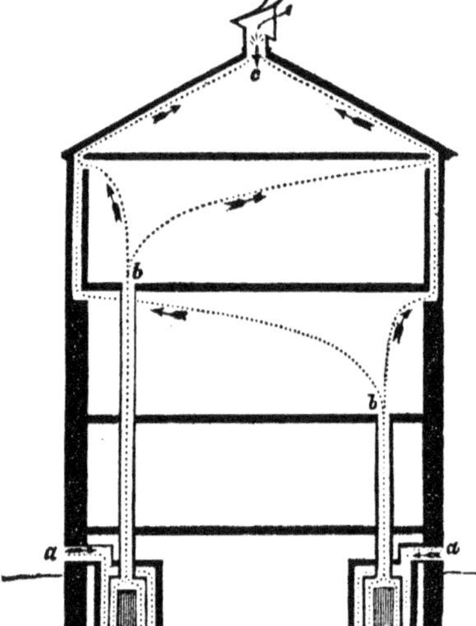

a. a. Cold air channels to furnaces.
b. b. Heated air.
The arrows show the currents of air from the furnaces to the outlet at the roof.
c. Gas burner.

This house was entirely without any external opening through the roof. The other arrangements in it presented nothing peculiar. The 'exits and the entrances' were all as deficient in capacity as usual. The first care was to perforate the roof. This was accordingly done, and an opening of sufficient size made to carry a turn-cap of two and a half feet in diameter in its smallest part. The cold-air shaft, with an area of only one hundred and forty square inches, was enlarged so as to measure six hundred, or about four times its former size. The necessary repairing of one furnace, gave us an opportunity to enlarge its air-chamber very considerably. Water, for evaporation, was placed within a chamber of the furnace. The registers in the rooms opening into the attic, being below the ceiling, were raised to the highest point, and increased in size.

Although we think the want of connection of the cowl at the roof with the registers from the rooms by closed tubes, a decided disadvantage, we were satisfied, on the whole, with the results; as the alterations gave great relief. These changes were made during the month of February, 1846, and the only inconvenience suffered during the winter, was the occasional rise of the temperature to five or ten degrees beyond the desired point. The atmosphere has lost its bad odor almost entirely, and is of course much more agreeable. A gas burner has lately been placed in the throat of the ventilator, for use when extra power is needed.

PLAN OF THE VENTILATION OF THE ENDICOTT SCHOOL-HOUSE.

This house, as well as the preceding, was heated by furnaces in the cellar, one for each room. Its ventilating flues were arranged in a better manner than usual, opening into little separate chimneys which pierced the roof near the copings. But they had proved to be insufficient, both on account of their size and situation. They were also affected sensibly by down-gusts, which completely reversed their action in certain states of the atmosphere and wind.

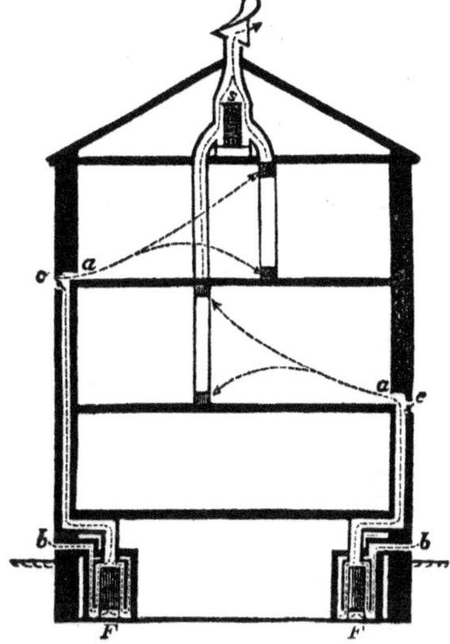

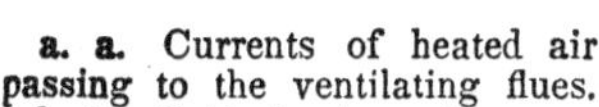

a. a. Currents of heated air **passing** to the ventilating flues.
b. b. Cold air channels.
c. c. Cold air valves opening **upon** the hot-air currents.
F. F. Furnaces.
S. Stove in ventilator in the **attic.**

After enlarging the cold-air shaft to a proper size, it was thought best, (as the hot-air pipe passed through the brick wall, so that it could not easily be altered,) to make an opening through the outer wall directly behind the register which delivered the hot-air into the room. An aperture of sixteen inches square, commanded by a revolving damper, was therefore cut. It has been found to answer exceedingly well; as we now get a much larger volume, of more temperate and purer air.

For the delivery of the bad air, the following arrangements were adopted. Large wooden boxes, or air-shafts, were carried from the floor of each story into the attic, where they communicate, by closed metal pipes of the same size, with a tin cylinder, three feet in diameter, which is continued to the roof, terminating there in a large cowl. There are openings, at the top and bottom of each room, into the ventilating shafts, which can be used separately, or together, as the state of the atmosphere requires.

An air-tight coal stove, placed within the drum, in the attic, completes the apparatus. This has been only recently constructed; but from results already produced, there is no doubt of its entire ability to accomplish all that is desirable.

The same general statements which have been made with regard to the Grammar School-houses, will apply to the Primary School-houses. They are undoubtedly in as bad a condition, to say the least; and from their smaller capacities in proportion to the number of pupils which they contain, require particular attention.

For ventilation of these, and the Recitation rooms, which resemble them in structure and size, your Committee recommend the use of the double fireplace* or the Ventilating Stove, which will be hereafter described. If the latter be used, ventilating flues, opening at the ceiling, must be carried out of the roof.

It only remains for your Committee to describe, more particularly, the system of ventilation which they consider to be, in its general features, best adapted for the school-houses under the care of the Board. Much of it has already been anticipated in other parts of this Report; and the following plan will show, at a glance, better than any description can do, its particular features.

* See page 38 of this Essay for a diagram and description.

DIAGRAM SHOWING THE BEST GENERAL PLAN FOR WARMING AND VENTILATING THE GRAMMAR SCHOOL-HOUSES.

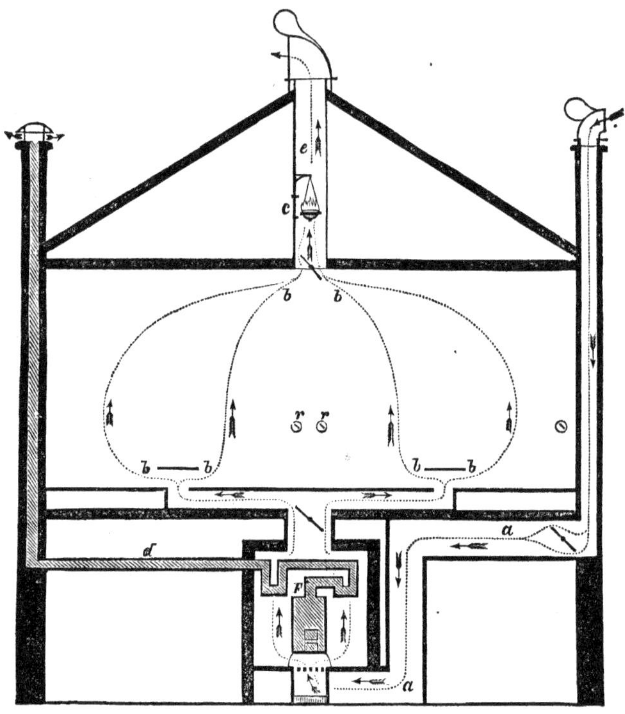

a. a. Cold-air channel, three feet in diameter, opening underneath the Furnace.

F. Furnace, three feet in diameter in a brick chamber ten feet square. The walls twelve inches thick.

d. Smoke flue, surmounted with Mr. Tredgold's chimney top.

b. b. b. b. Currents of warmed air, passing from the furnace, through a main flue of four feet in diameter, which supplies two branch flues. From these the air is diffused into all parts of the room, by means of the tablets which are placed over the mouths of the registers.

e. The ventilating shaft, two and a half feet in diameter, into which the foul gasses are collected, and from which they are finally discharged into the open air.

c. An Argand Lamp, to be lighted from the attic.

r. r. r. Registers, by means of which the whole circulation is controlled.

The Committee recommend attention to the following *general rules for Ventilation and Warming*.

1. The air must be taken from a pure source. The higher parts of the building are the best, as thereby all impurities, which often contaminate air taken from near the surface of the ground, are avoided.

2. In order to ensure a constant and abundant supply, the air shaft must be surmounted with a cowl or hood of some kind, with its mouth turned *towards the wind*.

3. The fresh air should in all cases be carried entirely beneath the furnace.

If the cellar is wet and the situation low, the underground culvert or channel should be of brick, laid in cement.

4. The furnace chamber should be so large that it can be entered at any time, without the necessity of taking down walls, for the purpose of repairs, or to observe the temperature. A large earthen pan for the evaporation of water should never be omitted. This should be kept always perfectly clean, and the water required to be frequently changed.

5. A thermometer should be constantly at hand, and the *temperature in the warm-air chamber should never be allowed to exceed that of boiling water.* A still lower temperature is often desirable. If this point is secured, the hot air can be conducted with perfect safety under floors, or into any part of the building, for its better diffusion.

6. The openings for the admission of the warm air into the rooms, should be as numerous as possible. The long platform occupied by the teachers, by being perforated in front for its whole length, would be an excellent diffusing surface.

7. Openings of ample size must be made in the highest points of the ceiling, to be connected at the top of the roof with a turn-cap or louvre, the former being always surmounted with a vane. It is better that the ceiling should be perforated at its centre, and there is no objection to running the ventilating shaft, at first, horizontally, if the perpendicular and terminal portion of it is of considerable length.

8. *It is highly important to have a power of some sort, within the apparatus at its top,* for the purpose of compelling constant action, and of increasing the force of the apparatus, whenever the state of the weather, or the crowding of the room, render it necessary.* For this purpose, the most convenient and economical means are furnished by a gas burner, an Argand lamp, or a stove; and one of these should be in constant readiness for use, when neither the velocity of the wind, or the low temperature of the external atmosphere are sufficient to produce the desired effect.

9. All the openings and flues for the admission of pure air, and the discharge of the foul air, should be of the *maximum* size; that is, they should be calculated for the *largest numbers* which the apartment is ever intended to accommodate.

10. Valves must be placed in all the flues, and so arranged as to be easily regulated without leaving the rooms into which they open.

11. The best average temperature for school-rooms, is from 64° to 68° Fahrenheit; this range including that of the healthiest climates in their best seasons.

For the purpose of summer ventilation, and for occasional use in moderate weather, fireplaces of good size should be constructed in all the new houses, at least. They should always be double, and furnished with large air chambers, which communicate with the open air. When not in use, they must be closed with tight boards or shutters, as they would otherwise interfere with the regular ventilation.

With these arrangements, intelligently controlled by the Teachers, your Committee believe that an atmosphere will be secured which will be perfectly agreeable and salubrious; which will lighten the labors of the Teachers, and promote the comfort, health, and happiness, of the thousands of children who are daily congregated in our Public Schools."

This Report was received, and the same Committee were "directed to adapt to each school-room such apparatus, if any, as may be required to secure to them proper ventilation in winter and summer, and to make such alterations and arrangements of the furnaces as may be required." To be able to execute this order, the Committee applied to the City Authorities for an appropriation of $4,000, which was readily granted, after an examination by a Joint Committee of the Board of Aldermen and Common Council, of the school-houses in which the improved ventilating apparatus had been introduced. The following is an extract from the Report of the Joint Committee:

* This in practice has not been found *necessary*, although it may be sometimes.

"In order to be fully satisfied, the Committee visited the Endicott School, where the apparatus was in operation. The day was exceedingly wet and disagreeable, and yet the air of the rooms was found in an unobjectionable condition. The masters fully sustained the representations of the petitioners; and from their statements, as well as from their own observations, the Committee were satisfied of the beneficial effects of said apparatus.

In order, however, to have a more full investigation of the matter, the Committee, on a subsequent day, visited the Johnson School and the Boylston School. The day was dry and cold, and they found the air in the Johnson School in a tolerably good condition. This is a girls' school; and it is well known that the pupils in such schools are neater, and attend in cleaner and more tidy apparel, than the pupils in the boys' schools.

In the Boylston School, however, the Committee found the air very disagreeable and oppressive; and they could not but feel the importance of executing some plan of relief."

If the Committee of Ways and Means,—or whatever the money-compelling power may be called—in every city, and town, and district, would satisfy themselves by actual examination, of the necessity of a more perfect system of ventilation in all school-rooms, or in all public halls where a large number of human beings are congregated for a considerable length of time, and where fires or lamps are burning, a reform would be speedily introduced in this respect.

With the means thus placed at their disposal, the Committee applied themselves diligently to the duty of ventilating the school-houses—and at the close of the year, they had the satisfaction of announcing in their Final Report, "that the Grammar School-houses of Boston are now in a better condition in respect to their ventilation, than any other Public Schools in the world." The Committee thus sum up the results of their labors.

"The diversity of arrangement and the modifications in our plans which we have been compelled by circumstances to adopt, have had their advantages, and enabled us to arrive at the best results, and to satisfy ourselves entirely in regard to the particular *set of apparatus* which we can recommend with confidence for future use as decidedly the most effective and convenient. We have therefore furnished drawings and specifications of the set of apparatus which we recommend.

Chilson's Furnace.

Your Committee have made themselves acquainted not only with all the Furnaces which have been manufactured in this place, and its neighborhood, but with all those which have been exhibited here recently. Most of them show much ingenuity of contrivance and excellence of workmanship; but are all, so far as we can judge, inferior in many respects, to the one invented by Mr. Chilson, a model and plans of which we now exhibit, and recommend as superior to all others.

It is simple in its structure, easily managed, will consume the fuel perfectly, and with a *moderate* fire. It is fitted for wood or coal. The fire place is broad and shallow, and is lined with soapstone or fire-brick, which not only makes it perfectly safe and durable, but modifies very materially the usual effect of the fire upon the iron pot.

The principal radiating surfaces are wrought iron, of a suitable thickness for service, while at the same time the heat of the smallest fire is communicated immediately to the air chamber. The mode of setting this Furnace we consider essential; more especially the plan of admitting the air to the furnace at its lowest point, as it then rises naturally into the apartments above. This process commences as soon as the temperature is raised even a single degree. The outer walls remain cold; the floor above is not endangered, and the whole building is rapidly filled with an atmosphere which is at once salubrious and delightful.

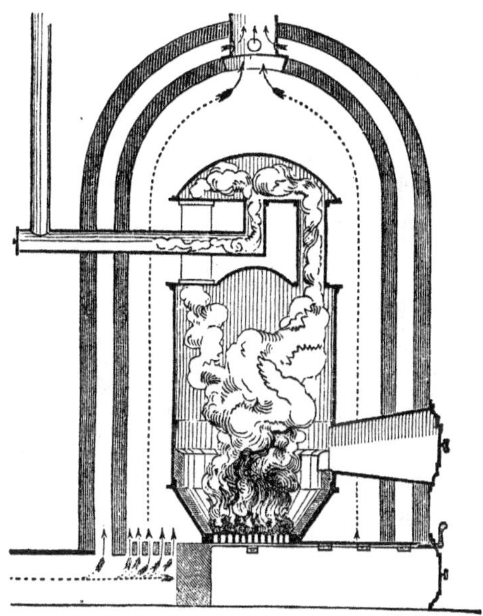

Section of Chilson's Furnace.

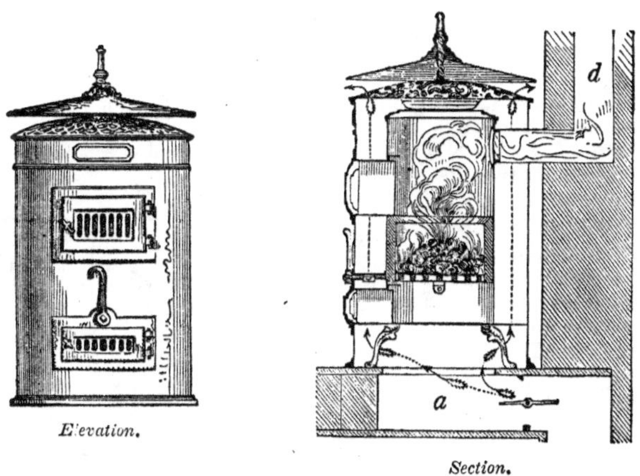

Elevation.

Section.

VENTILATING STOVE.

For the houses which we found without the Hot Air Furnaces, as also for the Recitation and other single rooms, the invention of a Stove which shoul answer the same purpose became essential. One was therefore contrived; and having been found in its earlier and ruder forms to be of great utility, it has since been improved in its appearance, as well as in the convenience of its management.

These Stoves are composed of two cylinders, the *inner* containing a fire chamber, which is lined with soap-stone or fire brick, while the *outer* constitutes a chamber for warming the air, which is introduced into it beneath the inner cylinder, from an air box directly connected with the external atmosphere.

They possess the following advantages:—

1. They are in fact *furnaces*, having distinct and capacious air chambers.

2. They insure, when properly set, that *supply of fresh air* which is *indispensable to the proper ventilation* of any apartment.

3. The Regulating Distributor, which is movable or fixed, as may be desired, determines with great accuracy the amount and temperature of the admitted air.

4. The outer cylinder is never hot enough to burn the person or clothing, or to be uncomfortable to those who are situated in its immediate vicinity.

5. They are constructed with the utmost regard to efficiency, durability, compactness, and neatness of appearance.

These Stoves have been furnished to the Schools whenever your Committee have required their use, and at manufacturers' prices, without any profit whatever to the inventor and patentee.

They may be used with advantage in the largest rooms, when the cellars are unfit for Furnaces, or when it is preferred to have the fire in the room itself. The Johnson, Wells, Hawes, and Winthrop School-houses are warmed entirely by them.

The discharging ventiducts have been made in various ways; some of wood, some of metal, and others of 'lath and plaster.' Some have opened at the ceiling only, and in but one part of the room, while others have been equally divided at opposite sides of the apartment. Our rule is this:—If the Heating Apparatus is at one end of an oblong room, the ventiduct is placed at the opposite. If the stove or furnace flue is at the middle of the longest side, the ventiducts are placed at each end, and are of course reduced to one half the size of the single one.

The *best* manner of constructing them is shown by the drawing, *Fig.* 1, and described on the following page.

There is great economy in carrying the boxes to the floor in all cases. In this way the room can be kept warm and the air pure in the coldest and most windy days.

The registers at the top and bottom can be used separately or together, as may be desired.

It is necessary and advantageous to apply some kind of cap or other covering upon the ventiducts where they terminate above the roof. It is necessary as a protection from the rain and the down blasts of wind, and it is also very advantageous to be enabled in this way to avail ourselves of the power of the wind to create an active upward current. We used at first the turncap or cowl invented by Mr. Espy, and with satisfactory results. It is undoubtedly the best movable top known; but is noisy, and somewhat liable to get out of working order. These objections to the movable tops have long been known, and various stationary tops have been invented, and have been partially successful. An improved Stationary Top, or Ejecting Ventilator, as it is called, has been invented during the past year by Mr. Emerson. It is shown in the drawing, and consists of the frustrum of a cone attached to the top of a tube, open in its whole extent, and surmounted by a fender which is supported upon rods, and answers the double purpose of keeping out the rain and of so directing or turning a blast of wind upon the structure, as that in what-

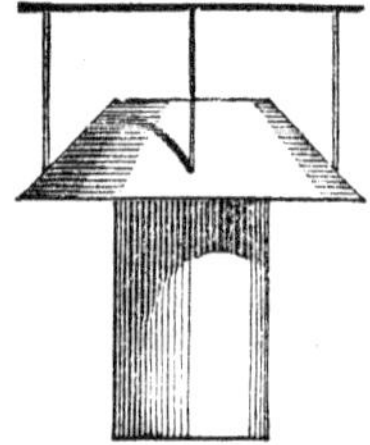
Ejecting Ventilator.

ever direction it falls, the effect, that of causing a strong upward draft, will be very uniform and constant.

Being satisfied that this Stationary Ejector possessed all the advantages of the best tops hitherto known, without the disadvantages of either of them, we have adopted it for several of the houses last ventilated, and find it in all respects satisfactory. We therefore recommend it for general use.

The Injector may generally be dispensed with, but in situations unfavorable for introducing air, it may be sometimes found convenient, or even necessary. [Mr. Emerson recommends the use of the Injector, whenever a ventilating stove or furnace is used, so as to secure the admission of a quantity of pure air, warmed by the heating surfaces of the stove or furnace, equal to the quantity of air rendered impure by respiration withdrawn by the Ejector. He refuses to allow his ventilators to be placed upon any school-house which is not supplied with fresh warm air.]

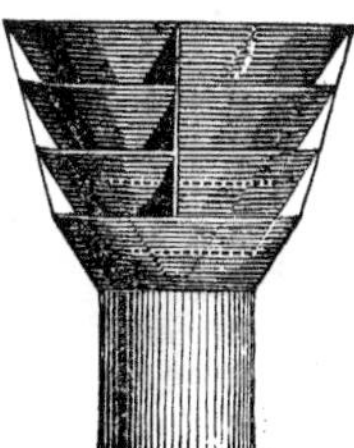

Injecting Ventilators.

Ventiducts.

The discharging ventiducts should be situated at the part of the rooms most distant from the stove or register of the furnace, and should always, if possible, be constructed in or upon an *interior* wall or partition, and an outer brick wall must, if possible, be avoided. They should be made of thoroughly seasoned sound pine boards, smoothed on the inner sides, and put together with two-inch iron screws. The outside finish may be of lath and plaster, or they may be projected backwards into a closet or entry, as shown in Figure 3. They must be carried entirely to the floor, and should be fitted at the top and bottom with a swivel blind, whose capacity is equal to that of the ventiduct into which it opens. This blind may be governed by stay rods or pulleys. The elevation gives a view of the ventiducts for a building of three stories, and shows the best mode of packing them, so as to avoid injuring the appearance of the rooms.

These ventiducts must be *kept entirely separate* to the main discharger at the roof, as any other arrangement would impair or destroy their utility.

The size of the ventilators and ventiducts must correspond to the capacity of the room, and the number it is intended to accommodate.

A room containing sixty scholars is found to require a discharging duct of fourteen inches in diameter. A room for one hundred scholars requires the tube to be eighteen inches; and a room for two hundred scholars requires it to be twenty-four inches.

The *fresh air ventiducts should exceed in capacity* those for carrying off the impure air by about *fifty per cent.;* so that there will then always be a surplus or plenum supply, and the little currents of cold which press in at the crevices of the doors and windows will be entirely prevented.

The section shown in Fig. 3 exhibits a very convenient mode of bringing the cold air to the ventilating stoves in a three story building in connection with the smoke flues.

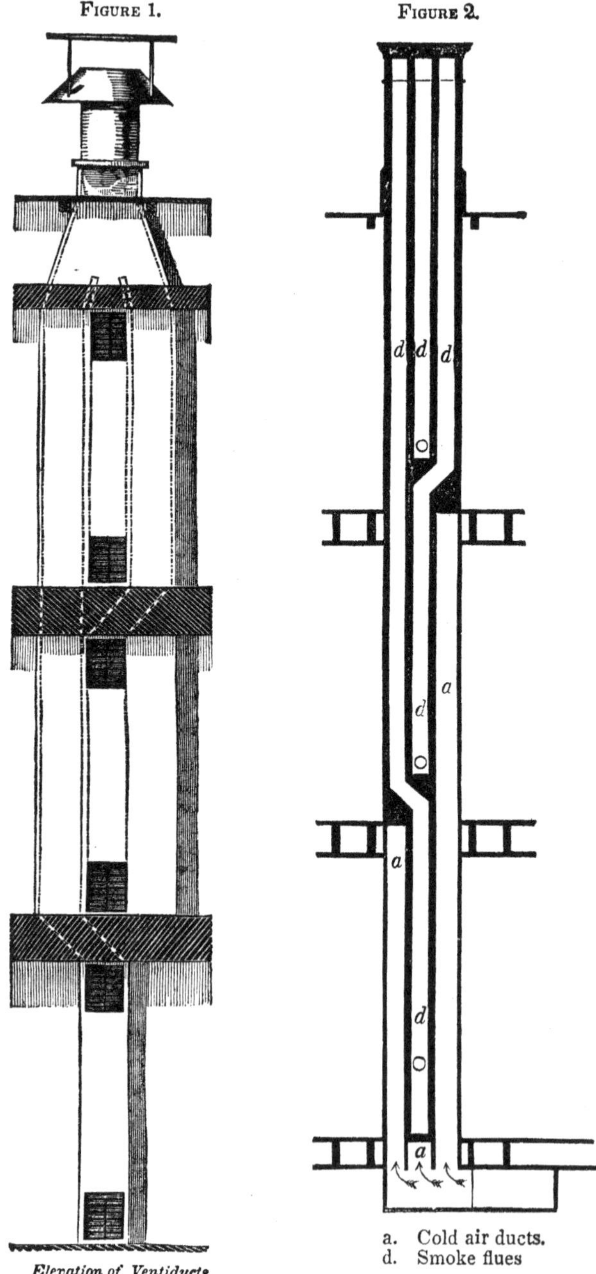

Elevation of Ventiducts.

The following section, (Fig. 3,) and plans (Fig's. 4 and 5,) exhibit at one view an example of a building of two stories warmed and ventilated by the apparatus and in the manner recommended.

FIGURE 3.

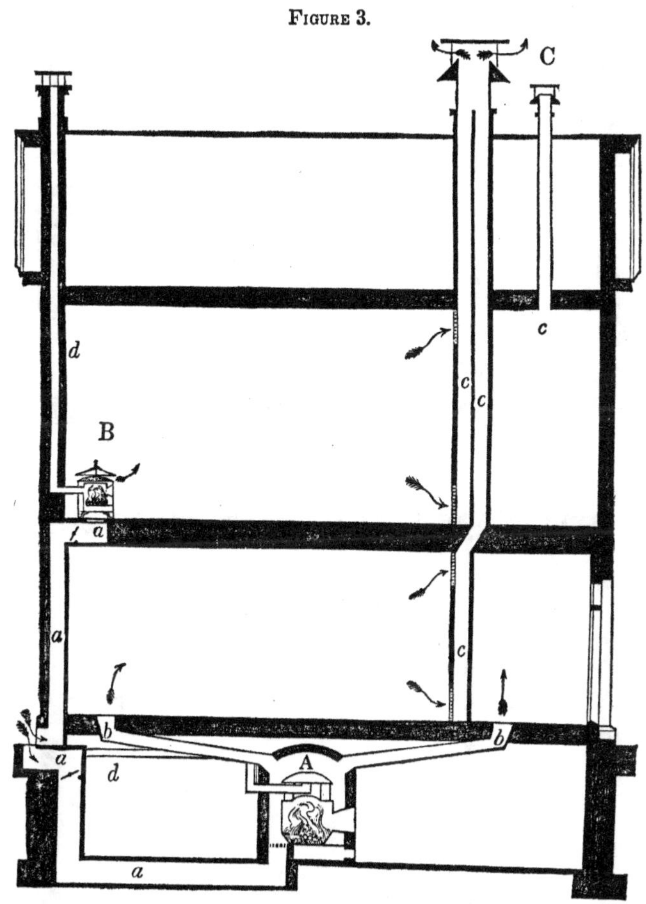

A. Chilson's Furnace.
B. The Boston School Stove.
C. Emerson's Ejector.
a. Cold or fresh air ducts.
b. Warmed air ducts.
c. Impure air ducts.
d. Smoke flues.

The letters on the plans correspond to those in the section.

Plans of First and Second Floors.

FIGURE 4.

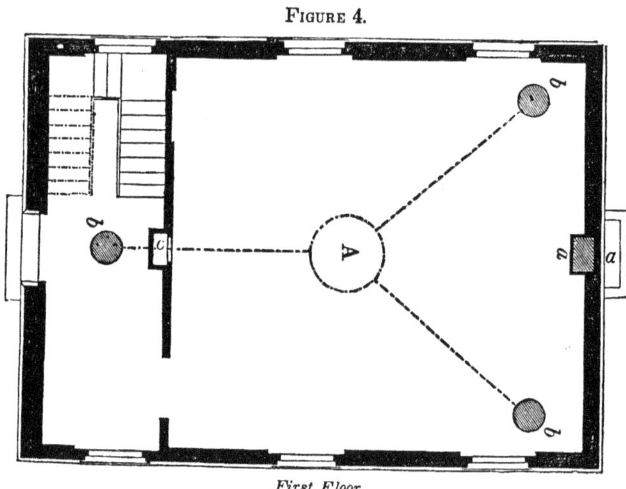

First Floor.

FIGURE 5.

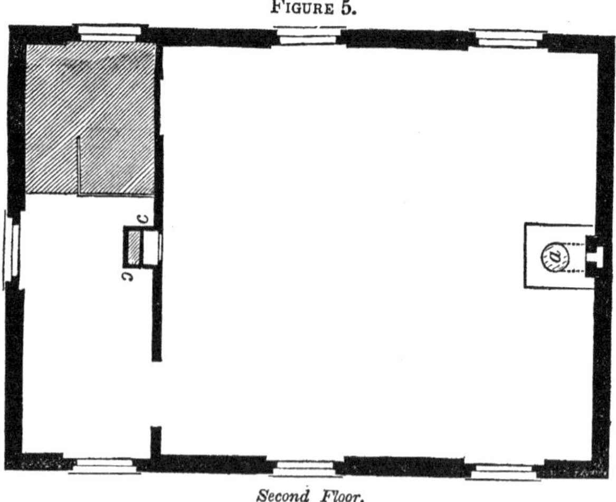

Second Floor.

A. Furnace. a. a. a. Fresh air ducts. b. b. b. Warm air registers. c. c. c. Impure air ducts.

The modes of ventilation and heating above described and illus trated, were unanimously approved by the school committee, and recommended to the city government, for introduction into the school-houses which may be hereafter erected.

The Committee append to their Report directions for the management of the Stoves, Furnaces and Ventiducts, to which they request the attention of the masters of the Public Schools, in conformity to the rule of the Board, which requires their attention to the Ventilation of the School-houses under their care.

Rules relative to the use of the Stoves, Furnaces and Ventilators.

1. *To kindle the fire.*—Close the upper, and open the lower registers of the ventiducts; close the upper door of the stove or furnace and open the lower door; place the cover of the stove one or two inches up.

2. *After the room becomes warm*—Raise the cover of the stove three or five inches; close the lower door of the stove and open the upper door; open the registers of the ventiducts about half their width.

3. *If the room become too warm*—Open the registers full width, and raise the cover of the stove high up, keeping the upper door of the stove or furnace open, and the lower door closed.

4. *If the room become too cool*—Close the upper registers, (for a short time only;) close the upper door of the stove and open the lower door; drop the cover down within two inches of the sides.

5. Never close the top of the stove entirely down, while there is any fire therein.

6. At night, on leaving the room, let the cover of the stove down within one inch of the sides; close the lower door, and open the upper one; place all the registers open about half their width.

7. Fill the water basins every morning, and wash them twice a week.

The fires should be kept, if possible, through the night, by covering the coal. The coal to be white ash.

Construction of Ventiducts.

Since the first edition of this work was published, the following note has been received from Dr. Clark, in relation to the structure of the discharging ventiducts.

BOSTON, Feb. 12th, 1849.

HENRY BARNARD, ESQ.:

My Dear Sir,—Will you allow me to ask your attention to a single matter relating to ventilation? I refer to the construction, situation, and proper materials of the ventiducts which are intended to carry off the foul air. In almost all instances within my knowledge, excepting in the buildings in this place, which have been ventilated within two or three years past, these discharging ducts are made of *brick* or stone, being often, therefore, also built in the outer wall. If there is any peculiar advantage in our school-house ventilation, its success is very much owing to the manner of locating and constructing these same ejecting ventiducts.

The brick ducts always operate *downwards;* that is to say, the air has a constant *tendency to fall* in them, and they will never "draw" in the proper or *upward* direction, with the best turncap or top known, unless there is a high wind, or unless *artificial* power, such as a *fire*, or a fan wheel be put in requisition. Now the contrary is the fact with the thin *wooden, or lath-and-plaster, interior ventiduct.* The current is always in the right or *upward* direction. They are warmed to the *temperature of the room*, and when provided with a proper top will operate *in all seasons.* Although the currents will *vary* in power and rapidity, yet, while almost all our ventiducts are provided, and should be, with means of heating by lamps or otherwise, I believe they have scarcely had occasion to light them. So that any impressions formed in relation to this part of the subject from the English, and particularly the French methods of ventilating school-houses, when the brick flues are always used, must be entirely erroneous. The days in which the fires in the French flues *would be forgotten* and omitted, or *be permitted to go out*, would far exceed the number of those in which our ventiducts would not act in the most perfect manner *without any power at all.*

I would not have troubled you, but that I know this point, from much practical experience, to be worthy of especial attention, and in case you should publish a new edition of your work on school-houses, I hope it may be considered.

I am, dear sir,

Yours very truly,

HENRY G. CLARK

Apparatus for Warming.

The thorough ventilation, the constant and regular change of the atmosphere of a school-room cannot be secured by simply providing flues or openings, however judiciously constructed and placed, for the escape of the air which has become impure from the process of breathing or other causes. These flues will not work satisfactorily, unless a mode of warming the room is adopted by which a large supply of pure fresh air, properly heated, is flowing in to supply the place of that which is escaping by means of the flues. Among the various modes of warming school-rooms and public halls, which we have seen in full and successful operation, we select a few, in addition to those described in other parts of the work, as worthy of the particular attention of committees and others, who are looking round for a heating apparatus. We shall use the cuts and description by which the patentees and venders have chosen to make their several modes of warming known to the public, without intending to decide on the relative merits of any one mode.

Culver's Hot-Air Furnace.

Patented and Manufactured by Culver & Co., 52 Cliff-street, New York.

Culver's Hot-Air Furnace, as described in the following diagram and explanations, is intended for hard coal, to be set in double walls of brick masonry in cellar or basement, below the rooms to be warmed.

Figure 1.

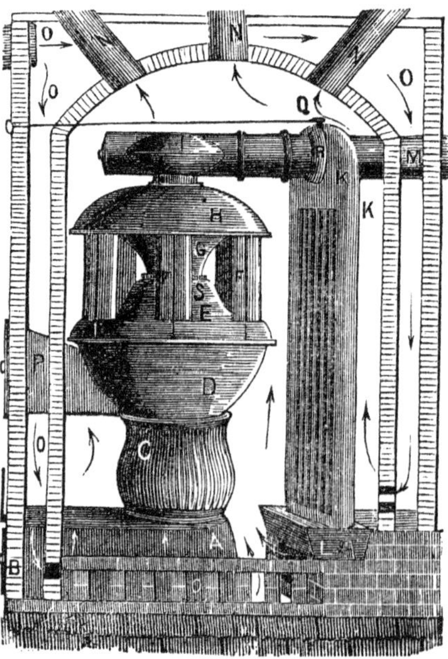

A. Iron or Brick Ash Pit.
B. Ash Pit door.
C. Pot, or coal Burner, with or without *soapstone* lining.
D. Fire Chamber.
E. Lower half of Tubular drum.
F. Elliptical tubes.
G. Upper half of Tubular drum.
H. Top of Tubular drum.
I. Cap and smoke pipe.
K. Flat Radiator.
L. Water bason or evaporator.
M. Smoke pipe to chimney.
N. Conductors of Hot Air.
O. Cold air conductor and chamber.
P. Feed door.
Q. Hot-Air chamber.
R. Damper in globe with rod attached.
S. Pendulum valve for cleaning.
→ Shows the direction of the currents of hot or cold air.

Culver & Co. also make, and put up, various sizes of Portable Furnaces, with metallic coverings, suitable for counting rooms, stores, school-rooms and small houses, warming the rooms in which they stand, as well as others in the same building, and they can be removed in summer as conveniently as stoves.

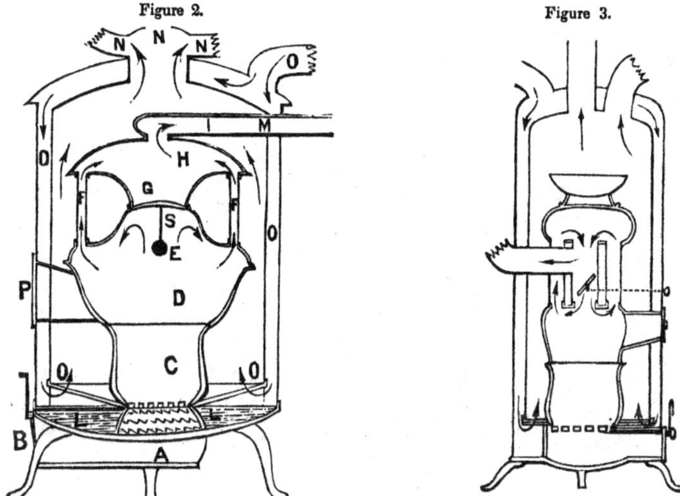

Figure 2 represents a section of large size Portable Furnace or double casings of sheet iron or zinc. The same letters for reference are used as in Fig. 1.
Figure 3 represents a smaller size Portable Furnace, with two metal coverings and an evaporating dish standing upon the top of the drum.

The peculiarities and advantages of the Furnace are thus set forth:

1. Its compact, convenient and beautiful form.

2. Its great *durability;* being in all its parts of cast iron, set within walls of brick masonry. The *pot* or burner being whole, is found by experience to be more durable than those made of rings or segments, and entirely prevents the admission of gas into the hot-air chamber.

3. The great radiating surfaces of this Furnace exceed those of any other, and being nearly all perpendicular, and so arranged as to afford no chance for the soot, light coal ashes or dust to collect on the plates and prevent the transmission of heat through them, for it must be obvious to every thinking mind, that if a radiating surface is of a zig-zag, or any other form that prevents the descent of dust or soot in a perpendicular line, it will certainly collect dust upon it, and just so much surface thus covered is destroyed for radiating purposes, and in the same proportion will a greater consumption of fuel be required to produce a given result.

These furnaces are so constructed that heat acts actively upon those surfaces within, and produces the immediate and powerful heating of the cold air that is admitted to the outer surface from the atmosphere, through the tubes for that purpose.

4. The great economy in the use of fuel, making and controlling more heat than by any other process of using it.

5. The *joints* of this Furnace are so constructed that the expansion and contraction of the metal cannot open them to admit gas into the hot-air chamber, and it can be cleaned of soot and ashes easily, without the necessity of taking down or breaking a joint; its action is simple, as easily understood and managed as a cylinder stove, and as readily repaired and kept in order, and the manner of "removing the deposits" is entirely novel and most efficient.

6. The constant current of the pure atmosphere into the air chamber, with

the evaporation for tempering it to any degree of humidity, gives a fine healthful ventilation, and a soft summer temperature, suited to the most delicate constitution, and without injury to the building or furniture.

The above described Air Heaters are manufactured and sold, wholesale and retail, by Culver & Co., who, when required, set them in double walls of brick masonry, with cast iron smoke pipe to chimneys, and conductors of hot air, of double cross tin, terminating with registers in the rooms, and secured safely from fire by tin or soap-stone linings.

Figure 4.

Figure 4 represents patterns of scroll work Registers manufactured by Culver & Co., and put in with their furnaces if desired. The registers have valves under the surface, which are easily controlled by means of the star centers. They can be used for ventilating purposes as well as for admitting warm air.

The following directions are given in Culver & Co.'s Circular for the use of their Furnace.

Directions for Use.—In kindling the fire, the valve should be opened by drawing out the Damper Rod R, so as to let the smoke pass directly through smoke pipe M to chimney.

Shavings, pine wood, or charcoal, should be thrown into the pot or coal burner C, and when well ignited, put in about half a hod of coal, and as soon as it also becomes ignited, fill the pot two thirds full of coal, and push the damper R partly in, so as to regulate the draught and heat as may be necessary. The valve may be entirely closed, if need be, so as to retain the heat, making it to pass through the Flat Radiator K.

In moderate weather, when little heat is wanted, put two shovels full of ashes on the centre of the fire, and by regulating the draught, you can make one fire last 24 hours without any alteration; and when you wish to renew the fire, poke out a portion of the ashes, and put on fresh coal, without turning the grate.

In cold weather, however, to secure a brisk fire, the crank should be turned so as to empty the pot entirely of ashes, and commence a new fire at least once in 24 hours.

When there is too much heat generated, the ash-pit door, B, should be closed entirely, and the damper rod partly drawn out, and if this is not sufficient, the Register in feed-door P may be opened; the heat in the different rooms may be regulated by opening or closing the Registers; all the Registers however should never be closed at the same time, unless the water door is opened to let out the hot air.

The cold-air conductor, O, should always be open when the Furnace is in operation.

Mr. Culver manufactures a Sand-Bath, with Water-Bath and Distilling Apparatus attached, which possesses the recommendations of efficiency, compactness, and economy of fuel. The following description applies to one erected by him in the Yale Analytical Laboratory, New Haven, as described by Prof. John P. Norton, in Silliman's Journal for July, 1851.

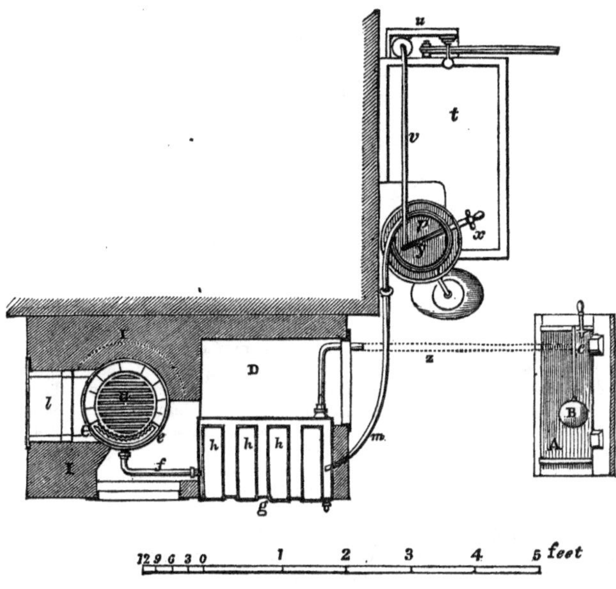

Fig. 1.—Furnace.

In fig. 1, *a* is the furnace, the position of which is also seen at *a* in fig. 2. The heat of the fire passes through the bed plate, *b*, *b*, fig. 2, heating the sand which lies upon its upper surface. All noxious fumes are conveyed away by the ventilator *c*, fig. 2, which opens into a chimney flue, and may be closed or opened at pleasure by the chain *d*. To this sand-bath, the water-baths and distilling apparatus are attached.

The furnace *a* is an iron pot, lined inside with firebrick as usual, *e*, *e*, fig. 1, where is inserted a water-back of large size. This communicates by the pipe *f*, with the water-bath *g*. There are two of these pipes, one above, and one below, as shown at *f*, *f*, in fig. 2, through the open door. The front elevation of the water-bath, which is of copper in all its parts, is shown at *g*, in fig. 2. Each of the doors seen on the front, opens into a separate compartment. The depth of these compartments is shown by the sections *h*, *h*, *h*, in fig. 1. At *i*, fig. 2, is a larger compartment, for receiving articles of considerable size.

At *j*, is a glass tube to show the height of water in the water-bath, and at *k*, a cock placed so low that all of the water contained may be drawn off, thus removing any small quantity of sediment which occasionally accumulates. These two parts are seen more clearly at *j*, and *k*, in fig. 3.

The furnace is fed through a door at *l*. A moderate fire is sufficient to establish a brisk circulation through the pipes *f*, *f*, and causes the water to boil violently in the water-bath, keeping it always full, up to 212° F. The steam formed escapes through the pipe *m*, fig. 1, also shown at *m*, *m*, figs. 2 and 3. At *n*, figs. 2 and 3, is a coupling, connecting the copper *m* with a blocktin pipe *o*, figs. 2 and 3, and worm *p*, fig. 1. This worm is contained in the condenser *q*, figs. 2 and 3. The distilled water thus produced, escapes at *r*, figs. 2 and 3, and runs into the receiver *s*, beneath. The condenser stands on a shelf over a sink *t*, figs. 1, 2, and 3, at the farther end of which is a force pump *u*, figs. 1 and 3. A pipe *v*, figs. 1

and 3, runs from the top of this pump into the condenser. The pump delivers cold water into the sink in the common way, but by closing the cock at *w*, fig. 3, will throw its stream into the condenser. This water, when warm, is drawn off at the cock *x*, figs. 1, 2, and 3. The pipe from this cock, seen at *y*, fig. 1, rises to within an inch or two of the top of the condenser, so that the warm water is drawn off first. By this arrangement, the very great convenience is obtained of a constant supply of hot water, delivered into the sink for washing.

As the well water at New Haven contains a considerable amount of solid matter, which soon incrusts the interior of vessels in which it is steadily boiled, rain water only is used in the water-bath. The supply is kept up through the pipe *z*, as shown in figs. 1, 2 and 3, running under the floor. Its whole course may be traced by these three figures. It rises into the box A, figs. 1, and 3, in which the water stands on a level with the upper part of the glass guage tube, shown at *j*, in fig. 3. Upon the surface floats a large, hollow, copper ball, B, fig. 1. As soon as the formation of steam, and its consequent passing off into the condenser, commences in the water-bath, the surface of course lowers, and a corresponding lowering occurs in the box A. The copper ball B sinks with the water, and gradually opens a valve at C, fig. 1. This admits a stream of water from an elevated cistern, which flows in just fast enough to supply that which passes off from the water-bath as steam.

This arrangement is only novel in its present application, being, I believe, quite common in some of our cities for regulating the flow of water into cisterns. It works admirably in the present case, and seldom if ever requires any attention. If the fire is very hot, so much steam is occasionally generated, that it is not condensed with sufficient rapidity; a partial flow of hot water back into the box A, has several times occurred under these circumstances, but has never been sufficient to overflow. This difficulty might be avoided by enlarging the conducting pipe *m*, and the worm *p*, or by reducing the size of the water-back *e*, *e*, fig. 1.

The space D, fig. 1, is a large, dry, hot oven, where quite a high heat is obtained. This is also shown at D, the door being taken off. In this oven a shelf is placed, perforated with holes for the insertion of funnels, tubes, &c. It is in constant use for drying, and is found to be of very great service in all cases where rapid drying is desirable, and a precise temperature is not required. The small door at E, fig. 2, is another means of access to this oven.

The water-bath is set in the brickwork, but may be taken out and reset without disturbing the rest of the apparatus; in fact, every part is accessible. The couplings to the pipes *f*, *f*, may be reached through the door F; those to the supply pipe *z*, at G, fig. 3, those to the escape pipe *m*, by taking out a brick at H, fig. 3. In order to obtain ready access to the interior of the furnace pot *a*, there is a large movable circular plate immediately above; its circumference is shown by the dotted line at I, I, in fig. 1.

The supply of water from the cistern to the box A, is cut off by a stop-cock at the cistern, and the water may be entirely drawn off from the box by a small cock at J, under the floor.

It will be seen that this arrangement is compact and simple. There is no part liable to get out of order, or that, once out of order, can not be easily reached for the purpose of repairs.

By means of one fire, and that not large, we heat the sand-bath sufficiently, maintain a large water-bath constantly at 212° F., make from ten to fifteen gallons of perfectly pure water per day, heat a large drying oven, and keep a constant supply of hot water over the sink for washing. Every thing takes care of itself, excepting the fire, and the occasional pumping of cold water into the condenser. I am unable, after two months of experience, to suggest any important improvement in these arrangements, and feel confident that any one who should put up a similar apparatus would not be disappointed.

The iron work is all japanned. The glass should be set with a putty made of boiled linseed oil, as that will harden under the heat to which it is exposed; the common putty made with fish oil remains soft, and the glass is constantly liable to get out of place.

Prof. Norton expresses his obligations to Mr. Culver, for the practical skill by which the difficulties in adjusting the different parts of this apparatus were overcome, and for the substantial and satisfactory manner in which the work was done.

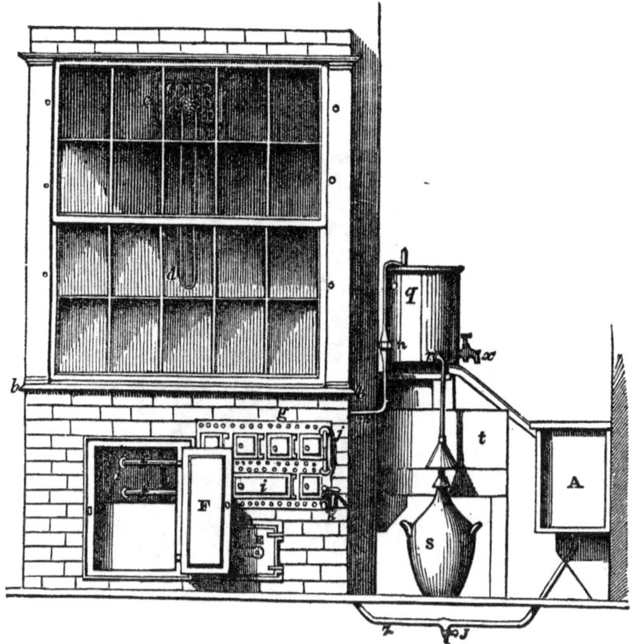

Fig. 2.—FRONT ELEVATION.

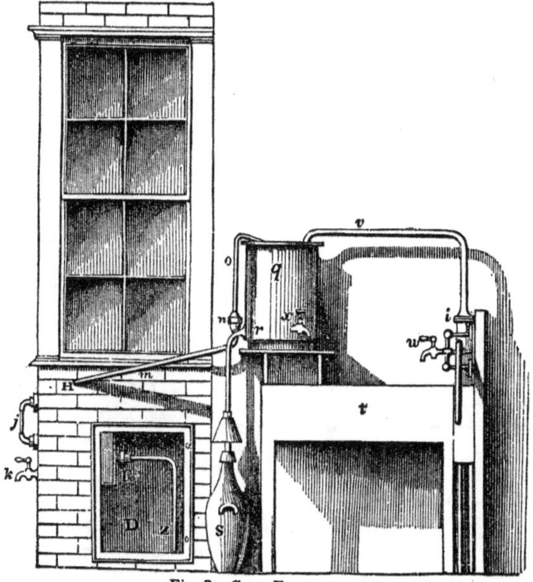

Fig. 3.—SIDE ELEVATION.

Mott's Ventilating School-Stove, for burning wood or coal.

Patented and Manufactured by J. L. Mott, 264 *Water-street, N. Y.*

By this stove the room is warmed by conducting a supply of moderatery heated pure air from without, as well as by direct radiation from the upper portion of the stove.

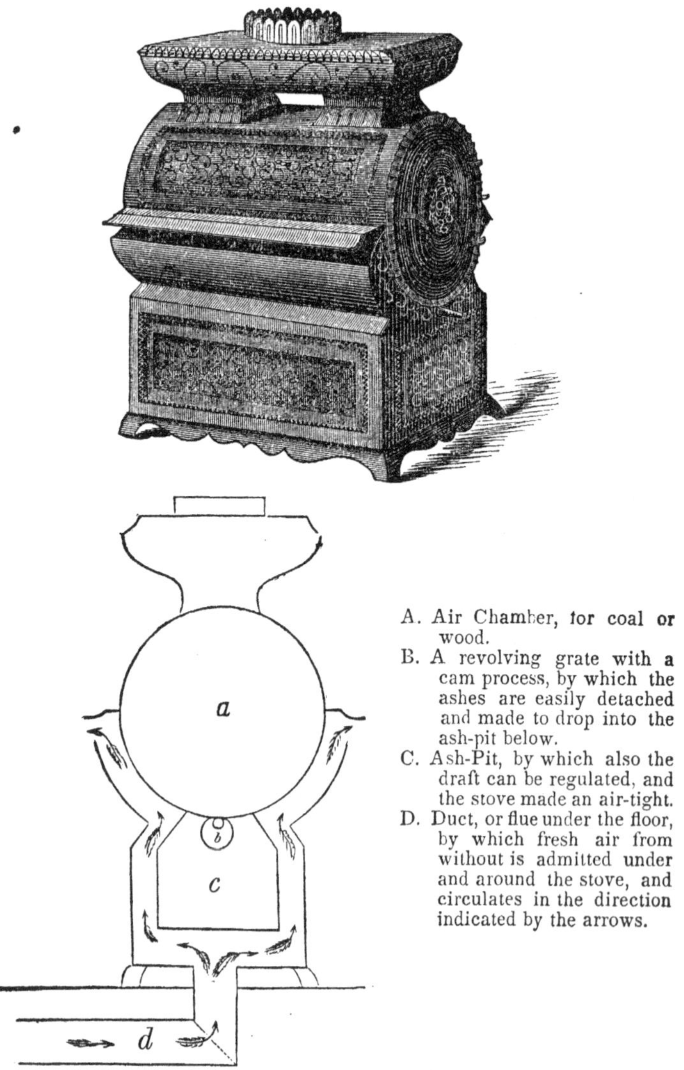

A. Air Chamber, for coal or wood.
B. A revolving grate with a cam process, by which the ashes are easily detached and made to drop into the ash-pit below.
C. Ash-Pit, by which also the draft can be regulated, and the stove made an air-tight.
D. Duct, or flue under the floor, by which fresh air from without is admitted under and around the stove, and circulates in the direction indicated by the arrows.

This, and all stoves designed to promote ventilation by introducing fresh air from without, will work satisfactorily only where a flue properly constructed is provided to carry off the air which has become impure from respiration.

CHILSON'S COAL VENTILATING SCHOOL STOVES.

The Boston Ventilating Stove, Fig. 1, designed and patented by Dr. Clark, and Chilson's Patent Trio Portable Furnace, Fig. 2, are composed of a cylinder of sheet-iron, inclosing a fire-chamber which is lined with soapstone, or fire-brick, and is so made as to present a large amount of radiating surface. The air to be warmed, is introduced beneath the fire-chamber by a flue from out of doors, and passing up, and around the heated surface, flows directly into the room, or into pipes to be communicated into other departments, as indicated by the arrows in the above drawings. These stoves and furnaces are intended to burn coal.

FIG. 1.

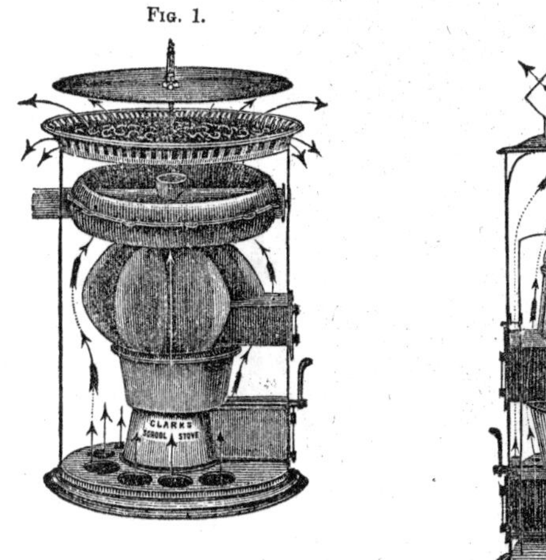

FIG. 2.

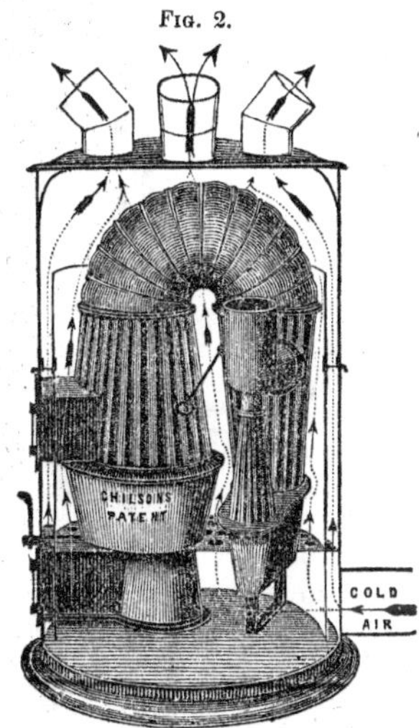

CHILSON'S WOOD VENTILATING STOVE.

Mr. Chilson has also patented a plan of stove for burning wood, Fig. 3, by which the air is introduced by a flue beneath the stove, and is warmed by circulating through cast-iron tubes, which constitute the sides and ends of the stove.

FIG. 3.

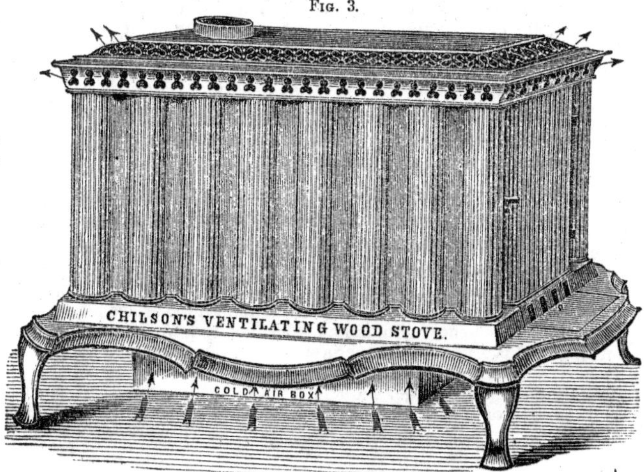

CHILSON'S AIR-WARMING AND VENTILATING FURNACE.

Patented and Manufactured by Gardner Chilson, Boston.

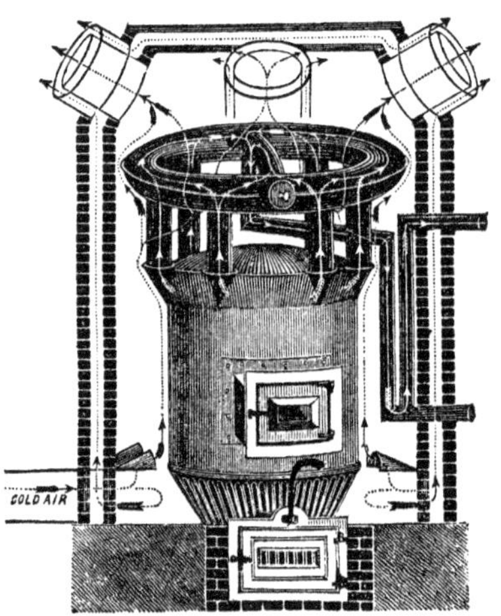

The construction of the *Air-Warming and Ventilating Furnace* was projected by the inventor, to obviate the serious, if not fatal, objections, so generally made, to the use of furnaces for warming apartments, where a fresh, healthful atmospheric air is required. From long experience in putting up furnaces, in which coal was consumed in deep iron pots, and the air which they warmed was made to pass over a large extent of iron surface, made and kept red-hot, he found that the occupants of the rooms thus warmed, complained that the air was not unfrequently filled with the gases of the burning coal, and was at all times dry and stagnant, causing, especially to persons of a nervous temperament, disagreeable sensations to the whole system, such as dizziness of the head, headache, inflammation of the eyes and lungs, dryness of the lips and skin, &c. He found, too, by his own experience and observation in the manufacture and use of furnaces of this kind, that there was an unnecessary consumption of coal, when burnt in deep, straight and narrow pots, causing the coal to melt and run to cinders, and at the same time burning out the pots, and loosening the joints of the furnace, by which the deadly gases escaped into the air-chambers, and hence into the apartments above. These objections, both on the score of health and expense, the inventor claims that he has thoroughly obviated in his *Air-Warming and Ventilating Furnace*, and at the same time preserved all the advantages heretofore realized from this mode of warming buildings. The advantages of the Furnace are—

1. The fire-pot is constructed on the most economical and philosophical principles. It is broad and shallow,—at least twice as broad and one third as deep as the common fire-pot;—is one third smaller at the bottom than at the top, and is lined with fire-brick or soap-stone. Thus the fire-bed is deep enough to keep the coal well ignited with a slow but perfect combustion, while the entire heat from the fuel is given out to act upon the radiating surface alone and the fire-pot can never become red-hot, and does not require renewal. This plan for burning coal is original with the inventor, and has met with universal approbation.

2. The radiating surface is large, and so placed that it receives the immediate and natural action of the heat, and at the same time imparts its heat in the

most direct and uniform manner to the fresh air from without, without suffering waste by absorption from the outer walls of the air-chamber.

3. The air-chamber is large, and the fresh air is admitted and discharged so readily and uniformly that no portion of the radiating surface can ever become overheated; and a delightful summer temperature is maintained in the rooms.

4. The joints of the furnace are so constructed, that, even if the iron-work was liable, like other furnaces, to crack from extreme expansion, by being overheated, (which it is not,) the gas from the burning coal cannot escape into the air-chamber.

5. There are no horizontal inner surfaces on which dust and soot can gather, which do not, at the same time, clean themselves, or admit of being easily cleaned.

6. The grate in the fire-pot is so constructed, that the ashes can be easily detached, and the combustion facilitated.

7. It has stood all the test which sharp rivalry and the most severe *philosophical* practical science could apply to it, and has thus far accomplished all that its inventor promised, and when tried in the same building with other furnaces, has uniformly received the preference.

Dr. Bell, Superintendent of the McLean Asylum for the Insane, who has given this whole subject his particular attention, in his Essay on the *Practical Methods of Ventilating Buildings*, published in the proceedings of the Massachusetts Medical Society for 1848, remarks as follows:

"The character of any variety of the hot-air furnace is measured, in my judgment, by the simplicity of its construction, its non-liability to be brought to an undue degree of heat in any part, and its ready receipt and emission of air. That made by Mr. Gardner Chilson, of Boston, with an air-chamber of brick, and an interspace of two or three feet in width, appears to me to combine all the essentials attainable of this mode of heating air, more fully than any other which has fallen under my observation."

In 1847, the School Committee of Boston sanctioned, by a unanimous vote, the introduction of this furnace into the new school-houses to be erected in that city, on the recommendation of a sub-committee, to which the whole subject of warming and ventilating the school-rooms had been referred. The following is the recommendation referred to.

"Your Committee have made themselves acquainted not only with all the Furnaces which have been manufactured in this place, and its neighborhood, but with all those which have been exhibited here recently. Most of them show much ingenuity of contrivance and excellence of workmanship; but are all, so far as we can judge, inferior, in many respects, to the one invented by Mr. Chilson, a model and plans of which we now exhibit, and recommend as superior to all others.

It is simple in its structure, easily managed, will consume the fuel perfectly, and with a *moderate* fire. It is fitted for wood or coal. The fire-place is broad and shallow, and is lined with soapstone or fire-brick, which not only makes it perfectly safe and durable, but modifies very materially the usual effect of the fire upon the iron pot.

The principal radiating surfaces are wrought iron, of a suitable thickness for service, while at the same time the heat of the smallest fire is communicated immediately to the air-chamber. The mode of setting this Furnace we consider essential; more especially the plan of admitting the air to the furnace at its lowest point, as it then rises naturally into the apartments above. This process commences as soon as the temperature is raised even a single degree. The outer walls remain cold; the floor above is not endangered, and the whole building is rapidly filled with an atmosphere which is at once salubrious and delightful."

This Ventilating Furnace may be seen in the Mayhew, Dwight, Hancock, Boylston, Bowdoin, and Ingraham school-houses, in Boston; also in several new school-houses in Cambridge, Roxbury, Dorchester, Springfield, in the Blind Asylum and House of Industry, South Boston, and in hundreds of private houses in Boston and its vicinity.

Directions for Setting Chilson's Patent Furnace.

In locating the furnace, choose a situation as equidistant from the registers as possible, so that the pipes may be of nearly equal length, and branch from two or more sides of the furnace.

Secure a proper foundation, by leveling the ground on which the furnace is to rest; and dig down a few inches preparatory to a foundation of brick work, which should cover two inches larger than the outer walls. Should the ground be soft or spongy, fill it with gravel or hard coal ashes; if it prove necessary from the lowness of the cellar to sink the base of the ash-pit below its surface, excavate a trench of corresponding depth, the width of which shall be that of the recess in the walls, and project out about three feet. Commence the walls as shown in the ground plan, figure 1.

Figure 1—Ground Plan.

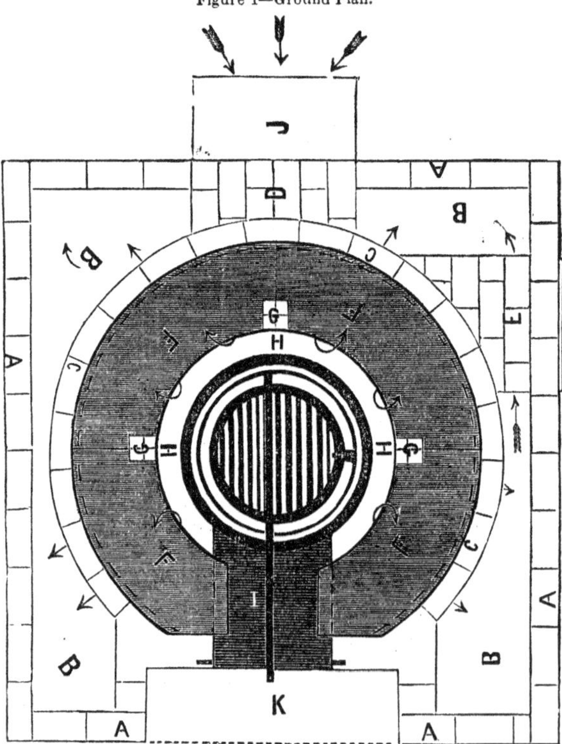

A A A—Outer Walls.
B B B B—Space, between outer and inner Walls, two inches at nearest point.
C C C C—Inner Wall.
D—Brick covering over Cold Air Channel.
E—Brick covering or floor from large Entrance Door.
F F F F—Iron Trench Plates.
G G G—Three four-inch Brick Piers, support under Trench Plates.
H H—Space between Trench Plates and base of Fire Pot, for ingress of Cold Air. Four and a half inches for Nos. 3 and 4; five inches for No. 5; six inches for No. 6.
I—Cast iron Ash-Pit, or Base to Furnace.
J—Cold Air Channel.
K—Set back, or recess in front Wall; for Nos. 3 and 4, thirty-three inches wide inside, and eight inches deep. For Nos. 5 and 6, thirty-seven inches wide, and twelve inches deep.

The outer wall should be four inches in thickness; that of the inner, eight inches from the base to the trench plates, and four inches above—made in the form of a circle, of such diameter as shall leave a space of two inches between it and the outer wall at the nearest point. Make the recess in the walls front of the door as shown by ground plan, No. 1, and of the dimensions described under same plan. Apertures must be made in the base of the inner wall, as shown in plan No. 1, to give the cold air free ingress into the space between the walls, and carry off the heat radiated from the inside wall into the perforated hot air pipe, and also to prevent the outer wall becoming hot and heating the cellar, causing a waste of heat, damage to vegetables, etc.

After the foundation has reached the height of the furnace base, the cold air channel, which is constructed to conduct the air directly to the space between the inner wall and the cast iron ash-pit, should be covered by means of iron bars overlaid with brick.

Figure 2—Sectional View.

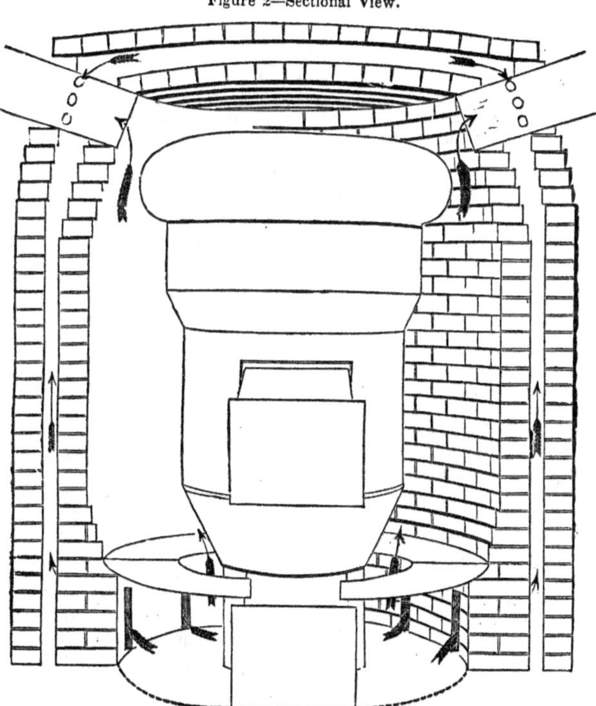

SIZE OF BRICK WORK.

No. 3—5-8 by 5-8, outside.	No. 5—6-6 by 6-6, outside.
" 4—6 feet by 6 feet, outside.	" 6—7 feet by 7 feet, outside.

Outside Walls, four incnes thick, for all sizes.
Inside Walls, eight inches thick, all sizes, to Trench Plates, and four inches above.
Eight apertures, eight inches high and two wide. in base of inner wall, for the passage of air between walls.

SIZE OF COLD AIR CHANNELS.

No. 3, Equivalent to 200 square inches, inside
" 4, " " 240 " " "
" 5, " " 325 " " "
" 6, " " 400 " " "

The entrance or man-hole door, should be built in the outer wall, as shown by ground plan, letter E, and a corresponding opening in the inner wall, for the purpose of entrance. On a level with the base, a covering, similar to that of the cold air channel, should be placed between them and the open space between walls, closed with brick, that the heat from the chamber may not escape through the openings.

Construct the inner wall, as shown in the sectional view, No. 2, allowing its line to follow outward, somewhat in the shape of the pot, for four or five courses, gradually receding until within two inches of the outside wall; from this point carry it uprightly to the level of the *dome* plate; then commence to draw in or decrease its size in the form of an arched cone, of such sweep, that when opposite the annular chamber, or ring of the furnace, it shall have a space of four inches between; carry this arched-shaped wall from eight to twelve inches above the furnace, according to its size, then place iron bars across covered with brick; finish by thoroughly and smoothly plastering the walls inside.

The outer walls are to be carried up as represented in the drawing, partially arched, and covered like the others; after the mason work has reached the height from which it is desired to carry the hot air pipes through the walls, place the ends even with the inner wall, and build them into it.

Also build in casings of sheet iron or tin in front of the clearing-out pipe and funnel, through both walls—two inches larger than the pipe, running through them; the ends outside are of course to be stopped with caps, in one of which a hole is made to admit the funnel.

The hot air pipes should be conducted from the *highest point* of the inner wall, as in sectional view, through the arch of the brick work; from which point they should gradually rise to the registers in the floor, always keeping in view the fact that the nearer the pipes can be carried to a perpendicular line from the wall of the furnace to the apartment above, the more readily and economically is heat obtained.

The size of the pipes and registers, and their general disposition, is a matter requiring the best judgment of the mechanic under whose supervision they come, and are determined by the size, position, and distance of the apartment from the furnace, and can not be subject to any fixed rule; as in two rooms of the same dimensions, we often use pipes and registers of different size, owing to their nearness or distance from the furnace in a horizontal line—their height above the basement—the relative position of other pipes, the purposes for which the rooms are to be used, and the amount of heat required, &c., &c. As a general rule, however, in rooms upon the *first* floor, whose dimensions are equal to fifteen feet square, and of ordinary height, use an eight-inch pipe, and registers eight by twelve inches; twenty feet square, ten-inch pipe, registers nine by fourteen inches; twenty-five feet square, twelve-inch pipe, registers ten by sixteen, or twelve by nineteen inches. For halls of *ordinary* size, use register nine by fourteen; ten-inch pipe. Adopt the same scale in rooms of different capacity.

If pipes or hot air tubes are carried into apartments above those of the first floor, they should be two inches smaller in size, than those used in rooms of the same capacity below; so that, should a lower room require a pipe of ten inches in diameter, that above would be eight inches, and still higher, six inches; supposing each room to be of the same size, and directly above the first.

In all hot air pipes that go *above* the first floor, a damper should be placed near the exit from the furnace, and kept closed when not in use, in order to economize the heat that would otherwise fill the pipes when the registers are closed.

It is often expedient to heat two adjoining rooms separated by a partition; in which case, it is our custom to use but one pipe for both; bringing it up to the partition, and placing a T or horizontal pipe across the top, projecting each side, into which registers are to be inserted, of a size corresponding with the rooms.

In double parlors, or rooms connected by sliding or folding doors, we usually place but one register, near their common opening, in case it is intended to use both apartments at once.

In many instances, it is required to heat rooms not in a direct line of communication from the furnace, and in which it seems difficult to introduce pipe without marring the building, or exposing them to view in their passage through other rooms. In such cases an ingenious mechanic will generally surmount the apparent difficulty by taking advantage of closets, spaces between partitions, chimney pieces, &c., or, if either are impracticable, by carrying the pipes upright through the corner of the room and hiding its unsightly appearance by finishing in front with wood, painting it in representation of a column, or in such a manner as will best suit the style of the apartment. As a *rule*, however, we do not carry pipes above the first floor, except it is designed to heat an apartment for use during the day, as the heat from the hall register will keep the chambers comfortably warmed by leaving the doors opened.

The smoke pipe should be carried directly to the nearest flue, and should it be necessary to carry it horizontally to a considerable distance, surround it by a casing, or pipe of tin, three inches larger in diameter than the smoke pipe itself, and the waste heat that radiates from the smoke pipe, may be used to warm any adjoining apartment, by continuing a hot air pipe into the room and inserting a *funnel register* which we manufacture for that purpose.

The cold air box should be constructed of wood, smooth-planed inside and out. Its opening should be from the north or west side of the building; carry it along the ceiling to the furnace, then drop it perpendicularly down to the base of the cold air channel. This box should contain a damper or slide, which in very cold weather, or when the fire is first kindling, can be *partially* closed; but so arranged that it shall never entirely shut out the air.

In speaking of a wooden cold air box, we do not by any means consider it imperative that this material should be used in its construction, as we often conduct the air in a brick trench covered with flat stones, smoothly plastered and thoroughly cemented, below the level of the ground. This method, when the cellar is dry, has the advantage of permanence, and occupies no room; but it is an additional expense which all are not willing to incur, and is not reckoned in making furnace estimates.

Perforate one or two of the hot air pipes with holes, two inches in diameter, in the part which goes between the walls, for the purpose of carrying off the heat that is collected in the space between.

If the cellar is wet, carry out the base on which the walls are to stand one foot larger than the walls themselves; use hydraulic or Roman cement in its construction; lay the brick two courses, and place a liberal supply of cement between; then, after the furnace walls are erected, carry up a barrier or guard wall from the edge of the brick base, a few inches above the level of the ground, and fill the intervening space between the barriers and the outer furnace wall with cement or clay; adopt also the same precaution around the trench; in fact, form a complete casing of brick, *thoroughly cemented*, all round the base of the furnace, which will prove a sufficient guaranty from water.

In public halls, or buildings where but a single register is required, carry up the inside wall to a perfect arch and lead the hot air pipe *directly from the top*, and use a hot air grate *without valves*, of the following sizes :—

No. 3	Furnaces—Grates	22	inches in diameter, and	Hot	Air	Pipes	18	inches in	diameter.
" 4	"	" 24	"	"	"	"	" 21	"	"
" 5	"	" 28	"	"	"	"	" 24	"	"
" 6	"	" 32	"	"	"	"	" 27	"	"

It is frequently desirable to have square or parallelogram shaped grates instead of round; when this is the case, use those sizes where capacity in square inches will be equivalent to those given above.

In speaking of grates *without valves*, we wish it especially understood, that in *no* instance where but *a single pipe* is taken from the furnace, should registers *with* valves be used, or *dampers placed in the hot air pipes;* but the amount of heat required, should be regulated by the fire itself; or, if an outlet be deemed expedient, carry it off by means of another pipe, into an adjoining apartment.

DIRECTIONS FOR USING CHILSON'S PATENT WARMING AND VENTILATING APPARATUS.

1st. In building a fire in the furnace, open the damper in the smoke-pipe.

2d. Clean out the old coal and ashes from the ash-pit, and also from the lever-grate; sift the old coal, ashes, &c., and preserve the coal siftings for covering over the fresh fire.

3d. Always keep the ash-pit, *under the grate*, *clear of ashes; this done, there is no possibility of burning out the grate.*

4th. Kindle the fire with a small quantity of either wood, bark, or charcoal. Dry hard wood preferable.

5th. When the kindlings are well charred, put on a small quantity of *white ash coal*, and when well ignited, (but before burning up clear,) add fresh coal, not exceeding six inches in depth.

6th. Close both the feed and ash-pit doors, also the small register in the ash-pit door, then *close* the *damper*, in the smoke pipe, as far as practicable to cause the fuel to be consumed slowly—or on the *air-tight principle;* this always to be done before the coal burns up *clear.*

7th. Cover over the fresh coal fire in moderate weather, with fine coal and the old coal siftings, keeping the draft *in the smoke pipe* well *shut off;* in this way, a fire may be kept for a great length of time without replenishing; thus greatly economizing in the consumption of fuel; but in extremely cold weather, do not cover over the fire with fine coal, but keep it bright, always checking the draft to keep the fire clear of clinker.

8th. Always have a large supply of cold air passing into the furnace. At no time have the damper, in the cold air-box, fully closed; even in very cold weather it should be at least one-half open. *The milder the weather, the more fresh air to be admitted for ventilation.*

9th. Never allow all the registers to be closed at the same time; and if the rooms become too warm, *regulate and lessen the fire*, and let there be constantly a free circulation of warm air from some, or all the registers; this is essential for the *ventilation* as well as warming of the rooms.

10th. Do not suffer the fire during the day, to get so low, before replenishing, as to require kindlings to bring it up.

11th. Where there is provision made for ventilation in the rooms, and ventiducts extending down to the floor, with apertures at the top and bottom, close the apertures at the top, and *open* those at the *bottom*, until the rooms become well warmed and ventilated, and when there is too much warmth in the rooms *open* the *upper* apertures, permitting the heat to run off, until the room becomes comfortable, then *close* the upper apertures; never *open* the *windows* or *doors* in cold weather to cool or to attempt to ventilate the rooms; if done, it will prevent the action or draft in the *foul air ventiducts;* there is also a liability to those sitting near the windows or doors to take cold, in consequence of the cold air falling upon their heads. The above directions are simple and easily followed, and if strictly adhered to, will be found very perfect in operation, and economical in the consumption of fuel, keeping the fire ignited a long time without replenishing, and giving out a large quantity of fresh, healthful, warm air, perfectly free from *red-hot iron heat.*

These ventilating flues or ventiducts, should always be located in an opposite corner of the room, from that at which the heated air enters, and should be carried up separately to the roof of the building. They should be fitted at the top and bottom with a door or valve, whose capacity should be equal to that of the ventiduct into which it opens.

The best material for their construction is, thoroughly seasoned, sound pine boards, planed smooth on the inner surface, and put together with iron screws.

It is indispensible to attach an ejecting ventilator to the ventiducts at their terminus. In this way, down blasts are obviated, the rain excluded, and, whenever there is a wind, no matter what its direction, it produces, in a properly constructed ejector, an active upward current.

The arear of the flues for *admitting* fresh air, should exceed those of its exit by about twenty-five per cent.

Bushnell's Patent Hot-air Furnace.

Manufactured by Ezra Clark, Jr., 61 Front street, Hartford, Conn.

Bushnell's Furnace is the only one constructed on strictly scientific principles, and bears any test either of theory or practice. Scientific gentlemen have endorsed its excellence, and successful practice approves and confirms their recommendation.

The radiating part of this furnace, being that portion which diffuses the heat, is distinguished from all others from the fact that the cold air is passed into the furnace chamber *between* horizontal cast iron pipes or tubes, *inside of which the hot gas of the fire is circulating*, and communicating its heat, as it passes off to the chimney; so that the cold air is brought in direct contact with the heated iron, and is actually heated before it reaches the inner chamber of the furnace. While the cold air is passing one way to be heated (between the heated iron pipes) the hot gas of the fire is passing the other way to be cooled, and thus the mean difference of temperature *is kept the greatest possible at every point.* The *greatest* amount of heat will be communicated in this way, by the *least* amount of iron surface; and as the radiator has a very large surface, it follows that *more* heat is extracted (from a given amount of fuel) *than by any other invention* yet offered to the public.

This furnace is so constructed that it *clears itself* of ashes and soot, never requiring to be disturbed, and consequently requires not as much care as an ordinary fire. A child can take care of it when in use, and it can stand from season to season, untouched, without trouble or expense, and be at any moment ready for immediate use.

Two kinds of pots are offered by the manufacturer, for use with this furnace; one similar to the most approved forms now in use, the other entirely different, and the invention of Dr. Bushnell. It differs from all others in allowing the fire to be *stirred above the grate*, and through the opening by which the coal is entered. This throws up the dead coals and cinders, which are then easily removed, and, as the grate *need never be dropped*, the dirty process of riddling is avoided. No ashes escape, and the cloud of dust which usually envelopes the tender in all other furnaces, is no where seen in this, and no uncleanliness results from renewing the fire. The fire may be stirred and cleaned when it is in full action, as well as at any other time; the coals will never rattle down to choke the fire, but will of necessity, by this method of stirring, *always* be thrown up into a light open cinder, giving free passage to the draft and facilitating combustion.

This furnace is offered in the entire confidence that it is *the best ever manufactured*, and this bold assertion is warranted and proved by the favorable testimony of those who have used it. A TRIAL IS ALL THE PROOF REQUIRED.

Three sizes of furnaces are made, viz.: No. 1 with 17 inch pot; No. 2 with 20 inch pot; No. 3 with 24 inch pot; which are now for sale in most of the larger cities and towns in the northern states.

Orders for Bushnell's Furnaces will be promptly attended to, on application by mail or otherwise, to Ezra Clark, Jr., Hartford, Conn.

Double Fire-Place for Warming and Ventilation.

The following plan of warming and ventilating a school-room is recommended by Mr. George B. Emerson in the School and Schoolmaster. The position of the proposed fire-place may be seen in the Plans of School-rooms by the same eminent teacher, published on page 50 of this work.

Warming.—In a suitable position, pointed out in the plates, near the door, let a common brick fireplace be built. Let this be inclosed, on the back and on each side, by a casing of brick, leaving, between the fireplace and the casing, a space of four or five inches, which will be heated through the back and jambs. Into this space let the air be admitted from beneath by a box 24 inches wide and 6 or 8 deep, leading from the external atmosphere by an opening beneath the front door, or at some other convenient place. The brick casing should be continued up as high as six or eight inches above the top of the fireplace, where it may open into the room by lateral orifices, to be commanded by iron doors, through which the heated air will enter the room. If these are lower, part of the warm air will find its way into the fireplace. The brick chimney should

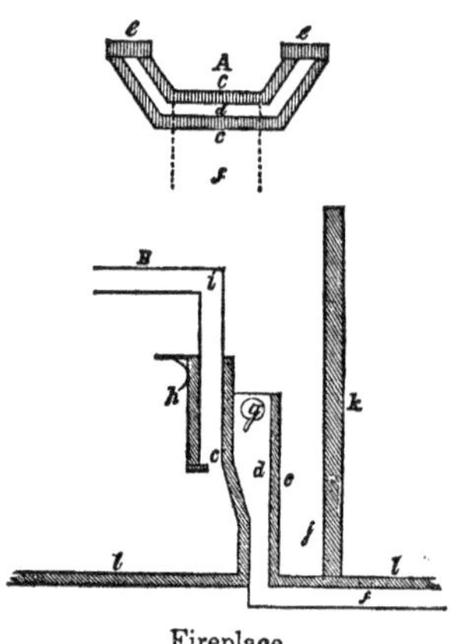

Fireplace.

A. Horizontal section. B. Perpendicular section. *c.* Brick walls, 4 inches thick. *d.* Air space between the walls. *e.* Solid fronts of masonry. *f.* Air box for supply of fresh air, extending beneath the floor to the front door. *g.* Openings on the sides of the fireplace, for the heated air to pass into the room. *h.* Front of the fireplace and mantelpiece. *i.* Iron smoke flue, 8 inches diameter. *j.* Space between the fireplace and wall. *k.* Partition wall. *l.* Floor.

rise at least two or three feet above the hollow back, and may be surmounted by a flat iron, soap-stone, or brick top, with an opening for a smoke-pipe, which may be thence conducted to any part of the room. The smoke-pipe should rise a foot, then pass to one side, and then over a passage, to the opposite extremity of the room, where it should ascend perpendicularly, and issue above the roof. The fireplace should be provided with iron doors, by which it may be completely closed.

The advantages of this double fireplace are, 1. the fire, being made against brick, imparts to the air of the apartment none of the deleterious qualities which are produced by a common iron stove, but gives the pleasant heat of an open fireplace; 2. none of the heat of the fuel will be lost, as the smoke-pipe may be extended far enough to communicate nearly all the heat contained in the smoke; 3. the current of air heated within the hollow back, and constantly pouring into the room, will diffuse an equable heat throughout every part; 4. the pressure of the air of the room will be constantly outward, little cold will enter by cracks and windows, and the fireplace will have no tendency to smoke; 5. by means of the iron doors, the fire may be completely controlled, increased or diminished at pleasure, with the advantages of an air-tight stove. For that purpose, there must be a valve or slide near the bottom of one of the doors.

If, instead of this fireplace, a common stove be adopted, it should be placed above the air-passage, which may be commanded by a valve or register in the floor, so as to admit or exclude air.

SCHOOL FURNITURE.

In the construction and arrangement of the furniture of a school, both for pupils and teachers, regard must be had to the following particulars:

1. The varying size of the occupant; so that not one shall be subjected to any awkward, inconvenient, or unhealthy position of the limbs, chest, or spine.

2. The grade of the school, the occupations of the pupils, and the methods of instruction, so that the objects aimed at may be secured in the best manner. A school composed of very young children, another in which drawing and sewing receive special attention, a third conducted on the monitorial plan, a fourth embracing a large number of pupils in a hall for study and lectures, under one principal teacher, with class-rooms, for recitations by assistants, and a fifth in which the pupils are classified under permanent teachers in separate rooms, will require different furniture and arrangements.

3. Facility of access, so that each pupil may go to and from his seat, with the least possible noise, inconvenience, and waste of time to himself and others.

4. The supervision of the whole school by the teacher, with a free passage for him to every pupil, as well as every facility for the accommodation of his books of reference, and the use of apparatus and diagrams, and his collective and class teaching.

5. Facility for sweeping and keeping the room neat.

The following diagrams and suggestions as to the details of construction and arrangements, will enable committees to furnish their school and class-rooms with appropriate furniture, which will answer the above conditions.

The wood portion of all school furniture should be made of clear, hard, well-seasoned material, like cherry, mahogany, or birch; the surfaces worked smooth, the edges and corners nicely rounded, and all the joints, as far as practicable, firmly morticed.

Each pupil should be allowed a desk with a top surface at least two feet long and eighteen inches wide, with a shelf, box, or drawer to receive books, &c.

The top surface of the desk should incline one inch in a foot toward the front edge, except three inches of the most distant portion, which should be level. Along the front edge of the level portion should run a groove, a quarter of an inch deep, to prevent pencils from rolling off; and on the opposite side an opening to receive a slate, and another for an inkstand, or a permanently fixed cast-iron box with a lid, in which a movable ink-well may be inserted. There should be no raised ledge on the front edge.

The shelf should be about two thirds as wide as the desk, and decline a little from the front. The opening to receive the books should be about four inches. A box, of which the top of the desk forms the lid, is a greater protection from dust, but the opening and shutting of the lid is a frequent source of noise. A portfolio case be attached to the inside of the lid, to receive drawings and manuscripts.

The standards to support the desk can be made of wood or cast-iron. The latter are to be preferred, because, without adding much to the cost, they have more strength and durability, and while presenting a variety of elegant forms they can be so curved as to admit of easy access to the seat, and facilitate the use of the broom in sweeping. A variety of patterns are presented in the following pages.

When made of wood the standards should be firmly fastened by a strong tenon into the sleepers of the floor or into a shoe, which can be made of cast-iron. The shoe can be made fast to the floor by numerous screws.

To secure the greatest firmness, the standards should not be more than four feet apart, and should be strengthened by bars extending between every two, or braces from the center of the standard to an equal distance on the shelf, or back of the desk above. For these purposes a socket for the bar or brace, should be cut in the middle of the standard.

The several parts of the standard must be adapted to their intended use. The top requires to be cast with a flange or stays crossing each other at right angles, to screw to the wood-work of the desk or seat for which it is intended. When it is practicable, the standard should receive the wood-work into a socket, arm, or lip, so as not to admit of being displaced by any rough usage, which will not at the same time shatter the iron. Several extra holes should be drilled in the standard to receive additional screws, as the old ones from time to time get loose.

The height of the standards, whether for desk or seat, will depend on the size of the pupils who are to occupy them.

Every pupil, young or old, should be provided with a chair (or bench having the seat hollowed like an ordinary chair) just high enough to allow, when properly occupied, the feet to rest on the floor without the muscles of the thigh being pressed hard upon the front edge of the seat.

In all cases, except in class-rooms fitted up specially for writing or drawing lessons, or when their occupancy will not exceed fifteen or twenty minutes without a change from a sitting to a standing posture, the seats should be provided with a support for the muscles of the back, and, as a general rule, especially for the majority of pupils, this support should rise above the shoulder blades, and should in all cases incline back as it rises, one inch in every foot.

The height of the seat from the floor, and the width, will depend on the age, or rather the size of the pupils; and, in providing seats for them, regard must be had to the grade of the school, and the varying size of the children. For a primary school, composed of children from four, and even three, years of age to eight or ten, the height should vary from eight to twelve inches, and the width from six to ten inches; and for a school for pupils ranging from ten to sixteen years of age, the height of the seats should vary from ten to seventeen inches, and the width from eight to thirteen inches.

To provide against the evil of seats too high for the smallest children, planks or suitable platforms should be furnished, to enable the teacher to seat that class of children properly, so that the feet can *rest* on the floor. If the children vary in age, and consequent size, in different seasons of the year an extra number of seats, both high and low, should be provided to meet the varying demand. Let the seats which are not required for immediate use be carefully stored away in the attic, and their places supplied by those which are.

Great difference of opinion and practice prevails as to the dimensions of the seats and desks for pupils of different ages. The following scale has generally been followed, in plans drawn or approved by the author of this treatise. For schools composed of children of all ages, from four years and under to seventeen years, eight different sizes have been adopted—and the number of each size has varied with the number of pupils. The aim has been to secure for each pupil an average space on the floor, of two feet long by twenty-six inches wide, besides the space occupied by teachers' desks, an open area of two or three feet around the room, and an aisle 16 inches wide between each range of desks.

	SEAT OR CHAIR.		DESK.	
NUMBER.	Height from floor to Front edge.	Width to the Support.	Height from floor to Front edge.	Width of top.
	inches.	inches.	inches.	inches
1	9½ to 10	9	19½ to 20	11
2	10½ to 11	9½	20½ to 21	12
3	12	10	22	13
4	13	10½	23	14
5	14	11	24	15
6	15	11½	25	16
7	16½	12½	26½	17
8	17 to 17½	12	27½ to 28	18

The scale of dimensions adopted in Wales' Improved School Furniture, will be found on page 364, and in Ross' American School Furniture, on page 368. The following table is taken from "*Richsons' School Builders Guide.*"

	FORMS.				DESKS.				DESK TOPS.
	HEIGHT.		BR'DTH.		HEIGHT.		BREADTH.		
	Upper Class.	Lower Class.	Upr. Clss.	Lwr Clss.	Upper Classes.	Lower Classes.	Flap.	Ink Brd.	Slope.
	ft. in.	ft. in.	in.	in.	ft. in.	ft. in.	ft. in.	in.	
Minutes of Committee of Council, 1839-40. pp. 54, 55.	1 4	...	9	..	2 6	...	1 0	3	1½in. in foot.
Battersea Village School, from a sketch by *Mr. Griffiths* ..	1 1	...	8	..	2 6	...	1 5	..	3in. in 1ft. 5 in.
National Society's Monthly Paper, No. XVIII, p. 11.......	1 6	1 2	6½	..	2 6	2 0	0 9	3	....
British and Foreign School Society, Plain Directions, p. 14.	1 4	...	6	..	2 4	...	0 9	..	....
Manchester National Schools. . .	1 4½	1 2½	9	9	2 6	2 4½	1 1	3	1½in. in foot.

Gallery and Furniture for Infant and Primary Schools.

The gallery, or a succession of seats rising one above the other, on which the children can be gathered at suitable times for simultaneous exercises, such as singing, lessons on real objects, pictures, simple operations of mental arithmetic, &c., has been found an economical arrangement, in respect to space and expense, in schools for a large number of very young children, variously modified; it is used in Great Britain, not only in infant and primary schools, but in national schools of the highest grade as to the age and proficiency of the pupils, for assembling the whole school for lectures, or for the collective teaching of large classes in writing, drawing, singing, and dictation.

The common mode, of constructing benches without backs, and without regard to the size of the pupils, for six or eight young children, or even a larger number, has nothing to recommend it but economy, and not even that, when the waste of the teacher's time, in discipline caused by the children's discomfort, is considered.

But the opposite extreme, of separate chairs for each child, especially if the chairs are set far apart for the purpose of preventing all communication and to secure quiet, is not therefore the best mode of seating a primary school. The social disposition of young children should be regarded, and their seats, whether the old fashioned form with the "new fangled back," or the neat chair with back and arms, should be contiguous, so that two can be seated near each other.

Even the youngest pupils should be provided with a desk, or with some facility for using the slate in drawing and printing. In the absence of a desk for each child, a leaf with slates inserted, or painted black, should be hung low against the wall for the use of primary classes.

Primary School Bench.

A movable bench for more than two pupils is an objectionable article of school furniture; but if introduced at all,

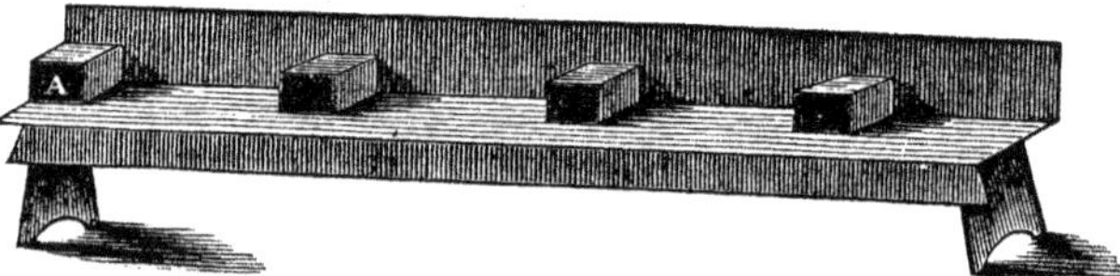

the above cut represents a style of this article which combines economy and convenience. The back is inclined slightly from a perpendicular, and the seat is hollowed. The scholars are separated by a compartment, or box, A, which serves as a rest for the arm, and a place of deposit for books.

Gallery and Sand Desk for Primary and Infant Schools.

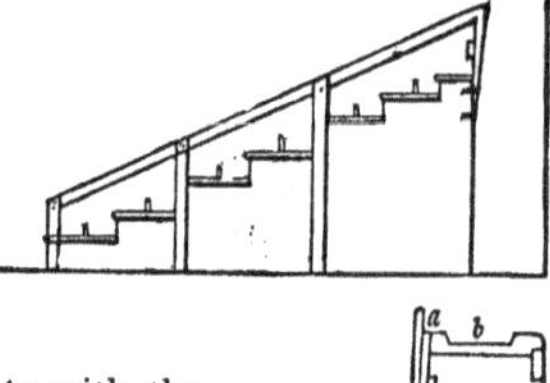

For very small children a *Gallery* consisting of a succession of seats rising above each other, varying in height from seven to nine inches, and provided with a support for the back. This arrangement, in large schools, affords great facility for instruction in music and all simultaneous exercises.

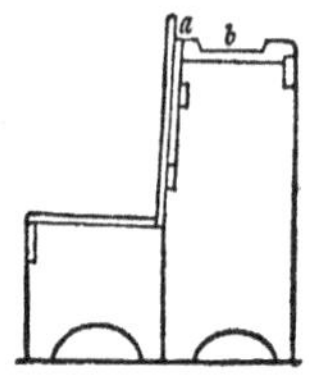

The *Sand Desk* having a trench (*b*) painted black, to contain a thin layer of sand, in which to trace letters and rude attempts at imitating forms, was originally much resorted to with the young classes, in schools educated on the Lancasterian or Mutual system. This style of desk is still used in the primary schools of the New York Public School Society, but very much improved by Mott's *Cast Iron Scroll Stanchions* and *Revolving Pivot Chair.* Every scholar is furnished with a slate, which is deposited in the opening (*a*) in the top of the desk.

The following cut, Fig. 4, represents a section of a gallery recommended in a memorandum of the Committee of Council on Education.

FIG. 4.

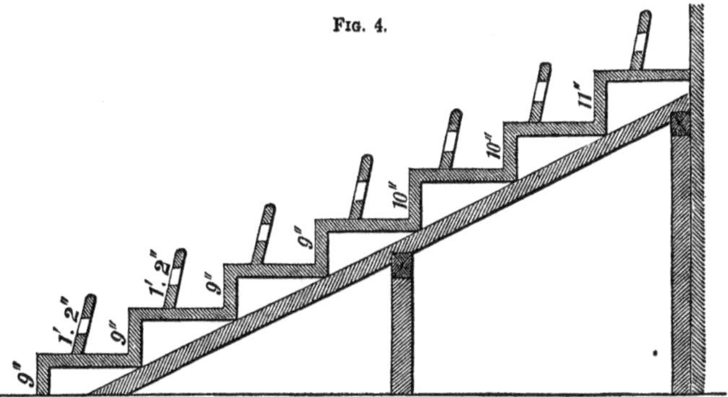

Fig. 5 represents a large gallery in the lecture-room of Borough Road School of the British and Foreign School Society; and Fig. 6, a small gallery in the corner of a class-room in the same school.

FIG. 5.

FIG. 6.

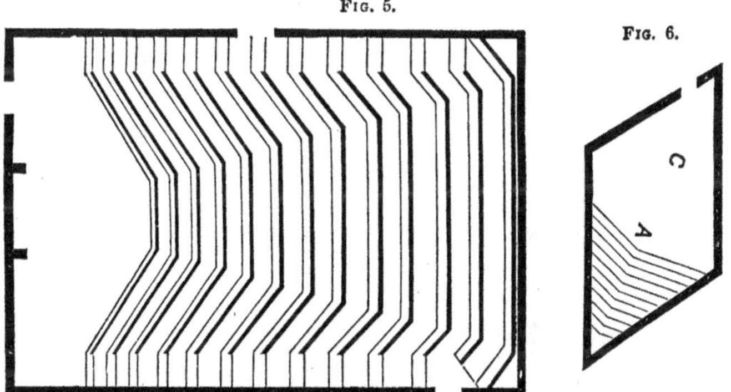

Figure 7 represents a *Closing Gallery*, designed for small rooms. Two steps, *b b*, are fixed, and two, *a a*, are made on rollers, and when out of use are pushed under *b b*. When used, they are kept in their place by a bolt to the floor.

FIG. 7.

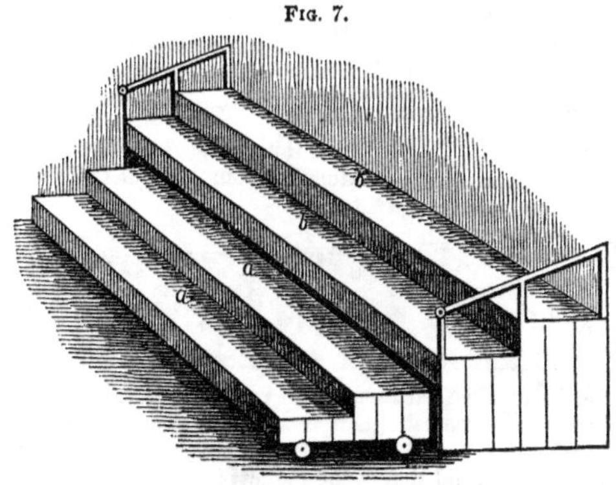

Desks and Seats of Wood.

The following cuts exhibit the cheapest mode of constructing a desk and seat of wood, for one or two pupils, the front part of the desk, constituting the back or support of the next seat. The height of the desk may vary from 28 to 29 inches

Fig. 8.

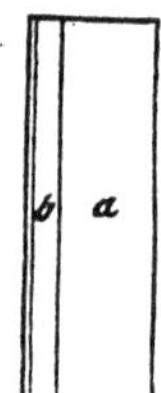

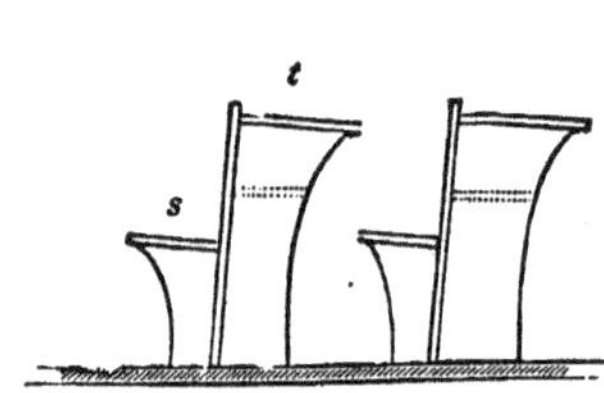

from the floor to the front edge of the top, for the oldest pupils, to 20 to 21 inches for the youngest. The corresponding seat may vary from 17 to 18 inches, to 9½ to 10 inches from the floor. The top of the desk and seat should be two feet long for each pupil. The upper surface (*a*,) except about three inches (*b*) of the desk, should slope one inch in a foot, and may vary in width, from 18 to 12 inches. The level portion of the desk has a grove (*a*) running along the line of the slope, to prevent pencils and pens from rolling off, and an opening *b* to receive a slate, and an opening *c*, (at the end, if the desk is for one pupil, and in the center, if for two pupils,) to receive an ink well, or box for an ink well, with a cover or lid. The seat slopes a little from the edge. The standard, of the desk and seat are curved, so as to facilitate sweeping and getting in and out. The standards may be set in a shoe, as shown on page 369, or made firm to the floor by cleats. Each desk is furnished with a shelf, for books, maps, &c.

Fig. 9.

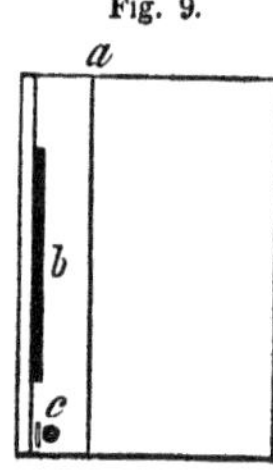

Fig. 10 is a section of a desk for two, with a chair for one pupil, on a standard of wood.

Fig. 10.

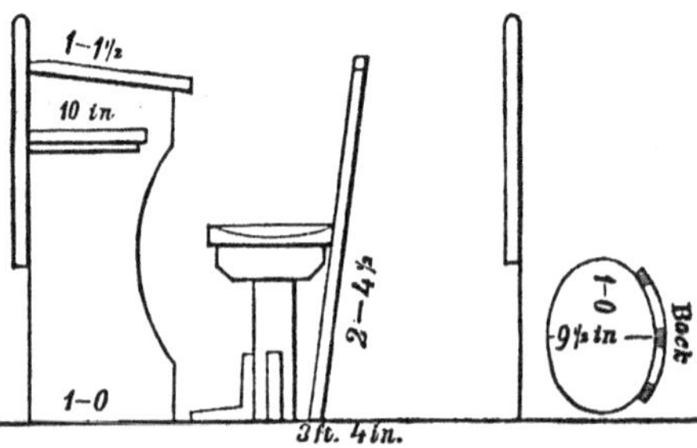

The following cut (Fig. 10) represents a range of seven desks and seats, divided by a partition (*a*) of matched boards, extending from the floor to three inches above

Fig. 11.

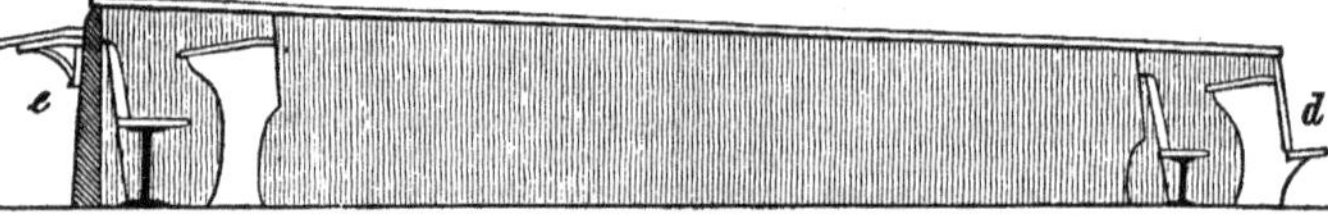

the surface of the desk. The partition gives great firmness to each desk, and separates each scholar more effectually than an aisle. The lowest seat is nine inches, and the chair, to the leaf desk (*e*,) is 17½ inches from the floor. The front edge of the lowest desk (*d*) is 19½, and that of the highest (*c*) is 28½ inches from the floor.

Hartford School Desk and Seat.

The following cut (Fig. 1,) represents a style of school desk, with a seat attached, which has been extensively introduced into village and country districts in Rhode Island, and the neighborhood of Hartford, and is recommended wherever a rigid economy must be observed.

Fig. 1.

The end piece, or supports, both of the seat and desk, are cast iron, and the wood work is attached by screws. They are made for one or two scholars, and of eight sizes, giving a seat from ten inches to seventeen, and a desk at the edge next to the scholar, from seventeen to twenty-six inches from the floor.

Fig. 3.

Fig. 2.

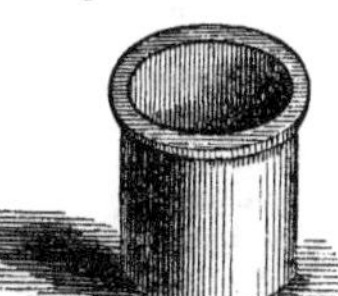

Each desk is fitted up with a glass ink-well (Fig. 2,) set firmly into the desk, and covered with a lid. The ink-well may be set into a cast iron box (Fig. 3,) having a cover; the box being let in and screwed to the desk, and the ink-well being removable for convenience in filling, cleaning, and emptying in cold weather.

Fig. 4.

The desk can be used, by detaching the support for the seat, with a convenient school-chair, made in the style represented in cut (Fig. 4,) or in any other style.

The cost of a desk and seat for two scholars, perfectly fitted up, varies from $1 37½ to $1 50 per scholar.

Manufactured by Messrs. Allen & Reed, Nos. 37 and 38 Pearl street, Hartford.

MOTT'S SCHOOL CHAIR AND DESK.

The following minute description of Mott's Patent Revolving Pivot Chair, and cast iron Scroll Stanchions for School Desks, is gathered from a circular of the patentee:

The seat of the chair is of wood: all the other parts, of cast iron. The desk stanchions are adjusted to the height of the chair—in the following scale, viz:

No. of the Chair.	Height of Chair Seat.	Height of front edge of Desk.	Width of Desk.	Length of Desk room for each scholar; (not less.)	Distance between the rows of Desks.
1	10 Inches.	17 Inches.	12 Inches.	17 Inches.	20 Inches.
2	12 "	19 "	12 "	18 "	22 "
3	14 "	22 "	14 "	20 "	24 "
4	16 "	24 "	15 "	22 "	25 "

The *first column* denotes the *number* of the chair, as also the number of the desk stanchions.

Second column, the height of the seat from the floor.

Third column, the height of the front edge of the desk from the floor.

Fourth column, the width of the top of the desk. The slope of the desk should rise 1¼ inch to the foot; the larger desks having 2½ to 3 inches level on top to accommodate inkstands.

Fifth column, the length of desk room required for each scholar. It should not be less than here given.

Sixth column, the distance that should be allowed between the desks, from the back of one to the front edge of the other. This space will allow a passage between the chair and the next rear desk. The number of scholars at a desk need not be limited.

The position of each chair, when screwed to the floor, should have two-thirds of the allotted desk room to the right of its centre, and be so near that the back of the chair, in its revolution, will barely clear the desk. By placing the chair as described, the body of the child is brought in close proximity to the desk, causing the back of the person to rest, at all times, and under all circumstances, against the back of the chair.

The chief peculiarity in the desk is, that in the place of straight wooden legs, there are substituted curved cast iron stanchions; the obvious advantages of which are, that they occasion no interference with the movements of the scholar seated opposite or near to them.

Two stanchions are necessary for a single desk. Two, also, will support a desk of sufficient length to accommodate three scholars; three, to accommodate six scholars; four, nine scholars; and so on for a greater number.

The expense of fitting up a room with this chair and desk, in the city of New York, varies from $1 50 to $2 00 a scholar, aside from the putting up of the desks.

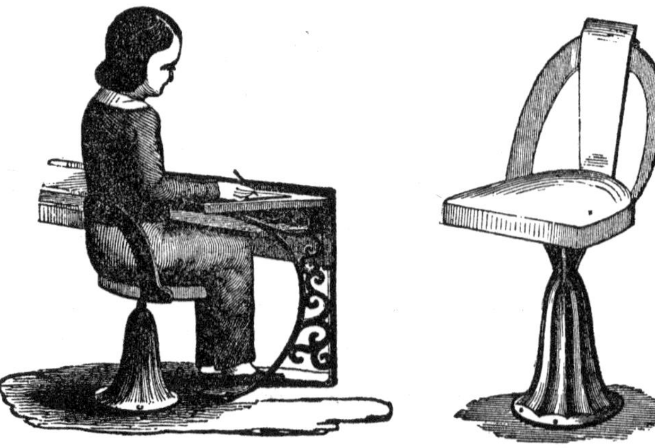

Since the foregoing style of chair and desk was introduced, much attention has been paid to the improvement of school furniture, with a view of securing convenience, durability, and economy, in the construction both of chairs and desks.

THE BOSTON LATIN HIGH SCHOOL DESK.

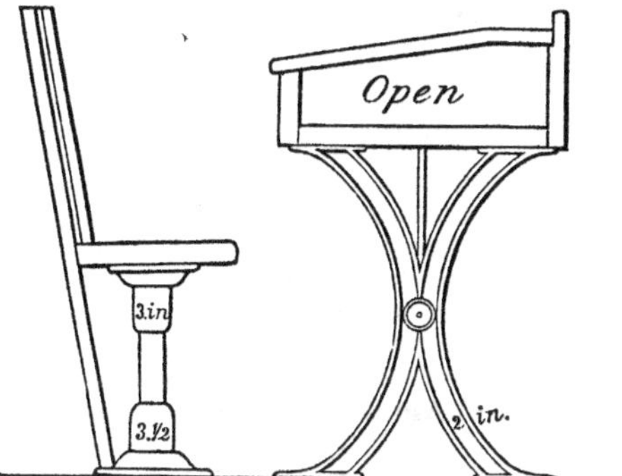

The above cut represents an end view of a new style of desk used in the Latin High School, in Bedford street, with a section of Wales' *Patent School Chair*. The standards of the desks are made of cast iron, and are braced in such a manner, that when properly secured to the floor, there is not the least motion. The curve in the standard facilitates the use of the broom in sweeping.

THE BOSTON PRIMARY SCHOOL CHAIR.

These Chairs were got up for the special benefit of the *Boston Primary Schools*, by JOSEPH W. INGRAHAM, Esq., Chairman of the Primary School Standing Committee; and have already been introduced, by order of the Primary School Board, into the greater portion of their Schools.

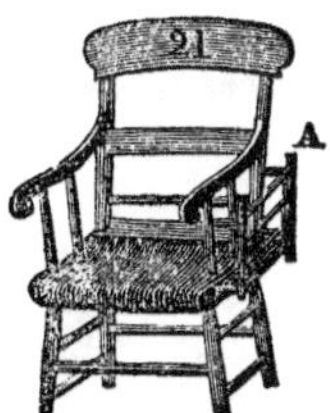

The first pattern, is a Chair with a *Shelf* (*s*) under the seat, for the purpose of holding the Books, Slates, &c. of the scholars.

The second pattern differs from the first, in having, instead of the *Shelf*, a *Rack* (A) on the back of the chair, for the same use as the Shelf in the preceding pattern. The third pattern is similar to the second, except that the *Rack* (A) is placed at *the side*, instead of *the back*, of the chair. The latter pattern (with the Rack on the side) is that now adopted in the Boston Schools.

These chairs are manufactured by William G. Shattuck, No. 80 *Commercial Street*, Boston. The price is fifty cents, each, for those with the Shelf, and *sixty-five* cents for those with the Rack.

Wales' Improved School Furniture.

The following cuts represent a large variety of improved school chairs, desks, and other furniture manufactured by Samuel Wales, Jr., at No. 14 Bromfield Street, Boston, Mass., from patterns of his own getting up, and with such facilities of experienced workmen, and ingenious machinery, as enables him to supply all orders for first-class work, with economy, precision, and promptness.

Wales' improved school chairs and desks embrace the following variety, and each variety is constructed on the following scale of height, so as to meet the varying proportions of scholars ranging from four years to twenty years of age:

No. 1.	Chairs,	10	inches	high;	Desks,	side	next	the	scholar,	20	inches	high.
" 2.	"	11	"	"	"	"	"	"	"	21	"	"
" 3.	"	12	"	"	"	"	"	"	"	22	"	"
" 4.	"	13	"	"	"	"	"	"	"	23	"	"
" 5.	"	14	"	"	"	"	"	"	"	24	"	"
" 6.	"	15	"	"	"	"	"	"	"	25½	"	"
" 7.	"	16	"	"	"	"	"	"	"	27	"	"
" 8.	"	17	"	"	"	"	"	"	"	28½	"	"

Wales' American School Chairs.

No. 1.

These chairs are plain and substantial. Each chair is based upon a single iron pedestal, which is secured to the seat of the chair at the top, and to the floor of the school-room at the foot. The center-piece of the chair-back descends directly into the foot of the iron pedestal, intersecting the back of the seat as it passes, in such a manner as to form a *back stay*, thereby producing in the chair, as a whole, the greatest possible degree of firmness and strength.

No. 2.

No. 2 represents an improved school desk for two scholars.

No. 3.

No. 3 represents an improved single desk for one scholar, on iron supports, with American school chairs to correspond. Each desk is furnished with an ink-well, and a metal cover of the best kind. The top is grooved, to accommodate pens, pencils, and other small articles, with a safe resting-place.

Wales' New England School Chairs.

No. 4.

Each chair is based upon a pedestal of iron, of great beauty and strength, which is firmly secured to the seat of the chair at the top, and to the floor of the school-room at the foot. An ornamental center-piece passes down into the base of the pedestal, forming the center of the chair-back and the *back stay*.

No. 5.

No. 6.

Cuts No. 5 and No. 6, represent an improved double school desk, the latter for one, and the former for two scholars, with the New England school chair to correspond.

Wales' Bowdoin School Chairs.

No. 7

These chairs are constructed substantially like those already described, with a tasteful scroll top. The following diagrams, Nos. 8 and 9, represent the chair in connection with a desk, both for one and two scholars.

No. 8.

No. 9.

WALES' WASHINGTON SCHOOL CHAIRS.

No. 10.

Nos. 10, 11, and 12, represent the eight sizes of another variety of the chair, with the corresponding desk, both single and double.

No. 11.

No. 12.

WALES' NORMAL SCHOOL DESKS AND CHAIRS.

No. 13.

No. 14.

The engraving represents a Normal School Double Desk, on iron supports, having two covers, with Washington School Chairs to correspond. Each cover opens a separate apartment in the desk, designed for the exclusive use of one scholar.

WALES' IMPROVED WRITING STOOLS.

No. 15.

For most educational purposes, chairs are highly preferable, and this seems to be the general opinion ; but, in cases where writing is taught in a separate department, the writing-stool is preferred, as being less expensive, and occupying less room.

WALES' PRIMARY SCHOOL CHAIR.

No. 16.

The engravings No. 16 and No. 17, represent a series of *three sizes*, suitable for scholars from four years of age and upward, comprehending all the sizes needed in primary and intermediate schools, to wit :—

No. 1,	. .	10 inches high.
" 2,	. .	11 " "
" 3,	. .	12 " "

Each chair is based on an iron pedestal, securely fastened to the seat at the top, and to the floor of the school-room at the foot ; thus becoming a permanent article of furniture, and completely avoiding the confusion, irregularity and noise, which are the unavoidable accompaniments of movable chairs in a school-room.

WALES' BASKET PRIMARY SCHOOL CHAIR.

No. 17.

The Basket Chair has a tastefully ornamented book basket of iron, into which the children can place their books, slates, and other utensils of study. As a whole, in view of their strength, comfort, beauty and adaptation to their object, these are regarded as the best Primary School Chairs extant.

Wales' Improved Settees.

No. 18.

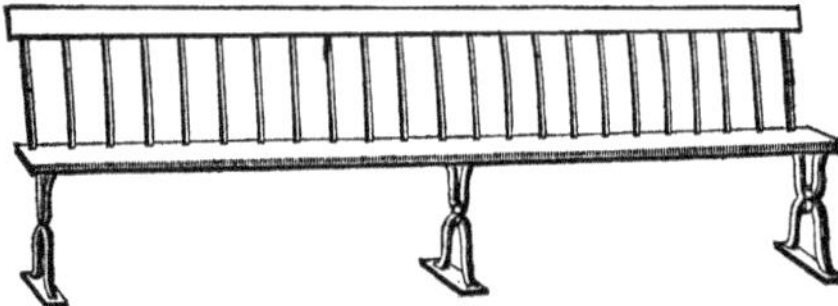

The engravings No. 18 and No. 19, represent an Improved Settee, eight feet in length, based upon iron supports, designed for that purpose. Such settees are well adapted for recitation-rooms, the walls of school-rooms, for the accommodation of visitors, or for any position where permanent settees are wanted. They are made of any required height, size, or length; often from forty to sixty feet in length, when placed on the walls of school-rooms; and, being without arms or other divisions, the whole length, in fact, forming a single settee, have been found to be very convenient, and of good appearance.

Wales' Improved Lyceum Settee.

No. 19.

The Improved Lyceum Settee is divided into five parts or seats, with fancy iron arms, made for that purpose.

Wales' Teachers' Arm-chairs.

No. 20.

The engravings, Nos. 20 and 21, represent two substantial, well-made, and comfortable arm-chairs, having no other claim to novelty than may be due to the fact that they are constructed entirely of hard wood, and are finished without paint of any kind; they will therefore wear well, and retain their good appearance without soiling or defacement, for a long period.

WALES' TEACHER'S ARM-CHAIRS, WITH CUSHIONS.
No. 21.

WALES' TEACHER'S TABLE, WITHOUT DRAWERS.
No. 22.

WALES' TEACHER'S TABLE, ONE DRAWER.
No. 23.

WALES' TEACHER'S TABLE, TWO DRAWERS.
No. 24.

Movable Skeleton Desk.
No. 25.

Portable Desk.
No. 26.

Wales' Teacher's Desk.
No. 27.

Wales' Teacher's Desk, three Drawers and Table Top.
No. 28.

Wales' Teacher's Desk, three Drawers and Top Desk.
No. 29.

WALES' TEACHER'S DESK, TWO DRAWERS AND TABLE TOP.
No. 30.

WALES' TEACHER'S DESK, TWO DRAWERS AND TOP DESK.
No. 31.

WALES' TEACHER'S DESK, FOUR DRAWERS AND TABLE TOP.
No. 32.

WALES' TEACHER'S DESK, FOUR DRAWERS AND TOP DESK.
No. 33.

WALES' TEACHER'S DESK, SIX DRAWERS AND TABLE TOP.

No. 34.

WALES' TEACHER'S DESK, SIX DRAWERS AND TOP DESK.

No. 35.

WALES' TEACHER'S DESK AND LIBRARY, FOUR DRAWERS, TABLE TOP AND BOOK-CASE

No. 36.

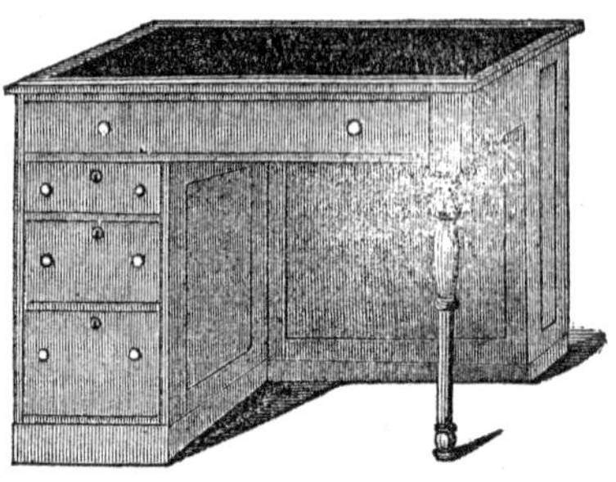

A.

A. The side occupied by the Teacher.

No. 37.

B.

B. The side facing the school, with a large drawer for maps, drawings, &c., and two doors which open a book-case, suitable for a school library.

WALES' TEACHER'S DESK AND LIBRARY, SIX DRAWERS, TABLE TOP AND LARGE BOOK-CASE.

No. 38.

A.

A. The side occupied by the Teacher.

No. 39.

B.

B. The side facing the school, with a large drawer for maps, drawings, &c., a small drawer for utensils of study, and three doors which open a large book-case, suitable for a school library.

As drawing is a regular study in our best conducted schools, suitable provision should be made, in the construction and arrangement of school furniture, for its convenient prosecution. If this branch is to be attended to at the desks usually occupied by the pupil, a light frame can be attached to the desk to support the model, or lesson copy, and a movable ledge provided, on which the upper part of the drawing board may rest.

A Leaf and Drawing Desk.

A drawing desk may be made, in connection with a fall or leaf desk, after the following plan, from Richson's School Builder's Guide.

In the fall or leaf desk, the leaf is attached to the level, fixed portion *b*, by hinges, and when turned up leans on an iron rod, or support *a*, and when turned down rests on a bracket (Fig. 1.) The bracket moves on iron pins, let into the under side of the desk above, and the strengthening bar *g*, below. The end of the arm of the bracket is made with a swivel joint, composed of two projecting points or pins, at right angles to each other, both of which fit into a hole *d*, on the under side of the desk, to prevent any movement of the bracket. When one of these points *f*, (Fig. 2,) is up, the leaf resting upon it forms an inclined desk, and when the other point *h*, is turned up, an extra height is gained and the leaf forms a level table.

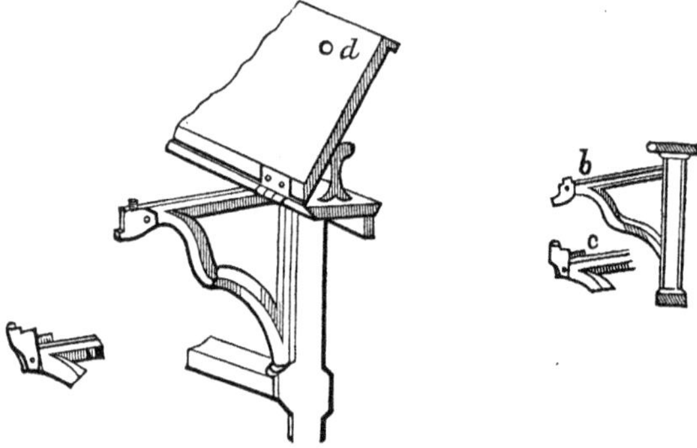

This form of study or writing desk is easily converted into a drawing desk, (Fig. 3,) by fitting to the under side *c*, of the leaf near the hinge, a wedge-

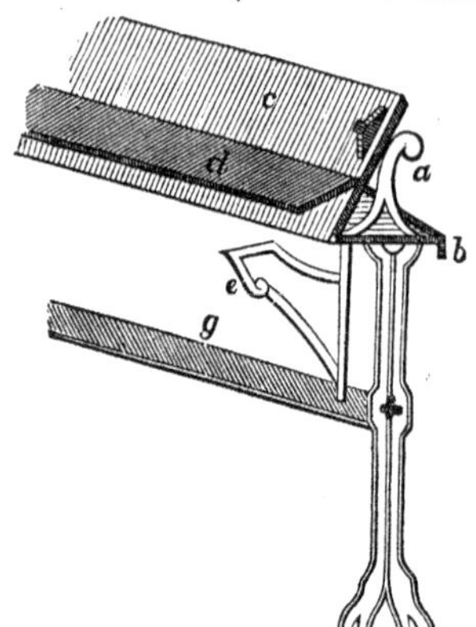

shaped ledge *d*, on which the upper end of the movable drawing board may rest, while the other end is placed on the pupils knees. The bracket *e*, is formed with a curve, in order to admit the ledge when the leaf is let down. The model or copy can rest on the ledge and against the leaf *c*. The bracket can be turned in when the leaf is thus used.

The annexed cut, Fig. 4, exhibits another method of forming the bracket in a cast iron standard. The upper portion of the standard is, in this specimen, provided with stays, into which the wood work is attached by screws.

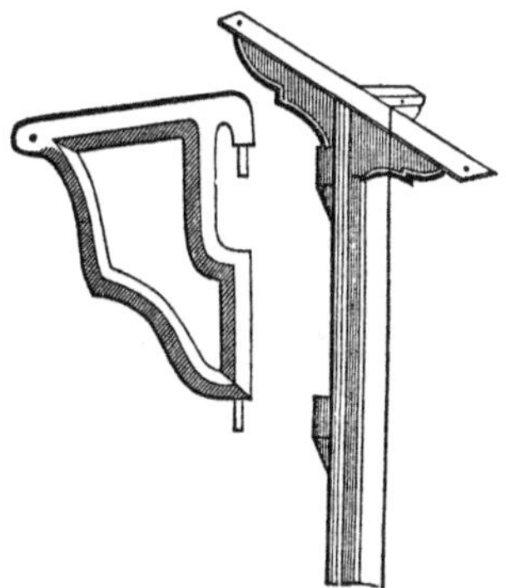

We give below the plan of a movable drawing desk, designed and manufactured by Joseph L. Ross, Boston.

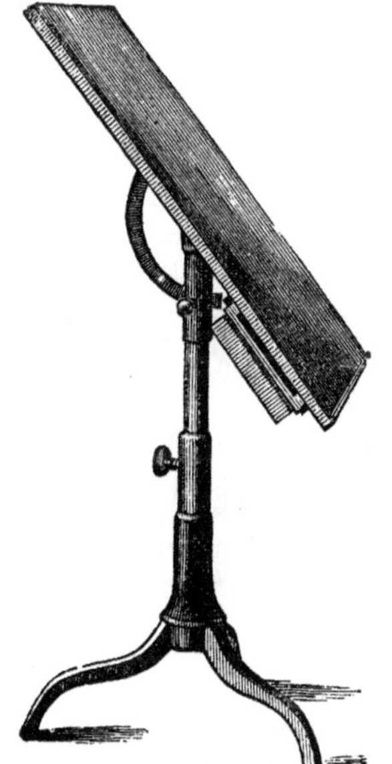

Ross' Movable Drawing Desk.

The standard consists of a hollow iron pillar, with a neat tripod base, on which it rests firmly on the floor. In this pillar is inserted a shaft, controlled by a screw, to raise or lower the desk at the pleasure of the pupil. The desk or drawing table is attached to the top of the shaft by hinges, on which it can be turned, and, by means of a circle, which passes through the shaft, and a screw, fixed at any angle required. Attached to the under side of the table is a drawer to receive the implements, &c.

The following cuts represent a front view (Fig. 1,) and end section (Fig. 2,) of the desk, and a front view and section of a drawing board (Fig. 3,) recommended for the use of the drawing schools in connection with the Department of Practical Art in the Board of Trade, England.

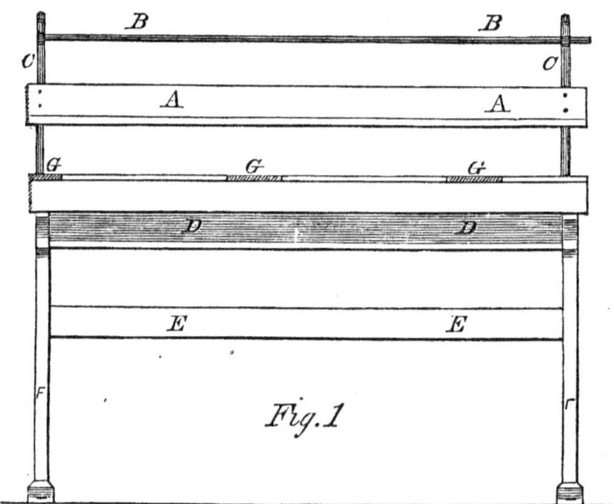

Fig. 1.—FRONT VIEW OF DRAWING DESK.

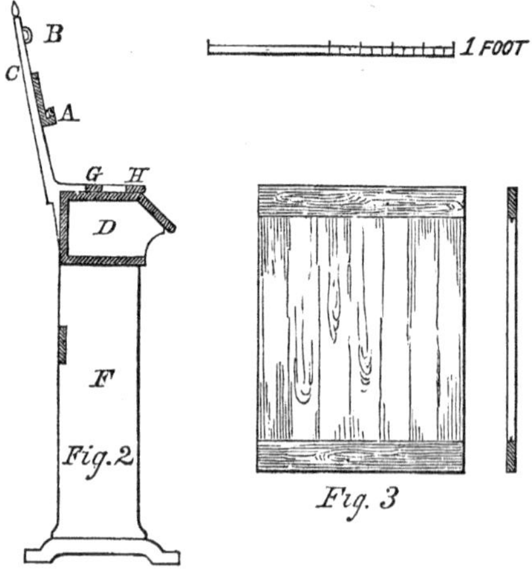

Fig. 2.—SECTION OF DRAWING DESK. Fig. 3.—DRAWING BOARD.

A, A, Fig. 1, A, Fig. 2—A wooden rail, screwed to iron uprights C, C, to hold the examples or copy.

B, B, $\frac{5}{8}$ inch rod, passing through eyes in $\frac{5}{8}$ inch iron uprights, C, C, C, to support the examples.

C, C, C, $\frac{5}{8}$ inch iron uprights, screwed to the desk at I, and punched at the upper end to receive the iron rod B.

D, D, hollow space to hold the students' pencils, knives, &c.

E, E, wooden rail to stiffen uprights, F, F, F, which are screwed to the floor.

G, G, (Fig. 1,) short fillets, as shown at G, (Fig. 2,) placed opposite each student, to retain the board, or example more upright if necessary.

H, (Fig. 2,) a fillet running along the desk, to prevent pencils, &c., rolling off.

KIMBALL'S IMPROVED SCHOOL CHAIRS AND DESK.

"These Chairs combine strength, comfort, and style of finish. They are made of different heights, varying from eight to sixteen inches, and for Primary as well as for Grammar and District Schools.

The School Desks are made of Pine, Cherry, or Black Walnut, and of heights to correspond with the chairs. The iron supporters are firmly screwed to the floor, and are braced in such a manner that there is not the least motion."

The above extracts are taken from the Circular of JAMES KIMBALL, 109 or 127 *Essex Street, Salem, Mass.*

The cuts below represent a view of the desk and seat, and of the frame for the same, used in the high school for girls in Newburyport, Mass. The frame is cast iron, to which the seat and desk is attached by screws. The frame is strengthened by a brace extending from each side below the seat.

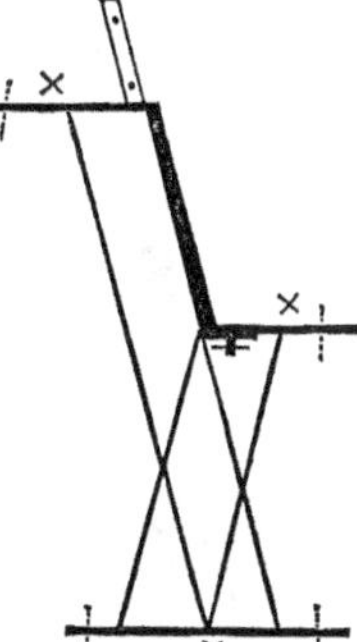

Ross' American School Furniture.

Although we have already published a variety of designs for desks and chairs for pupils and teachers, we gladly extend the liberty of choice by inserting a series of "practical illustrations of American School Furniture," manufactured by Joseph L. Ross, corner of Hawkins and Ivers streets, Boston, Mass. Mr. Ross was one of the earliest to embark in the enterprise of furnishing schools of every grade with graceful, comfortable, and durable furniture, and his chairs and desks may now be seen in public and private schools in every part of the country.

The chair are of seven different heights, the lowest being 10 inches, and the highest 17 inches. The seat is of hard wood, and is attached to a pedestal of iron which is attached to the floor by screws. The peculiarity of each style is sufficiently indicated by the diagrams.

The desks are also of different heights, and both chairs and desks can be ordered according to the following scale:

No.		Chairs		Desks, side next to the scholar	
No. 1.	extra Chairs,	17 inches high;	Desks, side next to the scholar,	29	inches high.
" 1.	Chairs,	16 inches high;	Desks, side next to the scholar,	27½	" "
" 2.	"	15 " "	" " " " " "	26	" "
" 3.	"	14 " "	" " " " " "	24½	" "
" 4.	"	13 " "	" " " " " "	23	" "
" 5.	"	12 " "	" " " " " "	22	" "
" 6.	"	11 " "	" " " " " "	21¼	" "
" 7.	"	10 " "	" " " " " "	20½	" "

No. 1. New England Primary School Chair.

No. 2. New York Primary School Chair.

No. 3. New England Primary School Basket Chair.

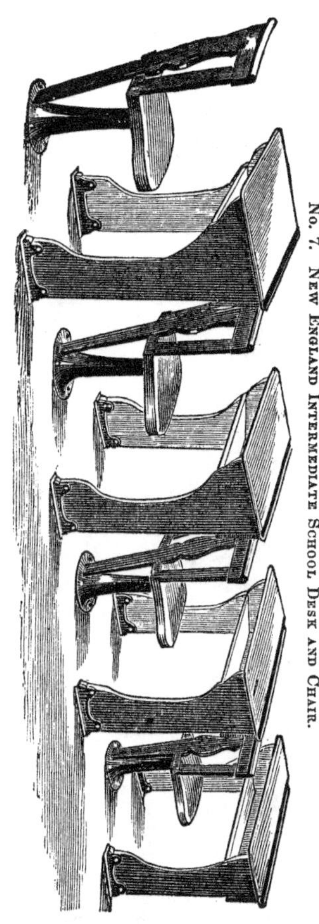

No. 7. New England Intermediate School Desk and Chair.

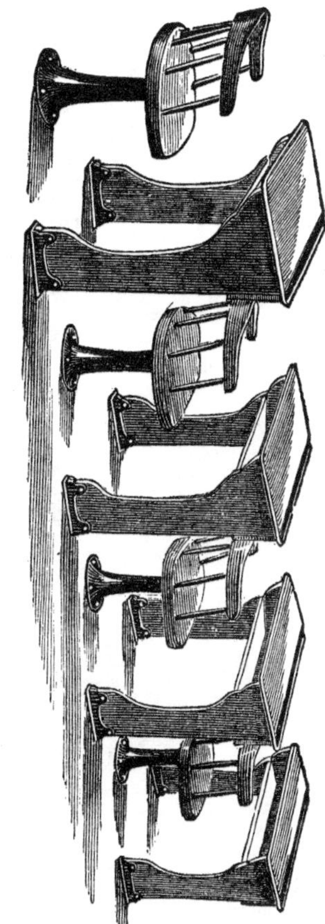

No. 5. New England Primary Desk and Chair.

No. 4. New England Single Primary School Desk and Chair.

No. 6. New England Double Primary School Desk and Chairs.

No. 8. New York Primary Double Desk and Chairs

No. 9. Village School Desk.

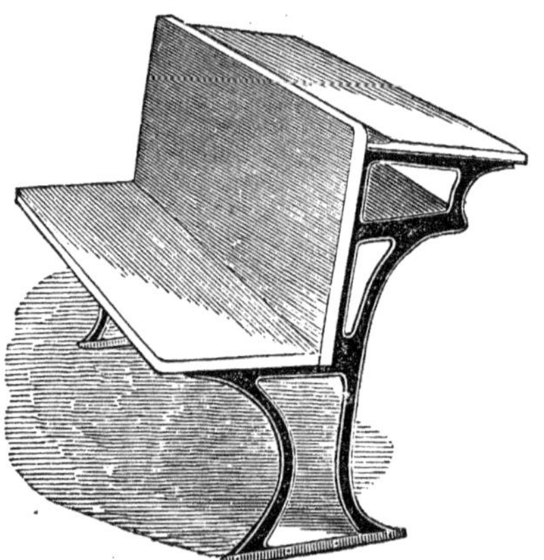

Nos. 1, 2, 3, represents different styles of chairs for primary schools, each of four different heights, viz., 10, 11, 12, and 13 inches. The basket for books, slates, &c., in No. 3, is made of cast-iron, and is free from any sharp corners.

Nos. 4, 5, 6, 7, represents the foregoing styles of chairs in connection with a desk for one or two pupils. The ends, or standards of the desks are wood, and are inserted and bolted in a shoe of iron, which is attached to the floor by screws. The chairs vary in height from 10 to 13 inches, and the desks to the scale on the foregoing page.

No. 8 represents a variety in the style of desks, the standard of the latter being cast-iron, of a neat pattern. These have been introduced into several of the primary and intermediate schools of New York.

No. 9 represents a school desk with seat for desk in advance, attached to the same standard. The standard or frame are of cast-iron, and are made of seven different sizes, varying from 10 to 17 inches.

Nos. 23 and 23 represents different styles of glass ink well, and metallic covers for the same.

No. 24 represents a settee for class-rooms, &c., and for visitors; made to order of any required length.

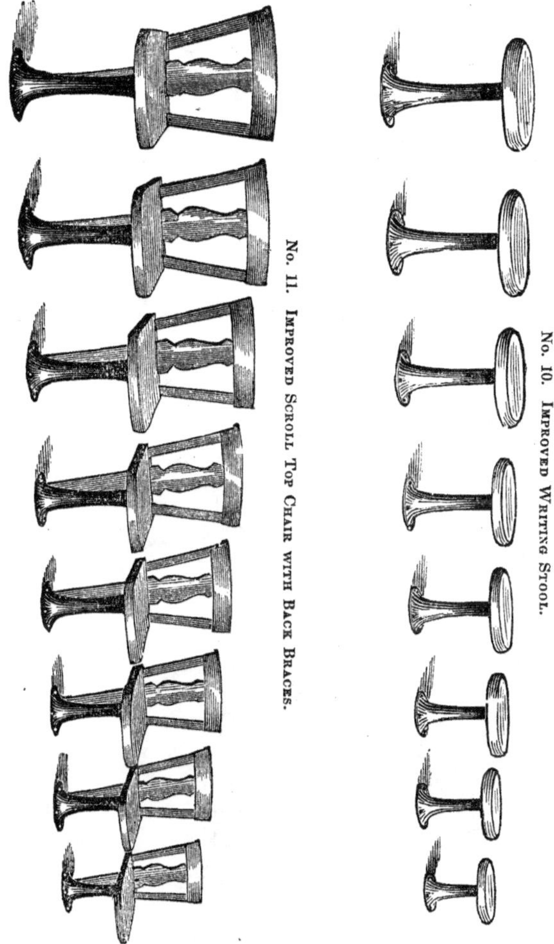

No. 11. Improved Scroll Top Chair with Back Braces.

No. 10. Improved Writing Stool.

No. 10 represents a stool or seat without a back, for writing and drawing, of eight different sizes, from 10 to 17 inches.

No. 11 represents a style of chair generally adopted in the grammar schools of Boston. The pedestal is of cast-iron, to which the seat is firmly attached by screws, and which is also attached to the floor in the same way. The center piece of the chair is let into the foot of the pedestal. There are eight sizes from 10 to 17 inches.

No. 23. Improved Metallic Ink Well Covers.

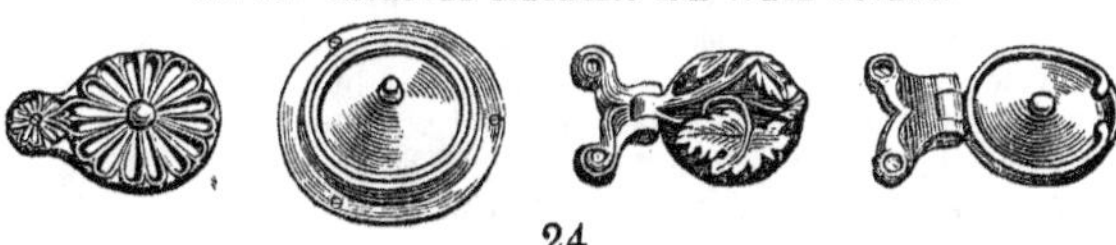

No. 12. Single Grammar School Desk and Chair.

No. 13. Double Grammar School Desk and two Chairs.

No. 23. Improved Ink Wells.

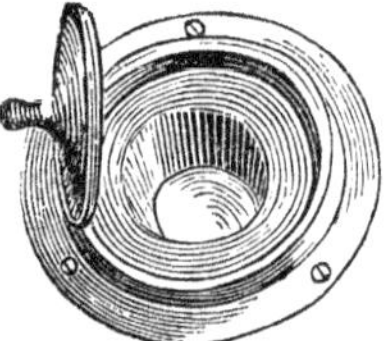

Nos. 12 and 13, represents a style of desk for one or two pupils, used in the grammar schools of Boston. The desk is 16 inches wide and 24 inches long for one, and 48 inches for two pupils. The desk is made firm by an iron brace, one end of which is screwed to the bottom of the desk, and the other to the iron standard. Along the back edge of the top of the desk is a hollow to receive pens, pencil, &c.; ink-pot or well is inserted with a lead or metallic cover.

No. 14. Single Desk with fall to lift and Chair for High Schools and Academies.

No. 15. Double Desk and two Chairs for two Scholars for High Schools and Academies.

No. 24. Settees for Recitation School Rooms, &c.

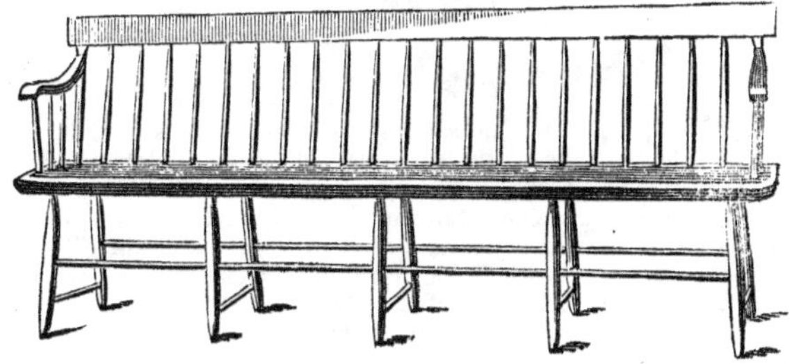

No. 16. Single Desk and Chair for Young Ladies' Seminaries.

No. 17. Single Desk and Chair for Young Ladies' Seminaries.

Nos. 14, 15, 16, 17, 18, present some modifications in the size, style, and finish of the desk. The top of the desk is covered with cloth, a portfolio with a clasp to keep it together, for drawings; an improved hinge; an improved metallic box with cover to receive a glass ink well, (see Fig. 22,) and the level portion of the top hollowed out to receive pens and pencil. Desks and chairs of this pattern have been manufactured for the Spingler Institute, Union Park, New York, and the City Normal School, Boston, and other schools of a higher character. The wood work of these and the other patterns are made of cherry, black-walnut or mahogany, according to order.

No. 18. Boston High School Desk and Chair.

No. 19. Double Desk and two Chairs for Young Ladies' Seminaries.

No. 21 represents a style of Drawing Desk, designed and manufactured for the Lowell Institute. The bottom of the desk is made of iron in a neat tripod form, with a hollow pillar inserted, in which is a shaft to raise and fall the desk at pleasure, that supports the top of the Drawing Table, and is confined to the same by hinges; with a circle affixed to the under side of the top and passing through the center of the shaft, which, by a set of screws, enables the person using the same, to raise the desk to any height or angle required. Attached to the under-side is a draw for the drawing instruments, made to draw out on either side.

No. 20. Double Desk and two Chairs for Young Ladies' Seminaries

No. 21. Lowell Institute Drawing Desk.

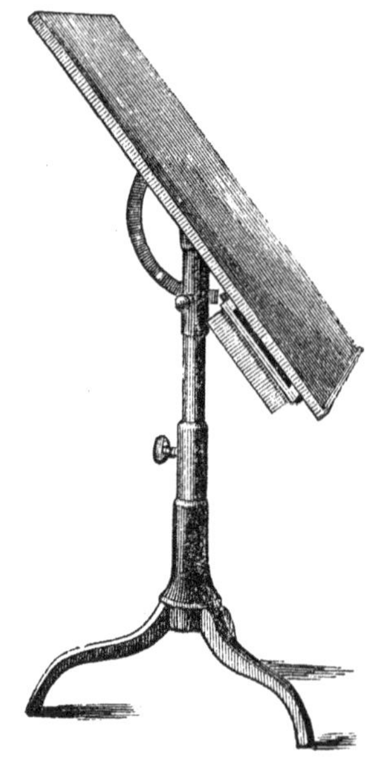

No. 25. Hard Wood Teacher's Chairs.

No. 26. A very neat and Comfortable Teacher's Chair.

No. 27. Oak Arm Chairs.

No. 28. Recitation Room Table.

No. 29. Primary School Table.

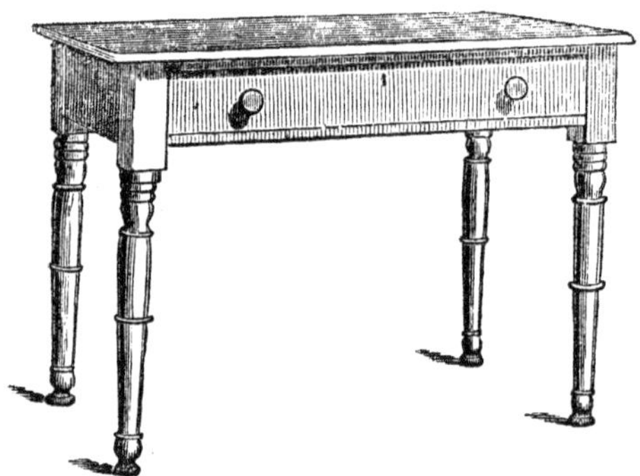

No. 30. Boston Primary School Desk.

No. 31. Teacher's Table, of various Sizes.

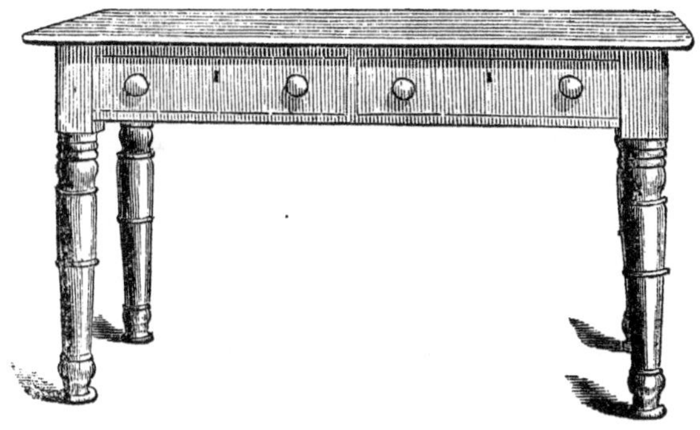

No. 32. Teacher's Desk, with two Drawers.

No. 33. Teacher's Desk, with four Drawers.

No. 34. Teacher's Desk, with a Movable Inclined Plane on Top.

No. 35. Teacher's Desk, Cloth Top, four Drawers.

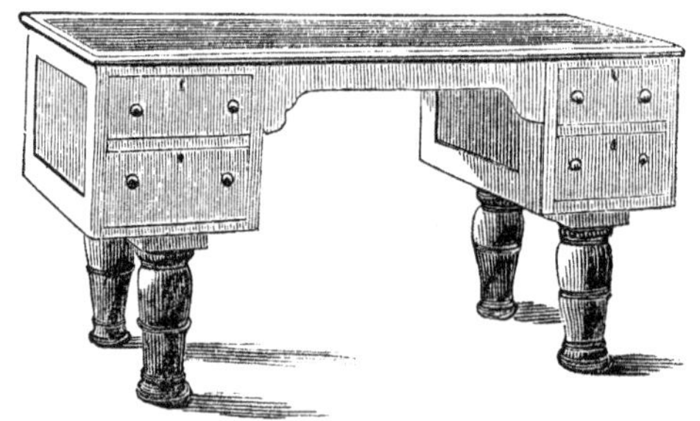

No. 36. Teacher's Desk, with four Drawers and Top esk.

No. 37. BOSTON TEACHER'S DESK, WITH NINE DRAWERS.

No. 38. BOSTON TEACHER'S DESK, NINE DRAWERS.

No 39. NEW YORK IMPROVED TEACHER'S DESK.

BOOK MANUAL.

The pupil should stand erect,—his heels near together,—toes turned out,—and his eyes directed to the face of the person speaking to him.

FIGURE ONE represents the Book Monitor with a pile of books across his left arm, with the backs from him, and with the top of the page to the right hand.

FIGURE TWO represents the Book Monitor, with the right hand hands the book to the Pupil, who receives it in his right hand, with the back of the book to the left; and then passes it into the left hand, where it is held with the back upwards, and with the thumb extended at an angle of forty-five degrees with the edge of the book (as in figure 2,) until a further order is given.

FIGURE THREE—When the page is given out, the book is turned by the thumb on the side; and, while held with both hands, is turned with the back downwards, with the thumbs meeting across the leaves, at a point judged to be nearest the place to be found. On opening the book, the left hand slides down to the bottom, and thence to the middle, where the thumb and little finger are made to press on the two opposite pages. If the Pupil should have thus lit upon the page sought for, he lets fall the right hand by the side, and his position is that of Fig. 3.

FIGURE FOUR—But, if he has opened short of the page required, the thumb of the right hand is to be placed near the upper corner of the page, as seen in Fig. 4; while the forefinger lifts the leaves to bring into view the number of the page. If he finds that he has not raised enough, the forefinger and thumb hold those already raised, while the second finger lifts the leaves, and brings them within the grasp of the thumb and finger. When the page required is found, all the fingers are to be passed under the leaves, and the whole turned at once. Should the Pupil, on the contrary, have opened too far, and be obliged to turn back, he places the right thumb, in like manner, on the left-hand page, and the leaves are lifted as before described.

FIGURE FIVE—Should the book be old, or so large as to be wearisome to hold, the right hand may sustain the left, as seen in Fig. 5.

FIGURE SIX and SEVEN—While reading, as the eye rises to the top of the right-hand page, the right hand is brought to the position seen in Fig. 4; and, with the forefinger under the leaf, the hand is slid down to the lower corner, and retained there during the reading of this page, as seen in Fig. 6. This also is the position in which the book is to be held when about to be closed; in doing which, the left hand, being carried up to the side, supports the book firmly and unmoved, while the right hand turns the part it supports over on the left thumb, as seen in Fig. 7. The thumb will then be drawn out from between the leaves, and placed on the cover; when the right hand will fall by the side, as seen in Fig. 2.

FIGURE EIGHT—But, if the reading has ended, the right hand retains the book, and the left hand falls by the side, as seen in Fig. 8. The book will now be in a position to be handed to the Book Monitor; who receives it in his right hand, and places it on his left arm, with the back towards his body. The books are now in the most suitable situation for being passed to the shelves or drawers, where, without being crowded, they should be placed with uniformity and care.

In conclusion, it may be proper to remark, that however trivial these minute directions may appear to some minds, it will be found on experience, that books thus treated, may be made to last double the time that they will do, under the usual management in schools. Nor is the attainment of a correct and graceful mode of handling a book, the only benefit received by the pupil. The use of this manual is calculated to beget a love of *order* and *propriety*, and disposes him more readily to adopt the habit generally, of doing things in a methodical and systematic manner.

The following remarks are from the "*Report of the Primary School Committee to the Board of Trustees of the Public School Society of New York, on the use of* SEATS WITHOUT BACKS :—

"On inquiry of the female teachers, several of the oldest and most experienced among them say, that instances of curved spine are often perceived among their scholars. Individual members of this Board have noticed similar instances; and it deserves to be mentioned, that a highly respectable and intelligent foreign gentleman, who is deeply interested in the cause of education, on a late visit to one of our schools, expressed his surprise on perceiving how large a proportion of the girls were round-shouldered and stooping in their figure."

* * * * * * *

"1st. It is a matter of notoriety to the medical profession, that, until about thirty or forty years ago, spinal curvatures were very little known. It is only since "the schoolmaster has got abroad,"—only since so great and universal an impulse has been given to education, that these cases have become sufficiently numerous to attract the particular attention of medical men. There is now to be found a distinct class of practitioners, and of machinists, who live and thrive by the treatment of spinal injuries.

2d. A large proportion of these cases can be distinctly traced to causes connected with school education. Among the illiterate in all countries, these injuries are scarcely known. They occur most frequently in schools where females are much confined to a sitting posture, with but a scanty allowance of those robust and active exercises which impart power to the muscular system, and invigorate the general health.

It should be here explained, that the trunk of the body is sustained in its erect position, solely by the action of muscles. Young and growing females who are but feebly endowed with muscular strength, experience such a sense of weariness in sitting upright, as to be induced, from necessity, to drop the body into a variety of curvatures; and one particular curve becoming habitual and long persisted in, finally ends in permanent deformity. The influence of exercise in preventing the evil, is precisely that which it has on the arm of a blacksmith; it augments the bulk, and redoubles the power of the muscles, and gives greater firmness and security to the joints.

3d. In all large cities there are many children, who, from infancy, are strongly predisposed to these affections, owing to a constitutional feebleness of muscle, or an unhealthy condition of the bones or joints. These require every precaution, during the course of their education, to prevent deformity.

Supposing the females attending our schools to be liable to spinal injuries, are these injuries owing to the use of seats without backs? The answer must be, that they are instrumental in causing them, just so far as they place the scholar under the necessity of seeking relief in the crooked and unhealthy attitudes into which she throws her body. Another question of similar import, is this:—*Would seats with back-supports tend to prevent these injuries?* A similar answer must be given. Such seats would act as a preventive, just in proportion as they removed the temptation and the necessity for indulging in injurious flexures of the body. When we see, as we often may, a girl of rapid growth, of yielding joints, and of feeble muscles, propping the weight of her body on her elbows, or, by way of change, bringing her sides alternately to rest on the desk before her, can we doubt for a moment, that, with a back-support, she would run less risk of injury to her figure? And in regard to those children, before alluded to, as having a natural predisposition to spinal distortions, seats of this kind would be indispensable to their safety."

APPARATUS.

In addition to the necessary furniture of a school, such as seats, desks, and other fixtures and articles required for the accommodation of pupils and teacher, and the order and cleanliness of the premises, every school-room should be furnished with such apparatus as shall enable the teacher to employ the hand and eye of every pupil in illustration and experiment, so far as may be practicable and desirable in the course of instruction pursued in the school. It is therefore important, in the internal arrangement of a school-house, to have regard to the safe-keeping, display, and use of such apparatus as the grade of the school, for which the house is intended, may require. A few suggestions will therefore be made on these points, and in aid of committees and trustees in selecting apparatus.

1. In a large school, and in schools of the highest grade, there will be need of a separate apartment appropriated to the safe-keeping of the apparatus, and in some departments of instruction, for the proper use of the same. But in small schools, and as far as practicable in all schools, maps, diagrams, and other apparatus, should be in view of the school at all times.

This will not only add to the attractions of the school, and make the school-room look like a workshop of education, but will awaken a desire in the pupils to know the uses of the various articles, and to become acquainted with the facts and principles which can thus be seen, heard, or handled.

2. Such articles as are liable to be injured by dust, or handling, must be provided with an appropriate room, or a case of sufficient size, having glazed and sliding doors, and convenient shelves.

The doors should not be glazed to the floor, on account of liability to breakage, and also to admit of drawers for maps and diagrams, and a closet for such articles as may be uninteresting or unseemly to the eye, although useful in their place.

The shelves should be movable, so as to admit of additions of larger or smaller specimens of apparatus, and also of such arrangement as the varying tastes of different teachers may require.

3. There should be a table, with a level top, and capable of being made perfectly firm, unless the teacher's desk can be so, for the teacher to place his apparatus on, when in use.

4. The apparatus of every school-room should be selected with reference to the grade of schools to which it is appropriated, and in Primary and District schools in particular, should be of simple construction and convenient for use.

5. As far as practicable, the real object in nature and art, and not a diagram, or model, should be secured.

The following list of articles is necessarily very imperfect, but it may help to guide committees in their search after apparatus.

Articles indispensable in Schools of every Grade.

A clock.

The cardinal points of the heavens painted on the ceiling, or on the teacher's platform, or the floor of the recitation room.

As much blackboard, or black surface on the walls of the school-room, and the recitation rooms, as can be secured. A portion of this black surface should be in full view of the whole school, for passing explanations; and another portion out of the way, within reach of the smallest pupils. One or more movable blackboards, or large slate, with one or more movable stands or supporters.

All the appendages to a blackboard, such as chalk, crayons, and a rubber of soft cloth, leather, or sheepskin, and a pointer.

An inkstand, fixed into the desk, with a lid, and with a pen-wiper attached.

A slate, iron-bound at the corners, and covered with list, or India-rubber cloth, for every desk, with a pencil-holder and sponge attached. A few extra slates for the use of the youngest pupils, under the care and at the discretion of the teacher.

A map of the district, town, county, and state.

A terrestrial globe, properly mounted, or suspended by a wire.

The measure of an inch, foot, yard, and rod, marked off on the edge of the blackboard, or on the wall.

Real measures of all kinds, linear, superficial, solid, and liquid; as a foot-rule, a yard-stick, quarts, bushels, an ounce, pound, &c., for the exercise of the eye and hand.

Vases for flowers and natural grasses.

Apparatus for a Primary or District School.

The apparatus for this class of schools cannot be specified with much minuteness, because the ages of the pupils, and the modes of instruction vary so much in different localities. The following list embraces the articles purchased for Primary and District schools in Rhode Island:

Movable Lesson Posts. These are from three and a half to four feet high, and are variously made of wood, and of cast-iron. It consists, when made of wood, of an upright piece of plank from two to three inches square at the bottom, and diminishing regularly to the top, where it is one inch, inserted in a round or cross base broad enough to support the lesson board, or card, which is suspended by a ring on a hook at or near the top of the post.

J. L. Mott, 264, Water street, New York, manufactures for the Primary schools of the Public School Society of New York, a very neat *cast-iron* lesson stand.

Reading Lessons. Colored Prints, and Diagrams of various kinds, such as of animals, costumes, trades, &c., pasted on boards of wood or strong pasteboard; some with, and others without printed descriptions beneath; to be suspended at appropriate times on the lesson stands, for class exercises, and at other times, on the walls, or deposited in their appropriate places.

In this list should be included the numeration table, tables for reading arithmetical marks, easy lessons, geometrical figures, punctuation marks, outline maps, &c.

Allen's *Education Table* will be found very useful in teaching the Alphabet, Spelling, Reading, and Arithmetic, to little children at home, and in Primary Schools.

Allen's Education Table consists of a board or table, along the centre of which are horizontal grooves, or raised ledges forming grooves between them, that connect with perpendicular grooves or compartments on the sides, in which are inserted an assortment of movable blocks, on the face of which are cut the letters of the alphabet, both capitals and small, the nine digits and cipher, and all the usual pauses and signs used in composition and arithmetic. The letters, figures and signs are large, so as to be readily recognized by all the members of a large class, and from even the extremity of a large school-room, and are so assorted and arranged as to be easily slid from the perpendicular grooves or compartments into the horizontal grooves, and there combined into syllables, words and sentences, or used in simple arithmetical operations. When the lesson in the alphabet, spelling, reading, composition, or arithmetic, is finished, the blocks can be returned to their appropriate places.

The experience of many teachers in schools of different grades, and of many mothers at home, (the God-appointed school for little children, next to which should be ranked the well organized Primary School, with a bright, gentle, affectionate and patient female teacher,) has demonstrated that by accustoming the child, either individually, or in a class, to select letter by letter, and move them from their appropriate case to the centre of the board, and there combining them into syllables and words, a knowledge of the alphabet, and of words, is acquired in a much shorter time and in a much more impressive and agreeable manner, than by any of even the best methods now pursued.

All of the advantages derived from the method of dictation, and the use of the slate and blackboard, in teaching children the alphabet, spelling, reading, and the use of capital letters and pauses, as well as the elementary principles of arithmetic, such as numeration, addition, subtraction, &c., can be secured by the introduction of this Table into our Primary and District Schools.

Manufactured by Edwin Allen *only, Windham, Conn., who will promptly attend to all orders for them.*

A *Moveable Black-board*, or prepared black surface of considerable extent, is indispensable.

The upper portion of the standing blackboard should be inclined back a little from the perpendicular, and along the lower edge there should be a projection or trough to catch the particles detached from the chalk or crayon when in use, and a drawer to receive the sponge, cloth, lamb's-skin, or other soft article used in cleaning the surface of the board.

Blackboards, even when made with great care, and of the best seasoned materials, are liable to injury and defacement from warping, opening of seams, or splitting when exposed to the overheated atmosphere of school-rooms, unless they are set in a frame like a slate, or the panel of a door.

By the following ingenious, and cheap contrivance, a few feet of board can be converted into a table, a sloping desk, one or two blackboards, and a form or seat, and the whole folded up so as not to occupy a space more than five inches wide, and be easily moved from one room to another. It is equally well adapted to a school-room, class-room, library or nursery.

f f Under side of the swinging board, suspended by rule-joint hinges, when turned up, painted black or dark chocolate.

a d Folding brackets, inclined at an angle of 75 degrees, and swung out to support the board when a sloping desk is required.

b c Folding brackets to support the swinging board when a bench or flat table is required.

h f f a b c d e e e e g g

e e e e Uprights attached to the wall.

g g Form to be used when the swinging board is let down, and to be supported by folding legs. The under side can be used as a blackboard for small children.

h A wooden button to retain the swinging board when turned up for use as a blackboard.

n Opening to receive inkstands, and deposit for slate, pencil, chalk, &c.

m Surface of swinging board when let down.

l Surface of form or bench.

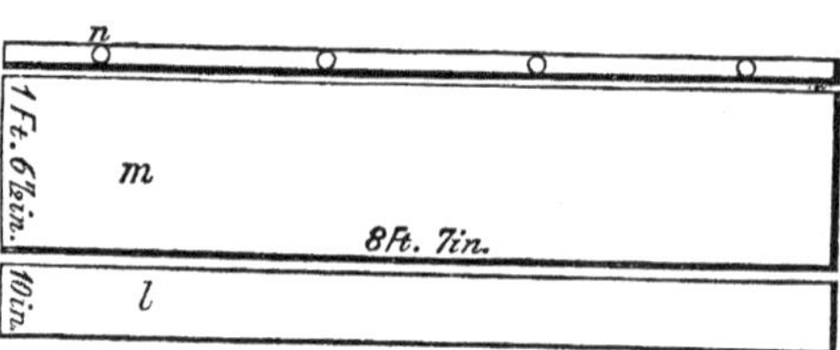

When not in use, or let down, the desk and form should hang flush with each other.

A cheap movable blackboard can be made after the following cut (Fig. 3.

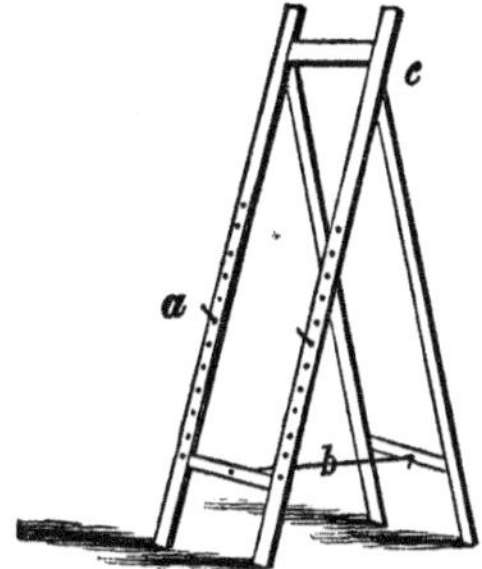

A movable stand to support a blackboard may be made like a painter's easel, as represented in the accompanying cut.

a, Pins for board to rest on. *c*, Hinge or joint to the supporting legs, which are braced by hook *b*, and may be folded up, and the stand put away in a closet. A stand of this kind is convenient to display outline and other maps, reading lessons and other diagrams.

A large movable blackboard may be made as represented in the accompanying cut. An upright frame, strongly braced by cross-pieces (*a*) is inserted into the feet (*b*,) or horizontal supports having castors, on which the whole may be rolled on the floor. Within grooves on the inside of this upright frame is a smaller frame (*c*) hung by a cord which passes over a pulley (*d*,) and is so balanced by weights, concealed in the upright parts, as to admit of being raised or lowered conveniently. Within this inner frame is hung the blackboard on pivots, by which the surface of the board can be inclined from a perpendicular.

A cheaper movable frame, with a blackboard suspended on a pivot, can be made as represented in the lower diagram. The feet, if made as represented in this cut, will be liable to get broken.

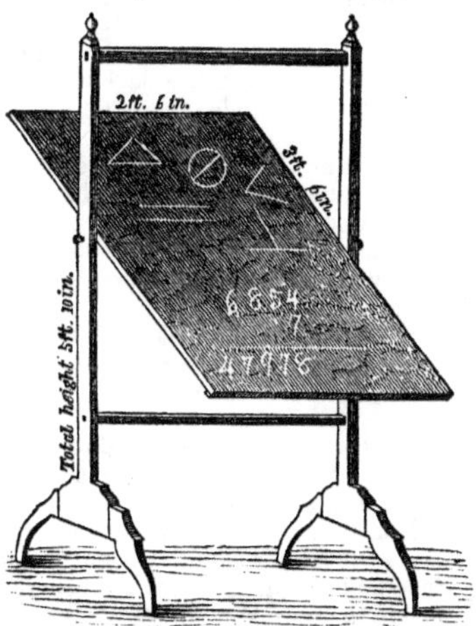

Composition for Blackboards.

Lampblack and flour of emery mixed with spirit-varnish.

No more lampblack and flour of emery should be used than are sufficient to give the required black and abrading surface ; and the varnish should contain only sufficient gum to hold the ingredients together, and confine the composition to the board. The thinner the mixture, the better.

The lampblack should first be ground with a small quantity of alcohol, or spirit-varnish, to free it from lumps.

The composition should be applied to the smoothly-planed surface of the board, with a common painter's brush. Let it become *thoroughly dry and hard before it is used.* Rub it down with pumice-stone, or a piece of smooth wood covered with the composition.

This composition may also be used on the walls.

Slate Blackboard.

In the class-rooms of the American Asylum for the Deaf and Dumb, and all similar institutions, where most of the instruction is given by writing, and drawings on the blackboard, large slates from three feet wide, to four feet long are substituted for the blackboard. These slates cost from $2 to $3, and are superior to any other form of blackboard, and in a series of years prove more economical.

Plaster Blackboard.

As a substitute for the painted board, it is common to paint black a portion of the plastered wall when covered with hard finish, (i. e. plaster of Paris and sand;) or to color it by mixing with the hard finish a sufficient quantity of lamp-black, wet with alcohol, at the time of putting it on. The hard finish, colored in this way, can be put on to an old, as well as to a new surface. Unless the lamp-black is wet with alcohol, or sour beer, it will not mix uniformly with the hard finish, and when dry, the surface, instead of being a uniform black, will present a spotted appearance.

Canvas Blackboard.

Every teacher can provide himself with a portable blackboard made of canvas cloth, 3 feet wide and 6 feet long, covered with three or four coats of black paint, like Winchester's Writing Charts. One side might, like this chart, present the elements of the written characters classified in the order of their simplicity, and guide-marks to enable a child to determine with ease the height, width, and inclination of every letter. Below, on the same side, might be ruled the musical scale, leaving sufficient space to receive such characters as may be required to illustrate lessons in music. The opposite side can be used for the ordinary purposes of a blackboard. When rolled up, the canvas would occupy a space three feet long, and not more than three inches in diameter.

Directions for making Crayons.

A school, or the schools of a town, may be supplied with crayons very cheaply, made after the following directions given by Professor Turner of the American Asylum for the Deaf and Dumb.

Take 5 pounds of Paris White, 1 pound of Wheat Flour, wet with water, and knead it well, make it so stiff that it will not stick to the table, but not so stiff as to crumble and fall to pieces when it is rolled under the hand.

To *roll* out the crayons to the proper size, two boards are needed, *one*, to roll them *on;* the *other* to roll them *with*. The first should be a smooth pine board, three feet long, and nine inches wide. The other should also be pine, a foot long, and nine inches wide, having nailed on the under side, near each edge, a slip of wood one third of an inch thick, in order to raise it so much above the under board, as, that the crayon, when brought to its proper size, may lie between them without being flattened.

The mass is rolled into a ball, and slices are cut from one side of it about one third of an inch thick; these slices are again cut into strips about four inches long and one third of an inch wide, and rolled separately between these boards until smooth and round.

Near at hand, should be another board 3 feet long and 4 inches wide, across which each crayon, as it is made, should be laid so that the ends may project on each side—the crayons should be laid in close contact and straight. When the board is filled, the ends should be trimmed off so as to make the crayons as long as the width of the board. It is then laid in the sun, if in hot weather, or if in winter, near a stove or fire-place, where the crayons may dry gradually, which will require twelve hours. When thoroughly dry, they are fit for use.

An experienced hand will make 150 in an hour.

We are indebted to Prof. Cook, of Rutgers College, New Jersey, for the following directions for making crayons which he finds, after long trial better for the uses of the black-board, than those made after the direction of Prof. Turner, or than those imported from Europe.

Take five pounds of whiting, four pounds of boiled plaster, and water enough to make the whole into a moderately thin paste. Mix these thoroughly and quickly. This compound will harden in a few minutes, when it may be dried and sawed into crayons.

Bolted Paris white is the best whiting, but the common kind may be used if care is taken to dry and pulverize it. The plaster used by masons, is sufficiently good. It should be fresh boiled. As it is the hardening ingredient in the compound, the crayons may be made more or less hard, by slightly increasing or diminishing the amount mentioned above.

The vessel in which the mixture is made, should be greased before using, to prevent adhesion. Any convenient one may be used, but a square or oblong box would be found most economical. The mixture is best dried at a common temperature; if artificial heat is used, it should not exceed that of boiling water.

Crayons made in this way are better than many of those found in market, and the materials from which they are made are both cheap and common. The square form, produced by sawing, is better for writing than the round.

Plaster Black Wall.

The following directions may be safely followed in making plaster black wall.

In the first place, the scratch coat, made with coarse sand, is spread upon the laths as usual, and the brown coat follows, being left a little rough under the "float." When the brown coat is perfectly dry, the black coat is laid on.

This is prepared of mason's "putty" and ground plaster and beach sand, mixed in the usual proportions for hard finish. The coloring matter is lamp-black, wet with alcohol or whiskey, forming a mixture of the consistency of paste. This is mixed with the other ingredients just as they are about to be spread upon the wall. The quantity of coloring to be used must be sufficient to make a black surface; *the sufficiency being determined by experiment*—no rule can be given. An intelligent mason can very soon try experiments so as to insure success. It is to be remembered that the black surface requires much more working with the smoothing trowel than ordinary white finish. It should be finished by being softly smoothed with a wet brush. When perfectly dry, it is nearly as hard as slate, and almost as durable, if carefully used. Great care should be taken not to put in *too much* lamp-black.

In building a new school-house it would be well to have a belt of this black surface pass entirely around the room, at the proper height. In a common school, when small children are to use it, its lower edge should be about two feet from the floor, extending thence upward from 3 to 5½ feet. At the lower edge there should be a "chalk trough," extending the whole length, made by nailing a thin strip of board to the plank, which bounds the black-board, leaving a trough two inches in width and depth, in which to place the chalk, brushes, pointers, &c.; this will also catch the dust which is wiped from the board. The upper edge should be bounded by a simple moulding.

The best thing for removing the chalk from the board is a brush, made of the size of a shoe-brush, with the wooden handle on the back, the face being covered with a sheep-skin with the wool on. This removes the chalk at a single sweep, without wearing the surface, and without soiling the hand of the operator. This is a great improvement over a dust-cloth or a sponge.

In all cases let the board be kept dry; never allow a pupil to wet the wiper when removing the chalk.

By long use, especially if the surface is ever cleaned with a wet wiper, this kind of black-board becomes too smooth and glossy upon the surface; the chalk passes over it without taking effect, and the light is reflected by it. A very simple wash, applied with a soft brush, will immediately restore it; this wash is made by dissolving one part of glue, to two parts of alum in water, so as to make a very thin solution. It is well to have the wash slightly colored with lamp-black. Care must be taken that this wash do not have too much "body."

A *map exhibitor*, consisting of a movable cross, (*c*) may be attached to a stand or easel, by being let into a groove, cut in the form of a dove-tail at the back (*a*) of the easel, just above the part where the movable leg is hinged. To suit the varying breadth of maps, the pins or hooks for holding them may be made to slide in a groove in the cross or horizontal part of the exhibitor. The same contrivance, the sliding hook, may be applied to a groove in a board or slip of board, on the side or end of the school-room, at the proper elevation, for the purpose of displaying maps or charts.

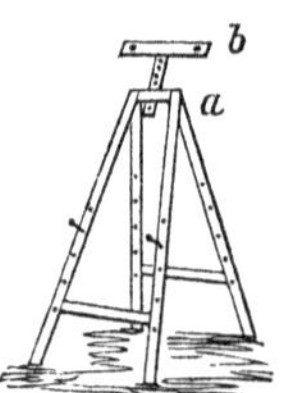

As ink must be provided in all schools, except those of the infant and primary grade, the material and shape of the pot or well to hold the ink, and the mode of inserting the same in the desk, and covering the mouth or top, so as to exclude dust and prevent evaporation, are points of considerable practical importance.

The inside material or lining should be glass, to prevent the ink being injured by corrosion. The conical shape, with a projecting rim slightly inclined towards the opening, will be found to have many advantages—such as facilitating its insertion in the desk, or the tray—the dip of the pen, without touching the side of the pot or well—the catching of any excess of ink thrown or jerked back by the writer, or thrown out by any sudden jar of the desk. Glass ink wells of various patterns can now be obtained at the principal crockery dealers, and are always furnished by the manufacturers of first class desks.*

The ink well should be movable, for convenience of filling and cleansing of sediment, and also for being emptied of ink when not in use, or of being emptied or removed, to avoid freezing in winter.

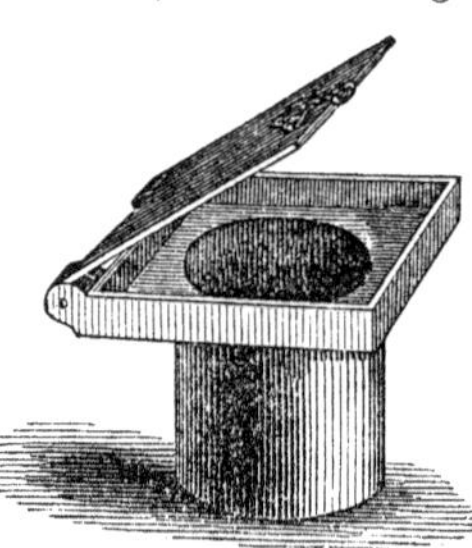

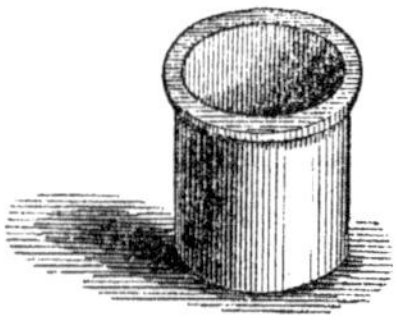

Each desk should be provided with a movable ink well, inserted in a cast iron or other metalic box having a cover, the box being set in, and secured firmly to the desk. The opening in a glass ink well, when not in use, will be protected by the lid, and the well itself can be removed for convenience in filling, cleansing, and emptying.

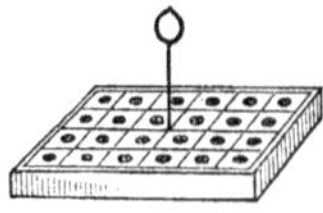

A *Tray for Ink Wells*, made of tin, of annexed construction, will be found very useful to collect the wells when not in use, or when they are removed for cleansing or other purposes.

A *Sponge Box*, for damping sponge without exposing the surface of the water, may be constructed after the following drawing from ***Richson's** School Building Guide*. To any desk standard (A) attach a box (B) lined with lead. On the inside of the box place a sloping cover, (C) lined on both sides with lead, having at the lower end two rows of perforations, and in the upper a broad slit or opening. Through this slit pass a strip of woolen list or flannel, one end (*n*) of which shall be in the water and the other extend to the perforations in the cover. The water which is taken up by the woolen strip, will filter down the inclined plane, and pass again into the box through the perforations. The surface of the strip will be kept sufficiently wet to damp a sponge without allowing the water to be exposed in the box.

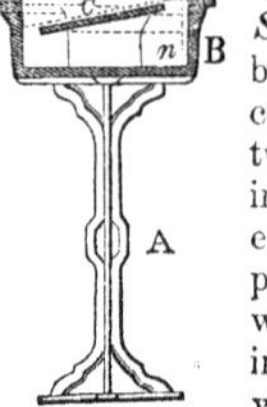

* J. L. Ross, corner of Ivers and Hawkins streets, Boston, has a very neat style of ink well, box, and cover, as illustrated on pages 371 and 372. Mr. Ross is also the agent of the Castleton Slate Company, and can furnish slates planed by machinery to a perfectly smooth surface, of any required dimensions, from eight feet long by five wide, and three-fourths of an inch thick, to any smaller size.

The Gonigraph is a small instrument composed of a number of flat rods connected by pivots, which can be put into all possible geometrical figures that consist of straight lines and angles, as triangles, squares, pentagons, hexagons, octagons, &c.

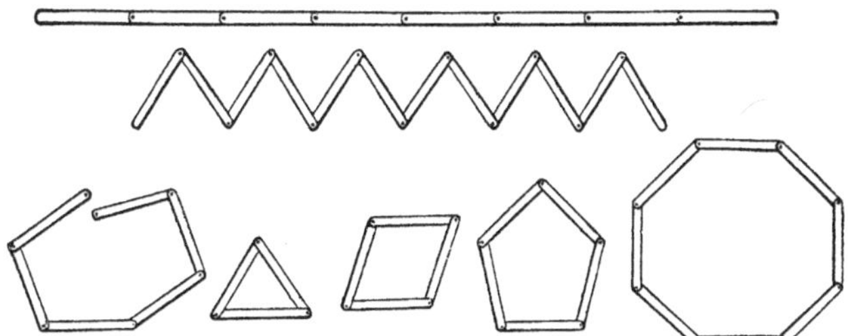

The Arithmeticon, represented in the annexed cut, is a most useful instrument. In an oblong open frame, twelve rows of wooden balls, alternately black and white, and of the size of a nutmeg or small walnut, and twelve in each row, are strung like beads on strong wires. The instrument, when fixed to a stand, is about four feet high, the frame being one-fourth part broader than it is high. It may be made much smaller, as in the cut. When it is used to exercise the children in arithmetic, the teacher or monitor stands behind, and slides the balls along the wires from *his* left to his right, calling out the number he shifts, as, twice two are four, thrice two are six, shifting first four balls, and then two more. As the children are apt to confuse the balls remaining with those shifted, a thin board covers half the surface on the side next the children, as marked by a line down the centre, so that they see only the balls shifted to the open side.

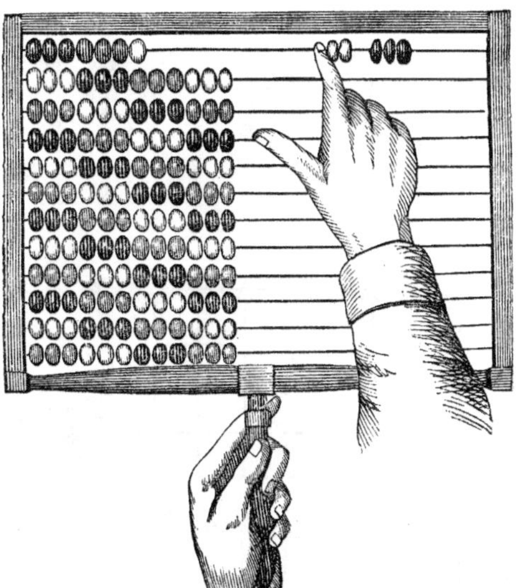

NUMERAL FRAME.

The *Arithmeticon* or *Numeral Frame* represented in the foregoing cut forms a part of *Holbrook's Common School Apparatus*, which embraces, in addition, the following articles.

For showing the figures, names, properties, and uses of various *Geometrical Forms and Solids*, the following blocks are made, accompanied with a sheet of diagrams.

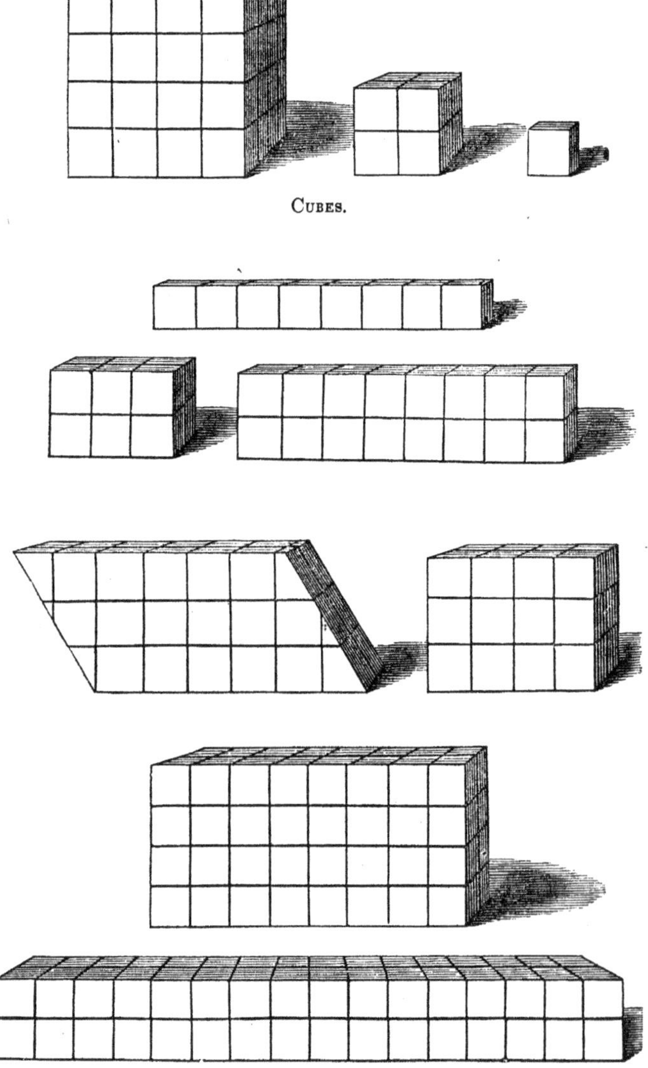

CUBES.

PARALLELOPIPEDS.

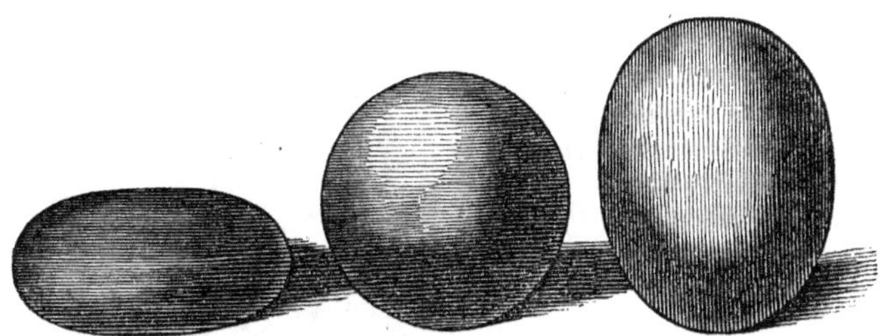

Oblate Spheroid. Sphere. Prolate Spheroid.

Hexagonal Prism. Prism. Triangular Prism. Cylinder.

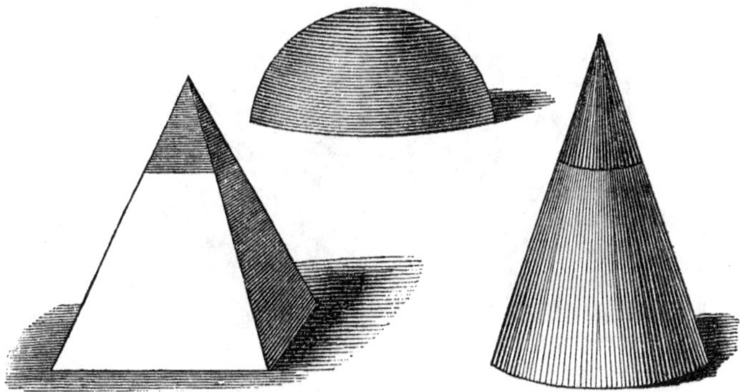

Pyramid and Frustrum. Cone and Frustrum.

A *Sectional Block*, to illustrate the extraction of the cube root.

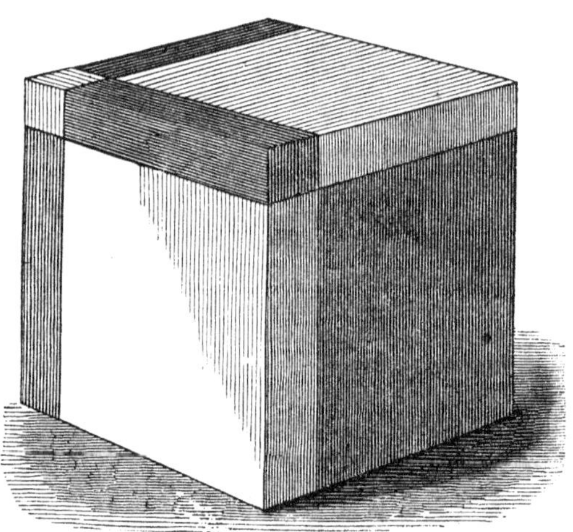

BLOCK TO ILLUSTRATE CUBE ROOT.

Accompanying this set is a *Drawing Slate*, designed particularly for young pupils. On the frame are a set of copies for writing and drawing, which are protected from injury in consequence of friction on the desk by cushions made of India rubber inserted in each corner. This slate is equally well adapted for the older pupils, and for all arithmetical operations, and its use is accompanied with less noise than any other form of slate.

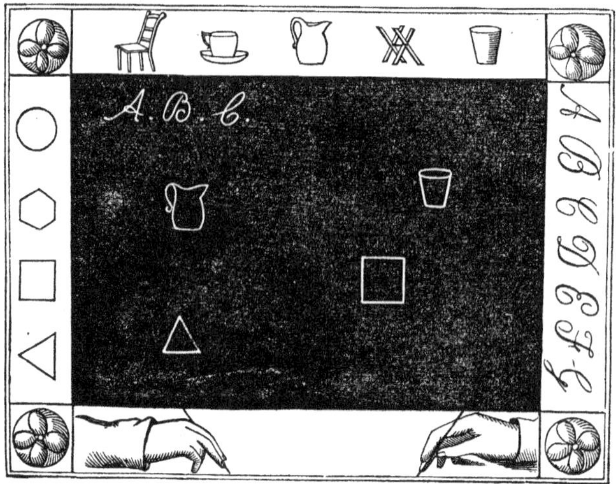

DRAWING SLATE.

A *Terrestrial Globe*, made of solid, firm material, and so mounted on a simple pedestal that it can be readily removed, and suspended by a cord—and thus be held in the hand, and displayed conveniently for familiar illustrations to a class. They are made from five to eight inches in diameter.

TERRESTRIAL GLOBE.

A *Hemisphere Globe*, cut in equal sections, and opening on a hinge, will solve at a glance many of the difficulties encountered by young pupils in the study of geography, and correct some fundamentally erroneous conceptions which even older scholars are liable to form of latitude and longitude, or from an exclusive use of maps.

HEMISPHERE GLOBE.

The *Tellurian* is designed to illustrate all the phenomena resulting from the relations of the Sun, Moon, and Earth, to each other—the succession of day and night, the change of the seasons, the change of the sun's declination, the different lengths of day and night, the changes of the moon, the harvest moon, the precession of the equinoxes, the differences of a solar and siderial year, &c., &c.

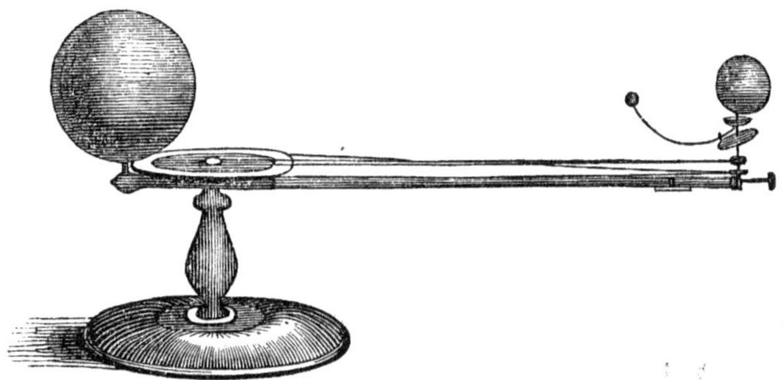

TELLURIAN.

The *Planetarium* or Orrery, gives the proportionate size and relative positions, and annual revolutions of the planets, composing the solar system, except the asteroids.

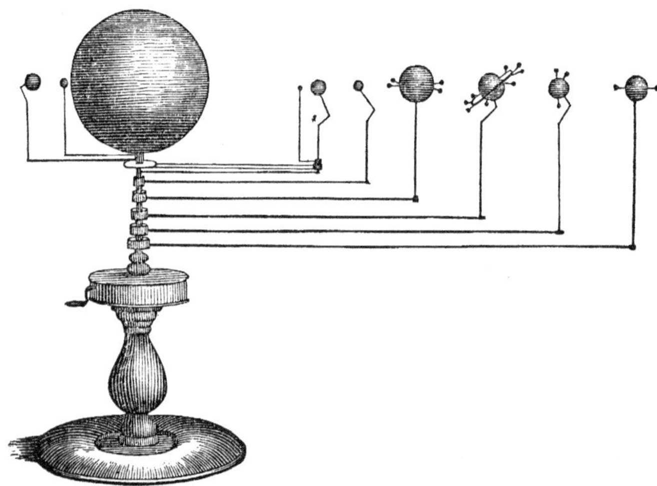

PLANETARIUM.

Holbrook's Common School Apparatus, is manufactured by the HOLBROOK SCHOOL APPARATUS MANUFACTURING COMPANY, at Hartford, Conn., and sold, securely packed for transportation, with a manual or text-book for the use of the teacher, for $20.00 a set.

APPARATUS FOR GRAMMAR SCHOOLS.

The School Committee of Boston, in 1847, adopted the following articles as a set of Philosophical Apparatus for the Grammar schools, which was selected and classified by Mr. Wightman, whose long experience in manufacturing apparatus for schools of every grade, admirably qualified him for the work:

Laws of Matter.

Apparatus for illustrating Inertia.
Pair of Lead Hemispheres, for Cohesion.
Pair of Glass Plates, for Capillary Attraction.

Laws of Motion.

Ivory Balls on Stand, for Collision.
Set of eight illustrations for Centre of Gravity.
Sliding Frame, for Composition of Forces.
Apparatus for illustrating Central Forces.

Mechanics.

Complete set of Mechanicals, consisting of Pulleys; Wheel and Axle; Capstan; Screw; Inclined Plane; Wedge.

Hydrostatics.

Bent Glass Tube, for Fluid Level.
Mounted Spirit Level.
Hydrometer and Jar, for Specific Gravity.
Scales and Weights, for Specific Gravity.
Hydrostatic Bellows, and Paradox.

Hydraulics.

Lifting, or Common Water Pump.
Forcing Pump; illustrating the Fire Engine.
Glass Syphon Cup; for illustrating Intermitting Springs.
Glass and Metal Syphons.

Pneumatics.

Patent Lever Air Pump and Clamp.
Three Glass Bell Receivers, adapted to the Apparatus.
Condensing and Exhausting Syringe.
Copper Chamber, for Condensed Air Fountain.
Revolving Jet and Glass Barrel.
Fountain Glass, Cock, and Jet for Vacuum.
Brass Magdeburg Hemispheres.
Improved Weight Lifter for upward pressure.
Iron Weight of 56 lbs. and Strap
Flexible Tube and Connectors for Weight Lifter.
Brass Plate and Sliding Rod.
Bolt Head and Jar.
Tall Jar and Balloon.
Hand and Bladder Glasses.
Wood Cylinder and Plate.
India Rubber Bag, for expansion of air.
Guinea and Feather Apparatus.
Glass Flask and Stop-Cock, for weighing air.

Electricity.

Plate Electrical Machine.
Pith Ball Electrometer.
Electrical Battery of four Jars.
Electrical Discharger.
Image Plates and Figure.
Insulated Stool.
Chime of Bells.
Miser's Plate, for shocks.
Tissue Figure, Ball and Point.
Electrical Flyer and Tellurian.
Electrical Sportsman, Jar and Birds.
Mahogany Thunder House and Pistol.

Hydrogen Gas Generator.
Chains, Balls of Pith, and Amalgam.

Optics.

Glass Prism; and pair of Lenses.
Dissected Eye Ball, showing its arrangement.

Magnetism.

Magnetic Needle on Stand.
Pair of Magnetic Swans.
Glass Vase for Magnetic Swans.
Horseshoe Magnet.

Astronomy.

Improved School Orrery.
Tellurian, or, Season Machine.

Arithmetic, and Geometry.

Set of 13 Geometrical Figures of Solids.
Box of 64 one inch Cubes, for Cube Root, &c.

Auxiliaries.

Tin Oiler.
Glass Funnel.
Sulphuric Acid.
Set of Iron Weights for Hydrostatic Paradox.

The foregoing Set is fully illustrated in "Wightman's Select Experiments," a valuable manual for the teacher.

The following illustrations of some of the articles enumerated in the above list, are taken from "Wightman's Illustrated Catalogue," which persons selecting apparatus will do well to consult before making their purchases. The address is Joseph M. Wightman, No. 33 Cornhill, Boston, Mass.

LAWS OF MATTER AND MOTION.

INERTIA APPARATUS.

This Figure represents a very convenient apparatus for illustrating Inertia, a stiff card being projected by the spring, and leaving the ball upon the pillar.

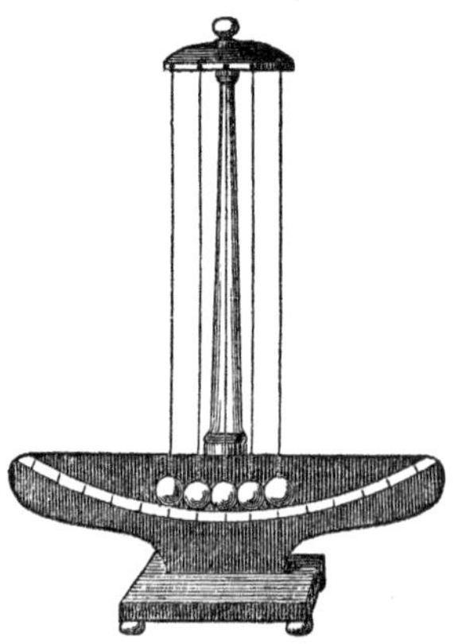

COLLISION BALLS AND STAND.

MECHANICALS.

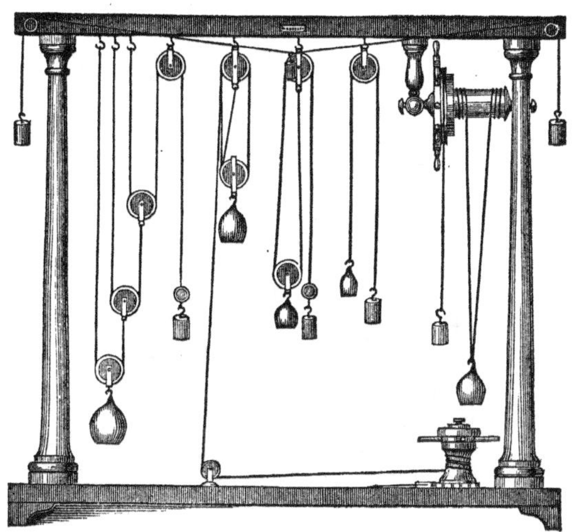

Pulleys, Wheel and Axle, Capstan.

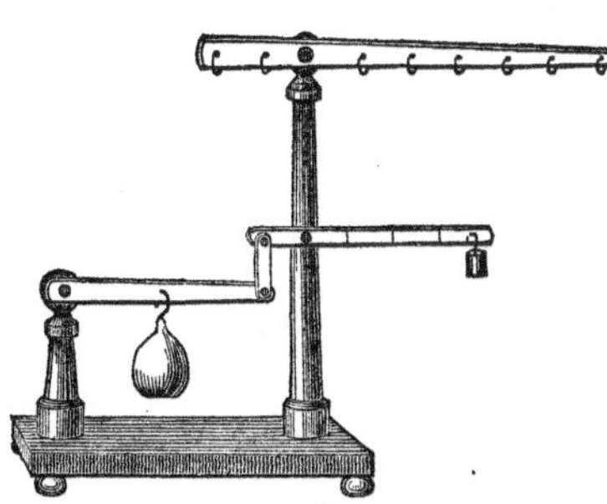

Simple and Compound Levers.

Screw.

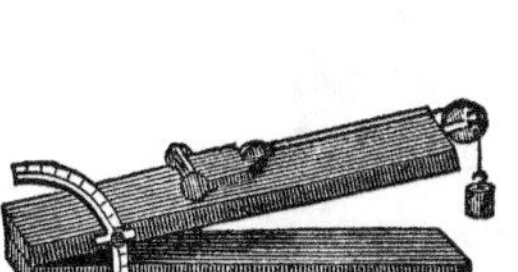

Inclined Plane.

Wedge.

HYDROSTATICS.

WIGHTMAN'S HYDROSTATIC BELLOWS AND PARADOX.

HYDRAULICS.

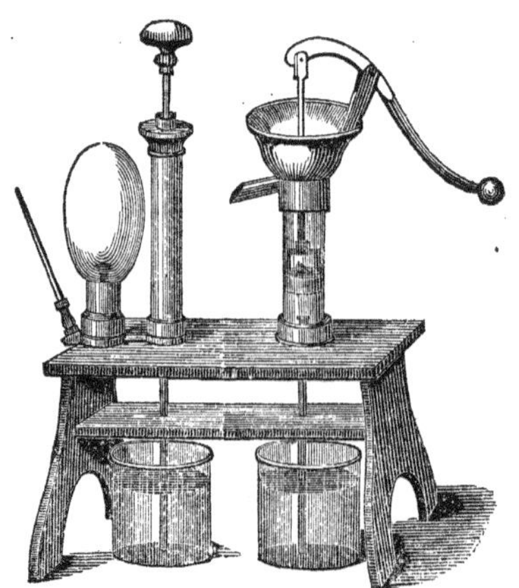

MODELS OF WATER PUMPS.

PNEUMATICS.

Patent Portable Air Pump.

Bolt Head Experiment.

Fountain in Vacuo.

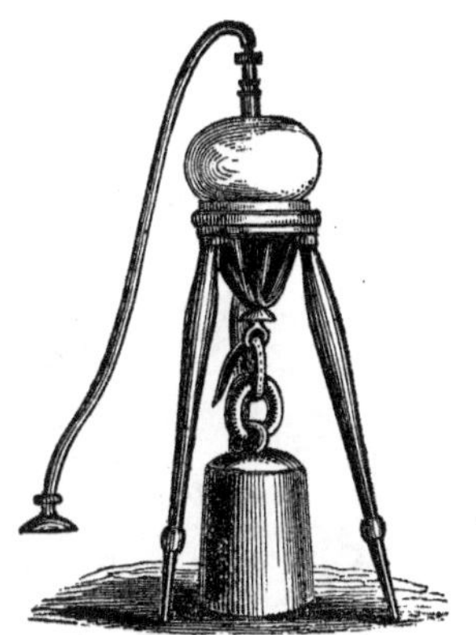

Wightman's Weight Lifter.

ELECTRICITY.

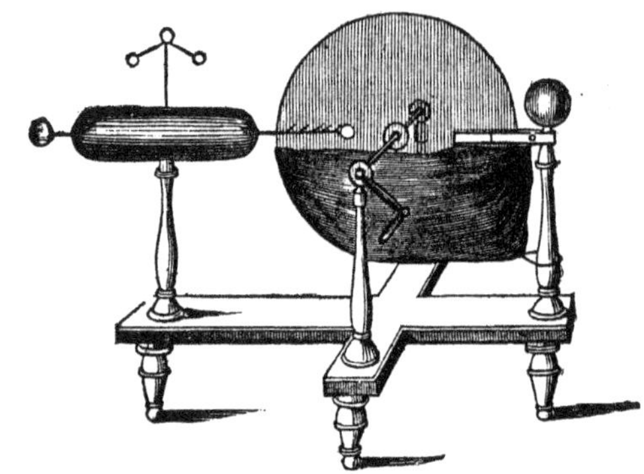

Plate Electrical Machine.

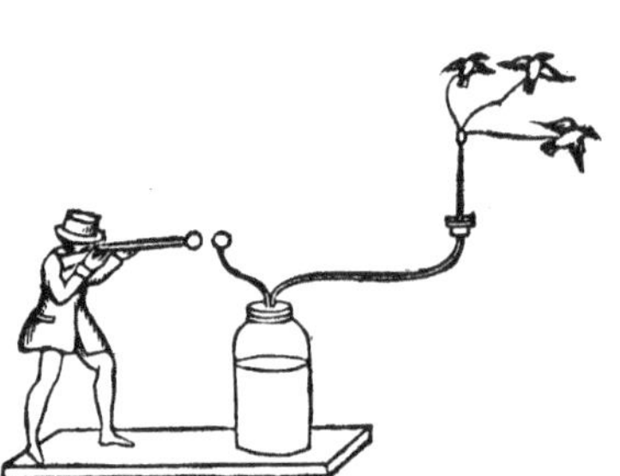

Electrical Sportsman.

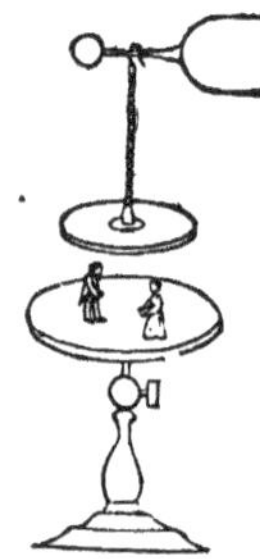

Dancing Images.

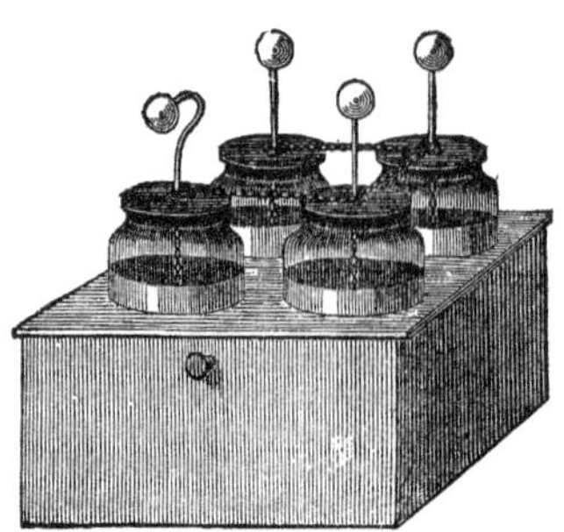

Electrical Battery.

Chime of Bells.

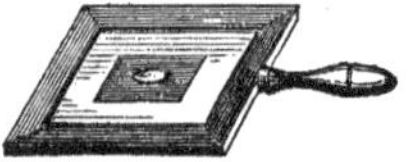

Miser's Plate.

PHILOSOPHICAL APPARATUS,

SELECTED FROM

CHAMBERLAIN & RITCHIE'S

CATALOGUES,

AND ARRANGED IN SETS CORRESPONDING TO THE SUMS ANNEXED.

It will be seen that the highest cost and largest sized instruments are not incorporated into the sets. The first and second sets have been made up for this Catalogue to meet the wants of common schools. See Preface.

SET OF PHILOSOPHICAL APPARATUS.

Item	Price	Item	Price
Cohesive Attraction Plates,	1.00	Orrery,	7.00
Pair Lead Hemispheres,	1.00	Tellurian,	7.00
Set of Capillary Tubes,	1.50	Set of Eight Cube Root Solids,	1.25
Inertia Apparatus,	1.00	Set of twelve Geometrical Solids,	1.00
Centre of Gravity Apparatus,	7.00	Set of ten Parallelopipeds,	1.00
Collision Balls,	3.00	U Magnet,	.50
Mechanical Powers,	25.00	Magnetic Needle and Stand,	.75
Prism,	.75		
Numeral Frame	1.25		$60.00

SET OF PHILOSOPHICAL APPARATUS.

Item	Price	Item	Price
Collision Balls	3.00	Electrical Machine, 18 inch plate,	25.00
Mechanical Powers,	25.00	Leyden Jar,	1.50
Prism,	.75	Discharger,	2.00
Orrery,	7.00	Spiral Tube,	2.50
Microscope,	4.00	Set of Bells,	3.00
		S. and point,	.50
Air Pump,	25.00	Pith Ball Electrometer,	.50
Brass capped Bell Glass, 8 quart,	3.50	Insulating Stool,	4.00
Straight Jar, for do.,	.75	Miser's Plate,	1.00
Tall Bell Glass and Jar,	2.25	Long Haired Man,	.50
Expansion Apparatus,	.75	Ether Spoon,	.75
Hand Glass,	.75	Box of Amalgam,	.25
Hemispherical Cups,	3.50	Stop Cock Leathers,	.25
Upward Pressure Apparatus,	5.00		
Rubber Hose, 4 feet with screws,	2.00	Electro Battery,	3.00
Set three Couplers,	1.50	Needle and Stand,	.75
Sliding Rod,	1.00	Terrestrial Helix,	1.00
Artificial Fountain,	3.00	U Magnet,	.75
Guinea and Feather Tube,	4.00	Vibrating Shocker,	4.50
Revolving Jet,	1.25	Handles and Wires,	1.75
Rubber Bag and Hook,	1.25		
Bell for Vacuum,	1.25		$150.00

SET OF PHILOSOPHICAL APPARATUS.

No. 3, marked [3] in Catalogue.

*Air Pump,	25 00
*Bell Glass, Screw Capped,	3 50
*Freezing Apparatus,	4 00
*Expansion,	75
Straight Glass Jar,	75
*Hand Glass,	75
*Tall Bell Glass and Jar,	3 00
*Mercury Tunnel,	75
*Glass Pan for do.,	25
Hemispherical Cups,	5 00
Upward Pressure Apparatus,	7 00
Set Screw Couplers,	2 50
Bell for Vacuo,	1 25
*Sliding Rod,	1 25
*Sheet Rubber Bag,	1 25
*Artificial Fountain,	4 00
*Guinea and Feather Tube,	6 00
*Barometer Apparatus,	3 00
*Weighing and Buoyancy of Air,	6 00
Syphon Vacuum Gauge,	2 50
Inertia Wheel,	1 00
*Philosophical Water Hammer,	3 00
*Condenser,	5 00
*Condensing Chamber and Cock,	3 50
Air Gun Barrel,	1 00
*Revolving Jet,	1 25
*Exploding Cup, Cap and Cock,	2 00
*Hose and Jet,	1 00
*Straight Brass Jet,	50
Stopcock Collars,	25
Pair Water Pumps,	12 00
Mechanical Powers,	35 00
Centre of Gravity Apparatus,	7 00
Electric Machine, 18 inch Plate,	25 00
Two quart Leyden Jar,	2 00
Diamond Jar,	3 00
Movable Coatings Jar,	3 00
Electrometer Jar,	1 50
Discharger,	2 50
Directing Rod,	2 00
Spiral Tube,	2 50
Bells,	3 00
S. and Point,	50
Pithball Electrometer,	50
Images and Plates,	2 50
Insulating Stool,	6 00
Box Pithballs,	25
Sportsman and Birds,	75
Powder Bomb,	1 25
Thunder House and Fixtures,	5 00
Hydrogen Generator,	3 00
Long-Haired Man,	50
Wheel and Point,	1 00
Seasons Machine,	1 50
Ether Spoon,	75
Wax Friction Cylinder,	1 00
Glass Friction Cylinder,	1 00
Box Amalgam,	25
Cylindrical Electro Battery,	3 00
Electro Magnet,	1 00
Electro Coil and Armatures,	2 50
Powder Cup,	25
Pair of Magnetic Needles and Stands,	2 00
Bar Magnet,	1 00
U Magnet and Armature,	1 00
Terrestrial Helix,	1 50
Revolving Electro Magnet,	5 00
Magnetizing Helix,	2 50
Compound Helices, with vibrating Armature for Shocks,	5 00
Pair Handles, for Shocks,	1 50
Set of Connecting Wires,	50
Galvanometer,	3 00
Pneumatics and Hydraulics,	$107 00
Electrics,	71 00
Mechanics, &c.,	42 00
Magnetics, &c.,	30 00
	$250 00

SET OF PHILOSOPHICAL APPARATUS.

No. 4, marked [4] in Catalogue.

Collision Balls,	3 00
Mechanical Powers,	35 00
Set of Eye Models,	12 00
Prism,	1 00
Compound Microscope,	7 00
Orrery,	7 00
Seasons Machine,	7 00
Pair ten inch Globes,	18 00
Double Barrel Air Pump,	40 00
Eight inch brass capped Bell Glass,	3 50
Tall Bell Glass and Jar,	3 00
Freezing Apparatus,	4 00
Expansion Apparatus,	75
Hand Glass,	75
Mercury Tunnel,	75
Glass Pan, for Mercury,	25
Straight Jar, for Bell Glass,	75
Hemispherical Cups,	5 00
Upward Pressure Apparatus	7 00
Dozen Bursting Squares,	1 50
Cap Valve for do.,	25
Wire Guard for do.,	75
Set of Screw Couplers,	2 50
Bell for Vacuo,	1 25

* Used in connection with Electric Apparatus.

Sliding Rod,	1 50
Sheet Rubber Bag,	1 25
Artificial Fountain,	4 00
Float Wheel,	1 00
Bacchus Illustration,	1 50
Guinea and Feather Tube,	6 00
Water Hammer,	3 00
Barometer Apparatus,	3 00
Weight and Buoyancy of Air,	6 00
Vacuum Gauge	2 50
Condensing Pump,	5 00
Condensing Chamber and Cock,	3 50
Air Gun Barrel,	1 00
Revolving Jet,	1 25
Jet Paradox Tunnel,	1 50
Water Pan and Tube,	75
Plate Paradox and Disks,	1 00
Pipe Paradox and Balls,	1 00
Water Hose,	1 00
Brass Jet,	50
Exploding Cup and Cock,	2 00
Stopcock Collars,	25
Pair Water Pumps and Fixtures,	12 00
Electric Machine, 18 inch Plate,	25 00
Battery of six three pint Jars,	10 00
Double Jar,	3 50
Diamond Jar,	3 00
Movable Coatings,	3 00
Electrometer Jar,	1 50
Discharger,	2 50
Directing Rod,	2 00
Spiral Tube,	2 50
Bells,	3 00
Pithball Electrometer,	50
S. and Point,	50
Pair Plates and Images,	2 50
Box Pithballs,	25
Insulating Stool,	6 00
Sportsman and Birds,	75
Powder Bomb,	1 25
Thunder House and Fixtures,	5 00
Hydrogen Generator,	3 00
Long-Haired Man,	50
Float Wheel and Point,	1 00
Seasons Machine,	1 50
Ether Spoon,	75
Wax Friction Cylinder,	1 00
Glass Friction Cylinder,	1 00
Electric Swing and Image,	2 00
Gasometers and Fixtures,	35 00
Flask, screw-capped for Oxygen,	1 00
Lead Conducting Tube,	1 50
Reflectors and Iron Ball,	6 00
Spirit Boiler for do.,	2 50
Pyrometer, Rods, and Lamps,	3 00
Conductometer and Rods,	1 00
Fire Syringe and Tinder,	1 50
Set of Wire Gauze,	50
Lamp Stand,	2 00
Spirit Lamp,	1 00
Grad. Oz. Measure,	1 00
Ten cubic inch do.,	1 00
Test Tubes, six,	75
Flasks, three,	75
Funnel,	20
Retorts, tubulated, three,	80
Evaporating Dishes, three,	60
Hydrogen Balloon,	2 00
Pair long-necked Matrasses,	60
Dozen Candle Bombs,	50
Dozen Prince Rupert's Drops,	50
Steam Globe and Jet,	1 50
Wollaston's Steam Apparatus,	3 00
Electro Cylinder Battery,	6 00
U Magnet and Armature,	50
Electro Magnet,	1 00
Bar Armature,	25
Y Armature,	50
Star Armature,	50
Magnetic Needle and Stand,	1 00
Powder Cup,	25
Coil and Hem. Armatures,	2 50
Magnetizing Helix,	2 50
Terrestrial Helix,	1 50
Revolving Magnet,	5 00
Vibrating Shocker,	5 00
Shocking Handles,	1 50
Set of Connecting Wires,	50
Pneumatics,	124 75
Electrics,	80 00
Chemicals,	68 20
Magnetics, &c.,	29 75
Mechanics, &c.	98 00
	$400 00

SET OF PHILOSOPHICAL APPARATUS.

No. 5, marked [5] in Catalogue.

Collision Balls,	4 00
Mechanical Powers,	35 00
Centre of Gravity,	7 00
Set of Eye Models,	12 00
Prism,	1 00
Microscope,	10 00
Orrery,	7 00
Seasons,	7 00
Pair of Globes,	30 00
Air Pump,	40 00
Open Swelled Bell Glass,	4 50
Brass screw-capped Bell,	3 50
Straight Jar for do.,	1 00
Freezing Apparatus,	4 00
Tall Bell Glass and Jar,	3 00
Expansion Apparatus,	75
Swelled Hand Glass,	1 00
Hemispherical Cups,	5 00
Upward Pressure Apparatus,	7 00
Dozen Bursting Squares,	1 50
Cap Valve for do.,	25
Wire Guard for do.,	75
Set of Screw Couplers,	2 50
Bell for Vacuo,	1 25
Sliding Rod for do.,	1 25
Sheet Rubber Bag, &c.,	1 25

Artificial Fountain, &c.,	4 00
Mercury Tunnel,	1 00
Glass Pan for Mercury,	30
Guinea and Feather Tube,	6 00
Barometer Apparatus,	3 00
Weight and Buoyancy of Air,	6 00
Syphon Vacuum Gauge,	2 50
Float Wheel,	1 00
Water Hammer,	3 00
Condensing Chamber and Cock,	3 50
Condenser,	5 00
Air Gun Barrel,	1 00
Revolving Jet,	1 25
Plate Paradox and Disks,	1 00
Pipe Paradox and Balls,	1 00
Hose and Water Jet,	1 00
Brass Jet,	50
Leathers for Stopcocks,	50
Exploding Cup, Cap, and Cock,	2 00
Jet Paradox and Balls,	1 50
Water Pan and Tube,	75
Pair of Water Pumps,	12 00
Electric Machine, 24 inch Plate,	50 00
Battery,	14 00
Double Jar,	3 50
Diamond Jar,	3 00
Movable Coatings,	3 00
Electrometer Jar,	1 50
Directing Rod,	2 00
Discharger,	2 50
Spiral Tube,	2 50
Pithball Electrometer,	50
Insulating Stool,	6 00
Set of Bells,	3 00
Dancing Image Plates,	2 00
Pair of Dancing Images,	50
Box of Pithballs,	50
Sportsman and Birds,	75
Powder Bomb,	1 25
Abbe Nolet's Globe,	3 00
Thunder House and Fixtures,	5 00
Hydrogen Generator,	3 00
Long-Haired Man,	50
Float Wheel and Point,	1 00
S. and Point,	50
Seasons Machine,	1 50
Ether Spoon,	75
Miser's Plate,	1 50
Electric Swing and Image,	2 00
Box of Amalgam,	25
Gasometers and Fixtures,	35 00
Retort for Oxygen,	2 00
Conducting Gas Tube,	1 50
Reflectors,	6 00
Spirit Boiler,	2 50
Pyrometer and Lamps,	3 00
Lamp Stand,	2 00
Conductometer	1 00
Pendent Spoon,	25
Fire Syringe and Tinder,	1 50
Set of Wire Gauze,	50
Gas Bag and Cock,	5 00
Chemical Thermometer,	2 50
Spirit Lamp,	1 00
Graduated Measure,	1 00
Test Tubes, six,	75
Flasks, three,	1 00
Funnel,	20
Flasks, flat bottom, three,	75
Tub. Retorts, six,	2 00
Evaporating Dishes, three,	75
Two Wedgwood do.,	50
Mortar and Pestle,	1 00
Hydrogen Balloon,	2 00
Stirring Rods,	25
Matrasses, two,	60
Candle Bombs, dozen,	50
Steam Globe, brass, with Jet,	1 50
Chemical Substances,	10 00
Electro Battery,	8 00
Bar Magnet,	1 00
U Magnet and Armature,	1 00
Electro Magnet,	2 00
Bar Armature,	25
Y Armature,	50
Star Armature,	75
Pair of Needles,	2 00
Powder Cup,	50
Coil and Hem. Armatures,	2 50
Magnetizing Helix,	3 00
Galvanometer,	3 00
Terrestrial Helix,	1 50
Revolving Electro Magnet,	5 00
Analysis of Shocks Apparatus,	12 00
Shocking Handles,	1 50
Set of Connecting Wires,	50
Thermo-Electric Arch,	5 00
Decomposing Cell,	3 00
Pneumatics,	135 30
Electrics,	110 00
Chemicals,	85 55
Mechanics, &c.,	118 00
Electro Magnets,	51 25
	$500 10

SET OF PHILOSOPHICAL APPARATUS.

No. 6, marked [6] in Catalogue.

Collision Balls,	4 00
Centre of Gravity Apparatus,	7 00
Mechanical Powers,	35 00
Lenses,	6 00
Prism,	2 00
Microscope,	12 00
Orrery,	7 00
Seasons Machine,	7 00
Globes,	45 00
Magic Lantern,	25 00
Astronomical Slides,	20 00
Air Pump,	85 00
Open Swelled Bell Glass,	4 50
Brass capped Bell Glass, 8 inch,	3 50
Straight Jar for do.,	1 00
Tall Bell Glass and Jar	3 00

Item	Price
Freezing Apparatus, ...	5 00
Expansion do., ...	1 00
Swelled Hand Glass, ...	1 00
Hemispherical Cups, ...	7 00
Upward Pressure Apparatus, ...	9 00
Dozen Bursting Squares, ...	1 50
Cap Valve for do., ...	25
Wire Guard for do., ...	75
Set of Screw Couplers, ...	2 50
Bell for Vacuo, ...	1 25
Sliding Rod for do., &c., ...	1 50
Sheet Rubber Bag, &c., ...	2 00
Artificial Fountain, ...	4 00
Bacchus Illustration, ...	1 50
Mercury Tunnel, ...	1 00
Guinea and Feather Tube, ...	6 00
Water Hammer, Cap, and Cock, .	3 00
Barometer Apparatus, ...	5 00
Weight and Buoyancy of Air, ...	7 00
Copper Condensing Chamber and Cock, ...	3 50
Condensing Pump, ...	5 00
Air Gun Barrel, ...	1 00
Jet Paradox and Balls, ...	1 50
Cock and Int. Ext. Jets for do., ..	1 50
Revolving Jet, ...	1 25
Plate Paradox and Disks, ...	1 00
Pipe Paradox and Balls, ...	1 00
Water Hose and Jet, ...	1 00
Brass Jet, ...	50
Water Pan and Tube, ...	75
Bladder, Cup, Cap, and Cock, ...	2 00
Stopcock Leathers, ...	50
Pair of Water Pumps, ...	12 00
Hydrostatic Bellows, ...	10 00
Electric Machine, 24 inch Plate, ..	50 00
Battery of six Jars, ...	14 00
Atmospheric Jar, ...	3 00
Diamond Jar, ...	3 00
Movable Coatings, ...	3 00
Electrometer Jar, ...	1 50
Directing Rod, ...	2 00
Jointed Discharger, ...	3 50
Universal Discharger, ...	8 00
Spiral Tube, ...	2 50
Pithball Electrometer, ...	75
Insulating Stool, ...	6 00
Set of Bells, ...	3 00
Dancing Image Plates, ...	3 00
Pair of Dancing Images, ...	50
Box of Pithballs, ...	50
Sportsman and Birds, ...	75
Powder Bomb, ...	1 25
Wax Friction Cylinder, ...	1 50
Glass Friction Cylinder, ...	1 50
Quadrant Electrometer, ...	2 00
Gold Leaf Electrometer, ...	3 00
Thunder House and Fixtures, ...	5 00
Hydrogen Generator, ...	4 00
Long-Haired Man, ...	50
Float Wheel and Point, ...	1 00
S and Point, ...	75
Abbe Nolet's Globe, ...	3 00
Seasons Machine, ...	1 50
Igniting Spoon, ...	75
Miser's Plate, ...	2 00
Bucket and Syphon, ...	1 00

Item	Price
Box of Amalgam, ...	50
Pair of Gasometers and Fixtures, .	35 00
Oxygen Retort, ...	2 00
Lead Conducting Tube, ...	1 50
Pair of Reflectors, ...	8 00
Spirit Boiler, ...	2 50
Radiating Cubes, ...	2 00
Pyrometer, ...	3 00
Lamp Stand, ...	2 00
Conductometer, ...	2 00
Pendent Spoons, ...	1 25
Fire Syringe and Tinder, ...	1 50
Set of Wire Gauze, ...	50
Large Gas Bag and Cock, ...	5 00
Crucibles, ...	20
Chemical Thermometer, ...	2 50
Spirit Lamp, ...	1 00
Dropping Tube, ...	20
Graduated Measure, Oz., ...	1 00
Measure, ten cubic inches, ...	1 25
Six Test Tubes, ...	75
Flasks, six, ...	2 20
Tunnel, Glass, ...	25
Flat Flasks, three, ...	1 25
Globe Receivers, two, ...	80
Tubular Retorts, six, ...	2 50
Glass Evaporating Dishes, three, .	60
Wedgwood Mortar and Pestle, ...	1 00
Hydrogen Balloon, ...	2 00
Stirring Rods, three, ...	25
Bologna Vials, six, ...	50
Rupert's Drops, dozen, ...	50
Matrasses, two, ...	70
Candle Bombs, dozen, ...	50
Steam Globe and Jet, ...	1 50
Wollaston's Steam Apparatus, ...	3 00
Marset's Steam Globe, ...	25 00
Chemical Substances, ...	15 00
Sulphate Copper Battery, ...	8 00
Bar Magnet, ...	1 00
U Magnet and Wheel, ...	3 00
Bar Armature, ...	25
Y Armature, ...	50
Star Armature, ...	75
Magnetic Needle and Stand, ...	1 00
Powder Cup, ...	50
Voltaic Pistol, ...	3 00
Electro Magnet, ...	2 00
Coil and Hem. Magnets, ...	3 50
Magnetizing Helix, ...	3 00
Galvanometer, ...	3 00
Terrestrial Helix, ...	2 00
De la Rive's Ring, ...	1 25
Bell Engine, ...	12 00
Revolving Electro Magnet, ...	5 00
Thermo-Electric Arch, ...	5 00
Analysis of Shocks Apparatus, ...	12 00
Shocking Handles, ...	1 50
Connecting Wires, ...	50
Decomposing Cell, ...	3 00
	173 00
Pneumatics, &c., ...	200 00
Electrics, ...	132 00
Chemicals, ...	120 00
Magnetics, &c., ...	75 00
	$700 00

SET OF PHILOSOPHICAL APPARATUS.

No. 7, marked [7] in Catalogue.

Item	Price
Set of Collision Balls,	6 00
Centre of Gravity Apparatus,	7 00
Whirling Machine, &c.,	8 00
Mechanical Powers,	35 00
Set of Lenses,	6 00
Prism,	2 00
Compound Microscope,	18 00
Orrery,	7 00
Pair 13 inch high-mounted Globes,	45 00
Magic Lantern,	25 00
Astronomical Illustrations,	20 00
Seasons Machine,	7 00
Air Pump,	85 00
Bell Glass, open, swelled,	6 00
Bell Glass, brass capped,	3 50
Tall Bell Glass and Jar,	3 00
Freezing Apparatus, 12 inch,	6 00
Expansion Apparatus,	2 00
Hand Glass, swelled,	1 00
Bladder Cup, Cap, and Cock,	2 00
Hemispherical Cups,	7 00
Upward Pressure Apparatus,	9 00
Dozen Bursting Squares,	1 75
Cap Valve for do.,	25
Wire Guard for do.,	75
Set of Screw Couplers, five,	2 50
Bell for Vacuo,	1 25
Sliding Rod for do.,	2 00
Vane Mill for Vacuo,	7 00
Sheet Rubber Bag, &c.,	2 00
Artificial Fountain and Jets,	4 00
Tall Bolthead and Cap,	1 50
Bacchus Illustration,	3 00
Mercury Tunnel,	1 00
Guinea and Feather Tube,	7 00
Water Hammer, Cap, and Cock,	3 00
Chamberlain's Barometer,	7 00
Vacuum Gauge,	3 50
Weighing Air Apparatus,	15 00
Buoyancy of Air Apparatus,	6 00
Double Transferrer,	10 00
Straight Jar,	1 00
Pear Gauge,	3 00
Syphon in Vacuo,	4 00
Glass Condensing Chamber,	10 00
Double Acting Condenser,	8 00
Air Gun Barrel,	1 00
Revolving Jet,	1 25
Stopcock, Int. and Ext. Jets,	2 00
Jet Paradox Tunnel, &c.,	1 50
Water Pan and Tube,	75
Plate Paradox and Disks,	1 25
Pipe Paradox and Balls,	1 25
Water Hose and Jet,	1 00
Straight Brass Jet,	75
Condensation Gauge Syphon,	3 00
Condensation Gauge Globe,	1 50
Condensation Gauge, graduated,	1 50
Dozen Crushing Squares,	1 00
Dozen Sinking Globes,	50
Bell for Condensed Air,	1 25
Thermometer for Condens. Cham.,	1 00

Item	Price
Stopcock Leathers,	50
Pair of Water Pumps,	12 00
Hydrostatic Bellows,	10 00
Hydrostatic Press,	25 00
Thirty inch Plate Machine,	85 00
Battery, six Jars,	14 00
Double Jar,	4 00
Diamond Jar,	3 00
Movable Coatings,	3 00
Atmospheric Jar,	3 00
Electrometer Jar,	2 50
Sliding Directing Rod,	3 00
Jointed Discharger,	3 50
Universal Discharger,	8 00
Spiral Spotted Tube	3 00
Spotted Star,	4 00
Revolving Bell Glass,	2 00
Pithball Electrometer,	1 00
Quadrant do.,	3 00
Gold Leaf do.,	3 00
Insulating Stool,	6 00
Stand, Bell, and Dancing Balls,	2 00
Set of Bells, three,	3 00
Dancing Image Plates,	3 00
Pair of Dancing Images,	50
Assortment of Pithballs,	1 00
Electric Sportsman and Birds,	1 00
Wax Friction Cylinder,	2 00
Glass Friction Cylinder,	2 00
Powder Bomb,	1 25
Thunder House and Fixtures,	6 00
Brass Cannon, &c.	4 00
Hydrogen Generator,	4 00
Long-Haired Man,	75
Float Wheel and Point,	1 50
Abbe Nolet's Globe,	5 00
Electric S. and Point,	1 00
Electric Bucket and Syphon,	1 50
Electric Swing and Image,	2 00
Electric Seasons Machine,	3 50
Electrophorus and Fixtures,	8 00
Electric Igniting Spoon,	1 00
Miser's Plate,	2 00
Inclined Plane and Wheel,	4 00
Pair of Gasometers,	60 00
Iron Retort for Oxygen,	3 00
Lead Conducting Tube,	1 50
Pair of 13 inch Reflectors, in case,	6 00
Spirit Boiler for do.,	2 50
Pair of Radiating Cubes,	2 00
Pyrometer, Rods, and Lamps,	4 00
Two Lamp Stands,	4 00
Conductometer, six Rods,	2 00
Pair of Pendent Spoons,	1 25
Fire Syringe and Tinder,	1 50
Set of Wire Gauze, three,	75
Blowpipe,	50
Elevating Stand, &c.,	1 50
Large Gas Bag and Stopcock,	5 00
Set of Crucibles,	20
Chemical Thermometer	2 50

Item	Price
Spirit Lamp,	1 00
Aphlogistic Lamp,	2 00
Dropping Tube,	25
Graduated Oz. Measure,	1 00
Measure, ten cubic inches,	1 25
Dozen Test Tubes, assorted,	1 50
Graduated Tube, cubic inch,	50
Condensation Tube,	75
Flasks, six, assorted,	2 20
Glass Funnels, two,	60
Flasks, flat bottom, six,	2 50
Globe Receivers, two,	80
Tubular Retorts, six, assorted,	2 50
Chemical Furnace,	10 00
Iron Tube for Decomposing,	1 00
Evaporating Dishes, three,	75
Wedgwood do., five,	1 50
Glass Mortar and Pestle,	1 00
Wedgwood do.,	1 25
Platina Spatula,	1 50
Hydrogen Balloon,	3 00
Stirring Rods, Glass, six,	50
Bologna Vials, dozen,	1 00
Prince Rupert's Drops,	50
Matrasses, three, assorted,	1 10
Alembic,	1 75
Steam Balls, dozen,	50
Brass Steam Globe and Jet,	1 50
Wollaston's Steam Apparatus,	3 00
Marcet's Steam Globe and Fixtures,	25 00
Chamberlain's Steam Flask and Fixtures,	8 00
Sul. Copper Battery,	3 00
Bar Magnet and Keeper,	1 00
U Magnet and Wheel Armature,	3 00
Bar Armature,	50
Y Armature,	50
Star Armature,	50
Magnetic Needle and Stand,	1 00
Galvanic Battery,	25 00
Powder Cup,	50
Voltaic Pistol,	4 00
Electro Magnet,	5 00
Coil and Hem. Magnets,	3 50
Magnetizing Helix,	3 00
Galvanometer,	3 00
Orsted's Galvanometer,	4 00
Terrestrial Helix,	2 00
De la Rive's Ring,	1 25
Bell Engine,	12 00
Revolving Electro Magnet,	5 00
Thermo-Electric Arch,	5 00
Analysis of Shocks Apparatus,	12 00
Shocking Handles,	1 50
Connecting Wires,	50
Magneto-Electric Machine,	40 00
Decomposing Cell,	3 00

Item	Price
Mechanics, Astronomical, Optics, &c.,	230 00
Pneumatics,	250 00
Electrics,	210 00
Chemicals,	200 00
Galvanic, &c.,	120 00
	$1010 00

Item	Price
Set of Chemical Substances, for use with the above Apparatus,	20 00

NOTE.—See page 347, Apparatus, figured and described in Pneumatics, but used in Chemistry.

SCHOOL APPARATUS.

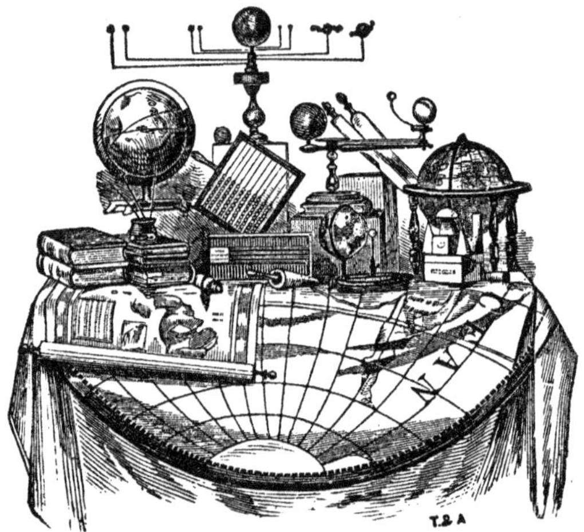

AIDS TO INSTRUCTION,

TO BE FOUND AT

IDE & DUTTON'S, 106 WASHINGTON ST., BOSTON.

Swain's Planetarium,	$15.00	Fowle's Outline Maps,	$4.00
Solar Telluric Globe,	7.00	do. Map of Massachusetts,	5.00
Cornell's Ter. Globe,	3.50	Pelton's Outline Maps,	25.00
Loring's Globes,	$2.50 to 50.00	Mitchell's do. do.	8.00
Copley's 16 in. Globes,	20.00 pair	Bliss's do. do.	7.00
Holbrook's School Apparatus,	$45.00 set	Astronomical Diagrams,	15.00
Numerical Frames,	1.00	Fowle's Physiol. Diagrams,	5.00
Allen's Game of Letters,	50c. to 10.00	Cutter's do. do.	7.00
Black-board Brushes,	50 cts.	Ide's Teacher's Register,	25 cts.
Chalk Crayons,	75 cts. gro.	do. do. Tokens,	25 per 100
Geometrical Solids,	1.25 set	School Rewards, all prices,	
Punctuation Tables,	25 cts.	Ide's Skeleton Maps,	36c. doz.

A Set for every Primary School.

Fowle's Maps,	$4.00
Loring's Semi Frame Globe,	2.50
Numerical Frame,	1.00
Black-board Brush,	50
Numeral Table, Sheet,	25
Punctuation Table, "	25
Articulation Table, "	50
Education Letter Table, Board,	1.50
	10.50

Persons enclosing us Ten Dollars, free of expense, will recive the above set sent as they may direct.

Large Grammar School Set.

Pelton's splendid Maps & Key,	$25.00
Fowle's large Map Massachusetts, (for use in Mass.,)	5.00
Loring's 12 in. Globes, (pair,)	25.00
Swain's Planetarium,	15.00
Fowle's Physiol. Diagrams,	5.00
6 Black-board Brushes,	2.25
1 gross Chalk Crayons,	75
1 set Geometrical Solids,	1.25
1 set Cube Root Blocks,	75
Tonman's Chart of Chemistry,	5.00
	$85.00

Persons enclosing us Eighty Dollars will receive the above set sent as they may direct.

We have also on hand the largest assortment of Maps (both ancient and modern), Atlases and Guide Books, to be found in the city, and a great variety of School Apparatus. Catalogues to be had gratuitous, by application by mail, post paid.

IDE & DUTTON.

Goodyear's Metallic Gum-elastic, or Vulcanized India rubber.

The fabric known as "*Goodyear's Gum-elastic*, or *Vulcanized India rubber*," invented and manufactured by Charles Goodyear, of New Haven, Conn., is capable of many highly useful applications in the school-room, and for educational purposes generally. By the changes wrought by Mr. Goodyear in the construction of his fabrics, all of the remarkable properties of the gum in its native state are preserved and improved, while its defects and objectional features are obviated. There seems to be no limit to the many useful purposes to which it may be applied, in every department of the useful arts, and of practical life, and the public is not yet apprised of its manifold adaptations to humane purposes, and to the protection of life and property. We shall here notice only a few of its many useful applications in the school-room, and for school purposes generally.

Book-binding or Covers.

Several styles of Goodyear's fabrics are admirably adapted to the binding, or covers of school-books. A cover of this material does not crack, or warp, is not injured by water or oil, is not easily soiled, and if soiled, can be readily cleaned. A school-book bound in this way, we have every reason to suppose, will outlast, in the ordinary "wear and tear" of a child's use, (except that of the knife, which ought never to be allowed in a child's hand in the school-room,) a dozen bound in the best style with any kind of leather.

School Books.

Its uses are not confined to covers, but school books can be printed on this fabric, which can be manufactured of suitable thinness for this purpose, and at the same time have a strength of texture, which will not tear, but outlast the best linen paper, and at the same time be readily cleaned when soiled.

When school books are printed on this fabric, and bound in covers of the same, one of the greatest items of educational expense will be reduced.

Maps and Charts.

We have seen beautiful specimens of maps printed on various specimens of a new fabric, recently invented, and called *vegetable leather*, *gum-elastic vellum*, and *metallic tissue*, which will admit of the roughest use, and are capable of being handled for years without any injury, and can be rolled or folded up when not in use. We see no difficulty in printing outline maps, charts, and diagrams of all kinds on this fabric, which can be rolled up when not needed, and which can be washed and wiped clean with sponge, if soiled from use, or from the dust and smoke of the school-room. Both sides of the fabric can be used for the purposes of printing. The outline maps, if made of suitable fabric, can be filled up by the scholar, and the pencil marks erased by the sponge. Maps of this material can be so made as to exhibit the elevations and depressions on the earth's surface.

Globes.

We have seen beautiful specimens of globes, celestial and terrestrial, and of a great variety of sizes, from three inches to three feet, made of the fabric above described, such as *vegetable leather*, or *gum-elastic vellum*. When embossed, they show the elevations and depressions, the mountains and valleys, and water-courses of the earth's surface. When inflated with gas lighter than atmospheric air, they float about the room. If soiled, they can be easily cleaned with the sponge, and will bear the roughest usage. If the great outlines of the globe only are printed, the pupil can be exercised in filling up the blank with a lead pencil. When articles made of this fabric come into demand, our schools can be furnished with globes almost at the price of children's toys, and thus the great objection of expense will no longer prevent the introduction of this piece of apparatus, and of visible illustration, into every school of every grade. When not inflated, the globe of three feet can be packed away in a space of about as many inches.

Floor Cloth, or Carpet.

This fabric is admirably adapted for carpeting the aisles of a school-room, both to prevent reverberation, and to secure cleanliness. It can be easily cleaned, and will wear as long as the floor itself.

Blackboard and Desk Covering.

By using different styles of this fabric, a suitable surface of any desirable size can be obtained for the lead or slate pencil, which can be attached permanently to a wall, or be made in a portable form.

It can be attached to the top of the desk, and thereby prevent all reverberation. When thus applied, it will not gather dust, or wear out, like cloth, but can be kept clean with a sponge, and will wear as long as the wood itself. The fabric used for covering a desk, can be of the same style of fabric as that used for a blackboard or slate, and thus answer all the purposes of either of these articles of apparatus.

Sponge.

An article is made of the gum, leavened and raised like bread, and called a sponge, from its close resemblance, in texture and uses, to the natural sponge. It is the best article which we have seen for erasing marks made by a lead or slate pencil, or chalk, on paper, slate, or blackboard, or prepared surface of any kind in the nature of the blackboard or slate. Besides answering all the purposes of the sponge in such applications, it will remove the oiliness which is frequently communicated to the slate by the hand, &c. It is also invaluable as a mop, or scrub, or shoe mat, at the door of the school-house, as it is not injured by exposure, or the roughest and most constant usage.

Pen and Pencil Wiper.

The article used for making the sponge can also be made into a pen-wiper, and can be attached to the inkstand, (which can also be manufactured of the same material.) It can also be attached to the end of the lead pencil, or to the port-crayon, or handle for the more convenient use of the crayon, chalk, or slate pencil. It will work much closer than the native gum, and is admirably adapted to drawing purposes.

Calisthenic Exercises.

Every school, and especially every school for girls and young ladies, should be supplied with swings, and other apparatus for developing, expanding, and strengthening the muscles of the chest, arms, &c., and for these purposes several styles of this fabric are admirably adapted.

Drawing and Writing Tablets.

One style of the improved metallic fabric is admirably adapted as a substitute for paper or slate, for introductory exercises in writing and drawing, as each impression of the pencil can be removed by the sponge, and a fresh, clean surface as constantly secured. The same material can be used for books for memoranda, records of attendance, returns of school committees, &c.

The excellence of this fabric for all school purposes, as compared with paper, and other materials used for similar purposes, consists in its durability and economy.

LIBRARY.

Every school should be furnished with a Library which should include,

1. Books on schools and school-systems, for the use of school officers and parents; and on the theory and practice of teaching, for the professional instruction of teachers.

2. Books of reference, for the use principally of teachers.

3. Books for circulation among the pupils.

4. Books for circulation among the parents, and inhabitants of the District, or neighborhood.

In the arrangement, and furniture of a school-house, provision should be made for the Library.

The following catalogue may assist those who are charged with the purchase of books:

Books on Education.

The School and School-master, by Alonzo Potter, (Bishop of Pennsylvania,) and George B. Emerson. New York: Harper and Brothers. Boston: Fowle and Capen. Price $1.00. 551 pages.

This volume was prepared at the request of the late James Wadsworth, of Geneseo, New York, with special reference to the condition and wants of common schools in that State. Its general principles and most of its details are applicable to similar schools in other parts of the country, and, indeed, to all seminaries employed in giving elementary instruction. Mr. Wadsworth directed a copy of it to be placed in each of the school libraries of New York, at his expense, and his noble example was followed in respect to the schools of Massachusetts, by the Hon. Martin Brimmer, of Boston.

CONTENTS. PART I. Introduction. Chapter I. Education of the People. *Sec.* I. What is Education. *Sec.* II. Prevailing Errors in regard to the Nature and End of Education. *Sec.* III. The same Subject continued. *Sec.* IV. Same Subject continued. *Sec.* V. What is the Education most needed by the American People. *Sec.* VI. The Importance of Education, 1. To the Individual. *Sec.* VII. The Importance of Education, 2. To Society.

Chapter II. Common Schools. *Sec.* I. Relation of Common Schools to other Means of Education. *Sec.* II. *Present State of Common Schools.*—1. School-houses. 2. Manners. 3. Morals. *Sec.* III. *Same Subject continued.*—4. Intellectual Instruction. 5. Irregular Attendance. *Sec.* IV. *How can Common Schools be improved?*—1. Discussion. 2. Female Teachers. 3. Union or High Schools. 4. Consolidation of Districts. *Sec.* V. *The Improvement of Common Schools continued.* Organization in Cities.—1. District System. 2. Monitorial. 3. Fächer System. 4. American system. 5. Diversity of Class-books. *Sec.* VI. *Same Subject, continued.*—Education of Teachers.

CONTENTS. PART II. Introduction. Book I. Qualities. *Chap.* I. Mental and Moral, important in a Teacher. *Chap.* II. Health. Exercise. Diet. Sleep. Recreation.

Book II. Studies. *Chap.* I. Laws of the Creation. *Chap.* II. Natural Laws. *Chap.* III. Independence of the Natural Laws. *Chap.* IV. Higher Studies. *Chap.* V. Advantages of a Teacher's Life.

Book III. Duties. *Chap.* I, To Himself. Self-Culture. *Chap.* II. To his Pupils, to give them means of Knowledge. *Chap.* III. To his Pupils, to form their Moral Character. *Chap.* IV. To his Pupils, Cultivation of their Powers. *Chap.* V. Communication of Knowledge. *Chap.* VI. To his Fellow-Teachers. *Chap.* VII. To Parents and the Community.

Book IV. The School. *Chap.* I. Organization. *Chap.* II. Instruction. General Principles. *Chap.* III. Teaching: 1. Reading. 2. Spelling. 3. Grammar. 4. Writing. 5. Drawing. 6. Arithmetic. 7. Accounts. 8. Geography. 9. History. 10. Physiology. 11. Composition. *Chap.* IV. Government.

BOOK V. THE SCHOOL-HOUSE. *Chap.* I. Situation. *Chap.* II. Size. *Chap.* III. Position and Arrangement. *Chap.* IV. Light. Warming. Ventilation.

THE TEACHER'S MANUAL, by Thomas H. Palmer. Boston: Marsh, Capen, Lyon & Webb, 1840. pp. 263. Price, 75 cents.

This work received the prize of five hundred dollars, offered by the American Institute of Instruction, in 1838, for "the best Essay on a system of Education best adapted to the Common Schools of our country."

CONTENTS. PART I. *Chapter* I. Introductory. *Chapter* II. Who are our Schoolmasters. *Chapter* III. Physical Education. *Chapter* IV. Intellectual Education. *Chapter* V. Intellectual Education, continued. *Chapter* VI. Moral Education. *Chapter* VII. Recapitulation.

PART II. *Chapter* I. Introductory. *Chapter* II. Physical Education. *Chapter* III. Physical Education, continued. *Chapter* IV. Physical Education, continued. *Chapter* V. Intellectual Education. *Chapter* VI. Intellectual Education, continued. *Chapter* VII. Intellectual Education, continued. *Chapter* VIII. Intellectual Education, continued. *Chapter* IX. Intellectual Education, continued. *Chapter* X. Intellectual Education, concluded. *Chapter* XI. Moral Education. *Chapter* XII. Moral Education, continued. *Chapter* XIII. Conclusion.

THE TEACHER TAUGHT, by Emerson Davis, late Principal of the Westfield Academy. Boston: Marsh, Capen, Lyon & Webb, 1839. pp. 79. Price 37½ cents.

This valuable work was first published in 1833, as "An Abstract of a Course of Lectures on School-keeping."

SLATE AND BLACKBOARD EXERCISES, By William A. Alcott. New York: Mark H. Newman. Price 37 cents.

The chapters in this little work were first published in the Connecticut Common School Journal, in 1841. The various suggestions and methods are highly practical.

THEORY AND PRACTICE OF TEACHING, by David P. Page, Principal of the New York State Normal School. New York: A. S. Barnes & Co.

CONTENTS. CHAPTER I. The Spirit of the Teacher. CHAPTER II. Responsibility of the Teacher. *Sec.* I. The Neglected Tree. *Sec.* II. Extent of Responsibility. *Sec.* III. The Auburn Prison. CHAPTER III. Habits of the Teacher. CHAPTER IV. Literary Qualifications of the Teacher. CHAPTER V. Right Views of Education. CHAPTER VI. Right Modes of Teaching. *Sec.* I. Pouring-in Process. *Sec.* II. Drawing-out Process. *Sec.* III. The more Excellent Way. *Sec.* IV. Waking up Mind. *Sec.* V. Remarks. CHAPTER VII. Conducting Recitations. CHAPTER VIII. Exciting an Interest in Study. *Sec.* I. Incentives. Emulation. *Sec.* II. Prizes and Rewards. *Sec.* III. Proper Incentives. CHAPTER IX. School Government. *Sec.* I. Requisites in the Teacher for Government. *Sec.* II. Means of securing Good Order. *Sec.* III. Punishments, Improper, Proper. *Sec.* IV. Corporal Punishment. *Sec.* V. Limitations and Suggestions. CHAPTER X. School Arrangements. *Sec.* I. Plan of Day's Work. *Sec.* II. Interruptions. *Sec.* III. Recesses. *Sec.* IV. Assignment of Lessons. *Sec.* V. Reviews. *Sec.* VI. Examinations, Exhibitions, Celebrations. CHAPTER XI. The Teacher's Relation to the Parents of his Pupils. CHAPTER XII. The Teacher's Care of his Health. CHAPTER XIII. The Teacher's Relation to his Profession. CHAPTER XIV. Miscellaneous Suggestions. *Sec.* I. Things to be avoided. *Sec.* II. Things to be performed. CHAPTER XV. The Rewards of the Teacher.

HINTS AND METHODS FOR THE USE OF TEACHERS. Hartford: Price 25 cents.

This volume is made up principally of selections from publications on methods of teaching, not easily accessible; and under each subject discussed, reference is made to various volumes, where additional suggestions can be found.

THE DISTRICT SCHOOL AS IT WAS, by one who went to it, (*Rev. Warren Burton.*) New York: J. Orville Taylor, 1838.

In this amusing picture of "the lights and shadows" of school life as it was in New England twenty years ago, the teachers and scholars of some of our District Schools as they are, will recognize the school-house, books, practices, and methods with which they are too familiar.

Confessions of a School-master, by Dr. William A. Alcott. New York: Mark H. Newman. Price 50 cents.

If our teachers will read these confessions of errors of omission and commission, and the record which it gives of real excellencies attained by the steps of a slow and laborious progress, they will save themselves the mortification of the first, and realize earlier the fruits of the last. Few men have the moral courage to look their former bad methods so directly in the face. Every young teacher should read this book.

CONTENTS. Chapter I. My Introduction to School Keeping. *Section* I. Preparation and Engagement. *Section* II. The Examination. *Section* III. My Cogitations.

Chapter II. My First Year. *Section* I. First day of School. *Section* II. General Course of Instruction. *Section* III. Particular Errors. *Section* IV. Religious Exercises.

Chapter III. My Second Year. *Section* I. Course of Instruction. *Section* II. Serious Mistakes.

Chapter IV. My Third Year. *Section* I. Complaint to the Grand Jurors. *Section* II. Introduction of a New School Book. *Section* III. Meeting of the Schools.

Chapter V. Fourth and Fifth Years. *Section* I. Modes of Punishing. *Section* II. Attending to other Employments. *Section* III. Late Evening Visits. *Section* IV. Studies and Methods.

Chapter VI. My Sixth Year. *Section* I. Teaching by the Year. Terms and Object. *Section* II. Description of the School and School-house. *Section* III. First Efforts at Improvement. Punctuality. *Section* IV. Methods and Discipline. *Section* V. Schools Neglected by Parents. *Section* VI. School Libraries. *Section* VII. Improper Company. Example.

Chapter VII. My Seventh Year. *Section* I. Divided Attention. *Section* II. Teaching on the Sabbath.

Chapter VIII. My Eighth Year. *Section* I. General Account of my School. *Section* II. Causes of Failure.

Chapter IX. My Ninth Year. *Section* I. A Novel Enterprise. *Section* II. Methods of Teaching. Discipline.

Chapter X. My Experience as a School Visitor. *Section* I. Examination of Teachers. *Section* II. Special Visits to Schools. *Section* III. Meetings for Improvement. *Section* IV. Introduction of a New Reading Book.

Chapter XI. My Tenth Year in School. *Section* I. Commencement of School. *Section* II. Spelling, Reading, Writing, etc. *Section* III. Teaching Geography. *Section* IV. A Practical Exercise. *Section* V. Experiment in Teaching Etymology. *Section* VI. Teaching Orthography. *Section* VII. Forcing Knowledge. *Section* VIII. Teaching Pupils to sit still. *Section* IX. My Moral Influence. *Section* X. My Ill Health. *Section* XI. Countenancing the Sports of my Pupils. *Section* XII. Discipline.

The School Teacher's Manual, by Henry Dunn, Secretary of the British and Foreign School Society, London. Hartford: Reed & Barber, 1839. pp. 223. Price 50 cents.

The American edition of this work is edited by Rev. Thomas H. Gallaudet, which is the best evidence that could be given of the general soundness of the views presented by the English author.

Teachers' Institute, by W. B. Fowle. Boston.

Teaching a Science: The Teacher an Artist, by Rev. B. R. Hall. New York: Baker & Scribner.

Corporal Punishment, by Lyman Cobb. New York: Mark H. Newman.

School Keeping, by an Experienced Teacher. Philadelphia: John Grigg, 1831.

The School-master's Friend, with the Committee-man's Guide, by Theodore Dwight, Jr. pp. 360. New York, Roe Lockwood, 415, Broadway, 1835.

The Teacher, or Moral Influences in the Instruction and Government of the Young, by Jacob Abbott. Boston, Whipple & Damrell, No. 9 Cornhill, Boston. Price 75 cents.

Theory of Teaching, with a few practical Illustrations, by a Teacher. Boston: E. P. Peabody, 1841. pp. 128.

District School, by J. Orville Taylor. New York: Harper & Brothers, 1834.

Lectures on Education, by Horace Mann, Secretary of the Massachusetts Board of Education. Boston: Fowle & Capen, 1845. Pp. 338. Price $1.00.

This volume embraces seven lectures, most of which were delivered before the Annual Common School Conventions, held in the several counties of Massachusetts, in 1838, '39, '40, '41, and '42. They are published in this form at the request of the Board of Education. No man, teacher, committee, parent, or friend of education generally, can read these lectures without obtaining much practical knowledge, and without being fired with a holy zeal in the cause.

CONTENTS. *Lecture* I. Means and Objects of Common School Education. *Lecture* II Special Preparation, a prerequisite to Teaching. *Lecture* III. The Necessity of Education in a Republican Government. *Lecture* IV. What God does, and what He leaves for Man to do, in the work of Education. *Lecture* V. An Historical View of Education; showing its Dignity and its Degradation. *Lecture* VI. On District School Libraries. *Lecture* VII. On School Punishments.

Locke and Milton on Education. Boston: Gray & Brown, 1830.

The Education of Mothers, by L. Aimé-Martin. Philadelphia: Lea & Blanchard, 1843.

Education and Health, by Amariah Brigham. Boston: Marsh, Capen & Lyon, 1843.

Dr. Channing on Self Culture. Boston: Monroe & Co. Price 33 cents.

Miss Sedgwick on Self Training, or Means and Ends. New York: Harper & Brothers.

These two volumes,—the first written with special reference to young men, and the last, to young women, should be read by all young teachers, who would make their own individual character, attainments, and conduct, the basis of all improvement in their profession.

The following works have special reference to instruction in Infant and Primary Schools:

Exercises for the Senses. London: Charles Knight & Co. Published under the superintendence of the Society for the Diffusion of Useful Knowledge.

Lessons on Objects: as given to children between the ages of six and eight, in a Pestalozzian School at Cheam, Sussex, by C. Mayo. London: Seeley, Burnside & Seeley, Fleet street, 1845.

Lessons on Shells, as given to children between the ages of eight and ten, and by the author of "Lessons on Objects." London: Seeley, Burnside & Seeley, 1846.

Patterson's Zoology for Schools. London.

Model Lessons for Infant School Teachers, by the author of "Lessons on Objects." Parts I. and II. London: Seeley, Burnside & Seeley, 1846.

Wilderspin's Infant System. London: James S. Hodgson, 112 Fleet street.

Wilderspin's Elementary Education. London: James S. Hodgson.

Chambers' Educational Course,—Infant Education, from two to six years of age. Edinburgh: W. R. Chambers.

Practical Education, by Maria Edgeworth. New York: Harper & Brothers, 1835.

The Teacher and Parent; a Treatise upon Common School Education. By Charles Northend. New York: A. S. Barnes & Co. Price 75 cents.

This is a valuable treatise, full of practical suggestions to teachers and parents, by one who has felt the want of such suggestions while acting as teacher of the Epes Grammar School in Salem, and more recently as Superintendent of Public Schools, in Danvers, Mass.

CONTENTS, PART I. Chapter I. Common Schools. II. The Teacher. III. Thorough Knowledge, Aptness to Teach, Accuracy, Patience, and Perseverance. IV. Candor, Truthfulness, and Courteousness. V. Ingenuity, Individuality. VI. Kindness, Gentleness, Forbearance, and Cheerfulness. VII. Common Sense, Knowledge of Human Nature, General Information, Desire to do Good, and Hopefulness. VIII. Correct Moral Principles, Exemplary Habits and Deportment; Diligence. IX. Neatness and Order; Self-Control. X. Earnestness, Energy, Enthusiasm. XI. Judgment and Prudence; System and Punctuality; Independence. XII. Professional Feeling and Interest; a Deep and Well-grounded Interest in Teaching. XIII. Means of Improvement. XIV. Teaching. XV. Discipline. XVI. Means of Interesting Pupils and Parents. XVII. Moral Instruction. XVIII. Emulation and Prizes. XIX. Primary Schools. XX. Lessons and Recitations. XXI. Examinations and Exhibitions. XXII. Multiplicity of Studies. XXIII. Reading. XXIV. Spelling. XXV. Penmanship. XXVI. Geography. XXVII. Grammar. XXVIII. Letter Writing and Composition. XXIX. Arithmetic. XXX. Book-Keeping; Declamation. XXXI. Singing. XXXII. Miscellaneous.

PART II. Chapter I. Introductory Remarks. II. School Houses. III. Children should not be sent to School too Young. IV. To Provide Good Teachers. V. School Supervision. VI. Parents should Encourage the Teacher. VII. Specific Duties. VIII. Candor and Charitableness. IX. High and Honorable Motives.

American Education; its Principles and Elements. By Edward D. Mansfield. New York: A. S. Barnes & Co., 1853.

This is a philosophical discussion of the principles, and not a practical treatise on the modes of instruction, in the several subjects treated of.

CONTENTS. Chapter I. The idea of a Republic. II. Means of perpetuating Civil and Religious Liberty. III. The idea of American Education. IV. The Teacher—his qualifications, teaching, and character. V. The idea of Science. VI. The Utility of Mathematics. VII. The Utility of Astronomy. VIII. The Utility of History. IX. The Science of Language. X. Literature a Means of Education. XI. Conversation an Instructor. XII. The Constitution the Law-book of the Nation. XIII. The Bible the Law-book from Heaven. XIV. The Education of Women. Elementary Ideas. The Future.

The Teacher's Institute; or, Familiar Hints to Young Teachers. By William B. Fowle. Boston: Lemuel N. Ide, 1849. Price 75 cents.

Mr. Fowle has had a long and successful experience as a teacher, particularly in the monitorial system, and has been eminently successful in conducting the exercises of Teachers' Institutes, or gatherings of young teachers for the purpose of instruction, in the matter and manner of teaching. This volume embraces the results of his experience, both as a teacher of children and of teachers.

CONTENTS. Reading. Spelling. Arithmetic. Mental Arithmetic. Writing. Drawing. Lectures on Geography. Remarks on Geography. Lecture on the Uses and Abuses of Memory. English Grammar. Composition. Letters on the Monitorial System. Remarks on the Use of Monitors. Neatness. The Opening and Closing of School. Music. Emulation and Discipline. Conclusion.

Popular Education; for the use of Teachers and Parents. By Ira Mayhew. New York: Burgess & Cady. Price 75 cents.

This Treatise was prepared and published in accordance with a resolution of the Senate and House of Representatives of the State of Michigan, by the author, while Superintendent of Public Instruction.

CONTENTS. Chapter I. In what does a correct Education consist? II. The Importance of Physical Education. III. Physical Education—The Laws of Health. IV. The Laws of Health—Philosophy of Respiration. V. The Nature of Intellectual and Moral Education. VI. The Education of the Five Senses. VII. The Necessity of Moral and Religious Education. VIII. The Importance of Popular Education. Education dissipates the Evils of Ignorance. Education increases the productiveness of Labor. Education diminishes Pauperism and Crime. Education increases human Happiness. IX. Political Necessity of National Education. The Practicability of National Education. X. The Means of Universal Education. Good School-houses should be provided. Well-qualified Teachers should be employed. Schools should continue through the Year. Every Child should attend School. The redeeming Power of Common Schools. Index.

LECTURES AND PROCEEDINGS OF THE AMERICAN INSTITUTE OF INSTRUCTION from 1830 to 1853.

These volumes embrace more than 150 lectures and essays, on a great variety of important topics, by some of the ablest scholars and most successful teachers in the country.

CONTENTS.—VOL. I, for 1830. Introductory Discourse, by *President Wayland*. *Lecture* I. Physical Education, by *John C. Warren*, M. D. *Lecture* II. The Development of the Intellectual Faculties, and on Teaching Geography, by *James G. Carter*. *Lecture* III. The Infant School System, by *William Russell*. *Lecture* IV. The Spelling of Words, and a Rational Method of Teaching their Meaning, by *Gideon F. Thayer*. *Lecture* V. Lyceums and Societies for the Diffusion of Useful Knowledge, by *Nehemiah Cleaveland*. *Lecture* VI. Practical Method of Teaching Rhetoric, by *Samuel P. Newman*. *Lecture* VII. Geometry and Algebra, by *F. J. Grund*. *Lecture* VIII. The Monitorial System of Instruction, by *Henry K. Oliver*. *Lecture* IX. Vocal Music, by *William C. Woodbridge*. *Lecture* X. Linear Drawing, by *Walter R. Johnson*. *Lecture* XI. Arithmetic, by *Warren Colburn*. *Lecture* XII. Classical Learning, by *Cornelius C. Felton*. *Lecture* XIII. The Construction and Furnishing of School-Rooms and School Apparatus, by *William J. Adams*.

VOL. II, for 1831. Introductory Lecture, by *James Walker*. *Lecture* I. Education of Females, by *George B. Emerson*. *Lecture* II. Moral Education, by *Jacob Abbott*. *Lecture* III. Usefulness of Lyceums, by *S. C. Phillips*. *Lecture* IV. Education of the Five Senses, by *William H. Brooks*. *Lecture* V. The Means which may be employed to stimulate the Student without the aid of Emulation, by *John L. Parkhurst*. *Lecture* VI. Grammar, by *Goold Brown*. *Lecture* VII. Influence of Academies and High Schools on Common Schools, by *William C. Fowler*. *Lecture* VIII. Natural History as a Branch of Common Education, by *Clement Durgin*. Prize Essay on School-Houses, by *W. A. Alcott*.

VOL. III, for 1832.—Introductory Discourse, by *Francis C. Gray*. *Lecture* I. The best Methods of Teaching the Living Languages, by *George Ticknor*. *Lecture* II. Some of the Diseases of a Literary Life, by *G. Hayward*, M. D. *Lecture* III. The Utility of Visible Illustrations, by *Walter R. Johnson*. *Lecture* IV. The Moral Influences of Physical Science, by *John Pierpont*. *Lecture* V. Prize Essay, on the Teaching of Penmanship, by *B. B. Foster*. *Lecture* VI. Nature and Means of Early Education, as deduced from Experience, by *A. B. Alcott*. *Lecture* VII. On Teaching Grammar and Composition, by *Asa Rand*.

VOL. IV, for 1833.—Introductory Lecture, by *William Sullivan*. *Lecture* I. On the Importance of a Knowledge of the Principles of Physiology to Parents and Teachers, by *Edward Reynolds*, M. D. *Lecture* II. The Classification of Schools, by *Samuel M. Burnside*. *Lecture* III. Primary Education, by *Gardner B. Perry*. *Lecture* IV. Emulation in Schools by *Leonard Withington*. *Lecture* V. The best Method of Teaching the Ancient Languages, by *Alpheus S. Packard*. *Lecture* VI. Jacotot's Method of Instruction, by *George W. Greene*. *Lecture* VII. The best Method of Teaching Geography, by *W. C. Woodbridge*. *Lecture* VIII. Necessity of Educating Teachers, by *Samuel R. Hall*. *Lecture* IX. The Adaptation of Intellectual Philosophy to Instruction, by *Abijah R. Baker*. *Lecture* X. The best Mode of Teaching Natural Philosophy, by *Benjamin Hale*.

VOL. V, 1834.—Introductory Lecture, by *Caleb Cushing*. *Lecture* I. The best Mode of Fixing the Attention of the Young, by *Warren Burton*. *Lecture* II. The Improvement which may be made in the Condition of Common Schools, by *Stephen Farley*. *Lecture* III. Duties of Parents in regard to the Schools where their Children are Instructed, by *Jacob Abbott*. *Lecture* IV. Maternal Instruction and Management of Infant Schools, by *M. M. Carll*. *Lecture* V. Teaching the Elements of Mathematics, by *Thomas Sherwin*. *Lecture* VI The Dangerous Tendency to Innovations and Extremes in Education, by *Hubbard Winslow*. *Lecture* VII. Union of Manual with Mental Labor, in a System of Education, by *Beriah Green*. *Lecture* VIII. The History and Uses of Chemistry, by *C. T. Jackson*. *Lecture* IX. Natural History as a Study in Common Schools, by *A. A. Gould*, M. D. *Lecture* X. Science of Government as a Branch of Popular Education, by *Joseph Story*.

VOL. VI, for 1835.—Introductory Lecture, by *W. H. Furness*. *Lecture* I. The Study of the Classics, by *A. Crosby*. *Lecture* II. Education for an Agricultural People, by *Samuel Nott, Jr.* *Lecture* III. Political Influence of Schoolmasters, by *E. Washburn*. *Lecture* IV. State and Prospects of the German Population of this Country, by *H. Bokum*. *Lecture* V. Religious Education, by *R. Park*. *Lecture* VI. Importance of an Acquaintance with the Philosophy of the Mind to an Instructor, by *J. Gregg*. *Lecture* VII. Ends of School Discipline, by *Henry L. McKean*. *Lecture* VIII. Importance and Means of Cultivating the Social Affections among Pupils, by *J. Blanchard*. *Lecture* IX. Meaning and Objects of Education, by *T. B. Fox*. *Lecture* X. Management of a Common School, by *T. Dwight, Jr.* *Lecture* XI. Moral and Spiritual Culture in Early Education, by *R. C. Waterston*. *Lecture* XII. Moral Uses of the Study of Natural History, by *W. Channing*, M. D. *Lecture* XIII. Schools of the Arts, by *W. Johnson*.

VOL. VII., for 1836.—*Lecture* I. Education of the Blind, by *Samuel G. Howe*, M. D. *Lecture* II. Thorough Teaching, by *William H. Brooks*. *Lecture* III. Physiology, or "The House I live in," by *William A. Alcott*. *Lecture* IV. Incitements to Moral and Intellectual Well-Doing, by *J. H. Belcher*. *Lecture* V. Duties of Female Teachers of Common Schools, by *Daniel Kimball*. *Lecture* VI. Methods of Teaching Elocution in Schools, by *T. D. P. Stone*. *Lecture* VII. Influence of Intellectual Action on Civilization, by *H. R. Cleaveland*. *Lecture* VIII. School Discipline, by *S. R. Hall*.

VOL. VIII., for 1837.—Introductory Discourse, by Rev. *Elipha White*. *Lecture* I. Study of the Classics, by *John Mulligan*. *Lecture* II. Moral Education, by *Joshua Bates*. *Lecture* III. Study of Natural History, by *John Lewis Russell*. *Lecture* IV. Comparative Merits of Private and Public Schools, by *Theodore Edson*. *Lecture* V. Elocution, by *David Fosdick, Jr.* *Lec-*

ture VI. Relation between the Board of Trustees and the Faculty of a University, &c., by *Jasper Adams*. *Lecture* VII. School Reform, or Teachers' Seminaries, by *Charles Brooks*. *Lecture* VIII. Teaching of Composition in Schools, by *R. G. Parker*. *Lecture* IX. Evils of the Present System of Primary Instruction, by *Thomas H. Palmer*. *Lecture* X. Reading and Declamation, by *William Russell*.

VOL. IX, for 1838.—*Lecture* I. Literary Responsibility of Teachers, by *Charles White*. *Lecture* II. The Head and the Heart; or, The Relative Importance of Intellectual and Moral Culture, by *Elisha Bartlett*. *Lecture* III. Vocal Music in Common Schools, by *Joseph Harrington, Jr.* *Lecture* IV. Model Schools, by *Thomas D. James*. *Lecture* V. Observations on the School System of Connecticut, by *Denison Olmsted*. *Lecture* VI. Teaching of English Grammar, by *R. G Parker*. *Lecture* VII. Mutual Duties of Parents and Teachers, by *David P. Page*. *Lecture* VIII. Man, the Subject of Education, by *Samuel G. Goodrich*.

VOL. X, for 1839 —Introductory Discourse, The Education of a Free People, by *Robert Rantoul, Jr.* *Lecture* I. Physiology of the Skin, by *John G. Metcalf*, M. D. *Lecture* II. Mind and its Developments, by *Emerson Davis*. *Lecture* III. A Classic Taste in our Common Schools, by *Luther B. Lincoln*. *Lecture* IV. Natural Theology as a Study in Schools, by *Henry A. Miles*. *Lecture* V. Division of Labor in Instruction, by *Thomas Cushing, Jr.* *Lecture* VI. The Claims of our Age and Country upon Teachers, by *David Mack*. *Lecture* VII. Progress of Moral Science, and its Application to the Business of Practical Life, by *Alexander H. Everett*. *Lecture* VIII. The Comparative Results of Education, by *T. P. Rodman*, *Lecture* IX. Physical Education, by *Abel L. Pierson*, M. D.

VOL. II, NEW SERIES, for 1840.—*Lecture* I. Intellectual Education in Harmony with Moral and Physical, by *Joshua Bates*. *Lecture* II. Results to be aimed at in School Instruction and Discipline, by *T. Cushing, Jr.* *Lecture* III. Duty of Visiting Schools, by *Thomas A. Greene*. *Lecture* IV. Objects and Means of School Instruction, by *A. B. Muzzey*. *Lecture* V. Courtesy, and its Connection with School Instruction, by *G. F. Thayer*. *Lecture* VI. On the Brain and the Stomach, by *Usher Parsons*, M. D. *Lecture* VII. Common Complaints made against Teachers, by *Jacob Abbott*.

VOL. XII, for 1841.—*Lecture* I. Best Method of Preparing and Using Spelling-Books, by *Horace Mann*. *Lecture* II. Best Method of Exercising the Different Faculties of the Mind, by *Wm. B. Fowle*. *Lecture* III. Education of the Laboring Classes, by *T. Parker*. *Lecture* IV. Importance of the Natural Sciences in our System of Popular Education, by *A. Gray*. *Lecture* V. Moral Culture Essential to Intellectual Education, by *E. W. Robinson*. *Lecture* VI. Simplicity of Character, as Affected by the Common Systems of Education, by *J. S. Dwight*. *Lecture* VII. Use of the Globes in Teaching Geography and Astronomy, by *A. Fleming*. *Lecture* VIII. Elementary Principles of Constitutional Law, as a Branch of Education in Common Schools, by *Edward A. Lawrence*.

VOL. XIII, for 1842.—*Lecture* I. Moral Education, by *George B. Emerson*. *Lecture* II. Universal Language, by *Samuel G. Howe*. *Lecture* III. The Girard College, by *E. C. Wines*. *Lecture* IV. School Room, as an aid to Self-Education, by *A. B. Muzzey*. *Lecture* V. Moral Responsibility of Teachers, by *William H. Wood*. *Lecture* VI. The Teacher's Daily Preparation.

VOL. XIV, for 1843.—*Lecture* I. The Bible in Common Schools, by *Heman Humphrey, D. D.* *Lecture* II. The Classification of Knowledge, by *Solomon Adams*. *Lecture* III. Moral Dignity of the Teacher's Office, by Prof. *I. H. Agnew*. *Lecture* IV. A few of the "Hows" of School-keeping, by *Roger S. Howard*. *Lecture* V. Advancement in the Means and Methods of Public Instruction, by *David P. Page*. *Lecture* VI. Reading, by *C. Pierce*. *Lecture* VII. Some of the Duties of the Faithful Teacher, by *Alfred Greenleaf*. *Lecture* VIII. Some of the Defects of our Systems of Education, by *R. B. Hubbard*. *Lecture* IX. Importance of our Common Schools, by *S. J. May*.

VOL. XV, for 1844.—*Lecture* I. The Religious Element in Education, by *Calvin E. Stowe*. *Lecture* II. Female Education, by *William Russell*. *Lecture* III. Some of the Obstacles to the Greater Success of Common Schools, by *Charles Northend*. *Lecture* IV. Some of the Dangers of Teachers, by *Daniel P. Galloup*. *Lecture* V. Natural History as a Regular Classic in our Seminaries, by *Charles Brooks*. *Lecture* VI. Classical Instruction, by *A. H. Weld*. *Lecture* VII. School Discipline, by *Joseph Hale*. *Lecture* VIII. Methods of Teaching to Read, by *Samuel S. Greene*. *Lecture* IX. The Duty of the American Teacher, by *John N. Bellows*. *Lecture* X. The Necessity of Education in a Republican Form of Government, by *Horace Mann*.

VOL. XVI, for 1845.—*Lecture* I. Dignity of the Teacher's Office, by *Joel Hawes*, D. D. *Address*. The Formation and Excellence of the Female Character, by *Joel Hawes*, D. D. *Lecture* II. The Duties of Examining Committees, by Prof. *E. D. Sanborn*. *Lecture* III. The Perfect Teacher, by *Denison Olmstead*, L. L. D. *Lecture* IV. Physiology, by *Edward Jarvis*, M. D. *Lecture* V. Intellectual Arithmetic, by *F. A. Adams*. *Lecture* VI. County Teachers' Institutes, by *Salem Town*. *Lecture* VII. Geography, by *William B. Fowle*. *Lecture* VIII. Vocal Music in Common Schools, by *A. N. Johnson*. *Lecture* IX. History, by *George S. Hillard*.

VOL. XVII, for 1846.—Journal of Proceedings. List of Officers. Annual Report. *Lecture* I. Home Preparation for School, by *Jason Whitman*. *Lecture* II. The Influence of Moral upon Intellectual Improvement, by *H. B. Hooker*. *Lecture* III. The Essentials of a Common School Education, and the conditions most favorable to their Attainment, by *Rufus Putnam*. *Lecture* IV. The Education of the Faculties, and the Proper Employment of Young Children, by *Samuel J. May*. *Lecture* V. The Obligation of Towns to Elevate the Character of our Common Schools, by *Luther B. Lincoln*. *Lecture* VI. Importance of Cultivating Taste in Early Life, by *Ariel Parish*. *Lecture* VII. On Phonotypy and Phonography, or Speech-Writing and Speech-Printing, by *Stephen P. Andrews*. *Lecture* VIII. On the Study of the English Language, by *D. Huntington*.

VOL. XVIII, for 1847.—Journal of Proceedings. List of Officers. *Lecture* I. On the Study of Language, by *Hubbard Winslow*. *Lecture* II. On the Appropriateness of Studies to the State of Mental Development, by *Thomas P. Rodman*.

VOL. XIX., for 1848. Journal of Proceedings. List of Officers. *Lecture* I. Failures in teaching, by *John Kingsbury*. *Lecture* II. Co-operation of Parents and Teachers, by *Jacob Batchelder*. *Lecture* III. Qualifications of the Teacher, by Rev. *Nathan Munroe*. *Lecture* IV. School Government, by *J. D. Philbrick*. *Lecture* V. The Improvement of Common Schools, by *Wm. D. Swan*.

VOL. XX., for 1849. Journal of Proceedings. List of Officers. *Lecture* I. The Defect of the Principle of Religious Authority in Modern Education, by *John H. Hopkins, D.D.* *Lecture* II. The Education demanded by the peculiar character of our Civil Institutions, by *Benjamin Larabee, D. D.* *Lecture* III. Earnestness, by *Roger S. Howard*. *Lecture* IV. The Essentials of Education, by *Thomas H. Palmer*. *Lecture* V. The Claims of Natural History, as a branch of Common School Education, by *William O. Ayers*. *Lecture* VI. Education the Condition of National Greatness, by Prof. *E. D. Sanborn*. *Lecture* VII. The Duties of Legislatures in relation to the Public Schools in the United States, by Rev. *Charles Brooks*. *Lecture* VIII. Practical Education, by *W. C. Goldthwait*.

VOL. XXI., for 1850. Journal of Proceedings. List of Officers. Annual Report. *Lecture* I. God's Plan for Educating Man, by *C. C. Chase*. *Lecture* II. Political Economy, as a Study for Common Schools, by *Amasa Walker*. *Lecture* III The Importance of Early Training, by *Solomon Jenner*. *Lecture* IV. Characteristics of the True Teacher, by *John D. Philbrick*. *Lecture* V. Influence of the Social Relations in the West upon Professional Usefulness and Success, by *Edward Wyman*. Appendix. Instruction in History. by *Elizabeth P. Peabody*. General Index, from 1830 to 1850. List of Members, Past and Present.

VOL. XXII., for 1851. Journal of Proceedings. List of Officers. Annual Report. *Lecture* I. Teachers' Morals and Manners, by *Henry K. Oliver*. *Lecture* II. The Supervision of Schools, by *D. B. Hagar*. *Lecture* III. The Teacher in the Nineteenth Century, by *Thomas Cushing, Jr.* *Lecture* IV. Importance of Moral and Religious Education in a Republic, by *William D Northend*. *Lecture* V. The Manifestations of Education in Different Ages, by *Samuel W. Bates*. *Lecture* VI. On the Present Condition and Wants of Common Schools, by Rev. *L. W. Leonard*. *Lecture* VII. Methods of Teaching Spelling, by *Christopher A. Green*. *Lecture* VIII. Physical Education, by Rev. *Darwin H. Ranney*.

VOL. XV., for 1852. Proceedings. List of Officers. Annual Report. *Lecture* I. The Incentives to Mental Culture among Teachers, by *James D. Butler*. *Lecture* II. Dr. Thomas Arnold, by *Joshua Bates, Jr.* *Lecture* III Self Reliance, by *William H. Wells*. *Lecture* IV. The School System of the State of New York, by *Joseph McKeen*. *Lecture* V. Essential Elements in American Educatian, by *Charles H. Wheeler*. *Lecture* VI. Drawing, a Means of Education. by *William J. Whitaker*.

VOL. XXIV., for 1853. Journal of Proceedings. List of Officers. Prize Essay, by *E. A. H. Allen*. *Lecture* I. Reading, by *F. T. Russell*. *Lecture* II. Life and Educational Principles of Pestalozzi, by *Hermann Kruisi*.

TRANSACTIONS OF THE WESTERN LITERARY INSTITUTE AND COLLEGE OF PROFESSIONAL TEACHERS, from 1834 to 1840.

The first General Convention of the Teachers of the West was held at Cincinnati, in June 1831, under the auspices of the "Academic Institute," and the proceedings and addresses were published in No. 1, of the Academic Pioneer. The second General Convention was held in October, 1832, at which the teachers organized a Constitution and officers under the name of the "College of Teachers," which held a meeting in October, 1833. In October, 1834, the fourth annual meeting was held at Cincinnati, the proceedings and lectures of which meeting were published, and constitute the first volume of the "Transactions," &c. A volume of Transactions was published every year, from 1834 to 1840.

VOLUME I., for 1834. Journal of Proceedings. Constitution. Names of Members. I. Opening Address, by *Albert Picket*. II The Philosophy of Family, School, and College Discipline. by *Daniel Drake*. III. Study of the Greek and Latin Languages, as a part in the course of a liberal education, by *T. M. Post*. IV. Neither the classics nor the mathematics should form a part of a scheme of General Education in our country, by *Thomas S. Grimke*. V. Utility of the Mathematics, by *E. D. Mansfield*. VI. Report on the question, "Ought the classics to constitute a part of Education," by *Alexander Kinmont*. VII. The application of Principles to Practice, in the various departments of Physical Science, by *Elijah Slack*. VIII. The Government of Public Literary Institutions. by *M. A. H. Niles* IX. The History and Moral Influence of Music, by *William Nixon*. X. The best method of Teaching Languages, by *William Hoopwood*.

TRANSACTIONS OF THE MASSACHUSETTS TEACHERS' ASSOCIATION. Edited by the Secretary. Boston: Samuel Coolidge, 1852.

CONTENTS.—VOL. I., for 1845 to 1847. Origin of the Association. Proceedings of the Association. First Annual Session Second Annual Session. Third Annual Session. *Lecture* I. On the Claims of Teaching to the rank of a Distinct Profession, by *Elbridge Smith*. *Lecture* II. On the first Principles of School Government. by Rev. *J. P. Cowles*. *Lecture* III. On the Management of the School-room, by *Ariel Parish* *Lecture* IV. On Thorough Instruction, by *Joseph Hale*. *Lecture* V. On the Relation of Education to its Age, by *Samuel W. Bates*. *Lecture* VI. On the Relation of Common Schools to Higher Seminaries, by Rev. *Charles Hammond* *Lecture* VII. On Teaching as a Profession, by *N. Wheeler*. Constitution. Index.

The following works will exhibit a pretty full view of the progress and condition of education in Europe.

SMITH'S HISTORY OF EDUCATION. Harper & Brothers. Price 50 cents.

This work is substantially an abridgement of the great German work of Schwartz, and is worthy of an attentive perusal, not only for its historical view of the subject, but for the discussion of the general principles which should be recognized in every system of education.

BIBER'S MEMOIR OF PESTALOZZI, and his plan of Education. London: I. Souter, 1831.

EDUCATIONAL INSTITUTIONS OF DR. FELLENBERG, with an Appendix containing Woodbridge's Sketches of Hofwyl. London: Longman, 1842.

REPORT ON EDUCATION IN EUROPE, by Alexander Dallas Bache. Philadelphia: Lydia R. Bailey, 1829. pp. 666.

REPORT ON ELEMENTARY INSTRUCTION IN EUROPE, by Calvin E. Stowe, D. D. Boston: Thomas H. Webb & Co. Price 31 cents.

SEVENTH ANNUAL REPORT of the Secretary of the (Massachusetts) Board of Education, Hon. Horace Mann, 1843. Boston: Fowle and Capen. Price 25 cents.

These three reports introduce the teacher into the school-rooms of the best teachers in Europe, and enable him to profit by the observations and experience of men who have been trained by a thorough preparatory course of study and practice at home, to the best methods of classification, instruction, and government of schools, as pursued abroad.

ACCOUNT OF THE EDINGURGH SESSIONAL SCHOOL, Edinburgh, by John Wood. Boston: Monroe & Francis, 1830.

COUSIN'S REPORT ON PUBLIC INSTRUCTION IN PRUSSIA, translated by Sarah Austin. New York: Wiley & Long, 1835.

WILLM ON THE EDUCATION OF THE PEOPLE, translated from the French by Prof. Nichol. Glasgow: 1847.

MANUAL OF THE SYSTEM OF PRIMARY INSTRUCTION pursued in the model schools of the British and Foreign School Society. London: 1839.

MINUTES OF THE PROCEEDINGS OF THE COMMITTEE OF COUNCIL ON EDUCATION, from 1838 to 1844. London: 8 vols.

STOW'S TRAINING SYSTEM, as pursued in the Glasgow Normal Seminary. Edinburgh: 1840.

AN OUTLINE OF THE METHODS OF TEACHING, in the Model School of the Board of National Education for Ireland. Dublin: I. S. Folds, 1840.

COUSIN'S REPORT ON PRIMARY INSTRUCTION IN HOLLAND. London: 1835.

GIRARDIN'S REPORT ON EDUCATION IN AUSTRIA, BAVARIA, &c. Paris: 1835.

HICKSON'S ACCOUNT OF THE DUTCH AND GERMAN SCHOOLS. London: Taylor and Walton, 1840.

INTRODUCTION TO THE SCIENCE AND ART OF EDUCATION AND INSTRUCTION FOR MASTERS OF PRIMARY SCHOOLS, by B. S. Denzel, President of Royal Training College for School-masters at Esslingen. 6 vols. Stutgard, 1839.

This is considered the most complete German Treatise on the subject

NATIONAL EDUCATION IN EUROPE; being an account of the Organization, Administration, Instruction, and Discipline of Public Schools of different grades in the principal States. By Henry Barnard. New York: C. B. Norton, 71, Chambers-street. 894 pages. Price $3.

This volume embraces not only the results of Mr. Barnard's observations in schools of different grades, and study of official documents during two visits to Europe, but the substance of the elaborate and valuable reports of Professor Calvin E. Stowe, D. D., to the Legislature of Ohio, in 1837; of President Alexander Dallas Bache, LL. D., to the Trustees of the Girard College of Orphans in Philadelphia, in 1839; of Honorable Horace Mann, LL. D., to the Massachusetts Board of Education in 1846; and of Joseph Kay, Esq., of the University of Oxford in 1850, on the subjects treated of: the nature and variety of which, can be seen in the following Index:

Reports and Documents relating to the Common School System of Connecticut. Hartford: Case, Tiffany & Co.

This Volume is made up of different numbers of the Connecticut Common School Journal, which contain separate documents of permanent value. It makes a large quarto volume of 400 pages, in double columns, and small type. Price $1.00.

I.—DOCUMENTS CONNECTED WITH THE COMMON SCHOOLS OF CONNECTICUT, FROM MAY, 1838, TO MAY, 1842.

Reports of the Board of Commissioners of Common Schools, for 1839, 1840, 1841, 1842
Barnard's Report—Legislative Document, 1838.
" Address of the Board of Commissioners of C. S. to the People, 1838.
" First Annual Report to the Board of C. C. S., 1839; Second do. for 1840; Third do. for 1841; Fourth do. for 1842.
" Report on Education in other States and Countries, 1840.
" " Public Schools in Boston, Providence, Lowell, Worcester, &c., 1841.
" Address on School-houses in 1839.
" Report on Public Schools of Hartford, 1841.
" Remarks on the History and Condition of the School Laws of Connecticut, 1841.
" Report on the Legal Provision respecting the Education and Employment of Children in Factories in various States and Countries.
" Letter to a Committee of the Legislature on the Expenses of the Board of Commissioners, 1841.
Reports of School Visitors in most of the Towns in Connecticut, for 1840 to 1842.
Summary of the Legislation of the State respecting Schools from 1647 to 1839.
Act to provide for the better Supervision of Common Schools, passed 1838.
Act giving additional powers to School Districts and School Societies, 1839.
Revised Common School Act, 1841.
Report and Act for repealing the Board of Commissioners, 1842.

II.—DOCUMENTS OR ARTICLES RESPECTING THE SCHOOL SYSTEM OF OTHER STATES AND COUNTRIES.

Condition of Public Education in Scotland, Ireland, England, and Wales, from various sources.
" " " Holland, by Prof. Bache, Cousin, and Cuvier.
" " " Prussia, by Prof. Bache, Cousin, Wyse, and Prof. Stowe.
" " " Duchy of Baden, and Nassau, by Prof. James.
" " " Austria, by Prof. Turnbull and Bache.
" " " Tuscany, from Qu. Review.
" " " Switzerland, from Journal of Education, and Prof. Bache.
" " " Bavaria and Hanover, by Hawkins.
" " " Saxony, by Prof. Bache.
" " " Russia, by Prof. Stowe.
" " " France, by Mrs. Austin and Prof. Bache.
" " " Belgium, from Foreign Qu. Review.

III.—NORMAL SCHOOLS, OR TEACHERS' SEMINARIES.

History of Teachers' Seminaries.
Essays on, by Rev. T. H. Gallaudet.
Address respecting, by Prof. Stowe.
Account of in Prussia, by Dr. Julius.
" " France, by Guizot.
" " Holland, by Cousin.
" " Europe, by Prof. Bache.
" " Massachusetts, by Mr. Mann.
" " New York, by Mr. Dix.
Normal Seminary, Glasgow.
Teachers' Departments, New York.
State Normal School at Lexington, Mass.
Borough Road School, London.
Primary Normal School, at Haarlem, (Holland.)
Seminary for Teachers, at Weissenfels, Prussia.
" " Potsdam, "
Primary Normal School at Stettin.
" " " Brühl and Neuweid
Normal School at Versailles, France.
" " Kussnacht, Switzerland
" " Beuggen, "
" " Hofwyl, "

IV.—ACCOUNT OF PARTICULAR SCHOOLS.

Infant Schools.
Model Infant School, Glasgow.
" " " London.
Quaker Street Infant, "
Infant School in Lombardy.
" " Rotterdam.

Evening Schools.—Schools of Industry, &c.
Evening School in London.
School of Industry at Norwood.
" " Ealing.
" " Lindfield.
" " Gowers Walk.
" " Guernsey.
" " Warwick.
" for Juvenile Offenders, Rotterdam.

Public Schools of Various Grades.
Primary School at the Hague.
Intermediate School at Leyden.
Borough Road School, London.
Sessional School, Edinburgh.
High School, Edinburgh.
School for the Poor, Amsterdam.
Primary School, Berlin.
Dorothean High School, "
Burgher School, "
Higher Burgher School, Potsdam.
Lovell's Lancasterian School, New Haven

Schools of Agriculture, &c., &c.
City Trade School, Berlin.
Commercial School, Leghorn.
Agricultural School at Templemoyle.
Institute of Agriculture, Wurtemburg.
School of Arts, Edinburgh.
Polytechnic Institute, Vienna.
Technical School, Zurich
Institute of the Arts, Berlin.
Mechanic Institutions, London.
" " Manchester.
Factory Schools.
Adult Schools. Sunday Schools.

REPORT ON THE PUBLIC SCHOOLS OF RHODE ISLAND, for 1845, by Henry Barnard, Commissioner of Public Schools. Providence: C. Burnett, Jr.

JOURNAL OF THE RHODE ISLAND INSTITUTE OF INSTRUCTION: commenced in 1845, and discontinued in 1849. Edited by Henry Barnard, Commissioner of Public Schools. The set consists of three volumes. Price $3.50 per set.

CONTENTS.—VOLUME I.

Report on the Public Schools of Rhode Island for 1845, and the following articles in *Extra Journal.*

Rules for the Care and Preservation of School-Houses.

The following provisions are included among the Regulations for the Government of Teachers and Pupils of Public Schools, adopted by School Committees in most of the towns of Rhode Island:

For Teachers:

There shall be a recess of at least fifteen minutes in the middle of every half day; but the primary schools may have a recess of ten minutes every hour: at the discretion of the teacher.

It shall be the duty of teachers to see that fires are made, in cold weather, in their respective school-rooms, at a seasonable hour to render them warm and comfortable by school time; to take care that their rooms are properly swept and dusted; and that a due regard to neatness and order is observed, both in and around the school-house.

As pure air of a proper temperature is indispensable to health and comfort, teachers cannot be too careful in giving attention to these things. If the room has no ventilator, the doors and windows should be opened before and after school, to permit a free and healthful circulation of air; and the temperature should be regulated by a thermometer suspended, five or six feet from the floor, in such a position as to indicate as near as possible the average temperature, and should be kept about 65 degrees Fahrenheit.

The teachers shall take care that the school-houses, tables, desks, and apparatus in the same, and all the public property entrusted to their charge, be not cut, scratched, marked, or injured and defaced in any manner whatever. And it shall be the duty of the teachers to give prompt notice to one or more of the trustees, of any repairs that may be needed.

For Pupils:

Every pupil who shall, *accidentally* or *otherwise*, injure any school property, whether fences, gates, trees or shrubs, or any building or any part thereof; or break any window glass, or injure or destroy any instrument, apparatus or furniture belonging to the school, shall be liable to pay all damages.

Every pupil who shall any where, on or around the school premises, use or write any profane or unchaste language, or shall draw any obscene pictures or representations, or cut, mark, or otherwise *intentionally* deface any school furniture or buildings, or any property whatsoever belonging to the school estate, shall be punished in proportion to the nature and extent of the offence, and shall be liable to the action of the civil law.

No scholar of either sex shall be permitted to enter any part of the yard or buildings appropriated to the other, without the teacher's permission.

Smoking and chewing tobacco in the school-house or upon the school premises, are strictly prohibited.

The scholars shall pass through the streets on their way to and from school in an orderly and becoming manner; shall clean the mud and dirt from their feet on entering the school-room: and take their seats in a quiet and respectful manner, as soon as convenient after the first bell rings; and shall take proper care that their books, desks, and the floor around them, are kept clean and in good order.

It is expected that all the scholars who enjoy the advantages of public schools, will give proper attention to the *cleanliness* of their persons, and the neatness and decency of their clothes—not only for the moral effect of the habit of neatness and order, but that the pupils may be at all times prepared, both in conduct and external appearance—to receive their friends and visitors in a respectable manner; and to render the school-room pleasant, comfortable and happy for teachers and scholars.

In the "*Regulations of the Public Schools in the city of Providence,*" it is made the duty "of the principal teacher in each school-house, for the compensation allowed by the Committee, to employ some suitable person to make the fires in the same when necessary, and to see that this important work is properly and economically done;" also "for the compensation allowed, to employ some suitable person to sweep the room and its entries daily, and dust the blinds, seats, desks, and other furniture in the same, and to clean the same once a quarter, and to see that this work is neatly and properly done."

The teachers must also "take care that the school-houses, the apparatus in the same, and all the public property entrusted to their charge, be not defaced, or otherwise injured by the scholars, and to give prompt notice to the Superintendant of any repairs and supplies that may be needed."

Practical Suggestions respecting Ventilation, Fires, Sweeping and Dusting.

The following suggestions are taken from the *Manual of the System of Discipline and Instruction for the Schools of the Public School Society of New York:*

VENTILATION.

Strict attention should be paid to all the means provided for temperature and ventilation. During the season of fires, the thermometer should be watched,—and the ventilating flues, windows, doors, and stoves, should be constantly attended to,—and every precaution taken, to give as pure an atmosphere to the school-room, as circumstances will allow. This is not only necessary, for a proper and free exercise of the physical powers,—but it will be found greatly to influence every mental exercise; for, both will partake of either languor, or vigor, according as ventilation is neglected, or duly attended to. In warm weather, the upper sashes should be down during school hours, and allowed to remain open about four inches during the night,—except, that on occasion of a storm, the windows against which it beats, may be closed. In winter, excepting when the weather is exceedingly cold and piercing, it may be of advantage to have two or more of the upper sashes down about an inch during the night; but these as well as the doors should be closed before kindling the fires. Two or more of the upper sashes should be drawn down at the end of the first half hour after opening school,—and again, for a short time at each successive half hour,—and whenever the thermometer rises to 70 degrees. At all seasons, the windows and doors should be thrown wide open for a few minutes during each recess, while the scholars are in the yard. The teacher should be careful to require all the scholars to go out, except such as may reasonably be excused on account of infirmity or sickness; and even these should be required to change their places, and to exercise themselves by walking to and fro in the school-room. At all seasons, at the close of school, all the doors and windows should be opened for a few minutes, in order that a pure atmosphere may be admitted and retained during the noon-time recess, or at night. A thermometrical diary must be kept during the winter season, and the temperature of the room noted at the opening, middle, and close, of each daily session. Further directions on this point are given in the instructions for making fires. The window-blinds and curtains are for the purpose of guarding against the sunshine, or observation from without. They should, therefore, be so managed, as only to exclude the direct rays of the sun, and kept open or shut accordingly. When required as a screen from observation, they should extend no farther than necessary for that purpose. Attention to these rules will give an air of cheerfulness within, so congenial to the young. It is important that this fact be impressed on all—that air, and light, are grand essentials in a school-room: let the first be freely admitted, and the second never causelessly excluded.

FIRES.

The ashes should be taken from the stoves in the morning only, leaving a layer of one inch in depth: then to proceed to build with the materials after the following manner: Place one large stick on each side; in the space between them, place the kindling wood; and above it, the small wood, somewhat crosswise; then, set fire to the kindling, and close the stove door. See that the draught is cleared of ashes, or other obstructions; and that the dampers are properly adjusted; (these are generally so arranged as to open the draught when the handle is parallel with the pipe). If the materials have been laid according tc the foregoing directions, the combustion will be free. Should the temperature of the room be as low as 40°, fill the stove with wood. Under ordinary circumstances, in thirty-five minutes the temperature will be raised to 60 degrees,—at which point it should certainly be, at the time of opening school; when the stove may be supplied with one or two large sticks. At all times, before supplying wood, draw forward the brands and coals with the fire-hook. If there should be too much fire, open the stove door, and if necessary, turn the damper,—or, what may be better for economy, effectually close the draft at the stove door with ashes. By attention to all these directions,* the temperature may be maintained, the wood entirely consumed, and the thermometer stand at 60 degrees, at the close of the school; which is desirable in cold weather, so as not to subject the pupils to too sudden a change of temperature on going into the open air. The evaporating pan should be kept *clean*, and filled with water when in use. In damp rooms it is not needed,—nor in damp weather:—but it should be emptied, and wiped dry, before it is set aside.

DUSTING AND SWEEPING.

For a large room, or one department of a Public School building, six brooms will be found sufficient to be in use. When half worn, they will serve for sweeping the yard; and when well worn down in that service, will still be useful for scrubbing, with water or sand; and, if properly used by the sweepers, will be evenly worn to the last. Before sweeping, pull down the upper sashes, and raise the under ones. Let the sweepers be arranged, one to each passage between the desks,—and, beginning at the windward side, sweep the dirt before them, till it is carried forward to the opposite side of the room. The broom should rest square on the floor, and, with the motion used in raking hay, should be drawn towards the sweeper, without flirting it outwards, or upwards, which raises unnecessary dust, and wears the broom irregularly. The dirt, when taken up, should be carried into the *middle of the street.* The dusting is to be done in the same regular manner, allowing a suitable interval after sweeping. If at noon, dusting should be done shortly before school time; if at night, dust the next morning. In out-door sweeping, the same rule is to be followed—the sweepers going in ranks, and sweeping from the windward. Let the scrubbing be done by a similar method. When once acquainted with these methodical plans, the cleaners will do the work, not only more effectually, but with more satisfaction and ease to themselves—and being a part of domestic economy, it will be, so far, an advantage to understand how to do it well.

Although not strictly within the design of this work, but as closely connected with habits of neatness and order, we insert from the Manual quoted above, the following directions for delivering, holding, and returning a book.

The Manual is soon to be enlarged, and well deserves a place in every teacher's library, although it has special reference to the organization and system of instruction adopted in the schools of the Public School Society.

* From a return recently made out respecting the quantity and cost of fuel used in the different schools of the Public School Society, it appears that the average cost of wood for a house like No. 17, (plans and description of which may be seen on p. 100,) having 13 stoves, including cartage, sawing, carrying in and piling, is $160. The lowest cost is $141, and the highest, $200. In a Primary house, (like that described on page 103,) having four stoves, the average cost is $33; the highest being $40, and the lowest $25. The difference in the cost is mainly to be attributed to the difference in the care and oversight of the fire by the teacher.

With a view of correcting the evil, the committee having charge of this business have prepared a table which exhibits at one view the quantity of wood furnished to each school, so as to enable every teacher to compare himself with every other in this particular.

The cost of heating a Primary building of the same size, by wood in a furnace, is $75, and of Ward school building, of the same size as No. 17, by coal in a furnace, is $260.

Regulations of Chauncy-Hall School, Boston.

The following Regulations of one of the best conducted Private Schools for Boys in New England, will furnish useful hints to teachers in framing regulations for their own schools, especially in reference to the *good behavior* of the pupils, and to the care of the school-room, furniture, &c.

REQUISITION.

Boys are required to be punctual at school.

To scrape their feet on the scraper, and to wipe them on every mat they pass over on their way to the hall.

To hang their hats, caps, coats, &c., on the hooks appropriated to them respectively, by loops prepared for the purpose.

To bow gracefully and respectfully on entering and leaving the hall, and any recitation room when a teacher is present.

To take their places on entering the hall.

To make no unnecessary noise within the walls of the building, at any time of night or day.

To keep their persons, clothes, and shoes clean.

To carry and bring their books for study, in a satchel.

To quit the neighborhood of the school in a quiet and orderly manner, immediately after dismissal.

To bring notes for absence, dated, and signed by persons authorized to do so, and stating the duration of the absence; also, notes for tardiness, and for occasions when pupils are wanted at home before the regular hour of dismissal.

To study lessons at home, except when inconvenient to the family—in such cases to bring a certificate of the fact in writing.

To present a pen by the feather end; a knife, by its handle; a book, the right side upward to be read by the person receiving it.

To bow on presenting or receiving any thing.

To stand while speaking to a teacher.

To keep all books clean, and the contents of desks neatly arranged.

To deposite in desks all books (except writing books,) slates, pencils, rulers, &c., before dismissal.

To give notice through the school Post Office, of all books, slates, &c., missing.

To pick up hats, caps, coats, pens, slips, books, &c., found on the floor, and put them in their appropriate places.

To replace lost keys, books, &c., belonging to the school, and make good all damage done by them.

To write all requests on their slates, and wait until called.

To close desks and fasten them before quitting school for the session.

To raise the hand as a request to speak across the hall or any recitation room.

To show two fingers when a pen is wanted.

To put all refuse paper, stumps of pens, &c., in the dust box.

To be accountable for the condition of the floor nearest their own seats.

To fill all vacant time with ciphering, as a general occupation; and to give notice to the teacher, before dismissal, in case of omitting the exercise wholly on any day.

To be particularly vigilant, when no teacher is in the hall.

To promote as far as possible, the happiness, comfort, and improvement of others.

To *follow* every class-mate while reading, and correct all errors discoverer in pronunciation, emphasis, or inflection.

To point the fore finger of the left hand, at each letter or figure of the slip of copy, while writing, and the feather of the pen towards the right shoulder.

To keep the writing book square in front.

To rest the body on the left arm, while spelling, and keep the eye directed towards their own slates.

To sit erectly against the back of the chairs, during the singing lessons, and to direct their attention to the instructor.

Transferrers to show reports finished as early in the week as 3 o'clock on Tuesday, P. M.

PROHIBITIONS.

Boys are forbidden to buy or sell, borrow or lend, give, take, or exchange, any thing, except fruit or other eatables, without the teacher's permission.

To read any book in school except such as contain the reading lesson of his class.

To have in his possession at school any book without the teacher's knowledge.

To throw pens, paper, or any thing whatever on the floor, or out at a window or door.

To go out to play with his class when he has had a *deviation*.

To spit on the floor.

To climb on any fence, railing, ladder, &c., about the school-house.

To scrawl on, blot, or mark slips.

To mark, cut, scratch, chalk, or otherwise disfigure, injure, or defile, any portion of the building or any thing connected with it.

To take out an inkstand, meddle with the contents of another's desk, or unnecessarily open or shut his own.

To write without using a card and wiper.

To quit school without having finished his copy.

To use a knife, except on the conditions prescribed.

To remove class lists from their depositories.

To meddle with ink unnecessarily.

To study *home* lessons in school hours.

To leave the hall at any time without leave.

To pass noisily, or upon the run, from one room to another, or through the entries.

To visit the office, furnace room, or any closet or teacher's room, except in class, without a written *permit*.

To play at *paw paw* any where, or any game within the building.

To play in the play-ground before school.

To leave whittlings or other rubbish in the play-ground, on the side-walk, or around the building.

To go out of the play-ground in school hours.

To carry out his pen on his ear.

To use any profane or indelicate language.

To nick-name any person.

To press his knees, in sitting, against a form.

To leave his seat for any purpose, but to receive class instruction.

To go home, when deficient, without having answered to his name.

To indulge in eating or drinking in school.

To go out in class, after having been out singly; or going out singly, to linger below to play.

To waste school hours by unnecessary talking, laughing, playing, idling, standing up, turning round, teazing, or otherwise calling off the attention of another boy.

To throw stones, snow-balls, or other missiles about the neighborhood of the school.

To bring bats, *hockey* sticks, bows and arrows, or other dangerous play-things to school.

To visit a privy in company with any one.

To strike, kick, push, or otherwise annoy his associates or others.

In fine, to do any thing that the law of love forbids—that law which requires us To do to others as we would think it right that they should do to us.

These regulations are not stated according to their relative importance, but as they have been adopted or called to mind. They are intended to meet general circumstances, but may be waived in cases of necessity, by special permission, obtained in the prescribed mode.

In a Lecture on Courtesy, delivered before the American Institute of Instruction at Boston, in August, 1840, Mr. Thayer, the Principal of the Chauncy Hall School, introduced the above regulations as the topics of his discourse. We extract portions of this admirable lecture, which may be found entire in the annual volume of the American Institute, published in 1842, and in the Massachusetts Common School Journal, Vol. II, for 1840.

Scraping the feet at the door, and wiping them on the mats. This should be insisted on as one of the most obvious items in the code of cleanliness. It is not only indispensable to the decent *appearance* of a school room, but, if neglected, a large quantity of soil is carried in on the feet, which, in the course of the day, is ground to powder, and a liberal portion inhaled at the nostrils, and otherwise deposited in the system, to its serious detriment. Besides, if the habit of neglecting this at school is indulged, it is practiced elsewhere; and the child, entering whatever place he may, shop, store, kitchen, or drawing room, carries along with him his usual complement of mud and dirt; and the unscraped and unwiped feet are welcome nowhere, among persons a single grade above the quadruped race.

I may be told, it is a matter little attended to by many adult persons of both sexes. To which I would reply, in the language of Polonius,

—— "'T is true—'t is pity;
And pity 't is—'t is true."

But this, instead of being an argument in favor of the non-observance of the wholesome rule in our schools, only points more emphatically to the duty of teachers in relation to it; for when, unless during the school-days, are such habits to be corrected, and better ones established?

I am fully aware of the difficulty of carrying rules like this into execution, even among children of double the age of those that form the schools of some who hear me; and do not forget how much this difficulty is increased by the tender age, and consequently greater thoughtlessness, of most of the pupils of the schools usually taught by females; but still, much may be done by proclaiming the rule, and placing at the school entrance one of the elder scholars, to remind the others of it, and see that it is observed, until the cleanly *habit* be established.

In the school above alluded to, the rule has grown into so general observance, that the discovery of mud on the stairs or entry leads immediately to the inquiry, whether any *stranger* has been in. For, though few carry the habit with them, all are so trained by *daily drilling*, that it soon becomes as difficult to *neglect* it, as it was at first to regard it.

Hanging up on the hooks, caps, outer garments, &c., by loops. It is not every school that is provided with hooks or pegs for children's caps, garments, &c. All, however, *should* be so provided with as much certainty as seats are furnished to sit upon. It not only encourages the parents to send the children in comfortable trim, but induces the children to take better care of their things, especially if a particular hook or peg be assigned to each individual pupil. It is one step in the system of *order*, so essential to the well-being of those destined to live among fellow-men. If dependent on the attention of mothers at home, I am aware that many children would often be destitute of the loops spoken of; but the children themselves could supply these, under the teacher's supervision; for I understand the use of the needle is taught, in many schools, to the younger pupils of both sexes, and has been found a very satisfactory mode of filling up time, which, among the junior classes, would otherwise be devoted to idleness.

The next in order is, on keeping clean the person, clothes, and shoes. This, I am aware, must cost the teacher a great deal of labor to enforce; for if sent from home in a clean condition, the chances are more than two to one, that, on reaching school, a new ablution will be necessary. And in how many families this business of ablution is rarely attended to at all, with any fidelity; and as to clean clothes and shoes, if insisted on, the answer might be in some such *pleasant* and laconic language as this: "He ought to be thankful that he can get *any* clothes, without all this fuss, as if he were dressing for a wedding or a coronation!" Still, the rule is a *good* one, and should be enforced, as far as practicable. *Water* can at least be had; and if a child seems a stranger to its application, one or two of the elder scholars should be sent out, as is the practice in some European schools, to introduce it to him, and aid him in using it. And if you can arouse him to feel some pride in keeping his dress and person clean, and his shoes well polished, or at least, in keeping them *free of mud*, you teach him a lesson of self-respect, that may prove his temporal salvation, and bring him to be, when out of school, instead of the squalid vagrant, a companion of pilferers and refugees from justice, the incipient worthy member of society, and perhaps a benefactor of his race. It is amazing to reflect how very slight a circumstance in the life of a human being, in the early stages, sometimes casts him on that tide, which leads to glory or to infamy!

Some one of note has said, that "he considers cleanliness as next to godliness;" and I have been accustomed to look upon one, thoroughly clean in the outward man, as necessarily possessing a clean heart, a pure spirit. Whether it may be adopted as a rule of judgment or not, need not now be decided. The claims of cleanliness are, without considering the deduction as infallible, too commanding to be resisted, and should ever be maintained.

The fourth relates to quitting the neighborhood of the school, on being dismissed. This is desirable for the safety of the children; it removes them to some extent, from temptation, and aids in the fulfillment of the reasonable expectations of parents, that their children will be at home at the appointed hour. It is a practical lesson in punctuality, which, as the young come into life, will be found of great service to them. It may be ranked with behavior, and considered as among those things which constitute the character of a good child. It is especially due to the families residing in the vicinity of the school. Do what you may to prevent annoyance, it is scarcely possible for a large school to be an agreeable neighbor to families within its hearing. They are subject to its petty disturbances, in all states of health and sickness, in trouble and in joy; and are surely entitled to the relief afforded by dismissal and sending the children to their homes. Shouting, screaming, and yelling, should be prohibited, and the children directed to go away in a quiet and orderly manner. Surely, every principle of courtesy, of kindness, and good neighborhood, demands it, and should not demand in vain. Who has not waited with the operations of some of the senses suspended, for the periodical abatement of an intolerable nuisance, and *felt*, in due time, all the joy of the anticipated relief?

"Every boy to be accountable for the condition of the floor nearest his seat;" that is, he is not to allow any thing, whether valuable or not, to lie on the floor, and, consequently, every thing contemplated in the preceding rule, as far as any individual's vicinity is concerned, is taken care of, and all worthless articles likewise removed. This making committee-men of all the pupils must have a very good effect on the condition of the school room, and promote that neatness and order, which are above recommended.

The next rule requires the pupils to be particularly quiet and diligent, when the teacher is called out of the room. This I regard as of very great consequence; for it involves a sentiment of magnanimity, which it should be the aim of all guardians of the young to implant, to develop, and to cherish. Children often infringe school regulations, and much is to be overlooked in them, especially when at a very tender age. Their little minds are scarcely able to entertain, for a long time together, the influence of many rules, except under the excitement of great hope or fear; and when the teacher is *present*, they often unconsciously offend, and should be judged with clemency; but when left as their own keepers, they should be early made to understand how discourteous, how dishonorable, how base, it is to transgress the laws of the school. Each should vie with each in good example, and thus convince the instructor, that confidence reposed in them can never be abused.

The last item, under the head of Requisitions, is this: "To promote, as far as possible, the happiness, comfort, and improvement, of others." If to the few exclusively moral and religious obligations, those of *courtesy* be added, this requisition cannot fail of being observed. I say, exclusively or *strictly* moral, because the notion of courtesy hardly enters the mind, when we speak of *moral* conduct; and yet, in nearly all the minor points, and in most which affect the happiness of others, in our ordinary intercourse with them, apart from the transactions of business, it is *courtesy* that influences us most. It may be denominated the *benevolence* of *behavior*. Aware I am that a hypocrite may be courteous; and hypocrisy in a child is inexpressibly loathsome. But hypocrisy is not a *necessary* attendant on courtesy. One may be as courteous as Lafayette, and yet as pure and upright as Washington. If, then, school-boys are kind-hearted and friendly to their mates, and evince it towards them in their manners, they will, by their example as well as by their words, fulfill the injunction of the rule.

The "*Prohibitions*" are in the same spirit as the *requisitions*, and seem to be much the same in substance, although thrown into a negative form of speech. The first is in these words: "No boy to throw pens, paper, or any thing whatever, on the floor, or out at a window or door." This refers to a *voluntary* act of the pupil,—the rule requiring boys to pick up whatever is found on the floor to those accidental scatterings, for which one would not be culpable. The prohibition is founded on that necessity for order and neatness, which must ever be maintained in a well-conducted institution, to whatever object, worthy of attention, it may be devoted. And this is urged thus repeatedly, because of the ineffable importance of *first steps*. BEGIN RIGHT, should be the motto and rallying word of every nursery and every school.

Spitting on the floor. This topic I would willingly avoid, but fidelity to my charge forbids it. The *practice*, disgusting as it is, is too prevalent in many of the families that furnish pupils for your schools, to be overlooked, or winked out of sight; and if the children could carry home new notions in regard to it, I am sure you would have furnished a good lesson to their parents.

The habits of large portions of society demand a reform. It is futile to expect any general amendment in those who have grown old in given practices; but with the children, those whose habits are, to a great extent, yet unformed, much may be done. And although the counteracting influences of home militate against your wholesome requisitions, happy is it for us, that a goodly portion of New England respect for teachers still remains, to give authority and weight to your well-founded and reasonable rules. In many, if not in most, families, of our own countrymen, the fact that the 'school-ma'am' said so, is sufficient to make the rule promulgated binding on the parents; the mother, especially, will exert her authority and influence on the teacher's side; and if the teacher possesses the qualities of judgment, discretion, a proper consideration for the circumstances of the families to which her children belong, to guide her in the adoption of her regulations, she will be able to exert a power for good, within the sphere of her daily duties, which will continue to be felt and acknowledged, long after she shall have rendered her final account.

Marking, cutting, scratching, chalking, on the school-house, fence, walls, &c., are forbidden, as connected with much that is low, corrupting, and injurious to the property and rights of others. They are the beginnings in that course of debasing follies and vices, for which the idle, the ignorant, and profane, are most remarkable; the first steps in that course of degradation and impurity, by which the community is disgraced, and the streams of social intercourse polluted. You mark the track of its subjects as you would the trail of a savage marauding party, by its foul deeds and revolting exploits; as you would the path of the boa constrictor, in its *filthy slime*, which tells that man's deadly enemy is abroad. And *we* are called on, by every consideration of duty, to ourselves, to our offspring, and to our race, to *arm* against this tremendous evil, this spiritual bohon upas, which threatens so wide-spread a moral death.

We cannot escape the evidences of this, which assail us on every hand, sometimes on the very walls of our school-houses and churches; but especially in places removed from *public* view, where the most schocking obscenity of language is displayed, to poison the youthful mind, illustrated by emblems, which, in the words of one who deeply mourns with us over the existence of this monstrous evil, this desolating curse, "*would make a heathen blush!*" These frightful assaults on decency demand reform. The deep, low murmur of insulted humanity will, I doubt not, unless this evil be checked, ascend to the tribunal of Eternal Purity, and invoke the malediction of our Judge, which may yet be displayed in the blasting of our fair land, like another Sodom! To avert so deplorable a catastrophe, let the thousands of the good and virtuous in your midst, formed into one indomitable phalanx, take the noble stand which belongs to them, and never abandon it, till the enemy be forever vanquished; forever banished from the now polluted, but ever to be cherished, land of the Pilgrims!

By these practices, the mind acquires such a hankering after, and morbid relish for mischief, that no tree, or shrubbery, or flowers, or public embellishments, or exhibitions of art or taste, however beautiful or expensive, are sacred from the marring or destructive touch. A sensibility to the beautiful needs to be cultivated among us; and may easily be done with the young, if a proper and sincere value be placed upon it by ourselves, and the children see that our admiration is a reality. It exists much more generally in continental Europe, than in our own country. There, the decorations of public walks, parks, and gardens; the galleries of the arts, and the magnificent structures which adorn their cities, are looked at, enjoyed, admired, by all classes; and rarely, indeed, is the Vandal hand of mischief or destruction found to desecrate these monuments of a nation's refinement. But how is it with us? No sooner has the artist given the last touch to the fluted column, than some barbarian urchin chips off a wedge of it, in wanton sport. How often is our indignation excited by the painter's boy, who, as he passes the newly-erected dwelling or recently-painted wall, daubs it with his black paint-brush, for yards in length, as he saunters heedlessly along. And what more common, in almost all public buildings, in cupolas, observatories, &c., especially, for persons, apprehensive of being forgotten by posterity, than to cut out their names or their initials, as if this were their only road to immortality!

The *use of knives* is the thing next prohibited. In mere *primary* schools, this rule, and the one last mentioned, would find, perhaps, little to do. Some, however, there are, I doubt not, even in such schools, who suffer from the too free use of knives, as their forms, desks, or benches, could testify. Nothing is more fascinating to a boy than a knife. And what pleasure can there be in possessing a knife, if one may not use it? Hence the trouble occasioned by the instrument. He early learns in imitation of his *elders* if not his *betters*, that wood was made to be cut, and that the mission of a knife is, to do the work.

This topic can hardly be thought out of place, by those who will look into the recitation-rooms of almost any of our colleges, where many a dunce, unworthy of any *degree*, soon, by his dexterity in this department, lays claim to that of master of the art,—of *hacking;* "and has his claim allowed."

I have already adverted to the *whittling* propensities of our people; but, with your permission, I will add a remark or two, with a view to placing this national peculiarity in a stronger light. So proverbial have we become, among foreigners, in this respect, that, if a Yankee is to be represented on the stage, you find him with a jackknife in one hand, and in the other a huge bit of pine timber, becoming every moment smaller, by his diligent handiwork. If he is talking, arguing, or, more appropriately, if he is driving a bargain, you find him plying this, his wonted trade, with all the energy and dexterity of a beaver; and, as it was once said of an English advocate, that he could never plead, without a piece of packthread in his hands, so the Yankee would lose half his thrift, unless the knife and wood were concomitants of his chaffering. But the habit is of evil tendency, and ought to be checked. He indulges in it without discrimination, upon whatever is cut-able; and, worse than the white ant, which saws down and carries away whole human habitations, when they have become deserted, the whittling Yankee would hack your dwelling in present occupation, until he rendered you houseless. Let the mischief be checked betimes; do it at school; showing, at the same time, the uselessness, the folly, and the annoying nature, of the habit. It is not merely at home, among our own people, that it is practiced by us; but we carry it with us wherever we go, and, even among strangers, establish our New England identity by it.

The *spirit* of the school rules at which we have glanced, should be carried into every family. It is not enough to present the summary at which we have arrived; we should also insist on minor particulars, by words and actions, not at school only, but *at home*, where great familiarity produces influences unfavorable to the exercise of courtesy,—such as the closing of all doors, especially in cold weather; the doing of it gently, without *slamming;* moving quietly over the floor; abstaining from shouting, whistling, boisterous plays, wearing the hat in the house, &c. Just in proportion as such habits can be secured by *your* labors, will you bring down upon your heads the blessing of mothers, worn by care, by sickness, and the rudeness of their offspring. Powerless themselves, to produce a reformation, their gratitude to you will be sincere and heartfelt.

Children should be taught to take leave of their parents and friends, on going to school, and to offer the friendly salute and kind inquiry, on returning home. Nothing tends more to strengthen the silken cords of family affection, than these little acts of courtesy; and their influence on the observer is highly favorable to benevolent feeling. If these points are attended to in our families, they will not fail of being carried into company, where they are always a coin of sterling value.

Dedicatory Exercises.

The opening of a new school-house is an occasion which well deserves a public and joyful commemoration. Out of it are to be the issues of life to the community in the midst of which it stands, and like the river seen in the vision of the prophet, which nourished all along its banks trees whose leaves were for the healing of the nations, the well-spring of all its influences should be a spot consecrated by religion. In prayer, and in praise to the Giver of all good, and the Author of all being,—in song, and hymn and anthem, and in addresses, from those whose position in society will command the highest respect for any object in whose behalf they may speak, and in the presence of all classes of the community, of pupils, and teachers, of fathers and mothers, of the old and young,—the school-house should be set apart to the sacred purpose of the physical, intellectual and moral culture of the children who will be gathered within its walls. We rejoice to see that these occasions are thus improved, and that so many of our most distinguished teachers, scholars and statesmen take part in the exercises. We have before us a large number of addresses, at once eloquent and practical, which have been delivered at the opening of new school-houses, and we shall select a few, not for their superiority to the rest, but as specimens of the manner in which topics appropriate to the occasion are introduced, and as fitting testimony to the importance of School Architecture.

School Celebration at Salem, Mass.

On the first of March, 1842, the occasion of occupying several new school-houses, was marked by a variety of interesting exercises, an account of which will be found in the Common School Journal for that year. We copy the addresses of Mr. George B. Emerson, and of G. F. Thayer.

Mr. Emerson said,—

"I congratulate you, my young friends, on this happy event. This pleasant day is like a smile of Heaven upon this occasion; and I believe Heaven always smiles on events like this. Many of us whom you see here have come from a distance, on the invitation of your excellent friend the Mayor, to show the interest which we feel in you, and in what has been done here for your improvement. We have taken great pleasure in looking over the buildings prepared for your use, the admirable arrangements and apparatus, so much superior to what is usually enjoyed by children in your position. We have been pleased to hear of the faithful teachers that are provided for you, and the excellent plan of your studies, and the excellent regulations.

Your fathers and friends have spared no pains to furnish you with all the best means and opportunities for learning. They now look to you to do your part. All that they have done will be of no avail, unless you are excited to exert yourselves,—to prove yourselves worthy of these great advantages.

I was gratified, in looking over the regulations, to see the course marked out for you,—to see the stress laid upon the great substantials of a good education,—to see the prominent place given to that most useful art, that most graceful accomplishment, *reading*. You cannot, my young friends, realize the great and manifold advantages of gaining, now, in the beginning of your life, familiarly and perfectly, the single power of reading distinctly, naturally, intelligently, with taste and interest,—and of acquiring a *love* for reading. There is no situation in life, in which it will not prove to you a source of the purest pleasure and highest improvement.

For many years, and many times in a year, I have passed by the shop of a diligent, industrious mechanic, whom I have often seen busy at his trade, with his arms bare, hard at work. His industry and steadiness have been successful, and he has gained a competency. But he still remains wisely devoted to his trade. During the day, you may see him at his work, or chatting with his neighbors. At night, he sits down in his parlor, by his quiet fireside, and enjoys the company of his friends. And he has the most extraordinary collection of friends that any man in New England can boast of. William H. Prescott goes out from Boston, and talks with him about Ferdinand and Isabella. Washington Irving comes from New York, and tells him the story of the wars of Grenada, and the adventurous voyage of Columbus, or the Legend of Sleepy Hollow, or the tale of the Broken Heart. George Bancroft sits down with him, and points out on a map, the colonies and settlements of America, their circumstances and fates, and gives him the early history of liberty. Jared Sparks comes down from Cambridge, and reads to him the letters of Washington, and makes his heart glow with the heroic deeds of that god-like man for the cause of his country. Or, if he is in the mood for poetry, his neighbor Washington Allston, the great painter, steps in and tells him a story,—and nobody tells a story so well,—or repeats to him lines of poetry. Bryant comes, with his sweet wood-notes, which he learnt among the green hills of Berkshire. And Richard H. Dana, father and son, come, the one to repeat grave, heart-stirring poetry, the other to speak of his *two years before the mast*. Or, if this mechanic is in a speculative mood, Professor Hitchcock comes to talk to him of all the changes that have befallen the soil of Massachusetts, since the flood and before; or Professor Espy tries to show him how to predict a storm. Nor is his acquaintance confined to his own country. In his graver hours, he sends for Sir John Herschel from across the ocean, and he comes and sits down and discourses eloquently upon the wonders of the vast creation,—of all the worlds that are poured upon our sight by the glory of a starry night. Nor is it across the stormy ocean of blue waves alone that his friends come to visit him; but across the darker and wider ocean of time, come the wise and the good, the eloquent and the witty, and sit down by his table, and discourse with him as long as he wishes to listen. That eloquent blind old man of Scio, with beard descending to his girdle, still blind, but still eloquent, sits down with him; and, as he sang almost three thousand years ago among the Grecian isles, sings the war of Troy or the wanderings of the sage Ulysses. The poet of the human heart comes from the banks of Avon, and the poet of Paradise from his small garden-house in Westminster; Burns from his cottage on the Ayr, and Scott from his dwelling by the Tweed;—and, any time these three years past, may have been seen by his fireside a man who ought to be a hero with school-boys, for no one ever so felt for them; a man whom so many of your neighbors in Boston lately strove in vain to see,—Charles Dickens. In the midst of such friends, our friend the leather-dresser lives a happy and respected life, not less respected, and far more happy, than if an uneasy ambition had made him a representative in Congress, or a governor of a State; and the more respected and happy that he disdains not to labor daily in his honorable calling.

My young friends, this is no fancy sketch. Many who hear me know as well as I do, Thomas Dowse, the leather-dresser of Cambridgeport.

and many have seen his choice and beautiful library. But I suppose there is no one here who knows a neighbor of his, who had in his early years the same advantages, but who did not improve them;—who never gained this love of reading, and who now, in consequence, instead of living this happy and desirable life, wastes his evenings in low company at taverns, or dozes them away by his own fire. Which of these lives will you choose to lead? They are both before you.

Some of you, perhaps, are looking forward to the life of a farmer,—a very happy life, if it be well spent. On the southern side of a gently sloping hill in Natick, not far from the place where may be still standing the last wigwam of the tribe of Indians of that name, in a comfortable farm-house, lives a man whom I sometimes go to see. I find him with his farmer's frock on, sometimes at the plough-tail, sometimes handling the hoe or the axe; and I never shake his hand, hardened by honorable toil, without wishing that I could harden my own poor hands by his side in the same respectable employment. I go out to look with him at trees, and to talk about them; for he is a lover of trees, and so am I; and he is not unwilling, when I come, to leave his work for a stroll in the woods. He long ago learnt the language of plants, and they have told him their history and their uses. He, again, is a reader, and has collected about him a set of friends, not so numerous as our friend Dowse, nor of just the same character, but a goodly number of very entertaining and instructive ones; and he finds time every day to enjoy their company. His winter evenings he spends with them, and in repeating experiments which the chemists and philosophers have made. He leads a happy life. Time never hangs heavy on his hands. For such a man we have an involuntary respect.

On the other side of Boston, down by the coast, lived, a few years ago, a farmer of a far different character. He had been what is called fortunate in business, and had a beautiful farm and garden in the country, and a house in town. Chancing to pass by his place, some four or five years ago, I stopped to see him. And I could not but congratulate him on having so delightful a place to spend his summers in. But he frankly confessed that he was heartily tired of it, and that he longed to go back to Boston. I found that he knew nothing about his trees, of which he had many fine ones,—for it was an old place he had bought,—nor of the plants in his garden. He had no books, and no taste for them. His time hung like a burden on him. He enjoyed neither his leisure nor his wealth. It would have been a blessing to him if he could have been obliged to exchange places with his hired men, and dig in his garden for his gardener, or plough the field for his ploughman. He went from country to town and from town to country, and died, at last, weary and sick of life. Yet he was a kind man, and might have been a happy one but for a single misfortune; he had not learned to enjoy reading. The love of reading is a blessing in any pursuit, in any course of life;—not less to the merchant and sailor than to the mechanic and farmer. What was it but a love of reading which made of a merchant's apprentice, a man whom many of you have seen and all have heard of, the truly great and learned Bowditch?

Our friends the young ladies may not think this which I have said exactly suited to them. But to you, my young friends, even more than to your brothers, it is important now to acquire a talent for reading well, and a taste for reading. I say *more important*, for, looking forward to the future, you will need it more than they. They are more independent of this resource. They have their shops, and farms, and counting-houses to go to. They are daily on change. They go abroad on the ocean. The sphere of woman, her place of honor, is home, her own fireside, the cares of her own family. A well-educated woman is a sun in this sphere, shedding around her the light of intelligence, the warmth of love and happiness.

And by a well-educated woman I do not mean merely one who has acquired ancient and foreign languages, or curious or striking accomplishments. I mean a woman who, having left school with a firmly-fixed love of reading, has employed the golden leisure of her youth in reading the best English books, such as shall prepare her for her duties. All the best books ever written are in English, either original or translated; and in this richest and best literature of the world she may find enough to prepare her for all the duties and relations of life. The mere talent of reading well, simply, gracefully,—what a beautiful accomplishment it is in woman! How many weary and otherwise heavy hours have I had charmed into pleasure by this talent in a female friend. But I speak of the higher acquisition, the natural and usual consequence of this, a taste for reading. This will give a woman a world of resources.

It gives her the oracles of God. These will be ever near her;—nearest to her hand when she wakes, and last from her hand when she retires to sleep. And what stores of wisdom, for this world and for a higher, will she gain from this volume! This will enable her to form her own character and the hearts of her children. Almost every distinguished man has confessed his obligations to his mother. To her is committed the whole formation of the character,—mind, heart, and body, at the most important period of life. How necessary, then, is it that she should possess a knowledge of the laws of the body and the mind! and how can she get it but by reading? If you gain only this, what an unspeakable blessing will your education be to you!

I need not, my young friends, speak of the other acquisitions you may make,—of writing, which places friends in the remotest parts of the world side by side,—or of calculation, the very basis of justice and honesty.

The acquisitions you may make will depend chiefly on yourselves. You will find your teachers ready to lead you on to higher studies whenever you are prepared to go.

These excellent establishments are emphatically yours. They are raised for your good; and, as we your seniors pass away,—and in a few years we shall have passed,—these buildings will become your property, and your children will fill the seats you now occupy. Consider them yours, then, to enjoy and profit by, but not yours to waste. Let it be your pride to preserve them uninjured, unmarred by the mischievous knives and pencils of vulgar children. Unite for this purpose. Consider an injury done to these buildings as an injury done to yourselves.

There is another thing which will depend on you, of more importance than any I have spoken of. I mean the tone of character which shall prevail in these schools. Your teachers will be happy to treat you as high-minded and generous children. Show that you can be so treated; that you are such.

Let me congratulate you upon the happy auspices of the name of him under whom, with the zealous co-operation of enlightened and patriotic associates, this momentous change in your school system has been effected,—a name which is borne by the oldest and best school in New Hampshire, and by one of the oldest and best in Massachusetts. It will depend upon you, my friends, to make the schools of Salem, equally, or still more distinguished, among those of the State.

Mr. Thayer said,—

Children: I did not expect that I should have the privilege of addressing you, on this most joyful occasion; for it was not till I met your respected Mayor, an hour ago, at the beautiful school-house we have just left, that I received an invitation to do so. You will not, therefore, anticipate a studied discourse, or any thing particularly interesting. Devoted, however, as my life is, and has long been, to the instruction and guidance of the young in no inconsiderable numbers, I shall, without further preface, imagine myself in the midst of my own school, and talk familiarly to you as I would, and do, to them.

And allow me to add my congratulations to those of your other friends for the ample, beautiful, and convenient arrangements that have been made for you, in the school-houses of this city; and especially in the new one we have just examined. I can assure you, it is superior in almost every respect to any public school-house in New England, if not in the United States. It, with others in the city, has cost your fathers and friends a great deal of money, which they have cheerfully expended as a means of making you wise and good. But you have incurred a great debt to them, which you can never repay while you are children, but must endeavor to do it to your children, when you shall become men and women, and take the place of your parents in the world. But before that period, you can do something. Now, immediately on entering upon the enjoyment of the precious privileges extended to you, you can acknowledge the debt, evince the gratitude you feel, not by *words*, but *deeds*;—by, (to use an expression well understood by all children,) '*being good.*' Yes,—by 'being good and doing good;'—by obedience to parents and teachers; by kindness to brothers and sisters, and all your young friends and companions; by fidelity in duty, at home and at school; by the practice of honesty and truth at all times; by refraining from the use of profane and indecent language; by keeping the mind and heart free from every thing impure. These are the means in your own hands. Fail not to use them; and although they will in fact be merely an acknowledgment of your obligation for the boon you possess, your friends will consider themselves well repaid for all they have done for you. It is from such conduct that the teacher's, as well as the father's, richest reward and highest satisfaction are derived. To see the beloved objects of our care and instruction appreciating our labors, and improving in all that is good and useful, under our management, affords the greatest happiness, lightens the heavy load of toil, relieves the aching head, and revives the fainting spirit.

There is, however, one great danger to which you,—to which all the young,—are especially exposed. I mean the influence of bad example. Example is omnipotent. Its force is irresistible to most minds. We are all swayed more or less, by others. Others are swayed by us. And this process is continually going on, even though we are entirely unconscious of it ourselves. Hence we see the importance of choosing good companions, and flying from the bad. Unless this is done, it will be in vain for your friends to give you wise counsel, or for you to form good resolutions. 'Who can touch pitch and be clean?' You will resemble those with whom you associate. You will catch their words, their manners, their habits. Are they pure, you will be pure. Are they depraved, they will corrupt you. Be it a rule with you, then, to avoid those who are addicted to practices that you would be unwilling your most respected friends should know, and regulate your own conduct by the same standard.

I would particularly caution you against *beginnings*. It is the *first step* that is the dangerous one; since it is obvious that, if you were to ascend the highest mountain, it could only be done by a step at a time, and if the first were not taken, the summit could never be reached. But, one successfully accomplished, the next follows as a matter of course. And equally and fatally sure is the *downward* track to crime and misery! If we suffer ourselves to be drawn in *that* direction, what human power can save us from destruction? This danger, too, is increased by the feeling of security we indulge, when we say, 'It is only a *little* thing; we shall never commit any great fault;'—not remembering that nothing stands still in life, in character, any more than in the material universe. We must be going forward or backward; up, towards improvement and glory,—or down, towards infamy and woe! Every thing accumulates, according to its kind; though it begins small, like the snowball you hold in your hand, it becomes, as you roll it on the ground before you, larger at every revolution, till, at last, it is beyond your power to move it at all.

I will illustrate this by a sad case which has recently occurred in Boston. But first, I wish to interest you in something of an agreeable nature, in connection with the faithful performance of duty.

I have spoken of some things that you should do, to show your sense of the benefits which have been conferred upon you, and I should like to dwell on each one of them separately; but I shall have time only to speak of one. It is, however, among the most important. I allude to *speaking the truth*,—the most substantial foundation of moral character. It has innumerable advantages, one of which is strikingly exhibited in the following story:—

Petrarch, an eminent Italian poet, who lived about five hundred years ago, secured the confidence and friendship of Cardinal Colonna, in whose family he resided in his youth, by his candor and strict regard to truth.

A violent quarrel had occurred in the family of this nobleman, which was carried so far, that resort was had to arms. The cardinal wished to know the foundation of the affair; and, calling all his people before him, he required each one to bind himself by a solemn oath, on the Gospels, to declare the whole truth. None were exempt. Even the cardinal's brother submitted to it. Petrarch, in his turn, presenting himself to take the oath, the cardinal closed the book, and said, '*As for you, Petrarch, your* WORD *is sufficient!*'

What more delightful reward could have been presented to the feelings of the noble youth than this, from his friend, his master, and one of the highest dignitaries of the church? Nothing but the peaceful whispers of his own conscience, or the approbation of his Maker, could have given him more heart-felt satisfaction. Who among you would not be a Petrarch? and, in this respect, which of you could not?

While, then, I would hold up for imitation this beautiful example, I would present a contrast as a warning to you.

There is now confined in the Boston jail a boy of fourteen years of age, who, for the previous six years, had been sinking deeper and deeper into vice and crime, until last October, when he was convicted, and sentenced to two years' confinement within the cold damp cell of a gloomy prison, for aggravated theft. In his own written account of his life, which I have seen, he says that he began his wretched course by playing truant from school. His second step was *lying*, to conceal it. Idle, and destitute of any fixed purpose, he fell in company with others, guilty like himself, of whom he learned to steal, and to use indecent and profane language. He sought the worst boys he could find. He became a gambler, a frequenter of the circus and the theatre, and engaged in various other corrupt and sinful practices. At length, becoming bold in his dishonesty, he robbed the post-office of letters containing very considerable sums of money, and was soon detected and condemned. If you were to visit that abode of misery, you might often see the boy's broken-hearted mother, weeping, and sobbing, and groaning, at the iron grating of his solitary cell, as if she would sink on the flinty floor, and die! 'And all this,' (to use the boy's own words,) 'comes from playing truant!'

Look, then, my young friends, on these two pictures,—both taken from life,—and tell me which you like best; and which of the two characters you propose to imitate. Will you be young Petrarchs, or will you adopt the course of the unfortunate boy in Boston jail? They are both before you. If you would be like the former, *begin right.* Resist temptation to wrong-doing, with all your might. Let no one entice you from the way which conscience points out.

This precept is applicable to all,—to both sexes and every age. Let me, then, I pray you, when I shall inquire, hereafter, respecting the habits and characters of the children of the Public Schools of Salem, have the satisfaction to hear, that the instructions of this occasion made an impression on their minds favorable to truth and duty, which subsequent time could never efface.

Dedication of the New School-house in Pawtucket, October 31, 1846

Address of President Wayland, of Brown University.

Ladies and Gentlemen,

There is something deeply interesting, both to the philanthropist and to the political economist, in the appearance of such a village as this, the abode of wealth, civilization and refinement. We find ourselves, as we look upon it, unconsciously reverting to the period, not very remote, when this whole region was a desert. Thick forests covered all these hills, and pressed down even to the water's brink. This river rushed over its rocky bed, or tumbled down its precipitous ledges, unnoticed by the eye of civilized man. A few savages from time to time, erected their transient wigwams upon its banks, as the season of hunting or fishing attracted them, and they alone disputed the claim of the beasts of the forest to this beautiful domain. The products of all this region were a scanty and precarious pasturage for game, a few canoe loads of fish, and, it may be, a few hundred pounds of venison. Whatever else the earth produced, fell and perished ungathered. Age after age, beheld this annual waste. Here was the earth with all its capabilities. Here were the waters with all their unexpended powers. But here was no man whose intellect had been instructed in the laws of nature. Here was neither continuous industry, nor even frugal forethought. Hence there could be no progress All things continued as they were from the beginning of the creation.

About two hundred years since, the first civilized man cast his eyes over this beautiful landscape. He brought with him the arts and the science of the older world, and a new era commenced in the history of that part of our country, since known as Rhode Island. The labors of agriculture soon began to work their magic changes. The forest was felled, the soil was tilled, and, in the place of the precarious products of the uncultivated field, rich harvests of grain waved over these plains. The beasts of the forest retired, and the animals given by the Creator to aid us in our toil, occupied their place. Instead of the graceful deer, the clumsy moose, the prowling wolf and the ravenous panther, these fields were covered with the lowing herds, the bleating sheep, the laborious ox, and the horse, in all latitudes the faithful servant of man.

This was a great and glorious transformation. From the moment that a civilized man first thrust his spade into this earth, or here yoked his oxen to the plough, the sleep of ages was broken, and the reign of progress commenced. From this moment the darkness had begun to pass away, and the sun was dispersing that night, which, since the deluge, ad brooded over this land. From that auspicious beginning, all the means of happiness that the eye beholds, have proceeded. Acre after acre has been reclaimed from barrenness. Every variety of product has been tried, in order to ascertain which would be produced by the earth most kindly. The smoky wigwam gave place to the log house, and this in turn, to the convenient farm-house, or the stately mansion. And thus another portion of the earth was added to the area of Anglo-Saxon civilization.

But still the river, to which all the distinctive prosperity of this region owes its origin, ran, as it ever had ran, to utter waste. This mighty and most productive means of wealth, remained wholly unemployed. A mine richer than that of gold, was yet unwrought. It was a mine of *mechanical power*, instead of *metallic treasure*, and let me add, a mine of incalculably greater value. At last it was discovered, that this little river, falling over its innumerable ledges, could do the labor of many thousand men. An accomplished manufacturer,* from England, whose name has made this village one of the most renowned spots in our country, came among us, and applied the power of this water-fall to the spinning and weaving of cotton. Who can measure the results of this one grand experiment? We hear of battles and sieges, of the defeat of armies, the capture of towns, the destruction of fleets; but what achievement of war was ever of such importance to a people, as that which was accomplished, when that wheel made its first revolution, and the first thread of cotton was here, in this very village, spun by water power? From this moment may be dated the commencement of general manufactures in this country, and that of cotton in particular. From that moment, every fall of water throughout our land became a most valuable possession. From that moment, this noble natural agent began, everywhere, to fabricate garments for our people. From that moment all the labor, of every age, throughout New England, could be profitably employed. From that moment it was certain that capital to any amount could readily find investment. The rich proceeds of one manufactory laid the foundations of a similar one by the side of it. As one branch of manufactures began to supply the demand of the nation, another branch was established. Thus we are every year adding millions to this form of investment, and employing additional thousands of hands in this mode of industry. We are entering into generous and successful rivalry with the nations of Europe. Already many of our cottons are preferred to theirs in the markets of the world. Soon, other branches of our manufactures will be brought to equal perfection. Nay, I anticipate the time when we, in this country, under a system of generous reciprocity, shall supply the continent and England herself with all those articles, for the fabrication of which we have special advantages.

But this chain of events by no means ceases here. Year after year every branch of manufactures is increasing its means, and distributing the proceeds of its labor over every part of our land. Wherever a fabric is sent, it is exchanged, in some form, for the productions of that region in which it is consumed. The common means for accomplishing these mutual and increasing exchanges, soon became utterly inadequate; more efficient modes of transportation must, from necessity, be invented. The business of the country could not be carried on without them. Our manufacturing prosperity, while it creates the necessity for internal improvements, also supplies the means for constructing them. The annual gains of manufacturing capital are next invested in canals and railroads, and thus the means of transporting these fabrics at the least cost, are at once

* Mr. Slater has even a higher claim to the gratitude and veneration of this country, than that which he derives from the introduction of the cotton manufacture. He established in Pawtucket the first SUNDAY SCHOOL that was ever opened in America; and for some time sustained it wholly at his own expense.

provided. Here is, then, another mode created, of advantageous investment. By means of internal improvement, the market of every producer is indefinitely extended, he also receives a fair remuneration for this very investment, by which his market is thus extended; and, at the same time the consumer receives whatever he purchases at a cheaper rate and in greater perfection. Thus, as we always observe, under the government of God, a real benefit to one is a benefit to all. And hence we learn, that to attempt to secure exclusive advantages to ourselves, is always labor lost. Nothing can be a real benefit to us, that is not a real benefit also to our neighbors.

And the illustration of all that I have said, is manifest every where around us. We behold how every other art has clustered around the art of transforming cotton into clothing. We see how one establishment has been the seed that has produced a multitude of those that resemble it. You see how manufactures have given rise to internal improvements; how the spindle has cut through the mountains, and filled up the valleys and graded the road, and stretched from city to city the iron rail. You see how loth these inseparable friends are to be parted from each other. The region of manufactures is the region of railroads. And you perceive, as the iron road that passes through this village, pursues its way toward the west, how it winds along through the valley of the Blackstone, greeting every village and waking every hamlet to renewed activity.

All this you readily perceive. You must be astonished yourselves, when you reflect upon the amount of capital which a single life time has added to the resources of this village, and the country in its immediate vicinity. But while we exult in the large measure of prosperity with which a bountiful Providence has endowed us, it may not be uninstructive to inquire, in what ways have these blessings been improved? Has it ever occurred to you, that almost all this capital has been invested in procuring for ourselves, the means of *physical* happiness? We erect houses, and we render them spacious, warm, and commodious. We furnish them with every means of physical luxury. We spread carpets for our feet. We stretch ourselves on couches of down. We temper the atmosphere at our will. We clothe ourselves with vestments wrought in every clime, and by people of every hue and language. We vary our dress with every fashion. We load our tables with luxuries imported from the tropics or the poles; we vex sea and land for new viands to stimulate our palates, already saturated with abundance. We please ourselves with every form of equipage, and tax the ingenuity of every artisan, that we may be enabled to roll from place to place without the fatigue of motion. But why need I proceed to specify any further. We all perceive, on the least reflection, that it is in expenditures of this kind, that almost all the expenses of living are incurred.

But if this be true, must there not be some grievous error in the principles of our conduct? Can this be a wise mode of expenditure for intelligent and immortal beings? In all that I have here recited, is there any thing in which, on principle, we have excelled, (excuse the homeliness of the illustration,) the *Beaver* that once inhabited these streams? The thoughtful animal expended all the treasures of his intellect or instinct, in rendering his dwelling commodious; and he accomplished it. Have we not done precisely the same thing? Has not all the expenditure of which I have spoken, been consumed for the convenience of the physical, the perishable, the material? Might not all this have been done, had we no consciousness of an immortal spirit?

But God has made us immortal. He has given to us a spiritual existence. Each one of us possesses a priceless mind. We are endowed with reason to discover truth, imagination to form conceptions of the beautiful and the grand, taste to delight in all that is lovely or glorious, and conscience by which we are allied to God the Father of all, and the holy and blessed throughout the universe. It is by the possession of these powers, that man claims precedence over the brute. It is by the cultivation of these, that we have become more powerful than the savage, who once dwelt where we now dwell. It is by the use of these powers, that all the wonders of art have been wrought, which we now behold around us. If such be the fact, it must certainly be true that this, the spiritual part of man, is by far the most deserving of attention, and that, in the cultivation of this portion of our nature, we can in the most appropriate manner invest our capital.

But while this is evident, does our practice correspond with these well established principles? We liberally expend our substance to preserve our bodies in health, and to cultivate in our children the full development of every power, and the outward manifestation of every grace. But do we bestow proportionate labor in developing every spiritual faculty, and protecting the immortal part from the spreading contagion of evil example, and the wasting results of evil habit? We expend whatever is necessary in furnishing our tables with every thing that may be desired for the sustentation of the body. Where is there the man among us, who would not blush to be considered an illiberal provider for the wants of his household? but is any man ashamed to confess, that he has made no provision for the spiritual appetites of his children? Who of us would permit tainted or unwholesome food to be brought into his house, or placed upon his table? and yet is not intellectual food of the most questionable character, daily read in the houses of many of our most excellent citizens? Who is ashamed to declare, that he has no library in his house, or that, he has never taken the pains to inquire whether the books that are read by his family, are useful or deleterious?

But this is not all. We know that the youthful mind is destitute of knowledge, and that it is strongly predisposed to the formation of improper habits. Every one knows that a child needs instruction, and that the labor of giving it instruction should be devolved upon those only, who are intellectually and morally qualified to impart it. The parent can rarely do this for himself. The principle of division of labor teaches us, that it can be much more successfully done by some one who will devote his whole attention to it. But, now, let us look over our own neighborhoods, and observe how very small, until quite lately, has been the amount of capital devoted to the education of our youth. Compare it with almost every other form of investment, and you at once perceive how small is its relative amount. Take, for instance, the railroad which passes within a stone's throw of the place in which we are assembled. Many of you and your fellow citizens, subscribed for its stock. You did wisely. It will, I presume, raise the value of every form of property here. Land will sell for a better price. You will thus become directly connected with the whole of the South, and with the whole of the East and West; and you can, at very little expense of transportation, exchange productions with the remotest extremities of our country. This is certainly an improvement upon your former means of communication, and you are willing to invest your capital in the effort to secure it. But suppose you had been assessed to an equal amount, in order to provide the means of education; suppose you had been called upon to subscribe the same sum in aid of an effort to give to the youth of this village the best education in New England, would you not have considered the demand excessive? Would you have believed that you could possibly have paid it? Yet, I ask, is not the education of your children as important an object as the improvement of your means of transportation? Suppose you were to unite in such an effort, would not the amount of which I have spoken be sufficient to accomplish the result, the giving to your children the best education in New England. Is it not evident, then, that we bestow upon the means of education, an attention very much less than they deserve?

I have spoken in this manner as though I were addressing you in particular. But this is not what I intend. I speak of the amount of attention which, until lately, has been given to this subject, here in this State, and throughout New England. I know as well as you, that you have not been specially behind hand in this matter. You have always been prepared to do your part, in every effort to improve the condition of education amongst us. I have, however, alluded to these facts and have presented these parallels, that you may be enabled to judge of the degree in which we have erred, in estimating the proportion of our income which is due to the cause of education.

I greatly rejoice, however, that indications of decided improvement in this respect, are visible every where around us. In Massachusetts, for several years past, no subject has appealed with greater success to the enlightened public opinion of her citizens. One of her most gifted and eloquent sons has consecrated his life to this noble cause, and the results of his efforts have become every where apparent. Nor have we of Rhode Island been wholly wanting to ourselves in this good work. Although for many years the people were indifferent to their true interests in this respect, yet, when they came to its importance, they pursued it with a manly steadfastness and a far-seeing liberality, which would do honor to any community in our country. The school system of Providence is acknowledged to be second to none in the land, in excellence and efficiency. The people in all our districts, agricultural and manufacturing, are seeking to know the best means of promoting the thorough education of their children; they are building school-houses on the best models that can be presented to them, and are raising money, with annually increasing liberality, for the purpose of accomplishing these results most perfectly.

It gives me great pleasure, Ladies and Gentlemen of Pawtucket, to be a witness to the enlightened zeal which you have manifested on this subject. From this village, first went forth the impulse which called into existence the most important manufacturing interest in this country. It is meet that as you have taught us how to supply our external, you should teach us how to supply our internal wants. You have taught us how we may clothe our bodies, it is well that you should teach us how to cultivate, and strengthen, and ennoble our minds. You have intended to render this school-house a model for your fellow citizens throughout the State. It is a noble and patriotic emulation, and we thank you for it. We hope that every village and district in the State will imitate your example.

I am delighted to observe that, in all your arrangements, you have in this matter acted with wise and thoughtful liberality. Instead of putting your school-house out of sight, in an inconvenient and unhealthy position, you have placed it on an eminence, in a desirable locality, and have determined to surround it with ample play-grounds. The building itself is exceedingly pleasing in its external proportions, and forms one of the most agreeable ornaments of your village. You thus associate education in the mind of the young with every thing gladsome and alluring; while, at the same time, you testify to your children, the importance which you attach to their intellectual cultivation.

The apartments of your house are large and convenient. The desks are constructed upon the most improved models, and the seats seem to me durable and neat, and, at the same time, comfortable to the pupil. Every thing in the school-rooms has the air of finish and completeness. The arrangements for illustration, by the blackboards, are, and I presume that those by every other means will be, ample. With such instructors as you have appointed, seconded by your own zealous and untiring efforts, I have no doubt that this school will be all that you desire to make it, one of the first model schools of New England.

But I perceive that your forethought has gone farther. You have determined that other habits, besides those of the intellect, shall here receive their appropriate share of attention. You have provided for each scholar an exclusive place for his own hat and outer clothing. You have furnished your apartments with convenient wash-rooms, an improvemen which I do not remember to have seen in any other school-house. Thus you have made it necessary for each scholar to cultivate habits of order and cleanliness. In all these respects, I do not see how your arrangements could be better made, or how any thing else could reasonably be desired.

How delightful an object of contemplation is such a school as this, when faithfully and zealously conducted. Here the slumbering germs of intellect will be quickened into life. Here talent, that would otherwise become torpid from inaction, will be placed upon the course of indefinite improvement. Here, the rough and uncultivated, arrested by the charms of knowledge, and allured by the accents of kindness, will lay aside their harshness, and assume the manners of refinement and good breeding. From hence the lessons of knowledge and the habits of order will be carried to many a family, and they will there awaken a whole circle to a higher and purer life. In a word, take the five hundred children, whom this building will accommodate, and suppose them destitute of the knowledge, the discipline and the manners, which this school will confer; trace their course through life in all its vicissitudes, and observe the station which each of them must occupy; and then, suppose these five hundred children imbued with the knowledge which you here are prepared to give, and the habits which you intend to cultivate, and follow them through life, and observe the stations which you have qualified them to occupy; and you have the measure of good which, year after year, you are accomplishing by the establishment of these means of instruction. Look at the money that it costs. You can calculate it to a single cent, both the principal investment and the interest which it would yield. But can you estimate the intellectual service, and moral advantages which will accrue to you and your children, by this expenditure? The one is to you as the small dust of the balance. Were it all lost, you would hardly think of it. You would not think it worth while to smile at a man, who should say, Pawtucket is ruined, for it has lost a sum equal to that which all its means of education have cost. But suppose that, what that sum has purchased were lost; suppose that your schools were shut up, and your whole population consigned to ignorance; that henceforth reading, writing, and all the knowledge which they unfold, should be taught or learned here no more for ever; then would Pawtucket in reality be ruined. Every virtuous and intelligent family would flee from your border, and very soon your name would be an opprobrium to New England. I ask, then, in view of all this, is there any money which you invest, that brings you in so rich a revenue, as that which you devote to the cause of education?

But I ought to apologize for occupying so much larger a portion of your time than I intended. I must, however, even now, break off abruptly, and give place to others who are much more deserving than myself to be heard on this occasion. I will therefore add but a single suggestion. Let this effort which you have made, be but the first step in your progress. Cultivate enlarged and liberal views of your duties to the young who are coming after you, and of the means that are given you to discharge them. A place as large as this, can perfectly well provide for all its youth of both sexes, as good an education as any one can desire.

What we are capable of doing in this respect, is so little known, that any public spirited and united population, as wealthy as this, can easily place itself in the vanguard in this march of improvement. It is in your power so to cultivate the mind and manners of your children, that wherever they go, they will take precedence of those of their own age and condition. Your example would excite others to follow in your footsteps. Who can tell how widely you might bless others, while you were laboring to bless yourselves? Are you prepared to enter upon so noble a career of improvement?

Remarks of Rev Mr. Osgood.

Mr. Osgood, of Providence, being called upon by the Chairman of the School Committee, spoke in substance as follows:

You will agree with me, friends, in deeming it a happy circumstance, that he, whose position places him at the head of the educational interests of this State, and whose name stands among the highest in the literature of our land, has favored us with his presence upon this occasion, and borne so decided witness to the importance of a far nobler popular education. After what we have heard, we cannot but recognize the common interests of all friends of sound learning, and rank the school and the university as helpers in the same good cause.

We have met to-day to consecrate this pleasant edifice to the service of popular instruction. Solemn prayer has been offered to the throne of mercy, and honest counsel has been addressed to you. This house is now consecrated as a temple of learning. Do we feel duly the significance of these exercises? Do we realize the common responsibility that we assume by participating in them? This afternoon has been spent in mockery, unless the parties here represented entertain and carry out serious convictions of duty.

Let us feel that in consecrating this house to the purposes of education, we consecrate it to the spirit of *order*. Without good order, education cannot succeed; and surely all will allow that good order cannot exist without the aid alike of master and scholar, parent and guardian. Let the teacher have your hearty co-operation in his endeavors to regulate his school. Let him not be left at the mercy of the unreasonable, who will call every act of discipline, tyranny; or of the quarrelsome, who will resent every restraint as a personality. Encourage in yourselves and your children the idea that good order has its foundation in the very nature of things, in the plan of the creation, and the hearts of man. There is order in God's works,—in the heavens above,—on the earth beneath. We imitate the divine mind when we strive to do our work in accordance with the best rules, and submit passing impulses and little details to a common standard of right. Let the child be taught to accept this idea, and to see in the order of the school not so much the teacher's will as the law of general good. Let this idea prevail, and a new day will come over our schools. Teachers will be more careful to place their passions under due control, by looking beyond present provocations to permanent principles; and parents and children will acknowledge the justice of proper discipline, even when its penalties fall upon themselves. Consecrating this house to education, we consecrate it then to the spirit of good order.

Akin to order is the spirit of *good will*,—that love that heightens every task, and cheers every labor. Let us feel that this building is set apart as the abode of good will. In the simple beauty of its walls, and the neatness of its arrangements, we see at once that it is intended to be a pleasant place, where the young shall come rather in love than fear. Let every thing be done to carry out this idea, and remove all gloom from the work that here is to go forward. Let the voice of music be heard in the intervals of study, and charm away weariness and discontent. Let courteous manners prevail between scholars and teachers. Let the law of love be supreme, and the good of each be regarded as the good of all. Let every thing be done to make knowledge attractive, without impairing its solidity. You have declared your principles upon this subject in the very structure of this edifice; virtually acknowledged the relation of the beautiful to the true, and applied to education that law of attraction that pervades all the plans of Divine Providence. Carry out these principles without fear and without extravagance. Let not your care be given merely to make your dwelling-houses attractive. Let there be no more school-rooms so rude and uncleanly as hardly to be fit to shelter well-bred cattle. Let children learn neatness, taste, and refinement, along with their alphabet and multiplication table. To good will, under every one of its attractive agencies, this house should be devoted.

Thus devoted, it will be a nursery of good works. *Utility* will go hand in hand with *good order* and *good will.* In this community, practical industry is the ruling power; utility is the prevailing standard. See to it that this standard is rightly adjusted, and that we do not confine our idea of usefulness to worldly or material interests. As we hear the sound of the spindle and the anvil, and see the spray of the waterfall, and the smoke of the furnace, let us rejoice at the large measure of enterprise and prosperity that have been granted us. But when we turn away from these things to look upon this house of learning, let us not think as some base souls do, that we have left utility behind, and are dealing only with what is visionary and unsubstantial. Next to the church of God, let us feel that the school-house is the most useful building in the community, and that from it should emanate the knowledge, principles, and habits that are to give life its direction and efficiency. Reckon in your estimate of the best wealth of your city, your schools, and, without them, regard all other wealth as disgraceful covetousness or mental poverty.

Let the idea of utility preside over the direction of this school, and all its studies tend not to fill the memory with loads of words, but to strengthen the mind, and invigorate and regulate the will and all the active powers.

Standing as it does in so sacred a seat of manufacturing industry, this house has a peculiar significance. Overlooking this prosperous town, it serves to express a generous creed—to say as if it were:—"We, the people of North Providence, think much of the importance of industry and wealth, but we think that some other things are of still greater importance, and however remiss in duty we may have been in time past, we mean to practice upon a more generous system, and this fair temple of learning, standing so far above the factory and workshop, is a substantial testimonial of our determination."

It is an interesting fact, that the first movement in this State in behalf of popular education was made, not by professional men, nor by merchants, nor any of the classes that might be thought, from their leisure or literature, to advocate the claims of sound learning, but by an association of mechanics and manufacturers in Providence. I read to-day, with great pleasure, the memorial which this association presented to the Legislature, in the year 1798. I honor those men for that document. But one of the original signers now survives. Who can meet that old man without respect? Who will not honor John Howland even more for taking the lead in that memorial, than for having served under Washington at Trenton, and braved death in the battles of the revolution? Peace to his sturdy heart, and many good days yet to that stout Saxon frame!

I must cease speaking with these few words as to the good order, good will and good works, to which this house of learning is devoted. May a good providence watch over it. Imagination cannot but conjecture the various scenes of its future history—picture to herself the groups of children who shall come to enjoy its privileges, and who in due time shall leave its walls for the pursuits of maturer life. Prophesy is not our gift, except the prophesy that calculates events by purposes and principles. Let this edifice be used faithfully for true purposes and for just principles, and its future history will be a blessed volume in the annal of your town It will tell of generations of noble men and women, who have been educated within these walls. And when this house shall have gone to dust, it will have performed a noble mission, by being the nursery of mental life that cannot die.

"Cold in the dust, the perished heart may lie,
But that which warmed it once, can never die."

Dedication of the Public High School-House, in Cambridge, Mass.

The edifice, which has just been erected (1848,) for the accommodation of the Public High School of the city of Cambridge, is built of brick, two stories high with a basement, and is a substantial, attractive and convenient school-house, of which the citizens of Cambridge may well feel proud. The cost, including land, furniture and apparatus, is $13,500. The plan of the interior is substantially the same as that of the High School in Hartford.

The following account of the Dedication of this house is abridged from the Cambridge Chronicle for June 29, 1848.

The services were commenced by the chanting of the Lord's Prayer by the scholars of the school.

Alderman Whitney, in behalf of the building committee, transferred the building to the care of the School Committee, through the Mayor of the city, with an appropriate address. After a dedicatory prayer by Rev. N. Hoppin, and another chant, of selections from Proverbs, by the children, the Mayor addressed remarks to the audience upon the relation of the High School to the other grades of schools, and to the cause of education generally in the city, and on some of the conditions on which the success of this and the other schools depended. Addresses were also made by gentlemen present, in which many pleasing incidents in the history of the public schools, and of the town and city of Cambridge, were narrated, and many valuable suggestions thrown out, by which children, teachers, parents and school officers can profit. We make the following extract from the address of Rev. Mr. Stearns, Chairman of the High School Committee.

"At the time of my settlement here as a clergyman in this place, in December, 1831, there were in the town 6 school-houses, 8 school-rooms, 8 teachers and about 400 scholars.

At this time, 1848, there are 17 school-houses, 35 rooms, 44 teachers, and 2136 children.

During this time, it is true, the population has more than doubled, but the interest taken in the schools, and their progress, has much more than tripled or quadrupled.

If at that period any school committee had seriously proposed the erection of such a building as this for a High School, they would undoubtedly have been excused from public service the coming year, if not immediately sent to Charlestown as insane. But the spirit of improvement has prevailed, and now we have all needed advantages for making good scholars, who shall be an honor to their parents, and to their generation.

But, Mr. Mayor, it cannot be too deeply impressed on the minds of our youth that the *means* of education, are not education itself. We may have good school-houses, fine libraries, superior collections of philosophical apparatus, and the best of teachers, with miserable scholars. There are means of improvement in creation all around us—good influences ascend to us from the earth and come down to us from the sky. The sun is a teacher, the evening stars impart knowledge, while every flower is eloquent with wisdom. But what intelligence do all these outward instructors communicate to the ox who grazes without reflection, or to the horse who eats his provender without thanksgiving? Hardly more will books, and maps, and pleasant seats, and air-pumps, and scientific lectures, do for a doltish mind. The outward may stimulate to improvement, but all good action springs from within. There must be in the scholar's own mind a strong desire for knowledge, a spirit aspiring to excellence, a force of moral purpose which no small difficulties can vanquish, or but little which is valuable will be accomplished.

Mr. Chairman, we have great hopes from the school now to be organized in this house,—and these teachers, and these parents, and these scholars, must see to it, that we and our fellow citizens are not disappointed.

This school is intended to carry forward and complete the education of our children—I mean complete it as far as it goes—for *education* never can be completed. It is a work which extends beyond the school-room into active life, all through time into eternity. It is the destiny of good minds to improve for ever. They will go on rising, expanding, increasing in true wisdom as the endless ages pass along, and their progress will be co-eternal with the eternity of God. We wish to begin right with the young in their earliest years, and to carry them forward in this school till they are prepared for service and usefulness in society, and the good beginnings of immortal advancement are firmly laid. We wish to attend here to the proper development of their faculties, to see that these unfold themselves in just proportions, and that our children are qualified to meet the demands of the age and devote their powers to life's best ends.

We establish this school, also, with our schools generally, as a preservative against vice. When I look round, as I do now, upon more than one hundred children fresh as a flower garden in the morning, it seems hardly in good taste, to suggest that any of them may become the victims of evil, and sink in disgrace from society. And yet, it is possible that among these young men and young women too, there may be some one or more who will live to be the objects of public indignation and of *self*-scorn. God forbid! But juvenile depravity has fearfully increased within a few years! And no one can tell who will be among the next victims. Mr. Chairman, I once had a dream—and it was among the most terrible dreams which ever troubled my sleeping imagination. I saw a bright and beautiful boy playing innocently upon the green, suddenly the grass began to move, the earth to undulate till it became water, and the boy went down in an instant, and nothing was left of him but three or four air bubbles on the surface. I awoke in horror, and was troubled all day by this midnight vision. I thought then, and I have ever since thought, that it was a vivid illustration of the course and end of many a youth. They sport thoughtlessly among the green and flowery fields of temptation. They begin to yield, principle gives way, and they go down and are lost as respects character for ever. We wish to render the treacherous earth under them firmer. We would change it into the hard granite of virtue, we would have them stand on the immovable rock of ages.

We hope, also, Mr. Mayor, from this school an advantage to the adult community. The benefits of an institution like this do not terminate with the children. By a reflex influence, they return to the families from which our children come. It is no unheard of thing for a rough, hard, uneducated man to be mellowed and transformed by the influences which his children and his children's children bring home from the churches and the schools. A good school does excite the adult mind; it awakens interest in education, and promotes improvement. If this school fulfills our expectations, it will be to the community a moral and intellectual sun, throwing light into every dwelling.

We believe also that it will act happily upon our younger schools. It will be to them an object of hope and honorable ambition. They will take their examples from it—and our little children from the first will be aspiring and reaching towards it. But I must stop, for I am impatient, as doubtless you and this assembly must be, for the instructions which are to fall from more eloquent lips than mine. Children, consider how much is depending upon you. Be determined to fix down to hard study, *to do right;* and on the first principle of all true wisdom, "Remember now thy Creator in the days of thy youth."

After appropriate introductory addresses by the School Committee and Mayor of Cambridge, Hon. Edward Everett, President of Harvard College, responded to an invitation to address the audience, as follows:—

May it please your Honor:—

Connected as I am with another place of education, of a kind which is commonly regarded as of a higher order, it is precisely in that connection, that I learn to feel and appreciate the importance of good schools. I am not so ignorant of the history of our fathers, as not to know, that the spirit, which founded and fostered Harvard College, is the spirit which has founded and upheld and will continue to support and cherish the schools of New England. I know well, sir, that Universities and Colleges can neither flourish nor even stand alone. You might as well attempt to build your second and third stories in the air, without a first floor or a basement, as to have collegiate institutions without good schools for preparatory education, and for the diffusion of general information throughout the community. If the day should ever come, which I do not fear in our beloved country, when this general education shall be neglected and these preparatory institutions allowed to perish;—if the day should ever come (of which I have no apprehension) when the schools of New England shall go down, depend upon it, sir, the colleges will go with them. It will be with them, as it was with the granite warehouses, the day before yesterday in Federal street, in Boston; if the piers at the foundation give way, the upper stories will come down in one undistinguished ruin.

I anticipate no such disaster, Mr. Mayor, though it must be admitted that we live in an age of revolutions, of which every steamer brings us some fresh and astonishing account. But our revolutions are of a more auspicious character, and it occurred to me as I was coming down with your worthy associate (Mr. Whitney,) and your respected predecessor (Mr. Green,) to whom we have just listened with so much pleasure, that we were traversing a region, in which a more important revolution commenced no very long time since, and is still in progress,—far more important for us and our children,—than any of those which have lately convulsed the continent of Europe. I do not now refer to the great political and historical events of which this neighborhood was the theatre; of which the monuments are in sight from these windows, but to a revolution quiet and silent in its origin and progress, unostentatious in outward manifestations, but imparting greater change and warranting brighter hopes for most of those who hear me,—for our young friends before us,—than any of the most startling events that stare upon us in capitals in the columns of the newspapers, after every arrival from Europe. The Reverend Mr. Stearns has beautifully sketched some of the most important features of this peaceful revolution.

When I entered college, Mr. Mayor, (and I believe I shall not tell the audience quite how many years ago that is; you can do it, sir, but I will thank you not to,) there were a few straggling houses, shops, and taverns along the Main street at Cambridgeport. All back of this street to the north, and I believe almost all south of it to the river,—the entire district in the centre of which we are now assembled, was in a state of nature; pretty equally divided between barren pasturage, salt-marsh, and what I must admit had no mean attraction for us freshmen, whortleberry swamp. Not one of the high roads had been cut, which now traverse the plain between Main street and the old road to Charlestown. East Cambridge did not exist even in the surveyor's imagination. There was not a church nor a public school east of Dr. Holmes' and Old Cambridge Common; and if any one had prophesied that within forty years a population like this would cover the soil,—with its streets and houses, and gardens, its numerous school-houses and churches, its conservatories breathing all the sweets of the tropics, its private libraries equal to the choicest in the land, and all the other appendages of a high civilization, he would have been set down as a visionary indeed. But this change, this revolution has taken place even within the life time of the venerable lady (Mrs. Merriam) introduced to us in such a pleasing manner by Mr. Stearns; and we are assembled this morning to take a respectful notice of what may be called its crowning incident, the opening of a High School in that primitive whortleberry swamp. I believe I do not over-state matters when I say, that no more important event than this is likely to occur, in the course of the lives of many of those here assembled. As far as our interests are concerned, all the revolutions in Europe multiplied tenfold are nothing to it. No, sir, not if the north were again to pour forth its myriads on central and southern Europe and break up the existing governments and states into one general wreck, it would not be an article of intelligence at all so important to us as the opening of a new school. No, my young friends, this is a day which may give an auspicious turn to your whole career in life; may affect your best interests not merely for time but for eternity.

There is certainly nothing in which the rapid progress of the country is more distinctly marked than its schools. It is not merely their multiplication in numbers, but their improvement as places of education. A school forty years ago was a very different affair from what it is now. The meaning of the word is changed. A little reading, writing, and ciphering, a very little grammar; and for those destined for college, a little Latin and Greek, very indifferently taught, were all we got at a common town school in my day. The range was narrow; the instruction superficial. In our modern school system, taking it as a whole composed of its several parts in due gradation,—viz. the primary, the district, and the High School,—the fortunate pupil not only enjoys a very thorough course of instruction in the elementary branches, but gets a good foundation in French, a good preparation for college, if he desires it, according to the present advanced standard of requirement; a general acquaintance with the applied mathematics, the elements of natural philosophy, some suitable information as to the form of government and political system under which we live, and no inconsiderable practice in the noble arts of writing and speaking our mother tongue.

It might seem, at first, that this is too wide a circle for a school. But the experience of our well conducted schools has abundantly shown that it is not too extensive. With faithful and competent teachers and willing and hearty learners, all the branches I have named and others I have passed over can be attended to with advantage, between the ages of four and sixteen.

Such being the case, our School Committees have done no more than their duty, in prescribing this extensive course and furnishing to master and pupils the means of pursuing it. I cannot tell you, sir, how much I have been gratified at hastily looking into the alcove behind us. As I stepped into it this morning, Mr. Smith, the intelligent master of the school, pointed out to me the beautiful electrical machine behind the door with the just remark that my venerable predecessor, President Dunster, would not have known what it was. No, sir, nor would the most eminent philosopher in the world before the time of Franklin. Lord Bacon would not have known what it was, nor Sir Isaac Newton. Mr. Smith reminded me of the notion of Cotton Mather (one of the most learned men of his day,) that lightning proceeded from the Prince of the Power of the Air, by which he accounted for the fact that it was so apt to strike the spires of churches. Cotton Mather would have come nearer the truth, if he had called it a shining manifestation of the power and skill, by which the Great Author of the Universe works out some of the mighty miracles of creation and nature. And only think, sir, that these newly discovered mysteries of the material world, unknown to the profoundest sages of elder days, are so effectually brought down to the reach of common schools in our day, that these young friends, before they are finally dismissed from these walls, will be made acquainted with not a few of the wonderful properties of the subtle element, evolved and condensed by that machine, and which recent science has taught to be but different forms of one principle, whether it flame across the heavens in the midnight storm, or guide the mariner across the pathless ocean;—or leap from city to city across the continent as swiftly as the thought of which it is the vehicle; and which I almost venture to predict, before some here present shall taste of death, will, by some still more sublime generalization, be identified with the yet hidden principle which thrills through the nerves of animated beings, and binds life to matter, by the ties of sensation.

But while you do well, sir, in your High School to make provision for these advanced studies, I know that as long as it remains under your instruction, the plain elementary branches will not be undervalued. There is perhaps a tendency in that direction in some of our modern schools: I venture to hope it will not be encouraged here. I know it is not to be the province of this school to teach the elements; but I am sure you will show that you entertain sound views of their importance. I hold, sir, that to read the English language well, that is with intelligence, feeling, spirit, and effect;—to write with dispatch, a neat, handsome, legible hand, (for it is after all, a great object in writing to have others able to read what you write,) and to be master of the four rules of arithmetic, so as to dispose at once with accuracy of every question of figures which comes up in practical life:—I say I call this a good education; and if you add the ability to write pure grammatical English, with the help of very few hard words, I regard it as an excellent education. These are the tools; you can do much with them, but you are helpless without them. They are the foundation; and unless you begin with these, all your flashy attainments, a little natural philosophy, and a little mental philosophy, a little physiology and a little geology, and all the other *ologies and osophies*, are but ostentatious rubbish.

There is certainly no country in the world in which so much money is paid for schooling as in ours. This can be proved by figures. I believe there is no country where the common schools are so good. But they may be improved. It is not enough to erect commodious school-houses; or compensate able teachers, and then leave them, masters and pupils, to themselves. A school is not a clock which you can wind up and then leave it to go of itself. It is an organized living body: it has sensibilities; it craves sympathy. You must not leave the School Committee to do all the work. Your teachers want the active countenance of the whole body of parents, of the whole intelligent community. I am sure you, Mr. Smith, would gladly put up with a little injudicious interference in single cases, if you could have the active sympathies of the whole body of parents to fall back upon in delicate and difficult cases, and to support and cheer you under the burthen of your labors, from day to day. I think this matter deserves more attention than it has received; and if so small a number as thirty parents would agree together, to come to the school, some one of them, each in his turn, but once a month, or rather if but 25 or 26 would do it, it would give your teacher the support and countenance of a parent's presence every day; at a cost to each individual of ten or eleven days in the year. Would not the good to be effected be worth the sacrifice?

I have already spoken too long, Mr. Mayor, and will allude to but one other topic. In most things, as I have said, connected with education, we are incalculably in advance of other days:—in some, perhaps, we have fallen below their standard. I know, sir, old men are apt to make unfavorable contrasts between the present time and the past; and if I do not soon begin to place myself in that class, others will do it for me. But I really think that in some things, belonging, perhaps, it will be tho ht, to the minor morals, the present promising generation of youth mi , learn something of their grandfathers, if not their fathers. When I first went to a village school, sir, I remember it as yesterday;—I seem still to hold by one hand for protection, (I was of the valiant age of three years) to an elder sister's apron;—with the other I grasped my primer, a volume of about two and a half inches in length, which formed then the sum total of my library, and which had lost the blue paper cover from one corner, (my first misfortune in life;) I say it was the practice then, as we were trudging along to school, to draw up by the road-side, if a traveller, a stranger, or a person in years, passed along, "and make our manners," as it was called. The little girls courtesied, the boys made a bow; it was not done with much grace, I suppose: but there was a civility and decency about it, which did the children good, and produced a pleasing impression on those who witnessed it. The age of village chivalry is past, never to return. These manners belong to a forgotten order of things. They are too precise and rigorous for this enlightened age. I sometimes fear the pendulum has swung too far in the opposite extreme. Last winter I was driving into town in a carriage closed behind, but open in front. There was in company with me, the Rev. President Woods, of Bowdoin College, Maine, and that distinguished philanthropist and excellent citizen, Mr. Amos Lawrence. Well, sir, we happened to pass a school-house just as the boys (to use the common expression) were "let out." I suppose the little men had just been taught within doors something about the laws, which regulate the course of projectiles, and determine the curves in which they move. Intent on a practical demonstration, and tempted by the convenient material, I must say they put in motion a quantity of spherical bodies, in the shape of snow balls, which brought the doctrine quite home to us wayfarers, and made it wonderful that we got off with no serious inconvenience, which was happily the case. This I thought was an instance of free and easy manners, verging to the opposite extreme of the old fashioned courtesy, which I have just described. I am quite sure that the boys of this school would be the last to indulge an experiment attended with so much risk to the heads of innocent third persons.

Nothing remains, sir, but to add my best wishes for teachers and pupils;—You are both commencing under the happiest auspices. When I consider that there is not one of you, my young friends, who does not enjoy gratuitously the opportunity of obtaining a better school education, than we could have bought, Mr. Mayor, when we were boys, with the wealth of the Indies, I cannot but think that each one of you, boys and girls, will be ready to say with grateful hearts, the lines have fallen to me in pleasant places; yea, I have a goodly heritage.

www.ingramcontent.com/pod-product-compliance
Lightning Source LLC
LaVergne TN
LVHW020938110826
845150LV00004B/893

* 9 7 8 1 4 2 5 5 5 1 5 2 0 *